DOVER *Pictorial Archive* SERIES

THE CRYSTAL PALACE EXHIBITION

Interior of the Crystal Palace, from a photograph by William Henry Fox Talbot.
Courtesy of the Victoria and Albert Museum, London.

THE CRYSTAL PALACE EXHIBITION

ILLUSTRATED CATALOGUE

LONDON 1851

AN UNABRIDGED REPUBLICATION OF

THE ART-JOURNAL
SPECIAL ISSUE

WITH A

NEW INTRODUCTION BY

JOHN GLOAG, F.S.A.

DOVER PUBLICATIONS, INC.

NEW YORK

Published in Canada by General Publishing
Company, Ltd., 30 Lesmill Road, Don Mills,
Toronto, Ontario.
Published in the United Kingdom by Constable
and Company, Ltd., 10 Orange Street, London
WC 2.

This Dover edition, first published in 1970, is
an unabridged republication of the work originally
published in 1851 by George Virtue for *The Art-
Journal*. This reprint also contains a new introductory essay by John Gloag, F. S. A.
*The Crystal Palace Exhibition Illustrated Cata-
logue* belongs to the Dover Pictorial Archive Series.

International Standard Book Number: 0-486-22503-8
Library of Congress Catalog Card Number: 74-115221

Manufactured in the United States of America
Dover Publications, Inc.
180 Varick Street
New York, N.Y. 10014

INTRODUCTION

TO THE DOVER EDITION

OF ALL contemporary records of the Great Exhibition of 1851, *The Art-Journal Catalogue* was easily the most interesting, by far the best illustrated, and quite different in character from other publications. That difference is emphasized by comparing it with such well-known works as the *Official Descriptive and Illustrated Catalogue*, issued, by authority of the Royal Commission that directed the Exhibition, in three ponderous volumes, useful for identifying individual exhibitors, lavishly illustrated, but marred by a complicated system of reference. Another three-volume work was Tallis's *History of the Crystal Palace*, badly illustrated by indifferent steel engravings, and packed with information, conveyed with the utmost tedium. In October 1851, a cheap popular work called *The Crystal Palace and its Contents* came out in fortnightly parts, sold at a penny, and continued until March 1852, when the last two parts appeared as a double number priced at two pence. Those parts were subsequently published in book form with over five hundred illustrations, fairly well engraved. Such works reflected the spirit of pious optimism generated by the Exhibition; but the editors of *The Art-Journal Catalogue* alone recognized a critical obligation, which is why their work is the most original and instructive as well as the best illustrated.

The *Catalogue* was dedicated to Prince Albert, whose energy and imagination had overcome the massive indifference of the government and the vociferous opposition of that large class of people who are always against any new project merely because it is new. In France many successful industrial expositions had been held; people with progressive ideas were conscious of the commercial advantages an industrial exhibition would bring to Britain; and in 1848 Prince Albert submitted a proposal to the government for a self-supporting exhibition of British industrial products, under the direction of a Royal Commission. He encountered lethargy rather than opposition, and when at last a few ministers were sufficiently roused to consider such a scheme they could only see and magnify the difficulties. *The Art-Journal Catalogue* is introduced by a compact and lucid history of the long battle to win support for the idea of the Great Exhibition that reveals not only the shifts and timid evasions of politicians, but the undaunted perseverance of the Prince, and the initiative of that enterprising and independent body, the Society of Arts.

The *Catalogue* is far more than an illustrated, descriptive account of selected exhibits; the editors offered a prize of 100 guineas for an essay on the Exhibition, which was awarded to Ralph Nicholson Wornum, (1812–1877) who wrote about "The Exhibition as a Lesson in Taste," a critical appraisement that occupies twenty-two pages at the end of the work, and provides an unbiased corrective to the laudatory descriptions that accompany so many of the illustrations. Wornum was an exceptional and penetrating art critic; his opinions, freshly minted by an analytical mind, were original, clearly expressed, and unclouded by the partial nationalism that invalidated the views of so many commentators on the Exhibition. In the "Battle of the Styles" he preserved the bland detachment of a neutral; uncommitted either to the Gothic revival or the classic idiom, he could observe and compare exhibits in those and other styles, and record the condition of British, European, American and oriental taste without the fervour of a partisan. There were other essays in the *Catalogue* on scientific and technical subjects by various authorities, which are now dated; but Wornum's essay has a timeless quality and, making allowance for differences in choice of language, might have been written today by some critic clear-minded enough to be uninfluenced by *avant-garde* theories or contemporary fashions.

Wornum had studied at London University and contemplated a career as a barrister, but soon abandoned that ambition and decided to become a painter. His father, Robert Wornum, a successful piano manufacturer who had invented the upright action for pianos, was willing to finance his son's artistic studies, so Ralph Wornum spent six years in Europe, visiting many museums and galleries, and returning

[vi]

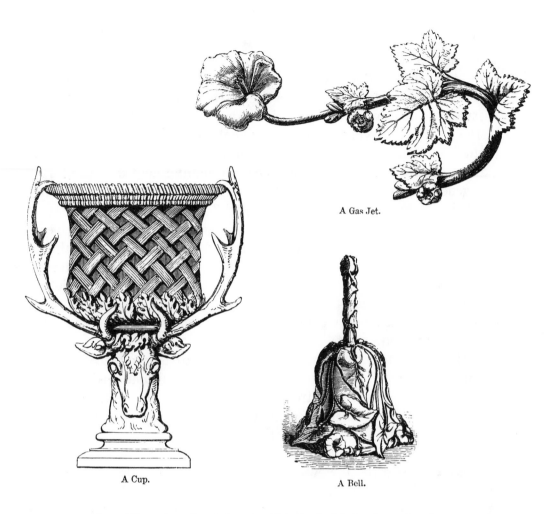

A Gas Jet.

A Cup.

A Bell.

FIG. 1. Three examples of the naturalist school of design. Reproduced from Ralph Nicholson Wornum's *Analysis of Ornament*, page 9.

in 1839 to London, where he attempted to establish himself as a portrait painter. He was unsuccessful, and soon discovered that his true vocation was art criticism. He contributed to various publications, including Smith's *Dictionary of Greek and Roman Antiquities*, and in 1846 joined the staff of *The Art-Journal*. As a result of some criticisms he made of the catalogues issued by the National Gallery, he was commissioned to compile an official catalogue for the Gallery, which was published in 1847. He became a lecturer on art in the government design schools; in that capacity he visited the chief towns in England, and the substance of the lectures he delivered formed the basis of his *Analysis of Ornament*, a book that still preserves his memory. It was

[vii]

first published in 1856, two years after his appointment as Keeper of the National Gallery and Secretary to the Trustees. The *Analysis of Ornament* became a best-seller, reaching an eighth edition in 1893, sixteen years after the author's death. In that work Wornum attacked a style that had appeared in Britain and Europe in the middle years of the century, a style without traditional roots, overwhelmingly ornamental in character, anarchical in composition, which blossomed in exuberant profusion at the Great Exhibition, and helped to accelerate the general decay of taste. "There is a class of ornament which has much increased of late years in England," he wrote, "and, by way of distinction, we may call it the *naturalist* school. The theory appears to be, that as nature is beautiful, ornamental details derived immediately from beautiful natural objects must insure a beautiful design. This, however, can only be true where the original uses of the details chosen have not been obviously violated; and one peculiar feature of this school is, that it often substitutes the *ornament itself* for the thing to be ornamented. . . ."*

He illustrated three examples, which are reproduced here in Figure 1 "in which the natural objects are so mismanaged as to be *principals:* flame proceeding from a flower, a basket on an animal's head to hold a liquid, a bell made of leaves! the elements chosen being so opposed to the proposed uses of the objects ornamented, as to make the designs simply aesthetic monstrosities, ornamental abominations." He had expressed those views about ornament, using almost the same phrases, in his essay on "The Exhibition as a Lesson in Taste" when he criticized the artistic faults of works whose designers had employed "imitations from nature as *principals* in the design, instead of mere accessory decorations, substituting the ornament itself for the thing to be ornamented: ornament," he continued, "is essentially the accessory to, and not the substitute of, the useful." In the *Analysis of Ornament* he repeated those words about the character of ornament, and added: "it is a decoration or adornment; it can have no independent existence."

Many exhibits at the Crystal Palace had shown how ornament had got out of control, and detailed engravings in the *Catalogue* illustrate the excesses of the *"naturalist* school" that Wornum condemned. Here is a small selection: the cup by Rudolphi of Paris, page 21, with an agate bowl, silver mounted and burnished, with grapes of enamel;

---

* *Analysis of Ornament*, Chap II, page 8.

the silverwork by Higgins of London, page 26; the tazza by Matifat of Paris, surrounded by a wreath of snakes, foliage, and flowers, page 49; the silver sugar ladles by G. W. Adams of London, page 67, "in which the vine and hop plants, with their respective foliage, are brought in most effectively"; the sideboard by Howard and Son, of London, page 79; the productions of T. Wilkinson & Co., of Birmingham, page 122; the soapstone cup supported by a foliated stand of ebony, designed by Mrs. Christopher Rawson, page 137; the teapoy, intricately carved in Irish bog-yew, by A. J. Jones of Dublin, page 263; and the perfume vase, page 283, by Gueyton of Paris, "the body ornamented with an embossed running pattern of oak-leaves, acorns, aqueous plants, and fish" and the lid "surmounted by a vulture, which seems ready to pounce on the prey beneath." Compared with the "naturalist school" rococo seemed almost sober and restrained; but then rococo, however fantastic, was composed within the framework of the classic tradition. Rococo might be fantastic and frivolous, madly gay and detached from reality, but it was never incongruous. Even the revived rococo style, which was much in evidence at the Great Exhibition, was still tenuously connected with the rules that determined the proportions of the classic orders of architecture.

In his essay on "The Exhibition as a Lesson in Taste," Wornum observed that classical Greek and Roman ornament adorned very few of the exhibits. "The taste so active fifty years ago, in this country at least, appears to have spread no further than its original promoters could extend it," he said; "in furniture it is scarcely represented, and in pottery it is still seemingly the great prerogative of Messrs. Wedgwood to exhibit pure specimens of the Greek style; and still for the most part in the exquisite productions of Flaxman, which appear more beautiful than ever, surrounded as they are by such endless specimens of the prevailing gorgeous taste of the present day, which gives the eye no resting-place, and presents no idea to the mind, from the want of individuality in its gorged designs." Such refreshing frankness about the shortcomings of contemporary taste, which was indeed "gorgeous," must have badly jolted the complacency of many readers of the *Catalogue*, and Wornum's view that in carving and modelling, English productions were, with only a few exceptions, "generally very inferior to those of the French and German carvers, and, in some cases, the Flemish and Italian," abraded national pride. He slightly softened the impact of his criticism by saying that "the very essence of this essay

[ix]

is the expression of opinion, without assuming any special value for our opinion. . . ." His objections to the character of English carving implied "every want but those of mere mechanical skill and means," for there was "want of definite design, and disregard of utility . . . an overloading of detail . . . a disagreeable inequality of execution, one part destroying the effect of the other." For example, one of the show pieces of the Exhibition came in for some rough treatment. "The so-called Kenilworth buffet, by Cookes & Sons of Warwick, is a massive and handsome piece of furniture, but it suffers materially in effect by the purely dramatic treatment of the figures, and the consequent sacrifice of symmetry; for which we have only a very feeble expression of a doubtful idea:—Ornamental Art, to be perfect, must engross the whole ability of the designer, it admits of no division of attention." (The carved oak Kenilworth buffet is shown on page 123. It is now in Warwick Castle.)

Wornum's strictures on another highlight of the Exhibition, the Mediaeval Court, disclose an un-Victorian attitude of mind. "We have in this collection," he wrote, "not an evidence of the application of a peculiar taste to modern and ordinary wants or purposes, but simply the copy of an old idea; old things in an old taste." He admitted that "Byzantine or Gothic symbolism, in as far as they generate beautiful forms, may claim our admiration," and instanced an inlaid table by Crace and Son, though he made no reference to the splendid vigour of Pugin's prie-dieu and carved oak cabinet, executed by that firm, and shown on page 318. Pugin almost alone of the Gothic revivalists rekindled the inspiration of mediaeval design; others were content to copy originals, and juggle with Gothic ornament. His name is excluded from the contents list; and though it appears in *The Official Descriptive and Illustrated Catalogue*, his influence on the arrangement and contents of the Mediaeval Court is not recorded, an omission corrected ten years later by his biographer, Benjamin Ferry.*

Wornum, preoccupied with the external evidence of style in ornament, made no mention of two exhibits that disclosed new technical achievements in the production of furniture, and although the editors of the *Catalogue* included them, they missed their significance. On page 152 two revolving chairs, with ornamental metal frames, made by the American Chair Company of New York were illustrated, described as

---

* *Recollections of A. N. Welby Pugin, and his father, Augustus Pugin.*
London: Edward Stanford, 1861.

"novelties," and praised for their comfort and elegant appearance. The editors missed the even greater significance of the table with the bentwood underframe, on page 296, by the Austrian designer Michael Thonet (1796–1871), and were concerned chiefly with the decorative character of the top, though they did notice that the legs were "bent from the solid piece. . . ." Thonet's bentwood chairs were ignored, and nobody apparently suspected that during the rest of the nineteenth century they would revolutionize the form of mass-produced seat furniture, compete with the popular traditional American forms of rocking chair, and challenge the use of cast iron for such household furnishings as hat and umbrella stands.

Wornum's conclusion that "The time has perhaps now gone by, at least in Europe, for the development of any particular or national style," is certainly supported by the array of designs adapted or copied from traditional styles, in nearly every branch of manufacture, from cast-iron fire grates and chimneypieces like those on pages 12, 35, 71,

Fig. 2.   Easy chair in papier-mâché with buttoned upholstery, designed by H. Fitz Cook and made by Jennings and Bettridge, of London and Birmingham. This was called the "Day Dreamer," and shown at the Great Exhibition of 1851. Reproduced, on a smaller scale, from the *Official Descriptive and Illustrated Catalogue*, Vol. II, plate 30.

75, and 205, to examples of revived rococo, such as the piano case, page 52; the silver toilet glass, page 113; the console-glass and table, page 257; the wine-cooler and pole screen, page 263; the console-table, page 267; and the Marlborough testimonial, page 309. The styles prevailing in the late sixteenth and early seventeenth centuries were also revived, and often labelled "Elizabethan," though the chair on page 66 thus described bears no resemblance to the joined back-stools or turned chairs of that period. Decorative motifs that had their origin in the Flemish and German copy books that circulated in England in the reigns of Elizabeth I and James I, were used lavishly. They appear on the "Kenilworth" buffet mentioned earlier, page 123; the marble chimneypiece and silver fire-irons, page 134; and the case of the table clock, page 213.

An original style was created when new uses were discovered for papier-mâché, for the material had been improved so that articles of large size could be made, including such decorative extravagancies as the "Victoria Regia" cot, on page 65, and the "Day Dreamer" chair, which is reproduced here (Figure 2) from the *Official Descriptive and Illustrated Catalogue*. The cane-seated single chair on page 156 represents a light and agreeable development of the Victorian vernacular style, made possible by an imaginative use of papier-mâché, wholly different in conception from the heavy-handed examples on page 209. The capacity for combining grace with luxurious elegance survived only in the design of vehicles, and those illustrated on pages 22, 148, 166, 196, 261, 276, 303 and 308 demonstrate that carriage-builders still retained a sense of style which designers and manufacturers in many other fields had lost.

In their Preface the editors of the *Catalogue* said: "The results of the Great Exhibition are pregnant with incalculable benefits to all classes of the community: the seed has been planted, of which the future is to produce the fruit: among the eager thousands whose interest was excited and whose curiosity was gratified, were many who obtained profitable suggestions at every visit . . . ." Wornum in his essay said that the Exhibition "is of all things best calculated to advance our National Taste, by bringing in close contiguity the various productions of nearly all the nations of the earth in any way distinguished for ornamental manufactures. The distinctive characteristics of each are so many elements of novelty of arrangements which every nation may appropriate according to its own views and practice."

Unfortunately, the Exhibition confused taste, strengthened the belief that design and ornament were identical, and the results of that confusion persisted until the beginning of the First World War in 1914. This reprint of *The Art-Journal Catalogue* has again made widely available a key work for studying the origins of late Victorian taste.

JOHN GLOAG

THE
CRYSTAL PALACE
EXHIBITION

ST. GEORGE

FROM THE MEDAL BY W. WYON, R.A., EXECUTED FOR

HIS ROYAL HIGHNESS PRINCE ALBERT

THE ART-JOURNAL ILLUSTRATED CATALOGUE.

THE INDUSTRY OF ALL NATIONS 1851

LUKE LIMNER DEL.

LONDON : PUBLISHED FOR THE PROPRIETORS, BY GEORGE VIRTUE.

BRADBURY AND EVANS, (PRINTERS EXTRAORDINARY TO THE QUEEN), WHITEFRIARS.

LONDON
BRADBURY AND EVANS (PRINTERS EXTRAORDINARY TO THE QUEEN), WHITEFRIARS.

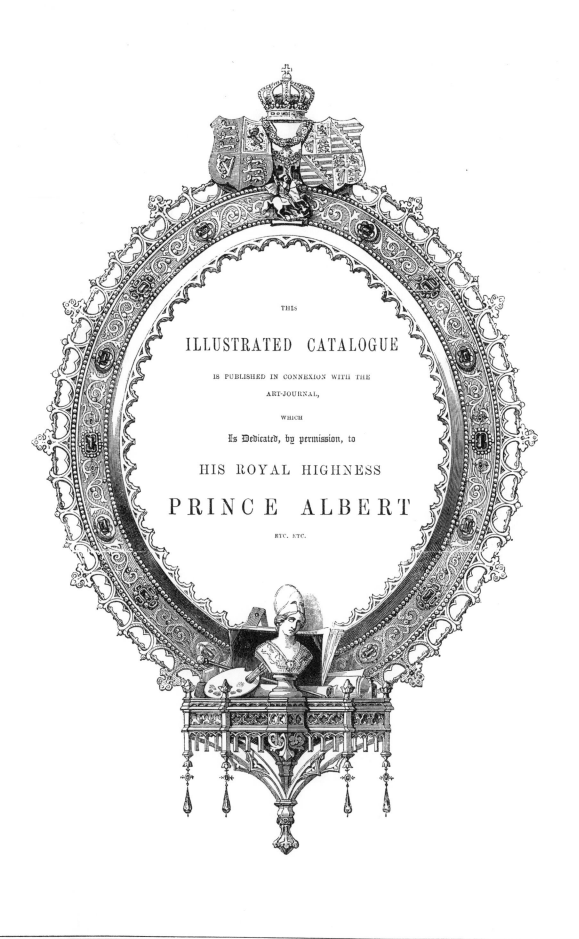

THIS

ILLUSTRATED CATALOGUE

IS PUBLISHED IN CONNEXION WITH THE

ART-JOURNAL,

WHICH

Is Dedicated, by permission, to

HIS ROYAL HIGHNESS

PRINCE ALBERT

ETC. ETC.

PREFACE.

E submit this Volume to the public in full assurance of its success. It will be obvious that neither cost nor labour has been spared to render it, in all respects, a worthy record of the great gathering of Works of Art and Industry to which an illustrious Prince invited all the Nations of the World—and to which there was a cordial and grateful response.

We have studied to introduce into this Catalogue, engravings, the most interesting and the most suggestive, of the various objects exhibited; to include, as far as possible, all such as might gratify or instruct; and thus to supply sources of after-education to manufacturers and artisans of all classes, and of all countries; rendering the Exhibition practically beneficial, long after its contents have been distributed. From the Exhibitors, universally, we received zealous aid and encouragement; and the result has been, we hope and believe, to satisfy them, generally, as to selection and manner of execution.

We have obtained from high and experienced authorities, Essays, such as might be permanently useful, in illustrating the leading objects of the Exhibition; and we close the Volume with the Prize Essay, for which we have awarded the sum of 100 Guineas. To the accomplished Professors who have thus co-operated with us, our best thanks are due: we are also bound to express our acknowledgments to Messrs. Dalziel, the eminent engravers, who superintended the engravings, and whose duty has been discharged with great ability, punctuality, and care; to Messrs. Nicholls and other artists by whom we have been assisted; to the Printers, Messrs. Bradbury and Evans, to whose exertions we are largely indebted for having placed at our entire disposal no fewer than thirty presses during a period of eight months, and who may refer to this publication as evidence not only of their skill in wood-block printing, but of the immense resources of their establishment; and to others by whose aid we have been enabled to complete a work which involved considerable toil, anxiety, and attention, on the part of all who were engaged in its production.

It may be permitted us to state that but for its association with THE ART-JOURNAL, it would have been impossible to have published this collection at less than four times the price at which it is now issued: and, perhaps, but for the experience and machinery possessed by the conductors of that Journal, it could not have been produced at all. We commenced our labours—and announced this Catalogue—immediately after the promulgation of the plan and the appointment of a Commission: personally visiting most of the principal cities of Europe: communicating with all the chief manufacturers of Great Britain: and arranging for such aids as might enable us to complete our undertaking with regularity, and as early as possible after the opening of the Exhibition.

The results of the Great Exhibition are pregnant with incalculable benefits to all classes of the community: the seed has been planted, of which the future is to produce the fruit: among the eager thousands whose interest was excited and whose curiosity was gratified, were many who obtained profitable suggestions at every visit: the manufacturer and the artisan have thus learned the most valuable of all lessons,—the disadvantages under which they had laboured, the deficiencies they had to remedy, and the prejudices they had to overcome.

But it is to the honour of Great Britain that, notwithstanding the generous risk incurred by inviting competitors from all the nations of the world—prepared as they had been by long years of successful study and practical experience—the fame of British manufacturers has been augmented by this contest: and there can be no doubt, that when His Royal Highness Prince Albert issues his summons to another competition, British supremacy will be manifested in every branch of Industrial Art.

In terminating our labours, we may hope that a project we have repeatedly and earnestly advocated in THE ART-JOURNAL, and which we presume to regard as, in some degree, the issue of our efforts to connect the Fine Arts with the Industrial Arts (a procedure originating with that Journal, having never been attempted elsewhere in Europe, and in which for a long period we had to contend against difficulties that seemed insurmountable), will derive some of its advantages from the Report thus made in this Illustrated Catalogue. Upon this topic it is unnecessary for us to dilate: the readers of THE ART-JOURNAL are well aware of our efforts to promote the interests of the manufacturer: to induce his advance, on the one hand; and, on the other, to lead the public to appreciate his improvements: to report his progress, and to make him acquainted with the progress of his competitors: to furnish him with such information as might be gathered from the best instructors —and, by immediately connecting him with the artist, to direct him to the safest sources of Art-education.

Our exertions have been fully appreciated: THE ART-JOURNAL has obtained a success unprecedented in periodical literature: we have the happiness to contrast the state of British Art-Manufacture in the year 1846 (when our labours in this direction may be said to have commenced), with its position in the memorable year 1851; and we trust that no one who has traced our course will consider us presumptuous in feeling that in the Great Exhibition of the Industry of All Nations, we have received our " exceeding great reward."

THE TABLE OF CONTENTS

ENGRAVINGS OF WORKS EXHIBITED.

TABLE OF CONTENTS.

TABLE OF CONTENTS.

ix

TABLE OF CONTENTS.

[TO THE BINDER.—This Table of Contents will be sufficiently instructive to the Binder as to the arrangement of the Pages: he will observe that each article is paged with a distinguishing mark; as thus, I*, I† ; and that the pages containing the "Engravings of Works Exhibited," are the only pages which contain no such mark.]

HISTORY OF THE GREAT EXHIBITION.

"IT IS MY ANXIOUS DESIRE TO PROMOTE AMONG NATIONS THE CULTIVATION OF ALL THOSE ARTS WHICH ARE FOSTERED BY PEACE, AND WHICH IN THEIR TURN CONTRIBUTE TO MAINTAIN THE PEACE OF THE WORLD."—THE QUEEN

WE commence this ILLUSTRATED CATALOGUE of the principal contents of the GREAT EXHIBITION with a brief but succinct History of the Building—and of the Project from its commencement up to the present time.

The experiment of an Exhibition of the Industry of all the civilised Nations of the World has been tried, and has succeeded beyond the most sanguine expectations of its projectors. It is, indeed, scarcely possible to instance any great enterprise of modern date which has so completely satisfied the anticipations which had been formed of its results. Differing from most other institutions for benefiting the great family of mankind, which have required time and experience to mature, it has sprung, like Minerva from the brain of Jove "full armed," into life and activity; resembling the goddess, however, only in her more pacific attributes; her love of the olive tree, and her patronage of the Industrial Arts. Other nations have devised means for the display and encouragement of their own arts and manufactures; but it has been reserved for England to provide an arena for the exhibition of the industrial triumphs of the whole world. She has offered an hospitable invitation to surrounding nations to bring the choicest products of their industry to her capital, and there to enter into an amicable competition with each other and with herself; and she has endeavoured to secure to them the certainty of an impartial verdict on their efforts. Whatever be the extent of the benefit which this great demonstration may confer upon the Industrial Arts of the world, it cannot fail to soften, if not to eradicate altogether, the prejudices and animosities which have so long retarded the happiness of nations; and to promote those feelings of "peace and good will" which are among the surest antecedents of their prosperity; a peace, which Shakspeare has told us—

> "Is of the nature of a conquest;
> For then both parties nobly are subdued,
> And neither party loses."

It forms no part of our present object to enter, with any degree of minuteness, into the history of exhibitions of this class; but a brief glance at the origin and progress of such associations in France and England may not be considered irrelevant. So far back as 1756-7, the Society of Arts of London offered prizes for specimens of various manufactures—tapestry, carpets, porcelain, among others—and publicly exhibited the articles which were thus collected; and in 1761 and 1762 the artists of Great Britain formed themselves into two societies for the exposition and sale of works of art. A few years afterwards (1768), the Royal Academy of Painting was established, as a private society, under the immediate patronage of the Crown, and Sir Joshua Reynolds appointed its President. Since then, numerous institutions of a similar character have been set on foot in this country, with considerable advantage to the branches of industry they were intended to benefit. France must, however, be regarded as the originator of exhibitions which are, in character and plan, most analogous to that on whose history we are about to enter. We gather from the historical essay of Messieurs Challamel and Burat, and the pamphlet of the Marquis d'Aveze on the subject, that, shortly after that nobleman's appointment to be Commissioner of the Royal Manufactories of the Gobelins, of Sèvres, and of the Savonnerie, in 1797, he found that two years of neglect had reduced the workmen almost to starvation, whilst it had left the respective warehouses filled with their choicest productions. In this crisis, the idea occurred to him of converting the chateau of St. Cloud, then uninhabited, into a bazaar, for the exhibition and disposal, by lottery, of the large stock of tapestry, china, and carpets, on hand in these establishments. Having obtained the consent of the government to his proposal, he set about arranging the various objects in the apartments of the chateau; but, on the day fixed for the opening of his bazaar, he was compelled, by a decree of the Directory, banishing the nobility, to quit France at a very short notice, and the project fell to the ground. On his return to Paris in the ensuing year, the Marquis planned another exhibition of an even more important kind. Having collected a great many objects of taste and *vertu*, he distributed them throughout the house and gardens of the Maison d'Orsay, Rue de Varennes, with a view to their sale. In looking over the catalogue of objects of which this collection was composed, we can hardly help being struck with its aristocratical character. The richest furniture and marqueterie produced by Boule, Riessner, and Jacob; the finest clocks and watches of L'Epine and Leroy; the superb china of Sèvres, of Angoulême, and of Nast; the most elegantly bound books, fully confirming the traditional excellence of Grolier and De Thou; silks of Lyons; historical pictures by Vincent and David; bronzes, and sculpture; served to show to what class of the community French manufacture had, up to that period, been mainly indebted for support. The success which attended the efforts of the Marquis led to the adoption of his idea by the government, and the establishment of the first official Exposition, on the very spot, on the Champ de Mars, on which the army had held a triumphal show of its splendid collection of Italian spoils. Six weeks after that fête, the nation erected on the same spot a Temple of Industry for the exhibition of more pacific trophies; an edifice surrounded by sixty porticos, filled with the most beautiful objects that had been manufactured in France. The system of deciding on the comparative merits of the various exhibitors by juries, composed of gentlemen distinguished for their taste, was then, for the first time, adopted. Prizes were awarded for watches, mathematical instruments, painting china, etc. The success of this Exposition was so great, that the government resolved to repeat it annually; but, in spite of the circular of the Minister of the Interior to that effect, the political commotions of the times prevented him from repeating it, until the year 1801, and then only at the instance of the First Consul, who visited the factories and ateliers of the principal towns in France, with several men of science, for the purpose of convincing the manufacturers of the importance to themselves of supporting such an undertaking. This second display took place in the quadrangle of the Louvre, in a temporary building erected for the occasion. Notwithstanding the difficulties which had attended its establishment, 200 exhibitors were competitors for the prizes. Upon this occasion, ten gold, twenty silver, and thirty bronze medals, were awarded; one of the last having been adjudged to the celebrated Jacquard, for his now famous machine.

It must not be overlooked that even at this early period the Juries awarded prizes for improvements in the quality of wool as a raw material, and for excellence in woollen and cotton fabrics. The third exhibition took place on the same spot in 1802; and on that occasion no fewer than 600 exhibitors competed for the prizes. The popularity of these expositions led to the formation of the *Société d'Encouragement*, which aided very importantly the industrial efforts of the French manufacturers. It is a remarkable fact, however, that whilst in France the Society of Arts and Manufactures owes its origin to these public expositions of the products of its industry, we are in England wholly indebted for exhibitions of this kind to our Society of Arts. The fourth exhibition of French industrial products took place in 1806, in a building erected for the purpose in front of the *Hôpital des Invalides*; when the exhibitors had increased to 1400, and it was found necessary to keep open the doors for 24 days. Here, for the first time, were displayed the printed cottons of Mulhausen and Logelbach; silk, thread, and cotton lace; blonde, cloth and mixed goods. Among the improvements for which prizes were awarded, were the manufacture of iron

by the aid of coke instead of charcoal, and that of steel by a process wholly unknown till then.

The disturbed condition of France, arising out of her wars with her European neighbours, prevented the fifth exhibition from taking place until 1819, when it was inaugurated on the fête of St. Louis, and continued open for thirty-five days. The number of exhibitors had increased to 1700. The sixth exhibition took place in 1823 on the same spot as its predecessor, and remained open 50 days. Great improvement was manifest in the manufacture of many of the articles; in machinery more especially. It was on this occasion that the model of the first French suspension bridge over the river Rhone, by M. Leguin, was exhibited by its engineer. The next Industrial Exposition occurred in 1827, when a large building was erected for it in the *Place de la Concorde*. The eighth was held in 1834; the ninth in 1839, when no fewer than 4381 competitors entered the field; the tenth in 1844, when 3960 manufacturers exhibited their productions; and the eleventh in 1849, in the Champs Elysées, when the number of competitors had increased to 4494. [Both these exhibitions were fully reported and extensively illustrated in the ART-JOURNAL.] It is true that other nations had followed the example of France, but without achieving her success. The Belgian and Bavarian governments have both had their industrial exhibitions [the Exhibition at Brussels was fully reported and illustrated in the ART-JOURNAL]; but neither of them call for especial notice.

In this country, during the last dozen years, there have been many exhibitions of this description; but, with here and there an exception, they have differed little in character from the ordinary Bazaar. Manchester, Leeds, and Dublin (the last so early as 1827) had all opened bazaars for the sale of the productions of the surrounding neighbourhood; but the first building in this country devoted expressly to the exhibition of manufactures, was that erected at Birmingham in 1849 on the occasion of the visit of the British Association. The building, on that occasion, included a space of 10,000 square feet, independently of a corridor of 800 feet, which connected the main exhibition room with Bingley House, within whose grounds it had been located; so that, including the rooms of the old mansion, the total area covered by the Exhibition was equal to 12,800 square feet. The cost of the building did not exceed 1300*l*. This and the Free Trade Bazaar, held in Covent Garden in 1845, approached nearer to the French expositions in the variety and extent of the national productions they comprised, than any of their predecessors in this country. [Both these exhibitions —that of the Free Trade Bazaar, and that held in Birmingham—were fully reported and extensively illustrated in the ART-JOURNAL.]

The idea of an Exhibition which should include specimens of the Industrial Products of various nations originated, in the early part of 1849, with M. Buffet, the French Minister of Agriculture and Commerce; and with a view to ascertain the opinions of the manufacturers on the subject, circulars were addressed by him to the Chambers of Commerce throughout France, proposing that specimens of the arts and manufactures of neighbouring countries should be admitted to the approaching exposition. The replies which were received to this suggestion were so unfavourable to its adoption, that M. Buffet was induced at once to abandon the idea. If, therefore, the merit of having originated exhibitions of her own manufactures belongs to France, it is to his Royal Highness PRINCE ALBERT that the more noble and disinterested plan of throwing open an institution of this description to the competition of the whole world, is exclusively due; and his suggestion has been carried out in a spirit every way worthy its grandeur and generosity.

The great success which attended the French Industrial Exposition of 1844 had caused representations to be made to the English government of the advantages which would accrue to our commerce from a similar exhibition in this country; but the efforts which were made to obtain its co-operation appear to have been wholly unsuccessful. In 1848, a proposal to establish a self-supporting exhibition of the products of British industry, to be directed by a

Royal Commission, was submitted by H.R.H. Prince Albert to the government, but with no better success; and it then became apparent that no reliance whatever could be placed upon the active support of Her Majesty's ministers for any such plan. They had, in all probability, no objection to see the experiment tried, but were evidently unwilling to commit themselves to any responsibility in behalf of a scheme which seemed to be beset by so many difficulties. Meanwhile, the popular feeling in favour of such an undertaking was rapidly strengthening, and the success which has attended the experiment may, in a great measure, be referred to the freedom of action which this dissociation from the timid councils of the government secured for its projectors. It may be proper, in this place, to remark that, excepting in facilitating its correspondence with foreign nations; the provision of a site for the building; and the organisation of the police; no assistance has been either sought or obtained from the government for the present Exhibition; whilst, in every case in which it has been attended by expense, the cost has been defrayed out of the funds at the disposal of the Executive Committee.

The initiative in those inquiries which were indispensable to the due consideration of the means by which the idea of an Exhibition for all Nations was to be carried out, was taken by the Society of Arts, a committee of whose members was formed in June, 1845, for the purpose; the funds for defraying the preliminary expenses of which were subscribed among themselves. An inquiry having been instituted for the purpose of ascertaining how far the manufacturers of Great Britain were favourable to such a design, with no very encouraging result, the idea was for a time abandoned. In 1847, the Council of the Society launched their pilot balloon in the shape of an Exhibition of British Manufactures, professedly the first of a series; and encouraged by its success, repeated the experiment in the ensuing year; when the intention of its executive was announced, to establish an annual competition of the same kind, with a view to the opening of a quinqennial exhibition for the industrial products of all nations to be held in 1851. As an accessory to their plan, the council

THE MEDAL OF MR. G. G. ADAMS.

THE MEDAL OF MR. LEONARD C. WYON.

THE MEDAL OF M. BONNARDEL.

sought to connect with it the various Schools of Design established in our larger towns, and obtained the co-operation of the Board of Trade, through its president, Mr. Labouchere, in that object. They also secured the promise of a site from the Earl of Carlisle, then Commissioner of Woods and Forests; who offered them the central area of Somerset House, or any other government ground at his disposal which seemed adapted for their purposes. The Exhibition of 1849, confined for the most part to works in the precious metals, several of the more important of which were contributed by Her Majesty, proved more successful than either of the two that had preceded it, and stimulated proportionally the exertions of the Council. A report on the French Exposition of the same year, by Mr. Digby Wyatt, had, moreover, strongly confirmed them in their conviction of the utility of such an exhibition in this country.

Meanwhile, H. R. H. Prince Albert was not only privy to, but entirely approved of these proceedings; and, on the termination of the Parliamentary session of 1849, took the subject under his immediate superintendence. But, indeed, for his indefatigable perseverance, his courageous defiance of all risks of failure, his remarkable sagacity in matters of business, and the influence which attached to his support, the whole project, notwithstanding the great exertions which had been made to secure its realisation, must have fallen to the ground. The maturely considered views of his Royal Highness, and the patriotic objects he proposed in making this great peace-offering to mankind, are admirably set forth in the speech delivered by him on the occasion of the banquet given by Mr. Alderman Farncomb, then Lord Mayor of London, to the municipal authorities of the United Kingdom in support of the project. "The Exhibition of 1851 would," he said, "afford a true test of the point of development at which the whole of mankind has arrived in this great task, and a new starting point from which all nations would be able to direct their further exertions." It is difficult to assign to Prince Albert the degree of praise which is really his due on this occasion without incurring the suspicion of being in some degree influenced by the exalted position he holds in the country. "It is," says Coleridge, "one of the most mischievous effects of flattery that it renders honourable natures more slow and reluctant in expressing their real feelings in praise of the deserving, than for the interests of truth and virtue might be desired." The remark applies with peculiar force to a person of His Royal Highness's rank. Rather than incur the imputation of sycophancy, his admirers have sometimes been led to do less than justice to the very prominent part he has taken in this project, and to the consummate skill with which he has smoothed down all opposition to it. In a word, for the World's Exhibition, the world is entirely indebted to the Prince Consort.

On the 29th of June, 1849, at a meeting, at Buckingham Palace, of several of the gentlemen, who afterwards became members of the Royal Commission, and Prince Albert, his Royal Highness communicated his plan for the formation of a great collection of works of Industry and Art in London, in 1851, for the purposes of exhibition, of competition, and of encouragement; when he proposed that these contributions should consist of four great divisions, namely : raw materials ; machinery and mechanical inventions; manufactures; and sculpture and plastic art generally; and the best proof we could adduce of the sagacity by which his suggestions were characterised is to be found in the brilliant success which has attended their almost literal adoption. At the second meeting for the same object, held at Osborne House on the 14th July, 1849, which was attended among other distinguished supporters of the project, by the late Sir Robert Peel, His Royal Highness gave a general outline of the plan of operations he recommended, which met with the unanimous approbation of his fellow labourers. These suggestions comprised the formation of a Royal Commission, its duties and powers; the definition of the nature of the Exhibition, and of the best mode of conducting its proceedings; the determination of the method of deciding the prizes, and the responsibility of the decision; and the means of raising a prize fund, and providing for the necessary expenses which the permanent establishment of quinquennial exhibitions would involve. The amount which it was proposed to distribute in prizes was 20,000*l*, and the lowest estimate for a suitable building did not fall below 50,000*l*. He also pointed out the advantages of the site which has since been adopted, and recommended an early application to the crown for permission to appropriate it.

Impressed with the truth of the proverb, *Ce n'est que le premier pas qui coûte*, the council of the Society of Arts, after much fruitless negotiation with other parties, entered into an engagement with Messrs. Munday, the well-known contractors, by which those gentlemen undertook to deposit a prize fund of 20,000*l*.; to erect a suitable building; to find offices ; and to advance the money requisite for all preliminary expenses ; and to take the whole risk of loss ; on the following conditions: The 20,000*l*. prize fund, the cost of the building, and five per cent on all advances, to be repaid out of the first receipts ; the residue to be divided into three equal parts; one part to be paid over at once to the Society of Arts, in aid of future exhibitions ; and out of the other two parts all other incidental costs, such as those of general management and preliminary expenses ; the residue, if any, to be the remuneration of the contractors for their outlay, trouble, and risk. Messrs. Munday subsequently consented, instead of this division, to receive such part of the surplus only, if any, as after payment of all expenses might be awarded by arbitration. An executive committee of four members, who became subsequently the executive committee of the Royal Commission, was then formed, who induced the contractors to allow them the option of determining the contract any time before the first of February, 1850. In such an event, however, Messrs. Munday's claims to compensation for their outlay and risk were to be adjusted by arbitration. After remaining out of their money more than a year, Messrs. Munday obtained very recently, an award of 5000*l*. with interest.

The pecuniary part of the undertaking having thus been provided for, the next object was to satisfy the government of the desire of the public for the proposed Exhibition, in order to warrant the issue of a Royal Commission for its management. With this view, a deputation from the Executive Committee proceeded to the manufacturing districts to collect the necessary information ; and after visiting sixty-five of the most important towns and cities of the United Kingdom, brought back with them strong manifestations of the popular desire in the shape of documents in which nearly 5,000 influential persons had registered their names as promoters of the project. About the same time Mr. Scott Russell, having occasion to visit several of the states included in the Zollverein, found that the advantages which it offered to the commerce of the world were everywhere appreciated, and received the most cordial offers of co-operation from a great number of influential persons in those countries. On the presentation of these reports to the government, the Royal Commission was issued, and at their first meeting on the 11th January, 1850, they decided on availing themselves of the election which had been reserved for them by the Society of

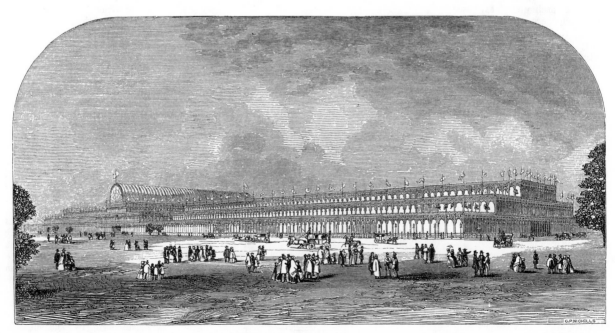

EXTERIOR OF THE BUILDING FOR THE GREAT EXHIBITION (SOUTH SIDE).

Arts, and rescinded the contract with Messrs. Munday; thus relying for their means of carrying out their views, in the first instance, wholly upon voluntary contributions.

How the appeal of the Commissioners to the country was responded to is sufficiently known. Meetings having taken place in all parts of the United Kingdom, subscriptions began to flow in, in a highly encouraging manner. On the 17th of October, 1849, the Lord Mayor of London called a meeting at the Egyptian Hall to receive a deputation of the members of the Society of Arts, charged by Prince Albert to explain the outlines of His Royal Highness's proposal for a Great Exhibition of the Industry of All Nations, to be held in London, in the year 1851. This meeting was attended by nearly four hundred of the most influential merchants, bankers, and traders, of London, and nothing could be more cordial than the spirit displayed by almost every person who assisted at it. Mr. Cole, who was the exponent of Prince Albert's views on the occasion, gave, in a speech of considerable ability, an interesting account of the reception the project had met with from the large body of manufacturers in the provinces, whose adhesion he had succeeded in obtaining. The feeling in favour of an international Exhibition appears to have been almost unanimous. Other meetings in the city, and other parts of the metropolis, were subsequently held, and a large amount of subscriptions collected. Whilst matters were progressing thus favourably, the Lord Mayor of London conceived the magnificent idea of inviting the chief magistrates of the various towns, cities, and boroughs, throughout the United Kingdom, to a grand banquet, at the Mansion-House, with the view of promoting the success of the Exhibition. The results of this *réunion* were, in the highest degree, satisfactory. Nearly the whole body of provincial Mayors accepted the invitation, and were thus inspired with something like a personal interest in the success of the undertaking. They had, moreover, the advantage of receiving Prince Albert's explanations from his own lips. Among the voices raised in favour of an international Exhibition on this occasion, were those of Lord John Russell, Lord Stanley, the Archbishop of Canterbury, the French Ambassador, and the late lamented Sir Robert Peel. On the succeeding day a meeting of the public functionaries who were present at the dinner, took place in the Egyptian Hall for business purposes, when the ball was set moving in good earnest.

The Commissioners having revised their original intention to give large money prizes, invited, by public advertisement, artists of all countries to compete for the designs for the reverses of three bronze medals intended to form the respective prizes, which should be illustrative of the objects of the Exhibition; and offered three prizes of 100*l.* each for the three subjects which should be selected for that purpose, and three prizes of 50*l.* for the three best designs which might not be accepted. In consequence of this advertisement no fewer than one hundred and twenty-nine designs were sent in, and were publicly exhibited in the rooms of the Royal Society of Arts. The judges appointed by the Commissioners were Lord Colborne, W. Dyce, Esq., R.A., J. Gibson, Esq., R.A., M. Eugene Lami, C. Newton, Esq., Herr J. D. Passavant, and Dr. Gustave Waagen; who on the 29th June decided in favour of the following gentlemen:—The first prizes of 100*l.* each, were awarded to, 1. Hyppolyte Bonnardel, of Paris. 2. Leonard C. Wyon, of London. 3. G. G. Adams, of London. The second prizes of 50*l.* each, were awarded to, 4. John Hancock, of London. 5. L. Wiener, of Brussells. 6. M. Gayrard, of Paris.

The medal of M. Bonnardel is decidedly the most ambitious of the three. It represents Britannia standing on a platform, with outstretched arms, and a crown in each hand with which she is in the act of decorating, simultaneously, the brows of Mercury, and a female he is holding by the hand, who may be presumed to be Industry. Flags of different nations make up the background. Motto—" Est etiam in magno quædam respublica mundo."

Mr. Wyon's design represents Britannia seated and in the act of placing a laurel wreath upon the head of a figure emblematical of Industry, whilst she extends her right hand as if to raise her up. Behind her are impersonations of the four quarters of the globe by whom Industry has been conducted to Britannia. To the right are emblems of the four sections : 1. The cotton plant and wheatsheaf; 2. A wheel ; 3. A bale of goods ; 4. A vase. Motto—" Dissociata locis concordi pace ligavit."

Mr. Adams's medal presents a gracefully modelled group of Fame crowning Industry, and Commerce looking on with approving eye. Industry has a distaff in her hand, and appears to be sitting on a cornucopia.

In July, 1850, letters patent were issued, incorporating the Commissioners under the title of "The Commissioners for the Exhibition of 1851," and the charter was accepted on the

WESTERN ENTRANCE TO THE GREAT EXHIBITION.

15th August. A guarantee fund of 230,000l. had been subscribed by a limited number of gentlemen, favourable to the Exhibition, one of whom opened the list with a subscription of 50,000l. Upon this security the Bank of England undertook to make the necessary advances. On the 21st of February preceding, the Building Committee ventured to recommend that upwards of sixteen acres should be covered in.

With a view to give Foreign nations as much time for preparation as possible, the Commissioners resolved, long before they had decided on the size and character of the building, to divide a certain large extent of space among foreign countries, amounting in the whole to 210,000 superficial feet, or rather more than the entire space which France had occupied for its two expositions of 1844 and 1849. Subsequently, the quantities of space allotted to foreign nations was increased; France obtaining 65,000 feet instead of 50,000. A definite amount of space proportioned to their presumed wants was also allotted to each of the British Colonies. With the view of avoiding, in the first instance, the confusion that would have arisen from the collection of duties for the

objects imported, the government was induced to treat the Exhibition as a bonded warehouse. On the 31st of October, 1850, the last day on which applications for space could be entertained, the whole of the demands for horizontal (floor and counter) space exceeded 417,000 superficial feet; being beyond the amount of available space for the United Kingdom, by about 210,000 superficial feet. Every class appears however to have been satisfied with the final allocations, which were the best that could have been made under the circumstances.

When the time arrived for making definite arrangements for the erection of the building, the Commissioners had only 35,000l. in hand; and, notwithstanding the guarantee to which they had themselves largely subscribed, they must have felt themselves committed to a very deep responsibility. Nothing daunted, however, an invitation was addressed, through the public prints, to architects of all nations, to furnish designs for an edifice, the roof of which was to cover 700,000 square feet; and the area of which, including the open spaces, was not to exceed 900,000 feet. Other conditions were enumerated which

SOUTHERN ENTRANCE TO THE TRANSEPT.

showed that the whole of the details had been carefully and judiciously considered. Although the time allowed for the preparation of the drawings was only a month, there were no fewer than two hundred and thirty-three competitors, many of whom sent in designs of a highly elaborate character. Of these, thirty-eight, or one-sixth of the whole, were from foreigners; 128 from London and its vicinity; and 51 from the provincial towns of England. The duty of examining, classifying, and comparing them, devolved on Mr. Digby Wyatt, who embodied the result of his investigation in a report. After fifteen protracted sittings, the Building Committee arrived at the "unanimous conclusion that, able and admirable as many of these designs appeared to be, there was yet no single one so accordant with the peculiar objects in view, either in the principle, or detail of its arrangements, as to warrant them in recommending it for adoption." This report was presented to the Royal Commissioners on the 9th of May. The rejection of the whole of the plans of the competing architects created, as was natural, no ordinary dissatisfaction; a feeling which was in no respect diminished by the fact that the Building Committee had prepared a plan of their own; and, assisted by Mr. Digby Wyatt, Mr. Charles Heard Wild, and Mr. Owen Jones, had completed extensive working drawings which they had caused to be lithographed. Their next step was to issue invitations for tenders to erect the building; requesting from the respective competitors, in addition, such suggestions and modifications, accompanied by estimates of cost, as might seem likely to effect a reduction in the general expense. The design of the Building Committee comprehended an edifice 2200 feet long, and 450 feet wide. Into any detailed description of it, however, it is foreign to our purpose to enter; suffice it to say that this child of many fathers was condemned, not less for its extraordinary ugliness, than that it would have been unnecessarily large, cumbrous, and costly, for a purpose avowedly temporary. Meanwhile, the contractors found some

difficulty in getting their tenders ready by the 10th of May. On that day, however, nineteen were sent in; but of these only eight professed to comprehend the execution of the whole of the work. The amounts of the remaining eleven competitors varied from 120,000*l.* to 150,000*l.*: and this, for the use only of the materials for the building. The Building Committee defended their edifice in an elaborate report, setting forth its economy and good taste. Public opinion was, however, decidedly against its adoption; and fortunately, a gentleman, not an architect, came "to the rescue."

Among the contractors who had accepted the invitation of the Building Committee, was the firm of Fox & Henderson, who, availing themselves of the permission to alter and amend the plan of the Committee, contained in the latter part of the report, presented a tender for a building of an entirely different character from that which had been suggested by the Committee. This, we need scarcely add, was the plan which, with certain modifications and additions, was ultimately adopted; and for which, notwithstanding all that has been said to the contrary, the public is wholly indebted to Mr. Paxton. He was, as he himself tells us, at that time occupied in erecting a house for the Victoria Regia, in the Gardens of the Duke of Devonshire, at Chatsworth, and to that circumstance the Crystal Palace may be said to owe its direct origin. The accounts which have been given by Mr. Paxton, Mr. Fox, and Mr. Barry, of their respective shares in the production of the accepted plan, are not strictly reconcileable with each other; but that the idea, in a state of maturity which demanded no great effort of mind to make it more complete, originated with Mr. Paxton, does not admit of a question. The very nature of that idea which rendered a single section of the building completely explanatory of the whole, would seem to have rendered elaborate plans of the proposed edifice, in its entirety, less a work of mind than of mechanical dexterity. A single bay of 24 feet square would,

INTERIOR OF THE TRANSEPT, AS SEEN FROM THE SOUTH ENTRANCE.

if we except the transept and its semicircular roof, supply the means of making a correct drawing of the whole; and if it be correct, as stated by Mr. Paxton at the dinner given to him at Derby, on the 6th of August, that his original sketch on a sheet of blotting paper indicates the principal features of the building as it now stands as much as the most finished drawings which have been made since, there can be no excuse for attempting to deprive him of any portion of the merit of the invention. But he appears to have done considerably more than merely furnish the idea. In nine days from that on which he had made the blotting paper sketch, he was in possession of nine plans, all, with a single exception, prepared by his own hand. And although his suggestion to Messrs. Fox & Henderson was offered so late as the 22nd June, 1850, his plan was engraved and published in the *Illustrated News* of the 6th July. There can be no doubt that the great experience of Mr. Fox enabled him, after consulting with

Mr. Cole, to adapt the drawings more to the arrangements adopted by the Committee in the plan they had themselves prepared, than Mr. Paxton had done: but in a case like this, the first idea is considerably more than half the battle. Mr. Fox prepared, he tells us, the working drawings, and made everything ship-shape; but to the fullest extent he admits that all the leading features of the plan, including each progressive improvement of any importance, were suggested by the originator of the general idea. At one of the meetings of the Building Committee, it was suggested that the transept, at the sacrifice of not dividing the building into two equal parts, should include the larger trees; but there appeared to be a good deal of difficulty in adopting such a recommendation, as at that time the whole of the roof was intended to be flat. Having promised to see what could be done in the matter, Mr. Paxton accompanied Mr. Fox to his office, and whilst he was occupied in arranging the ground-

THE TRANSEPT, FROM THE NORTH SIDE.

plan, so as to bring the trees into the centre, he "hit upon the idea of covering the transept with a circular roof, similar to that on the great conservatory at Chatsworth, and made a sketch of it, which was copied that night by one of Mr. Fox's draughtsmen." In a recent letter to the "Times" newspaper, Mr. Barry, in reference to this statement, declares that at the first presentation of Mr. Paxton's design to the Building Committee, as well as to the Royal Commission, and before he had offered any suggestion on the subject, he recommended, very strongly, the addition of a vaulted roof, not only to the transept, but also over the nave; and submitted to the Commissioners a sketch showing the effect of such an addition. The probability, therefore, is, that the two gentlemen hit upon the same idea at pretty nearly the same moment. There is, however, at all events, no pretext for imputing to either of them a desire to claim for himself a merit which does not belong to him. The Royal Commissioners themselves, in their official report, distinctly acknowledge the services which were rendered to the edifice by Mr. Barry's judicious suggestions, and whilst they compliment Mr. Paxton on the "grand effect produced by his happy idea of raising the semi-cylindrical vault of the transept above the tiers of terraces which extend on either side of it," acknowledge that, "for much of its grace of proportion and beauty of form, the building is indebted to Mr. Barry;" and that "upon the form and distribution of the arches and filling in frames, as well as of the columns, the suggestions of that gentleman exercised a happy influence." We doubt, however, if the adoption of these suggestions should be allowed to detract in any respect from the *éclat* due to Mr. Paxton as the legitimate parent of the Crystal Palace.

After consulting the iron masters, glass manufacturers, and others, on whose co-operation they were compelled, in a great measure, to depend for their means of fulfilling their proposals, Messrs. Fox & Henderson sent in their tenders, and on the 16th were verbally informed that they were accepted. On the 26th July, the Committee expressed a wish that they should commence operations; but as no Royal Charter could be obtained until the succeeding year, and as the solicitor to the Treasury was of opinion that until that had been obtained, the Commissioners could not legally act, the works must have stood still, but for the good understanding and mutual confidence, which subsisted between Messrs. Fox & Henderson and themselves. Rather than that any delay should take place, they agreed to proceed at once, and to incur the risk whatever it might be of waiting for the Royal Charter. To avoid unnecessary complication, Mr. William Cubitt was invested with absolute power to arrange with Messrs. Fox & Henderson all the details connected with the arduous task on which they were about to enter. On the 30th July, they obtained possession of the ground, and proceeded to take the necessary levels and surveys, and to fix the position of the various points. The working drawings, all of which he made himself, occupied Mr. Fox 18 hours a day for seven weeks; and as these left his hands, his partner Mr. Henderson directed the preparation of the iron work and other materials required for the construction of the building. As the drawings proceeded, calculations of strength were entered into; and so soon as a number of the important parts were prepared, such as the cast-iron girders and wrought-iron trusses, Mr. Cubitt was invited to witness a set of experiments illustrative of the correctness of these calculations. The greatest load it was possible for it to receive having been placed upon each part, it was distinctly shown that it would bear four times that weight without a fracture. As the works advanced, the safety of the edifice was much discussed in the public prints, and grave doubts of its stability having been

THE MAIN AVENUE—WEST.

suggested by Mr. Turner, the constructor of the large conservatory in Kew Gardens, and by Professor Airey the Astronomer Royal, a series of experiments was decided on which should set any such question wholly at rest. Tests had, as we have shown, been applied in the course of the work which had satisfied the scientific men who witnessed them that the iron girders would bear a strain upon them four times as great as they could ever be called upon to bear; but it was resolved to subject them to a still severer ordeal.

The first of these more elaborate experiments, which took place in the presence of Her Majesty, Prince Albert, and several scientific persons, was to ascertain the extent of oscillation that would be produced in the galleries by the regular motion of large bodies of persons. Three hundred workmen were accordingly deployed over the platform, and then crowded together as closely as possible. The load borne by the planks laid across the platform represented the degree of pressure that would be occasioned by the crowding of the bays of the galleries. The amount of deflection produced by this experiment was scarcely perceptible. The men next walked regularly and irregularly, and finally ran over the temporary floor, with little more effect. Even when packed in the closest order, and jumping simultaneously for several minutes, the play of the timbers and the wrought-iron work, was admirably developed, and the extreme deflection of any one girder did not exceed a quarter of an inch. As, however, the workmen were unable to keep military time in their step, the whole corps of Sappers and Miners employed on the ground, arranged in close order, marched several times over and around the bays without producing any other effect than is observable in a house in which dancing is going on. The crowning experiment suggested by Messrs. Maudslay & Field, the eminent civil engineers, rendered any further test wholly unnecessary. Seven frames, each capable of holding 36 cannon-balls, of 68lbs each, were constructed, and drawn with their contents over the floor. In this way a pressure on the flooring of seven and

a-half tons was obtained; the probable pressure from a crowd not exceeding 95lb. The pressure of an ordinary crowd, however, at a public meeting or a theatre does not exceed 60lbs. to the square foot.

During the entire progress of the building, Mr. Fox was present daily at the works, to assign to each part, as it arrived upon the ground, its proper position, without which it would have been impossible that the building should have been completed in time; and so unlimited was the confidence displayed by his firm in the Royal Commissioners, that it was not until the 31st of October that the contract with them was completed; up to which time they had not only received no order for the building, and no payment on account of the work they had done, but had incurred the risk of expending upwards of 50,000l. without being in a legal position to call upon the Commissioners for the repayment of any portion of it. There was, however, no ground for apprehension on the score of finance; for whilst the work was yet in progress, funds were flowing in to the exchequer of the executive with a rapidity altogether unlooked for, and to an amount which was calculated to silence all further anxiety on the subject. To anticipate, in some respects, the order of our narrative, we may mention that before the Commissioners had opened their doors to the public, that is to say on the 29th of April, they had in hand 113,044l. :—namely, 64,344l. arising from public subscriptions; 3200l. from Messrs. Spicer & Clowes for the privilege of printing the Catalogues; 5500l. from Messrs. Schweppe, for the privilege of supplying refreshments; and 40,000l. arising from the sale of season tickets. The last item afforded a tolerable notion of the probable prospects of the Exhibition, in a financial point of view; nor have those expectations, sanguine as they were, been in any respect disappointed.

It is now time to enter upon the history of the building itself, and of the manner in which the contractors have fulfilled their duty to their employers and to the public at large.

The site of the Great Exhibition is the one originally

THE MAIN AVENUE—EAST.

proposed for it by H.R.H. Prince Albert. It consists of a rectangular piece of ground in Hyde Park, situated between the Queen's Drive and Rotten Row, and contains about 26 acres, being 2300 feet in length, by 500 feet in breadth. Its principal frontage extends from east to west. Several lofty trees which stretch across the centre of its length have been allowed to remain, and it is to them we are indebted for the magnificent transept and semicircular roof, suggested after the first plans had received the approval of the Commissioners. The ground although apparently level has a fall of from 1 to 250 inches from west to east. Among the most striking advantages of the spot were the facilities of access from all parts which it presented, and the ease with which it could be drained and supplied with gas and water; whilst the beauty of the neighbourhood can scarcely be exceeded within the same convenient distance from the metropolis. Indeed, however strong may have been the private objections urged against the adoption of this site, in the first instance, it is now universally admitted that a more desirable locality for the purpose to which it has been converted could not have been selected. The plan of the building forms a parallelogram 1848 feet long and 408 feet wide; independently of a projection on the north side, 48 feet wide and 936 feet long. The principal entrance is situated in the centre of the south side, opposite to Prince of Wales' gate, which forms one of the main openings into Hyde Park. After passing through a vestibule 72 feet by 48, the visitor finds himself in the transept, which is 72 feet wide, 108 feet high, and 408 feet from south to north. The roof springs in a semi-cylindrical form from an elevation of 68 feet from the ground, and occupies a diameter of 72 feet. The *coup d'œil* of the exterior of the building from the Prince of Wales' Gate is exceedingly striking. On each side of the space covered by the transept runs an aisle 24 feet wide. The nave or grand avenue, 72 feet wide by 64 feet high, occupies the centre throughout the entire length of the building, and

is 1848 feet long. On either side smaller avenues or aisles run parallel with it 24 feet in width, and at a height of 24 feet from the ground are galleries, which not only extend the whole length of the building, but which are carried completely round the transept; thus opening a direct communication throughout the whole of that floor. Beyond the nearest aisles and parallel with them at a distance of 48 feet, are second aisles of similar width, with galleries over them, which are on the same level as those by which the outside aisles are surmounted. To facilitate access from one line of galleries to the other, bridges, at frequent intervals, span the 48-feet avenues, and, at the same time, divide them into courts, most of which have been so arranged as to be open to the spectator, who may happen to be in the gallery above. The width of 48 feet thus subdivided, and the second aisles, are roofed over at a height of 44 feet from the ground. The remaining portion of the building comprises in width only one story 24 feet high, in which, of course, there are no galleries. Access to the galleries is obtained by ten double staircases, 8 feet wide. About its centre, the grand avenue, at a point determined by the position of three large trees which it was resolved to enclose, is crossed by the transept. Two other groups of trees, whose immolation was also interdicted, have rendered open courts necessary; but they are, nevertheless, included within the building. The entire area enclosed and roofed over comprises no fewer than 772,784 square feet, or about 19 acres; thus presenting an edifice about four times the size of St. Peter's, at Rome, and six times that of St. Paul's. We have already described the principal entrance at the south front. Besides this, there is one at each end, and, at convenient intervals, no fewer than fifteen places of egress. The horizontal measure of 24 feet, which formed a leading feature of the design of the Building Committee, is also preserved in the present plan. The avenues into which

THE UNITED STATES' DEPARTMENT.

the building is divided are formed by hollow cast-iron columns, 24 feet apart, which rise in one, two, or three stories respectively. In the lower story these columns are 19 feet high, and in the two upper ones 17 feet. Between the different columns short bars of iron, 3 feet in length, called "connecting pieces," from the use to which they are applied, are employed as supports to the girders in horizontal tiers, dividing the building, at its greatest height, into the three stories to which we have already referred. The girders, of which, some of cast, and some of wrought-iron, are all of the same depth, namely, 3 feet, with the exception of four; an arrangement by which the horizontal lines are preserved throughout.

The first impression conveyed to the mind of a visitor, inexperienced in the science of architecture, on entering the building, is a sense of insecurity, arising from the apparent lightness of its supports as compared with the vastness of its dimensions. But this feeling is soon dissipated when he is informed how severely the strength of every separate part has been tested, and with what extreme care the connexion of all the supports with each other has been considered, so as to present the greatest possible combination of strength. The ratlines of a ship of war, and the wires of a suspension bridge, may have little retentive power *per se*, but when judiciously connected with other supports, offer a resistance which a superficial observer would be little likely to understand. The lightness of its proportions indicates, at a glance, the nature of the material which forms the main supports of the building; and whilst those which are vertical consist entirely of cast-iron, the horizontal "connecting pieces" and girders are constructed both of wrought and cast-iron. Of wrought-iron 550 tons have been employed; but of cast-iron Messrs. Fox and Henderson have used no fewer than 3500 tons. The whole

of the roof above the highest tier or story of iron frame-work, consists of wood and glass, and the external enclosures and face-work are composed, for the most part, of the same materials. In the entire edifice there have been employed 896,000 superficial feet of glass, and, including the flooring, 600,000 of wood. In those parts of the building which are two or more stories or tiers in height, the upper tiers do not support galleries, being only intended to give additional stability to the columns. The highest tier is in all cases devoted to the support of the roof; an arrangement which forms a rather remarkable feature of the edifice. Among other striking examples of the ingenuity of the originators and constructors of the Crystal Palace is the ridge-and-furrow roof, by which the rain water is distributed into equal portions, and all ordinary chances of overflow averted; and the peculiar formation of the floor, which is a "trellised wooden pathway," with spaces between each board through which, on sweeping, "the dust at once disappears, and falls into the vacuity below." It may also be thoroughly washed without discomfort, for the water disappears as fast as the dust through the interstices; and the boards become fit for visitors almost immediately afterwards. There is one drawback on its adoption, however, of which most visitors to the Exhibition must have had experience; wherever it is laid transversely it is extremely troublesome to walk over, be the boards ever so evenly placed. Into technical minutiæ connected with the erection of the building, and the simplification of labour by its constructors, it is no part of our design to enter. Those who may be interested in such details, will find them duly set forth in the official records of the Commissioners. Many of them deserve praise for their ingenuity; and the speed enforced upon Messrs. Fox & Henderson, in the construction of the Crystal Palace, is the

THE HALL OF THE ZOLLVEREIN.

less to be deplored, as it necessitated experiments which have created important facilities for the builders of future edifices of this description. There are, however, some details yet to be recorded, without which the present sketch, although addressed to the general reader only, could hardly be considered complete. The total area of the ground floor is, as we have already stated, 772,784 square feet, and that of the galleries, 217,100 square feet. The extent of the latter is nearly a mile. The total cubic contents of the building are 33,000,000 feet; there are nearly 2300 cast-iron girders, and 358 wrought-iron trusses for supporting the galleries and roof; 30 miles of gutter for carrying water to the columns; 202 miles of sash bars; and 900,000 superficial feet of glass.

The decoration of the Exhibition of the Industry of all Nations was entrusted to Mr. Owen Jones, and some apprehensions were entertained, in the first instance, that the combination of deep blues, reds, and yellows, would produce too glaring an effect upon the eye. Mr. Jones has, however, by toning down his colours, and calculating the effect of a long perspective upon them, produced a result which has met with very general approbation. The outside of the building, which has not afforded him the advantages presented by the perspective of the interior, has not been considered quite so successful. At the east and west ends considerable spaces have been enclosed for the exhibition of objects, the weight and dimensions of which precluded their admittance within; among them, large blocks of marble, stone, slate, coal, asphalte pavements, and garden and monumental ornaments. At the western end, and considerably beyond the recognised precincts of the Exhibition, is the fine colossal model for a statue of Richard Cœur de Lion, of the Baron Marochetti. About 155 feet from the north-west angle is an engine-house, 96 feet by 24, for generating the steam which gives motion to the various machines which require to be exhibited in operation. The external appearance of this

structure is similar in character to that of the main edifice. It contains five boilers, of 150 horse power, and a large tank, serving as a balance head to the water supply. With this is connected a six-inch main, which runs completely round the Exhibition, on which, at intervals of 240 feet, are placed fire-cocks; and, at different points in its circuit, 16 four-inch branch pipes supply the water requisite for the purposes of the building. The mains, which run along the north and south sides of the building, are connected across the transept by a five-inch main, from which, near the centre of the building, pipes branch out for the supply of the various fountains erected on the central line of the nave; nor has the more substantial convenience of the visitors been overlooked; large refreshment rooms and counters, with corresponding waiting-rooms, have been provided around the trees at the northern extremity of the transept, and adjoining the open courts, at the eastern and western ends. The official business of the Exhibition demanding the services of a large staff of clerks, ample accommodation has been provided for them in offices placed on each side of the southern entrance; whilst, for money and check-takers, venders of Catalogues, etc., a considerable space has been appropriated at the eastern and western extremities of the building, as well as on each side of the principal entrance.

Although all objections to the use of the site in Hyde Park by the Commissioners vanished as the building advanced towards completion, they had been compelled to bind themselves by a deed of covenant to remove it, and resign the ground into the hands of the Commissioners of Woods and Forests, within seven months after the close of the Exhibition. This agreement rendered an appeal to parliament indispensable. After much discussion, in both houses, and elsewhere, a respite of one year has been granted; an arrangement which appears to have been perfectly satisfactory to all, save a few dissentients who either reside or possess property in the immediate neighbourhood. Mr. Paxton's notion from the

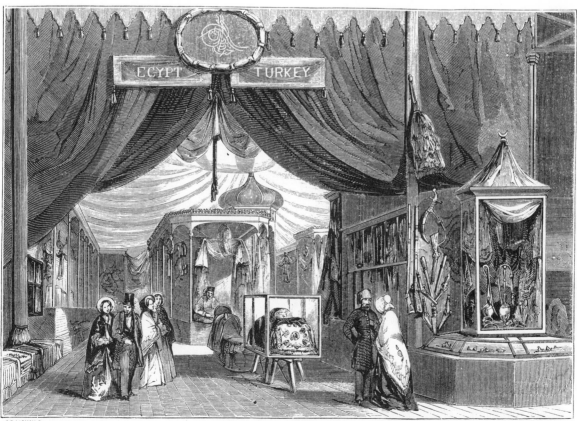

ENTRANCE TO THE TURKISH DEPARTMENT.

first appears to have been to convert it into a winter garden when it shall have answered its present purpose.

Whatever credit may be claimed by the Executive Committee, much is due to the contractors, Messrs. Fox and Henderson, for the almost superhuman exertions which were made by them to enable the commissioners to open the Exhibition on the 1st of May. Such was the extraordinary eagerness of the public to be present at its inauguration, that upwards of 40,000l. of season tickets were disposed of on the 29th of April; and but for the restriction that the holders of season tickets only should be admitted to this ceremony, the place would doubtless have overflowed with visitors. It is not our intention to enter into minute details of the circumstances which attended its inauguration; they were in every respect worthy of the occasion. It was opened by Her Majesty in person, accompanied by the Royal Family, and attended by the members of her cabinet, and by all the officers and ladies of her court. So soon as the music which hailed her entry had ceased, H.R.H. Prince Albert, as President of the Royal Commissioners, read a report of their proceedings since their appointment. This manifesto mentions that "for the suggestion of the principle of this structure, the Commissioners are indebted to Mr. Joseph Paxton, and expresses a hope that the undertaking, which has for its end the promotion of all branches of human industry, and the strengthening of the bonds of peace and friendship among all nations of the earth, may, under God's blessing, conduce to the welfare of Her Majesty's people, and be long remembered among the brightest incidents of her peaceful and happy reign."

To this address, Her Majesty returned a most gracious answer, and the Archbishop of Canterbury having invoked the blessing of the Almighty on the undertaking, the ceremony terminated with the performance of the Hallelujah chorus by the united choirs of the Chapel Royal, St. Paul's, Westminster Abbey, and St. George's Chapel, Windsor. The procession included all the persons who had been officially engaged in the work; the royal and foreign commissioners, Her Majesty's ministers, the whole of the lords and ladies of the court in waiting, and the foreign ambassadors. The vast but elegant proportions of the building, the richness and tastefulness of

INTERIOR OF THE MEDIÆVAL COURT.

the costumes, and the large number (25,000) of well-dressed persons assembled on the occasion, rendered its inauguration one of the most imposing sights that had ever been witnessed in this country. But it is not in her regal capacity alone that Her Majesty has deigned to honour the Great Exhibition with her countenance. Day after day, accompanied by her children, and often at much personal inconvenience, has she flattered the various exhibitors by careful examinations of their productions; until it may fairly be presumed that there is scarcely one of her subjects who has more thoroughly inspected all that is worthy of attention within its walls than she has done. Whatever may have been the weather, or however crowded the interior, Her Majesty has devoted, almost daily, until the close of the session of parliament released her from attendance in London, several hours to visits to the Crystal Palace; inspecting each department in succession, and selecting from many of them such objects as gratified her taste, or were, for other reasons, considered to possess claims upon her attention.

On entering the building, for the first time, the eye is completely dazzled by the rich variety of hues which burst upon it on every side; and it is not until this partial bewilderment has subsided, that we are in a condition to appreciate as it deserves its real magnificence and the harmonious beauty of effect produced by the artistical arrangement of the glowing and varied hues which blaze along its grand and simple lines. After passing through the southern entrance, the whole extent of the transept, interrupted only by the magnificent glass fountain of Messrs. Osler, and the groups of sculpture and tropical plants and trees, that are intermixed throughout, flashes on the eye more like the fabled palace of Vathek, than a structure reared in a few months by mortal hands. On either side, as well throughout its centre, are ranged groups of statuary by Baily, MacDowell, Foley, Marshall, Lough, Bell, Marochetti, Wyatt, Watson, Weekes, Hollins, Legrew, Earle, and other well-known English sculptors. Forming the centre, or nearly so, of the entire building, and dividing alike the transept and the nave, rises the gigantic fountain of Messrs. Osler, the culminating point of view from every quarter of the building; whilst at the northern end the eye is relieved by the verdure of tropical plants and the lofty and overshadowing branches of forest trees.

On the right, looking from Messrs. Osler's glass fountain up the Eastern Division of the Nave, towards the American organ and its enormous eagle, a combination of splendours bursts upon the sight of overpowering magnificence. Here, as in the Transept, the objects which first attract the eye are the sculptures, which are ranged on every side; some of them of colossal size and of unrivalled beauty, by Kiss, Simonis, Monti, Du Seigneur, Duchesne, Muller, Schwanthaler, Powers, and others. The Western Division of the Nave, devoted to the products of England and her Colonies, if less showy, on a superficial view, than its rival, has much of sterling merit to recommend it. Here, too, are interspersed statues, fountains, mirrors, organs, and other large ornamental objects.

Crossing the Transept, and pursuing our course to the left, we enter the western division of the nave. We have here the Indian Court, Africa, Canada, the West Indies, the Cape of Good Hope, the Mediæval Court, and the English Sculpture Court, including works of Gibson, Baily, Mac Dowell, Foley, Carew, Marshall, Behnes, Hogan, Bell, Jones, Stephens, Thornycroft, Watson, etc. To these succeed Birmingham, the great British Furniture Court, Sheffield, and its hardware, the woollen and mixed fabrics, shawls, flax, and linens, and printing and dyeing. The long avenue leading from the Mediæval Court to the end of the building is devoted to general hardware, brass and iron-work of all kinds, locks, grates, etc.; whilst behind it, and parallel with it, but occupying three times its breadth, is the department for agricultural machines and implements. At the back of this division is the long narrow gallery occupied by the mineral products of England. Passing the small compartment of glass which runs transversely under the great organ gallery, across the nave, we have the cotton fabric and carriage courts, leather, furs, and hair, minerals and mineral manufactures, and machinery; including cotton and woollen power-looms in motion. The next is the largest compartment in the

building, comprising machinery in motion, flax, silk, and lace, rope-making lathes, tools, and mills; minerals and mineral manufactures, furniture, marine engines, ceilings, hydraulic presses, steam hammers, fire engines, etc. Then follow paper and stationery; Jersey, Ceylon, and Malta, with the Fine Arts Court behind them; railway and steam machinery in motion; building contrivances, printing, and French machinery, occupying the whole of the last compartments on both sides the nave, as well as those which face the transept. Crossing to the left of the Crystal Fountain, we have Persia, Greece, Egypt, and Turkey, Spain, Portugal, Madeira and Italy, musical instruments, and chemicals; France, its tapestry, machinery, arms, and instruments, occupying two large courts; Belgium, her furniture, carpets, and machinery; Austria, with her gorgeous furniture courts, and machinery furniture; the Zollverein, with its octagon room, the most tastefully-arranged compartment in the building; North of Germany and Hanse Towns; Russia, with its malachite doors, vases, and ornaments; and the United States, with its agricultural implements, raw materials, etc., occupying all that part of the nave which terminates with its organ, if we except a small gallery on the north-east side, devoted to English paper-hangings. From this extremity of the building, and from the organ gallery more especially, the finest *coup d'œil* of the nave and its adjoining galleries may be obtained.

Crossing once more the nave on our return, we pass from the United States to Sweden, part of Russia, Denmark, another division of the Zollverein, Russian cloths, hats, and carpets, Prussian fabrics, Saxony, and the Austrian sculpture court; Austria runing back side by side with Belgium, the whole way. Next succeeds another division of France, with its splendid frontage of articles of *virtu* and ornamental furniture, its magnificent court for plate, bronzes, and china; its tasteful furniture, and carpets, its jewels, including those of the Queen of Spain; its laces, gloves, and rich embroideries; Switzerland, China, and Tunis, terminate this half of the nave.

Among the more striking objects in the south-eastern gallery, in the British half of the nave, are the silks and shawls, abutting on the transept; lace and embroideries, jewellery, and clocks and watches; and behind them military arms and models, raw produce, substances used as food, and chemicals. Traversing the gallery for naval architecture, by the organ, we have philosophical instruments, civil engineering, architecture and building models, musical instruments, anatomical models, glass chandeliers, decorations, etc.; china, cutlery, and animal and vegetable manufactures, and china and pottery above the left side of the northern part of the transept. On the opposite side, in the north-eastern gallery, are perfumery, toys, fishing materials, miscellaneous articles, wax flowers, stained glass, British, French, Austrian, Belgian, Prussian, Bavarian, and American products.

Clear passages under the galleries, of eight and ten feet broad, run the whole length of the building. Upon the extreme north and south sides, there are also longitudinal passages of similar width; the former interrupted by the offices of the commissioners and the entrances, and the latter by the refreshment rooms. With the exception of the offices, staircases, entrances, refreshment courts, and the various avenues and passages, including the transept, the whole of the ground-floor and galleries are available for exhibitors. As we have already shown, foreign countries, including the United States of America, occupy the east side of the transept above and below; whilst the United Kingdom, the East Indies, and the British Colonies are confined to the west side; with the exception of the United Kingdom, which extends into parts of the north and south galleries, on the east side of the transept. The productions of England and her Colonies occupy thirty separate sections. Of the four main departments into which it is divided, machinery occupies the north side, raw materials and produce the south side, and manufactures and the fine arts the centre. Along the central passage, to the west of the transept, a frontage on each side, of seven bays, or 168 feet, is devoted to the production of the Colonies.

In retiring from the contemplation of this magnificent edifice, the extraordinary expedition with which it was constructed must be regarded as one of the marvels of the age.

The tenders of the contractors were not, it is stated, accepted by the Royal Commissioners until the 26th of July, 1850; the possession of the site was only obtained on the 30th of the same month, and the first column was not fixed until the 26th of September, leaving only seven months for its completion. When we remember the elaborate calculations that were necessary before the iron and wood-work of the building could be put in hand, the machines for economising labour that had to be devised and manufactured, and the contracts for materials to be entered into, and the thousands of hands that had to be set to work, the celerity with which the building was completed is one of the most remarkable features of its history.

In the sketch which we have here given of the history of the Great Exhibition, from its origin to the present time, we have confined ourselves exclusively to facts; having carefully avoided making it the vehicle of opinions of any kind. This restriction, and the limited amount of space at our disposal, have prevented us from entering upon many topics which might otherwise have diversified our narrative, and relieved the monotony inseparable from the compression, into a few pages, of the great body of facts we have been called upon to enumerate. All questions inviting discussion would have been out of place in a narrative like this, which aims simply at presenting a brief, but faithful, history of one of the most splendid and remarkable undertakings that has ever been attempted in this or any other country. We have left all controversy on the plans and arrangements of the Royal Commissioners, and the officials with whom they have associated themselves, to the *Art-Journal*, without the aid of whose staff it would have been impossible for us, or, indeed, for any one else, to have produced the present volume, at anything like the price at which it is now published. With the composition of the juries, or the principle on which they arrive at their verdicts, and all the topics to which such an enquiry would of necessity conduct us, we shall have nothing to do on the present occasion. The *Art-Journal* has displayed no want of courage in dealing with such subjects, or in protecting the interests of the great body of British exhibitors from the effects of that overstrained courtesy which seems to consider that the rights of hospitality demand sacrifices on the part of their English competitors, which are alike inconsistent with reason or with justice. We have, moreover, no official knowledge of the manner in which the respective prizes have been awarded, and possess, therefore, no correct data for speculation on the subject; much will depend not only on the impartiality, but competency of the various jurors for the duty they have undertaken, and their perfect freedom from national jealousy or bias of any kind. Whether or not this great enterprise will be productive of the unmixed good which has been anticipated from its present success, its effects on the general trade and commerce of the country cannot have been as injurious as some persons profess to think; but it may be questioned if it have not

benefited some classes at the expense of others. How far the glut on the English market, of all kinds of ornamental goods, when the Exhibition has closed, may be atoned for by the increased stimulus which their excellence may have given to the British manufacturer remains to be seen. The question has been often asked, what is to be done with the Crystal Palace; but the graver inquiry would seem to be, what is to be done with its contents? A very large proportion of them will, in all probability, be sold for what they will fetch; and if so, with what effect upon the trade of the British metropolis? —A partial injury at most: whilst the benefits arising out of the Exhibition are certain to prove both important and permanent. It will encourage us in the prosecution of those arts in which we are in the ascendant, and show us our weakness in those branches of industry in which we may be behind our neighbours. To be aware of our deficiencies is the first step towards amending them; and there is no maxim safer than that which teaches us not to undervalue our rivals: our Industrial Exhibition will have had this good effect at least.

The extent to which this congress of the world's genius and industry has already promoted the objects of civilisation and of peace, may be seen in the cordial feelings with which England and France are now inspired towards each other; and the noble spirit of emulation, devoid of its former rancorous prejudices, which it has generated between them. We need scarcely refer more particularly to the splendid and cordial reception given by the great body of savans and men of science of France to a large assemblage of English gentlemen (most of them identified in some way or other with the Exhibition), at the Hôtel de Ville of Paris, in the early part of August; and the strong and grateful impression it has left upon the minds of all who had the opportunity of participating in it. So noble a demonstration of mutual good feeling cannot fail to form an era in the histories of both countries; realising, as it did, so completely the language of Beranger's charming song, written when the prejudices and antipathies of the two nations were at boiling heat:—

" J'ai vu la Paix descendre sur la terre,
Sémant de l'or, des fleurs, et des épis,
L'air était calme, et du dieu de la guerre,
Elle étouffait les foudres assoupis.
' Ah!' disait-elle, ' égaux par la vaillance,
Français, Anglais, Belge, Russe, ou Germain,
Peuples formez une sainte alliance,
Et donnez-vous la main!

" ' Oui, libre enfin, que le monde respire,
Sur le passé jetez un voile épais,
Sémez vos champs aux accords de la lyre,
L'encens des arts doit brûler pour la paix.
L'espoir riant au sein de l'abondance,
Accueillera les doux fruits de l'hymen.
Peuples formez une sainte alliance,
Et donnez-vous la main!' "

The Art-Journal
ILLUSTRATED CATALOGUE
of the
INDVSTRY
of all nations

THE Works of Mr. Alderman Copeland, for the manufacture of Porcelain and Earthenware are at Stoke-upon-Trent,—the principal town of the Staffordshire potteries: his London establishment is in New Bond Street. The artist who presides over the works is Mr. Thomas

commonest article of earthenware—manufactured for exportation by tens of thousands. The

compartment allotted to Mr. Copeland in the Exhibition cannot fail to be universally attractive,—not alone because of the grace and beauty

Battam, whose taste, judgment, and experience have been largely exercised to secure for this manufactory the high reputation it enjoys, not only in England, but throughout Europe, in Asia, and in America. The list of the Alderman's productions comprises all classes of "goods"—from the statuary porcelain figure and the elaborately decorated vase, to the

of the articles shown, but as exhibiting our progress in a class of art upon which much of our commercial prosperity must depend. The collection will be carefully examined, and by foreigners especially, who will find much to admire, and much

that will by no means suffer in comparison with the best productions of Dresden and Sèvres—always bearing in mind that at these Royal works objects are occasionally produced at national cost: such as those now to be found upon the stalls allotted to these famous factories; and that to expect private enterprise to enter into competition with them would be neither reasonable nor fair. At the same time it is only right to say, that Mr. Copeland challenges a comparison between his productions and those of either Dresden or Sèvres—in so far as concerns articles made especially for trade—and that from such comparison he does not shrink as regards either the materials, its ornamentation, or its price. We have devoted to the works of Alder-

man Copeland a larger space than we shall be able to accord generally even to manufacturers of the first order; but his works are very numerous and excellent, and although we assume to have selected the best, we have left unrepresented a mass of interesting and beautiful productions. For instance, out of forty statuettes in statuary

man. The statuette of SAPPHO is from the

porcelain, we engrave but two—the "Sappho," after Theed; and the "Bacchus and Ino," after Foley: setting aside the "Sabrina," after Marshall; the "Indian and the Negro," after Cumberworth; the "Venus," after Gibson, and

others of great merit and beauty formed in this valuable material. The tazza, called "THE DOVE TAZZA," which commences the preceding page, is a superb ornament, peculiarly adapted for general purposes of elegant decoration; it is

original, by M. Theed,—an artist of high ability,

executed in fine porcelain: the doves, from the celebrated doves of the Capitol, together with the festoons of flowers, and the embossment generally, are richly gilt. On the same page,

are a PINE-STAND, formed of the foliage of the pine, and a BRACKET, called the IVY BRACKET. The EWER AND BASIN which commence this page are in the Greek style, with outlines after Flax-

who has been for a long time resident in Rome.

The figure is, we believe, the largest yet

attempted in this style of Art-manufacture, being

about thirty-four inches high. The PANEL FOR

a FIREPLACE, is one of a series of admirable

designs in this class of manufacture, for which this house is so justly eminent: the foliated

and the outer borders enriched with chased and

extremely rich and harmonious. The concluding

scroll panels and works are enamelled on a gold ground, the centre subjects in colours on black.

burnished gold, relieved with blue: the effect is

object on the second page is a JUG of Etruscan

form, graceful in outline, and ornamented with floriated decorations and antique enrichments.

The first subject on the third page is a BRACKET, called the "Cupid Bracket." It is followed by a TRIPOD FLOWER-STAND, a very meritorious production, and one which, with reference to its size as well as merit, we have

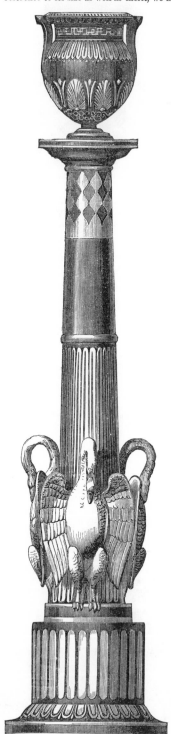

not seen equalled in the beautiful material of which it is composed, viz., statuary porcelain; there is much classic elegance in this design, and the execution of its components is, in the highest degree, satisfactory. Following this is a VASE of much beauty: and on the succeeding columns are pictured, first the "Bacchus and Ino," of Foley—a very triumph of Art;

and next a GROUP OF OBJECTS FOR THE CONSERVATORY, consisting of Vases, Flower-pots, and Pedestals for the same. The uses to

which these useful ornaments are intended to be applied require no explanation; it is sufficient to point out their merits as elegant

luxuries for the wealthy. The first engraving on this page is a VASE and PEDESTAL, of blue and white porcelain, standing together

about five feet high; the proportions of the column have been well studied, and the base of a triangular form, exhibits at each angle

a Stork of considerable dimensions. These objects are succeeded by a TAZZA in the Italian style, a kind of AMPHORA, or water-bottle, of antique form and decoration, and by a GARDEN SEAT, the latter ornamented with a bas-relief of classically-designed figures. The last subject is a PANEL for a fireplace, simply but tastefully embellished with coloured designs: this ap-

plication of the plastic arts to domestic architecture, is now becoming very general in houses of a superior class.

In all the examples here brought forward there is undoubted evidence that the mind of the artist has been at work to accomplish the task of uniting beauty with utility, by a skilful adaptation of what may be gathered from the past to the tastes and requirements of the present generation, however varied and exacting.

We engrave on this page two beautiful objects contributed by M. LE PAGE-MOUTIER, of Paris,—a FOWLING-PIECE and a SHIELD, both exquisitely wrought. The stock of the former is elaborated with designs, in which the ivy forms a prominent feature; the lock is chased, and represents a dog and a fox, and the barrel is also richly chased in vine leaves and grapes: the

work is altogether worthy of the best period of the middle ages, when offensive weapons of all kinds seem to have been made as much for ornament as for use. The shield is an extraordinary piece of workmanship, chased by the artist VECHT in metal, in the boldest and most vigorous style.

The subject represented is the "Massacre of the Innocents," and the designs are copied from some of the best works of the old masters,—Raffaelle, Poussin, &c.; it seems, therefore, almost unnecessary to dilate upon what has emanated from such sources, the fountain of all that is great and noble in Art. The theme is one calculated to elicit no other feelings than those of

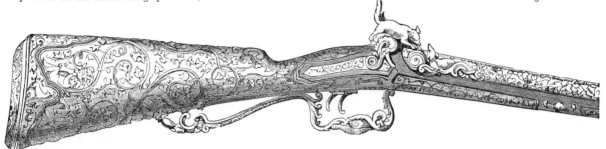

horror and detestation, but it affords abundant scope for the display of bold action and most effective grouping. Unlike a field of military combatants, where man meets man in deadly struggle, and each feels that life or death depends, perhaps, on the strength of his own right hand, the rage and fury are here on one side only, the

despair and agony on the other. Still there is no quiet submission—no resistless surrender of the little ones, to those who are executing the commands of the tyrant. It is this mingling together of men, women, and children, their variety of attitudes, induced by the difference of purpose which places them in action, the strength of arm

that emboldens the warrior, the power of maternal love that animates the mother, which make any representation of the "Murder of the Innocents" a picture such as no other historical event can furnish. M. Le Page-Moutier has acquired as a manufacturer of the most costly and excellent fire-arms, swords, &c., the reputa-

tion of being among the first, if not the very first, in France; we visited his establishment a few months ago, when a large variety of his

productions were submitted to our inspection; the only regret we felt on the occasion was, that so much talent and labour should be bestowed

on the art that destroys, instead of upon that which assists to preserve mankind, and to elevate the moral and social condition of humanity.

The establishment of MR. HANDYSIDE, of Derby—the "Britannia Foundry"—is principally represented by the elegant Iron VASE which we engrave. It is of very large size and elegant character. The body of the Vase is decorated with an elaborate interlaced design, which we

Among the specimens of excellent iron-work contributed by M. OVIDE MARTIN, of Paris, are some beautiful CROSSES, of which we engrave

have engraved above it. The base is an octagon, having eight open-work screens hanging in front of the pedestal, which give singular lightness and elegance to the entire object. As an example of the taste and improvement which characterise the iron manufactures of our own

two, chiefly as suggestions in ornamental design for our own manufacturers. They are charac-

country, we believe our readers will consider this work deserving of much attention : it is an excellent design, as excellently worked out, and reflects credit on the establishment from which it has emanated—one that from the magnitude of its operations is second to none in England.

terised by much lightness and elegance of outline, while the main portions are "filled in" so as to add to the general richness of the design.

The appended engraving is of the plinth of a CANDELABRUM, manufactured by M. BROCHON, Paris, for the Strasbourg Railway. It is of cast iron, and will be much admired for its elegant proportions, and its artistic details; the shaft rises in gothic flutes from a floriated base, which is again followed by ornamental work of a similar character, but varied in form and design, having fruit inter-

mixed with the leaves. The pedestal exhibits several projecting ornaments, terminating at the top by what would seem to be the heads of the panther. The whole column shows that much artistic taste has been expended upon its construction; it is of very considerable height, and altogether reflects great credit upon M. Brochon's establishment, which is one of the most important, for iron-work of all kinds, in Paris.

Munich, famous for its school of PAINTING ON GLASS, contributes no example of it to the Exhibition; the fame of Bavaria in this department of Art is upheld only by Messrs. KELLNER, of NUREMBERG, who contribute a copy of the "Volkhamer Window,"—the glory of the Lorenzo Kirche, of that renowned city. It is not known who composed this votive offering of the Volkhamer family, but the general opinion seems to be that when the design was decided upon, several artists assisted in preparing it. The figure-subjects are taken from the Old and New Testa-

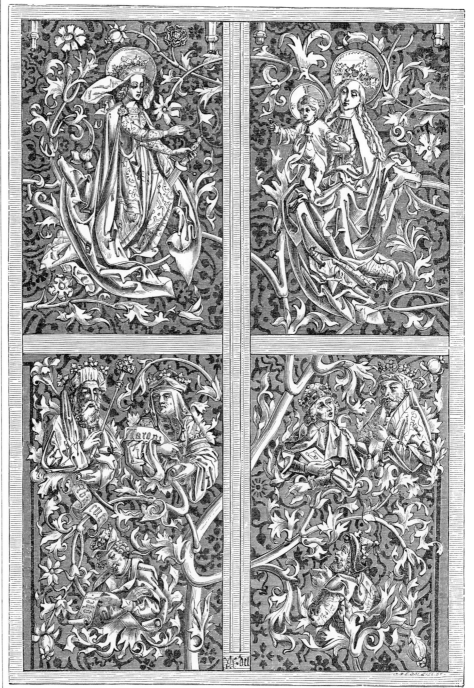

ments. The figures kneeling at the lower portion of the window represent the various members of the Volkhamer family. The minor divisions are filled up with florid architectural ornaments and scriptural illustrations; and in the upper compartment is represented the Holy Trinity, surrounded by a choir of angels. The dimensions are 30 feet by 12 feet; we engrave only a part of it. In this work, whether we regard its technical superiority, the richness of its composition, or the extraordinary blending of colour which it presents, all has been achieved which

could possibly be expected even from the gifted days when it was created. It was a deep sense of these excellencies that induced M. Stephen Kellner to make a copy of the window, as faithful as possible, both in drawing and colour; and all who have seen the beautiful original, must consider that he has succeeded to admiration. He is one of the sons of Jacob Kellner, of Nuremberg, whose family are much renowned as glass-painters, and have produced some of the most beautiful specimens

of modern art. They are thoroughly acquainted with the style and characteristics of the middle ages, as the many excellent copies they have executed testify. Their prices are very moderate, being from twelve to fifteen florins (20s. to 25s.) per square foot, according to the nature of the design. Their establishment in Nuremberg, —which we visited in the summer of 1850—is well worthy the attention of church-builders, and, indeed, also of private gentlemen who desire to decorate their houses.

The productions of Mr. W. G. ROGERS, of London, in WOOD CARVING are by no means new

to our readers, comprising as they do the most perfect of modern efforts in this branch of art. Mr. Rogers's fame, as it is well known, rests mainly on his imitation and extension of the style

adopted by his great forerunner in wood-carving, Grinling Gibbons; but he has recently diversified his labours by adding to the works of the character described, such as may be truly called the *bijoux* of the art, consisting of small and

delicately finished objects, chiefly in box-wood, and in the Italian style. From among these

minute performances, executed with the co-opera-

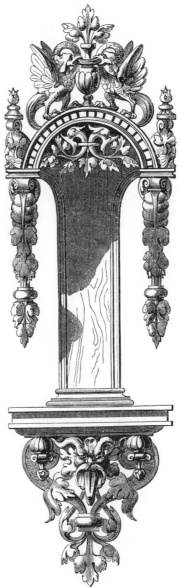

tion of his son W. Harry Rogers, as designer, we have

principally selected the illustrations of our great carver's contribution to the Exhibition; believ-

ing them to be not only interesting subjects to the general reader, but useful suggestions to the manufacturer. Upon the present page will be seen a carved BOX-WOOD BRACKET, with canopy,

intended to receive a thermometer; two perforated PANELS belonging to a work-table, composed of the foliated ornament; a BRACKET in satin-wood; an ORANGE CUP, covered with subjects and inscriptions connected with the career

of William III.; and a box-wood SALT-CELLAR enriched with columns and elaborate sunk panels. The last subject is accompanied by its corresponding SPOON, which, from its ornamentation, we have deemed worthy of two separate views.

Continuing our illustrations of Mr. Rogers's early Italian character, and have been converted by Mr. Rogers (for G. Field, Esq.) into BRACKETS, by the addition of plafonds and masses of heart-shaped foliage. We introduce these four original conceptions, believing that they will prove prac- the page, is a large oval FRAME of the Venetian

carvings, we here offer to our read-ers a selection of various objects, all of which are very perfect both in design and execution. The two oval MINIATURE FRAMES at the top of the page are in box-wood and in different styles. The first is a sim-ple border of pinks arranged round a moulding and carved literally from nature; while the second is in the quaint conventional style which is generally known as "Eliza-bethan." Following these are four grotesque masks, which have an

tically suggestive, because while in many styles of ornament the mask is a very prominent fea-ture, it is rarely executed with the spirit and vigour which are evinced by the present exam-ples. The next subject, that in the centre of

school, made for the Hon. Arthur Kerr, and kindly lent by that gen-tleman for exhibition. The two remaining works here engraved are GROUPS OF STILL LIFE, intended for the decoration of dining-rooms. Both are studies from original frag-ments by Grinling Gibbons, restored and extended; and are favourable examples of a style of art, the pro-secution of which has mainly tended to raise Mr. Rogers's reputation to its present position. One is a NET, in and about which fish and shells are arranged with studied negligence ; as a finish to the whole, sprigs and flowers of aquatic weeds are plentifully introduced. The other is a TROPHY, consisting of a pheasant and a woodcock hung up together, and

accompanied by a profusion of fruit and flowers. The feathering of the birds' plumage, produced by a remarkably few touches, is eminently successful, and the eyes and general expression of the heads afford a striking contrast to those of

some birds by the same hand, in which life is attempted to be portrayed. Mr. W. G. Rogers's most important contribution to the Exhibition (if magnitude be a criterion) is a carved frame, 11 feet high by 9 feet wide, boldly relieved in lime-tree, in the style of Gibbons. It is entirely composed of English fruits and flowers, mounted upon a moulding of polished walnut-wood. Of this frame we engrave the upper portion, which is admirably grouped, and in which appear many kinds of English flowers which Gibbons never introduced into his productions. In the centre of the page is the celebrated boxwood cradle, executed for her Majesty the Queen, and with the details of which our readers are already familiar. We conclude our selection from Mr. Rogers's works with engravings of three miniature frames of various designs. The first consists merely of a garland of different flowers,

frame, intended to receive miniatures of the Royal Family of this country. The design,

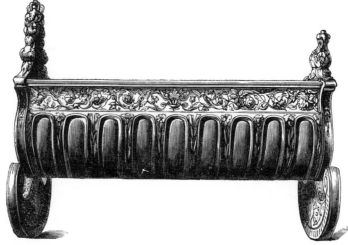

which is surmounted by a regal crown, contains

and interlaced with the motto, "Dieu et mon Droit." The third and last subject is a small frame, in the style of the period of Elizabeth or James I. Here the curious strap ornament, which prevailed at that epoch, is made a good use of, and happily blended with cords supporting masses of fruit. It is with much satisfaction that we find Mr. Rogers offering so excellent a display of the perfection to which England has attained in the beautiful but long-neglected art of carving in wood. This art, unquestionably, owes no small portion of the excellence it has reached among us at the present time to the success which has attended his efforts, and to the example of his energetic perseverance and ability in pursuing it. There cannot be a doubt that many of the admirable specimens that our wood sculptors exhibit in the great Exposition may be traced, indirectly if not directly, to his influence. A large share of merit is

bound by twisted ribbon, and placed round a simple bead moulding. The second is an oval

the letters V. A. R., monogrammatically arranged,

therefore due to a true artist who has been the means of again resuscitating an almost forgotten Art.

The COALBROOKE-DALE IRON WORKS, as might be expected, from the magnitude and high character of the establishment, are worthily represented in the Exhibition. The first of our examples is a GARDEN VASE, of cast iron, with masks and handles of novel design; it

feet nine inches high, finished in white and gold, with branches for six lights; the pattern of this

stands on a marbled pedestal, measuring altogether about three feet in height, and is adapted for flowers or for a fountain. This is followed by another GARDEN VASE, with serpent handles, in

which is placed an earthen pot for flowers. The next object is an Elizabethan LOOKING-GLASS, two

frame merits all commendation. Below this is an ornamental FLOWER-POT STAND, four feet high,

complete with the pots in china. The first two engravings on the next page are copied from an

elegant VASE and PEDESTAL, in which floriated decoration and stags'-heads form the principal features of the ornament. But the most important contribution of the Coalbrooke-dale Company is an ornamental CHIMNEY-PIECE and GRATE,

and the mouldings are of imitation marble; the grate consists of burnished steel fronts and ornaments in bronze electro-gilt, and the whole is so

seven feet high and four feet wide, with decorations illustrative of deer-stalking, boar-hunting, and hawking. The figures are of cast-iron gilt,

arranged that the ornamentation connects in one design the fender, ash-pan, and grate. The fire-brick for the back is in one piece, including the bottom of

the grate on which the fire rests, and is constructed to give the greatest heat with a small fire. The fender, ash-pan, and grate are removed in one piece, to afford greater facilities for the operation of sweeping the chimney. The entire work is a beautiful example of manufactured Art.

The COVENTRY "TOWN RIBBON," of which we append an engraving, is the result of a town subscription, and may, we presume, be accepted as an example of the combined skill of several workers in the ancient and venerable city, famous for the fabric of ribbons since the commencement of the sixteenth century, or from even an earlier date. This specimen is exceedingly effective, creditable not alone to the designer, but to the various workmen engaged in its production; it "tells" well in black and white, a severe test for an article of this kind; but the reader will be pleased to imagine a large number of colours, harmoniously combined into a production of much grace and beauty. The ribbon is designed by M. CLACK (a pupil of the Coventry School of Design), and draughted by R. BARTON, requiring in its manufacture 24,000 cords and 10,000 cards.

An IRON BEDSTEAD, and CHILD'S COT, also of iron, contributed by M. DUPONT, of Paris, will attract attention from the rich and elaborate designs which they exhibit, especially the former object. This has a kind of frieze in basso-rilievo, running round one of the sides and the end, representing a hunting party; the flat terminating pillars are also similarly ornamented. The whole is of cast-iron, produced from a mould that brings out the figures and details of the design with remarkable sharpness and decision. The frame-work of the cot is very light and elegant, and the introduction of a young angel at its foot, as if keeping watch over the little sleeper, is a pretty idea: the basket and fringe are made of netted wool. We may, perhaps, be allowed to take an objection to the practical convenience of the bed, although we may unequivocally express approbation of its ornamental design.

THE INDUSTRY OF ALL NATIONS.

Etruria—the celebrated establishment founded by JOSIAH WEDGWOOD, and where the knowledge of Bentley and the classic taste and genius of Flaxman, combined with his own ability, gave a world-wide reputation to its founder—has sent its *quota* of beautiful works through its present occupants, Messrs. WEDG-

WOOD & BROWN, who have reproduced some of the best articles originally designed or executed by its famous founder. There are still in the establishment many designs of high quality which have not yet been worked out, and we may instance the group of the

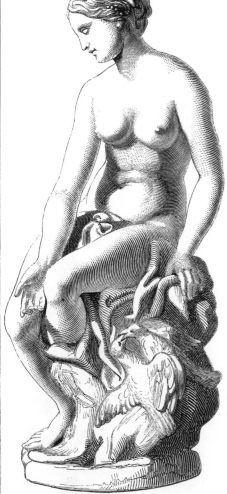

Infant Hercules strangling the Serpents, said to be the work of Flaxman, and now first made for the

Exhibition in Hyde Park. The VENUS, which we engrave, is also produced for the first time

on the same occasion, as well as the CUPID; both charming figures. The entire series of works displayed by the present firm are of the

classic form and style of decoration, so well known to connoisseurs; the ground of each

article being of a lavender tint, the figures and ornaments, in pure white clay in relief upon the surface, have the delicate and beautiful shades of the tint faintly appearing through the more

delicate parts. Many of these Vases are of large size, and some have figures directly copied from the antique; others being designed in strict accordance with those upon the Greek and Roman gems. Indeed, the Wedgwood imitations of these rare and costly articles have always been highly prized. There is much

simplicity in the general character of the floral and other ornament which decorate the sur-

its position among the principal Art-manufac-

turers of the present day; attesting to the deserved character obtained for the establish-

face of these choice works; and we rejoice to see this eminent house again prepared to assert

ment by the famous Josiah Wedgwood. These works are all carefully and beautifully executed, and deserve the high praise they will

command; and the re-awakened attention which will be insured, to one of the most famed and tasteful of

English establishments, in connection with plastic art.

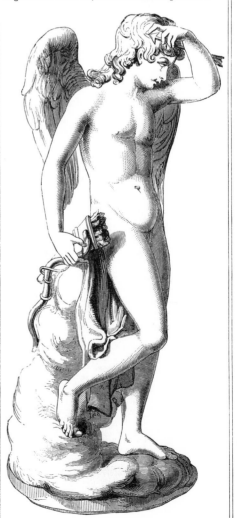

We commence this page with a group composed of CANDELABRA, TABLE-LAMPS, and a GAS-CHANDELIER, selected from a variety of articles of a similar description contributed by Messrs. SALT & LLOYD, of Birmingham. In all these objects the designer has had recourse to nature for the ornaments with which they are enriched. It would not, probably, be very difficult to point out where these ornaments might have been more effectively and tastefully disposed; but still there is much in the general character of the designs that will meet approval, and exhibit

the advance which, within a few years, has been made by the manufacturers of Birmingham. One great error against which it is necessary to guard British manufacturers of ornamental articles, is the too free introduction of decoration: elegance is more often united to simplicity than allied with abundance: symmetry and beauty of form must never be sacrificed to a profuse display of adornment. These remarks are not made with reference to the objects here engraved, but are thrown out as hints to our manufacturers generally. The edifices and works of Art which Greece produced, when she had reached the highest point of refinement and civilisation, were remarkable for their elegant simplicity. It was not till luxury had enervated her powers, and wealth had created an over abundance, that she lost her purity of taste and became lavish, even to prodigality, of the resources at her command. It is to the earlier periods of the history of that country one looks for all that is great in Art.

A SIDEBOARD of mahogany, selected from the contributions of MESSRS. JOHNSTONE & JEANES, of London, is entitled to high commendation for the pure taste which the manufacturers have exhibited in its construction. The style is Italian of the best period, not over-ornamented, yet showing an abundance of chaste decoration, which may be thus briefly described. At each end is a young Bacchus; one, placed on a lion, holds up a bunch of grapes to the other, who, stretches out a cup to receive it; these figures are carved with much spirit. In the centre of the back-piece is a medallion of a Bacchante, and at each corner one of a Bacchanal, the interstices being filled in with wreaths of the grape-vine and its fruit.

The WINE COOLER, exhibited by M. EICHLER, of Berlin, is of terra-cotta; it may be accepted as a proof of the great excellence so frequently given by competent artists to ordinary objects of commerce. In composition, grouping, drawing, and entire arrangement, few more perfect works than this have been produced in the precious metals; yet, upon this common material, so much fine taste and intellectual labour have been expended as to give it high value as a work of pure and true Art.

A silver-mounted MEERSCHAUM, by M. HELD, of Nuremberg, representing St. George and the Dragon. We have selected for engraving this out of several drawings sent us by one of the most successful manufacturers of Germany. The article is one upon which much ingenuity is expended; it is often embellished with great skill and taste, and is not unfrequently made costly by the exercise of artistic talent; indeed, a very large proportion of the young Art of Germany is employed in modelling, carving, or decorating these meerschaums. In Germany there are few more productive articles of trade; they are exhibited in the gayest shops; and their ornamentation is generally expensive as well as beautiful.

The FRAME of CARTON PIERRE, with the brackets and medallions enclosed in it, are the contributions of Messrs. GROPIUS, of Berlin. Their establishment is renowned throughout Germany; they have obtained repute for the quality and durability of their material as well as for the excellence of their models; it is known, indeed, that they are assisted by several accomplished artists. When we visited their extensive works and show-rooms, in the summer of 1850, we examined a vast variety of fine compositions in brackets, statuettes, picture and looking-glass

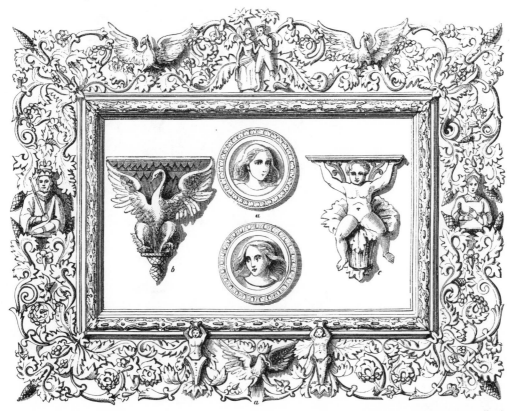

frames, &c.; as in all such cases of manufacture, a large portion of the merit of the manufacturer consists in the skill with which he composes his materials—the judicious mixture of the component parts; still, as in this instance, celebrity is to be obtained also by employing good artists to produce good models; the collection exhibited by Messrs. Gropius cannot fail to be appreciated; its introduction into England is desirable.

Mr. BATTAM, of Johnson's-court, Fleet-street, Enameller of Porcelain and Glass, contributes various TAZZE, VASES, &c., imitations of Etrus-

can art, in form and ornamentation. These imitations are of rare excellence; in many cases,

indeed, they cannot be distinguished, except upon minute scrutiny, from the originals. The

vases are of various sizes; the third upon this column is of considerable height—nearly 4 feet.

The FAIR LINEN CLOTH, which commences this column is intended for a cummunion-table; it is one of the contributions of Mr. GILBERT FRENCH, of Bolton, to whose manufactures of a similar description we have, on more than one occasion, referred with great satisfaction. Mr. French exhibits a pure taste and an accurate knowledge of what is essential to appropriateness of design in his various productions of church linen; and spares no expense in procuring suitable patterns, and in working them out in the finest qualities of fabric. The improvements he has effected in these articles of ecclesiastical use are such as must be manifest to all who had observed the inelegant, and often offensive, designs which formerly covered the altars of our churches; many of them better adapted for a dining-hall than a sacred temple. The cloth here engraved bears on it the symbols of its application; in the centre is the "Lamb," surrounded by the evangelists.

The TABLE-TOP, formed chiefly of the MARBLE OF DERBYSHIRE, is contributed by Mr. G. REDFERN, of Ashford, by whom the work is manufactured, and who has established a high reputation for various admirable productions in the spars and marbles of the county in which he flourishes; these objects comprise cups, vases, chimney-ornaments, and the ordinary "toys" of the material, with articles of greater value and importance. The table-top here engraved is unquestionably the best production that has been yet manufactured in Derbyshire. It is composed of various marbles, from the common limestone to the costly lapis lazuli, verd antique, malachite, &c. The ground-work is of the ordinary black marble, a marble found remarkably pure in this district, often in large slabs, without a single speck of white. The design introduces several birds of varied plumage, and ornamentation of a graceful character. As a specimen of mosaic, it may vie with examples of the costliest order that have been produced in modern Italy; the table will rank among the most satisfactory proofs of what may be achieved by British taste and skill, and will also afford evidence of the value of home materials judiciously applied.

The picturesque village of Ashford, in which Mr. Redfern has his establishment, is situated in one of the beautiful dells of Derbyshire, not far from princely Chatsworth, and in the neighbourhood of the best quarries of the county; whence the largest variety of British marbles is obtained.

M. VANDERKELEN-BRESSON, of Brussels, a lace-manufacturer—who has, by his untiring ability, greatly aided the celebrity of the Belgian capital in this branch of the textile Arts—has contributed an exquisite specimen of patient industry in a LACE VEIL, the border of which we here engrave. It possesses novelty in its design, as well as in its fabrication. We do not engrave the *fond*, or groundwork of the lace, except in some portions

of the scroll, which will better enable our readers to judge of the taste and elegance of the design. It is meritorious and more than usually suggestive.

The three VASES are from the establishment of M. VILLEMSENS, of Paris, worker in bronze, and manufacturer of church ornaments; the latter branch of business especially, being largely carried on, by this house. During our visit to Paris towards the close of the past year, we saw in his extensive show-rooms a vast variety of objects, exhibiting more or less taste in composition, and ingenuity of workmanship; these were principally executed in bronze and in brass, and were adapted as well for the embellishment of the private dwelling as for purposes of ecclesiastical

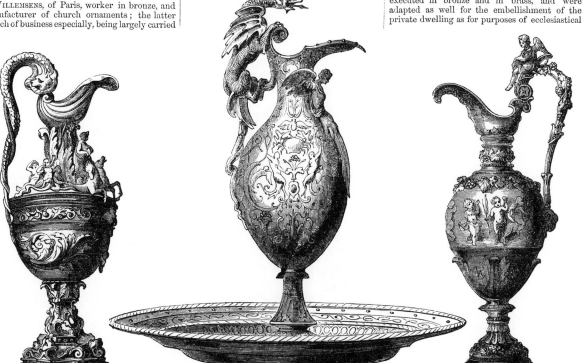

use and decoration,—statues, vases, chandeliers, candelabra, delicate rail-work, &c. The three bronze vases and dish selected from the contributions of this firm, are distinguished by beauty of outline and elaborate ornament, approaching very closely to the best antiques.

Messrs. WATERHOUSE, of Dublin, have contributed the various specimens of BROOCHES which appear

on this page. They are all, more or less, remarkable, as well for the peculiarity of their

museum of the Royal Irish Academy and elsewhere. The largest and finest of the series, "the royal Tara

brooch," has been very recently discovered near Drogheda; it is of bronze, ornamented with niello and gems,

character, as for their history, and the ability shown in their fabrication. They are, in fact, copies of

and is the most remarkable work of the kind that has yet been procured. In these objects, Messrs. Waterhouse

The pillar engraved below is of TERRA COTTA, the production of FEILNER & Co., of Berlin. Its height is above seven feet; it is from the design of an eminent Prussian architect. In the establishment of the Messrs. Feilner we saw many admirable examples of this beautiful art, and regretted to learn that their contributions to the Exhibition were to be limited. Their "Industry" relies for its recompense, however, less upon articles which more closely appertain to Fine Art than to those necessaries of life, the fire-stoves, which in Ger-

the most curious antique brooches which have been found in Ireland, and are preserved in the

have been singularly successful; the great beauty of their works cannot fail to insure their extensive popularity.

many are so frequently found beautifully and elaborately ornamented. Yet these gentlemen have produced works of far higher moment. There is in the garden of Professor Wichmann, a doorway copied from a medieval design, of which the whole of the arch and side column mouldings are of terra-cotta; it is also used for figure and arabesque bas- and alt-relief enrichments of considerable size, and with admirable effect in front of ordinary dwelling-houses.

The CENTRE-DISH and two VASES which occupy this column, are from the establishment of Mr. MELLISH, of London. They are of glass, silvered by Mr. Hale Thomson's process, described at length

in the "Art-Journal" for March of the present year, to which we would refer such of our readers as feel an interest in this truly beautiful manu-

facturing Art. There is a peculiarity in the manufacture of the glass used by Mr. Mellish in his process, which merits particular notice, from its

novelty and ingenuity; all the articles, whether goblets, vases, or others, have double sides, between which the silver solution is precipitated.

The TOILETTE GLASS and the CUP, underneath, are exhibited by M. RUDOLPHI, of Paris. His works, generally, are on a small scale, but valuable

even more for their beauty, than for the materials of which they are composed, though these are of a costly kind; gems and intaglios set in the purest gold of elaborate workmanship, and gold and silver ornaments exquisitely wrought. The

TOILETTE-GLASS is small in dimensions, about thirteen inches high; it is of silver intermixed with enamels of various colours, to represent fruit and foliage: the object is of rare taste in conception, and of great merit in execution. The design of the CUP, though not altogether novel, is carried out with much ingenuity: the base exhibits a boy assisting another to climb a vine. The bowl is of agate, and the mounting of silver burnished and matted, with grapes of enamel: the diameter is about nine inches.

The small VASE is the contribution of Mr. HEMPHILL, of Clonmel; and is formed of ivory, in what he has termed the Elizabethan style. It is five inches in diameter, and four in height, and is entirely turned in the lathe. The intention of the designer has been to produce a work graceful in outline, and sufficiently ornamental without being heavy. There is a commendable originality in the decoration of the lower parts.

Messrs. H. & A. HOLMES, carriage-builders, of Derby, contribute a LIGHT PARK PHÆTON, of which the accompanying is an engraving: it upholds the high reputation which these gentlemen have acquired in all parts of Europe. The phæton is elegant in outline, light and simple in construction, free from unnecessary carvings and ornamental iron-work; and, moreover, inexpensive to keep in repair, and not difficult to clean.

The IRON LETTER POST is manufactured by M. VANDENBRANDE, of Brussels. These posts serve the purposes in Belgium that a receiving-house does in England. The letter-collectors open them several times during the day, and each time affix a notice, on a tablet, of the time of the last "Levée," or taking out. They stand about three feet in height;

The CHIMNEY-PIECE and BOOKCASES, intended for the side of a Library, are contributed by Messrs. HOLLAND & SONS, of London, and have been executed by them from the designs, and under the superintendence of, Mr. T. R. Macquoid, architect. The style is founded on that of the cinque-cento, with a free adaptation of natural forms introduced with judgment and taste. The work is exquisitely carved in walnut-wood, and

and are made to serve also as posts at the corners of the chief streets.

inlaid with green and red marbles; the doors are of perforated brass, and all the materials are of British growth and manufacture. The size is about twenty feet long by thirteen feet high; we engrave only the half.

Mr. POTTS, of Birmingham, has long been distinguished as a manufacturer of LAMPS, CLOCK-STANDS, CANDELABRA, and articles of *virtu*, displaying pure taste in design and refined skill in manufacture. It is not, perhaps, too much to say, that his abilities and exertions have done much to elevate the character of the Birmingham bronze and brass works. The whole of his numerous contributions are entirely the work of English hands: we select, we believe, the best. The first engraving is from an elegant little

priate and well-studied design, and most careful execution. It will well bear the closest scrutiny.

The centre subject at the bottom of this page is a grand CANDELABRUM for ten lights, designed

HAND-BELL, the handle of which introduces "Puck," seated on a snail, and directing his course. The next is a CANDELABRUM, which he calls the "Heron Candelabrum," from the birds

from the story of Daphne and Apollo: the figures are vigorously and expressively grouped,

CANDELABRUM, made to hold four lights; its

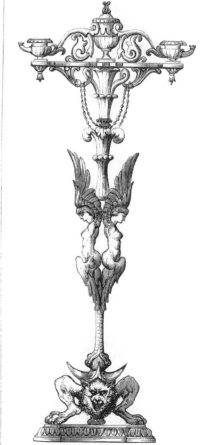

that support the stem. A very elegant CLOCK STAND claims attention from its truly appro-

displaying great artistic skill in the modeller. The last engraving on this page is from another

principal ornaments are grotesque winged figures.

Resuming the contributions of Mr. POTTS, we introduce first on this page a TRIPOD FLOWER

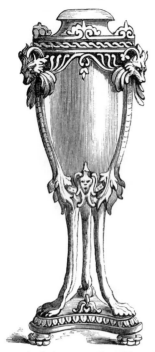

the two columns, on the top of the page, is a GAS LAMP, with three burners, exhibiting considerable novelty in design; it is bold in character, yet not heavy. An exceedingly pretty

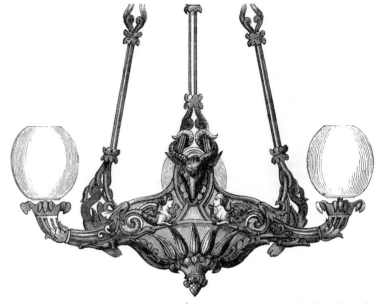

CARD DISH follows; it is of metal, and the designer has introduced birds of Paradise as supporters of the tray. Below this is a FLOWER VASE, formed after the antique model, yet not

STAND, simple in construction, with much of the character of the antique. Following this is

an actual copy. We have engraved the whole of the bas-relief forming the decorative part of the

the general appearance of this design is peculiarly agreeable; it has little ornament, but that little

body of the vase; the subject is a youthful sylvan, "Pan," kneeling at the altar of Hymen, where he is crowned by Flora: it is termed by

a CANDLE LAMP, the pedestal composed of elephants' heads, very skilfully wrought. Across

the maker, "A Festival in honour of Spring." The other engraving is from a CANDLE LAMP:

is judiciously applied, and executed with much spirit. There are few objects of manufacturing art which have exhibited, during some years past, more manifest improvements than the table candle-lamp in all of its many varieties of form.

We stated, in our preliminary remarks on Mr. POTTS's contributions, that no one had done so much to advance the character of the Birmingham bronze and brass-works as this intelligent and enterprising manufacturer. To him must be accorded the merit of having first introduced a new combination of artistic media, which has

since been followed up by others with no little success, though Mr. Potts has still kept the lead in his hands. We allude to the application of a ceramic substance, statuary porcelain, for ornamental purposes in conjunction with metal, in

chandelier lustres, lamp brackets, and numerous other objects of utility and decoration. This introduction has given a vast impulse to the Industrial Arts, presenting as it does a valuable auxiliary which may, in interwoven or appended ornament, minister most felicitously to elevate

and enrich the particular branch to which it may be applied. But it is requisite to use it with the utmost discrimination and judgment, inasmuch as it might otherwise lead to the perpetration of much that is offensive to the taste. The charm of novelty taxes the talent of the designer most severely, and often compels him to pro-

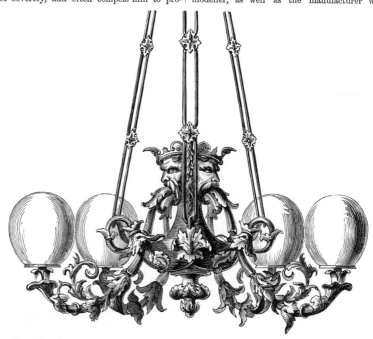

determines what is, and what is not, to be produced, should be well skilled in those principles by which such desirable ends may be attained: each should habituate himself to considering the effect of every pattern in different materials and articles. Above all, the designer should be

selected from Mr. Potts's contributions as exhibited on this page. The first is a light and elegant CANDELABRUM for two or four lights; it is designed after the best examples of the antique. By its side is a richly ornamented GAS CHANDELIER in the Italian style of decoration,

duce, for the sake of change, and to please a public too exacting on this point, that which his judgment and matured experience would impel him to withhold. But inasmuch as novelty is worth nothing without beauty and correctness of form, it is necessary that the designer or modeller, as well as the manufacturer who

taught that his principles are to be found only in the very highest art. The designer must, in mental power, be raised to the level of the artist, and must emulate him, not only in skill, but in range of information. But we must proceed to notice the remaining objects we have

the scrolls being surmounted by grotesque marks. The two engravings below these represent another GAS CHANDELIER and its PULLIES: the style of this work displays a bold arrangement of curves, and angles, and is altogether a beautiful example of metallurgical manufacturing art.

The silver works of Mr. Higgins, of London, are such as come within the province rather of a spoon and fork manufacturer than of a maker of

silver plate. From his very numerous contributions we select several, chiefly commending

those designs which are taken exclusively from natural objects; and we may remark that

the articles which Mr. Higgins exhibits, as specimens of his best ordinary production, are worthy of more public attention than such as have been

prepared expressly for the present occasion. Our illustrations commence with an APOSTLE SPOON, surmounted by a figure of St. Peter, being one of a series of twelve, which are elevated on a rotatory pedestal. With this is a simple but graceful DESSERT FORK, of which the stem and prongs are of silver in imitation of twisted

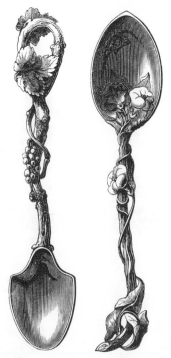

branches, and the handle composed of agate. On the opposite side of the page are a DESSERT-

SPOON and a DESSERT-FORK taken from different sets, one composed of vine branches and the other of conventional ornament. In the centre

column we engrave a light and elegant CREAM-LADLE, the design of which appropriately consists of stems, leaves, and flowers of the common buttercup. The plant is fashioned for its purpose

with the best possible taste, and the effect of the work is greatly enhanced by the gilding, which is only introduced in the cavities of the flowers. Underneath the cream-ladle which, when per-

forated in the bowl, may be employed as a sugar-sifter, are two small spoons, one a TEA-SPOON, ornamented with convolvulus, and the other an EGG-SPOON, chiefly remarkable for the novel form of the bowl, which is both pleasing to the eye and agreeable to the lip. The two remaining subjects are CADDY-SPOONS, of beautiful sim-

plicity. We especially admire the shell, to which clings a sprig of weed resembling the small water-lily. The flowers and the interior of the shell are gilt. Its companion is also worthy of

much praise, though a mere wild anemone gathered in the fields, and copied with as much fidelity as its application to the form of a caddy-spoon would permit. The first group on the present page are two KNIFE-HANDLES; the first made of ivory, and decorated with vine leaves and bunches of grapes: the second of

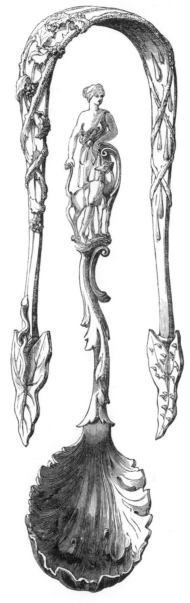

silver, with ornaments of a conventional character: both are distinguished by considerable elegance. Next follows a SKEWER-HANDLE, in the Italian style; the introduction of the birds

is very effective and graceful. On the top of the second column are a PAIR OF ICE-TONGS and a

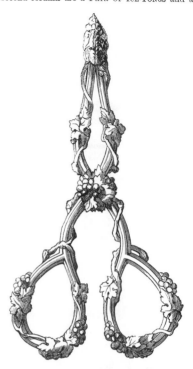

SPOON for helping this article of luxury; the form and ornamentation of the first of these objects exhibit great originality; the second, with the figure terminating the handle and its leaf-like bowl, possesses much beauty of design. A PAIR OF SUGAR-TONGS commences the third column; they are decorated with the vine-branch, its foliage, and fruit. A TAPER-STAND succeeds to this: in it the designer has also had recourse

to the productions of nature for the form and character of his subject. The page is completed by a FISH-CARVER of massive design, somewhat assimilating to the Moorish: we admire this as a deviation from the ordinary forms of such objects, as well as for its own intrinsic merit. There is not one of the subjects we have engraved in these

two pages that is not worthy of the best period of manufacturing Art wheresoever practised; an undoubted proof of the advanced state of taste and ingenuity on the part of our designers and those associated with them in carrying out their

intentions. It is gratifying to see British manufacturers taking advantage of the often inculcated maxim that "to nature alone must we look for beauty, and the nearer the approach to

her creations the more striking the success:" it is a truth ever to be remembered by the designer.

THE INDUSTRY OF ALL NATIONS.

We occupy the present page with some examples of INDIAN MANUFACTURE, exhibited by Capt. H. C. JAMES, of the Bengal army. They were brought by him from India, and are curiously characteristic of Eastern taste. The papier-mâché tray was made in Cashmere, and is entirely painted by hand, in a most elaborate style, labour of this kind being of very little value there. The vase beneath is constructed of

over apartments; it was taken at the capture of Lahore, and is believed to have belonged to some of Holkar's household. The brooch is used by the women in Chinese Tartary to fasten their plaid shawls over their shoulders. It is generally made of brass; its chief curiosity consists in its size, which, in the original, is nine inches and a half by seven inches. The gold ring

being peculiar to that country. On the opposite side of our page is the case of a small compass, carried by Mahomedans in India when travelling. It is made of a kind of bronze, inlaid with silver; the inscription contains the names of Mahomet and his two brothers. The compass within it is in the shape of a flying bird, whose head points to the west or Mecca, and tells in what direction the bearer

a composition of metal and clay, called "biddur," of a very dark tint, and is inlaid with thin pieces of silver; such vessels are generally used to hold water, and are chiefly manufactured at Ninga-

ought to turn his face to pray. The magnet is, of course, in the right wing of the bird.

The cut at the foot of the page exhibits the pattern of a Cashmere covering for a couch;

pore, in Bengal. The very elegant silver vase, with the chain attached, is used to sprinkle rose-water is of the fashion of those commonly worn by the better class of natives in Cashmere, the pattern the ornament is stitched over a light blue silk, which gives it a peculiarly delicate tone.

Mr. J. S. Evans, of London, contributes two ALBUM COVERS, the work of his son, Mr. J. W. Evans. The first is a small quarto, richly illuminated in gold and various colours on brown leather; and we should, perhaps, mention that while the black, which forms the field, is a positive dye, the remaining colours are enamelled. The design is taken from an original specimen

The CURTAIN-PIN and CORNICE POLE-ENDS in this column, are contributed by MR. HANDS, of Birmingham, whose manufactory is eminent

for all kinds of stamped metal goods, such as those we have engraved, door-furniture, coffin-furniture, &c. In the subjects we have selected,

floral decoration has been resorted to with considerable success, and with sufficient taste to give the flowers a true and natural position, as

of the time of Henry II., of France. The interior of each cover is of white vellum, elegantly tooled in gold, from a pattern by Mr. W. Harry Rogers.

The second is a royal quarto, of brown Russia, inlaid with black kid, a novel process as applied to rich workmanship, though not unusual in

we see in the blue-bells introduced into the third design, and the bunches of hops in that which precedes it. In the manufactured articles them-

simple book-binding. The design, in harmony with the colours of the materials employed, is in the Etruscan style, and is from a drawing by

Mr. Rogers. A vase occupies the centre, and the border and corners are composed of Archaic foliage, in which the honeysuckle is prominent.

selves, we find a sharpness and accuracy of detail that prove the amazing power of the stamping-machine to produce so desirable a result.

This and the following pages are devoted to the contributions of PORCELAIN, from the ROYAL MANUFACTORY AT DRESDEN, or, rather, at Meissen, a small town on the Elbe, about fifteen miles from the capital of Saxony. The Dresden china, for it has always borne the name of the city though made at a distance from it, acquired through the past century high distinction for the beauty and variety of its fanciful decorations, and for the costliness of its workmanship; nor has its value become much lessened even at the present time, although it may, perhaps, be doubted whether its progress has kept pace with that of many other branches of manufacturing art. During our recent tour through Germany, we had an opportunity of visiting this establishment, and were supplied by the Director, through the Minister of the Interior, with the drawings from which our engravings are taken. We confess to have felt a little disappointment at the comparatively limited scale on which these royal porcelain works are conducted, and still greater surprise at the small amount of wages paid to their artists and workmen, many of whom are men of first-rate talent, who do not receive more than fifty shillings per month. If the English manufacturer, therefore, had this low rate of wages to contend against, he would stand no chance of a successful competition; but inasmuch as the monopoly exercised by the government keeps up the prices of the productions, both are placed, so far, on a tolerably

department. The peculiarities of manufacture which distinguish the collection of this porcelain

equal level. The total number of persons engaged in the manufactory at Meissen is about three hundred and fifty, and each respective room is set apart for a particular division of the process. Thus, in one apartment, the simpler vases and table-services are moulded; in another, flowers are exclusively manufactured, each leaf being inserted separately; in a third, birds and the more delicate ornaments, and so forth; while the painting and gilding form a separate

ware are relieved floral and bouquet agroupments; figures round and relieved; and many varieties of the famous hawthorn pattern; all

GLASS, the frame of which is adorned with birds, flowers, and fancy ornaments. The next two are of VASES from four to five feet

these are the characteristics of the Dresden manufacture. The first engraving on the opposite page is from an enormous LOOKING-

high, exceedingly elegant in form, and decorated in a chaste and pure style of art. The first two engravings on this page are also of VASES, the

former an imitation of the antique Grecian, but decorated with enamelled paintings; the latter of a floral character, and filled with porcelain

flowers. The group contains objects of very great elegance and beauty; the contributions altogether uphold the character of modern Dresden.

The extensive GLASS works of Messrs. BACCHUS and SONS, of Birmingham, furnish some beautiful examples of their manufacture, of which we engrave two groups, remarkable both for their novelty of form and of ornamentation. Several of these objects, it will be readily supposed, lose no little portion of their rich appearance in the engravings, where black only is made to take the

The three COAL-VASES, or, as such articles of domestic use are generally called, coal-skuttles, are from the establishment of Mr. PERRY, of Wolverhampton, who has, with much good taste, endeavoured to give a character of elegance to these ordinary but necessary appendages to our

place of the most brilliant colours; this is especially to be observed in the large vase in the first group, where, if we imagine the lozenge-shaped ornaments of a deep ruby colour, cased with white enamel, and the wreaths of green ivy, we may form some idea of the rich effect produced. There are few objects of British manufacture which have, of late years, been marked by more decided im-

"household hearths." Hitherto, in whatever room of a dwelling-house one happens to enter, the coal-scuttle is invariably thrust into some obscure corner, as unworthy of filling a place

among the furniture of the apartment, and this not because it is seldom in requisition, but on account of its unsightliness. Mr. Perry's artistic-looking designs, though manufactured only in japanned iron, may, however, have the effect of drawing them from their obscurity, and assigning them an honourable post, even in the drawing-room. It is upon such comparatively trivial matters

provement than is to be found in our "glass-houses;" and Birmingham is now a formidable rival to London in this branch of industrial art: moreover, it is rapidly, and rightly, advancing.

that art has the power to confer dignity; and, notwithstanding the absurdity—as we have sometimes heard it remarked—of adopting Greek and Roman models in things of little importance, they acquire value from the very circumstance of such pure models having been followed.

The decorative articles of various kinds in EMBOSSED LEATHER, executed by Messrs. LEAKE, of London, exhibit the applicability of that substance to very many articles of luxury and convenience used in domestic life. As a simple decoration it possesses the tone and effect of wood-carving, at a considerable diminution of expense; and it may be applied to cornices of rooms, or portions of furniture as massive as cabinets and book-cases usually are, with the best possible effect. The flower-wreaths of Gibbons, or the fanciful grotesques of the *cinque cento*, may be reproduced with remarkable precision. Of course, we do not venture to say that wood-carving can be equalled in this fabric, but it may be approached closely. The process of ornamenting leather is one

ornamented with embossed work of a rich and beautiful kind. The works of Messrs. Leake are, in some instances, excellent reproductions of antique designs; and in others, equally

good original works, or adaptations of good forms. It will be seen that fruit, flowers, and the human form are produced by this process, as well as all the varieties of orna-

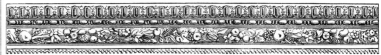

of a very early date; indeed, it may be traced back some three thousand years, to the days of the ancient Pharaohs, and, singularly enough, we then find it embossed much in the same manner as practised at the present time. The extraordinary durability of leather gave it much value in the eyes of our forefathers; defensive armour was frequently constructed therefrom, and mediæval writers abound with notices of very many useful and ornamental

ment. Great boldness and vigour, and, occasionally, extreme delicacy, are visible in all the works of these manufacturers. The chair

on our present page exhibits the applicability of the Art to the decoration of furniture. The picture-frame is a happy rendering of

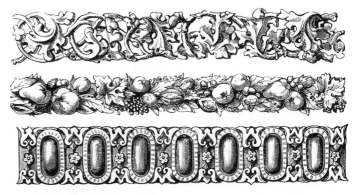

articles made of *cuir-boulli*, as this manufacture was then called. The cuirass of the knight and the casket of the lady were equally constructed of leather, and

the style of the seventeenth century. The panel, executed in the taste of the Renaissance, re-produces the vigour and fancy of the gro-

tesque works of that period to the eye, as successfully as the fruit and flowers recall the works of the famed wood carvers of yore.

MR. MORANT, of London, whose reputation and that of his father, for cabinet-work and house decoration have been established for nearly half a century, contributes a variety of

elegant objects—of which we have selected three. The first is the top of a CONSOLE GLASS.

The next is a small TABLE, supported by storks, | the top is of plate glass painted to imitate Floren-

tine mosaic. The last subject is also a TABLE, from a design furnished by the Duchess of Sutherland, for whom Mr. Morant executed it. The column of this table exhibits swans and aquatic plants.

The VASE and four POKALS, or DRINKING CUPS, upon this and the succeeding page, are the contributions of the Royal Porcelain Manufactory of MUNICH; and, they are nearly the only aids which the Exhibition receives from the renowned capital of Bavaria. They are designed by NEUREUTHER; and are intended to hold the famous

and potent Beer, the favourite beverage of all classes of Bavarians. M. Neureuther is at the

head of the government establishment, and we received direct from him the drawings from which these engravings are executed, with expressions of regret that his country will not be more

worthily represented. The cups are of Por-

celain, formed upon the old German models, and

beautifully ornamented in colours and gold, portions of the decoration being in relief.

The two FIRE-GRATES engraved on this page are from the manufactory of Messrs. STUART and SMITH, known as "Roscoe Place," SHEFFIELD, an establishment which ranks high among those of that famous industrial town. They are made upon the principle known as "Sylvester's," whose invention formed an era in domestic economy

directly opposed to health and comfort; it is obvious that the principle of construction must be best which throws the greatest heat where it is most required, and this is mainly effected by the invention of Mr. Sylvester. The first ex-

been to create a style of decoration from nature, without the introduction of mere conventional forms. The other, in the mediæval style, is designed by Mr. H. Duesbury, an architect of ability, who has shown much taste and ingenuity

and comfort. Their superiority over the old-fashioned grates has become widely tested by their very general use; these latter were so constructed that the larger portion of the heat passed up the chimney, from the fuel being placed so high, and, as a consequence, the lower part of the room was invariably cold, a condition

ample engraved is denominated by the makers a "Trefoil Grate," from the shape of its outer frame; it is composed partly of "dead" steel, and partly of burnished, with or-molu enrichments. The object of its ornamentation has

in adapting this style to its required purpose. The extensive collections of Messrs. Stuart and Smith exhibit a large variety of this description of manufactures, displaying enterprise, taste, and clever mechanical execution.

The five engravings of KEY-HANDLES, on this column, are selections from the contributions of Mr. JOHN CHUBB, London; whose safety locks and improved keys have become famous, not only in England but throughout Europe. He

has devoted much attention to those improvements which may be described as restorations;

taking the best antique models, and, in some instances refining even upon them: he has thus

substituted forms of much elegance for the ungainly shapes to which we have been accus-

tomed, yet in no way to lessen the ease with which the object may be used. The articles

he contributes cannot fail to augment the high reputation he has laboured for and acquired.

The CUT GLASS DISH and COVER which we here engrave are productions of M. DIERCKX, of Antwerp, and are chiefly remarkable for the peculiarity of design which they present, and which is of a novel

character. Glass is peculiarly susceptible of angular decoration; and this dish and cover are ornamented with figures designed to give the fullest amount of prismatic beauty of which the material is capable.

The establishment of MM. GAGNEAU, Fréres, Paris, has attained deserved celebrity for the manufacture

of CANDELABRA and LAMPS of every description, exhibiting a very large amount of that artistic

talent in design for which the French have long since made themselves famous. We are well acquainted with the show-rooms of this firm, and can truly state that we have rarely seen so many beautiful objects, of their kind, brought together as they exhibit; the metals used are principally bronze, brass, and or-molu. The candelabrum engraved below is exceedingly rich in ornament, but by no means overloaded; the tripod forming the base has at each angle a demi-figure of grotesque character; above this, to conceal the plain shaft, are three females standing on an ornamental platform, which figures may be regarded as caryatides or supports to the higher parts of the composition:

these we consider very elegant both in form and decoration. The lamp which forms the subject of the other engraving is intended to be fixed to a wall; the design scarcely belongs to any definite school or period, but is rather of a mixed character, yet so harmoniously put together that no incongruity is apparent in it. The contributions of this class from France are numerous, and, many of them, highly suggestive; it is, however, needless to point attention to this fact; the works sufficiently commend themselves by their variety and excellence.

The ZINC CASTINGS of GEISS of Berlin are very numerous, although his contributions to the Exhibition are limited; they comprise a variety of objects, chiefly for the purposes of the archi- tect,—capitals, cornices, &c. Zinc has been hitherto very little used in England; in Prussia, however, it has been resorted to, more or less, in nearly every structure of modern erection. M. Geiss has devoted his attention chiefly to the produce of statues in zinc; the purity of the casts, the perfection of the chiselling, and durability of the material, combine to recommend it, while the cost of zinc, thus adopted, is about one-eighth of the cost of bronze. We select for engraving the famous "Amazon" of Professor Kiss, of Berlin; the original, in bronze, faces the entrance to the New Museum, at Berlin. The copy exhibited is life-size; one of half life-size has been also produced by M. Geiss. We have no doubt that the exhibition of these statues, so admirably calculated for gardens in England, will be followed by a large importation of similar works. We counted above twenty in the ateliers of M. Geiss; among them Baily's "Eve," "The Boy and Swan" of Kalide, the Stags of Rauch, with several copies after Canova, Thorvaldsen, and the more famous works of the antique.

We engrave on this page two of the CAST IRON BRACELETS of DEVARANNE, of Berlin; works as meritorious in their way, and as true examples graceful productions of Berlin have for a very we are rightly informed, to the peculiar nature of the sand into which the metal is poured; for the iron principally used is obtained from English

of Art, as the great life-size statue of Professor Kiss. M. Devaranne contributes not only these miniature wonders in cast iron, but also mines. The collection exhibited by M. Devar- annes will attract universal attention; they consist of necklaces, brooches, bracelets, pins, and

gigantic castings in zinc, of which some specimens appear in another part of our Journal. These long period retained celebrity; nothing of iron has been cast so skilfully elsewhere, owing, if other objects so skilfully designed and delicately wrought as to be absolute marvels of Fine Art.

The PILLAR, surmounted by a group, and the TABLE which commences the next column, are from the ROYAL IRON FOUNDRY OF BERLIN; they are, of course, made of cast iron. This establishment is under the immediate direction of the Government. The pillar is designed by Professor Strack; the base shows a claw tripod, from which rises a shaft encircled upwards by a triad of graceful figures, terminating with a flat top whereon is placed a highly-spirited Amazon group, the work of Professor Fischer,

figures, in bas-relief, form a kind of entablature below its surface, which is supported by four winged demi-figures, springing from the shaft.

This is moulded and ornamented with considerable elegance; indeed, the entire object is one of much artistic beauty in its several parts.

The annexed engravings form portions of a BRIDLE, contributed by Mr. PENNY, of London, a metal chaser, who has executed the whole of the ornamental work in electro-plated silver. He calls it the "Prince of Wales's Bridle," having made it with a view to its being adopted by his Royal Highness. The emblems with which it

is decorated, therefore, bear reference to the position of the Prince in connection with a great maritime power. The ornamental outer edge of the winker, here engraved, is composed of dolphins, sea-horns, and foliage; the inner edge has an anchor, with foliage entwined; the centre of this part, which is not engraved, shows the

also of iron. The dark tone of this metal is greatly relieved by an inlaid thread of silver, beautifully wrought into one of the most chaste and simple of the antique configurations. The Table is unique in its design; a series of antique

heraldic arms of the Prince, his coronet, &c. The rosettes, which form the centre-piece in the engraving, have a foliage border surrounding the coronet. The buckles, head-stall, face-piece,

loops, &c., are also ornamented. The leather-work is manufactured by Mr. LANGDON, of London. The design of the harness, altogether and in detail, is by Mr. W. Harry Rogers.

The EMBROIDERED ALTAR-CLOTH is by Mr. T. HARRISON, of London; it is a very elaborate specimen of gold embroidery upon a field of rich crimson velvet. In the centre is the monogram I H S surrounded by a "gloria" of twelve principal rays and stars. In the spaces are introduced two conventional roses surrounded by stars. A flowing pattern of trefoil and gothic pine-apples forms an elegant border to the cloth, and the whole is edged by a massive fringe of gold four inches in depth. The design for the embroidery is the work of Mr. W. Harry Rogers.

The BIT for a horse, commencing this column, is contributed by Messrs. ASHFORD, of Birmingham, extensive manufacturers of what is termed "saddlers' ironmongery," such as steel-bits, stirrups, whips, and whip-mounts, but all of a superior quality. The example here introduced is intended for the use of a lady; it is of pierced

The BOOK COVER, the back of which appears on the opposite column, is exhibited by Messrs. BONE & SON, of London. They are designed by Mr. W. Harry Rogers, and cannot fail of being

steel, highly polished, is exceedingly light in construction, and may be regarded as a novelty.

admired for the lightness and elegance of the composition, which is entirely of a floriated character, an arrangement of the ivy, holly, and other evergreens worked into a pattern with much taste. It is almost as effective in what the trade call "blind-work," as when richly gilt.

A FOWLING-PIECE, contributed by M. SAUER, of Suhl, Saxony, shows some exquisite carved work, emblematical of its uses, on the stock. The gun itself is of peculiar construction in its manufacture, tending to obviate the dangers attending any sudden explosion; we have before us diagrams of its mechanical arrangement, but which we cannot afford space to introduce into our pages.

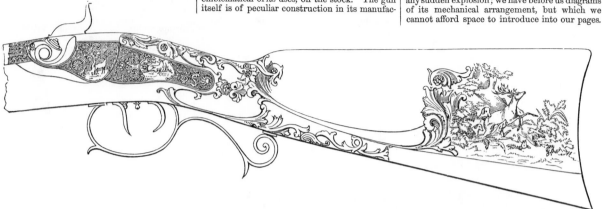

The CHATELAIN-HEAD is exhibited by Mr. THORNHILL, of London; it is entirely produced by hand, in hard steel, chiefly by means of minute files. The principal portions are flat, perforated and engraved, but a slight projection is given to the more important ornaments or emblems introduced. The design which is by Mr. W. Harry Rogers, is in the Italian style, consisting of foliage surrounding an oval compartment. This has the monogram V.A., and is surmounted by the royal crown; beneath are the Prince of Wales' feathers, and a label inscribed 1851. Six medallions contain the crests of the illustrious promoter of the Exhibition.

IVORY POKAL, by CHRISTIAN FRANK, Fürth, near Nuremberg. The pokal is of gothic form, and beautifully carved in relief, illustrative of subjects taken from the old German Niebelungen Lied, after the paintings of Jul. Schnorr von Carolsfeld. The relievos are: From the fourth adventure, 'Sigfried with the Saxons;' seventeenth adventure, 'Sigfried mourned and entombed;' twenty-second adventure, 'Briemhild received by the Huns;' thirty-seventh adventure, 'The death of Rudiger.'

The SCISSORS are also by Mr. THORNHILL; the ornamentation is an adaptation of the Italian style. They are highly to be commended as examples of the taste of the designer, whoever he may be.

Messrs. CORK & EDGE, of Burslem, Staffordshire, manufacturers of earthenware, supply the markets in England and on the Continent with ordinary articles of domestic use, in which they endeavour to combine utility with an amount of ornament, that will not prejudice economy. Our first cut represents a TEAPOT of brown glazed ware, of very cheap construction, but not without its peculiar grace in design. A patented branch of their business

is devoted to the ornamentation of similar articles by inlaying clays of various tints, thus producing an indestructible colouring for the leaves and other ornaments, such as appear

upon our second specimen of their works. The WATER-JUG, which completes our selection of articles from this establishment, is a tasteful arrangement of forms; the water-lily being

introduced in the base of the jug with very good effect. It must be borne in mind that all these articles are constructed only for the cheapest market; and we give them as instances of improvement in such branches of our national industry, as were but a few years ago, as must be acknowledged, most inartistic in taste.

Messrs. FAUDEL & PHILLIPS, of London, exhibit a STATE BEDSTEAD, of needlework, produced principally from British materials worked

entirely by Englishwomen in London; it includes almost every description of ornamental needlework commonly called "Berlin," and embroidery. A lengthened description of this costly and beautiful piece of furniture would fill half our page; we must therefore be content with speaking of it as a work in every way honourable to the taste and enterprise of the manufacturers, who have long been famous in their trade.

The two specimens of CARPETS on this page are from the factory of MESSRS. HENDERSON & Co., Durham, whose establishment produces a large variety of Venetian and damask stair-carpets, as well as of Brussels carpets for all purposes—distinguished by beauty of design, brilliancy of colour, and fineness of quality; while the prices which we understand they command in the market, testify to the high character they hold

among the "trade." For the last seventeen years this house has worked entirely from drawings expressly designed for them, and thus at an early period they materially contributed to give effect to that principle of property in design, the justice of which is now universally admitted. The establishment of a woollen manufacture in Durham, dates back as far as the commencement of the seventeenth century, with funds

supplied out of a charitable trust connected with the city, but the manufacture languished till 1619, and was then abandoned. In 1780, another attempt was made, and was equally unfortunate, two successive parties having failed in working it out; but in 1813, Mr. Gilbert Henderson, the father of the present enterprising proprietors, undertook the task of establishing a manufactory confined to the production of these carpets only.

The CHATELAINE, which, with its various details, occupies this page, is the contribution of Mr. DURHAM, of London; it is an excellent example of steel-manufacture, displaying considerable taste and fancy in the entire composition; while the various articles which form the a fine effect. The modern chatelaine is but a reproduction of an article of decorative ornament, worn by ladies in our own country more

than a century and a half ago. The watch, the scissors, *etui*, pincushion, &c., were then ostentatiously appended to the dresses of the ladies,

quite as much for ornament as for use. The elegant and ornamental character of the object may

pendant group are designed with much taste, and worked up with considerable skill. The numerous *facets* upon the ornamental knobs and enrichments which cover the entire surface of the chatelaine, give to it again ensure its favourable reception; and the beauty of such as that we now engrave must recommend it even to the fastidious utilitarian.

The RICHLY-EMBROIDERED MUSLIN DRESS, of which we engrave a part, is one of the many contributions of Messrs. BROWN, SHARPS, & CO., of Paisley. These manufacturers have long been famous; having obtained eminence not only for the excellence of their work, but for the purity and beauty of their designs,—and it is known that they have employed in the production of subjects for their numerous workers, artists whose reputations have not been merely Provincial. Our engraving can of course afford but a limited idea of the skill of the designer : in this, as in

many others of the articles contributed by the firm, he has aimed at copies of natural flowers, and has avoided those conventional forms which for a long period were considered indispensable to workers in muslin. The dress to which reference is here made, will be found among the richest and most elaborate productions of the

needle. It will readily be supposed that patterns of this description unavoidably lose much of their true effect, by the necessity that compels us to have them drawn on a greatly reduced scale, to suit the size of our pages. Hence, what seems to possess a redundancy of ornament in the engraving, although delicately and carefully drawn on the wood, takes a far less crowded, and a bolder, form on the manufactured article ; this will be understood when we state that the pattern measures, in the original, upwards of three feet in height by four in width.

A LINEN BAND, designed by S. M'CLOY, a pupil of the Belfast School of Design, and produced by Mr. M'CRACKEN, manufacturer of linen

ornaments, Belfast, presents a pattern of much elegance. The subject is derived from the hawthorn in its autumnal or ripe state, when the

berries assume their deep red colour. The arrangement of this composition is exceedingly well managed ; and in the manufactured article

it has a rich and brilliant appearance, the foliage being embossed in gold, with the red berries on a blue ground ; the centre shows the hawthorn

in bloom, coloured after nature on a white ground. To this design was awarded the first prize of three pounds, offered last year by Lord

Dufferin to the Belfast School for the best design for ornamental linen ; it is a work uniting simplicity of subject with great skill in adaptation.

We engrave one of three drawings transmitted to us by PROFESSOR KÄHSZMANN, of Vienna; it exhibits HEBE OFFERING NECTAR TO THE EAGLE OF JOVE. The Professor, we understand, occupies a high position in Austria: his works are generally of a poetical order; but he has been entrusted with some "for the nation" which are in closer proximity to actual life. Happily for the sculptors of the Continent, their governments find them frequent employment; private "commissions" are rare.

how much of grace, dignity, and manly vigour may be sacrificed, to render homage to the so-called "jolly god." These examples of his manufacture are highly creditable to Mr. Meigh; they are works of a right good order,

From the contributions in PORCELAIN and EARTHENWARE of Mr. CHARLES MEIGH, of Shelton, Staffordshire Potteries, we select three objects: the

and exhibit marked improvement in one of the most extensive and best conducted of the factories of Staffordshire. It is only of late that

one, a CLOCK CASE, of very elegant and appropriate design, executed in statuary porcelain; the next, a VASE, also in statuary porcelain—copied, we believe, with some alterations, from a French model; and next, one of those Bacchanalian DRINKING CUPS, ornamented with figures after Poussin—which seem to have been invented for the purpose of showing

Mr. Meigh has paid attention to the better class of goods; but for many years he has enjoyed high repute as a producer of admirable works in earthenware; and he is among the largest exporters in the kingdom.

In the production of CAMEI the continental artists have achieved a well-deserved reputation: we engrave three very beautiful works of this class, the productions of M. JULIN, of Liege. The first is a copy after Horace Vernet of his "Chasse au Faucon," very delicately and beautifully rendered.

The same artist's well-known picture of "Mazeppa" has furnished the second subject; the third is a charming group of "Galatea and the Sea-Nymphs." The grades of tint in camei are fortunate aids to the sculptor in producing striking and interesting effects; these advantages were so highly appreciated by the ancients, that they endeavoured

to imitate them in their glass-works—of which a well-known instance may be cited in the Portland Vase. The works of the ancients in this department of Art were frequently cut upon onyx of large dimensions; one of the most celebrated is preserved at Vienna, and represents the apotheosis of Augustus. The antiques differ from the modern

camei, being cut upon tinted stones, and not on shells (conchylie); the latter being an imitative art in another material, and the result of a comparatively modern era,—the taste for camei having been resuscitated by the famous family of the Medici, and perfected, under their auspices, in Florence.

The TERRA COTTA works of Mrs. MARSH are situated at Charlottensburg distant about four miles from Berlin; the lady by whom they are conducted is the widow of the manufacturer who formed the very admirable establishment. Here are produced works of the highest artistic merit, works designed by the best artists of Prussia, who do not "shame" to dedicate genius to the improvement of the humblest articles of

daily use. We select for engraving four of the productions of Mrs. Marsh;—the Pokal, or

drinking-cup is a copy ; the gothic vase is from the design of Professor Strach. But the most beautiful of the objects contributed by Mrs. Marsh is a Fountain, which we also engrave. This work was produced expressly for the Exhibition.

The VASE, filled with artificial FLOWERS OF SILVER, is the production of STRUBE AND SON, Jewellers, and Silver and Gold Workers, of Leipsic. The Vase is an object of much delicate beauty : the flowers are not made in dies, but are the production of the artist's hand, and are accurately modelled from nature.

We saw at the establishment of Messrs. Strube much that was rare and valuable, but in this particular branch they are unrivalled.

The composition of this fountain is purely classical in design ; the plinth supporting the basin is surrounded by a group of Cupidons ; and the basin itself is ornamented with the leaves of various aqueous plants.

The works of M. FALLOISE, of Liege, in wrought metals, are of the highest order of merit ; the cover of a SNUFF-BOX we print on this page ; and works of great ability on subsequent pages.

This page, and the two pages which follow, are devoted to a few of the contributions of M. MATIFAT, of Paris, an extensive manufacturer of bronze articles, both useful and ornamental. In our illustrated notice of the Exposition in Paris of 1849, we engraved a number of the objects contributed by this most ingenious artist, being particularly struck with their beauty of design and very superior style of workmanship. We have reason to

lead of all other nations in bronze casting; still it is only within a few years comparatively that she has made any considerable move in advance of the old routine system of manufacture; while among those who have quitted the

beaten track, and have introduced new ideas and new arrangements of the best models of antiquity, M. Matifat may take his stand with the very foremost, throwing into his profession a zeal, energy, and perseverance which, united

with skill and taste, could not fail of success, and to elevate him to a high position in his especial branch of manufacture. Having thus awarded him the praise to which he is justly

entitled for his productions generally, we proceed to remark upon the objects we have engraved from a few of his numerous contributions. The first is a FOUNTAIN, of somewhat

small dimensions, suitable for a conservatory; among the floriated ornaments are birds, a squirrel, and a snake; all of which are introduced with the skill of an artist who desires to

make his design both natural and elegant. The first on this column is a VASE or TAZZA, of the style of Louis XIV., cast in iron, its diameter is eight feet, and its height five feet;

know that in this we conferred a benefit upon more than one of our own manufacturers, to whom our pages introduced M. Matifat, and who have availed themselves of his talent and experience to raise the character of their own productions; for this gentleman, like all men of true genius, is influenced by none of those petty and unworthy feelings which would cause him to "hide his lamp under a bushel," fearing lest others should derive light from it. France has for a long time taken the

the form of this vase is exceedingly elegant, and its ornamentation simple, but of pure taste. Underneath are two smaller engravings, one of a DRAWER-HANDLE, and the other a portion of an ESCUTCHEON. Next follows a JEWEL CASKET, of embossed steel, the joints are of iron, damascened with gold, the frames are of silver.

Paris, for some years past, has been regarded as the great manufactory for the finest productions in bronze, calling into employ many excellent artists and the most skilful workmen; for it must be borne in mind that the majority of the best works are sculptured by the hand from the model, as it comes rough from the mould.

To resume, however, our notice of M. MATIFAT'S contributions. The present page commences with a TAZZA and COVER, of chased iron; the flowers in the centre are enamelled, the foot and

Then follows a FLOWER-BASKET, which, being of silver, may be used as a centre-piece for a

the interior are inlaid with gold damascene work, imparting to the object a rich and costly effect.

dessert service: the numerous figures in this

The next object is a TAZZA, of considerable dimensions, and exquisite in form and workman-

ship. The body is surrounded with a wreath of snakes, foliage, and flowers; and other snakes are twisted into the forms of handles: the base and pedestal are decorated in a similar manner.

lesign are judiciously distributed throughout

the composition. An ITALIAN ARCHITECTURAL ORNAMENT, executed in bronze, concludes the

can celebe, exhibiting on the side we have engraved a combat between a man and a centaur.

enamels. The next is a EWER of very elegant form, and highly embossed in the manner of the

We come next to a VASE, the style of which the artist terms Assyrian; it stands two feet and a half in height, and is beautifully studded with

antique. The last engraving exhibits a CHANDELIER of simple but pure character, in which the relative proportions of the different parts are

page; it is distinguished by great beauty of proportion and elaborate chiselling. A GAS PILLAR,

of chaste design, is introduced above; to which succeeds a small VASE, modelled after the Etrus-

evidence that the design has emanated from an artist well instructed in those

principles on which are based the beauty and harmony of curved lines.

A drawing-room CLOCK, made of or-molu, is contributed by MESSRS. HOWELL & JAMES, of London. It is designed by MR. ADAMS, an artist of talent, who has in this produced an elegant work of Art, with emblems most appropriate to the subject. Below the dial are four bas-reliefs of children, representing the "Seasons," and on each side are female groups symbolising Childhood, Youth, Womanhood, and Old Age. A basket of flowers crowns the top, from which hangs a wreath encircling the dial. The scroll work at the base is exceedingly bold, while the pedestal exhibits more delicate ornamentation.

We next introduce an engraving from a splendid horizontal grand PIANO-FORTE, one of the specimens which we have selected from the contributions of MESSRS. COLLARD & COLLARD, of London. The case and the music-stand are richly carved, and the instrument altogether accords well with

the reputation this house has acquired for their instruments among professors and amateurs. Where expense is not an object to the purchaser, we see no reason why the piano-forte should not more frequently exhibit the skill of the carver in wood than we are accustomed to see in it; there is always abundant space for the display of much elegant decoration, without, as may be presumed, detracting from its higher value in the estimation of the performer; and being, generally, an appendage to the drawing-room, ornament, as well as utility in its construction, merits consideration.

From the contributions of Messrs. HARCOURT BROTHERS of Birmingham, we select three—two

BELL-PULLS, and a VASE of bronze. These gentlemen are eminent manufacturers of the several

objects for which the great factory of hardware has been long famous. Their manufactory of

"household" metal furniture is very extensive.

We introduce on this page another engraving of one of the PIANOS of MESSRS. COLLARD & COLLARD, of London. It is richly decorated, and forms a most elegant work of art-manufacture.

The engraving underneath is from one of the carpets contributed by JAN HEUKENSFELDT, of Delfdt. It is or a good order of Art, and will do credit to this long established and justly

celebrated manufacturer, who presides over a very extensive factory of the best Dutch carpets.

Among the fine DIAPERS and damask linens received from Dunfermline, are some singularly rich and beautiful TABLE-CLOTHS, manufactured by Mr. BIRRELL, from designs furnished by Mr. Paton—an artist who has for upwards of a quarter of a century aided the manufacturers of that famous and venerable town. We have engraved one of them on this page—bold and elaborate in design, and in all respects worthy of

covering a regal table. In the corners of the border we discern the "St. George," and in the centres of the same part, the badges of the Order, the Thistle, and St. Patrick. In the centre of the cloth is a medallion bust of Her Gracious Majesty. This table-cloth is made from the finest Flemish flax.

We introduce here four copies of the backs of WATCHES,—the watches contributed by Messrs. ROTHERAM & SON, of Coventry. They exhibit marked improvement of style, and do great credit to the extensive establishment from which they emanate. The designs are good, and the workmanship is excellent. They are enamelled, and tastefully set with jewels, so disposed as to give much beauty and agreeable effect to the forms.

While Sheffield contends successfully with the metropolis in the manufacture of steel goods, she unquestionably takes the lead of all other towns for the excellence displayed in her silver and plated articles adapted for ordinary use; and even goes so far as to rival many of her competitors in what is more especially intended for ornamental purposes, and is moreover executed in the more costly metal. In two or three recent numbers of the *Art-Journal*, we made our readers acquainted with a few of the most important manufacturers of this populous and busy town, introducing, at the same time, numerous engravings copied from their productions. The FISH-KNIFE and FORK, inserted below, are manufactured by Messrs. MAPPIN, BROTHERS, of Sheffield, and will bear comparison with the best examples of a similar description of metal work.

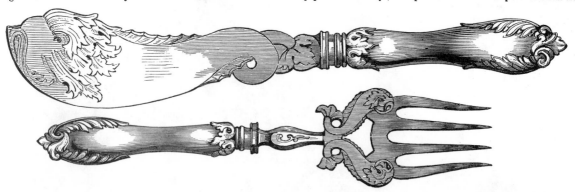

A STATE CHAIR and a STATE BANNER SCREEN, by M. JANCOWSKI, of York, are rich and costly examples of embroidery and decorative furniture. The CHAIR is embroidered on ruby-coloured silk velvet; on the back is the royal coat of arms, the lion raised in gold, the unicorn in silver, with a gold coronet; the crown is worked in gold, silver, silks, and jewels. From the ribbon which shows the motto, a wreath of the rose, shamrock, and thistle, worked in silks, is suspended, and the roses are raised so that every leaf may be lifted up. The seat exhibits the plume of the Prince of Wales, worked in a new style of silk embroidery, having the appearance of silver; the coronet is in gold, silver, and jewels; the motto in gold and silver.

numerous assistants, by whom, we are informed,

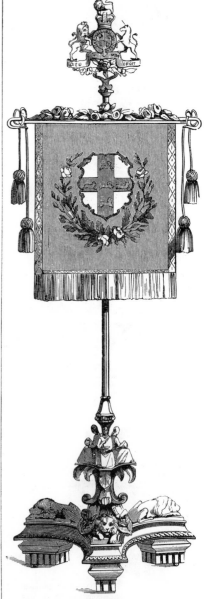

The chair is made up in a splendid carved and gilded frame, trimmed with solid gold bullion fringes. The BANNER SCREEN is embroidered on pale blue satin, with gold, silver, and silks trimmed with rich bullion; it represents the York City Arms; the pole, six feet ten inches in height, is surmounted by the Royal arms finely carved; the pedestal is also richly carved. Both these gorgeous objects reflect the highest credit on the taste and judgment of M. Jancowski and his they have been entirely designed and carried out.

A Shawl, from the manufactory of Messrs. John Morgan & Co., of Paisley, has a rich and most elaborate pattern, reminding us of some of the best designs that are imported from the East—but greatly improving upon them. Besides Shawls, the manufacturers are also producers of printed and tartan fabrics to a large extent, specimens of which are likewise to be found in the Exhibition. In all these cases, the patterns are designed, and the goods are manufactured, dyed, and finished on the premises of Messrs. Morgan.

From the establishment of M. Gabain, of Berlin, which we visited during our late tour through Germany, have been forwarded a large variety of Silk Stuffs. We engrave on this page one example, of a graceful palm-pattern, designed by Professor Bötticher, of Berlin. This pattern is about five feet in height, by twenty-seven inches in breadth, when it is repeated. This weaving is done on a satin ground, and it is produced in various colours, as well as in different tints of the same colour. We may, hereafter, introduce other productions of this house.

We fill up this page with one of the contributions of Messrs. Hoole & Robson, of Sheffield.—A Fender, remarkable for the grace of its design, as well as for the beauty of its execution—qualities for which this eminent firm have obtained much celebrity; deservedly so, as we shall be enabled to show in our engravings from others of their works in subsequent pages. The combination of steel and bronze adapted by them is, in many instances, productive of the happiest effects. Perhaps there is no class of our native manufacturers, who have made greater advances in the field of improvement than those connected with the polished steel trade.

A PEDIMENT, designed and modelled by Mr. C. Fox, of Brighton, shows an effective arrangement of the figures introduced into it. The subject is intended to represent the "Arts, Commerce, and Manufactures, promoted by the Great Exhibition." The first group to the left represents Navigation, the next Industry bringing her offerings to Peace. In the centre is the Queen, holding out wreaths of laurel to the various contributors, and to the right the Fine Arts and Science are symbolised in respective groups.

A CARYATIDE, sculptured in oak by M. CRUCHET, of Paris, is a bold and not inelegant conception of an architectural ornament which, of itself, has generally little to recommend it as a decorative object. Used as substitutes for columns, they possess neither the elegance of outline, nor the symmetry of proportion, that render the latter important and interesting features of the edifice with which they are connected. It would seem that the origin of these figures appertains to Egyptian architecture, for they are recorded in all the traces of this style of building that have come down to us; and they were adopted, though sparingly, by the Greeks, from whom we have derived one, now in the British Museum among the Elgin collection,

We engrave here one of the contributions of Professor RIETSCHEL, of Dresden—a dead CHRIST, over whom mourns the VIRGIN MOTHER. The artist holds rank among the most eminent sculptors of Germany: to him has been confided the task of executing the principal national monuments of Saxony; and the sculptured decorations of the Theatre of Dresden are the production of this master-mind of his country. His sculptures will excite in England the admiration so universally accorded to them throughout the rest of Europe. We had—in 1850—the privilege to see this accomplished

which was taken from the Acropolis, at Athens. artist at work upon this, the latest, and perhaps the greatest, of his many admirable productions.

Few knowing the vast resources and the long experience of the eminent firm of Messrs. HUNT & ROSKELL, of London, who now conduct the business formerly carried on by Messrs. Storr & Mor-

timer, will be surprised to find them making a display in the Exhibition commensurate with the reputation of an establishment that produces many of the most costly manufactured articles in the precious metals. Without disparagement to any other house in London, in a similar branch of business, it may be said that Messrs. Hunt & Roskell have no rival in the extent of their transactions, and a visit to their show-rooms is like inspecting a museum of Art. We, therefore, feel that we do not pay an unmerited compliment to these manufacturers in gold and silver works of

merits of foreign and English silver-work, it has been stated that the inferiority of the latter has been in a great measure attributable to the absence of good designs, and to the superior taste and delicacy of finish in the foreign workmen. Recent

political events abroad have, however, brought over a number of the latter to this country, and there cannot be a doubt that we have greatly benefited by this fusion of adventitious aid with English energy, perseverance, and capital. More-over, manufacturers have found it essential to their interests to seek the assistance of other heads than those of the mere artisan, however skilful as a workman, to invent, and suggest, and improve. Hence from these two causes a decided change

every kind and description, by devoting two or three pages of our Catalogue to a notice of their contributions. In the remarks we have occasionally made in the *Art-Journal* upon the comparative

for the better has, within the past few years, been perceptible in every branch of this department of Industrial Art; and we may add, without egotism, that the pages of the *Art-Journal* have had some influence in effecting this amelioration,

by means we need not now enlarge upon. With

these few brief introductory observations we

proceed to the notice of the various subjects selected from Messrs. Hunt & Roskell's contributions. The first page commences with two bronze STATUETTES; the former represents a Hindoo girl plucking the sacred moon-plant (*sarcostema viminalis*), and the latter depositing her lamp in the waters of the Ganges. The originals of these statuettes are, we believe, executed in silver, and formed a part of the Ellenborough testimonial. The group that succeeds form the ORANGE GOODWOOD PLATE, for the year 1846; it represents William of Nassau at the Battle of Nieuport. This is followed by the TESTIMONIAL presented to Mr. B. Lumley, lessee of Her Majesty's Theatre; it is designed and modelled by Mr. A. Brown; the figures, appropriately introduced, are those of the sister muses who preside over dramatic and musical festivals. The column on

the second page commences with a DESSERT STAND, showing a Hindoo flower setter under a banyan tree; the succeeding objects are two ICE-PAILS, formed by the lotus, supported by other Indian plants; these three objects are from a service presented to the Earl of Ellenborough. The large engraving on the same page is a massive and costly CANDELABRUM in silver, a testimonial presented to the Marquis of Tweeddale. The subject of the group is taken

from Buchanan's "History of Scotland," and illustrates the historical fact connected with the rise of this noble family; a countryman, named Hay—the family name—is, with his two sons,

leading the Scots to the defeat of the Danes, A.D. 980. The composition, which evinces remarkable spirit, is also designed and modelled by Mr. A. Brown. At the head of the third

page is an elegant CUP, followed by a silver-gilt CASKET, in the style of the cinque-cento period, set with antique gems; and below this is a CUP to correspond. A group in silver, of Mazeppa,

to Sir Moses Montefiore. It is scarcely necessary to remind our readers that Sir Moses is of the Hebrew persuasion, and that the design, which is by Sir J. Hayter, has reference to certain events connected with the past and present history of the Jews. Thus, the sphinxes indicate the captivity of Israel in Egypt; the figures are Moses,

comes next; great spirit is imparted to this work by the animals being "relieved" from the ground, the horse, especially, appears as if flying. The last engraving is from a TESTIMONIAL presented

Ezra, the great deliverer of the people, a Jew of Damascus, loaded with chains, and one released; under them are appropriate texts in Hebrew, with the vine and the fig-tree overshadowing. The group on the summit represents David rescuing the lamb from the jaws of the lion, and the bassi-relievi show the Passage of the Red

Sea, and the Destruction of Pharaoh's host; Lawless Violence in the world, typified by wolves devouring the flocks; the Millenium as spoken of by Isaiah; Sir Moses and Lady Montefiore landing at Alexandria; Sir Moses obtaining the firman from the Sultan; and two other subjects.

THE INDUSTRY OF ALL NATIONS.

The SILVER CUP, engraved below, is designed, modelled, and embossed by the exhibitor, Mr. SHARP, of London; he terms it the "Justice Cup." It exhibits round the body in bas-relief, Justice protecting the Innocent, and driving from the earth Violence, Fraud, and Discord.

A PANEL, carved in wood, and *carton-pierre* by M. CRUCHET, of Paris, will attract attention, not only from its position, but for the artistic arrangement of its various groups, and the bold execution of the work. The centre is filled with a design modified from Albert Durer's "St. Hubert," and the lower composition shows a group of children engaged in agricultural operations.

The CARPET pattern engraved below is from the manufactory of Messrs. PARDOE & Co., of Kidderminster, one of the largest establishments in that town; it produces an infinite variety of goods, from the costly velvet to the commoner kinds, but all of more than ordinary excellence.

Mr. BIELEFELD, of London, the extensive manufacturer of ornaments in PAPIER-MACHE, exhibits a large variety of his manufactures, from which we have selected five specimens for engraving, namely, two corbels, one bracket, a

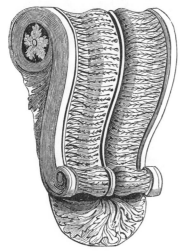

centre-piece, and a cornice or moulding, all of them designed with true artistic taste, and executed with very considerable sharpness and delicacy. Mr. Bielefeld manufactures almost

exclusively for the trade; or, in other words, supplies architects, builders, and decorators with the ornaments required for the edifices they may be erecting; and, in the present day, these papier-mâché manufactures have, in a great measure,

superseded the use of plaster ornaments, and are not unfrequently used instead of the more costly

designs; the facility with which it may be put together and fixed up; its lightness, and, lastly,

it above every other employed in interior decoration. We have, on more than one occasion, visited and reported Mr. Bielefeld's most interest-

materials of stone and wood. Its hardness, durability, and ready assumption of all forms and

its cheapness, are all qualities highly desirable in a manufacture of the kind, and which recommend

ing establishment, and have had opportunities of inspecting the very extensive variety of ornamental productions constantly issuing from it.

Perhaps there are few branches of British Industrial Art in which greater advance has been made during the past few years than our

glass manufactures exhibit: in quality of material, in form, and in design, the works of the present day manifest a decided superiority over

those of a quarter of a century ago. The three GLASSES on this column, manufactured by Mr. CONNE, of London, are in themselves sufficient

evidence of this progress; the ornamental design in the first and second examples is characterised by delicacy, and in the third by boldness, while the form of each respectively is in good taste.

From upwards of one hundred specimens of DAMASK TABLE LINEN and COLOURED TABLE CLOTHS, manufactured by Mr. BEVERIDGE, of Dunfermline, we have selected six for introduc-

tion on this and the two following pages. Mr. Beveridge's manufactory is among the first, if not the most extensive, in the town and its neighbourhood, employing about fifteen hundred

pair of hands out of some five or six thousand engaged in this branch of trade. The varieties of fabric woven in Dunfermline may be stated to consist of damask table-linen, table-covers,

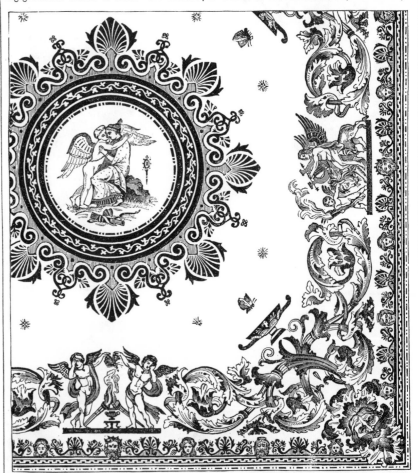

linen floor-cloths, and diapers of all descriptions; more than one half of the goods so manufactured, and these chiefly of the finer sorts, are disposed of in the home market, the remainder being exported, principally to the United States. Table linen has greatly benefited by the introduction of the Jacquard loom, which is used for every description of cloth, from that made expressly for her Majesty's table, to the coarsest "whitey-brown," destined to cover the pine-board of some American backwoodsman. Some idea may be

formed of the present advanced state of the manufacture, when it is known that for the design of a table-cloth and napkin, such as some of those represented on our pages, as much as one hundred pounds are frequently paid. Our

A CIMITAR and SCABBARD, by Messrs. WILKIN-SON and SON, of London, is a most elegant speci-men of manufacturing art. It is of silver, chased and gilt, and is ornamented with one hundred and four precious stones, consisting of emeralds,

first engraving is from a TABLE-CLOTH of damask, woven in an arabesque pattern, of great boldness. The second is also a damask TABLE-CLOTH, with napkins to correspond; they are of classic design,

the centre exhibiting figures of Cupid and Psyche. This page commences with a TABLE-COVER of arabesque pattern, in various colours; it is made of silk, cotton, and wool. This is followed by a

linen damask TABLE-CLOTH, with napkins to correspond; the border is Gothic, having the figures of St. George, St. Andrew, and St. Patrick in the corner niches, with St. George and the

Dragon in the centre. This pattern is singularly beautiful. The articles confer honour upon the manufacturer. They are, we understand, prin-cipally designed by Mr. Paton, of Dunfermline.

rubies, turquoises, jacynths, carbuncles, &c., &c., inserted in arabesque patterns. The blade is of the finest temper; it combines embossing with engraving, blueing, and gilding, so as to form two elevations of an highly ornamental pattern.

We resume on this page the contributions of Mr. BEVERIDGE, of Dunfermline. The first engraving is from a linen damask TABLE-CLOTH, having napkins and doyleys to correspond. The pattern introduced is borrowed from the vine. The next is a TABLE-COVER, in what the manufacturer terms the French style; it is woven in a variety of rich colours, in wool, silk, and cotton. It seems almost unnecessary to add that the circumscribed space to which we are compelled to limit our engravings, detracts somewhat from the boldness of the designs. There is a curious history attached to the introduction of this art into Dunfermline—from Drumsheugh, near

Edinburgh, where it was secretly practised at the beginning of the last century. A man, named Blake, feigning to be of weak intellect, found his way into a weaving-shop, and was permitted to amuse himself underneath a loom, where he carefully observed the manner in which the cords and other parts were arranged, and, by the aid of a good memory, and some previous knowledge of the general mechanism of the loom, he brought away the grand secret, and was not long in reducing it to practice. In no branch of Art-Manufacture do we perceive such unequivocal signs of advancement as in the damasks produced of late years in Scotland and in Ireland; of this our

Catalogue supplies sufficient proof; those of Belfast, engraved in subsequent pages, are honourable to Ireland; the great manufacturing capital of the island is, in all respects, worthily represented; while the ancient renown of "gray Dunfermline" is more than sustained by the productions of its looms, which find their way, common or refined, to every country, and almost every district, of the civilised world. In such articles as those under notice, we can have no dread of foreign competition; neither in the material, its fabrication, nor even in the decoration to which they have been subjected, shall we be surpassed by the manufacturers of Germany, Belgium, or France.

On this column are engravings from two exquisitely beautiful CASKETS, manufactured by Mr. WERTHEIMER, of London. The engraved work on these objects is of the most elaborate and delicate description; they are adorned with malachite and precious stones, and are, in every way, worthy of finding

a home in the most sumptuous boudoir. The lower one is placed on a superbly gilt stand, the base of which has also malachites inserted. While so many exquisite works—worthy rivals to the best of those which "the great era" produced in Germany and France—are contributed from

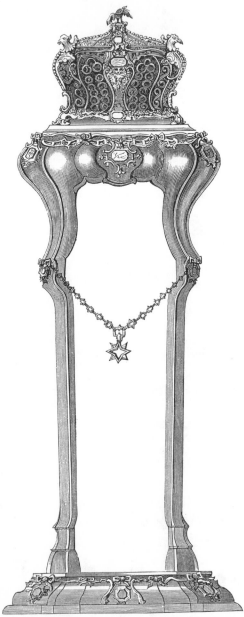

the Continent, it is with exceeding pleasure we direct attention to those which have been created in England; Mr. Wertheimer is, we understand, a German, but one who is to be regarded as a British subject. We believe the coming of such men among us to be the surest way to benefit ourselves.

The RIBBON patterns occupying this column are from the manufactory of Mr. C. BRAY, of Coventry. The

former of the two designs has a quaint yet elegant

border, and the centre shows two light and graceful patterns. The latter contains a greater variety of beautiful subject, disposed in a highly effective manner.

The manufacture of PAPIER-MÂCHÉ into a great variety of useful articles of large size is the result of the efforts made, within a comparatively recent period, by the various artisans who have devoted their attention to this important branch of the industrial arts.

It is not many years since the limits of the trade were circumscribed to a tea-tray, but now we find articles of furniture, not only of a slight and ornamental character, such as ladies' work-tables or boxes, but of a more substantial kind, in chairs and sofas for the draw-

ing-room, or the entire casings of pianofortes. All such examples of the variety and comprehensive nature of *papier-mâché* works are exhibited by Messrs. JENNENS & BETTRIDGE, of London and Birmingham, and our pages testify to their beauty. These manufacturers have earned a reputation by their unceasing endeavours to improve the character of such productions,—a reputation which is certainly well deserved, and which will be increased by their contributions to the Great Exhibition. We commence our series of illustrations with an INKSTAND, designed by H. M'Carthy, a sculptor of great ability, the animals being in oxidised silver; the entire surface of the inkstand is black, and the base upon which the stag stands is ingeniously designed for an envelope-box. We follow with the most novel and beautiful of the series of these manufacturers' works. The "VICTORIA REGIA" COT, designed by Mr. J. Bell, the eminent sculptor. The body of the cot is nautilus-shaped; it is of a dark tint, upon which is richly emblazoned the rose, nightshade, and poppy. The flowers of the *Victoria regia* decorate the base,

and gracefully curl over the cot as supports for the curtain. The entire fittings are sumptuous in character, but in the best possible taste. Our next example exhibits a very novel and graceful adjunct to the boudoir, in the LOTUS-TABLE, also designed by Mr. J. Bell; it is, perhaps, one of the most original conceptions contributed by the manufacturers whose works we are describing. The floriated decoration which covers its surface is eastern in character, possessing all its elaboration of form, and all its vivid beauty of colour, the effect of the whole being gorgeous in the extreme, but not by any means offensively gaudy, a qualification that is not always duly considered, though it always should be, in works of this class. An improvement is effected by constructing the shaft of the table in the style of a telescope, and allowing each part to be

lifted for use as required. The ELIZABETHAN CHAIR is a favourable specimen of the success

which may attend the manufacturer who fear-

second group comprises a VASE, originally designed for the late Princess Sophia; it is richly

lessly carries out his conceptions in any material, however discouraging it may appear in the outset. The peculiar character of decoration embraced by this style has been effectually preserved, but it has been rendered very light and elegant by the perforated work, and the colouring and gilding, which adorn it. It is remarkably firm and strong, but the ornamentation prevents it from appearing heavy. Of a totally different character is our second CHAIR, in which lightness and gracefulness of contour have been entirely considered, and are well carried out. It is termed the "Légère Chair," and has been provisionally registered by its makers, who seem

to be aware of its claim to popularity. Our

inlaid with mother-of-pearl and gilding on a pink ground. The ladies' WORK-TABLE is decorated in the same taste, and is of very novel form. The POMPEIAN FLOWER-STAND is a graceful and elegant ornament to the drawing-room. The WRITING-DESK seen in the foreground is inlaid with imitative gems by the patented process, employed exclusively by this establishment with the happiest effect. The small CROCHET-BOX beside it is ornamented with a classic bas-relief, electro-silvered by Elkington, the subject being the story of Niobe. Our last engraving shows a group of TRAYS, the old staple branch of the trade, which are designed with freedom and decorated with good taste; we give an example of the simplest as well as the most fanciful, that we may fairly represent these works. The centre one was made for the Duchess of Sutherland; its shape was expressly designed to admit the tea-urn nearer to the dispensers of "the cup which cheers but not inebriates;" the tray to the left is richly inlaid with patent pearl ornaments; the design of the other is plainer.

Mr. G. W. ADAMS, of London, exhibits numerous objects of silver, and silver-gilt plate, of more than ordinary excellence in design. We have selected from his contributions, of which, by the way, he is also the manufacturer, a DESSERT FORK and SPOON, and two DESSERT SUGAR

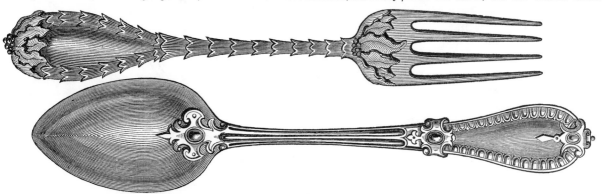

LADLES. The patterns of the former are remarkable for their simple elegance; there is little ornamentation in them, but what there is, shows the best taste. The latter are richer and more elaborate in their design, in which the vine and hop plants, with their respective foliage, are

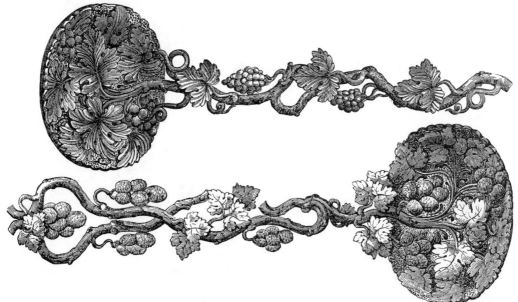

brought in most effectively. The works of our silversmiths undoubtedly exhibit great progress during the last few years; they have certainly kept pace with the increasing taste of the age and the demand for the beautiful, in all matters connected with the chief manufacturing arts.

Liége, for many years famous for its manufactory of fire-arms, shows well in the great Exhibition. We engrave here a most elegantly ornamented PISTOL, made by M. MANDAN, of that city; it is certainly as fine a specimen of elaborate engraved work as we remember to have seen so applied. The design of the decoration is in the Romanesque style, and is displayed with considerable taste.

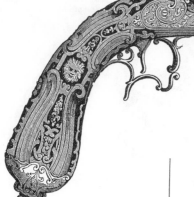

M. GEERTS, of Louvain, who has been extensively employed by the Belgian government in decorating the town-hall of that city with statuary, and the stalls of the Cathedral of Antwerp with groups of wood-carving, contributes a group of angels, carrying the slaughtered innocents of Herod's massacre heavenward, and comforting an un-

The three WATCHES, the backs of which we engrave on this column, are manufactured by Mr. W. H. JACKSON, of Clerkenwell; they are

elegantly designed and elaborately engraved.

The internal construction of these watches shows,

we understand, several important improvements.

fortunate mother. It is executed in light wood, and expresses a novel and poetic idea embodied in the taste of the medieval artists who flourished in the Low Countries in the fifteenth and six-teenth centuries; indeed, the eminent sculptor has been singularly happy in catching the style and spirit exhibited in works of that period, but in a great degree refining upon the school.

MR. URLING, of London, for many years well known as an extensive manufacturer of lace, contributes a white LACE SCARF, in imitation of Brussels point, ornamented with British plants and flowers in needlework. The date, 1851, is encircled by the rose, thistle, and shamrock. The straight lines of the border are embroidered in gold, and worked upon a fine clear net, for which Mr. Urling long ago obtained a patent. The design for this scarf was, we believe, made expressly for the manufacturer by Miss Gann, a clever pupil of the Government School of Design.

The CLARET-JUG and TEA-SERVICE are contributed by MR. DODD, of London, whose taste and knowledge in the art of design are, if we mistake not, the results of considerable artistic experience, which is abundantly manifested in the objects before us. These are manufactured of silver, richly chased; a series of medallions. illustrative of different subjects, occupies the body of each, and the spaces between them are filled in with enrichments, elaborately executed. When we compare such forms and ornaments as these with the works of half a century back, there can be but one opinion as to the progress made.

Some rich and elaborate carving will be seen in the SIDEBOARD, manufactured by Messrs. TROLLOPE & SONS, of London. There is considerable novelty of design in the pillars that form the frame-work of the glass, while the whole of the carving shows great elegance of design united with exceeding delicacy in the manipulation; it has been executed at a very large cost.

This column is devoted to a series of VASES, executed in white terra-cotta, by Messrs. DOUL-

TON & WATT, of Lambeth, whose attention has only recently been directed to objects of an

artistic character; those we have engraved may be regarded as a prelude to further success,

which increased experience must insure. The use of terra-cotta, or of artificial stone, as applied

to objects of art and of decoration, is by no means new in this country, although such appli-

From numerous specimens of engraved and cut GLASS, contributed by Mr. W. NAYLOR, of London, we have selected several and formed them into a group, which will exhibit their

various forms and ornaments to great advantage. | The patterns are cut with extreme minuteness. | cation has been of late very limited. Half a century since, it was carried on to a great extent by Messrs. Coade, of Lambeth.

The SERPENTINE MARBLE WORKS, established at Penzance, in Cornwall, contribute many examples of this beautiful material. We select a few specimens more illustrative of form than of colour,

Two of the richly decorated and admirably constructed FIRE-GRATES of Messrs. HOOLE & ROBSON of Sheffield, are introduced on this page; other of their productions will appear elsewhere.

These gentlemen are foremost among the best manufacturers of the kingdom; their establishment has been long celebrated, not only for its large extent but for the admirable skill of its

the latter being the most striking recommendation these works possess. The slender VASE at the head of our page, the FONT in the centre,

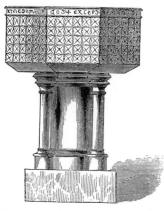

and the VASE at the base, are all beautiful, and are considerably enhanced by the variegated colours which pervade the marble. The geolo-

productions, and their contributions cannot fail to attract very general attention. They were among the first to introduce that happy mingling of brass and or-molu with iron, which, under judicious management, is so effective in giving

grace and elegance to the fire-side; and they have taken especial care to obtain all the advantages which can be derived from the proper application of art to their purposes, employing thoroughly educated artists in the superintend-

gical riches of our own land are, in very many instances, well displayed throughout the British departments of the Exhibition, and strongly testify to their value and beauty.

ence of their works. In this class of manufacture England stands pre-eminent; regard being had, however, to the fact that the English fire-

grate is comparatively unknown upon the continent, and that consequently none of its fabricants have attempted to enter into competition with us.

The art of glass-painting is carried on in | England principally at Birmingham and at New-

A group of the VIRGIN and CHILD, by M. VANDER HAGEN, a Belgian sculptor settled in London, will remind those who have studied ecclesiastical sculptures of some of these classical

castle-upon-Tyne; each of these towns boasts of possessing extensive establishments for these beautiful productions, and each is a formidable rival to the other. The ILLUMINATED WINDOW is from the manufactory of Mr. GIBSON, of New-castle-on-Tyne; its ornamentation is derived from the early Norman style; fillets of ruby and green, interlacing on a stone-coloured ground, form geometrical compartments; in the top one is the cross, and in the centre of the others are

bosses composed of rich colours; the whole design resulting in tracery filled with elaborate ornament, is worked in black outline relieved by shadow; the border is in enamel on a blue ground. This window will be much admired for its gorgeous, yet simple and unpretending effect.

and well-modelled compositions. It is very symmetrical in its proportions, and the drapery is arranged in an easy flowing style, that gives grace and firmness to the principal figure.

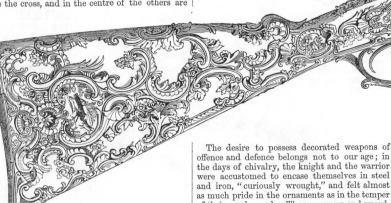

The desire to possess decorated weapons of offence and defence belongs not to our age; in the days of chivalry, the knight and the warrior were accustomed to encase themselves in steel and iron, "curiously wrought," and felt almost as much pride in the ornaments as in the temper of their good swords. The armourers and sword-

cutlers of Brabant competed then with those of Madrid, Toledo, and Damascus, to produce the most elegant examples of their workmanship, many of which are still preserved. Even the introduction of gunpowder only changed the application of their art from armour and swords to guns of every size and description. The GUN-STOCK here engraved is by M. TOUREY, of Liége. It is very elaborately carved and inlaid with gold, silver, and platina, in the enriched style of the time of Louis the Fourteenth.

A very beautiful example of wood carving is exhibited in a BENETIER by M. KNECHT, of Paris. Its character is well adapted to the style usually followed in ecclesiastical structures, being an arrangement of the vine in Gothic forms ; the centre shows the "Virgin and Child," the former treading on the serpent.

The group—the FORTUNE-TELLER—is contributed by Professor WICKMANN, of Berlin, a sculptor of eminent rank in Germany. He is an artist who especially studies grace ; his works exhibit exceeding refinement, yet in combination with rigid adherence to truth. This work he has executed in marble ; it was designed expressly for the Exhibition. The intention of the sculptor is to tell the story of a young girl "spaeing" the fortune of another.

The work is happily conceived, and wrought with the highest finish. During our visit to Germany in 1850, in the atelier of M. Wickmann, we had the pleasure to examine many other fine examples of the admirable artist's genius, and it will be our privilege to engrave some of them hereafter for the *Art-Journal*. With that view we have received copies from the sculptor, whom we shall hope thus to make better known than he is in England.

A FRIEZE sculptured in wood, by M. LIENARD, of Paris, represents a boar-hunt in the olden time ; the party have just come on the lair of the wild animal, and are preparing to attack him. The design is very spirited, the figures are grouped with much pictorial effect, and the work

is boldly yet delicately carved in alto-relievo. M. Lienard is, we believe, a young artist who has acquired very considerable reputation in Paris as a designer, and, judging from the specimens he has sent to the Exhibition, of his own handy-work, he can execute with as much skill as he invents. We understand that not a few of the leading Parisian manufacturers of ornamental articles are indebted to him for some of their best designs.

The FLORAL ORNAMENTS, executed in leather, and contributed by MESSRS. ESQUILANT & CO., of London, are excellent specimens of this description of manufacture. They are made of the stoutest material, and may be readily mistaken for wood-carvings; hence their peculiar applicability for the internal decoration of houses, and for the saloons of steam ships, for which it is perhaps more especially adapted, as less liable to split or break off than wood; in fact, where cheapness, durability, and ornament are required, these leather productions are valuable.

AN EMBROIDERED CHEMISETTE, designed by J. WAUGH, pupil of the Belfast School of Design,

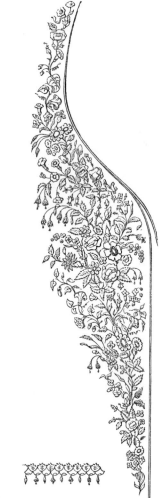

An example of CARVED WOOD, also by M. LIENARD, of Paris, shows it to be the work of an artist. It is sculptured in alto-relievo; the design has reference to field sports, the three compartments and manufactured in muslin by Mr. J. HOLDEN, of Belfast, is in good taste; it gained the first prize

exhibiting respectively, foxes, deer, and partridges; the sides of the centre-frame, birds and hunting implements; while the base supports two or three dogs. Festoons of leaves encircling the frames enrich the composition, and impart to it much elegance by their graceful arrangement. of five pounds, offered by Lord Dufferin last year to the Belfast School, for the best drawing suited to this elegant portion of a lady's dress.

The Ironworks of M. ANDRE, of Paris, are of great magnitude, furnishing every kind of ornamental objects which the manufacture of this metal supplies, principally of an importance commensurate with the large resources of the establishment. We have selected, as examples of their productions, a cast-iron group intended for a FOUNTAIN, which is very original in design; all the materials of the composition are drawn from objects associated with water, amphibious

There is a class of manufacturers in France, whose artistic talents are more frequently called into requisition than in England,—the makers of window fastenings and long window bolts; we have seen in Paris a large variety of these objects, on which taste and talent of no ordinary kind have been expended. We engrave here a

animals, and aquatic plants. Among the former the chief is a crocodile holding a fish in his mouth, beneath this is an otter to the right, a tortoise to the left, and a large frog at the third

angle: from the mouths of these animals the jets of water are intended to rise, and they are surrounded by the water-lily, floating reeds, and bending rushes. The other example is from a

WINDOW BOLT, by M. COUDRUE, of Paris, as an excellent example of this kind of manufacture; it affords, in its various details, suggestions of which other producers may profitably avail themselves.

The WORK-TABLE which concludes this page is manufactured by Mr. C. F. GRUBB, of Banbury, Oxfordshire. As the production of a self-educated artisan, it shows considerable taste in design, and ingenuity of execution. A wreath of flowers is

cast-iron CHIMNEY-PIECE, in what is called the Louis Quatorze style, a style still much in vogue among the French: such an object so manufactured is a novelty in this country, so far as our observation has extended, and it is one from

which our own manufacturers may, we should think, borrow an idea with no little advantage, though it may be doubted whether iron would ever be extensively used as a substitute for marble in the decoration of first-rate domestic edifices.

carried round the top, from which are suspended sprigs of ivy reaching to the pedestal; this is formed of dock leaves, and at the end of these are seen rabbits that constitute the feet of the table; a novelty in ornament worthy of notice.

We select from the works of MESSRS. GRAINGER, of Worcester, a series of articles which exhibit a

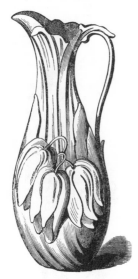

peculiar fancy in design, combined with much

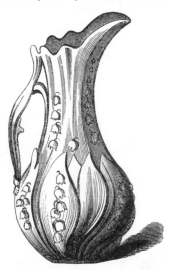

simplicity of decoration. The JUGS are covered

with leaves and flowers, or appear as if constructed with interlaced leaves, a style of ornamentation for which Messrs. Grainger have a peculiar reputation. The difficulty, however, of adapting this mode of decoration to the forms and uses of the articles is considerable : it has been combated with judgment but not always

simplicity; the few water-leaves which decorate it being applicable and unobtrusive, and the general contour graceful. The COFFEE-SERVICE is a quaint and curious group, designed after the style of the old continental china, but possessing

handles are formed of wheat-ears, with their stalks and leaves. The same decoration forms the boundary line of the tray, also made in china. As a light and elegant service for the boudoir, it possesses attraction; and though

with success. We consider some of the objects we engrave as among the curiosities of earthenware manufacture, but are not prepared to enforce their claim to unqualified approval. The EWER and BASON is agreeable, from its entire

some originalities of its own, in the form of its outlines. It is covered with an open honeycomb pattern, which shows the rich blue ground through its perforations; a style of decoration in great vogue more than a century ago. The

presenting the appearance of its costly prototype, it is manufactured at a comparatively small cost; indeed, this remark will apply to the generality of works issued from the extensive manufactory of Messrs. Grainger.

The great improvements made of late in all the appointments of "an Englishman's fireside," are visible to the least observant. Stoves of all kinds and forms, fenders of the most fanciful designs, and enrichments of the most classical description, have been freely used in their decoration. We here present a specimen of good taste in FIRE-IRONS, the originals of our group

We present two groups of the works of Messrs. BROADHEAD & ATKIN, manufacturers of silver and plated goods, of Sheffield; they embrace some very good examples of Decorative Art applied to objects of ordinary use, or to those which form the ornamental adjuncts to the

dinner-table. The tea and coffee-pots, with the cream-jug and sugar-basin *en suite*, exhibit a happy rendering of forms with which we are in some degree familiar, but with ornaments presenting the charm of novelty. In the series of illustrations which occupy our Catalogue, a large

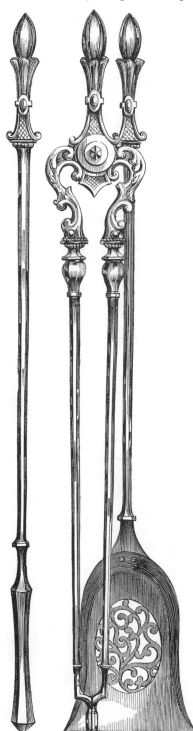

number of designs will appear, that have been executed both in clay and metal, to give variety to the breakfast service, and most of them prove

an anxiety to leave a beaten track. Our larger group contains flower-stands, a cake-basket, a claret-jug, and a bottle-stand, all of good design.

We fill this page with a FENDER, to which the manufacturers have given the name of the "snake fender," made by Messrs. JOBSON & Co., Sheffield,

for Mr. W. S. Burton, of London. Other works of Messrs. Jobson, for which we could not arrange in this division, will appear in subsequent pages.

being the work of Messrs. H. & W. TURNER, of Sheffield, who have adopted a style of decoration which gives a sufficient amount of ornament, without detracting from the rigid utilitarian principle, so necessary in producing works of this class, and which ought ever to be borne strictly in remembrance by the designer.

THE INDUSTRY OF ALL NATIONS.

We commence this page with an engraving from the back of a very elegant WATCH, manufactured by MR. JONES, of London. It is ornamented in a rich, elaborate, and tasteful style.

MR. A. PELLATT, of London, exhibits a TEA-SERVICE with its TRAY, designed by Mr. Binns, which he designates the "Bridal Breakfast Service," and especially intended for a bridal present. It is painted with emblems, adapted to such an auspicious event, in the language of flowers.

The BAROMETER is manufactured by MR. DOBBIE, of Falkirk; it claims merit as being made on a plan by which the least possible rise or fall

A piece of TAPESTRY, for a screen, worked in heraldic patterns by MISS BIFIELD, of Islington, aided by a large number of her pupils, is a very ingenious and clever specimen of needlework. It is unnecessary to explain the armorial bearings, which are sufficiently well known, except perhaps the two lowest; these

of the mercury is ascertained with the greatest precision. The case is richly and carefully carved.

are the arms of the Duke of Wellington and of the late Sir Robert Peel, significant of the great military and political leaders of the present age. Each quartering is worked on a separate portion of velvet, and afterwards carefully united so as to form an entire piece.

We may presume to say that there is no class of manufacturers whose talents seem to have been brought out with more success than those engaged in the various branches of cabinet-work; and there is, perhaps, no description of manufacture in which taste, ingenuity, and artistic skill may be more effectively exercised. Furniture, whether useful or merely ornamental, at once reveals its own story of the degree of talent and the length of time devoted to its execution; all connected with it, to use a homely phrase, is plain and aboveboard, and the eye cannot be deceived by false appearances, nor lured to admire by the display of glittering colours, as is the case in many other operative arts. The SIDEBOARD introduced here is manufactured and exhibited by Messrs. HOWARD & SON, of London; the back and front are inlaid with fine plate glass, enriched by carved floriated ornaments of "cunning workmanship" in the Italian style.

Our next subject is a CARPET contributed by WATSON, BELL, & Co., of London; the ground-work of this carpet is simple but in good taste: the centre, however, and the border are rich and massive in design, and most effective in the arrangement of their well-selected colours.

This page contains specimens of JEWELLERY, produced by Messrs. WATHERSTON & BROGDEN, of London; eminent manu-

facturers, who have studied to combine richness of material with beauty of design and skill in arrangement. The

contributions exhibited are of great value, but they will attract attention less from their actual worth than from the ability they manifest; they will be worthy competitors with those continental pro-

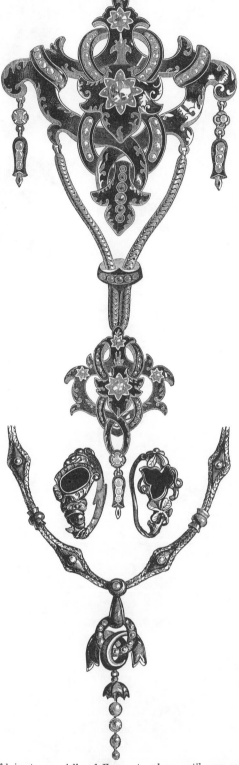

ductions which have established the fame of so many

fabricants, especially of France, to whom, until very re-

cently, we appeared willing to yield the palm without dispute. The bracelet which heads the page was suggested by one of

the Nineveh monuments; the brooches, or more properly, breast ornaments which follow, several of which are deduced from

flowers and leaves, are chiefly composed of enamels united with precious stones.

The STATUE of Cupid is the work of Mr. P. MAC DOWELL, R.A., whose well-earned reputation as a sculptor of high merit it is unnecessary to dilate upon. He here represents the winged boy in the act of drawing a shaft from his quiver.

Few of our readers who may not have seen the original of the annexed engraving will have any idea from what it has been copied; it is, in fact, a CAKE, from the celebrated establishment of Mr. GUNTER, of London, who has employed a

clever Italian artist, M. Conté, to design it for him, and to model the elegant little figures which ornament the base. The work reflects credit to all parties concerned in producing it, and is worthy of being perpetuated in more enduring material.

The CHIMNEY-PIECE is exhibited by Messrs. BRINE, BROTHERS, of London, and manufactured after a design by Mr. T. Sharp. It is elaborately carved in statuary marble, with cast metal ornaments, electro-gilt, mounted on the pilasters, frieze, and spandrils. In the last are the initials

of the Queen and Prince Albert, formed with the stems of the rose, shamrock, and thistle, which entwine them. The work is nine feet high.

The beautiful decorative IRON CUP here intro- | duced is by M. FALLOISE, of Liége. The upper

The Jewellery of M. LEVY PRINS, of Brussels, has achieved celebrity in the capital of Belgium; and will not be without many admirers in our own. There is much of novelty in the arrange-

shows the interior, with its varied enrich- | ments. The ornamentation is of the time of

ment of the leading lines, which give the contour to each of his bijoux; and there is also considerable fancy in the combination of flowers, leaves, and jewels, that make up the composition.

The taste for floral ornament in jewellery has been very prevalent of late; and it is a good and a happy taste, inasmuch as the brilliant colouring of an enamelled leaf or floret is an

Francis I., a period when the arts of all kinds | had reached a high point of civilisation.

excellent foil to a sparkling stone; and we have scarcely seen the designs for jewellery at any period more tasteful, elegant, and appropriate, than they are at the present day. There is a wholesome novelty about these designs, which tends to strengthen the well-grounded belief that the manufacturer in brooches is about to leave the beaten track, and to study for himself,

and give the result to the world in a free untrammelled spirit. The demand for novelty in such articles as these is incessant, and we are sure that the workman who can best supply that

demand in a really original as well as tasteful manner, will surely meet his reward. The continental manufacturer has hitherto had the largest share of merit awarded to him for design, but for

execution and sterling goodness of material, we believe our own workmen to be as unrivalled in this as in other branches of Industrial Art. There cannot, however, be a doubt that he may still learn the other qualifications from his continental neighbour, which, when he has achieved, may make him regardless of dangerous rivalry.

This Cup, by M. Falloise, of Liége, is of iron; the ornament

upon it is of the most delicate and fanciful kind, and is produced by

cutting the surface away into the various forms | required, and inlaying it with gold and silver;

the variety of tint obtained by this means is very | pleasing; the Shield is also similarly enriched.

The china-works of Messrs. CHAMBERLAIN, of Worcester, will uphold the reputation of the long-established "Royal Porcelain Works,"—an industrial foundation which belongs to the his-

tory of English ceramic manufactures, and which has flourished for more than a century in "the faithful city" of its location. It would be difficult, in the present day, for new manufacturers

to obtain the same amount of *éclat* which attached itself to some of "the old houses" in by-gone times; a fact which may be accounted for in the quality of the competition everywhere

around them. Achieving a celebrity so long since, the Messrs. Chamberlain have retained it in the specimens they now contribute to our Industrial Congress in Hyde Park, inasmuch as

they are elegant in form, and beautiful in decoration. Our cuts will give faithful ideas of their *contours*, although they can but hint at the

at the head of our page are of antique simplicity, appropriately decorated with scriptural scenes, their general surface being entirely covered with

ing another of our groups, the SCENT-BOTTLE being an exceedingly graceful and elegant adjunct to the boudoir. The honeycomb pattern is, we

will not fail to note the excellence of the painting in many of the articles contributed by this firm.

the praise of substantial excellence to the productions of Messrs. Chamberlain, and are glad to

colours which enrich them. The VASES are generally of good form, and present much variety. The COMMUNION-CUPS and WINE-FLAGON

an open honeycomb pattern, giving them great delicacy and richness. The same style of enrichment has been adopted in the articles form-

believe, peculiar to this establishment; we are not aware that examples of its peculiar character have been produced elsewhere. The observer

They have, indeed, always aimed at superiority in this department. Altogether, we can award

see our elder fabricants still vigorous in the field, and still upholding the honour of our native trade.

MR. WOODRUFF, of Bakewell in Derbyshire, contributes some TABLES constructed of the

We engrave underneath the centre of a COUNTERPANE, which exhibits considerable improvement over the ordinary style adopted with so

monotonous an effect in articles of the kind. It is the work of a hand-loom weaver, JOSIAH LUDWORTH, of Bolton. The peculiar description

of bed-cover, called counterpane (from *countre-point*) is not now made extensively, except of a very low quality; it is of the most durable kind, but has been supplanted by *quilts*, on which the pattern is produced by the Jacquard loom. The knots or loops which form the pattern engraved

are pulled up by the hand with a small steel instrument, similar to a shoemaker's awl. This operation has been performed on this counterpane no fewer than 844,800 times. The article is creditable to the industry of an ingenious workman; and as such we have engraved it.

spars of the county, in Mosaic. We engrave a Vase of black marble, and the border of a CHESS-

TABLE, both remarkable for simplicity and taste.

A TABLE-TOP executed in glass mosaic by Mr. H. STEVENS, of Pimlico, is an example of the artist's ingenuity in adapting his materials to the composition of a good design, and of his patient industry in perfecting his work. Mr. Stevens exhibits several objects of a similar character, heraldic designs, pedestals, &c., all of

which have a brilliant effect in the variously coloured glass of which they are made. This glass mosaic is coming into fashion for ornamenting fire-places in drawing-rooms, and for decorative objects in large halls, for which it seems to be adapted, and where the colours are introduced with judgment, the work is very beautiful.

THE INDUSTRY OF ALL NATIONS.

The two pages which follow, contain the contributions in PORCELAIN and EARTHENWARE of Mr. JOHN RIDGWAY, of Cauldron Place, Staffordshire Potteries. They exhibit examples of the useful rather than the ornamental; Mr. Ridgway's attention having been more especially

directed to improvements in the forms and decoration of objects which are the wants of every day. The establishment of Mr. Ridgway is one of the largest, and among the best conducted, of the many factories of Staffordshire; and there is no manufacturer who has obtained higher reputation for the excellence of the materials employed. The works exhibited by him will demand consideration on this ground. We first engrave two of several "Fountain Handbasins"—objects which Mr. Ridgway devised in order to meet a suggestion of the Board of Health, for a frequent and easy supply of pure water, and facilities for the rapid disposal of water that has been used. "These vessels may

and discharge pipes attached, and to be screwed down to the floor." But it will be perceived that although the usefulness of these articles has been the primary consideration, their elegance has also been properly cared for, and they are really graceful additions to the dressing-room, free of the trouble attendant on the use of the ordinary ewer and basin. Another novelty

appears on our page, a STAIR-RAIL, also made in earthenware, and susceptible of much that is ornamental in painting and gilding; there is a lightness and an elegance in this object, not without a peculiar value, when used appropriately, for terraces, &c. The large group delineates a graceful TEA-SERVICE, remarkable for its simplicity. The amount of decoration is but small, but it is good of its kind, and as symmetry of contour has been chiefly considered, as well as that recommendable quality, economy, we cannot but think it has claims to attention on these heads. We must be understood, in some instances, to be doing what we trust the public may also do, when we award due merit to all manufacturers who endeavour to improve ordinary articles of domestic use, while they do not, at

they generally are, at prices which confine them exclusively to the rich. We have always fully appreciated the value of decorative Art, and, sometimes, had to deplore the want of a judicious acquaintance therewith in our manufactories; yet, while we are willing to bestow

commendation, when deserved, on the ornamental articles which now meet the eye at every turn, and testify to the enlarged acquaintance of our mechanical designers with the leading principles of elegance, we are not the less prepared to give the meed of praise to the simple, the tasteful, and the economic works, which are to render pleasure as well as service to the humbler classes. We also frequently see, with satisfaction, a simple treatment adopted even for expensive works; it is not elaboration of ornament which makes elegance, or gives dignity to design, a fact with

be fixed by any plumber conversant with such work. They require neither wood nor brickwork about them, but simply to have the supply

the same time, too greatly tax the buyer. There is as great a merit in this as in the production of articles of higher elaboration, produced, as

which all who have studied Classic Art are sufficiently familiar. The principal pieces of a DINNER-SERVICE, which fill another of our columns, are equally remarkable for the simplicity with which they are designed. The ornament upon them is of the most unpretending kind, and all the better for its unobtrusiveness. It consists entirely of a few simple scrolls and fanciful leaves,

which form the handles or encircle the bases of the various articles upon which they are introduced. The general form of each article is well preserved, and its elegance enhanced by the contrast afforded in the ornament thus sparingly in-

troduced; and the result is exceedingly satisfactory. The FOUNTAINS are of a more ambitious character, and they may also be considered as novelties. The purity of well-glazed pottery gives it a peculiar applicability for such a purpose, and

the happy manner in which its surface might be rendered agreeable to the eye, by the decoration so readily placed on it, should give it a claim to the attention of persons of taste. Flowers and foliage, or tints of varied hue, might give variety

and beauty to such decorative adjuncts to the garden, of which none of the generally-used materials are equally susceptible; and the "coolness" of their appearance, a particularly acceptable quality in those seasons when gardens and fountains are especially agreeable, is also considerably enhanced, when formed of porcelain. The upper fountain of the two which we engrave, is designed in the taste of the seventeenth century, and is, therefore, to be considered as a type of a peculiar style, which was sometimes introduced

with good effect on old Delft ware, and occasionally appeared as a centre for the dinner-table. It is susceptible of bright masses of colour, the boldness of its surfaces, as well as their occasional angularity, affording full scope for this. Our second example is more classic in its outline, and elegant in its proportion; floral ornament is sparingly

introduced on its surface, and its general effect is that of chaste simplicity. It will at once be apparent that there is a decided "opening" for such a branch of pottery-manufacture; one that will much add to the reputation of the Staffordshire manufacturer if taste be properly directed; and one that will be welcomed in the present day, when so much is required and patronised by persons of refinement; we trust

the "fitness" of articles for the localities to which they are to be devoted may be more carefully studied than has been our wont in years gone by; this object, which should be scrupulously considered and provided for by the manufacturer, would achieve entire success. Mr. Ridgway is an extensive as well as a valuable contributor to the Exhibition, as they who know his establishment might have expected.

THE INDUSTRY OF ALL NATIONS.

A BOOK-COVER, manufactured by Mr. LEIGHTON, of London, from a drawing by his son, is worthy of commendation. It was designed for an edition of Thomson's "Seasons;" the four great divisions of the year are, there-

THE GIRL WITH A HOOP is a charming little figure, sculptured in marble, by Mr. WEEKS, of London. The statue stands about four feet high, and is the portrait of a young lady; but the composition is

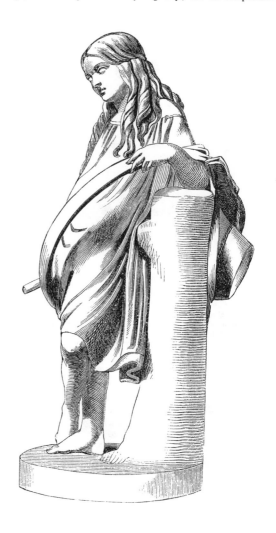

fore, stamped upon it round a circle, on which appear the twelve signs of the zodiac; in the centre, a floral group, comprises the crocus of spring, the rose of summer, the ripe corn of autumn, and the holly of Christmas.

purely ideal, and intended to show that portrait-sculpture may be so treated as to contain as much fancy as works that are entirely inventive. Mr. Weeks holds high and deserved rank among British sculptors.

We introduce on this page one of the RIBBONS contributed by Messrs. Cox & Co., of London and Coventry; the design is graceful and effective, and may be accepted as one of the proofs of our progress in competition with our more advanced neighbours of the continent.

The two subjects which occupy this page are from a TABLE-COVER and a CARPET, manufactured by Messrs. TEMPLETON & Co., of Glasgow. They are termed by the makers, "Patent Axminster," from their close resemblance to the costly and well-known carpets first made at Axminster; the

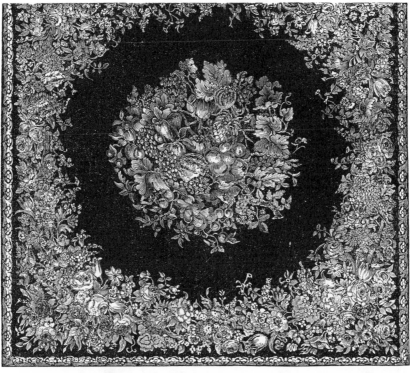

difference being that the latter are composed of separate "tufts" tied in by the hand, while Messrs. Templeton's manufactures are entirely woven, a process which originated in their establishment. We need scarcely remark that the softness, beauty, and richness of these fabrics

are all that the most luxurious can desire. The first of our engravings exhibits a most elaborate pattern of floriated ornament; that of the other consists of flowers and scroll-work, in Louis Quatorze style. About four hundred pairs of hands are employed in this establishment.

Mr. J. SPARKES HALL, of London, exhibits many improvements in modern BOOTS and SHOES, together with a curious series of well executed

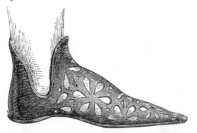

fac-similes of ancient ones. The first and second of our cuts are copied from originals of the

fourteenth century; the third is a fac-simile of the late Duchess of York's shoe, which was re-

markable for its smallness. His modern improvements exhibit an ingenious adaptation of

Honiton lace to ladies' shoes; we engrave a slipper of blue satin thus decorated for the Queen;

also the front of a shoe in vulcanised india-rubber, upon which a rich pattern is imprinted in gold;

and a model slipper of perforated leather, showing blue silk beneath the ornament decorated with tambour stitching and lace rosettes.

The bronze manufactory of M. VITTOZ, of Paris, supplies the GROUP OF VASES and the CLOCK engraved below. The former are modelled after the best antiques, presenting great beauty of outline, and are embellished with some exqui-

sition are strikingly apparent; there is an entire absence of everything approaching to *petitesse* in its details, the introduction of which would have marred the noble simplicity of the design. The

sitely wrought classical designs. The latter forms the centre-piece to a candelabrum; the figures are of bronze, the ornaments and dial of plain gold, the hands and indices of burnished gold. The boldness and breadth of the compo-

base of the clock serves as a pedestal to a well-modelled figure of Michel Angelo. The whole is placed on a stand of black marble, of sexagonal form. At the establishment of M. VITTOZ

are produced some of the largest bronze works made in Paris, as well as the more delicate and elaborate objects for merely ornamental pur-

poses. Among these, we saw a few months since a large number of fine statuettes, and a life-size figure of a dead Christ, from the model of Priault.

The engraving that commences this page is a portion of a TABLE-COVER, designed by Mr. Gruner, (of high reputation as a designer,) and executed by MRS. PURCELL and her assistants, in silks and wools. The pattern, in all its varied compart- ments, is very beautiful, full of subject, yet clear, distinct, and carried out with a definite purpose; there is no portion of it which may not be made suggestive to a variety of manufactures. The execution of the tapestry by Mrs. Purcell is most perfect; this, however, might be looked for in one who, we believe, was trained in the school of the late Miss Linwood, whose exhibition of needlework was, it will be remembered, for many years, among the popular sights of the metropolis.

The group below consists of GLASS objects, contributed by MR. J. G. GREEN, of London; they are of the purest crystal, engraved in the most elaborate and artistic style; the forms are borrowed from the best antiques. The large Jug to the left is termed the "Neptune Jug," a re- presentation of that deity being depicted upon it: next to this is a Cream-jug, ornamented with a kind of arabesque pattern. The two large Jugs

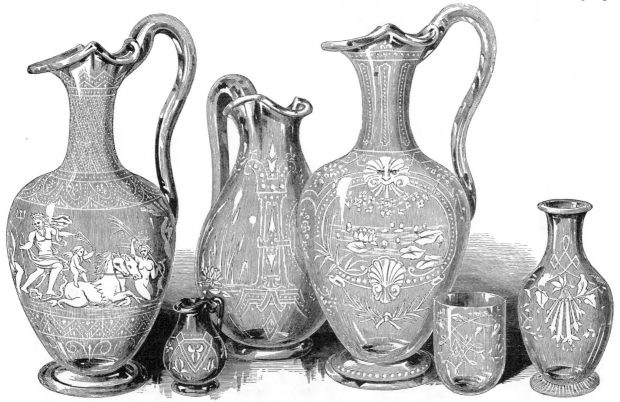

that succeed are beautifully decorated with various devices, in which the water-lily takes a prominent place. The other objects are a Water-caraft and Tumbler, adorned with the fuschia-plant. We scarcely ever remember to have seen glass more exquisitely engraved than in these specimens.

The group of CUPID and the NYMPH is by Mr. THRUPP, of London, one of the most rising sculptors of the English school; the subject is treated with considerable originality as well as with much artistic feeling. The Nymph seems to be persuading the boy to direct his shaft towards a certain object, which Cupid appears averse to do; it is evidently a matter for consideration.

The designs for BERLIN WOOL-WORK which fill the present column are exhibited by Mr. ANDREW HALL, of Manchester, and are constructed on an improved plan, which places the outline on the canvas or foundation to be worked, together with many of the colours indicated in their

places; only leaving it to the worker to increase the number of shades by which the requisite softness will be produced. By this means the constant necessity for counting the threads is obviated, errors in counting are avoided, and the

sight is less taxed. The interlaced patterns we select are simple and good in design; the slipper is decorated with ivy leaves and berries, and is novel and effective. The taste for embroidery has ranked high amongst the elegant arts of

The three DECANTERS which are next introduced are from Mr. SUMMERFIELD, of London, whose manufactory is at Birmingham, and is carried on under the name of Lloyd & Summerfield. These

objects are of the purest cut crystal, ornamented with much novelty of design, the forms whereof being in very bold relief, bring out the colour of the glass in an exceedingly brilliant style.

refined life in past ages, and modern experience teaches us that it still maintains its position; it well becomes the manufacturer therefore to devote his attention to this widely-spread taste, and endeavour to obviate any tendency to commonplace imbecility of design in its pursuit.

To the contributions of Messrs. FEETHAM, of London, we shall endeavour to do justice in other pages of our catalogue. They consist of hardware, and comprise the ordinary productions

of the trade,—of excellent design and manufacture. We occupy part of the first column of this page with a few of the minor articles of this

firm : an IRON KNOCKER, the heads of FIRE IRONS, and three metal BELL-PULLS. It is scarcely necessary to say that if our selections were not thus

limited, we should be able to afford a far more adequate idea of their works; they add considerably to the exhibition of British Industrial Art.

SHEFFIELD has been long famous for its manufacture of cutlery, and the improvement exhibited in all its various branches of the trade we have already had occasion to note. Mr. G. WILKINSON, one of its best SCISSORS-MAKERS, has contributed some specimens of his own peculiar art which

formed of the lily of the valley and its leaves, are very tasteful. There is quaintness, as well as elegance, in the other designs. In fact, restricted as design may appear to be when applied to so simple

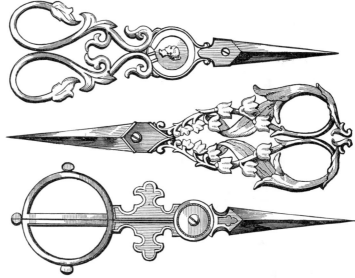

as a coat-of-arms to this purpose. The arms, supporters, crest, and motto of the Cavendish family are made to do duty in this way without any disagreeable result. We conclude our series

a century. We have no fear of its losing the rank it has obtained. During a recent visit, we were offered, by one manufacturer of scissors, the means to examine no fewer than 7000 exe-

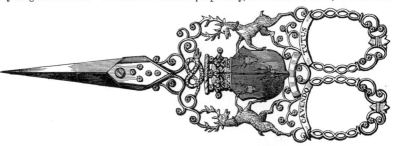

fully bear out the deserved reputation of that enterprising town. The first on our page has been manufactured by him for the "Indian Steel Company," and is of much delicacy and elegance of design. The group which follows presents great novelty of form ; the flowing curves of the handle,

a thing as the handle of a pair of scissors, it is surprising how varied it may be made through the aid of a clever designer. We present an ingenious adaptation of so unpromising a subject

with a large pair of scissors, which also have "the charm of novelty." Sheffield, in this branch of Industrial Art, has maintained its supremacy, and defied the world, for more than

cuted designs. Mr. Wilkinson has not only studied to improve the forms of objects of a comparatively costly character; he has very essentially improved the commonest articles of

his produce, so as to make them more convenient as well as more elegant. This advance is especially shown by comparing the tailor's shears of his manufacture with those in ordinary use, and especially the scissors constructed with a very simple spring, so as to open and close with facility.

From a variety of fine SCULPTURES exhibited by Mr. THOMAS, of London, we have selected five examples, to show his diversified talent and taste in those objects to which this branch of the fine arts is most generally applied. Mr. Thomas has for a series of years been engaged under Mr. Barry, in

unwearied, and his success has kept pace with his exertions. Many of the

modelling the ornamental details of the New Palace of Westminster, and in sculpturing several of the figures with which it is already decorated, and others which are destined hereafter to find a place in that magnificent edifice. His labours in this important and arduous undertaking have been

aristocratic mansions throughout this country can also testify to the varied

character of his natural and acquired endowments as an architect, sculptor, decorator, and designer, in all of which professions he seems equally at home. The first group we have here engraved is entitled CHARITY, it is intended for part of a monumental group; the treatment of the subject is most artistic, and the sentiment conveyed is perfectly in unison with the title. By the side of this is an engraving of a bronze figure from Shakespeare's "Tempest," ARIEL DIRECTING THE STORM; Mr. Thomas's conception of the character is very spirited. Below these figures is a CHIMNEY-PIECE for Preston Hall, the new mansion of Mr. E. L. BETTS; the subjects on it are Dorigene and Griselda, from Chaucer, with a medallion of the poet in the centre, and on either side of the principal figures a bas-relief carrying out the incidents of each: the stove and fender which are to be placed here, we purpose engraving elsewhere. The statue of FAIR ROSAMOND follows on this page, a work of goodly proportions, telling its own pathetic tale: and lastly a FOUNTAIN, of which the subject is "Acis and Galatea" surrounded by Tritons; this, like the chimney-piece, has been executed for Mr. Betts's mansion.

ROSOMONDA.

A PIANO-FORTE, by Messrs. BROADWOOD, of London, the eminent makers, is an elegant example of the taste they frequently display in the manufacture of their instruments. The legs, and such portions of the case as admit of decoration, have been judiciously supplied with it in the rich

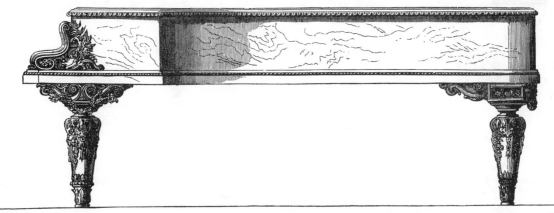

style of Italian ornament. The case of this instrument, which is made of the beautiful Amboyna wood, was manufactured by Mr. Morant, of London.

This page commences with a PORTFOLIO-TABLE, carved and inlaid; and an EBONY TRIPOD, both manufactured by Mr. WILLIAM JONES, of Maescalad, Dolgelly, N. Wales, from designs furnished by a gentleman of that neighbourhood, Mr. H. Reveley : these contributions, from a place so far removed from the great marts of operative industry, are highly creditable to the parties who have brought them forward. The table is

intended for displaying a portfolio or book of large prints; the top of it lifts up like a reading-desk, as seen in the engraving, and its great recommendation is that it avoids the necessity of stooping. By removing the ledges in the front and sides, it is converted into a table for the purposes of writing, drawing, &c. Mr. Jones is, we understand, a person who has raised himself from the condition of an ordinary carpenter to one of considerable provincial eminence as an ornamental carver in wood.

Among the numerous contributions from Germany is a SECRETAIRE, by M. VON HAGEN, of Erfurt. It is made of walnut-wood, the design is in

Our next subject is a HOT-AIR STOVE, made by Messrs. LEARNED & THATCHER, Albany, United States; it is intended for a drawing-room or parlour, and consequently is manufactured with a considerable amount of tasteful ornament to render it suitable for its destination. There is doubtless some peculiarity in its internal construction with which we are unacquainted, for the drawing supplied to us from America speaks of the

stove being patented. The basin at the top holds, we presume, water, as we have seen in similar articles in our own country; and in this basin is placed a small vase of coloured glass, probably for the same purpose : the latter gives a judicious finish to the entire object, which is one highly creditable to the manufacturers as both useful and ornamental.

the Renaissance style, and it is beautifully ornamented with inlaid ivory, ebony, and brass, forming altogether a good example of manufacturing art.

This engraving is from an improved ventilating STOVE GRATE, manufactured by Mr JEAKES, of London: we introduce it chiefly on account of its excellent ornamental character, but it possesses recommendations that entitle it to extensive use; the principle of these is that, when heated, it emits no unhealthy effluvium.

A musical instrument called a GUITARPA occupies this column: it is invented and constructed by DON JOSE GALLEGOS, of Malaga. The tone of this ingenious piece of mechanism comprises that of the harp, guitar, and violoncello; it has thirty-five strings, twenty-six of which and twenty-one pegs act upon the harp,

We introduce here a REVOLVING TABLE, for the use of sculptors and modellers, manufactured by PALMER & CO., Brighton, after a model by San Giovanni, the

sculptor. It is to enable sculptors to turn round with facility any object upon which they may be at work. It is equally applicable for showing busts or statues.

producing in their full extent the diatonic and chromatic scales: six strings belong to the part of the Spanish guitar, while the violoncello part has three silver strings and eighteen pegs. The pedestal by which it is supported is so constructed that the instrument may be either elevated or depressed at pleasure.

MESSRS. RANSOME & PARSONS, of Ipswich, exhibit, among other articles, the VASES, in artificial stone, which we have selected for engraving:

we do this, however, rather with reference to the material than to the forms, which, though

good, are not new. The material differs from all other artificial productions for similar pur-

poses, flint forming its basis; it may be made to imitate any description of stone, from the finest marble to the coarsest and commonest sandstone.

The town of Wolverhampton is a formidable rival to Birmingham in the extent of its manufactures in papier-mâché, and its light iron-ware productions of every kind. It is almost impossible to enumerate the variety of articles included in this category; but we may in particular, allude to tea-trays of every description, coal-vases, candlesticks, bread-baskets, ornamental baskets,

&c., &c. The business transactions in these and similar manufactures, are most extensive, both for the home market and for exportation. Messrs. WALTON & Co., of Wolverhampton, are among its chief manufacturers, and, consequently, their contributions to the Great Exhibition are on a proportionate scale of magnitude and importance, including a large variety of trays, sundry

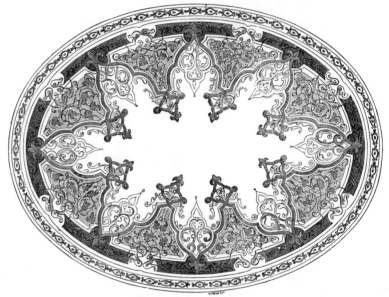

vases, tazzi, coal-scoops, dish-covers, &c. On this and the following columns we engrave six subjects —a Tazza, a Coal-vase, and four Trays, all, excepting the second, made of papier-mâché. The TAZZA is decorated with Roman ornaments in gold and colours; the COAL-VASE is also ornamented with the same materials. The Trays show the several styles of the Byzan-

tine, the German Gothic, the Rénaissance, the Alhambresque, and the Elizabethan, worked in gold, pearls, and colours. Many of the manufactures contributed by Messrs. Walton are painted with much taste and elegance, as representations of landscapes, and historical and fancy scenes. The perfect adhesion of an opaque glass fused by heat on the surface of wrought iron, so as to produce a smooth and even enamel, capable of withstanding the effects of the atmosphere,

A FLOWER-HOLDER, manufactured by Mr. BALLENY, of Birmingham, is well and appropriately designed; the cup exhibits grapes and leaves of the vine, the stem of which is twisted into a handle.

has long been considered a great desideratum by all manufacturers of hardware; this object | Messrs. Walton & Co. seem to have successfully attained. The articles shown are covered with

A CARRIAGE-LAMP, contributed by Messrs. HALLMARKE, ALDEBERT, & Co., of London, forms the subject of the annexed engraving. It is made of the finest and most massive glass, beau-

two kinds of enamel; that intended for better purposes is of a pure white colour, that upon | more common goods is black, and is applied to coat the articles both inside and out. It is less

expensive, and is equally effective and durable : | the contributions of this firm are very attractive.

tifully cut and set in silver; it is, altogether, one of the richest and most creditable specimens of such articles we remember to have seen.

A piece of SILK. contributed by the Committee of the SPITALFIELDS SCHOOL OF DESIGN, shows much beauty of pattern, which is composed of groups of flowers, with fern leaves and trails of ivy; it is designed by the present assistant-master, Mr. BROWN, who was a pupil of the school.

A BEEHIVE, designed by Mr. W. WILSON, of Berwick-upon-Tweed, exhibits a novel and good form, applied to a

We introduce here a HALL STOVE, manufactured by M. H. C. GRAAMANS, of Rotterdam; it possesses nothing new in its shape, but the ornamentation is in good taste, and stands out in bold relief from the flat. The Dutch have long been celebrated for

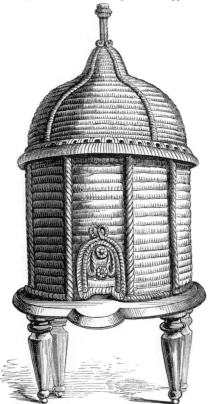

common object; one that might be made an ornament to the garden. It is the work of a highly ingenious artisan.

their decorative furniture of every description; much of their carved work finds its way to England, and several contributions in this style will be found in the Exhibition.

The Vase beneath, and the Fan-light, or, as the French term it, the *Oeil de Bœuf*, commencing the next column, are made of white terra-cotta, by M. Garnaud, Jun., of Paris. The former is of considerable size, presenting an agreeable adaptation of somewhat novel ornament to an antique form. The fan-light is, of course, intended to surmount a doorway; it is about five feet in width, by three feet and a half in height. The material is very durable, and possesses the advantage of being far cheaper than stone, to which it bears a strong resemblance; it is much used in Paris for all kinds of architectural decoration.

The engraving that follows is a portion of a very elegant Carpet, contributed by Messrs. White, Son, & Co., of London. The pattern of the ground consists of a few well-arranged sprigs, and is, accordingly, very simple; but the centre, the corners, and the border present features of great boldness and beauty. The wreaths of flowers on the last portion, and the shells and scroll-work on the corners, exhibit taste in the

designer of no common kind; nor will the pattern of the inner border fail to attract the attention of all who estimate purity of character in ornamental work. This design emanates from Messrs. White & Co., who are, consequently, its proprietors; they exhibit several other excellent productions.

A fine damask linen TABLE-CLOTH, manufactured by Messrs. HUNT and SON, of Dunfermline, is here introduced. It was made expressly for the use of Her Majesty when sojourning at her home in the Highlands, and is, therefore, most appropriately adorned in the centre with a view of the Castle of Balmoral. The borders present illustrations applicable to the healthy and manly amusements pursued by Prince Albert and the visitors to the Royal residence, especially that of deer-stalking, and the spaces are filled with some of the natural productions of the mountain and the glen.

On this page we exhibit another of the RIBBONS manufactured by Messrs. Cox, of London and Coventry. Those who are acquainted with the ancient and venerable city are well aware of the immense advances they have made of late years, not only in design, to which we believe the Government school has very largely contributed, but in the study and application of colours, and especially in the process of dyeing.

Mr. BLAKELY, of Norwich, contributes some splendid SHAWLS, woven expressly for the Exhibition. Our space does not permit us to enlarge upon the beauty and merits of those we have here engraved; it must suffice to say they are of the very best order of design, material, and

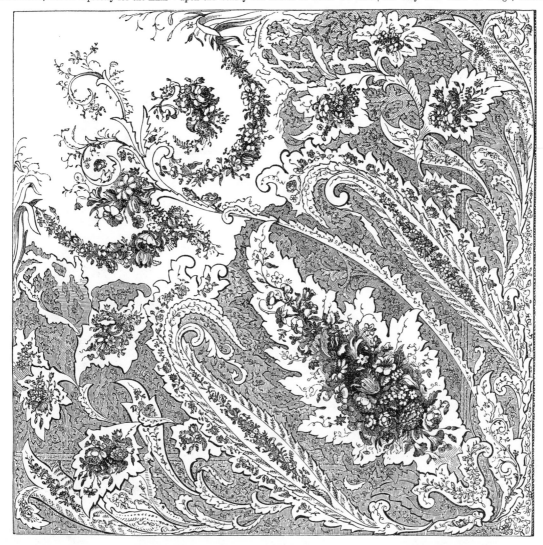

workmanship. Norwich has long been famous for this description of manufacture; it will lose none of its credit in the Great Exhibition.

Messrs. PAYNE & SONS, of Bath, contribute a VASE, in silver, after a marble antique in the Capitoline Museum. It is enriched with bold and highly relieved foliage and interlacing flower scrolls, the handles springing from Silenus' heads. The work is a very elegant specimen of art, and highly creditable to a provincial manufacturer.

We follow with a VASE formed of very different material: it is of terra-cotta, designed by the distinguished sculptor, and architect, Mr. John Thomas, and is contributed by EDWARD BETTS, Esq., who, having discovered a valuable vein of rich clay on his estate, at Aylesford, in Kent, has established a pottery there in order to make it serviceable to Art as well as for purposes

of utility in agriculture and in manufactures. We shall heartily rejoice if this project succeed; at present, it is notorious that in England with "all appliances and means," we have, of late years, almost entirely neglected this branch of Art.

M. FRAIKIN, the eminent sculptor of Brussels, has contributed some of the poetical works for which he is so justly famed. Among others, he has sent to the Exhibition the kneeling figure here engraved; it represents a damsel, quaintly habited in the taste of the fifteenth century, in an attitude of devotion; the figure is remarkable for its purity of treatment and delicacy of expression.

The musical instrument is manufactured by Messrs. LUFF & Co., of London. It is termed an HARMONIUM. We, of course, have had no opportunity of testing its merits as a musical instrument, but, knowing that this long-established firm bears good repute in the profession,

there is no doubt of its possessing excellencies in this respect, which we must leave to others more competent than ourselves to decide. We can testify to the elegance of its external appearance.

Throughout the task we have undertaken, to prepare this "Illustrated Catalogue," we have scrupulously avoided instituting a comparison between the works of any one manufacturer and those of another, whether of our own country or from foreign lands. Our object is to select, according to our best judgment, whatever is most beautiful and most worthy of being singled

out from the great mass of contributions for especial notice, let who may be its producer.

On this occasion the critic's pen is used only to describe and to eulogise ; were it desirable to

use it as generally applied, we might sometimes be tempted to enter upon the comparative merits of many of those works we have had the opportunity of inspecting, both in the Exhibition and in the ateliers of the fabricators. It will, however, be thought by all who are fortunate enough to get a sight of the most ex-

quisite TEA AND COFFEE SERVICE, manufactured by M. DURAND, of Paris, that any work of a similar character brought into competition with it will be put to a severe test, so pure is the taste that has designed, and so skilful are the hands that have been engaged in working it out. The whole service is of massive silver, modelled, chased, and engraved in the very first style of

placed ; the body of the tripod forms a tea-urn, and on the plateau at its base stand the coffee-pot and the tea-pot ; the tea-cups and coffee-cups are ranged round the bottom. It may readily be imagined, when the whole are "placed in position," how superb an appearance is presented by such a combination of truly rich and costly

art. It is valued at forty thousand francs. The centre-piece stands about four feet high; the figures introduced into it are of bronze, which affords a striking and effective contrast to the white metal. Midway in the centre-piece are four baskets for cakes, &c.; the angles of the tripod support each a small vase, on which the cream-jug, sugar-basin, and water-basin are

objects. Besides the centre-piece, we have engraved the cream-jug, the sugar-basin, and the tea-pot ; it will, of course, be seen that neither of these is engraved to its proper scale of size, but drawn to suit our column. The coffee-pot and water-basin are *en suite*. We regret we could not arrange for their introduction also.

The next engraving is from a piece of WOOD-CARVING, exhibited by Mr. RINGHAM, of Ipswich. It is composed of wheat and wild flowers, and is executed with considerable spirit and freedom.

A GLOBE, manufactured by Messrs. JOHNSTON, of Edinburgh, is a beautiful work of manufactured art, showing some fine carved work, the principal features of which apply to the subject.

The corner of this page is occupied by an engraving of a HALL or OFFICE STOVE, manufactured by Messrs. ROBERTSON, CARR & STEEL, of the

This engraving is from a group, the work of a true artist, SAN GIOVANNI, of Brighton; whose models from nature are of the purest and best order of Art. It is the only object he has sent.

Chantrey Works, Sheffield. Other of their excellent and useful productions, on a larger scale, will be found in subsequent pages of this catalogue.

The CARPETS here engraved are from the manufactory of Messrs. HENDERSON & WIDNELL, of Lasswade, near Edinburgh, successors to the well-known firm of Whytock & Co. This establishment is celebrated for its make of the finer sorts of carpet, those termed "tapestry" and "velvet-pile," and also of carpets similar to the Axminster, Persian, and Tournay fabrics, woven in one piece. We have seen carpets produced by this firm equal in texture, richness of colour, and beauty of pattern, to any foreign fabric of a similar description; engravings from some of these, with a lengthened notice of the extensive manufactory, were introduced into the *Art-Journal* about four or five years since. The

improvements introduced by Mr. Whytock and his successors into the process of weaving and printing these carpets have been the result of much study and long experience; we may adduce as one instance as regards the weaving, the new method of applying the shuttle. Those who have seen the workmen at the Gobelins, in Paris, employed on similar carpets, must have observed how the shuttle is thrown from hand to hand; instead of which Mr. Henderson uses the crossbow, to draw it at once across the largest carpets, thereby saving a considerable portion of the

workman's time. Again, the necessity for expensive block-cutting and engraving has been superseded, and the process greatly simplified by the plans adopted by the present proprietors of this establishment. Among the other advantages arising from their new method, not the least important is that there is scarcely any limitation to the number of colours that may be used in line without increasing the expense; more than twenty are not unfrequently thus introduced, while a good opportunity is afforded to the considerate artist to vary his colours or shades.

THE INDUSTRY OF ALL NATIONS.

A TABLE-COVER, of which we introduce the half, is worked in tapestry by MDLLE. HUNSON and her assistants, of Paris. The design is in the Arabesque style, and was furnished by M. Clerget, a most elegant designer and skilful draughtsman, especially for textile manufactures; he carries on an extensive business, in conjunction with Mdlle. Hunson, in the production of tapestries. In the centre of this table-cover is the well-known Arabic inscription, "God is great;" the pattern is executed in the finest silks and wools.

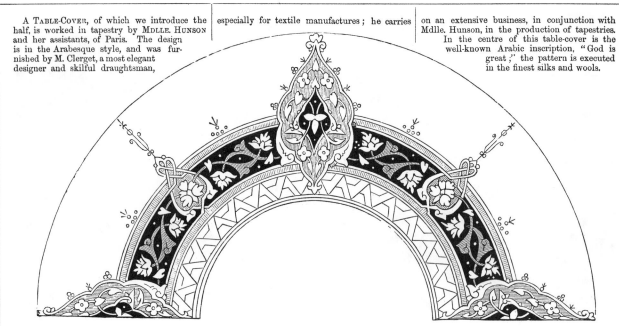

A STATUE of Saher de Quincy, Earl of Winchester, to be executed in bronze, is by MR. J. S. WESTMACOTT; it is intended to be placed in the House of Lords.

MADAME GRUEL, who conducts one of the most *recherché* book-binding establishments in Paris, exhibits several specimens of the Art which has made her house celebrated among the bibliopolists of the French metropolis. We engrave on this page an Ivory BOOK-COVER.

A damask TABLE-CLOTH, manufactured and exhibited by Mr. JOHN HENNING, of Waringstown, near Belfast, shows a clever floriated pattern. The design is by Hugh Blain, of the Belfast School of Design, to whom was awarded Lord Dufferin's first prize for a table-cloth.

An ALBUM-COVER, by Mr. BUDDEN, of Cambridge, is highly creditable

to the taste of a provincial binder; it is executed in gold and colours.

Messrs. S. R. & T. BROWN, of Glasgow, extensive manufacturers of embroidered muslins, exhibit several truly beautiful designs, principally

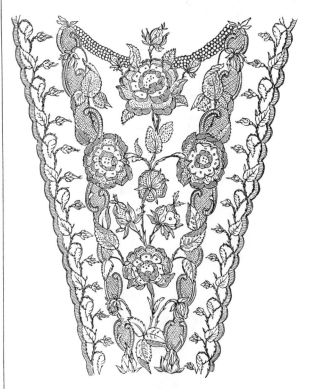

adapted to ladies' dresses. We engrave from their various contributions a CHEMISETTE of a simple but very elegant pattern of roses and leaves.

The four engravings which occupy these two columns represent COAL-BOXES, to use the only term that seems applicable to their purpose, although it is inappropriate, when the form of these objects is regarded; they are manufactured in japanned iron by Mr. H. FEARNCOMBE, of Wolverhampton. The first, the shape of which assimilates to that of a tureen, is ornamented in the Italian style, and is worthy of being imitated in silver. The two following are of the form of vases; both

In conformity with our plan of representing every meritorious producer of articles which exhibit improvements derived from the influence

are very elegantly designed, especially in their pedestals. The last represents a nautilus shell set on a piece of coral rock; the handle of the lid represents a sea-horse. The novelty and beauty of this design must challenge approbation; indeed, the entire set quite merits being

of art, we introduce upon this and the succeeding column four examples of the EMBROIDERED WAISTCOATS contributed by Mr. J. W. GABRIEL,

devoted to a more honourable, though not more useful, purpose than that for which each is intended. They are designed and modelled by Mr. F. Wright. Wolverhampton has long been cele-

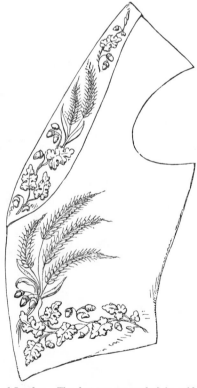

of London. The first two are worked in gold on rich silk, and are designed mainly for court dresses; the other two are wrought in silk upon

brated for its japanned iron ware: such works as these must tend to increase its reputation.

black cloth : the ornamentation is derived principally from natural flowers. The style of modern male attire affords little opportunity

for the embroiderer and ornamentist to display their skill; the only garment which admits of the least approach to elegance being the vest;

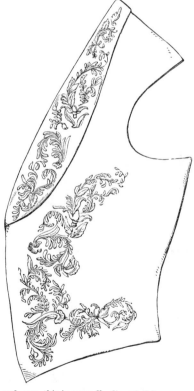

and even this is generally discarded by persons of good taste. In the patterns here engraved, however, we see much that is truly graceful.

Mr. TOMLINSON, of Ashford, Derbyshire, one of the many ingenious manufacturers of the native spars and marbles of the county, contributes, among other articles, the TABLE here

An INKSTAND, or to designate it more correctly according to its varied contents, a com-

engraved. The stem as well as the top is made of black marble; a wreath of flowers and leaves in their natural colours encircles the top; the table is entirely formed of the spars of Derbyshire.

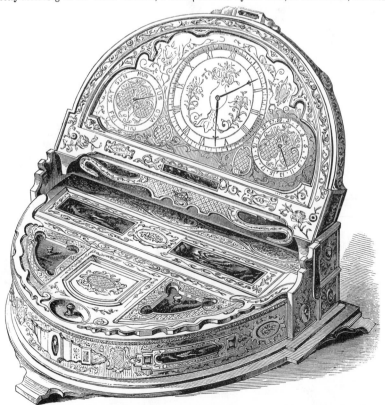

pendium for the writing-table, made and contributed by Mr. COLE, of Clerkenwell, is a most

useful and elegant work of manufacturing art; novel in character when the variety and arrangement of its "fittings" is considered, and most elaborately engraved and richly ornamented.

In the notices which have appeared from time to time in the *Art-Journal*, descriptive of the progress of manufacturing design, we have found occasion to notice those productions of foreign houses remarkable for ability and taste, and among the rest that of M. MOREL, who has, however, for the last few years become a resident in London. His works are equally deserving of high praise, as well for design as for execution, and display great and varied fancy combined with the highest artistic finish. We furnish three

elaborate ornamental taste of the East, the quatrefoils containing views of the principal buildings in Constantinople; it is a very brilliant

production. Not less so is our second example, an AGATE CUP, the mountings richly chased in gold, and their effect heightened by the most

examples from his contributions to the Crystal Palace. The first is an ENAMELLED CUP, executed for the Sultan; it is richly decorated in the

vivid enamels. Our third engraving is from a rich COFFER, jewelled, chased, and enamelled, and intended to contain the original manuscript

of M. Guizot's "Life of Washington." We shall engrave elsewhere other of the productions of M. Morel, which are all of the highest merit.

We continue on this page engravings from the contributions of M. MOREL. The first is a VASE, in the style of the sixteenth century; the bowl is made of agate, and the setting of gold enamelled; the handle is composed of drapery attached to a single figure at the top; a group of a Triton and a Nereid form the stem. The beauty of the foot is enhanced by the

the top, bowl, and stem are made of separate pieces of rock crystal, richly mounted in enamelled gold. The CUP in the

centre is a truly elegant piece of workmanship; the dragon which forms the handle is one of the most perfect

introduction of pearls. The next is a TOILETTE-GLASS, of massive silver, with six branches for lights; the style is that of

specimens of modern enamelling in gold; some of the colours are exceedingly difficult to produce. The shell-like bowl is one entire piece of lapis-lazuli; the stem is formed

is a statue of Queen Elizabeth on horse-

Louis the Fifteenth, with flowers, birds, and squirrels introduced. The CUP and COVER to the left at the bottom of the page is in the style of the sixteenth century;

of struggling sea-nymphs, with their tails entangled, and resting on a bed of coral; the foot is enamelled in the best Italian taste of the Cellini school. The last subject is a FLAGON of gold and silver, enamelled; the body is of rock crystal. There

back, by M. Morel, which is a fine example of silver embossed with the hammer.

The Porcelain manufactory of Messrs. HERBERT MINTON, & Co., is at Stoke-upon-Trent, the principal town of the famous district known as the "Staffordshire Potteries." The establishment has long been eminent for the production of admirable works. The head of the firm is a gentleman of accomplished mind, and of refined taste, and his large resources have been made available to obtain good models, and valuable assistance, wherever they could be found, in all parts of Europe. His collection at the Exhibition consists,

of an extensive variety of objects, all of which are of the highest merit; it is not too much to say, that the corner of the gallery in which they are placed has

been a point of attraction to visitors, and that here, at all events, foreigners have been enlightened as to the capabilities of British producers to encounter competition with the whole world. We engrave several of Messrs. Minton

& Co's. productions, commencing with the DESSERT-SERVICE, purchased by Her Majesty. The series (which is entirely original in the models, arrangement, and decoration,) is one of exceeding beauty, designed with pure artistic skill, and exhibiting, in manipulation and finish, a degree of refinement that has rarely, if ever, been surpassed in modern art. The subjects have been elaborately treated; it would seem as if the utmost

very novel combination. Our first cut is of a JELLY or CREAM-STAND; the companion to which is an "ASSIETTE MONTÉE;" between them is a FLOWER-

amount of labour had been expended upon them,—yet nowhere do they seem crowded or overladen; a result which arises, no doubt, mainly from the delicacy of the material, the figures and ornamentation being of "Parian," slightly gilt, and the baskets of richly decorated porcelain,—a

BASKET, supported by four figures, representing the seasons. A TRIANGULAR FRUIT-BASKET, and an OVAL FRUIT-BASKET, follow, and fill this page. The second page devoted to the works of Messrs. Minton & Co. commences with the SALT-CELLAR and small FRUIT-DISH,

or compotier, and terminates with the SUGAR or CREAM-BOWL,—parts of the beautiful dessert-

service, of which the leading objects are pictured

on the preceding page. The two groups of chil-

of the last century, and it is not too much to say that the delicacy of the modelling, and the grace and truthfulness of the attitudes have been seldom equalled. The two small FIGURES are elegantly formed; they are in gilt Parian, with

the stands in porcelain tastefully decorated, and serve as candlesticks. They are original designs in the style and costume of Louis Quinze. On the third page are pictured, first, a VASE

dren sporting with goats are in Parian,—that exquisite material in which England remains unrivalled,

FOR PLANTS, of terra cotta, designed expressly for Messrs. Minton & Co. by the Baron Marochetti; it is of very large size. The second is likewise for plants, and also of terra cotta; a fine com-

and which is only second to marble. They are original designs, executed in the style and spirit

position, executed with exceeding care. The third cut is from a WINE-COOLER, which forms the centre-piece of the dessert-service, and is, on the whole, the most meritorious object of the collection; our limited space does not permit us to describe it; and our fourth is from one of the numerous admirable STATUETTES, in Parian, ex-

hibited by this house. Of these Messrs. Minton & Co. have produced many, from original sources;

the whole collection, we find abundant evidence of that matured judgment, and refined taste, by

which the manufacturers of Great Britain have been, of late years, elevated; and which, in the

some after eminent foreign sculptors, but chiefly from the leading artists of our own school. In

present Exhibition, have so largely contributed to uphold, and will extend, our national repute.

The silver manufactures of Mr. M. EMANUEL. of London, evince great taste in design, and some very excellent workmanship. He exhibits a variety of objects besides those we have here engraved, such as gilt candelabra, gilt plateau,

with china racks and medallions, processes of gold manufacture. The first we introduce is one of a pair of rock crystal CANDLESTICKS,

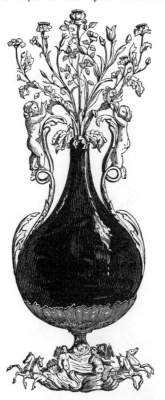

silver, and gilt, with figures of children, sea-horses, and marine objects, composing the base. The next is a FLOWER-VASE, of richly coloured glass, mounted in silver; the handles are made to represent boys climbing upwards to the

flower stems. and the pedestal is composed of groups of figures and horses. The two objects commencing the other columns are silver DESSERT STANDS. The vine forms their stems. at the

base of which children are at play with animals; the dishes are supported by a sort of trellis-work of the leaves and fruit of the vine. But the

attributes; and, surmounting the top, is Phœbus driving the chariot of the sun; the composition of this group is full of spirit, and the whole of

most important contribution of this manufacturer is a large silver CLOCK, designed by Mr. Woodington, the well-known sculptor: it is, truly, a fine work of art. Between four figures,

indicating the "Seasons," is one of "Time," in the attitude of repose; above the dial is a bas-relief, representing the winds and their various

the figures are exceedingly well modelled. Mr. Emanuel has done wisely in securing the services of an artist of acknowledged talent and repute.

The appended engraving of a SIDEBOARD is from one manufactured and contributed by Mr. T. W. CALDECOTT, of London. The material of which it is made is old English oak, and it is carved, in the Renaissance style, with much taste and spirit; this style, when freed from the affectation with which designers are too apt to deform it, is well adapted for displaying a bold and effective ornamentation, such as we find in the work before us. There is here no breaking up of the general character of the ornament into unmeaning details, for the sake of gaining an apparent richness. The great merit of the decoration is its close adherence to the style adopted.

The CARPET is manufactured and exhibited by Mr. HARRIS, of Stourport. It is termed a "Brussels velvet pile," and is one of several, equally excellent, which this extensive manufacturer contributes. The design is a cordon of leaves of the *Clitoria arborescens*, enclosed by a trellis work of flowers, among which the *Lilium tigrinum* is conspicuous. This is among the best productions of British manufactured art.

The contributions of our fellow-subjects in Canada are not without a considerable portion of interest, but they are chiefly of a character which does not come within the scope of our plan of illustration; indeed, are not of a description to admit of it, even with less limitation. The wealth of Canada lies in her agricultural and mineral productions, of which she contributes to the Exhibition a large variety of examples. Among her textile fabrics are several specimens highly creditable to her manufacturers, and there are some engineering objects worthy of notice, especially a powerful and most elegant fire-

community exhibit no little taste, and spare no expense. to put their carriage and all its appointments, into suitable condition. The

to exclude as much as possible the severity of the cold, are often very costly. There are

harness of the horses is generally very gay. and beautifully ornamented; while the fur robes in which the riders envelope themselves

some choice specimens of all these objects in the Canadian department of the Exhibition,

engine. We have selected, from the few productions that we deem would make effective engravings, a SLEIGH, of elegant proportions, manufactured by

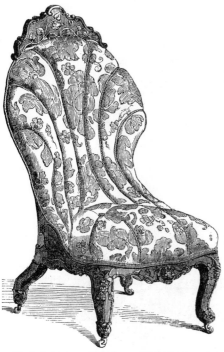

which are worthy of minute inspection. The rides and drives round about Quebec, Montreal,

Toronto, &c., are, during the winter months, quite lively with the showy equipages, and

Mr. J. J. SAURIN, of Quebec. "Sleighing," as it is termed, forms one of the principal amusements of the Canadians of all ranks, who can afford to keep one of any description, and the wealthier part of the

musical with the bells suspended from the heads of the horses. The FURNITURE, also engraved on this page, is manufactured by

Messrs. J. & W. HILTON, of Montreal. They are made of black walnut, boldly carved, the chairs are covered with crimson and gold damask.

We introduce here the pediment of a FIRE-PLACE, manufactured of Derbyshire black marble, by Messrs. JOHN LOMAS & SONS, of Bakewell. The caps and bases of the columns are of Sienna marble; the frieze is inlaid with an elegant scroll, executed in marbles of various beautiful colours.

The three ancient KNIFE-HANDLES are from the collection of the GRAND DUKE OF SAXE WEIMAR, who possesses several thousands, ranging from the thirteenth to the eighteenth centuries. Many of these are both curious and very costly.

The CHANDELIER is manufactured by Mr J. FARADAY, of London. It is constructed upon a principle for which a patent has been obtained, whereby all noxious vapours arising from the gas are carried off, by means of the descending draught; the lights

Messrs. B. R. & J. MOORE, of Clerkenwell, exhibit an eight-day CLOCK, with lever escapement, striking the quarters and hours on fine cathedral-tone bells. The plate upon which the clock stands is steel, highly polished and enamelled.

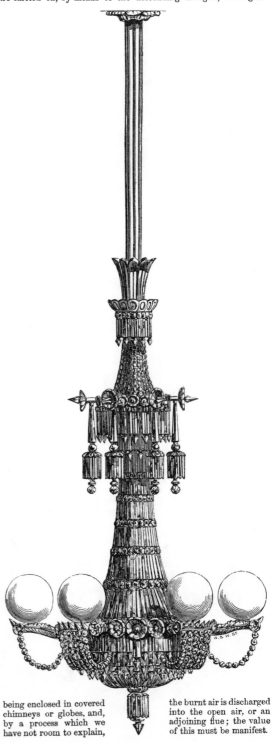

being enclosed in covered chimneys or globes, and, by a process which we have not room to explain, the burnt air is discharged into the open air, or an adjoining flue; the value of this must be manifest.

The ALTO-RELIEVO, by Mr. NELSON, of London, is a portion of a monument proposed to be erected to the memory of the officers and men of the fiftieth regiment of the line, who fell on the banks of the Sutlej, in 1845-6.

We insert on this column another KNIFE and SHEATH, from the collection of the GRAND DUKE OF SAXE WEIMAR.

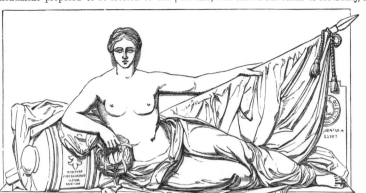

A BOOK-COVER, carved in box-wood, by Mr. Rogers, forms one side of a magnificent Bible, exhibited by Mr. NISBET, of London. The subject of the beautiful design in the centre, is "The Brazen Serpent in the Wilderness."

The handle exhibits busts of Gustavus Adolphus, and Christina, king and queen of Sweden.

We fill this page with engravings from the productions of Messrs. T. WILKINSON & Co., of Birmingham,—works which entitle these manufacturers to much praise. A scene from Paul and Virginia, "that

gentle story of the Indian isle," furnishes the theme for the first of our examples; the incident chosen from the tale is Paul's expostulation previous to Virginia's departure for France, the flowers of the Indian

page is a poetic conception admirably adapted to its uses; the subject, Prometheus endeavouring to regain the fire taken by Jupiter. The TEA-URN,—a vase of Etruscan form resting on a rock, has the novelty of a

basement decorated by figures of children playing musical instruments. These works are very creditable to the establishment from which they

plant which overshadows them forming a graceful receptacle for lights. The centre-piece, with tritons and sea-nymphs under a canopy of real coral, is an attractive work. The second CANDELABRUM at the foot of our

emanate, and are satisfactory testimonials of the zeal with which the manufacturers of our large and celebrated industrial marts are determined to uphold the character they have so long enjoyed, and desire to maintain.

The first engraving on this page is from a carved BOOK-COVER, by Madame GRUEL, of Paris. It is a beautiful example of the taste which this celebrated house displays in all matters of art.

A state CARRIAGE-LAMP, by Mr. B. BLACK, of London, is richly ornamented in chased silver.

One of the most costly and admirable works of its class in the Exhibition is the BUFFET, designed and manufactured by Messrs. COOKES & SONS, of Warwick. Any attempt to describe this elaborately carved piece of workmanship would, in our limited space, be out of the question. All we can do is to explain that the designs are chiefly suggested by Scott's "Kenilworth." It is, altogether, a work of manufacturing art, that reflects the highest credit on the producers.

The two engravings which commence this page are from the iron-foundry of M. DUCEL, of Paris. The first is a FOUNTAIN, of large dimensions, exhibiting dolphins supporting a shell, in which stands a figure, springing from aquatic plants. The other is an iron VASE, to be placed in a garden; it stands four feet and a half high, and is richly decorated. At each end of the three angles, above the pedestal, is a winged figure.

The subject underneath is from a CLOCK-CASE, executed in terra-cotta by Messrs. PRATT, of Burslem. It is of large size, and intended for the exterior of a building, for which its truly excellent design peculiarly adapts it. The figures, which have an antique character, and are elegantly posed, are well modelled, and the entire composition is conceived in an artistic spirit. We should be pleased to see greater attention paid to this branch of manufacturing art, for which there is, indeed, ample room.

A brocaded SILK, designed and exhibited by Messrs. LEWIS & ALLENBY, of London, and manufactured for them by Messrs. Campbell, Harrison, & Lloyd, of Spitalfields. The elaborate nature of the pattern, and the unusual number of colours (fifteen) with which the silk is brocaded, require for its production nearly thirty thousand cards, and ninety-six shuttles. As a specimen of weaving, it is of the best order.

This page is completed by the introduction of an engraving of a piece of RIBBON, manufactured by Mr. J. C. RATCLIFF, of Coventry. The pattern is suggested by the convolvulus plant, and shows a good adaptation of its graceful forms. The ribbon is termed by the manufacturer a "bro

caded damask-figured lutestring." It is made in a nine hundred Jacquard machine, employing fifteen hundred cards, and it has in it three thousand eight hundred and sixty-eight threads of warp silk. We engrave it as much for the "curiosity" of its manufacture, as for its design.

The productions of Mr. ASPREY, of London, are among the most remarkable for good taste, beauty of design, and excellence of execution. We think they

need fear no comparison that may be instituted with other works of their class in the Exhibition. Our selection comprises a TOILET-GLASS, with an

open framework and handle of a highly ornamental character, in flat chased work, richly gilt. The MINIATURE GLASS beneath it is provided with a prop,

and is constructed in the lightest manner,—so as at once to be elegant and useful; the framework is fanciful in design, but it will be seen that its general character is

good and useful, and convenient for the boudoir table. The TAPER-STAND is an equally elegant article; the entire bowl is cut from cornelian;

cabinet, is equally sumptuous in its fittings; it is richly chased and gilt, a large malachite

stone beneath. The INKSTAND is a fanciful composition; the large slab upon the top is a

which the richly-gilt open-work mountings have a singularly good effect, the arrangement of tints being further aided by the introduction

the receptacle for the taper, the little figures, and the ornamental handle and foot, are chased and gilt. A JEWEL-CASKET, in the form of a

decorates the lid; the doors beneath are in gilt open work, displaying slabs of the same costly

rare bloodstone. The CASKET is, perhaps, the best of the series; it is formed of ebony, upon

ot coral cameos. The groups of entwined serpents which cover the lid, and form the feet, are happily conceived and well executed.

We consider the ORNAMENTAL JEWELLERY of Messrs. C. ROWLANDS & SON, of London, suffi-

Hence we have now imitations of flowers, either

taste, are essential to work out such designs. The jewellers of Paris have long been without

ciently important and beautiful to devote a page to the illustration of a few of their contributions. The business of the manufacturing jeweller has undergone a great change during the last few years, for there is a fashion in the works of his hands, which, perpetually changing, compels him to seek new methods of exhibiting his taste and skill. We may instance, as an example, the manufacture of watch-seals, a branch of their art

singly or in groups, in which not only their forms are closely followed, but oftentimes successful attempts are made to produce natural colours

rivals in this description of art-manufacture, and, it must be admitted, have taught our fellow-countrymen many lessons, which they have profitably turned to account. The first subject we introduce of Messrs. Rowlands' contributions is a BRACELET, set with rubies, in gold, of exquisite workmanship. The next three subjects are from BROOCHES; the first of these is in a style which, we believe, the French jewellers originated; the setting of this is of gold, the large stone between

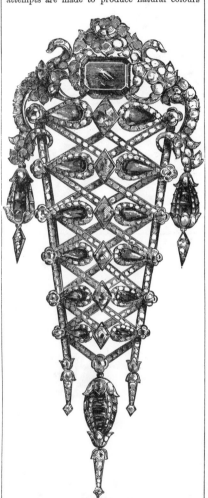

that is now rarely called into exercise; a few years since, a gentleman was seldom seen without two or three of these appendages glittering on his person. And again, in such objects as ladies' ear-rings, which are almost wholly out of date, except as worn on what may be termed "state occasions." These alterations in the style of ornamental dress have compelled the manufacturer to devote his attention chiefly to bracelets, ornaments for the head, and brooches. The

by the introduction of precious stones; it will, therefore, be easily conceived that great

the figures is a carbuncle, and brilliants decorate the drops; it is a very rich and elegant ornament. The second brooch is composed of rubies and brilliants in a costly setting; while the third is little else than a mass of diamonds, strung together in the most graceful form, in imitation of a bouquet of flowers. The last subject is a BRACELET. This bracelet is made up of diamonds and enamels; the large stone in the centre is a carbuncle. All of these jewelled ornaments are not only of a most costly description, but they

last-mentioned objects, though of distant origin, have assumed a totally varied form and feature from even their more immediate predecessors.

delicacy of workmanship, as well as considerable

exhibit taste on the part of the designer, combined with ingenuity and skill on that of the artistic workman of a more than ordinary character.

The two subjects commencing this page are contributed by M. PAILLARD, a bronze manufacturer of Paris. The first is a CLOCK of massive design, which, however, from its being pierced or open towards the bottom, loses much of the heaviness it would otherwise present. The dial is surmounted by a group of children playing with birds; they form a most pleasing picture. The other object is a GIRANDOLE, corresponding in style with the clock, but the child is at the base, and the birds are perched among the branches.

America, among her consignments of manufactured objects, contributes several worthy of being introduced into our pages. The United States present a wide field for the operations of skilful artisans in ornamental articles; as their wealth increases, so do also their taste for the elegant and the beautiful, and their desire to possess what will minister to the refinements of life. This is ever the case with nations, as they advance in intellectual power, and in the just appreciation of what confers real dignity on a people; and their moral strength keeps pace with their pro-

gress in intelligence. The PIANO-FORTE here introduced is designed and manufactured by Messrs. NUNN & CLARK, of New York. It is richly carved in rosewood, and the execution of the work is creditable to the skill and ingenuity of the workmen who have produced it.

Messrs. WOOLLAMS, of London, exhibit a great variety of new and beautiful designs in paper-hangings, a branch of the industrial arts which has received much improvement during the last quarter of a century in England; perhaps we may safely assert that there is scarcely any one trade in which greater progress is visible. The and very deservedly, inasmuch as the character of each style, and the taste of each age, have been studied, and its most characteristic features applied with success to the adornment of our walls. The series upon the present page are good examples of this fact, and exhibit much

variety of style; the elongated panel, is a free translation of the best Italian period, when a Raffaelle did not disdain to devote his transcendant genius to the walls of a Loggia, and produce a style which has never been surpassed, amid all the changes of fashion. The gorgeous taste of Persia has furnished the theme of the second of our series, the fanciful and brilliant hues of which are, of course, but to be guessed at without the aid of colour; the same remark

reputation for good design and tasteful colouring which the continental houses almost monopolised, is now abundantly shared by the home producer: must apply to our third example, in which the style of the decoration adopted in that far-famed building—the Alhambra—has been chosen, and re-produced with great success, and at a cost which enables the moderately-wealthy to rival the dearly-purchased luxuries of the East.

The visitor to the Great Exhibition may search in vain through the whole length and breadth of the vast edifice for works more truly beautiful of their class, than those contributed

by M. FROMENT-MEURICE, the eminent goldsmith and jeweller of Paris. There is a certain point

at which the productions of the industrial artisan, as we are accustomed to call every one engaged

in handicraft, cease to be manufactures, and are entitled to be classed, absolutely, among works of Art; but we are too apt to draw the line of distinction between the artisan and the artist, where none, in truth, should exist. Thus, for instance, if one man sculptures a large figure

have performed. This is an injustice of comparatively modern date; it was not practised centuries ago, when the respect due to art of all kinds was greater than it is now. It was not so much the "Perseus" of Cellini, that won that

or ornament in marble he is ranked with the latter; while, if another does a similar work on a diminutive scale, in some metal or in wood, he most frequently finds himself placed in no higher grade than the former, without any regard to the real excellence of the work that either may

accomplished sculptor his rank, as his salvers, and his cups, his dagger-hilts and sword-handles, —these it was that made the artist. Wherever mind is brought to bear upon matter, so as to leave upon it the impress of genius, not mere

mechanical ingenuity, the result becomes entitled to the highest award that can be accorded to it. We would, therefore, in accordance with these preliminary remarks, claim for M. Fremont-Meurice, as also for many others whom we

could name, both British and foreign producers, that position which, in our judgment, they merit, and we feel assured that all who are able to appreciate art, must see in this and the following page, which contain engravings from

his contributions, that we are not arguing upon false premises. The first subject is an exquisitely wrought TOILET TABLE in silver, inlaid in parts with a kind of niello-work: it is intended as a present from the Legitimists of France to

page at the bottom is from a BRACELET, of the early mediæval style; in a rich gothic frame-work are three compartments, containing, we first page, the upper is an elegant little LOOKING GLASS, in an elegant silver frame. and the lower a CLASP of novel design. On this page the first two subjects are BROOCHES, with jewels in their centres, and the frame-work supported by

presume, representations of scenes in the life of St. Louis; the centre or chief one, seems to represent his death. Of the other two subjects in the

winged figures: below these is another CLASP, in a similar style to the preceding. The JUG and SALVER, are the same, on an enlarged scale, as those seen on the table in the former page; they are full of elaborate workmanship of the highest

the Duchess of Parma. The whole design of this object is singularly rich and beautiful; any description would be superfluous, as it sufficiently tells its own tale of the taste and well-directed study bestowed upon it. The engraving across the

order. The CASKET is also to be found on the table; this, perhaps, is the finest of the works this eminent goldsmith exhibits; it would do

honour to his renowned Florentine prototype, and France may well plume herself on her artistic skill when she sends forth such productions.

The following DESIGN, is intended to ornament the top of a box of sewed muslins or cambrics. It was designed by S. M'CLOY, of the Belfast School of Design, for Mr. M'Cracken, an extensive manufacturer in that town, and it obtained the first prize of two pounds given by Lord Dufferin at the recent exhibition of the works executed by the pupils of the above School. The convolvulus plant has suggested this very graceful pattern.

The BRACKET and SCREEN are among the contributions of the PATENT WOOD CARVING COMPANY, of London, whose operations are chiefly conducted by the aid of machinery. We have engraved, either here or elsewhere, for the original of the screen stands about sixteen feet high, occupying a conspicuous place near the transept, while the bracket measures about as many inches.

not adopted a uniformity of scale in the objects

The works of Messrs. ELLIS & SON, of Exeter, to which we devote this page, exhibit a great

which this desirable end is attained is one great merit of the invention: the point of the pin is received into a sheath to which a chain is attached, and this chain being drawn tight and passed through a notch, cannot by any possibility slip. We engrave three specimens of

amount of taste, combined with much sensible utility, particularly in brooches, where the "patent safety chains" enable the wearer to use

these BROOCHES, the two upper ones in plain silver, the third a more expensive combination of gold and jewels, especially remarkable for the beauty of its setting, which is quite worthy of the

best days of artistic jewellers-work. It is not only in productions of this kind that Messrs. Ellis command attention; the JEWEL-BOX, which forms the third of our series is very richly deco-

them without fear of their becoming unfastened when once properly secured; the simplicity with

rated, particularly with filligree work, which we have it not in our power to exhibit in a woodcut. The FISH-KNIFE at the bottom of our page is remarkable for the applicability of the figures and or-

nament which enrich its surface, and adds another to the many proofs of well-directed study exhibited in all branches of modern British manufacture, and which was never so well developed as now.

We occupy this page with examples of the ability of a London house, in a branch of manufacture that has given high reputation to Sheffield, Rotherham, Birmingham, &c., and to which places we generally look for the supply of such articles. London is scarcely acknowledged as a manufacturing city, except for objects of furniture or luxury; for metallic works we expect to look elsewhere. Yet London contains

in its streets many establishments of much extent, skill, and power, scarcely known to the busy throng which pass their doors,—some of whom, using the articles there made, imagine they have been fabricated in provincial towns. Mr. PIERCE, of Jermyn-street, has contributed STOVES, FENDERS, and the appurtenances of the fire-place, of a very tasteful and yet sumptuous kind. The latter term may especially apply to the STOVE we have

selected for engraving. The chimney-piece is in marble of various delicate hues; the fender, fire-irons, and ornamental adjuncts to the grate, are formed of massive silver. This costly work is of large proportions, and has been executed for the Earl of Ellesmere. The FENDER at the head of the page is a graceful design, comprising figures and ornaments equally well disposed. The same remark will apply to the one

beneath, in which dogs and deer bound forth from enriched scroll-work of elaborate convolution. The brilliancy and beauty of these works entitle them to high praise. The combinations of polished steel, gilding, and marble, are altogether in the happiest style, and will uphold the reputation which the manufacturer has enjoyed for many years: there is no question that England stands unrivalled in this branch of art.

The engravings on this page are from CARPETS contributed by Messrs. TURBERVILLE SMITH, & Co., of London. It is very difficult to form anything like a correct notion of the richness and beauty of these fabrics, when the colours are represented only by graduated shades of black, but the patterns, however delineated, speak for themselves. In the first, we have only the fern-plant, one of the most graceful productions of

the woods and hedgerows, and, as seen, worked out in this carpet in shades of the liveliest green, nothing can be more ornamental. For the second pattern, the flower-garden seems to have been rifled of its gayest and choicest flowers, to furnish the designer with materials for his work, so much that it almost requires one well instructed in botany to make out a list of its contents; and yet there is nothing overdone, nor any absence

of the most elegant harmony. Therein lies the skill of the designer in bringing all his selections into one mass of beautiful colouring without offending the purest taste. We think it will be generally conceded that our best carpet-manu-facturers have not come into the field of com-petition without being fully prepared for the contest. The carpets engraved on this page were designed for Messrs. Smith by Mr. E. T. Parris.

Messrs. H. WILKINSON & Co., of Sheffield, exhibit the CENTRE-PIECE we here engrave; it is a clever combination of figures and foliage, standing on a pedestal of enriched character. The branches

We have, ere this, found occasion, in our pages, to recommend to favourable notice the beautiful "ILLUMINATED GLASS" of Mr. KIDD; that term has not been inaptly used by him as its designa-

for candles bend forward from the main stem with an easy lightness, and the glass dish in the

tion. The most brilliant effects are produced by the ornaments being cut on the under side,

centre is of good form. "The IONIC INKSTAND," in the Elizabethan style, is a simple but graceful necessary for the library table. The manufacturers uphold the high reputation they have acquired. and filled with silvering, giving them the effect of embossing. Many of the forms are good.

CHINA—"the central flowery Nation"—is

represented through the contributions of various

persons, chiefly European. By far the most

important portions of the collection are sent by Messrs. HEWETT & Co., of Fenchurch Street, and comprise a large quantity of articles remarkable for their value and beauty. The IVORY BASKET which we engrave is an elegant example of taste,

and action predominates. With a little more ease in the flow of its lines it might be made an elegant and desirable addition to the boudoir of the European belle, reflecting the fair face as

stand of ebony; it is used as a medicine-cup. The entire design has much freedom and fancy, combined with the peculiar taste of the fabricant and the nature of the foliage. Beneath is a Japanese sweetmeat box on wheels; it is con-

combined with the patience and care for which the Chinese workmen are celebrated. The LOOK-ING GLASS, on its carved stand, has more freedom of design than we find in works coming from China, where mathematical precision in thought

pleasantly as it now reflects the Crystal Palace.

The other articles on our page are contributed by Mrs. CHRISTOPHER RAWSON: the upper one is an elegant CUP cut in soap-stone, upon a foliated

structed of a red lacquered ware; the boxes being formed to fit into each other in a variety of shapes. The archaic taste of a peculiar nation, schooled into a certain precise tone of mind, is strikingly visible in all these works.

The manufactory of Messrs. RICHARDSON, at Stourbridge, is chiefly famous for its productions in CRYSTAL GLASS, which they have carried to the utmost extent of brilliancy and purity. An examination of their contributions in decanters, wine-glasses, goblets, cream-bowls, butter-coolers, &c., will at once carry conviction that in this branch of the art England excels every other country of the world. Bohemia asserts, and probably maintains, its supremacy in the manufacture of coloured glass, but it cannot enter into competition with us as regards that which is colourless.

We are rapidly gaining upon them on their own ground, and it will be seen, by comparison, that,

of late years, we have so far studied forms and ornamentation as to have already far surpassed

them in these most essential matters. There is one point which, in justice to Messrs. Richard-

son, we must not omit to notice : all the articles they have sent to the Exhibition are produced

by British workmen; so that whatever merit they possess, and it is unquestionably great, is

due to the taste and talent of our own countrymen : the principal designer and engraver in

their establishment is Mr. W. J. Muckley. Among the objects emanating from this factory

seen in the Exhibition, and forming portions of

the contributions of other manufacturers, are the glass pillars and domes to the bronze and

other candle-lamps exhibited by Messrs. Blews & Son, of Birmingham, which are exceedingly novel in style and rich in colour; of these we shall

engrave specimens. The two DECANTERS with which we commence our illustrations, are of the purest crystal; the lozenge-shape cuttings bring out the prismatic colours with exceeding brilliancy: the GOBLET at the head of the second column is elegant in form, and the introduction of the vine upon the cup,

of the cutting, while it retains all its boldness. The next subject is a BUTTER DISH of crystal.

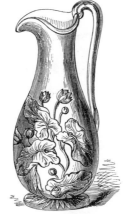

designed after the style of the antique. The VASE that follows is very elegant; it is manu-

enamel colours. The DECANTER completing

that page is most lustrous, and the lozenge-shaped cutting exceedingly bold. All the objects introduced in this page are of crystal of the purest kind; the beauty and variety of the cutting in the

though not a novelty, is appropriate. The FRUIT DISH and STAND that follows is of ruby glass covered on flint, and then cut through, showing the two colours to great advantage. The WINE GLASS is very elaborately ornamented, and the stem, which looks a little heavy in the engraving, loses this appearance in the original object, by the style

factured in opal; the scroll and band at top and bottom are gilt; the flowers and fruit painted with vitrified

whole of these works cannot fail to secure to them unqualified admiration. The large group at the bottom consists of one of each articles in a set of glass for dessert purposes, consequently they are all of a similar pattern, except the CLARET JUG, which is cut in a similar style, but is somewhat varied in its decoration.

Messrs. LAMBERT & RAWLINGS, of London, exhibit a variety of objects in the precious metals, adapted for useful and decorative pur-

poses; such as soup tureens and stands, ruby glass cups with silver mountings, designed after the antique, all characterised by a taste ac-

quired by long years of experience. We have selected from their contributions a pair of massive WINE FLAGONS, each standing twenty-two inches high, and holding eleven quarts:

they are richly chased and partly gilt, their style is antique, and they are hammered out of the

winged horse; and this is followed by an elaborately chased silver twelve-light CANDELABRUM

ounces; the design is appropriate to the Great Exhibition—Britannia, with the olive-branch of

plate. The next illustration is from a SALT CELLAR, the model of which is a Pegasus, or

and DESSERT CENTRE combined; its height is four feet, and its weight nearly twelve hundred

peace, is welcoming the representatives of the four quarters of the earth, heralded by Tritons.

The ornamental FRINGE for a window is the manufacture of Mr. R. BURGH, of London, who conducts an extensive business of this description; one of considerable importance, as connected with domestic furniture, and in which he finds ample room for the display of good taste.

The annexed engraving is from a COUTEAU DE CHASSE, by M. DEVISME, of Paris; it is a beautifully decorated piece of workmanship. The handle is of carved ivory, the hilt of polished

A CLOCK, manufactured by Mr. J. WALKER, of London, merits high commendation, from the truly elegant and artistic character of the design. The case is electro-gilt; the pedestal, of turquoise-blue glass, is surmounted by a group of figures, representing Britannia, in the robes of peace, directing attention to the progress made by Time and Science in the civilisation and

steel, chased, and the scabbard of dark steel ornaments on a grey ground. There are many elegant objects of this description by the French exhibitors, equally meritorious in character.

happiness of the people of Great Britain; this is illustrated by a series of seven subjects, revolving, by the aid of machinery, in the base of the clock. The several parts of this work might be described at length; altogether, there are few more meritorious productions in the Exhibition.

Birmingham has recently made great progress in the production of the better sort of plated and silver manufactures, so much so, indeed, as to have become a formidable rival to Sheffield, a town whose supremacy in this department of business was, till now, indisputable; however,

there is ample room for the manufacturers of both these important places to display their ingenuity and skill to the best advantage, and so contend for the palm of excellence. We engrave on this page some of the works contributed by the establishment of Messrs. PRIME & SON, of Birmingham. The first subject represents a BUTTER-KNIFE; the handle is in the Italian

the industrial arts, are in nothing more manifest than when seen in

metallic manufactures. The various processes of electrotyping, magneto-

style, and the blade is ornamented with an open floriated pattern. The LIQUOR STAND that follows offers considerable novelty in its design, which shows the utmost harmony in the ornamentation of its several component parts. To this succeeds a CAKE BASKET, the form of which is decidedly good, and the chasing in excellent taste. The TOAST RACK shows also a

very meritorious design; and the TRAY underneath it is equally entitled to commendation. Lastly, the ASPARAGUS TONGS, which complete the page, are sufficiently enriched with ornament to render them an elegant appendage to the dinner-table. We believe that all these manufactures are executed in magneto-plated silver. The results of scientific research, when applied to

plating, and others, have greatly tended to produce this satisfactory result.

Messrs. HORNE, ALLEN, & Co., of London, among other examples of PAPER-HANGING, exhibit the panelling, a portion of which we engrave. A richly-composed group of flowers and foliage runs round the entire design, which is executed with much care and precision, and exhibits considerable taste in the arrangement of colours. Floral decoration is exceedingly well applied to works

In our report of the recent exhibition of the works from the Government Schools of Design, at Marlborough House, published in the April

number of the *Art-Journal*, we noticed the important fact of the utility of such schools for artistic education, which rendered it unnecessary

for the British manufacturer to call in foreign aid. This was vividly exemplified in the instance

of Mrs. TREADWIN, of Exeter, an eminent lace-manufacturer, who had prepared for a continental

of this class, and when carefully studied, and truthfully rendered, is more gratifying to the eye than any other style of border ornament.

journey to procure designs. Fortunately, she first visited Somerset House, when the design for a LACE FLOUNCE was made the subject of a com-

petition among the students. The successful design was by Mr. C. P. Slocombe, which has since been worked out, and is here engraved.

The two BAROMETERS occupying this column are manufactured by Messrs. GRAY & KEEN, of Liverpool. The cases are made of English

walnut-wood. The first is of Gothic form, and has an elaborated dial plate, in which the architecture of the florid style is represented. The

second was designed for the "Sailors' Home," in Liverpool; it is a fac-simile of a patent anchor, the flukes of which support the ornamental disc.

The two IRON BEDSTEADS, introduced on this page, are from the establishment of Messrs. PEYTON & HARLOW, of Birmingham and London,

houses where we would, possibly, least expect to find them. The great points which should be aimed at in the manufacture of these bedsteads are lightness and elegance, in almost direct

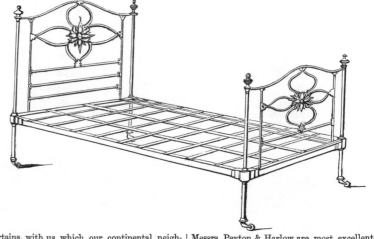

curtains, with us, which our continental neighbours seldom or never use. The productions of

very extensive manufacturers of these articles of domestic furniture, the use of which has, within the last few years, become very general, even in

opposition to those of French make, where solidity is chiefly required. This variation arises from the difference of construction in the two styles, and the adoption of hangings, or

Messrs. Peyton & Harlow are most excellent of their kind, and excellent examples of metal work.

In the course of our continental tour last year, undertaken for the purpose of ascertaining what preparations were making there for this

year's Great Exhibition, we visited the extensive establishment of M. CAPPELLMANS, at Brussels, and, in the course of our report, made an inci-

dental mention of his varied and important manufactory, which is devoted not only to com-

mon earthenware and pottery, but to porcelain of a better kind, and to glass work, in plain

sheets, or in "*verres filigraines*," rivalling in beauty the ancient Venetian works. Among the

common pottery we discovered imitations of popular English forms, and, among the plates,

filled with examples of the CHINA and EARTHEN-WARE contributed by M. Cappellmans. The large

characterised the pottery of the Low Countries two centuries since. The FRUIT-BASKET at the

our old friend, the much-patronised and much-abused "willow pattern." The present page is

VASE is of very fanciful design, exhibiting much of the peculiar and somewhat whimsical taste which

foot of the page, with its supporting angels, is a very graceful and elegant work of its class.

The CHIMNEY-POTS, in the Tudor style, are manufactured

The model of a group of a Scottish deer-hunter and his dogs, is by H. M'CARTHY, of London. It is a spirited performance, well composed, and does credit to the designer. It is executed in silver for ornamental purposes.

by Messrs. H. DOULTON & Co.

of Lambeth, who also con-

tributed the terra cotta vases engraved on a former page.

The CARPET is engraved from a portion of one manufactured by Messrs. A. LAPWORTH & Co., of London, for the state drawing-room of Buckingham Palace; it is a costly and elegant work of textile manufacturing art.

The two FIRE-PLACES are excellent examples of the manufactures of Messrs. ROBERTSON, CARR, & STEEL, of Sheffield, a firm conducting a most extensive business in that town. The latter of the two must attract attention from the novel construction of the fire-basket, which seems of a form calculated to hold a large body of com-

The engraving on this column is from a portion of a SUMMER-HOUSE, made of zinc; it is from the manufactory of M. DEYDIER, of Vaugirard, near Paris.

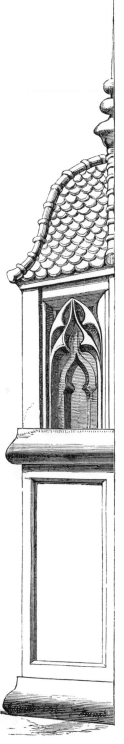

bustibles, as well as to throw out very considerable heat; the fire-basket of the other is of a more familiar form. The ornamental parts of both are unexceptionable in design and of highly enriched patterns; the whole seems to combine the double purpose of chimney-piece and stove. On looking at such works of manufacturing

Art as these, we are sometimes induced to institute a comparison between them and the famous "Dutch tiled fire-places," the glory of our forefathers; we scarcely need add our opinion as to which are the most esteemed. Although our examples are somewhat similar, the productions of Messrs. Robertson & Co. are very varied.

His establishment is on a very extensive scale, producing a large variety of articles, of a similar description to those we generally find wrought in other ordinary metals.

THE INDUSTRY OF ALL NATIONS.

We may certainly compliment Messrs. SILK & BROWN, of London, on their very elegant park PHAETON, engraved on this page. It is suspended upon a "swan-necked" carriage, on C and under springs, the whole exhibiting a study of graceful lines and curves. The body panels are painted a rich emerald-green colour, of a dark shade; the carriage and wheels a pale primrose, delicately picked out with green and red. The inside of the phaeton is trimmed in a rich but chaste manner, with green and white velvet lace: the mountings are all of silver.

Messrs. HOOPER & Co., of Boston, America, exhibit the elegant EPERGNE, which is here engraved. It is of very tasteful design, and possesses much brilliancy of effect. The amount of decoration which is included in the general design, is neither too sparing in its character, nor too profuse; the vine and its fruit are clustered around the base, or depend gracefully from the

branches, and the infant bacchanals below give life to the composition. The works of Messrs. Hooper are among the most attractive of those exhibited by their fellow-countrymen, both as regards their position in the building, and their general excellence. They deserve the approbation they obtain, and do the manufacturers much credit for the skill manifested in their production.

The Baron MAROCHETTI exhibits an emblematic igure of the ANGEL OF SLEEP, with bat-like wings, and gesture expressive of silence. It is

designed to be placed above the doors of a mausoleum, for which it is a suitable emblem.

A Vase, or fruit-cup, manufactured and exhibited by Messrs. J. Wagner & Son, distinguished artists of Berlin, is an exquisite example of metallic sculpture. The various figures are admirably modelled, and the ornamentation is altogether in the best taste. It is executed in oxidised silver.

The piece of Silk represented in the annexed engraving is manufactured and exhibited by Messrs. Stone & Kemp, of Spitalfields, who are noted for associating art with their productions. There is evidence of this in the design before us, which, we believe, emanated from the School of Design in the locality referred to. It is satisfactory to find manufacturers avail themselves of the assistance of such institutions.

The circular engraving which appears underneath is from a Table-top, forming a portion of

From among the variety of objects manufac- | tured and exhibited by B. Schreger, of Darm-

the costly and attractive contributions from the Austrian dominions. The table is manufactured by M. Karl Leistler, of Vienna; it is inlaid with various woods, arranged in a novel pattern.

stadt, we have selected a Paper-Weight, which represents a boar-hunt, placed not very appro- | priately, but yet ornamentally, upon a base designed like a foot-stool in a scroll frame-work.

The English carriage-builder still maintains, in his various contributions to the Exhibition, the high position universally acceded to him in this branch of industrial art. We engrave here a most elegant PARK PHÆTON, manufactured by Messrs. HALLMARKE, ALDEBERT, & HALLMARKE, of London. The body of the carriage has a form similar to that of the nautilus shell; and the vehicle, altogether, is remarkable for its lightness.

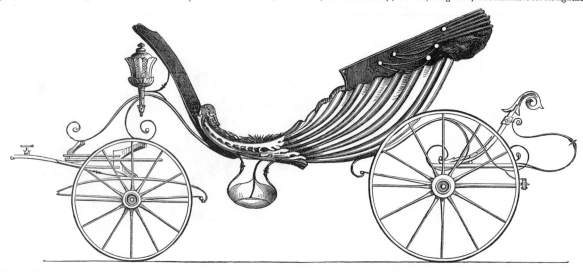

The two SWORDS on this column are the manufacture of Messrs. REEVES, GREAVES, & Co., of Birmingham. The longer one is an officer's FIELD-

The BOOK-COVERS of Madame GRUEL, of Paris, are so truly artistic in design and execution, that we feel no apology need be offered for introducing another of them into our pages. This, like

SWORD; the hilt and mounting of the scabbard are richly chased and gilt. The other is a Highland CLAYMORE, of good, yet elaborate, workmanship.

the preceding, is carved either in ivory or box-wood. The centre of the design shows the Virgin, crowned; the surrounding ornamentation exhibits a kind of trellis-work, partially covered.

Messrs. TOWLER, CAMPIN, & Co., of Norwich, exhibit some of the exquisite textile fabrics which have given character and reputation to that ancient city. A magnificent fillover scarf with a silk ground, is one of their contributions. It measures four yards in length, and two in width. The sobriety of colour which prevails in these elaborate productions is a proof of the good taste of the manufacturers. We engrave

the centre of one of the SHAWLS, which is but a small portion of the whole, the entire pattern being of the most intricate design, which it would be utterly impossible, adequately, to represent in our pages; it is like exhibiting a leaf from a tree,—but, as that is enough for a botanist to determine its character, so our cut may be received as an assurance of the taste which characterises these beautiful articles of female dress.

The group, in marble, of VENUS AND CUPID, life-size, is by Mr. E. DAVIS, of London. The subject is one that has engaged the sculptor and painter of almost every age, so that it seems impossible to invest it with any sentiment or action approaching to novelty. Mr. Davis has represented Cupid interceding with his mother for his bow, which Venus appears unwilling to place in his hands. The two figures are exceedingly well modelled, and arranged with much grace.

The CANDELABRUM, to hold nine lights, is exhibited by Mr. G. BROWN, of London, an extensive manufacturer of composition articles. It stands eight feet high, and is manufactured in wood and *carton-pierre*, gilded to imitate or-molu.

America has long been noted for the luxurious easiness of its chairs, which combine in themselves all the means of gratification a Sybarite could wish. The AMERICAN CHAIR COMPANY, of New York, exhibit some novelties, which even

increase the luxury and convenience of this necessary article of furniture; instead of the ordinary legs conjoined to each angle of the seat, they combine to support a stem, as in ordinary

music-stools, between which and the seat the SPRING is inserted; this we exhibit in our first cut. It will allow of the greatest weight and freest motion on all sides; the seat is also made

to revolve on its axis. The design and fittings of these chairs are equally good and elegant, and certainly we have never tested a more easy and commodious article of household furniture.

The TABLE-COVER engraved below is exhibited by Mdlle. HUNSON & Co., of Paris, from a design by M. Clerget. It is worked in wools and silks of various rich colours and shades, well selected.

M. DETOUCHE, of Paris, a most extensive manufacturer of clocks and watches, exhibits a superb CLOCK, which is the subject of the annexed engraving; it is manufactured of bronze, gilded. The design of the base is exceedingly bold, and the figures introduced have a purpose

beyond mere ornament, they are pointing upwards to indicate the flight of time. The upper part of the clock shows much elegant and elaborate decoration arranged in unquestionable taste.

The first engraving on this page is from the COVER OF A BIBLE, bound and exhibited by Mr. A. TARRANT, of London. It is an elaborate specimen of the art of book-binding; the ornament is beautiful in design, skilfully worked out, and is highly suggestive for other purposes.

The CARPET is from the manufactory of Messrs. TEMPLETON & Co., of Glasgow, of whose contributions we have given examples in a former page of our Catalogue. We have never seen any fabric of this description richer and more elegant than this: the pattern is full of "subject," displayed with exceeding taste and judgment,—groups and wreaths of flowers, scrolls, and border-ornaments, presenting a combination of beautiful forms.

Messrs. SIMCOX & PEMBERTON, of Birmingham, contribute many admirable specimens of the variety of useful articles which go towards the

fittings of a house, and which, until of late years, were considered beneath the thought of the artistic designer. The CURTAIN-BAND is an excellent sample of the applicability of floral nature

to ornamental art; the BELL PULL, which succeeds, may be also traced to the same fertile source of decoration, as modified by the particular taste of the architect. An Elizabethan CURTAIN-BAND succeeds, and shows how well the character of

internal decoration of any period may now be carried out in all minor accessories. The DOOR-HANDLE is of much lightness and elegance; and

the CORNICE and CURTAIN ORNAMENTS present an attractive novelty of form. They are all

highly favourable examples of manufacturing art, applied to the exigencies of every-day life.

M. GILLE, of Paris, contributes the porcelain works engraved in our present column, which

are remarkable for novelty and taste. The handle

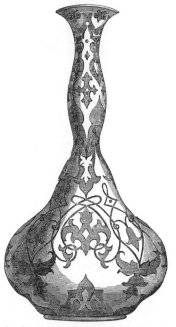

of the JUG is ingeniously formed of a lizard.

The TOILET-BOTTLE is in the elegant taste of the East. The VASE is that of the old Venetians.

The two objects which occupy this column are from the contributions of M. LA HOCHE, of Paris, who is eminent for the taste he invariably displays in the manufacture of porcelain clocks, and what are termed articles of *virtu*. Indeed, it may be said that his reputation in these departments of manufacturing art is second to none in the French metropolis. The first of

The National Manufactory established at Beauvais is represented by a series of works in tapestry for chairs, sofas, screens, and carpets. The extreme beauty of these productions is worthy of attention, particularly the skilful arrangement of colour they present, which,

our selections is a very elegant CLOCK, which appears in a vase-like form. The figures are designed with much grace and playfulness of action; the pediment is tastefully decorated with flowers, and the vase, of dark blue porcelain, equals the finest Dresden. The WINE-

though vivid, is so exquisitely toned as to be most grateful to the eye. The woodwork of the furniture is by M. DUVAL, one of the most famed of the Paris upholsterers, and who is specially appointed to mount all the tapestries issued from the National Manufactory, as well as to

COOLER, of light blue porcelain, is another work of great artistic beauty. We cannot speak too highly of the productions of this manufacturer.

We are well acquainted with his establishment in Paris, which is full of admirable works, arranged for show in the most attractive manner.

superintend other government work. The ornamentation he has executed with much perfection of finish, combining boldness of form with delicacy of handling, the whole being characterised by good taste. We select a CHAIR and a SCREEN as examples of these national works.

The manufactures in PAPIER-MÂCHÉ, of Messrs.

M'CULLUM & HODGSON, of Birmingham, deservedly

stand in high repute. Their productions in this

light and elegant material are characterised by excellent design and great richness in the variety

which it is unnecessary to particularise, as they sufficiently explain their own application. The

of colours introduced. We engrave on this page a number of these useful and ornamental objects,

TABLE is especially unique in its ornament, and the CABINET is most elaborately decorated. There

is no question that England stands unrivalled in this branch of industrial art, and her manufac-

turers seem determined to maintain their supremacy, if energy and perseverance can effect it.

The white terra-cotta productions introduced on this column are by Mr. BLANCHARD, of Lambeth. The first is a VASE and PILLAR, highly ornamented,

and executed with a sharpness and clearness equal to the sculptured stone. The second is a VASE, less decorated than the preceding, but equally

deserving of favourable notice. We should be glad to see this beautiful material brought into more general application, for which it is well adapted.

A most successful attempt to imitate the style and effect of the real Cashmere shawls may be seen in the subjoined engraving from a

most elaborate character, and aims at producing, on the lighter fabrics, suitable for summer wear, the qualities which have hitherto been

SHAWL, designed by Messrs. LEWIS & ALLENBY, of London, and printed for them by Messrs. Swaisland, of Crayford. The design is of the

found only in the more weighty and costly manufactures of the Asiatic producer. The shawl exhibits much rich harmony of colour.

If we desired to convince a foreigner of the immense wealth which this country possesses in the shape of manufactured articles, we would

invite him to accompany us for a day's stroll through the leading thoroughfares of our vast metropolis, to inspect the contents of the nume-

rous establishments for the manufacture and sale of works in the precious metals; or, what would be as effectual, and cost less time and labour, we would take him to the south-west gallery of the Great Exhibition edifice, to point

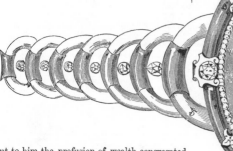

out to him the profusion of wealth congregated there in glittering heaps, almost, if not quite, realising the dreams of eastern fable. But it is not so much the value of the mere metal to which importance should be attached, as indi-

cating the riches that England contains within

her, as it is the amount of skill and labour

which are brought to bear on the production of

articles of luxury alone, and which must necessarily increase their value tenfold. Thus, the stranger would be led to reflect that, where so

much capital is expended on the production, there must be still larger means at the disposal of the buyers, to call for such an outlay; consequently, his ideas of our wealth receive a two-

fold impression. Among the mass of contributions that make up the costly piles to which allusion has been made, the silver ornaments and the jewellery manufactured by Messrs. S. H. & D. GASS, of London, must, from their

magnitude and beauty, attract observation. The most important of these is a SILVER DESSERT SERVICE, of novel character and design, modelled from plants growing in the Royal Gardens at Kew; of this service, five of the objects are engraved on the preceding page, and two on this column. It is quite needless to expatiate upon the taste displayed in the adaptation of these natural forms to manufacturing art. On the second column of the preceding page we have also introduced a jewelled BROOCH, in the style of the *cinque-cento* period; this object requires

close examination ere one can appreciate the beauty of its design. At the bottom of the same page is a BRACELET, set with diamonds and carbuncles, with portraits of the Queen and the Prince of Wales, after Thorburn, A.R.A., and executed in *niello*, engraved by J. J. Crew. A

CHRISTENING CUP, embellished with angels keeping watch over a kneeling child, designed by R. Redgrave, R.A., completes our illustrations of the contributions of Messrs. Gass; but we may hereafter find occasion to pay their stand another visit, as we observed among their pro-

ductions several objects deserving of notice; a silver gauntlet niello bracelet, designed by D. Maclise, R.A.; a silvered and jewelled dessert set, in the Elizabethan style; numerous articles of jewellery, of various kinds, and in diversified style; and a large vase, most ingeniously composed of human hair, executed by J. Woolley.

Messrs. COWLEY & JAMES, of Walsall, exhibit the brass CHANDELIER here engraved, and which consists of floral ornament, of a light and graceful character, well calculated to relieve from weighty monotony, an article which, in the

or even weightiness of appearance, a very objectionable quality, whenever exhibited. In some instances, the style or character of the apartment for which they are intended may demand a certain "weight," but the prevailing idea to guide the

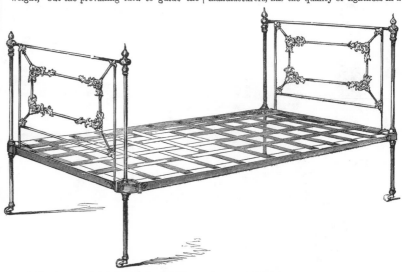

remarkable degree, the design and ornamentation being of the simplest kind; and, we must say, we prefer it to much of the overwrought and highly-elaborated articles, which we are not unfrequently called upon to notice. We are

hands of a tasteful designer, may be made an elegant adjunct to the drawing-room. However elaborate or beautiful the design and execution of such articles of modern furniture may be, we must confess that we think heaviness of construction,

artisan should be the construction of a receptacle for light, which, like that element, should be ethereal, and graceful, and ponderosity be especially eschewed. The BEDSTEAD, by the same manufacturers, has the quality of lightness in a

convinced, from long experience, that it is far easier to produce such works, than to confine decoration to that which is simple and appropriate; the former may be done by the ornamentist, the latter only by the artist of taste.

The two CHAIRS and the large SIDEBOARD which appear on this page are the work of Messrs. HUNTER, of London. The chairs are of very elegant design, and are beautifully carved; they are, however, as remarkable for their comfort as for their elegance, and present all that is requisite for the beauty or the ease of the drawing-

wood for decorative purposes. The embellishments of this large and important work are all indicative of its use; the laden branches of the vine encircle it, from between which peep the

The VASE in the centre is a foreign contribution; it is one of the valuable productions of Russia. It is entirely constructed of Jasper, and though good in form, its great recommendation is its large value. The wealth of the Russian mines and quarries has long been a celebrated feature of the country; and the contributions it

room. The sideboard is carved in a bold and massive style, entirely from the wood of the walnut tree, which has been chosen by the manufacturer to show the capability of English

heads of bacchanals; and the cornucopiæ, filled to overflowing with the plentiful fruits of the earth, give large promise of abundance. It is, altogether, a well-conceived production.

has sent us testify abundantly to the truth of "travellers' tales" connected therewith. We purpose engraving, in a future number, other subjects worthy of notice from this vast empire.

It is rather surprising that the English manufacturer of carpets should, till within the last few years, be so far behind his foreign competitor as, it must be acknowledged, he has been, seeing that the use of these fabrics is so much more general here than elsewhere; and it is an axiom among the trading community, that not only the supply of an article should keep pace with the demand, but also that a stimulus should be given to the demand by every kind of improvement of which the object in question is capable. Now there is scarcely an article of ordinary

domestic use better calculated to develope the artistic resources of the manufacturer's mind than those to which we are now referring, whether they are intended for the dwellings of the middle classes, or the mansions of the wealthy, and, in consequence, we have latterly noticed they exhibit a far greater degree of refinement and taste than we were wont to see shown in them. Among the contributors of carpets of various degrees of quality, some rich, and others suited to more common purposes, are Messrs. A. LAPWORTH & Co., of London,

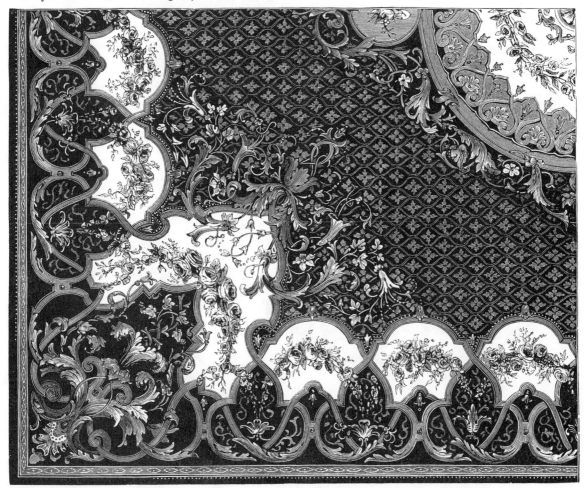

from whose contributions we have made some selections. The first engraving represents an elegant HEARTH-RUG, designed for Messrs. Lapworth by Miss Gann, a clever pupil of the School of Design at Somerset House. The design is simple, but very elegant, being nothing more than wreaths of white and red roses, upon a dark, claret-coloured ground; in the border, a white ribbon is entwined with them. The other subject is from a rich Axminster CARPET; the borders, corners, and centre of this are exceedingly fanciful, but they manifest much beauty.

The palm of excellence in gold and silver ornamental works has hitherto, almost universally, been conceded to the manufacturers of France; but those who have attentively examined British works of this class, and, among others. the productions of Mr. J. ANGELL, of London, will be inclined to qualify their admiration of the contributions of foreign rivals; this, too, with-

engine that either multiplies the labours of man's ingenuity, or disperses them throughout the world, is a witness to the fact. Capital, taste, and skill have been liberally expended to bring about such improvement. The application of the Fine Arts to manufactures has made rapid strides within the last few years; science has kept pace with them, developing new

resources of colour and material to realise every new artistic conception of beauty and elegance. The manufacturers have bestirred themselves manfully; in earthenware. porcelain, glass, iron, and metal work generally, and in the textile fabrics, the progress has been marked and rapid; and what is of still greater importance, the labours of the producer have been met by

out any disparagement of their merits. If we had no other examples in the Exhibition whereby to prove the immense progress made in this department of industrial art we could confidently appeal to these works as evidences of our advance. The present is unquestionably the age of improvement as well as of invention, and every object of ornamental or useful application, from the toy with which childhood amuses itself, to the gigantic steam

the appreciation of the public: hence have arisen renewed efforts on the part of the former to carry still further his improvements, and to invite the patronage of the latter. But we must not exhaust our space with preliminary remarks, to the exclusion of a description of Mr. Angell's beautiful productions. Among the objects for which we could not find room are several groups,

and salvers in silver and silver gilt, richly wrought, and finely designed; the subjects we have especially noticed as worthy of being recorded are—"The Battle of Alexander and Darius," on a chased shield; "The Labours of Hercules," on a salver; groups of "Sir Roger de Coverley and the Gipsies," and "Arab Merchants Halting in the Desert." Our selection has been chiefly from works of less magnitude, but not of less value as works of high art. The first is a SILVER CUP, excellent in form, and richly embellished with floriated patterns; the base exhibits an elegant novelty. By the side of this is a CAKE-BASKET, of silver-gilt; the border is enamelled work, as are also the orna-

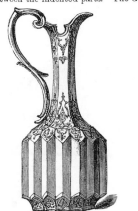

ments between the indented parts. The GROUP

at the bottom of the page is composed of some

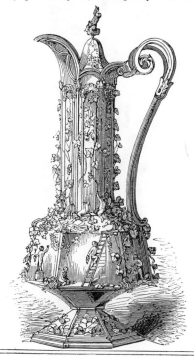

very splendid objects; the large cup to the left

is in gold and enamels; it stands a considerable height, and is most exquisite in its elaborate and delicate workmanship; the centre-piece is

one of a set of four table ornaments, intended by their designs to represent the four seasons. The large VASE to the right is of silver enamelled;

it is a truly beautiful example of the chaser's skill. The smaller objects in the process are scarcely less worthy of favourable remark. On this page we first introduce a SILVER JUG, of a

fluted pattern, graceful in its proportions: this is followed by another in gold, of Etruscan form, a present to Dr. Elliotson from one of his patients; and the third in the same column,

called the "VINTAGE JUG," is of gold, with the ornaments in silver; the combination of the two metals, one burnished and the other "matted," produces a brilliant effect. The first

TEA AND COFFEE SERVICE is of silver-gilt and enamelled in the richest style; the GROUP underneath it is composed of various objects in silver, glass and silver, and silver enamelled;

and the last TEA AND COFFEE SERVICE is of silver, set with enamels. While adverting to the taste which has produced the whole of the objects we have engraved, we are bound to

notice especially the beauty of the enamelling, which we scarcely remember to have seen equalled. The difficulty of enamelling upon silver is, we are assured, not easily surmounted.

We introduce on this column the CAPITAL OF A PILLAR, and a PINNACLE, manufactured by Mr. BLANCHARD, of Lambeth. They are executed in white terra cotta. The former, though ex-

hibiting no originality in design, is wrought with a sharpness and delicacy, as if cut from the solid stone. The latter is one of the largest architectural ornaments hitherto made in this material.

Messrs. SMEE & SON, of London, exhibit the CANOPY BEDSTEAD, of which an engraving appears below. It is manufactured of mahogany, boldly carved, and the hangings are of rich crimson Spitalfields silk. There is sufficient ornament in this object to constitute it an ele-

gant article of domestic furniture, but the manufacturers have not aimed at producing an elaborate work of industrial art. The CABINET that succeeds is also from the same establishment. It is inlaid with very beautiful marquetrie; the sides have plate-glass inserted.

The CANOE is one of the contributions from Canada. It is made of the bark of a tree, and is exceedingly light in its construction. There is, likewise, in this department of the Exhibition another canoe, much larger in size, capable of holding twenty men. It was brought, through lakes and rivers, twelve hundred miles, to be shipped for England. As we observed in a former page, with reference to the contributions from Canada. there are few having any pretensions to ornamental works; utility, rather than display, being the object of the colonial manufacturer. The canoe is an example of native ingenuity.

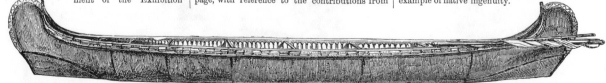

This engraving represents the centre of a DAMASK TABLE-CLOTH, designed by Joseph Blain, pupil of the Government School of Design in Belfast; and manufactured by Messrs. CORRY, BLAIN, & Co., of the same town, on the new system of steam-loom weaving, which is, we believe, the first successful effort made to manufacture linen damask by steam power. There is also a novelty in the purpose of the design

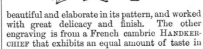

here introduced, which admits of some explanation; each group being figurative and expressive of an object according to the language of flowers. Our space will not permit us to go into the details of the matter, which we must leave to the reader's ingenuity to decipher.

The two subjects occupying the latter half of this page are exhibited by Messrs. B. SALOMONS & SONS, of London; the first is a CANZOU, or LADY'S CAPE, of embroidered needle-work, most beautiful and elaborate in its pattern, and worked with great delicacy and finish. The other engraving is from a French cambric HANDKERCHIEF that exhibits an equal amount of taste in its design, and of superior execution; it also displays every known description of stitch in this kind of embroidery. It would almost seem that ingenuity and patient industry could go no farther in such matters than have been expended on these textile fabrics, which must have occupied

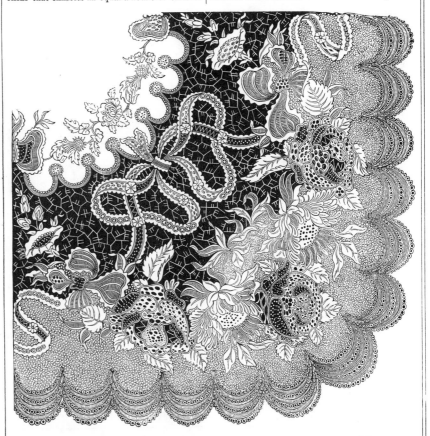

no inconsiderable time in their production. Hitherto the foreign manufacturer has held almost the entire command of the English markets; but the contents of the south-eastern gallery of the Exhibition shows much in no way inferior to the best fabrics of the continent.

The VASE OF FLOWERS is a well-executed specimen of wood-carving, by Mr. PERRY, of Taunton. The contents of the vase, so to speak, is a bunch of roses only, but the vase itself is ornamented with an allegorical composition, in which the artist's idea has been to show the probable effects of the Great Exhibition upon the whole world. In this Mr. Perry has evinced considerable ingenuity, but it would far exceed the limits of our space to enter upon any lengthened descriptive explanation. The design

On this and the two succeeding pages we engrave some beautiful specimens of DAMASK TABLE LINEN, from the extensive and far-famed manufactory of Mr. M. ANDREWS, Ardoyne,

Belfast. The first two examples are styled the "Clarendon Pattern," having been made for presentation to the Earl of Clarendon by the Royal Society for the Promotion and Improve-

upon the stand is a circle of flowers and plants, emblematical of various countries of the globe. We think the artist's intention in his allegorical design would have told better, if done on a larger scale; it is too full of subject for its size.

ment of the Growth of Flax in Ireland. Both the NAPKIN and TABLE-CLOTH bear appropriate designs and ornaments; the former contains the arms of the Lord Lieutenant, encircled by a

wreath and inscription, with an elegant floriated border; the centre of the latter shows the star of the Order of the Garter, in a garland of the rose, shamrock, and thistle, with other devices.

That our American friends, with all their apparent dislike of pomp and parade, are not

insensible to the luxuries and conveniences of life, is evident from the elegant CARRIAGES they

exhibit. The one engraved is manufactured and exhibited by Messrs. CLAPP & SON, of Boston.

We introduce on this column another of the contributions from Canada, an elegantly-built and tastefully ornamented single SLEIGH, built by Messrs. M'LEAN & WRIGHT, of Montreal.

On this column are STATUETTES, executed in statuary porcelain, at the works of Mr. COPELAND,

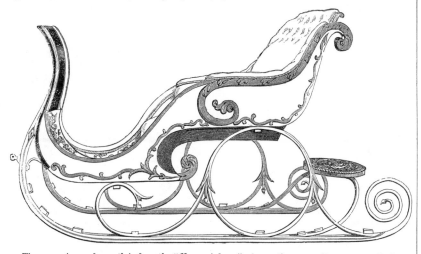

The engraving underneath is from the "Clarendon" DAMASK TABLE-CLOTH, by Mr. ANDREWS, described on the preceding page. It is an admirable specimen of his art-manufacture.

from models by Cumberworth, of Paris; the sub-

jects are the Indian Fruit-girl, and Water-bearer. The attitudes of these figures are very graceful.

Another description of American carriages is copied from a single horse phaeton, manufactured by Mr. WATSON, of Philadelphia. One peculiarity we notice in it, is the unusual size of the fore-wheels compared with the hinder, so contrary to the practice of our carriage-builders, but there is no doubt this causes it to run easily. The body of the vehicle seems very light in its construction.

A wicker GARDEN-CHAIR, contributed by Mr. TOPF, of New York, possesses much novelty, and no little taste, in its ornamental design.

The TABLE-CLOTH called the "Ardoyne Exhibition Pattern," is another of the beautiful fabrics of Mr. M. ANDREWS, of Belfast. It was designed, in competition, by J. Mackenzie, of the Belfast School of Design, who richly merited the prize he obtained for a composition so excellent.

On this and the three following pages, our readers are introduced to illustrations from far-famed establishment, which has now been in existence for more than a century, stands about seven miles from Paris, and its extensive museum and show-rooms have long been points of attraction to every visitor to the French Metropolis. The number of workmen employed in the manufactory is about one hundred and

some of the PORCELAIN WORKS exhibited by the Government Manufactory at SÈVRES. This fifty, and the artists engaged in the ornamental department are of the first merit, as those who are acquainted with

direction of the affairs of the establishment is undertaken by

the Sèvres porcelain must readily acknowledge ; while the general

a body of some of the most able artists and scientific men in the country.   The present administrator-general is M. Ebelmen.   M.

Dieterle, to whom we are indebted for the drawings supplied to us, has charge of the artistic department, under the council ; and

M. Vital Roux superintends the ateliers. Our space precludes us from giving a list of the

numerous staff of artists, male and female, by whom these gentlemen are assisted; it is

sufficient to say they are, in every way, qualified for the important duties devolving upon them. Our first engraving represents a LAMP, designed and executed by M. Klagmann; TAZZA, of elegant proportions, with a light, floriated border under the rim; and this is followed by a VASE of Etruscan form, ornamented with flowers. A covered VASE succeeds this,

on the shade are figures emblematical of Evening, Morning, Silence, and Sleep; on the body are little genii of various kinds. The second column commences with a small, flat-shaped with Alhambresque borders, exceedingly graceful in shape, and covered with elaborate painting; and the column is completed by a CUP, in the Cellini style, ornamented with designs of

Raffaellesque character. The second page opens with a VASE of ancient form, embellished with bold and rich groups of flowers; by its side stands another VASE, entitled the "Agricultural Vase;" on the side seen in the engraving is a labourer conducting his plough, attended by the

four Seasons; the opposite side shows a horse, with its characteristic qualities of strength, beauty, courage, description, to do it justice, would far exceed our limits. The GROUP on the fourth

and swiftness; this vase is designed by M. Klagmann. Underneath these is a large VASE, called the "Vase of Labour," symbolised by an elegantly-designed frieze, in which Agriculture, Industry, Study, and Religious Education are represented; the medallions indicate Ceres, Vulcan, and Minerva; the figures on the plinth are the Fates. On the third page is a VASE of Chinese form, decorated with birds and flowers; and, by its side, a TABLE, the top of which has flowers painted by M. Schiltz; the bronze stand is by M. Matifat.

page is composed of a number of very beautiful objects. The covered VASE that

follows is designed in the best taste; the ornaments are in the style of Raffaelle.

A BAPTISMAL FONT succeeds, nearly six feet in width; it is a noble work of ceramic art, but a lengthened

The three objects filling the last column are in the highest degree meritorious.

Messrs. POUSSIELGUE & RUSAND, are extensive manufacturers, in Paris, of every kind of furniture for ecclesiastical purposes, such as chandeliers,

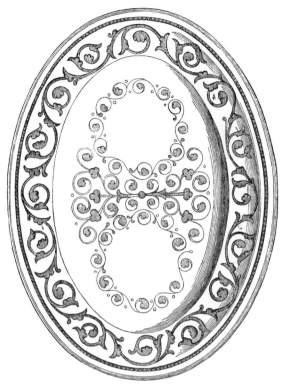

shrines, monstrances, lamps, cups, &c.: this page is devoted to a few of

the ornament is in keeping with the use to which they are applied. The OSTENSOIR, or confessional screen, is an elaborate and rich piece of work-

manship of very elegant scarcely necessary for us and novel design. It seems to remark that, in every-

their contributions, commencing with a communion SALVER and CHALICE of silver, with gilt ornaments. The two EWERS are more decorated, but thing connected with the forms and ceremonies of the Roman Catholic worship, there is more external magnificence than in any other church.

On this and the following page will be found engravings from a large variety of objects, manufactured by Messrs. APSLEY PELLATT & Co., of the Falcon Glass-Works, London. The first is

a VASE for flowers, forming part of a dessert-service; the cutting is peculiar; fine splits cross each other at right angles, and these, being set into sunken pannels, leave raised flat squares, or

diamonds; the shadows produced by them alternating with the brightness of the splits, produce a beautifully-varied and prismatic effect; the whole of this dessert-service is a fine specimen of modern glass and glass-cutting. A CLARET-JUG, to be mounted in silver, follows; it affords an excellent contrast between the bright ground and the dead engraving. A WATER-JUG

of pure form and cutting, succeeds; the material of which it is made is exquisitely transparent.

chandeliers composed of white glass, the one prominent object in their manufacture should produce the splendid natural prismatic colours. Great attention seems to have been paid to this

The whole construction of the next object, a CHANDELIER, is novel, and very effective: in all be, by the form and cutting of the parts, to break and refract the rays of light, and thus to

essential matter in this chandelier, the whole body appearing one entire mass of glass, cut into large diamond-shape pieces. Underneath this is a GROUP, the centre object of which is the ETAGERER of the dessert-service already referred to; the others are CLARET-JUGS of elegant work-

manship, and SALT-CELLARS, broad and massive in design. This page commences with a CLARET-JUG of antique form, and richly ornamented

with florid engraving. Of the engraving on the first WINE-DECANTER we cannot speak too highly, the deep intaglio of the fruit presenting a roundness of form and delicacy of outline

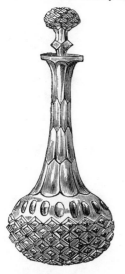

quite unique. The other DECANTER exhibits a style of cutting calculated to bring out the brilliancy of the glass. A CHANDELIER of colossal dimensions is one of the most effective

we have seen for a long time; the drops are very large, although their magnitude is lost in the vast size of the chandelier itself; the fan ornaments, formed of independent drops of different lengths set together, are novel;

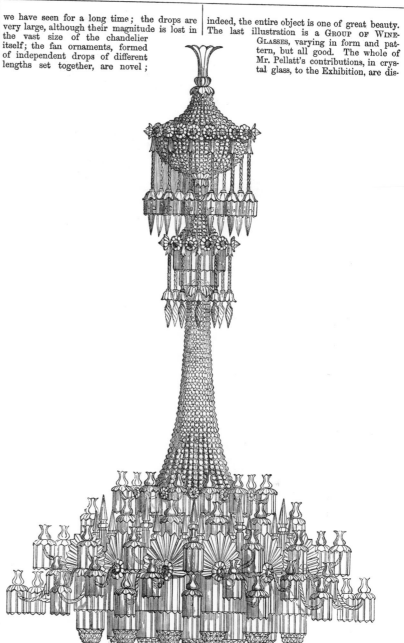

tinguished by sound and pure taste, and by material and workmanship of a most superior

great degree, attribute the prominent position it has held, of late years, in Great Britain, defying

indeed, the entire object is one of great beauty. The last illustration is a GROUP OF WINE-GLASSES, varying in form and pattern, but all good. The whole of Mr. Pellatt's contributions, in crystal glass, to the Exhibition, are dis-

character. To this gentleman the art is largely indebted, and to his exertions we may, in a

the competition of the world, and excelling, in most particulars, the works of the old Venetians.

Among the contributions in silver and electro-plate, exhibited by Messrs. SMITH & NICHOLSON, of London, are the objects from which engravings appear on this page. Our space permits only a very brief description of them. A SALVER, supported by two figures, carrying baskets, repre-

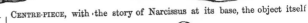

senting Spring and Autumn; these are intended for FRUIT-DISHES. A CENTRE-PIECE, with the story of Narcissus at its base, the object itself

being modelled from the leaves and flower of the plant; and the SHAK-SPEARE TESTIMONIAL, presented to Mr. Macready, which is designed in a manner highly complimentary to that great master of the histrionic art. In front of the salver is a FRUIT-BASKET of a very simple form.

The Austrian department has, since the opening of the Great Exhibition, been one of its principal points of attraction. Indeed, for a considerable period before that time, the announcements made as to the various articles intended to be sent had excited much interest. The furniture for a suite of palatial rooms by Mr. CARL LEISTLER, of Vienna, favourably known from the works he had executed for Prince Leichtenstein, was spoken of as a *point d'appui.* Expectation has been gratified, and the originality and beauty of his productions have obtained for him due applause. We have

selected for engraving the principal objects of the series; and commence with two CHAIRS, both carved from the beautifully-veined and richly-tinted wood of the locust tree. The execution of the carved work upon these chairs merits high praise; it is exceedingly sharp and well-defined; the

designs are bold and massive. The PIANO is constructed of dark rosewood, inlaid in buhl-

work, of gold, silver, and copper tints, producing an exceedingly gorgeous effect; which is further

heightened by the figures on each side; the sockets for candles, and the consoles being richly gilt.

The TABLE which follows is also of dark rose-wood; the stem is of a singularly original and

beautiful character. The great work of the series, however, is the STATE BEDSTEAD, most elaborately

carved in locust-tree wood; it is decorated with a series of statuettes and bas-reliefs in the same material, typical of man's career, commencing with figures of Adam and Eve, on the foot-board, and ending with scenes of his regeneration, at the head. An abundance of carved work of a fanciful kind is

spread over its surface; the hangings are constructed of crimson damask and velvet of various depths of tint, fringed with gold lace, and the work altogether is as sumptuous as it is thoroughly artistic.

The glass manufacture of Bohemia has obtained high celebrity for the taste of its form and the beauty of its colour; and the manufacturers of that country have in no wise done their European celebrity any discredit by their contributions. We select a few examples from the contributions of M. WILHELM HOFFMANN, of Prague.

They occupy a prominent position in the transept—a place of honour their intrinsic excellence deserves. They comprise a great variety of articles, as well for the every-day use of life as for the more luxurious ornament of the boudoir, or its needful elegancies.

There is a delicate appreciation of tender hues of colour in these productions well worthy of attentive study; this elevates the simplest of them far above the gaudy vulgarities occasionally fabricated, and termed "Bohemian glass," and which are chiefly remarkable for the strong contrasts of deep colour, and abundant display of gilding upon their surface. M. Hoffmann's works have no such defects. The large vase and its pedestal is nearly four feet in height, and is entirely of pure white, except where the leaves bend over, and they are tinted with pale green. Altogether M. Hoffmann's display is as satisfactory as that of any manufacturer in the Exhibition.

The TABLE is another of the works of M. Leistler, it is carved from the locust tree wood

The elegant marble CHIMNEY-PIECE—and GLASS, the frame of which is constructed of the same material—is the work of GUISEPPE BOTTINELLI, of Milan, the figures being executed by DEMOCRITE GANDOLFI, a brother artist of the same city. The design is of much elegance, and highly suggestive.

there is much fancy displayed in the arrange- | ment of the ornament upon the central support,

which is of a quaint and original character. The | design and execution are both alike excellent.

This CHAIR is the production of M. AUGUST KITSCHELT, of Vienna; it is of free and fanciful design, more remarkable for the taste of the upholsterer than the wood-carver. It is covered with velvets of delicate hues, pink and blue predominating; the arrangement of the colours is very tasteful; the trimmings are of a pale golden hue. There is a lightness and fancy in its construction which bespeaks the best taste.

The carved TABLE is by M. LEISTLER; the stem is very elegant in design, exhibiting floriated ornament of an exceedingly tasteful kind. The top is richly inlaid with various coloured woods; this has been engraved on page 149 of our present Catalogue. The BOOKCASE exhibits much

novelty of design; it is constructed of white lime-tree wood, relieved by panels, &c., of satin-wood. The group of children which surround the canopy are very beautifully carved, and the entire portion of the ornamental work is executed with force and elegance. It is as beautiful an example of manipulative skill, as of general ability in design. The Italian taste of the renaissance is the predominating character of style

chosen; it has been successfully adapted, in the present instance to a portion of furniture, which "coarse or unskilful hands" have generally made square and unsightly, but which, in the hands of a skilful manufacturer, may be converted into an elegant piece of ornamental furniture.

From the ROYAL PORCELAIN MANUFACTORY of Copenhagen is exhibited a large variety of works of a useful and ornamental character; among the latter, some beautiful figures, busts, &c., in biscuit china, after Thorwaldsen's models. We introduce here his famous group of GANYMEDE.

We have already described and engraved some of the works produced at the Royal Porcelain Manufactory at Dresden, and must refer to former pages of the Catalogue for a description of this establishment. We now add two more

A very tasteful radiating HALL-STOVE is exhibited by Mr. J. HAYWOOD, of Derby, sufficiently rich in its ornamental work to grace the most aristocratic mansion in the land. As it is very

specimens of their works, both of which are remarkable for vigour of conception, in styles the most opposite to each other—the one partaking of the fancy of the east, the other charac-

probable some critical eye may discover a little inaccuracy of perspective in the drawing of the hearth-plate, it is necessary to state that it has been so placed the better to show the design.

teristic of the period when Dresden china first became celebrated throughout Europe for its beauty of form and fabric,—characteristics which appear upon the works we have selected.

On this and the subsequent page we introduce engravings from some of the numerous contributions of Messrs. RICE HARRIS & SON, of the Islington Glass Works, Birmingham. Some estimate may be formed of the extent and importance of this establishment, when we enumerate among its contributions articles in flint-glass, cut and engraved; pressed and moulded glass tumblers, goblets, wine-glasses, sugar-basins, butter-coolers, door-knobs, &c.; orna-

is a VASE, black coated, with white enamel, richly cut, and ornamented with gold and silver. The

mental glass, of various colours, gilt and enamelled, cut and engraved, consisting of tazzas, compotiers, liqueur-services, toilet-bottles, claret-jugs, vases; specimens of colours combined by casing or coating; specimens of threaded or Venetian glass; in short, examples of almost every kind of object into which this beautiful material is capable of being manufactured. The

small VASE at the head of the succeeding

column is ruby-coloured, with cut gilt lines,

space we have, therefore, devoted to illustrating a portion of them, is not greater than their excellence demands, and we regret our inability to find room for a more lengthened description than we are able to give of what are introduced. The first group consists of VASES and GOBLETS, elaborately engraved and cut; in the centre of the second group of VASES, GOBLETS, and a JUG, and the next is an opaque yellow VASE, cut and scalloped with chased gilt flowers; the VASE

that follows is deeply cut in a novel style of

ornament. In the upper group on this page, to

the left, is a VASE of ruby glass, with cut plates,

and gilt chased ornaments; and by its side a large GOBLET and COVER, of ground crystal, covered with ruby and white, richly cut in three

centre of the lower group is a large alabaster VASE, nearly five feet high, elegantly and

opaque white, enamelled, heightened with gold in the ornament and handle; and in the left of the group is a VASE of dark, opaque blue, cut

shields; on one are the royal arms of England, and on the other two the monograms of the Queen and Prince Albert respectively. In the

tastefully ornamented with gilt scrolls; on either side stands a JUG and GOBLET. of

and scalloped, and ornamented with oak-leaves and acorns in silver. The whole of these works are executed in the highest degree of finish.

We have, on former occasions, made ourselves acquainted

with the manufactured works of Messrs. MESSENGER & SONS, of Birmingham, who are contributors to the great Exhibition

of an extensive variety of useful and ornamental productions

in iron, bronze, &c., distinguished by elegance and correctness of design, and excellent workmanship. Of these we might have

ful in form and character: the next is a GROUP, in bronze and or-morlu, of the Queen

is, in all respects, a good example of English casting. A stair-case BALUSTRADE, in or-

beneath it is equally entitled to commendation, and the VASE, of open-work, is both

selected a large number for illustration, if our space had been less limited. The CANDLE-STICK, which commences this page is grace-

and the Prince of Wales, modelled by Mr. John Bell,—the distinguished sculptor. It

morlu, is an admirable piece of work in form, colour, and casting. The INKSTAND

light and elegant. The firm of Messenger and Sons has amply sustained its reputation.

We should most assuredly have omitted one of the *greatest* features of the Exhibition had we neglected to introduce into our Catalogue the colossal statue of the renowned crusader, GODFREY OF BOUILLON, modelled by M. SIMONIS, of Brussels. It is a work conceived in a noble spirit, and as admirably carried out.

Some objects of manufacture, novel in this country but much practised by

the continental jewellers, are exhibited by Mr. F. ALLEN, of Birmingham; we engrave two FLOWER-VASES, of fillagree-

The SCROLL underneath is another of the many valuable contributions of Messrs. MESSENGER & SONS, of Birmingham; it is intended for a gas-bracket, and shows a very graceful arrangement of curved lines.

work, made of fine gold threads throughout; they are exquisitely delicate.

Messrs. JACKSON & GRAHAM, the eminent upholsterers, of London, are large contributors

to the Great Exhibition of many important articles of their manufacture. We engrave on

this column a portion of a BOOK-CASE, the panels of which are fitted with plate-glass, and the end

of a SOFA, showing a demi-figure, boldly carved. The SIDEBOARD and CHEVAL-GLASS, with their

underneath are good in their respective styles. The BOOK-CASE on the next page exhibits the best

taste in its design; the artist has evidently aimed to combine simplicity of idea with a due

bronze candlesticks and ornaments, are beautiful in design, and admirably carved; the CHAIRS

regard to richness of detail. The CARPET shows a bold and well-tilled pattern, arrayed in bright

and harmonious colours. It is quite evident, from the examples here shown, that Messrs.

Jackson & Graham employ artists of no common order to furnish them with designs for their

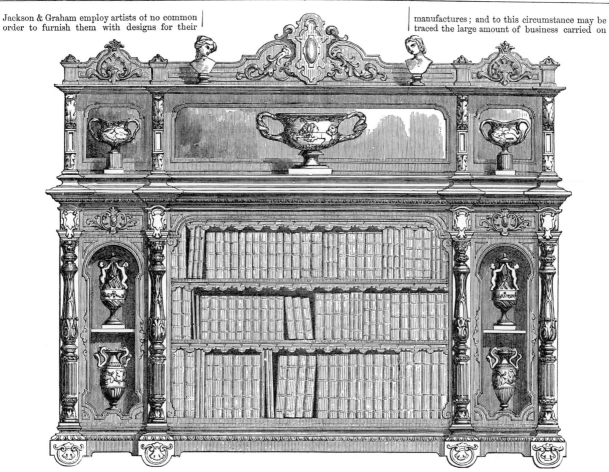

manufactures; and to this circumstance may be traced the large amount of business carried on by the firm. Public taste has, of late years, increased to such an extent, that mediocre productions find little chance of sale; hence the best producer is certain of being recompensed in proportion to the spirit and taste with which he may conduct his manufacturing transactions.

The manufacture of the particular kind of earthenware generally known as "BEAUVAIS

WARE," is carried on in places far distant from that ancient town. The three objects occupying

this column are from the factory of M. DE BOISSIMON, of Langeais, in the Department of Indre et

Loire; he is also the producer of other objects, applicable to mere purposes of utility. The VASES are beautiful examples of the "ware."

The musical instrument shown in the appended engraving is from the manufactory of Messrs. LUFF & SON, of London; it is called by the exhibitors an "Albert Cottage Pianoforte HARMONIUM;" the design of the case is elegant, being carved with much elaborate workmanship.

The engraving underneath is from a printed cloth TABLE-COVER, commemorative of the Great Exhibition, manufactured and exhibited by Mr. W. UNDERWOOD, of London, from a design by Mr. Slocombe. It is exceedingly rich in its ornamental work, conspicuous among which are the

royal arms of England, surrounded, in the centre and border, by those of the principal nations contributing to the grand display of industrial art; appropriate mottoes enclose the whole.

From one of our most picturesque and fashionable provincial towns, we have a display of plate

and jewellery unsurpassed by places of greater celebrity. Messrs. MARTIN, BASKETT, & MARTIN,

of Cheltenham, are the contributors of the objects introduced on this page. The first is a richly

chased CLARET-JUG, after Cellini, a sufficient guarantee for its beauty. The next is a SALT-CELLAR, showing great novelty and elegance in its design, and very skilful execution. The two

subjects heading the other columns are respectively termed a PORTE-MONTRE and CHATELAINE; they are made on such a principle as to suit watches of any size, besides having the advantage

of keeping the watch secure and steady. A BUTTER-COOLER succeeds; the dish for the butter is of white marble, the ornament, consisting of leaves and butter-cups, is of silver, the interior of the flowers being gilt; the combination of

these materials produces a very chaste effect. The last illustration is from a BRACELET, formed of gold, enamels, diamonds, and carbuncles, in the following style: the diamonds are placed

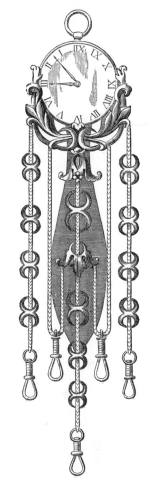

over the carbuncles; the gold cross-bands connecting the precious stones are slightly enamelled in scroll-work of a rich turquoise-blue colour, forming altogether a brilliant and perfect ornament. Other contributions of these tasteful manufacturers are some beautiful pearl ornaments, an ink-stand on which is modelled a group of Milton and his daughters, a silver-gilt toilette stand, tea-services, centre-pieces, and a

large variety of chronometers and watches. One would scarcely expect to see such productions emanating from a place having no manufacturing notoriety; but the call upon our national industry seems to have been answered from every quarter, even where the least expected.

M. REGOUT, of Maestricht, Holland, exhibits some tasteful FLOWER-STANDS of bronze; articles

of elegant luxury, which we are glad to know are becoming more generally adopted for the

decoration of our houses. We engrave two specimens, one in the form of an antique tripod, the other in a more free and fanciful style.

We have elsewhere found occasion to notice the great improvement visible in the papier-mâché works of the present day, as contrasted with those of a few years since; this improvement characterises the works of nearly every manufacturer in this branch of trade.

and gilding, on the dark ground usually adopted, cannot be by us represented. The DRESSING-TABLE beneath is a very light and tasteful pro-

article is obviated, and a positive gain in the general appearance effected. The CHAIR has also the merit of grace and lightness, and the FOOTSTOOL is of a novel and agreeable form. Mr. Clay deserves this meed of praise for the skill he has displayed in the selection of designs

The PAPIER-MÂCHÉ works exhibited by Mr. H. CLAY, comprise tea-trays and articles of furniture of much lightness and elegance. An elaborate and beautiful design for one of these TEA-TRAYS we here engrave, premising that we can give the design only; the brilliancy of colour

duction; the glass swings freely from scrolls which spring from each side, and thus the ordinary objectionable stand for this necessary

for manufacture in this material. It is pleasant to know that manufacturers of such old standing are willing and able thus to exert their capital and ability in upholding the character they have obtained. It is a good and healthy tone of mind, which we are glad to recognise generally.

An EMBROIDERED VEST, manufactured and exhibited by Messrs. McGEE & Co., of Belfast, from a design by J. B. Wilkinson, of the School of Design in that town, combines neatness with elegance of pattern. The drawing gained the prize of 5l., offered by the manufacturers for the best design.

This engraving is from a piece of SILK, manufactured by M. GABIAN, of Berlin, with whose establishment we were much interested on our recent tour of inspection through Germany. The pattern displays great boldness; the silk itself, we presume, is intended chiefly for Royal use, as explained by the black eagle of Prussia, with its spreading wings.

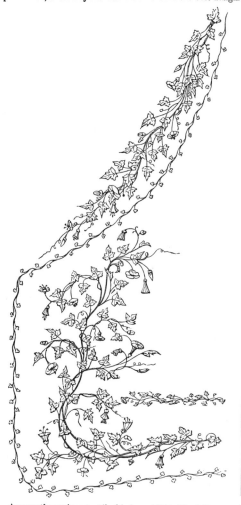

Among the various textile fabrics exhibited by Messrs. REDMAYNE & SON, of London, is a piece of RIBBON, the pattern of which we here introduce; the design is very graceful, consisting of floriated wreaths, in which is the passion-flower, one of the most beautiful productions of the garden.

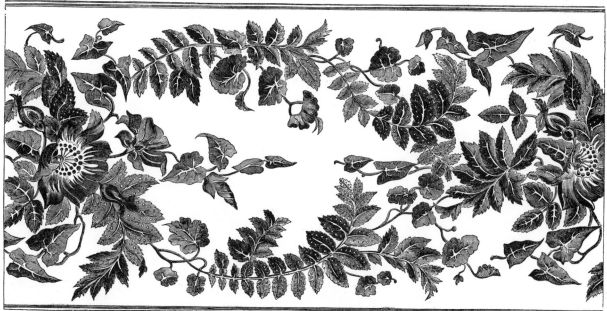

A small but well-selected display of silver work and jewellery is made by Mr. R. Atten-

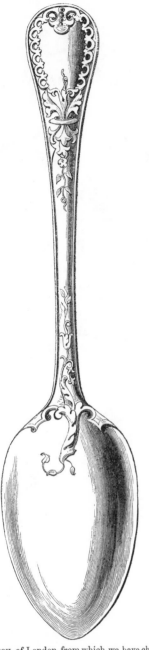

compliment to the gentleman whose name is so worthily associated with the vast undertaking in Hyde Park; the design of the spoon is in pure

classic taste. The BRACELET that follows this is of very choice workmanship; the cable is of massive gold, and the pendent consists of vine-

leaves set with brilliants. The TAZZA with its top is excellent and novel in form, and exhibits some very elaborate engraving; it also shows

the effect that can be produced by the various methods of working upon silver, gilding, and chasing. The TEA-SERVICE, called the "Albany,

BOROUGH, of London, from which we have chosen a few examples for introduction on this page.

or Bachelor's Pattern," is worthy of commendation from its simple but pure form; the only attempt at ornament is in the handles, and

the borders, or rims. Besides the objects we have engraved, Mr. Attenborough exhibits a silver centrepiece for the table, an agricultural

The first is a SPOON, to which the manufacturer has given the title of the "Paxton Spoon," in

prize cup, &c., all of which are highly creditable to his taste, and to the skill of those whom he employs to work out his designs. He is one of

the many who uphold the reputation of England in a branch of the industrial arts, in which we are so rapidly advancing in every department.

Messrs. ELKINGTON, MASON, & CO., of London and Birmingham, are extensive contributors of their celebrated electro-plate manufactures, a

branch of industrial art which has made immense strides since the patent for the various processes of gilding and plating metals by the agency of

electricity was granted to this firm in 1840. Messrs. Elkington alone employ about five hundred work-people in their establishment, and about thirty other British manufacturers have

licences to use this process, which is also extensively adopted in foreign countries; thus some

dilate upon the advantages which electro-plating possesses, as there must be few persons who

selection from the numerous objects which the glass cases of Messrs. Elkington in the Exhibition contain, but we think our examples will

ornamented with subjects taken from English national games—cricket and archery; the figures on these objects are well modelled, and the composition of each is very effective. The COM-

idea may be formed of its importance to the trading community. It is unnecessary for us to

have not practically tested its use and excellence. We have found some difficulty in making a

sufficiently illustrate the variety and artistic qualities of their productions. We commence with two TABLE ORNAMENTS, or FRUIT-DISHES,

MUNION-SERVICE, commencing this page, is designed in the ornamented Gothic style. The TEA and COFFEE-SERVICE, which follows, is an elegant adaptation of the arabesque pattern;

and the lower one is of richly-engraved Gothic.

the CANDLESTICK and FLOWER-VASE; the former shows much originality of design. The next

engraving is from a large CENTRE-PIECE for eight

lights, in the style of the fifteenth century, with winged figures supporting baskets for fruit. The

CRUET-FRAME has an arabesque pattern, and the

A JUG and three VASES appear on this

column, each excellent of its kind; as are also

CENTRE-PIECE which follows it is modelled from the "Crown imperial" plant. A very elegant

CLARET-JUG completes the next column; its form

and enrichments are highly to be commended.

We come now to what must be considered, for

design and workmanship, the most important

contribution of Messrs. Elkington,—a VASE, intended to represent the triumph of Science and the Industrial Arts in the Great Exhibition; the style is Elizabethan enriched. Four statuettes on the body of the vase represent Newton, Bacon, Shakspeare, and

Watt, commemorating Astronomy, Philosophy, Poetry, and Mechanics respectively. On the four bas-reliefs, between these figures, the practical operations of Science and Art are displayed, and their influences typified by the figures on the base, indicating War, Rebellion, Hatred, and Revenge, overthrown and chained. The recognition and the reward of peaceful industry are symbolised by the figure of Prince Albert surmounting the composition, who, as Patron of the Exhibition, is rewarding the successful contributors. The height of the vase is four feet; it was designed and modelled by Mr. W. Beattie. Among the other manufactures of this firm, is a group, in silver, representing "Queen Elizabeth entering Kenilworth Castle."

THE INDUSTRY OF ALL NATIONS.

The two CARRIAGES engraved below are contributed by Messrs. JONES, BROTHERS, of Brussels, extensive manufacturers and exporters of carriages of all descriptions; employing in their different departments upwards of a hundred men. They have obtained five medals

The appended STOVE, from the manufactory of Mr. MAUND, of London, in no degree detracts from the elegance of the most classically-furnished hall, or other apartment, in which it may be placed. The general form is that of an antique urn, and is another proof of

for their productions at various exhibitions in Belgium, and in 1847 they gained the "Gala" medal.

These medals have been found of the greatest use as a stimulus to inventive industry among continental manufacturers, but, until the present period, they have been unknown in our own country. The rewards of this kind intended to be bestowed on native ability contributed to the Great Exhibition, will test its applicability to our own land, and, we have very little doubt, will be found as effective here, as they have certainly been proved to be upon the continent.

the great and universal applicability of the graceful designs of antiquity,—forms studied with perfect truth and beauty, which are capable of being reproduced for new purposes, unthought of by the men who imagined them, but whose pure taste has rendered their ideas immortal.

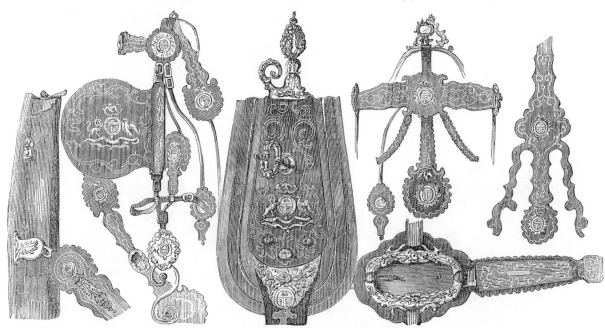

The various examples of decorative HARNESS, exhibited by Messrs. LACEY & PHILLIPS, of Philadelphia, exhibit manipulative skill, and are tasteful and elegant additions to the well-appointed equipage. The mountings are of silver, and the decoration is executed with very great care.

This is another of the CARPETS, manufactured by Messrs. T. SMITH & Co., of whose contributions we have inserted two examples in a former page. The pattern of this is very bold, and rich in colours, and the fabric itself is of the most luxurious character, uniting elegance of decoration with great warmth, the two grand desiderata requisite in manufactures of this description; we cannot possibly award them higher praise.

Our continental neighbours, on the other side of the Straits of Dover, have undoubtedly made a most excellent display in every kind of cabinet-work; this will not be thought singular by those who are acquainted with the demand which exists in France, and in Paris especially, for every description of decorative furniture. There is scarcely a house of public entertainment, of the better kind, in the French metropolis, that cannot show numerous articles in which the skill of the wood-carver and the taste of the designer, are not abundantly manifest; while the

private residences of the middle classes, and of the more wealthy, are supplied according to the means of each respectively. The CABINET engraved here is manufactured by M. RINGUET LEPRINCE; its chief interest, in our estimation, lies in the elegant simplicity of its ornament.

The Spoons and Sugar-ladle, manufactured and contributed by Mr. W. R. Smily, of London, will please exceedingly by their novelty, and a rich and graceful style of ornament; the running foliage on the handles of the spoons is a pretty idea, and the bowl of the sugar-ladle is good.

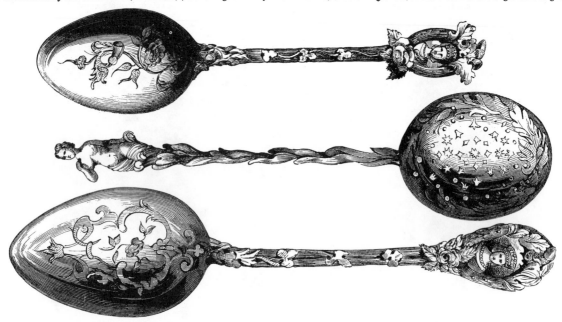

Mr. Jeakes, of London, is the manufacturer of the Stove and Fender which occupy the remainder of this page. The designs of the former object especially are most elaborate, and were, we are informed, supplied by Messrs. Lawford and Heneker, architects. The narrow

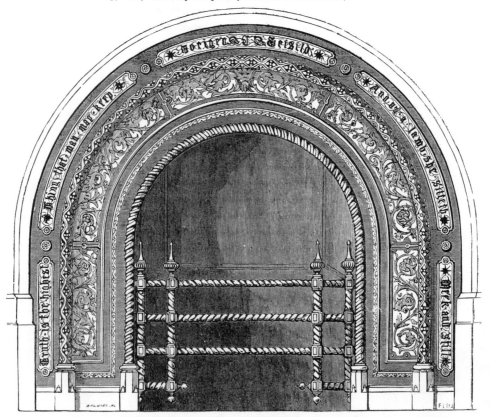

mouldings of the arch are fancifully varied, and form an agreeable contrast to the broader one, which shows a light, Raffaellesque kind of pattern.

The style and form of the twisted bars are un- common, adding considerably to its novelty. The fender harmonises well with the stove.

The CHAIR is one of a set, manufactured by Messrs. W. & B. HILTON, of Montreal, in Canada, as a present to the Queen, from the ladies of that place, who have worked the tapestry.

The illustration underneath is from a damask TABLE-CLOTH, manufactured by Mr. BERRILL, of Dunfermline, especially for the American market. The medallion in the centre is intended for a portrait of Washington; it is surrounded by devices bearing reference to the part he acted in asserting the independence of his country. The border shows a bold and well-filled pattern.

From several CARPETS, manufactured and exhibited by Messrs. H. BRINTON & SONS, of Kidderminster, we have selected one for the purpose of engraving. It is a Brussels velvet, of an exceedingly bold and effective pattern, consisting of scrolls and the leaves of the palm-tree,

with some smaller floriated ornaments. There is infinite variety in the arrangement of the forms introduced, and great ingenuity and skill must have been exercised in combining them into an harmonious composition; notwithstanding which, the artist has succeeded in his object.

A set of polished steel FIRE-IRONS, with ormolu handles, by Messrs. H. & W. TURNER, of Sheffield, have as much elegance imparted to them as can be exhibited on objects affording but little scope for the exercise of the designer's taste.

Messrs. HANCOCK, RIXON, & DUNT, of London, exhibit a CHANDELIER, of cut glass, for thirty-two lights. The section of the body forms a star; the upper part is composed of drops, which are arranged in the shape of banners. It will present a brilliant appearance when lighted.

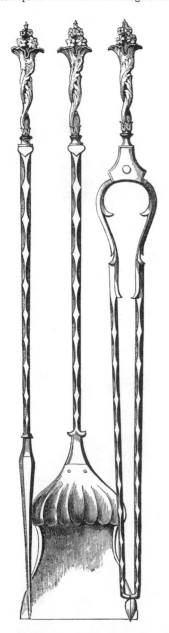

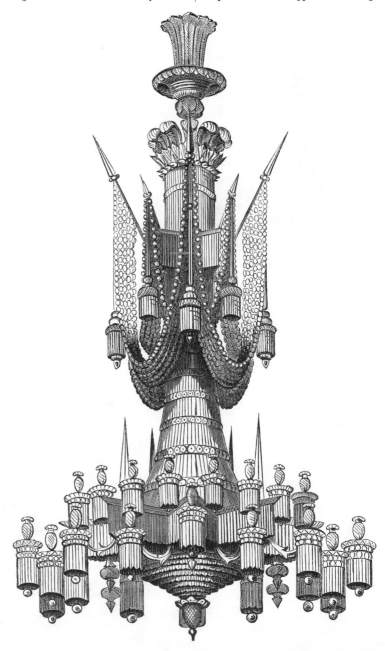

The illustration that fills the lower part of the page is from a piece of EMBROIDERED CLOTH, from the establishment of Messrs. HOULDSWORTH & Co., Manchester. The pattern is worked in what appears to be gold thread, on a deep moreen ground, presenting altogether an ex-

ceedingly rich effect, as the pattern stands out in bold relief. The cloth is intended for a table-cover, and a very splendid table-cover it makes.

Messrs. W. HARGREAVES & Co., of Sheffield, exhibit a large and well-selected assortment of cutlery, as table-knives, carvers, game-carvers, dessert-knives, from which we introduce here four examples of ornamental handles. The first two are of TABLE-KNIVES, in a bold style of workmanship, and carefully executed; the last is from a GAME CARVING-KNIFE, with a brace of birds at its termination; the third is an ivory-handled BREAD-KNIFE, which, in form, is a manifest improvement upon most of those in general use. All these handles are of fine ivory elaborately carved and mounted with silver ferules, and the blades are of the highest polished steel.

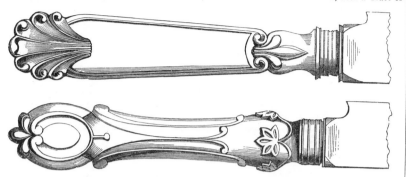

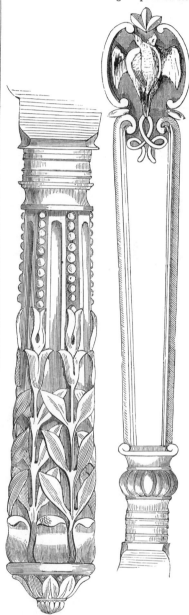

The engraving immediately underneath is from the hilt of a COUTEAU DE CHASSE, manufactured by M. DELACOUR, an extensive armourer, of Paris. The design is very elegant in all its details, but its merits are likely to be overlooked, without a close inspection of the work, which is of iron, bronzed and richly gilt.

A FRIEZE, modelled in plaster by Mr. J. HARMER, Jun., of Pentonville, shows considerable taste in the art of design as well as skill in the manipulation. The scroll is judiciously ornamented with flowers, leaves, and wheat-ears, and a variety of other natural objects, and it encloses some admirably arranged groups of fruit, &c.

The appended design is from a piece of SILK, exhibited by Messrs. REDMAYNE & SON, of London; it shows a graceful running pattern of natural objects—the rose, shamrock, and thistle.

Messrs. MESSENGER & SONS, of Birmingham, have a CANDELABRUM for ecclesiastical purposes.

A LIBRARY TABLE, manufactured by Messrs. GILLOW, of London, is worthy of the high position which the firm holds as cabinet-makers; it is of very simple construction, but elegant in its design: the *chimeræ* at the angles are boldly carved; the other ornaments are in excellent taste.

DANTE'S LOVERS are embodied by Mr. MUNRO in a touching and characteristic style; worthily depicting the simplicity and earnestness which the immortal poet has made the prevailing traits of those whose course of love "never did run smooth." The quaint costume gives an air of much truthfulness to the group, which is excellently composed.

A Rhenish legend has furnished M. ENGELHARD, of Hamburg, with the theme for a very lovely statue of LURLINE, the dangerously-beautiful resident of the Lurley-berg, who woos the boatmen to destruction.

The SIDEBOARD, by Mr. GILLOW, of London, is of bold design and spirited execution; it is an excellent specimen of the ability of our manufacturers in wood-carving, as well as of taste and fancy in composition. It shows a freedom from too great slavishness of idea, a determination to get rid of the trammels of conventional styles, which is very cheering to all who have felt its primary importance to native interests.

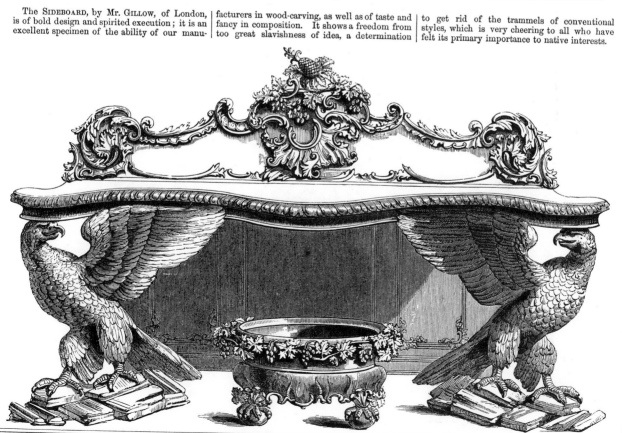

Messrs. MAPPIN, of Sheffield, some of whose contributions appeared in a former page of our Catalogue, are the manufacturers and exhibitors of the DESSERT KNIVES engraved underneath.

Mr. JAMES EDWARDS exhibits a gracefully-conceived bas-relief, which he terms "The Last Dream" in life, of a fair and delicate female, and illustrative of the passage, "her sun went down while it was yet day, but unto the upright there ariseth light in the darkness." The young girl has sunk to rest, peacefully and trustingly; the volume upon which her hope is founded rests on her bosom, and her last earthly imaginings are of the ever-living spirits who welcome her.

The manufacturers of BILLIARD-TABLES have recently introduced a great improvement into them, by the substitution of slate tops for wood.

That engraved is of this description; the frame is of Spanish mahogany, boldly carved. The manufacturers are Messrs. THURSTON & Co., of London.

The exquisitely beautiful STOVE, enclosed in a mantel-piece of white statuary marble, is manufactured by Messrs. YATES, HAYWOOD, & Co., of the Effingham Works, Rotherham, from the design of one of the artists of that establishment, Mr. George Wright. It is certainly one of the most superb objects of this kind which we remember to have seen. The hearth-plate slopes upwards, and is so contrived that the ashes, falling upon it, run through and are concealed. The andirons are composed of groups of foliage and rustic appendages, in the midst of

which are seated a shepherd and wood-nymph, charmingly modelled. The material of which it is made is steel, very highly polished, set with or-molu ornaments; we may add, that its construction is such as to require no fender. Messrs. Yates & Co. exhibit other articles—all designed and produced on their own premises, by their own workmen; a merit of no common value, and which augments the worth of their contributions.

The contributions from our fellow-countrymen in the Channel Islands are comparatively few, and of these, still fewer which attract attention as objects of manufacturing or decorative art. The only work we have found available for our purpose is a CHEFFONIERE, or sideboard, manufactured by Mr. G. C. LE FEUVRE, of Jersey; it is made of oak, a portion of the wood being the produce of the island; the designs in the compartments are worked in tapestry. The upper part of the sideboard is omitted—as by no means so good as the portion we have engraved.

Messrs. H. C. McCrea, of Halifax, exhibit numerous specimens of Furniture Damasks, table-covers, poncho stuffs, &c.: we here engrave a piece of the first-named—the furniture-damask—of a bold and good pattern.

The Candelabrum is one of a pair formed of the purest crystal, by Messrs. F. & C. Osler, of London and Birmingham, for her Majesty the Queen: each of them stands eight feet high, and is made to hold fifteen lights.

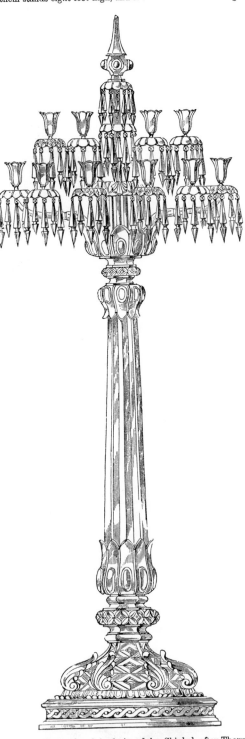

This engraving is also from a piece of Furniture Damask, manufactured by Mr. W. Brown, of Halifax, an extensive producer of table-covers, &c.

The Pediment of a fire-place, of bronzed | iron, is from the foundry of M. Egell, of Berlin, | and is designed by Shinkel, after Thorwaldsen.

The engraving underneath represents a STAINED GLASS WINDOW, executed by Messrs. BALLANTINE & ALLAN, of Edinburgh. It is intended for the entrance-hall of Glenormiston, the property of Mr. W. Chambers. This estate is held direct from the Crown, on condition that the proprietor, when required, shall present the sovereign with a red rose on the festival of St. John. The design in the centre of the window represents this ceremony, which, according to local tradition, was last performed in 1529

Mr. W. HASLAM, of Derby, exhibits a specimen of IRON WORK, intended for the door of a church. It is, as far as can be ascertained, a fac-simile of that placed, in the year 1251, on the door of the chapel in which Prince Edward, afterwards Edward I., and his wife, Eleanor, attended divine service. This attempt on the part of Mr. Haslam to imitate the style of

the ancient church-wrought iron-work, which was carried to such high perfection during the period referred to, has been eminently successful.

an heiress of that period, supported by a knight, is offering a rose to the monarch; in the background, a retainer displays the banner of St. John. The picture, as well as the entire window, is surrounded by a rich border of ruby and gold, studded with imitations of gems. The background is pale blue, with gold bands, stencilled in white enamel, with the united national emblems—the rose, shamrock, and thistle. In the upper corners is the legend—"HE THAT THOLES (*i.e.* endures) OVERCOMES."

A WINE-COOLER, manufactured in terra-cotta, and exhibited by Mr. W. MARSH, of Longport, Staffordshire, merits commendation from the excellence of its design; in its form and ornament it displays taste of no ordinary kind. The chimeræ forming the handles are fanciful, but of a fashion which reminds us of some of the best antiques, both in mineral and metallic substances. The work is designed by one of the pupils of the Hanley school—an establishment that, with others of a similar character in the neighbouring locality, has done good service among the "potters."

Brussels Lace, that magnet of attraction to ladies, is contributed in great abundance and beauty, by many famed manufacturers of the Belgian capital. We have already engraved the contribution of one celebrated house; we now add another, by M. DELEHAYE, the successor to the well-known firm of Ducpetiaux & Co. It is a portion of the border of a LACE VEIL, and is remarkable for the delicacy and grace of its design, in which flowers, wreaths, and scrolls, are ingeniously combined to form an enriched pattern, through which a ribbon is entwined;

the line of this is prevented from becoming monotonous, by its combination with a leafy spray, introduced with the best possible taste. The same manufacturer exhibits some exquisite examples of handkerchiefs of equally graceful design, and remarkable for the extreme delicacy of their fabric. The patient labour and perseverance necessary to complete these exquisite additions to the toilette of beauty can scarcely be understood by those who have not witnessed their slow growth in the manufactory, in which years are consumed in the product of a single veil.

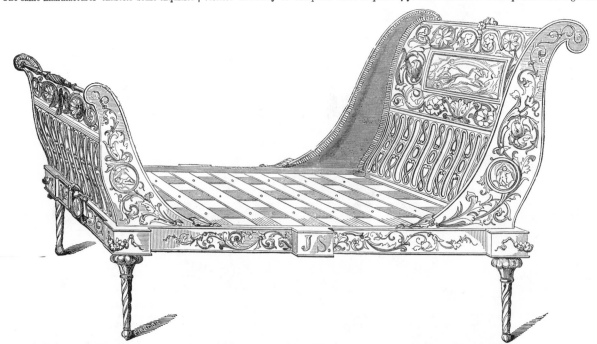

The IRON BEDSTEAD is a Spanish contribution, and is the work of TOMAS DE MEGNE, of Madrid. It presents some peculiar features of a graceful character, besides being well designed for its use. The great improvement in articles of this class, both at home and abroad, cannot fail to attract the notice of the most unreflective, the Crystal Palace alone contains a great and striking variety, both in construction and ornament.

The engravings on this column are from the papier-mâché contributions of Messrs. M'CULLUM and HODSON, of Birmingham, who have already

been noticed in one of the preceding pages of our Catalogue. The first is a LADIES' CABINET,

fitted with writing-desk, and drawers for various purposes, such as holding jewels, envelopes, &c.;

the second is a JEWEL-BOX of elegant form; underneath this is another LADIES' CABINET,

inlaid with pearl, containing work-box, &c.; and the last is a WORK-TABLE, also inlaid with pearl, with papier-mâché work-bag; the bag is somewhat of a novelty as regards its material.

The two subjects on this column are from the electro-silver-plate manufactory of Messrs. CARTWRIGHT & HIRONS, of Birmingham. Their establishment is, we are informed, of comparatively recent date, but there is no doubt, from the taste

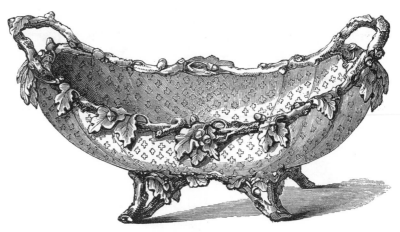

ornamented in a chaste style; it is mounted in a floriated pattern of carved oak. The other is

is entirely new in construction, the bottles and handle being made to revolve within the border, while the frame remains stationary; the orna-

exhibited in the few objects they have contributed to the great emporium of industry, that it will, ere long, become favourably and widely known. The first of our engravings is from a BASKET, for cake or fruit, of good form and a large revolving LIQUEUR-STAND, to hold five bottles, with glasses between each. This frame ment bears the same character with the preceding; the two objects, thus harmonising, being evidently intended to be used at the same time.

Messrs. GRAY & Co., of Birmingham, exhibit a variety of new designs for chandeliers and lamps,

constructed in the brass-work for which that city is famed. The free use of foliage in works

of this class is not without great value, in break- | ing stiff and monotonous lines, and aiding the

general elegance of the entire composition. The | only danger—and it is one, we confess, we often

see and regret—is the too free use of this ornamental adjunct; the *juste mileu* is not so easy to obtain as may be generally considered, and good taste only can ensure it; this is to be

acquired only by much study and experience, by a constant striving after a knowledge of the great leading principles which governed the art-manufacturers of past times. The CHANDELIER in the style of the renaissance, is a successful work, presenting an attractive general form, the

details being well studied from original authorities. We are most pleased, however, with the CARRIAGE-LAMP, an exceedingly graceful design, the leading lines of which are all good; and the elegance of its general form proves how a common-place article may be elevated into a tasteful and beautiful work. The small HAND-LAMP beneath is a quaint and not inelegant conception, greatly superior to the ordinary deformities,

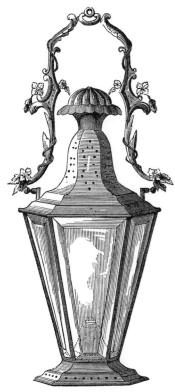

which, at one period, completely usurped the place of utility. Another graceful HANGING-LAMP appears on this column, uniting the necessary qualities of beauty and usefulness. The LAMP affixed to a scroll underneath is intended

for the interior of a carriage, and possesses also its own peculiar merit. The BRACKET-LIGHT and the lower half of a CHANDELIER, on the former page, are light and very elegantly decorated ornaments: the patterns of the two being *en suite*, we presume they are intended for the same room.

Mr. JAMES HEATH, of Bath, exhibits some of the INVALID CHAIRS which are named after that

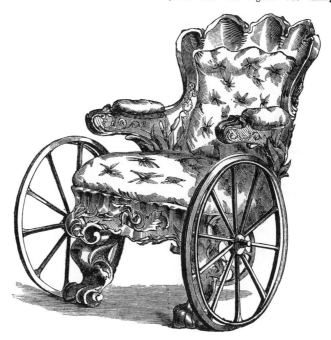

upper one constructed to move about a room at the pleasure of the sitter, unassisted by an

amount of luxurious elegance by no means inapplicable to a work of the kind. On the side panels,

The SKATE, by Mr. LOY, of London, presents features of great novelty in form and construction. The spring across the instep secures it on the foot without screwing; and a simple con-

city, and universally welcomed by all who need their aid. We engrave two examples, the

attendant. The lower, for open air exercise, is very elaborately painted and gilt, combining an

and at the back, are paintings: the one indicated in our engraving is from the "Aurora" of Guido.

trivance of plug and socket does the same for the heel. It is made of satin wood, enriched by plates of gilded metal work; the swan's neck in front is a graceful and appropriate ornament.

The FISH SLICE and RAZOR which appear on this page are from the well-known manufactory of Messrs. JOSEPH RODGERS & SONS, Sheffield, whose cutlery goods have acquired a reputation for excellence throughout the world. Their

Two elegant examples of the Art-manufactures of America may be found in a pair of GAS CHANDELIERS, made and contributed by Messrs. CORNELIUS & BAKER, of Philadelphia. They stand about fifteen feet and a half high, by six

feet wide, having fifteen burners with plain glass globes, and are of brass lacquered. The design is very rich in ornament, and possesses some novelty in the succession of curves ingeniously and tastefully united: the gas-keys represent

show of knives, razors, scissors, &c., of all descriptions, is, as would be expected, commensurate with the extent of their establishment; and it embraces not only the finished articles, but the several processes or stages of manufacture, from the raw material to the polished blade.

bunches of fruit, thus combining beauty with utility. Besides these objects, the manufacturers exhibit a number of patent solar lamps, which they have named the "damask lamp," from the rich damask colour they have succeeded in imparting to the brass: the designs in these lamps can be varied at pleasure. Messrs. Corne-

lius & Baker are the most extensive manufacturers of lamps, chandeliers, gas-fixtures, &c., in the United States, employing upwards of seven hundred persons in the several departments of the establishment, which has been in existence for upwards of a quarter of a century; if we may judge from their contributions to the Exhibition their celebrity is not undeserved.

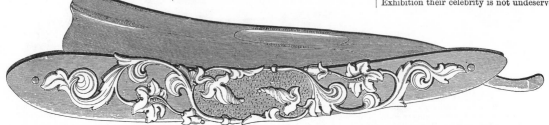

This engraving is from another of the admirably constructed and beautifully designed STOVES, manufactured for Messrs. Gray and Son, of Edinburgh, by Messrs. HOOLE & ROBSON, of Sheffield, the whole of whose works have been objects of very general admiration,—and of great attraction to all who desire to combine elegance with comfort "at home."

The CLOCK, for a table, or to be placed on a bracket in a hall, is manufactured by Mr. BENNETT, of London; the case shows some bold carving, executed with considerable taste. A large number of horological objects are exhibited by Mr. Bennett, particularly a model watch on a large scale, constructed to show the most compact form of the modern time-piece, with all its many recent improvements.

We have given in a former page of our Catalogue, one of the CARPETS contributed by WATSON, BELL, & Co., of London, we now introduce another equally worthy of attentive notice, and high estimation. It is made of a determinate shape, the centre being filled with a rich group of flowers; the double borders are very light and elegant; the outer one, by its delicacy, contrasting well with the dark ground-work.

The large engraving is from a FLOOR-CLOTH of a good, bold pattern, manufactured by Mr. R. Y. BARNES, of London. We introduce it no less as a correct and appropriate design, than from a desire to give examples, so far as they appear suitable, of every description of industrial art.

Mr. WOODRUFF, of Bakewell, in Derbyshire, has already been noticed by us, and some of his works engraved. We then stated that his ability had brought him to the notice of royalty, and that he had been commissioned to construct a CONSOLE TABLE-TOP, in coloured marbles of the county, from a design by Mr. Gruner; this beautiful work we here engrave; it is an excellent example of native talent and ingenuity.

The productions of Mr. HALL, of Derby, have been heretofore noticed in our pages as admirable examples of ability in a class of manufacture of great local interest; and by which

that interest has been extended far and wide as the result of the excellence of the works produced. Derbyshire is as much celebrated for the mineral spars it contains, as for the beauty

of its scenery, and within the shire live many ingenious workmen, who well know how to convert these natural advantages into objects which rival in attraction the productions of

Italy. The black marble, which forms, in most instances, the basis of their work, is nowhere found more pure in its colour and stratification, than in Derbyshire; while the

fluor spar is unsurpassed in its beauty of tint. The advantage of good material has, therefore, always been ready, in this favoured county, to the hands of its workmen; yet they have been,

ever, they have seen the necessity of progress; have studied the best examples of the antique; have called invention to their aid; and the consequence is, that they have found markets for

and may direct attention to the works of Mr. Hall as in all respects admirable. This page contains several of his contributions; they exhibit the taste and judgment by which he has been guided in the choice of appropriate and

for many years, too content with this alone, and have not paid the attention to elegance of form which the articles they produced only required, to insure universal appreciation. Of late, however, they have seen the necessity of progress;

their commodities in all parts of the world. We have already engraved some satisfactory proofs of the success which may attend works of this class, by native artists, from native products;

elegant "authorities." His establishment in Derby has been fully described in the *Art-Journal* for September, 1850; it is extensive, and admirably conducted, and sends forth a variety of works, chiefly of the marbles of Derbyshire.

We introduce here another of the CARPETS manufactured by Messrs. HARRIS & Co., of Stour- port. It is of the quality termed "Brussels velvet pile." The border is designed by Mr. I. K. Harvey,

Messrs. BLEWS & SONS, of Birmingham and London, are extensive manufacturers of brass candle and ship lamps, candlesticks, bells, imperial weights and measures, &c.

We engrave on this and the succeeding column four examples of their CANDLE-LAMPS: the first is called the "armorial

from the *Magnolia grandiflora*, with the flower-buds in their different stages of advancement, and the *Ipomœa*. The centre is a large wreath of exotic and other flowers, on a rich crimson ground, and the corners are occupied by the national emblems. The borders and corners are on a maroon ground.

lamp;" the second, termed the "vine-wreath foot," shows that graceful plant climbing up the shaft and over the shade; the leaves and fruit being coloured. In the third example the convolvulus forms the principal ornament at the base. The fourth has a very elegant pedestal of leaves, dogs' heads,

and birds; the pillar is of richly-cut ruby glass, with centre groups of flowers. The glass, it is

sufficient to say, is from the factory of Messrs. Richardson, of Stourbridge; the bronze and brass castings are exceedingly sharp and brilliant.

The engraving which occupies so large a portion of this page is from a STAINED GLASS WINDOW, manufactured and exhibited by the ST. HELEN'S GLASS COMPANY, Lancashire. The subject is "St. Michael casting out the great red Dragon,"

from a design by Mr. Frank Howard; and instead of being produced on numerous pieces of glass, as is usually the case, it is painted upon one entire piece upwards of nine feet in height, by nearly five feet in width, whereby the dark

stiff lines of lead and metal that disfigure the ordinary pictures are avoided. It may be remarked that the colours themselves are all glass, and have been repeatedly fired to "flux" them;

no varnish or other perishable colours are employed, but all have passed together through the fire. The establishment by which this work is contributed is of high repute and of great extent.

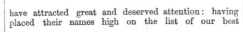

Messrs. T. & R. Boote, of Burslem, have attained considerable eminence as producers of earthenware of a fine order. We

have attracted great and deserved attention: having placed their names high on the list of our best

giving the effect of bas-reliefs, without being raised; the second Jug is of Parian,

have engraved on this and the succeeding

with the bouquet in high relief; and the

manufacturers. The first, fourth, and fifth Jugs are

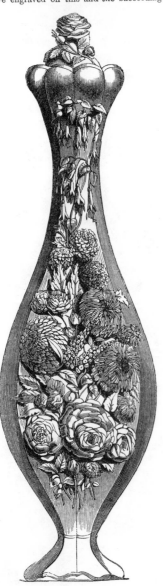

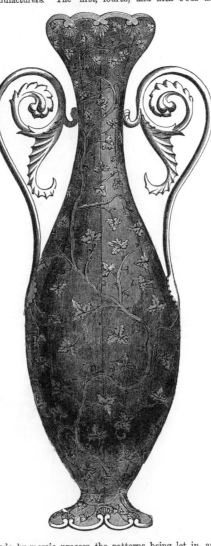

page several of their productions—which

made by mosaic process, the patterns being let in, and

third, also of Parian, of a fawn colour,

with white figures, is of Gothic form. The two large VASES, somewhat similar in form, are of drab-coloured Parian, the flowers and fruit, which

are beautifully modelled in high relief, being white; the centre VASE, of mosaic character,

has a rich jet tint; the pattern is of a deep mazarine blue, traced in gold. The FLOWER

VASE on this column is in the Gothic style; stained glass is introduced on certain of the perforated parts. Our limited allotment of space prevents our rendering, by our remarks, full justice to this very admirable establishment.

The DAMASKS of Messrs. J. HOLDSWORTH & Co., of Halifax, are rich and beautiful fabrics. We engrave one—which, for its combination of delicacy and boldness is worthy of especial notice.

The GROUP underneath is another of the contributions of Messrs. T. & W. BOOTE, for whom it was modelled by Mr. Gillard; it represents Repentance, Faith, and Resignation, respectively

symbolised by their attitudes. The work is well arranged; it stands nearly two feet high, and is of Parian. Another group—the Mother—is entitled to high praise. Both are original productions.

The luxurious decoration of fire-arms may be said to have commenced when the practice of war declined as an exhibition of mere force, and became a science, whose principal stratagems and modes of operation were studied in military schools. Spain and Italy first adorned their weapons with artistic decoration, and many costly and elaborate works of the kind grace our museums. The PISTOL, by M. GAUVAIN, of Paris, here engraved, rivals in beauty of execution many of these old works, and is a good specimen of modern art applied to such purposes.

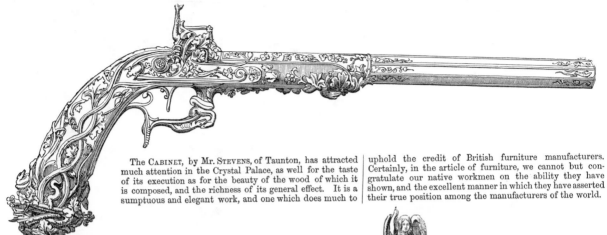

The CABINET, by Mr. STEVENS, of Taunton, has attracted much attention in the Crystal Palace, as well for the taste of its execution as for the beauty of the wood of which it is composed, and the richness of its general effect. It is a sumptuous and elegant work, and one which does much to uphold the credit of British furniture manufacturers. Certainly, in the article of furniture, we cannot but congratulate our native workmen on the ability they have shown, and the excellent manner in which they have asserted their true position among the manufacturers of the world.

Messrs. RETTIE & SONS, of Aberdeen, exhibit some curious specimens of persevering ingenuity successfully exerted in a material the most unpromising. The hard and impracticable character of GRANITE would seem to defy delicacy and

minutiæ of workmanship, and to preclude its becoming an article of personal decoration. Yet the BRACELETS here engraved are cut with much labour and patience from this material, the various parts being mounted and linked together

in silver. A choice of granite has been made from Aberdeen, Balmoral, &c.; and, by dint of labour, a comparatively valueless article is elevated into the position of a precious stone, and placed among the fancy articles of a jewel case.

When Raffaelle was embellishing with his immortal pencil the walls of the Vatican, he, perhaps, had little idea what a legacy he was leaving for the use of future decorators, not alone for actual copyists, but for those to whom his beautiful designs serve as suggestions to be moulded

Messrs. ARROWSMITH, of London, exhibit their patent WINDOW-CURTAINS,—a novelty. It is an application on a net-work ground, giving it the effect of Brussels lace, and on moreen, or other common material, of velvet. into whatever forms may be required. The two engravings on this page, which the reader will easily distinguish from the others,

The elegant carved zebra CABINET, which we also engrave, has its panels decorated with paintings, illustrating the phases of "Woman's History." It is a remarkably agreeable example of English furniture.

are from a decorative PANEL, exhibited by Messrs. HINCHLIFF & Co., of London; they are of the genuine Raffaellesque character, and that is sufficient to attest their excellence.

The number of hands employed upon the production of a single article, even of common use, is greater than would be supposed by one unacquainted with the art and mystery of manufacture; but when the object assumes a strictly ornamental character, it naturally embraces a wider range of operation. Sheffield, from the extent and variety of its decorative manufacturers, must employ no inconsiderable number of designers and artists on the knife-handles produced there. That here engraved is the HANDLE of a silver FISH-SLICE, from the establishment of Messrs. HILLIARD & THOMASON, of Birmingham.

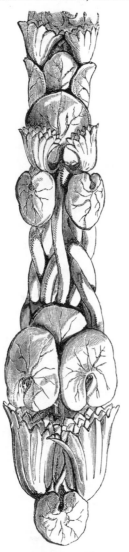

The CONSOLE TABLE and GLASS are contributed by the GUTTA PERCHA COMPANY, of London, and, of course, the ornamental portions are manufactured of that material. The design of the frame shows an elaborate composition of fruit, leaves, and flowers, arranged with much elegance and artistic effect. The panels of the table are decorated with antique shields.

The RAZOR that terminates the illustrations on this page is from the manufactory of Messrs. HAWCROFT & SONS, of Sheffield, and is exhibited under the title of the "Sheffield Town Razor," from its having been made for the express purpose of showing the skill of the artisans of that place, in the production of such objects. The handle is fancifully inlaid with a design of no small excellence, and the blade has engraved upon it an exterior view of the "Crystal Palace."

The continental manufacturers of fictile ware have not been slow in answering the demand upon their industrial classes; many of them have forwarded contributions which evince a large amount of artistic design and mechanical

The TABLE is from the manufactory of Messrs. | GILLOW & Co., of London. It is boldly carved.

skill. From some quarters these productions are adapted for ordinary use in the particular localities where they are manufactured, and other contributions may be designated as "for all nations," inasmuch as Art, by its high qualities,

The CONSOLE TABLE, and FRAME for a glass, with the BRACKET, are of gutta percha, contributed | by the company by which this novel material for manufacturing purposes has been introduced.

makes itself universal, and welcomed everywhere. The three objects on this column, are manufactured by MM. VILLEROY & BOCH, of Wallerfangen, near Mannheim; the first is a BEER-JUG, without a handle; it is made of brown clay, the figure in white; the profits arising from its sale

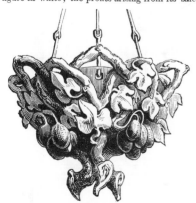

are to go towards defraying the cost of repairing the cathedral of Cologne. The next is another BEER-JUG, of variously-coloured clays, with some grotesque ornaments upon it; and the last a HANGING VASE, of terra cotta, silver mounted.

THE INDUSTRY OF ALL NATIONS.

The stand of MESSRS. F. & R. PRATT, of Burslem, exhibits several excellent examples of earthenware, printed in a peculiar style, some of them after the pictures in the Vernon Gallery; and also a dessert-

service with designs from the works of our best English painters. We have selected, from their more

miscellaneous contributions, four objects, engraved in this column, of a less decorative character, but never-

theless most excellent of their class; the forms Messrs. Pratt have adapted to objects of general use, have

been, in some instances taken from the Etruscan, and exhibit, therefore, the good taste of the manufacturers in resorting for suggestions to the best sources.

Among the contributions of cabinet-work received from France, not the least excellent are some specimens forwarded by M. J. P. JEANSELME, of Paris, consisting of sideboard of oak, dressing-room furniture, arm-chairs, the whole a rich and unique effect. The ornament exhibits, perhaps, little that is novel in design, but it is of the highest charac-ter and is executed with a delicacy and pre-

and chairs in the Louis Quatorze style, and the CABINET, which we have here engraved. It is manufactured of dark wood, highly polished, and inlaid with beautiful marbles and stones of different colours, which give to

cision that show it to be the work of a well-practised craftsman. Nowhere has the general "breadth" been destroyed by an overlaying of decoration, as we sometimes see it.

The HERALDIC CHAIR, upon the surface of which are sculptured the arms borne by the ancestors of her most gracious Majesty in the Saxon line, was made by G. SHACK-

The graceful figure of ANDROMEDA, from the sculpture by Mr. J. A. Bell, has been excellently rendered by the COALBROOK DALE COMPANY, and is a work every way honourable to British Art-manufacture. As an example of casting, it may take rank with the best specimens in the Exhibition. The figure is very elegantly conceived,

LOCK of Bolsover, near Chesterfield, in Derbyshire. It is a work of considerable merit.

Professor RIETSCHEL of Dresden, exhibits his bas-relief of CUPID ON A PANTHER, whose headlong flight has alarmed the youthful god, and disarranged his arrows.

and has a charming simplicity of treatment. The pedestal is a work of much fancy, and is in the highly-wrought style of the Cellini period. It is emblematical throughout of the story connected with the figure it supports.

The manufacturers of Sheffield have contributed well and ably, asserting their due position, and maintaining it by their works in a marked manner. The reputation enjoyed by that town for plated goods has been of long duration, and we hope to see it of as long continuance. The group we engrave is from the manufactory of Messrs. HALL & Co., and consists of a series of graceful articles for the breakfast-table, executed with much care; a TEA and COFFEE-SERVICE, possessing the necessary requisites of utility, combined with elegance of form and delicacy of ornament. The TOAST-RACK beside it is a "registered" novelty; it occupies less space upon the table than the elongated form so generally adopted for such articles, and is better in every way. The bars, formed of the wheat-ear and leaf, are very graceful and most appropriate.

The group of the EAGLE AND CHILD, by M. AUG. LE CHESNE, the French sculptor, whose works have attracted much attention during their exhibition among us, is a powerfully-told story, but of somewhat too painful a kind. The mother has fallen in a deep and troubled sleep in the prairie, her infant clings to her side, holding an arum flower in his hand, and endeavouring to rouse her aid against the eagle, which, attracted by the hope of prey, has seized, and will speedily carry away, the alarmed infant. The work is characterised by strong expression, as well as great care in execution. It is the intention of the sculptor to continue the story in a bas-relief on its pedestal, representing the mother awakened, strangling the eagle, and saving her child.

The CAR engraved below is manufactured by Messrs. HUTTON, the celebrated carriage-builders of Dublin; in it a body of the shape of an ordinary Irish car is adapted so as to obviate some of the objections to that kind of carriage, while it has the effect of making it more commodious and better suited to general purposes. Messrs. HUTTON exhibit other descriptions of carriages.

The BASKET, in silver filagree, belongs to those delicate and beautiful works which must be seen to be fully appreciated. It is one of the contributions sent to us from Tunis, and exhibits all the patient manipulation and elaborate ornament which we associate more with eastern climes than with our own northern latitude.

The very elegant MARBLE CHIMNEY-PIECE, by M. LECLERCQ, of Brussels, has been made expressly for his Majesty the King of the Belgians, and is one of the most chaste and beautiful works in the Exhibition; the excellence of its workmanship fully equals the taste of its design: the ornaments and figures are executed in a similarly admirable way. We have little doubt that this result is obtained through the constant connection preserved between artist and manufacturer on the continent. We perfectly remember, on the occasion of our visit to Brussels last year, calling on M. Leclercq while he was preparing this chimney-piece, and finding M. Simonis, the great sculptor of the principal public work in Brussels—the statue of Godfrey de Bouillon—tendering his advice and assistance to M. Leclercq. The absence of this union of powers as supplied by the artist and artisan, so to speak, has long been felt in England, and has, doubtless, operated injuriously upon British manufacturing art: it will not long continue.

The annexed engraving and that which follows are cabinet-work, manufactured by M. TAHAN, of Paris; the first is a FLOWER-STAND, appropriately ornamented with leaves. The CABINET has

much florid ornament in dark walnut wood, which is agreeably relieved by the coloured paintings in the panels; copies of Ary Scheffer's popular pictures of Mignon reflecting on her country.

Mr. CRICHTON, of Edinburgh, exhibits the beautiful CLARET-JUG, in silver, decorated with enamel, which has been deservedly placed in the Fine-

Art Court of the Crystal Palace. The mantle of the famous silversmith, George Heriot, seems to have again descended on the city of his birth.

The illustration underneath represents the top of a carved rosewood WARDROBE, by M. JOLY-LECLERC, of Paris; the Italian style of furniture decoration has been here well applied.

The VASE by M. VITTOZ, of Paris, is an elaborate and artistic work, one which may bear comparison with its earlier prototypes, in design.

The KNIFE-HANDLES here introduced are from the manufactory of Mr. W. T. LOY, jun., of London. The first and fifth are from BREAD-KNIVES; they are of ivory, with small figures bearing wheat in their arms; the blades are of highly-polished steel, ornamented on each side with ears of wheat, in open-work. The second is from a DESSERT-KNIFE; it shows the figure of Silenus, carrying grapes and other fruits. The fourth, from a TABLE-KNIFE, exhibits a female dancing-figure; it has a gold ferule, and a richly embossed blade. The centre engraving is from a CHEESE-SCOOP; it shows a boy, supporting on his head a basket of fruit, &c.

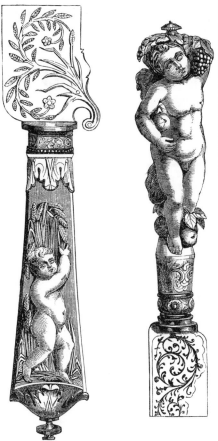

The engraving underneath is from a BATH, manufactured of slate, by Mr. G. E. MAGNUS, of Pimlico; it is of large proportions, the two wings projecting to a sufficient extent to take in the basin between them, as seen in the shaded part of the engraving, at the base of the centre. The design is in the Italian style, and the slate is enamelled in

imitation of various beautiful marbles. In the establishment of Mr. Magnus we have seen many objects of this material, vases, chimney-pieces, &c.

There are many individuals too apt to entertain an idea that the manufacturers in provincial towns, excepting always those places especially distinguished for certain classes of productions, as Birmingham, Sheffield, Manchester, &c., are very far behind those of the metropolis. This opinion cannot justly be entertained after the display which the provinces have made in the Exhibition. Here, for instance, we have, in the CABINET of Mr. FREEMAN, of Norwich, a specimen of work that would do credit to the first house in London. It is made of walnut-wood and ebony, richly carved, from a bold and well-studied Italian design.

Mr. F. H. THOMSON, of Glasgow, exhibits some beautiful specimens of electro-plating, two of which we select for engraving—a CUP, supported by a figure of Cupid, and a TEA-URN by that of Time. There is much ability displayed in these

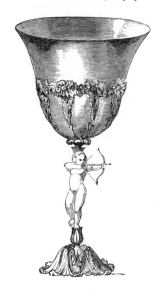

and other works exhibited by this firm; and it is something to find manufacturers forsaking the worn-out paths of their predecessors for new ones, even though they do not exactly reach those we should wish to see them pursuing.

The FENDER is manufactured and contributed by Messrs. ROBERTSON, CARR, & STEEL, of Sheffield, some of whose beautiful stoves have already been illustrated by us, and to which the present object is a suitable addition to the fireside. The curved outline flows gracefully from the centre.

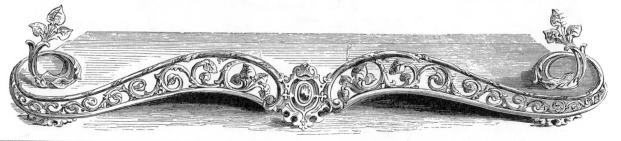

The FONT is of terra-cotta, from Switzerland, made by J. ZIEGLER-PELLIS, of Winterthur, in the canton of Zurich. The general arrangement of the architectural ornament is in the best taste of the later Gothic style.

The ALMS-BASINS by Mr. J. WIPPELL, of Exeter, are carved from the wood of the walnut tree; they are lined with crimson or scarlet silk

velvet. Inscriptions in medieval characters surround the moveable lids, such as "All things come of thee, and of thine own have we given

thee,"—"Freely ye have received, freely give." The ornament appears of a very graceful and appropriate character for ecclesiastical purposes.

Among the Viennese manufacturers, few have exhibited more ability in designs for furniture than M. KITSCHELT, whose LADIES' WORK-TABLE we here engrave. The flow of line throughout its composition is very free and elegant; there is also much taste displayed in the arrangement of the draperies in the centre which are of delicate and varied tints.

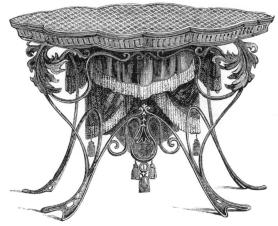

M. CARL LEISTLER, of Vienna, is the maker of the PRIE-DIEU below, which is remarkable for the finished elegance of its details; constructed of costly and beautiful woods, its value is enhanced by the artistic taste of its design; it possesses some claim to originality of style, following no

particular school of ornament. These devotional pieces of furniture are unknown among us, but are very common on the continent; the Exhibition furnishes several beautiful examples of this kind of manufacture.

Messrs. Doe, Hazleton, & Co., of Boston, U. S., exhibit an admirably carved Table of ebony.

Mr. Hopkins of Wimborne contributes a Door Handle of Gothic design, lined with coloured glass and china, a combination of new materials.

We introduce here two out of the numerous Carpets contributed by the distinguished firm of Messrs. Requillard, Roussel, & Choqueil, of Paris.

Messrs. BAILY & SONS, of London, exhibit a large number of artistic works

included in the general denomination

of "hardware," which are deserving of

high praise from the great amount of care bestowed upon their design and

execution. The ornamental cast-iron is particularly good; the DOOR-HANDLES, KNOCKERS, and BELL-PULLS, a few of which we

have selected for engraving, will testify fully to this fact; they embrace much variety of style, but each style is admirably

rendered. The HALL-STOVE is novel in design and bold in its details. The

wrought-iron BALCONY has been placed

by the Royal Commissioners in the Fine

Art court,—a very marked testimony to the merit of a really beautiful work.

The statue engraved on this column is by M. GEEFS, of Antwerp, and is entitled by the sculptor "THE FAITHFUL MESSENGER;" the story being told with graceful simplicity. It is that

Messrs. M'ALPIN, STEAD, & Co., of Cummers-dale, near Carlisle, contribute several specimens

of CHINTZ-FURNITURE, manufactured of cotton-velvet and of cotton, and printed by blocks

of a young Greek girl separated from her lover, who is refreshing the carrier-pigeon, returned from conveying to him her missive of affection.

The Austrian department shows various examples of INLAID FLOORING, by MM. LEISTLER and SON, of Vienna; we introduce here one of their patterns—a star upon a ground of dark wood.

and machinery. Two of their patterns are engraved on this page; they are both excellent.

The FOUNTAIN, which presents many features of novelty and gracefulness of general construction, is by Professor KALIDE, of Berlin, whose group of "The Boy and Swan," which forms the centre,

The three glass VASES are by Messrs. NEFFEN, of Winterburg, in Austria. They

principally differ from those by Hoffman, which we have already engraved, by a

more frequent use of polished surface, and the introduction of gold rims. Many of

appears in more instances than one in the Crystal Palace, and is a favourite work of the artist. The fountain ornaments the gardens of Charlottensberg, the summer residence of the King of Prussia.

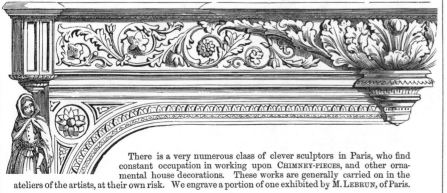

There is a very numerous class of clever sculptors in Paris, who find constant occupation in working upon CHIMNEY-PIECES, and other ornamental house decorations. These works are generally carried on in the ateliers of the artists, at their own risk. We engrave a portion of one exhibited by M. LEBRUN, of Paris.

the forms exhibit much elegance. The prevailing colours are pink, green, and white; some of them are richly engraved.

MESSRS. J. & M. P. BELL & Co., proprietors of | the Pottery Works Glasgow, exhibit the various

objects illustrated in this column; they are | made principally of Parian and terra-cotta,

and are designed after some of the best antique | models. The TOILET SET is especially elegant.

The Sculptor RAUCH, of BERLIN, exhibits the Statue of VICTORY—a work remarkable for its freedom from ordinary conventionalities of treatment, and for general vigour of conception. The action is that of the Genius suddenly awakened to the merit of the victor, and about

to raise the laurel crown for his due reward. The entire pose of the figure is original; she turns half round in her seat, the action being that of sudden thought and prompt attention, with a willing promptitude to acknowledge merit.

The above pattern exhibits that adopted for one of the INLAID FLOORS of coloured woods, designed and executed by M. LEISTLER, of Vienna.

Messrs. JACKSON & SONS, of London, are ex- tensive manufacturers of works in papier-mâché,

relief, the subject a dog attacking a duck's nest; the other, of a similar description, shows two

carton-pierre, and composition, for decoration and furniture. We introduce on this page four

dogs fighting over the nest of a heron; these subjects are very cleverly modelled. A CANDE-

of their contributions to the Exhibition, different in character. The first is an ORNAMENT in high

LABRUM exhibits a very pretty design; and the DECORATION that follows it is a bold example of the Italian style, with its grotesque ornaments.

Among the silver works manufactured and exhibited by Messrs. HILLIARD & THOMASON, of

The graceful statue of the youthful BACCHUS gazing on the inviting grape, is by LEOPOLD

NENCINI, of Florence, and is the production of one who has perfected his taste in the best school.

Birmingham, is a prettily designed INFANT'S CORAL, in which appears a child ringing a bell.

The appended engraving will be easily recognised by hundreds of visitors to the Exhibition, as the INTERIOR OF HER MAJESTY'S THEATRE,

drawn from a model made of card-board by Mr. T. D. DEIGHTON; the ornaments are painted by Mr. Powell. The representation is most accurate.

Among the large variety of objects in silver, manufactured and contributed by Mr. G. R. COLLIS, of Birmingham, are the CANDELABRUM and CENTRE-PIECE engraved on this page. Without any attempt at originality

The TABLE introduced underneath is from the manufactory of Mr. J. FLETCHER, of Cork; he terms it the "Gladiatorial Table," from the figure of a gladiator supporting the top. The idea exhibits great originality.

of idea, the arrangement of the scrolls and floriated ornament in each is good and effective. In the lower object we should have preferred to see a less massive introduction of the scroll-work, which would give it a

The most valuable contributions from the vast empire of Russia are, unquestionably, her mineral and other natural productions. Of manufactured objects we notice only a few specimens, except in textile fabrics.

greater degree of lightness. We notice, among the contributions of Mr. Collis, a solid silver table top, weighing nearly nine hundred ounces, for the Governor of Aleppo; and numerous other specimens of silver manufacture, many of which are deserving of illustration, had our space permitted.

The engraving above is from a small model of a CATHEDRAL-DOOR, executed in bronze by Count TOLSTOY, of St. Petersburg. The original of this, also in bronze, thirty feet in height, adorns the cathedral of Moscow.

The engraving which occupies so conspicuous a place on this page, is from a piece of exquisite WOOD-CARVING, executed and contributed by Mr. T. W. WALLIS, of Louth, in Lincolnshire. It is the first of a series of four that the sculptor purposes to execute, representing the four seasons. This is intended for "Spring," symbolised by flowers, the growth of that season, among which birds are introduced; these are arranged with an elegance and natural disposition

The manufactory of Messrs. CHARLES MEIGH & SON, of Hanley, is one of the largest and oldest in the pottery districts, having been established by the father of Mr. Meigh, Sen., about seventy years back; in proof of its extent,

we may remark that upwards of seven hundred hands are employed there in the various departments; that more than two hundred and fifty tons of coals are consumed every week; and

that, during the same short space of time, eighty tons of clay are made up into their various articles of manufacture. Of these, which consist exclusively of earthenware, Parian, and stone-

of their several forms that can scarcely be surpassed, and are carved with exceeding boldness of relief, some of the objects projecting twelve inches from the background. The work stands five and a half feet high, by nearly three feet wide; it contains forty-seven varieties of plants.

ware, about two-thirds are for the home market, and the remainder for exportation. We introduce on this column a CANDLESTICK, adapted from a celebrated wine-cup by Cellini, and two JUGS.

The subjects on this column are also from the contributions of Messrs. MEIGH & SON. The

JUG adorned with the vine exhibits a young Bacchanal imbibing the juice of the grape; the

BUTTER-COOLER is covered with a trellis-work, overgrown with creeping plants; the other two

objects are FLOWER-POTS, differing greatly in form and style of ornament, but both excellent

and appropriate to their purpose; the idea of the basket among the leaves, in the latter, is good.

The CENTRE-PIECE, serving the double purpose of an epergne and a candelabrum, is manufactured by Messrs. HAWKESWORTH, EYRE, & Co.,

the manly game of cricket, for which Sheffield has, within the last few years, become celebrated.

of Sheffield. It is a testimonial presented to Mr. M. J. Ellison, of that place, by his fellow-townsmen, for his exertions in promoting there

The TUREEN, by the same manufacturers, is an adaptation of what is generally known as the

"melon pattern," with scroll handles and feet, &c., in the Louis Quatorze style; it is elegant

in form, and far more consistent with our ideas of beauty than if more elaborately ornamented.

The contributions of Mr. W. WINFIELD, of the Cambridge-street Works, Birmingham, occupy a prominent position on one side of the "Birmingham Court" in the Exhibition. They consist of articles of a similar kind, the majority of which are distinguished by tasteful design and most excellent workmanship. On this and the two following columns will be found illustrations from a few we have selected to demonstrate the variety and importance of the manufactures of this establishment. The first column exhibits three BED-PILLARS, good in design, and of a rich and handsome appearance. The GAS-LAMP and BRACKET is one which, we understand, has been purchased by the Queen, a fact that supersedes the necessity of any further reference, as it bears ample testimony to the excellence of the work: the figures introduced are of parian.

The two CURTAIN-BANDS are graceful appendages to the windows of the elegant drawing-room.

principally of metallic bedsteads, of which Mr. Winfield is one of the oldest and most extensive manufacturers, gas-fittings of every description, window-cornices, curtain-bands, and a multitude

The two CLARET-JUGS on this column are manufactured by Messrs. LISTER & SONS, of Newcastle-upon-Tyne, silversmiths and jewellers.

These objects derive their value less from the metal of which they are made than from the taste displayed in the designs and the skilful work-

Resuming here our notice of the works of Mr. WINFIELD, of Birmingham, we commence with a CHILD'S COT, which he terms the "Angel Cot," from the figure very happily introduced into it, suggested by the traditional idea that, in

these unseen beings are present to watch over and protect us; the body and frame of the cot are very elegant. The BEDSTEAD that follows is excellent in the character of its design; the fluted taper pillars are drawn by a new process.

the earlier stages of our existence especially,

that enables a tube of this description to be made with the same facility as an ordinary parallel one. On the next page is a wall BRACKET, ornamented with the figure of "Dorothea," modelled by Mr. Bell: by its side is a

manship bestowed on them. They differ greatly in their styles, but the delicacy and boldness displayed in both are worthy of commendation.

LAMP, of more than ordinary excellence in the arrangement of its composition; while the superb BEDSTEAD that completes our illustrations is one

of the best objects of its kind ever brought before our notice. The style of this production is *renaissance*, and it abounds in all those rich

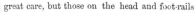

features peculiar to that period of decorative

art; the figures on the pillars are modelled with

great care, but those on the head and foot-rails

are objectionable from their unartistic attitude.

The contributions of M. RUDOLPHI, the eminent jeweller of Paris, are so truly beautiful

that we cannot resist the temptation of adding another column of illustrations to those already

given in preceding pages. The three BROOCHES are exquisite in design, and of the most delicate

workmanship; and a close examination of the TABLE will show how much artistic taste and

skill have been expended on its production.

The PIANOFORTE engraved is an American contribution, the manufacture of Mr. J. PIRSSON, of New York; it is of extraordinary size, being intended for four performers, two at each end. Its instrumental qualities are spoken of in high terms; and it is said to have been used at the concerts of Mademoiselle Lind.

The very elegant BAPTISMAL FONT, sculptured in Caen stone, is designed and executed by Mr. J. CASTLE, of Oxford, and is one of the principal ornaments

The LOCK and KEY are exhibited by Mr. J. GIBBONS, Jun., of Wolverhampton; he terms it an improved lock for doors, park-gates, &c.

of the English Fine Art Court. Symbolical figures of angels decorate its sides, bearing emblematic devices, the entire being covered with foliage and fruit.

The BROOKLYN FLINT GLASS-WORKS, situated at New York, U. S., contribute a well-filled

THE CRUSADER CHESS TABLE, is the work of Mr. GRAYDON, of Dublin; the pieces represent the chief characters of the Crusades, under Cœur-de-Lion. These pieces were carved in ivory by Mr. Slaight, of London.

stand, which occupies a central position in the American de-

partment of the Great Exhibition. There is enough novelty of form in these works to

Messrs. C. W. DOVE & Co, of Leeds, exhibit a number of beautiful velvet-pile Brussels, Kidderminster, and Threeply CARPETS; we engrave an elegant and exceedingly rich pattern, designed for them by Mr. Harvey.

assure us that our transatlantic brethren are fully aware of the mercantile value of Art.

Messrs. GOUGH of Sheffield exhibit articles of electro-plate, from which we select a group possessing much gracefulness of contour. The CANDLESTICK is of novel decoration, and the EPERGNE of light and elegant form, the ornament being well adapted to the objects manufactured.

Mr. BENNET, of Dublin, exhibits the very

Mr. BATTAM, of London, some of whose successful imitations of antique vases, &c., are engraved on a former page of our Catalogue, has adopted the appropriate and picturesque method of exhibiting his works, in a fac-simile of an ETRUSCAN TOMB, the various niches containing their urns, and the ground covered with pateræ and sacrificial vessels of a characteristic kind.

graceful CLARET-JUG, in silver, here engraved.

Mr. T. Earle has embodied the story of Jacob and Rachel in a gracefully conceived group. The shepherd stands by the well where the maiden fills her water-vessel, and tells his tale with simple earnestness.

The Vase in Terra Cotta, is produced at the works of Messrs. Ferguson, Miller, & Co., of Neathfield, Glasgow, and contains figures typical of the great gathering in 1851. In colour and manipulation it is decidedly good.

Mr. Whitwell of Dockray Hall Mills, Kendal, | a carpet manufacturer of eminence, contributes | among many other very excellent specimens, the

Kidderminster Carpet we here engrave. The fabric | is double cloth, not twilled in the warp, and the | colouring is produced by change of the shuttle.

This engraving is from a TABLE-COVER, de- | signed and executed by Messrs. Webb & Son, of | Spitalfields, for Messrs. DEWAR & Co., of London.

The two objects filling the lower part of this page are from examples of the cabinet work of Mr. J. M. LEVEIN, of London. The first is an ESCRITOIRE, of satin-wood, in the Louis Quatorze style, inlaid with tulip-wood in flowers and scroll-work. The other combines a JEWEL-CASE and STAND; it is made of the tulip and kingwoods, ornamented with or-molu, and inlaid

with Sèvres china. Another of the contributions of M. Levein, which our space would not allow us to illustrate, is a very beautiful sideboard formed of a wood, the growth of New Zealand.

A TABLE, in papier-mâché, which, we presume, is intended for a ladies' work-table, is from the manufactory of Messrs. HALBEARD & WELLINGS, of Birmingham. Its vase-like form is a novelty in this description of cabinet manufacture.

The SLEIGH, from which the engraving underneath is copied, is an American production, manufactured by Messrs. J. GOOLD & Co., of Albany, U.S. It is a double-bodied carriage, of excellent workmanship, to be drawn by two ponies, for which its construction admirably fits it.

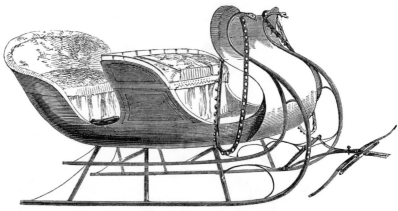

From the numerous articles of merit in ALTAR-CLOTHS, hangings, &c., exhibited by Messrs. NEWTON, JONES, & WILLIS, of Birmingham, we select two—engravings of which occupy the lower part of this page. That underneath is a portion of the ORPHREY of an archbishop's cape, designed for the Anglican church; the whole of the enrichments are worked by hand in gold and silk.

The second engraving on this column is from the other contribution of Messrs. NEWTON, JONES, & WILLIS, to which allusion is elsewhere made.

It is a portion of an ALTAR-CLOTH, embroidered by hand, in gold and silk; in the design is a dove, drawn in the style of the ancient illuminators.

The simplicity of the worship of the English church is most striking, when compared with that of the church from which it sprung; even in our highest festivals, there is little room for that "outward adornment," to which the subjects here engraved are meant to be applied.

The original of the appended engraving is a CLOCK and INKSTAND for a library table; it is exhibited by Mr. J. HUX, of London, the manufacturer of the clock; the case and stand are beautifully carved by Mr. W. G. ROGERS, the eminent sculptor in wood, who has also executed several other clock-cases for Mr. HUX, that appear in the Exhibition, and which are well worthy of his high reputation. The work before us forms an elegant and useful ornament.

On the opposite page is an illustration from the papier-mâché TABLES of Messrs. HALBEARD & WELLINGS, of Birmingham; another, of a different character, appears underneath; both in its form, and its ornamentation, it exhibits a taste that qualifies it for a place in the boudoir.

One of the great defects we have frequently noticed in decorative furniture is the inapplicability of ornament to the purpose of the object on which it appears; and another is the combination of styles, sometimes the most distinct from each other, so as to form an incongruous mixture, showing how little of the true principles of decoration have been acquired by the designer; and also how much labour, time, and cost of workmanship, may be expended fruitlessly. The architecture, if the term may be permitted, of a piece of furniture should be as pure as that of an edifice, otherwise it offends rather than pleases the eye which can detect the slightest want of harmony. No such charge, however, can be brought against the splendid

SIDEBOARD of M. E. P. DURAND, of Paris, which, in design and execution, may compete with the best which the Exhibition has called forth. The leading idea of this work is eminently good, while the several details of which the ornaments are formed, at once declare its intended purpose.

A GIRL AT A SPRING is a favourite subject with English painters and sculptors; Mr. W. F. WOODINGTON has here brought forward a figure which displays considerable elegance of attitude.

The two engravings placed in this column are from an imperial quarto BIBLE, bound in morocco, by Mr. R. NEIL, of Edinburgh, and ornamented in a very costly manner, with the

Cathedral, St. John's, Edinburgh, and St. Giles's, Edinburgh; the whole sketched from the buildings, and wrought with the hand. Mr. Neil is

description of work known among bookbinders as "blind tooling," enriched with embossing and illuminated colouring. On the gilt edges are representations of three churches—Glasgow

almost self-taught, and he has executed the entire work by gas-light, after business hours: it is highly creditable to his industry and taste.

The PIANO FORTE is a contribution from the manufactory of Mr. CHICKERING, of Boston, United States; his instruments have obtained

high reputation, even among European professors who have tried them, for their brilliancy of tone

and their power. That which we have here

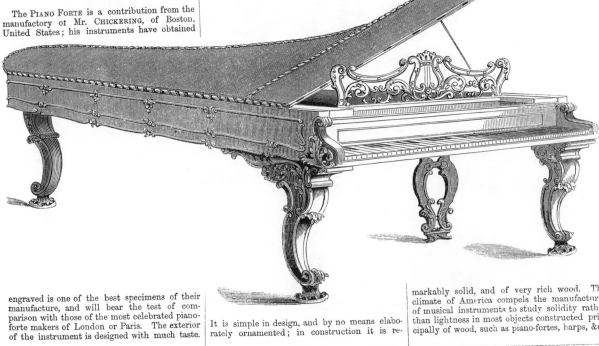

engraved is one of the best specimens of their manufacture, and will bear the test of comparison with those of the most celebrated pianoforte makers of London or Paris. The exterior of the instrument is designed with much taste.

It is simple in design, and by no means elaborately ornamented; in construction it is re-

markably solid, and of very rich wood. The climate of America compels the manufacturer of musical instruments to study solidity rather than lightness in most objects constructed principally of wood, such as piano-fortes, harps, &c.

The engraving underneath, stretching across the page, shows the top of a SOFA-BACK, manufactured by M. JEANSELME, of Paris, whose name has appeared in other parts of our Catalogue. The work is beautifully carved in the style of the best period of Italian sculptured art, and merits high praise for design and execution.

The contributions in papier mâché of Messrs. SPIERS & SON, of Oxford, are numerous; they consist of tables, work-tables, writing-desks,

being sufficiently subdued, and regard being had, generally, to harmony of composition. They derive much of their interest and attraction

The piece of EMBROIDERY intended to decorate the front of a waistcoat, is exhibited by Mdlles. DANIEL and CORSINS of Hoxton; the pattern exhibits a Cornucopia, round which flowers are clinging: the work is executed with great delicacy, and exhibits considerable taste in design.

tea-trays, albums. fire-screens, portfolios, &c., all of which are in good taste; the ornamentation

from the paintings with which they are embellished, consisting of some of the most picturesque or celebrated edifices in Oxford, as well as sketches taken from its outskirts.

The CHAIR is another of the contributions of Messrs. GILLOW, of London, to whose works we have frequently referred. It presents a solidity of construction that would have appeared too

massive, if not lightened by the character of the ornament with which it is judiciously relieved.

The town of Paisley maintains the reputation it has long enjoyed for the manufacture of woollen and worsted textile fabrics, in shawls, plaids, tartans, &c. We here engrave one of the woven long SHAWLS, exhibited by Messrs. J. & A. ROXBURGH, of this place; the design is a very elaborate composition of floriated forms, arranged in a most intricate pattern, yet exhibiting little or nothing of that confusion which might be looked for in such a multiplicity of details. The

On this and the succeeding column, are introduced illustrations of some of the silver goods manufactured by MM. CHRISTOFLE & Co., of

Paris, who are entitled to take rank with the best silversmiths of the French metropolis, for

purity of taste in the designs they have here furnished. Our first subject is a CREAM-JUG of

task of the engraver is rendered intelligible, without the aid of colour, although to combine such a variety of forms is by no means easy; and even with all his skill, a mere black and white transcript of the pattern does but meagre justice to this rich and beautiful object of manufacturing art, one of the best among the many excellent productions emanating from Paisley.

very elegant form, slightly ornamented in a good style: the next is a FLOWER-STAND, showing much originality of design, as regards the combination of the two principal parts. The engraved work on the COFFEE-POT is executed with

great delicacy in the *Renaissance* style. The CANDELABRUM is gracefully modelled, and shows

considerable lightness in the design. The VASE, concluding the series, is a bold composition.

Occupying the central place in the Crystal Palace, the GLASS FOUNTAIN, by Messrs. OSLER, of Birmingham, is, perhaps, the most striking object in the Exhibition; the lightness and beauty, as

well as the perfect novelty of its design, have rendered it the theme of admiration with all visitors. The ingenuity with which this has been effected is very perfect; it is supported

by bars of iron, which are so completely embedded in the glass shafts, as to be invisible, and in no degree interfering with the purity and crystalline effect of the whole object.

Many of the manufacturers of our country towns have succeeded in enforcing that general claim to notice, which, while awarded to them in their own locality, they might have failed to have obtained, but for the great and general competition called forth by the invitation of 1851. The TABLE by Mr. PALMER, an eminent upholsterer of Bath, is an excellent example of provincial manufacture; it is very graceful in design, and the execution is of a most satisfactory kind.

The CHAIR is engraved from one manufactured by M. BALNY, of Paris, who contributes numerous articles of furniture, manifesting good taste. and no little ingenuity of workmanship. The style of this chair is Elizabethan, well carried out.

A terra-cotta VASE, from the works of Messrs. FERGUSON, MILLER, & Co., of Heathfield, near Glasgow, shows, among its other ornaments, a

Mr. C. J. RICHARDSON is well known by his excellent works on Elizabethan ornament and furniture, in which he has, with much perseverance and ability, pointed out the peculiarities, and rich fancies, visible in that school of design. He has now practically realised his knowledge,

by the production of various ARTICLES OF FURNITURE, possessing all the picturesque richness of the style, combined with the knowledge of its leading principles, which elevate these works.

nuptial procession, designed in the style of the antique. These figures are modelled with great accuracy, and are arranged in an artistic manner.

The CONSOLE-GLASS and TABLE combined, are designed and manufactured by Mr. S. LECAND, of London; the frames are carved in American pine and lime-tree woods, and double gilt in matted and burnished gold.

The style is a variation of the *Louis Quatorze*; birds, flowers, and winged horses being mingled with the other description of ornamental work, and giving to the whole more novelty than we are often accustomed to see.

These VASES are the productions of Captain BEAU-CLERC, and are formed in terra-cotta, of two tints. The

body of each vase is of deep red, the figures of a much

Among the numerous objects of cabinet-work manufactured by Messrs. GILLOW & CO., of London, is a SOFA, termed a "Wanstead Sofa." It has little carved work, but it is of a good order; the griffins at each end, forming the legs, are sculptured with boldness.

yellower clay, both being the production of Ireland.

THE INDUSTRY OF ALL NATIONS.

The GOTHIC HINGE is manufactured and exhibited by Messrs. BARNARD and BISHOP, of Norwich. It is of wrought iron, and is a well-directed attempt to revive the ancient iron smith-work, of which many of our old ecclesiastical edifices and baronial mansions furnish fine examples.

The manufactory of Messrs. J. ROSE & Co., of

A STATE-BED, designed and manufactured by Mr. T. FOX, of London, is a fine example of this description of furniture. The design is in the Elizabethan style, but showing greater lightness than we usually find in the carved works of that period. It is made of walnut, relieved by

Coleport, Shropshire, has obtained considerable

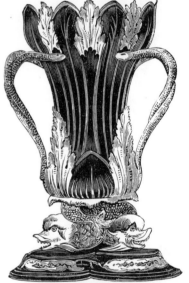

eminence for its productions in embossed porce-

gilding; the footboard is divided into panels, and in the centre is a shield, on which appears a Bacchanalian mask; carved figures are placed at each corner. The backboard is stuffed, and the furniture is of light blue silk with satin margin and white trimmings. It is of good workmanship.

lain, which bear comparison, for beauty of material and skill of workmanship, with the best of the Pottery districts of Staffordshire. Some idea of the

variety and originality of their patterns, combined with other good qualities, may be received from the examples

we have here introduced. The first column commences with a DESSERT-PLATE, the border of which shows a

pleasing novelty, while the groups of fruit are painted with much taste. The FLOWER-VASE that follows is also

new in design, and appropriate; and the EPERGNE is entitled to favourable notice. On this column we engrave

specimens of TEA and COFFEE-CUPS, all of which are characterised by novelty of design in their ornament;

a JUG in this column is justly entitled to a similar remark. The

group which follows is composed chiefly of FRUIT-DISHES, de-

signed in the character of the style known as the "Louis Quatorze." The GROUP OF

FIGURES—Puck throned on a mushroom

—is of Parian. It is a clever design and

the figures are capitally modelled: it is,

we believe, the work of the late admirable sculptor, Mr. Pitts, and finished by his son.

The figure placed on this column is from another of the models exhibited by Mr. F. M. MILLER. The sculptor has given it the title of SPRING, symbolising that season by the doves perched on the hand of the figure, and the plough, modelled after an antique agricultural implement, on which it rests. The embodiment of the idea is carried out in a graceful manner, and the pose of the figure is remarkably easy.

The illustration above is a portion of a Gothic | CHIMNEY-PIECE sculptured by M. LEBRUN, of Paris.

The engraving underneath is from a piece of EMBROIDERY TRIMMING, exhibited by Messrs. BENNOCH, TWENTYMAN, & Co., of London.

A CONSOLE CHEFFONIER is exhibited by Messrs. TRAPNELL & SON, of Bristol: it is made of En- | glish walnut-wood, the top is of statuary marble, set in a rich moulding of ebony and tortoiseshell.

The CARRIAGE here introduced is manufactured by Messrs. R. & E. VEZEY, of Bath; it belongs to the class usually termed "sociables." The general appearance of this carriage is very elegant, and all the springs being fixed with india-rubber bearings, it "rides" very easily. The body, &c., is painted in rich ultra-marine blue, relieved with white and amber, in delicate lines; and it is lined with drab silk and lace.

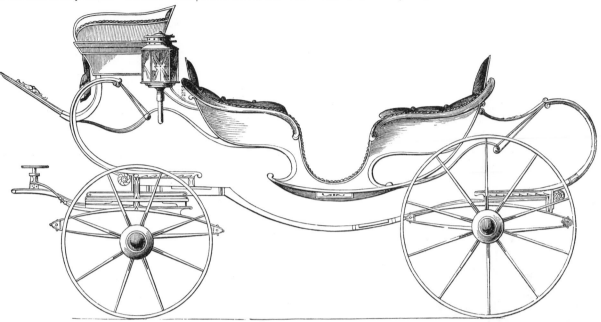

Messrs. HILLIARD & THOMASON, of Birmingham, are the contributors of fish-knives and forks, The engraving underneath shows the pattern of a BRUSSELS CARPET, printed by patent machinery, at the factory of Messrs. J. BRIGHT & Co., of Crag, near Macclesfield. The composi-

taper-stands, &c. We engrave here the HANDLE OF A FISH-KNIFE, very excellent in design. tion of this design is exceedingly bold, though we cannot assign to it much originality of inven- tion. Messrs. Bright are also exhibitors of velvet pile carpets, tapestries, furniture-covers, &c.

We occupy this page with works by M. LEISTLER, who may be, with justice, considered the most important Austrian manufacturer; that he claims high rank, as well for the artistic taste as for the beauty with which his

tures, and other objects of art, which may thus be conveniently and elegantly arranged over their surface. The figures who hold them, the

fanciful foliage, and the equally fanciful group of horned serpents forming the base, are all remarkable for the vigour and delicacy with which

they are carved. The small SETTEE beneath is equally good in execution, but is less graceful in

design, and is not redeemed from heaviness. In some instances, parts are better than the whole

of these articles of furniture, and many that might be passed by as ordinary looking, deserve

study in detail; we engrave the central portion of a SOFA-BACK as an illustration of this, which

works are executed, will be readily admitted by those who inspect the four palatial apartments he has furnished for the inspection of "the world," in its Exhibition. A very grace-

ful novelty is represented in our first cut; it is an ORNAMENTAL STAND, of a fanciful and original design, the large framed boards of rosewood being intended for the exhibition of small minia-

possesses elegance. The TABLE beneath is intended for a drawing-room; it is of the finest-coloured and most costly wood. The CHAIR is

of sumptuous construction, whether its carved work, or its upholstery, be considered; it is constructed with the strictest attention to comfort.

The engravings on this page are from a *suite* of carved decorative furniture, consisting of about twenty objects; they are manufactured

are made is Irish bog-yew. The FAUTEUIL, or arm-chair, shows at the back busts of ancient Irish warriors, supporting the ancient arms of

chanalian busts at the angles; a figure of Hibernia surmounts the top, with the accessories of the wolf-dog, harp, &c. The POLE-SCREEN, one of a pair, stands on a tripod composed of three busts with helmeted heads; the looking-glass panels

by Mr. A. J. JONES, of Dublin, from his own designs, which are intended to illustrate Irish history and antiquities; the wood of which they

Ireland; the elbows are represented by wolf-dogs, one in action, the other recumbent. The TEA-POY, being a receptacle for foreign produce,

is appropriately ornamented; its base exhibits the chase of the giant deer by wolf-dogs. A

sarcophagus WINE-COOLER is elaborately sculptured on the four sides, and enriched with bac-

form the field on which is sculptured, in demi-relief, an ancient Irish Kern, or light-armed warrior, on the one, and on the other, the Gallowglass, or heavy-armed Irish warrior.

It was reasonably to be expected that Germany, so rich in musical talent, would furnish some examples of her skill in the manufacture of MUSICAL INSTRUMENTS. We have, therefore, engraved several from the establishment of Messrs. F. GLIER & SON, of Klingenthal, in Saxony.

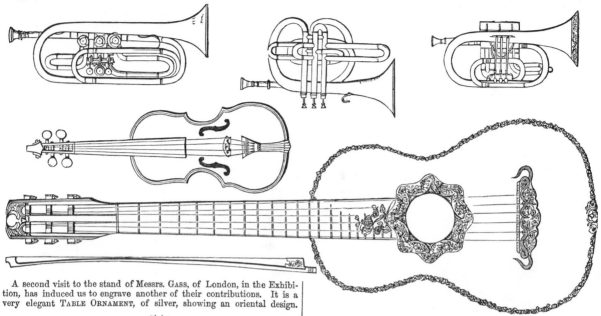

A second visit to the stand of Messrs. GASS, of London, in the Exhibition, has induced us to engrave another of their contributions. It is a very elegant TABLE ORNAMENT, of silver, showing an oriental design.

The three engravings which complete this page are selected from a

large variety of useful and ornamental articles, manufactured by Mr. T.

HARRISON, of Sheffield, chiefly in electro-plate on imperial metal and

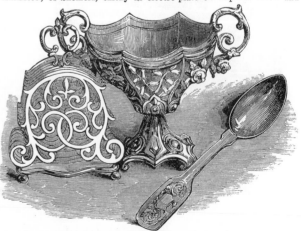

Two Indian water-bearers are placed beneath a palm-tree; at each corner of the triangular base is a sphynx, between which is a wreath of flowers.

nickel silver; many of these are designed with very considerable taste.

On this column we introduce a VASE of silver for perfume, and a TANKARD of silver gilt, from

the manufactory of M. VITTOZ, of Paris; each of these objects are exquisite examples of the taste

displayed by the French designer in producing models for the manufacturer in costly metals.

A valuable auxiliary to the amateur sketcher

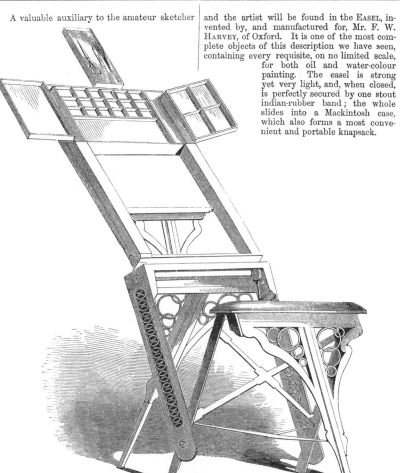

and the artist will be found in the EASEL, invented by, and manufactured for, Mr. F. W. HARVEY, of Oxford. It is one of the most complete objects of this description we have seen, containing every requisite, on no limited scale, for both oil and water-colour painting. The easel is strong yet very light, and, when closed, is perfectly secured by one stout indian-rubber band; the whole slides into a Mackintosh case, which also forms a most convenient and portable knapsack.

Mr. HANICQ, of Malines, has furnished a pyramid

of glazed cases, containing the important and beautiful devotional books for which he is celebrated as one of the most extensive continental publishers.

A CHIMNEY-PIECE of marble, designed and manufactured by Messrs. JOSEPH BROWNE & Co., of London, is a well-executed work, from a light and graceful composition, to which the two principal figures impart a novelty that is carried out by the ornamentation of the other parts.

The Russian contributions to the Crystal Palace evince a large amount of costly splendour combined with quaint and characteristic design,

showing much fancy in the Art-manufacturers who have been engaged in their fabrication. In other pages of our Catalogue, many of the

The BRONZE FOUNTAIN is the production of Mr. JAMES, of Lambeth, and is of very appropriate design, inasmuch as all the accessories are really, or mythologically, connected with the element it is destined to display. It is a small work, a model, in fact, but all the details are carefully carried

out, and it is worked by a miniature steam-engine, of singularly excellent construction.

larger Russian works appear; we here devote two columns to specimens of the silver cups which occupy so important a position in the department devoted to this great empire. There is a very free and fanciful taste prevalent in

these articles, which gives to them a strong individuality of character. This is particularly

visible in the first and second of our engravings; the others, however, call to mind the German

works of the fifteenth century, to which they are nearly allied. They are the productions of the goldsmith, PAUL SAZIKOFF, of Moscow.

A CONSOLE-TABLE, by M. JEANSELME, of Paris, | is a good example of the Louis Quatorze style.

The engraving underneath is from the model | of a SARCOPHAGUS with GOTHIC CANOPY, sculp-

tured by Mr. W. PLOWS, of Foss Bridge, York, in | stone from the quarries at Heldenley, near Malton

The appended engraving is from a piece of EMBROIDERY, for a Priest's robe; it is manufactured by MM. LEMIRE & SON, of Lyons; the cross is worked in gold, upon a ground of purple.

A statuary group under the name of "THE SUPPLIANT" is exhibited, with other works, by Mr. WEEKES, the distinguished sculptor; the figure is presumed to represent a female in distress, who, with her infant, is soliciting charity.

The CHAIR introduced below is made by MR. G. W. ENGLAND, of Leeds; it is manufactured

A TABLE, of walnut wood, is another of the contributions made by MR. PALMER, of Bath; it shows some bold carving, executed from a design of considerable novelty, especially in the

form of the cross-piece connecting the legs. The manufacturer is entitled to very high praise.

of mahogany, the grain ot the wood running in one uniform direction: the design is good.

The sword here engraved is from the manufactory of Messrs. REEVES, GREAVES & Co., sword cutlers of Birmingham. It is a cavalry dress Sabre, the hilt, blade, and scabbard mountings of which are entirely of steel, elaborately engraved, in designs that show considerable ele-

The subject of the annexed illustration is a CARVED FRAME, for a looking-glass, manufactured by Messrs. GILLOW, of London; it is a very elegant production

of its class. and a pleasing contrast to the *Louis Quatorze* style so much in vogue, and which we should be glad to see superseded by one of greater simplicity.

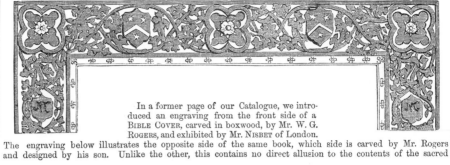

In a former page of our Catalogue, we introduced an engraving from the front side of a BIBLE COVER, carved in boxwood, by Mr. W. G. ROGERS, and exhibited by Mr. NISBET of London. The engraving below illustrates the opposite side of the same book, which side is carved by Mr. Rogers and designed by his son. Unlike the other, this contains no direct allusion to the contents of the sacred

gance of composition. The manufacture of these weapons from the rough metal to the finished object is highly interesting and curious, employing, as it does, a variety of workmen, each of whom must possess a greater or less amount of artistic skill and mechanical ingenuity to perfect his portion of work.

volume; the border is similar, but the centre ornament exhibits only a graceful arrangement of wheat,

grapes, and other devices. The execution of this work is exceedingly delicate and masterly in all its parts.

The CABINET here introduced is manufactured by Mr. HARRISON, of the Wood-carving Company, Pimlico, whose operations are conducted by a process of burning the wood into the required

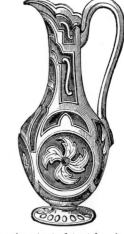

ornamented, while the latter possesses the pure outline of the antique without anything of a de-

corative character to detract from its simplicity

pattern, so as to imitate carving. The cabinet engraved is of oak and it shows some excellent ornamental work: the contributions of this establishment are numerous and exceedingly varied.

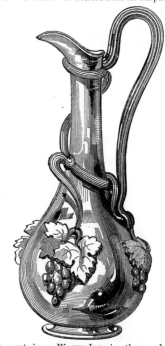

the next is a WATER-JUG in the mediæval

MESSRS. LLOYD & SUMMERFIELD, of Birmingham, are the contributors of the productions in Glass represented on this page. The group exhibits JUGS and a VASE; the former are richly style; the CLARET-JUG and decorated DRINKING-GLASSES show considerable novelty in design.

The FLOWER-STAND, one of a pair, and BRACKET, in this column, are by M. FLEISCH-MANN, of Sonneberg, in Germany; the latter object is of *papier mâché*, from a very bold

The readers of the *Art-Journal* must be well aware of the interest we have always evinced in the welfare of the various schools of design established throughout the kingdom—institutions that we doubt not are destined to exercise an important influence on British Manufacturing Art. The fruits of the exertions which are made for sustaining these schools begin now to be manifested in a way that must be very gratifying to all who, like ourselves, have advocated their establishment, and augured their prosperity. One of these pleasing results is

design. The flower-stand is chiefly constructed of iron, modelled in a new way, and combined with *papier mâché*, and covered with glass; it represents two vines, each with a bunch of

golden grapes. The pedestals consist of roots of trees thickly covered with grass and herbs.

developed in the CABINET here engraved, which is the work of A. HAYBALL, a young woodcarver of Sheffield, and educated in the school of design attached to that town. It is made of English walnut-wood; the design is of the pure Italian style, abundantly rich in ornament, and free from many of the monstrosities that too frequently deface similar productions; there is indeed scarcely a single part of the work open to reasonable objection. We understand that Mr. Hayball undertook the task from a desire to uphold the character of the Sheffield School.

THE INDUSTRY OF ALL NATIONS.

Messrs. DIXON & SONS, of Sheffield, are extensive manufacturers of silver and plated goods, and in what is known as Britannia metal; we have engraved on this page a few of the numerous appears in these designs. The silver and gilt TEA AND COFFEE SERVICE possesses considerable novelty in form and composition; the various pieces are modelled from the pitcher-plant, and the waiter on which they are placed from a leaf

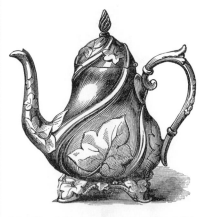

articles they contribute to the Exhibition. In the TUREEN and DISH we have examples of the plain but truly elegant Grecian style adapted to objects of ordinary use; and it is certainly not of the *Victoria Regia*. The COFFEE-POT on this column has a floral ornament in high relief; the CAKE-PLATE is modelled as from a single leaf, in

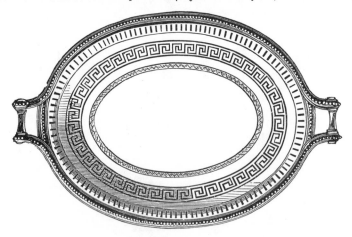

a little refreshing to the eye, somewhat over- wearied with the constant recurrence of the an elegant form; and the POWDER-FLASK, which concludes the page, shows an embossing in the Italian style, forming a frame and displaying in

elaborate and often over-decorated patterns of the Italian style, and those founded upon it. The absence of a *plethora* of ornament is amply atoned for by the simple beauty of that which the centre a group of dead game. The flask has a stopper, very ingeniously and effectively contrived to facilitate the sportsman in loading his gun.

The TABLE, manufactured by Messrs. JOHNSTONE & JEANES, of London, is circular, and made on the expanding principle; by a simple process, the quaternions of which the top is composed draw out, and sectional pieces being introduced, the table is increased to double its original size. The tripod is very massive; it looks disproportioned as seen in the engraving, but not so when the table is expanded.

A model, in bronze, of a FOUNTAIN is exhibited by M. GASSER, of Vienna; it would be highly effective on a large scale.

The GROUP OF FURNITURE introduced underneath is from the establishment of Messrs. SNELL & CO., of London. As might be expected, the invitations to exhibit have been answered by contributions from the most eminent cabinet-makers in Great Britain and on the continent, each of whom appears to have striven worthily in the production of works calculated to uphold their own individual reputation, and that of their respective countries. The CABINET and GLASS are much to our taste; the frame of the latter is especially good,

and possesses novelty. The oval TABLE has a rich marquetrie border, and the other objects that appear in our illustration deserve attention.

The BROOCH engraved underneath is manufactured by M. RUDOLPHI, of Paris; the design of the beautiful setting is of the Renaissance period.

The city of Lyons, as might be expected, contributes a large, varied, and costly supply of the silk manufactures for which she has long been celebrated throughout Europe. It is not our province, here at least, to institute comparisons between the productions of France and those of our country; but we may nevertheless be permitted to add that, unfortunately for our own manufacturers, fashion has arbitrarily set a value upon the fabrics of the continent, to which they

The group, by M. LECHESNE, of Paris, which he terms THE FAITHFUL FRIEND, is remarkable for the vigour with which the story is told by the

sculptor. A boy is accompanied by his dog, both are attacked by a serpent, but the faithful animal is on the defensive, and destroys the reptile.

are not always entitled. Of the two illustrations on the lower part of this page the first is from a piece of RIBBON, made by Messrs. COLLARD & Co., of St. Etienne; the pattern is simple, but

arranged with considerable grace. The second is from a silk SCARF, which presents a combination of elegant and novel forms most skilfully composed; it is a superb fabric from the manufactory of Messrs. BERTRAND, GAYET, & DUMONTAL of Lyons, an establishment of high reputation.

This group—THE DELIVERER—is a sequel, by M. LECHESNE, to that which we engrave on the opposite page. The dog has destroyed the aggressive serpent, and is receiving the caresses of the boy who has been saved by his prowess.

We introduce here another BROOCH by M. RUDOLPHI, of Paris; it is an exquisitely-delicate piece of workmanship; the mounting shows the leaves and bunches of grapes, elegantly arranged; the centre is a very charming enamel painting.

The engraving underneath is from a piece of SILK DAMASK, made by Messrs. MATHEVON & BOUVARD, of Lyons; the design is truly excellent.

The velvets of Lyons are no less distinguished by beauty of fabric than the silks manufactured in the same place; we engrave here one of the costly FIGURED VELVETS made by Messrs. MATHEVON & BOUVARD.

The CARRIAGE, or "Pilentum," as it is designated by the manufacturer, Mr. MULLINER, of Northampton, is an excellent specimen of provincial carriage-building, which may vie with the best of metropolitan manufacture; the panels are painted to resemble cane-work, and so successfully as almost to deceive the eye. The body of the vehicle is suspended on elliptical springs.

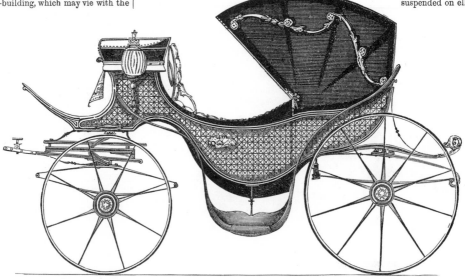

We introduce here two engravings from the manufactures of Lyons; the first is a cloth of silk, called "Drap d'Or," made by Messrs. MATHEVON & BOUVARD; it is an exquisitely beautiful fabric, in which the design and its arrangement are equally good, while the gold and colours weaved into it present a most rich appearance. The second is from the manufactory

of Messrs. LE MIRE & SON; it is a piece of gold brocade, showing great originality in the disposition of the pattern, which consists of flowers, both wild and cultivated, mingled with ears of rye-corn, bound together.

M. ROULÉ, of Antwerp, a wood-carver of eminence, who has been employed by his Government in the reconstruction of the ornamental Gothic wood-work of the stalls of Antwerp Cathedral, has sent some of his beautiful works in furniture to the Exhibition. A Gothic sideboard is a fine specimen of his art, in which his knowledge of the style and power of treating it, fully prove how wisely the choice of his Government has fallen on him. The BEDSTEAD we engrave is a more free and fanciful work in the Italian style; it is carved in ebony, and is very boldly and beautifully wrought,—a work that reflects the greatest honour on its fabricant.

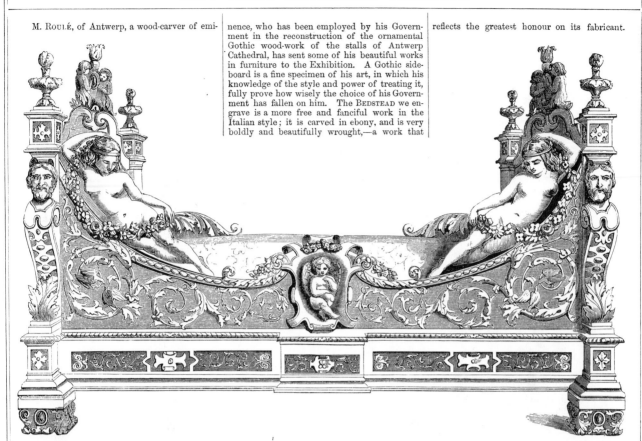

From the Sherwood Iron-Works, situated at Mansfield, Mr. F. WAKEFIELD, the proprietor, has sent a variety of stoves, and some other examples of metallic work. We introduce here a specimen of his design for wrought-iron RAILING, exhibiting a pattern equally novel, artistic, and effective for its purpose. The STOVE-GRATE, as it is termed by the manufacturer, is a laudable attempt, successfully carried out, to produce a chaste and simple style of ornament, in combination with a new and effective mode of diffusing heat throughout an

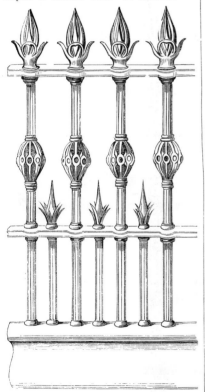

apartment, a desideratum too often lost sight of in the construction of stoves and grates; that here engraved is of highly polished steel, beautifully wrought. Among other manufactures contributed by Mr. Wakefield, but which are not altogether suitable for our pages, are various cooking apparatuses, adapted to the means of the three grades into which the community is generally divided, the higher, middle, and lower.

From the very few examples of Russian furniture, which appear in the Exhibition, we have selected a CABINET, manufactured by M. GAMBS, of

The CANDELABRUM is one of a pair, also from a Russian manufacturer, M. KRUMBIGEL, of Moscow. They are of bronze, gilt; the height of the

St. Petersburgh; it is made of tulip-wood, ornamented with bronze and inlaid with porcelain. The design is good, simple, and without pretension.

pedestal looks a little disproportioned to that of the shaft; in all its other parts the design is unexceptionable, and, in some respects, original.

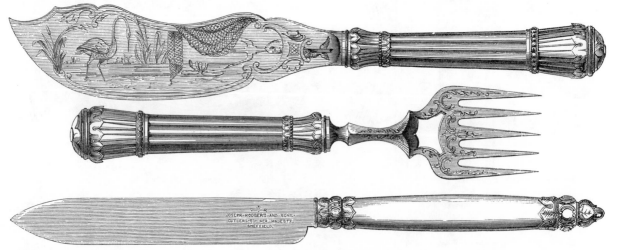

Messrs. J. RODGERS & SONS, of Sheffield, are the manufacturers of the FISH-SLICE and FORK, and DESSERT-KNIFE, which appear above. The

blade of the first-named shows an engraving of a subject that is suggestive of the intended use of the article itself; a kingfisher is standing

in a stream, surrounded by aqueous plants, while a fishing-net is tastefully brought into the composition. The handles are simply designed.

Mr. F. M. MILLER exhibits a bas-relief, the subject being from "Comus"—and exhibiting THE ATTENDANT SPIRIT descending on a glancing star. It is a gracefully conceived rendering of a highly poetic image, and reflects honour on the young sculptor who has so successfully executed it. We hope to see it in marble.

Mr. J. E. JONES exhibits a portrait-statue which he terms "THE FAVOURITE," in allusion, we presume, to the dog, upon which the left hand of the lady reposes so trustingly, and which appears to return her confidence

The LUSTRE, engraved below, is intended for the display of sixty lights, and is manufactured by BERNSTORFF & EICHWEDE of Hanover. It is very sumptuous in its en-

with a due amount of attachment on his part. There is a natural simplicity about the figure that renders it extremely pleasing; the drapery is tastefully disposed, and the entire composition is altogether graceful and attractive.

richments, and good in general design. The contributions from Northern Germany are not large, but the present is one of the best, and may be suggestive to manufacturers at home, who sometimes display too much floral ornament in works of this class.

One of the parquetage FLOORS by M. LEISTLER of Vienna; the woods are of various tints, from the white lime to the dark rose-wood; they give variety and beauty to the pattern.

A STATUARY GROUP, modelled by Mr. JONES BARKER, of London, is a highly spirited production. We presume it to be the dying Marmion of Sir Walter Scott, shaking the "fragment of his blade." We have frequently thought this a good subject for the sculptor, and should like to see it carried out on a large scale. Mr. Barker's group is small, but it tells its story effectively.

A SILVER SCENT-BOTTLE is another of the contributions of M. RUDOLPHI, the eminent silversmith of Paris, and, like all the works produced by him, it manifests a pure feeling for art.

Every visitor to the Austrian department of the Exhibition, will at once recognise the annexed engraving as the magnificent oak BOOK CASE. manufactured by MM. LEISTLER & SON, as a present from the Emperor of Austria to the Queen of England. The work is well worthy of

the Imperial donor and the Royal recipient, while it does infinite credit to those who have produced it. The Gothic carving is beautifully decorated.

In a former page of the Catalogue we introduced several engravings from the jewellery manufactured by Messrs. WATHERSTON & BROGDEN, of London; we are induced to devote another page to the contributions of this firm, principally for the purpose of giving an illustration of the magnificent VASE of gold, jewelled and enamelled, which occupies so prominent a

festoons of diamonds, representing the rose, shamrock, and thistle; and, surrounding the body of the vase, are relievos, which express the ancient progenitors of the British nation; other appropriate devices are introduced. Still

lower are two figures of Fame, crowning England's most renowned warriors, poets, and men of science; while, on the lower part of the cup, as an expression of British character,

are the figures of Truth, Prudence, Industry, and Fortitude. The vase weighs ninety-five ounces, and is richly decorated with diamonds, pearls, rubies, carbuncles, sapphires, and eme-

position among their works in the Exhibition. It is designed by Mr. Alfred Brown: the group surmounting the cover represents the United Kingdom as symbolised by the figures of Britannia, Scotia, and Hibernia; around the edge of the cup are four heads emblematical of the four quarters of the globe, in all of which Great Britain possesses colonies. Below these are ralds, relieved by a cinque-cento ornamental ground, in enamel. The work is surpassed by nothing in the Exhibition, in reference either to design or execution. The BROOCHES engraved on this column are elegant specimens of jewellery.

The Gallery of Art exhibited in the Austrian department has attracted great attention since the Exhibition first opened, and it has continued throughout to be one of the most crowded portions of the building. This is due as well to the excellence of the works exhibited, as to the striking peculiarities which some of them display; such as the "Veiled Vestal," purchased by the Duke of Devonshire, or the BASHFUL BEGGAR, by GANDOLFI, of Milan, which we here engrave. The veil over the face is so rendered as to appear transparent; the fingers are also dimly seen through the thin drapery that covers the hands of the figure.

Mr. WEST, of Dublin, an eminent gold and silversmith of that city, exhibits a variety of BROOCHES, made after the fashion of

those worn by "the daughters of Erin" some centuries ago.

Messrs. MINTON, & Co., of Stoke-upon-Trent, Staffordshire, exhibit some excellent FLOWER-VASES, coloured after the style of the old Majolica. The quiet tone of

That at the foot of our page is an entirely new design, and is the

colour he has adopted for their fanciful surfaces evinces the very best taste.

brooch presented by the people of Dublin to Miss Helen Faucit.

Another of the most extensive silversmiths and jewellers of Paris, M. GUEYTON, contributes to the Exhibition a very large variety of his manufactures, consisting of almost every descrip-

tion of *bijouterie* and *virtu*. We engrave on this page a few we have selected from the many. The first is an unique ORNAMENT for the corner of a

centre ornament. The large engraving is from a PERFUME VASE, in which the handles are not

the body is ornamented with an embossed

plants, and fish; the lid is surmounted by a

less distinguished by novelty than by good taste, though they may here seem somewhat too large:

running pattern of oak-leaves, acorns, aqueous

vulture, which seems ready to pounce on the

book-cover; next follows a HAND LOOKING-GLASS of very elegant pattern. The BRACELET on the top of the page is a beautiful specimen of jewellery, with its winged figures supporting the

prey beneath. The CASKET is an admirable specimen of the cinque-cento style: the pattern

is engraved with much delicacy, while the figures of the key-escutcheon are in bold relief.

The OTTOMAN, exhibited by M. BALNY, of Paris, is a very elegant and novel mode of treating an article of furniture which, in general, has nothing to recommend it but unadorned utility.

M. Balny has shown how such objects may be made elegant and artistic, by using the centre of the ottoman as a pedestal for a statue; the idea has both novelty and ingenuity to recommend it.

M. VITTOZ of Paris contributes a BRONZE CLOCK, the design embracing a group of emblematical figures supporting a starry globe, upon which the hours are indicated by a serpent.

The establishment of Messrs. BROADWOOD of London has a reputation all over the world for its manufacture of pianos; and it would be superfluous to offer any observations as to their merited celebrity. Our business is less with the quality of the instrument than with the appearance of its case; and the GRAND PIANO we engrave is for this reason alone deserving of especial attention. The inlaid and ornamental work upon its surface is of the best

kind, and is very tastefully arranged; it is composed of ebony inlaid, the ornaments in gold relief; the legs are particularly novel and elegant.

The manufactory of Messrs. H. & W. TURNER, of Sheffield, is exclusively devoted to the production of the best description of FIRE-IRONS, for which it is famous in "the trade." We have, in former pages of our Catalogue, given some examples of their works; we now give one of a form equally novel and graceful. These fire-irons are termed by the makers "Cyma-Recta," and they certainly present in their curved lines a more elegant appearance than the old-fashioned straight irons now in common use. This will occur to all who examine the objects, which we expect to see very generally adopted.

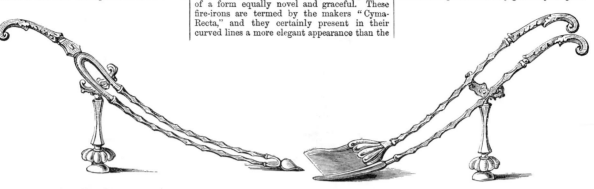

Undoubtedly one of the most superb specimens of cabinet-work to be seen in the Exhibition, is the SIDEBOARD, of carved walnut-wood, by M. FOURDINOIS, of Paris. Whether we consider the elaborate richness of the design, or its skilful execution, we must award it the very highest merit. The multiplicity of details that make up the composition entirely preclude the possibility of our giving anything like a satisfactory description of the work; but the artist and engraver have each done his work so well, that our engraving amply supplies any deficiency of explanatory remark. The style of the Renaissance has certainly never been more successfully carried out in an article of furniture, than in this example of French taste and skill. It is beyond question one of the most meritorious articles of its class in the Exhibition, whether we regard the varied beauty of the design, or its execution.

From the manufactory of Count HAR-RACH, in Bohemia, many fine specimens of

the richly-coloured GLASS which gives the

country a peculiar reputation, are exhi-

bited. They show much quaintness of form as well as brilliancy of colour.

The bronze TABLE and VASE underneath are designed by Signor BERNARDI, of Milan, and are executed at the Prince of Salms' foundry, at Vienna; the FLOWER-STAND is executed by M. LEISTLER, in zebra-wood; the POTS are in coloured porcelain. The SIDEBOARD, also by M. LEISTLER, is magnificently carved in the wood of the locust tree; the top is a slab of *rosso antico*; the LAMPS on each side are designed by M. BERNARDI, and executed

by M. HOLLENBACH. The GLASS in the centre has a metal frame of rich design, and is by M. H. RATZERS-

DORFER, of Vienna. The Austrian department is one of the most attractive features of the Exhibition;

we have endeavoured to render it justice by the number and the quality of our various illustrations.

The establishment of M. Odiot ranks among the largest of the silversmiths in Paris. The visit we paid to France in the autumn of the past year afforded us an opportunity of inspecting the immense stock of manufactured articles

displayed in his show-rooms; and we must do M. Odiot the justice to say that his productions do him infinite credit in every way. We fill this page with five engravings, selected from his important contributions to the Exhibition; the

and truthfulness; the floriated ornaments on the handles are novel. The next subject is

composed of fish, and objects appertaining to the sport of angling, and the sides of the ink-

an INKSTAND, which is altogether a novelty in design; the ornamental group on its top is

stand are in harmony with them. The two TUREENS and DISHES that make up the remaining

illustrations are widely dissimilar, but each presenting features of beauty and novelty (we are

compelled to repeat the last word once more) that cannot fail to attract attention; the former,

reader will receive gratification from the novelty presented by the major part of them. Our first example is from a COFFEE-POT, of very elegant form and ornamentation. The CUP underneath is of exquisite workmanship; the figures on it are modelled with much freedom

though richly engraved and sculptured, presents in its ornaments a unity of idea, that seems

wanting in the latter, which, nevertheless, is a magnificent piece of sculptured silver-work.

The group of DESSERT SERVICE is contributed by Messrs. DANIELL, of London: it is remarkable not alone for much grace and elegance of design, but as a triumphant attempt to restore to fictile art the once famous rose colour, named after the favourite of Louis Quatorze, "Du Barry." In the works exhibited by Messrs. Daniell, and manufactured at Coalbrookdale, this beautiful colour is unquestionably improved upon: it has a far finer and richer tint, and perhaps may be regarded as one of the triumphs of the Exhibition. The PARIAN VASE is also a contribution by Messrs. Daniell.

The figure engraved underneath is from the statue of the FISHER BOY, by HIRAM POWERS, the distinguished American sculptor; it is a work in every way worthy of its high repute.

The eminent sculptor, GEEFS, of Antwerp, contributes a group designed from the old and beautiful national legend of GENEVIEVE OF BRABANT; who, wrongfully accused of infidelity, is

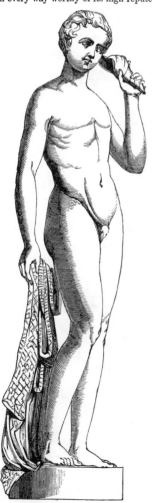

driven by her lord to the wilds of the forest, where she and her infant are succoured by a fawn until her innocence is established, and she is again sought by her deceived husband. The story is simply and touchingly told, and the group well composed by the accomplished artist.

The two objects which form the illustrations on the upper portion of this page are produced by Messrs. WHITE & PARLBY, of London, who carry on an establishment for the manufacture of ornaments in composition, principally for the decoration of rooms, but also, as our engravings show, for the lighter description of furniture. They exhibit the model of a room, as prepared for the gilder, painter, and upholsterer, with

groups of other productions, which must be regarded more as models than as finished works. The TABLE is one of such; it has long pendent leaves

ornamenting the column. The LADIES' WORK-TABLE is very elegant in design; its style is Italian, well arranged in all its various details.

In an earlier page of the Catalogue we introduced two single examples of the BRONZES of M. PAILLARD, of Paris; we now bring forward a GROUP, composed from his numerous contributions in the Exhibition. In the centre is a noble VASE, of porcelain, in the Louis Quatorze style, with bronze ornaments, festoons of flowers, and

figures. To the right is the well-known group of the "CUPIDS STRUGGLING FOR THE HEART."

The remainder of the composition is made up of statuettes, candelabra, vases, and other objects.

One is so apt to associate the manufacturing productions of Manchester with cotton and calicoes, as to feel some surprise to see an exhibition of beautiful GLASS-WORK emanating from that busy town. The engravings introduced on this page sufficiently testify to the position which the "metropolis of the north" may assume in the manufacture of fictile objects; moreover, it is not generally known that not less than twenty-five tons of flint-glass are, at

the present time, produced weekly in Manchester, where the establishment of Messrs. MOLINEAUX, WEBB, & Co., takes the lead in this department of industrial art. This house has now existed for nearly a quarter of a century,

other manufacturers in localities where such

glass is in no way inferior to the best in the

and its proprietors have paid such attention to the production of ornamental coloured glass, that it may be affirmed, without prejudice to

business is now carried on, that the Manchester

country. The first object we have engraved is

a SUGAR-BASIN, of cut prisms; by its side are a Grecian-shaped ruby JUG, and GOBLET to correspond, with richly-cut sunk diamonds; in the centre of the third column is a ruby gilt CHALICE,

in the mediæval style. The opalescent VASE at the bottom of the page is engraved after Flax-

man's design of "Diomed casting his spear at Mars;" and in the middle of the group to the

left of this are a ruby antique JUG and GOBLET, on which has been engraved the lotus-plant.

The Duchy of Saxe-Coburg has made great exertions to be worthily represented in the Exhibition. This might be looked for from the connection existing between that country and the Prince who has rendered such efficient service in bringing the vast industrial display to its present satisfactory condition; the land of his birth would naturally feel a double interest in doing her best to second his laudable efforts.

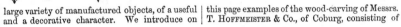

Hence we find, among her numerous contributions, many valuable natural productions, and a large variety of manufactured objects, of a useful and a decorative character. We introduce on this page examples of the wood-carving of Messrs. T. HOFFMEISTER & Co., of Coburg, consisting of

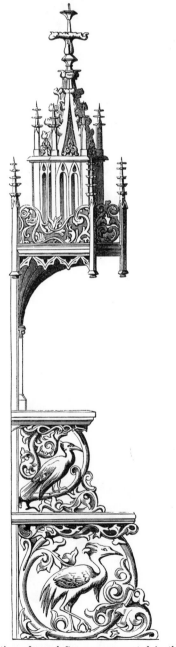

portions of an oak SIDEBOARD, executed in the German-Gothic style of the middle ages, and one of a series of four ARM-CHAIRS to match. The CROSS-PIECE at the top of the page is the upper part of the CANOPY seen underneath. The workmanship of these objects is exceedingly good.

The illustrations on this page form a portion

of the contributions from Malta, and are from

the sculptured works which have made the

Maltese department so attractive a part of the

Exhibition. The artists whose taste and skill have wrought out these truly beautiful productions are MM. Deccsaro, Dimech, Soler, S. and F.

Testa; we place them together because we have selected our engravings almost indiscriminately from their contributions, and because we consider them of equal excellence. Our space, moreover, precludes us from entering upon any

particular description of each illustration; it will be sufficient to remark that the mantles of some of the old Italian masters seem to have fallen on the shoulders of these Maltese sculptors, who exhibit so much "cunning workmanship" in their art. We would instance, as examples of rich and bold sculpture, the Vase with eagles, and the vine-leaf Jug, on the first

column, the former by S. Testa, and the latter by J. Soler; while, in the whole of the illustrations, the elaborate ornamentation of the Italian school is abundantly manifest. While we confess that our taste inclines more to the simplicity and elegance of the Greek compositions, we most readily award to these all the merit, and it is undoubtedly great, which belongs to them.

The gracefully-conceived group of EVE NURSING THE INFANTS CAIN AND ABEL, is by EUGENE LE BAY, a French sculptor of eminence; he has given it the title of "Le Premier Berceau," a

poetic term. appropriately applied to the group he has so tastefully designed and so well executed.

The RAZORS contributed by Mr. FENNEY, of Sheffield, are remarkable for the enriched character of the blade and handle; the former being a novelty with which we are but little

most extensive and meritorious in the kingdom; the whole process of forming the razor, from the rude materials of iron, horn, ivory, and tortoise-

acquainted; it is an additional proof that our manufacturers are studying the beauty of ornament, and its general applicability to all purposes. The establishment of W. Fenney is one of the

shell, is there conducted, and few more interesting works are to be seen in the emporium of the steel fabricants with which Sheffield abounds.

The very elegant COLOUR-BOX engraved below is exhibited by Messrs. ACKERMANN, of London, whose names have been so long associated with the Fine Arts. The outer bands and outlines of the running decoration are of gold; the flowers pink; the ground pale blue. The darkest parts of the ornament are of a deep grape colour, producing a rich and chaste effect. The box contains an extensive assortment of drawing materials.

The Stoves by Messrs. Jobson & Co., of Sheffield, are from designs by Mr. Walton, and manufactured for Messrs. Barton, of London. The first is especially designed to give due effect to polished steel, and has a very brilliant appearance, owing to the twisted ornament adopted for its decoration. It is one of those designs so expressly adapted for the peculiarities of the

Messrs. T. J. & J. Mayer, of the Dale-hall Pottery, near Burslem, exhibit, among numerous

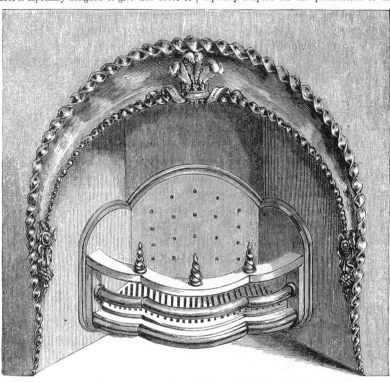

material in which it is to be constructed, that it is only fully to be appreciated by viewing it thus worked out. Our second cut exhibits a new design for the patent light and heat-reflecting stoves, which have given Mr. Jobson a peculiar reputation; the power possessed by the circular

other contributions, the Tea-Urns, Vases, and Cup, delineated on this and the succeeding

reflector which surrounds the fire-grate is very great, and more effective in throwing forward and economising heat, than any previous invention of the kind with which we have been made acquainted. It is also elegant in form, and the ornaments are judiciously connected with it.

column. We are so accustomed to see the first-named objects manufactured in metal, that any of a ceramic substance must be regarded as a novelty: they are made, however, of a highly

vitrified stoneware that will resist the action of

extreme variations of temperature, and are,

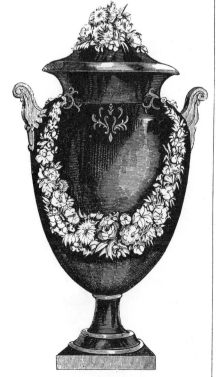

consequently, well adapted to their purposes.

The DECORATIVE PANEL, in the style of Edward I., is designed by Mr. W. F. D'ALMAINE, of London. In the centre is a figure of Queen Eleanor, executed on a gold diapered ground.

Among the SILK manufactures of Messrs. WINKWORTH & PROCTERS, of Manchester, is a piece, from which we take the annexed engraving; the convolvulus and wheat are well arranged.

This artistic design for a LAMP, fitted for the court-yard of a palace, is by the architect BERNARDO DE BERNARDIS, and has been executed in bronze at the foundry of the Prince of Salms at Vienna. It is executed with considerable ability, as good an example of manufacture as of design, both being in their own way excellent. The TABLE on the upper portion of our page is by MICHAEL THONET, of Vienna, its top is elaborately inlaid with woods of various colours; we give one half of this to display the beauty and intricacy of the design. This top lifts and a receptacle beneath of a semi-spherical form is

opened which has some peculiarities of construction: it is formed of rosewood, so bent that the grain of the wood invariably follows the line of the curve and shape required, by which means lightness and elasticity is gained, with the least possible material. The legs are similarly bent from the solid piece; the table being entirely constructed of rosewood and walnut, slightly inlaid with delicate lines of brasswork, as an outline to the principal forms.

The large TABLE at the foot of the page is by M. LEISTLER, and is of rosewood and locust tree in the sumptuous style of later Venetian taste. We have engraved several other contributions by M. Leistler, in previous pages of our Catalogue, all of them testifying to the ability which

guides his hand-labour, and, more than all, to the right direction of taste in the primary forms of design exhibited in the varied works he has sent to England. The massive scrolls, forming the legs of this table, are carved with great boldness of execution combined with delicacy.

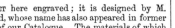

M. RINGUET LEPRINCE, of Paris, exhibits, with other objects of decorative furniture, one of which we have previously introduced, the large

CABINET here engraved; it is designed by M. Lienard, whose name has also appeared in former pages of our Catalogue. The materials of which

The objects on this column are from the orna-

mental STONEWARE, contributed by M. MANSARD,

of Paris. They are similar to the Beauvais.

it is constructed are ebony and pear-tree wood : | the design and workmanship are excellent.

The Cup is by Mr. GARRARD, the eminent silversmith; its principal feature is a group of St. George and the Dragon.

M. SIMONIS, of Brussels, the distinguished sculptor, whose colossal figure of Godfrey de Bouillon has attracted such marked attention, has contributed some familiar transcripts of nature, which, although of much smaller dimensions, are to many equally attractive. "THE HAPPY CHILD" which we here engrave is one of these works; the infant is playing with a toy Punchinello. The statue is life-size, executed in marble.

Mr. J. E. CAREW, the eminent sculptor, realises very charmingly WHITTINGTON LISTENING TO THE BELLS OF LONDON.

Messrs. ACKROYD & SON, of Halifax, exhibit the elaborate DAMASK for hangings, a portion of which we engrave. It is designed in the style which pervades the Alhambra, and is carefully and exactly carried out, in strict accordance with its peculiarities. The pattern we have selected is red upon a ground of rich deep blue.

"THE UNHAPPY CHILD" below is the work of M. SIMONIS, of Brussels, a companion figure to "The Happy Child," which we have also engraved. The boy has broken his drum. and, in a violent fit of temper, has kicked his clothing about his feet till they have become entangled, and add to his ebullition of rage. The work is most truthful.

The TESTIMONIAL CUP, of silver, by Messrs. GARRARD, of London, is a most spirited and artistic work of its class.

The DAMASK CURTAIN is also by MESSRS. T. ACKROYD & SON, of Halifax; it is very rich in colour, the flowers being white, the leaves and ornaments in various tints of

A graceful statue, by PUTTINATI, of Milan, which he

orange, on a ground of deep crimson. It is a very successful and artistic production, quite worthy of being placed beside the best works of this class in the Great Exhibition.

terms MORNING PRAYER, is full of the best feeling generated by the choice of a subject replete with sentiment.

The importation of foreign WATCHES into England is carried on to a considerable extent,

although, we believe, that since our manufacturers have learned to combine cheapness with

excellence, a large diminution has taken place in the number imported. The watch-makers of Switzerland have long maintained their pre-

A CHEVAL SCREEN, carved and gilt. is exhibited by Mr. T. NICOLL, of London; it is so constructed that by a simple process it may be converted into a stand for lights, a music-stand,

eminence in this branch of industrial art by the ingenuity and skill which they have brought to bear on their productions; so that the watches

of that country find a ready sale throughout the continents of Europe and America. We have engraved on this page six out of several which

M. PATEK, of Geneva, has contributed to the Exhibition. By a simple and ingenious mechanism, the use of watch-keys is rendered unnecessary in

and a table. In the centre is a Pastil painting, by Mr. A. Blaikley, representing Peace and Plenty; the composition of the picture is highly pleasing, while the design of the frame is good.

some of them; a screw in the handle, when turned, winds up the watch, and, by another movement, equally simple, regulates the hands.

A CHESS-BOARD and CHESS-MEN, in silver and gold, richly ornamented with jewels, enamels, &c., is exhibited by MESSRS. PHILLIPS. of London, but made by Messrs. C. M. Wieshaupt and Sons, of Hanau. Germany. The figures were modelled by M. E. Von Launitz, the sculptor, of Frankfort.

The female figure is from one of the "Queens" in the set of Chess-Men; she is habited in the

A Statue, in plaster, entitled "THE BATHER," is exhibited by Mr. J. LAWLOR, a clever sculptor,

One of the "Kings" of the Chess-Men is here introduced, whose costume is in harmony with

costume worn in the early part of the sixteenth century by the royal princesses of Germany.

who has executed several excellent productions.

its companion on the opposite side. The whole of this work is singularly unique and beautiful.

The above engraving illustrates the lower portion of the CARVED FRAME, of which we gave the upper part in a preceding page. It is carved by Professor ALBERTY, of Berlin, from a design by M. Stüler.

Messrs. LITHGOW & PURDIE, of Edinburgh, exhibit the very chaste and beautiful design for

A carved MANTEL-PIECE, by M. CONTÉ, of London, deserves to be highly commended for its chaste style of ornament. M. Conté is an Italian

artist, who has long resided in London, where, in his atelier, we have seen very many most elegant works in marble, especially some statuettes.

The SIDEBOARD by Messrs. HINDLEY, of London, is in the later Gothic style, and is peculiarly appropriate for one of those mansions in

which that form of decoration predominates. For a work of this kind, however, the style presents peculiar excellencies, as it has a singu-

the PANELLING of a saloon, indicative of "The Seasons." The style is Italian, of the best order.

larly solid character, and is capable of the boldest relief of light and shade. Floral decoration, in

conjunction with geometric form, has advantages which may be of great value to the designer.

A CARRIAGE, termed "The Diorapha" by the inventors and builders, Messrs. ROCK & SON, of | Hastings, possesses the advantage of being used either as a close carriage, a barouche, or entirely | open; it is therefore well adapted for all seasons and weathers. The transformations are easily made.

The VASE or Cup engraved underneath is sculptured in marble by M. VANLINDEN, of Antwerp. The body shows four bas-reliefs

A GOTHIC VASE of rich pale red terra-cotta, excellent in design, and of admirable workmanship, is modelled and exhibited by Mr. J. PULHAM, of

designed from Spenser's Faerie Queene, "Cupid trying his bow," "Cupid the conqueror of the mighty," "Fidelity," and "The end of his occupation;" at the top of the vase Cupid is represented as captive to Venus, who has bound the "mischievous boy" with roses.

Broxbourne, Hertfordshire. It stands on a granulated pedestal of similar character, which, like the vase, shows great sharpness and delicacy of execution.

Mr. BROOKER, of Maryport, exhibits the FIGURE-HEAD OF A SHIP, representing Ceres in search of Proserpine, discovering the veil she has dropped. It is a very meritorious attempt to elevate the character of such works.

The FOUNTAIN below is of iron, and is from the manufactory of Mr. HANDYSIDE, of Derby, whose beautiful vase we have already engraved.

Mr. WALLER, whose work on "Monumental Brasses" has rendered his name familiar to the antiquary, has exhibited a BRASS, exemplifying the adaptation of modern costume to monumental design. It represents a female figure, with a greyhound at her feet, beneath a canopy of enriched pointed architecture. In the shafts, which on either side support the canopy, are compartments, containing subjects from the six works of mercy, according to Matthew, xxv., 35, 36. The subject which occupies the centre of the canopy, is that of "The Good Samaritan." That on the apex is a group representing "Charity," and the two brackets each contain a subject from Psalm lxxxv., 10, "Mercy and truth are met together; righteousness and peace have kissed each other."

The two knives are from the well-known establishment of Messrs. J. RODGERS & SONS, of Sheffield. The first is a silver-handled BOWIE-KNIFE, and the second a silver DESSERT-KNIFE with engraved blade; the designs of both are good. This firm well sustains its reputation.

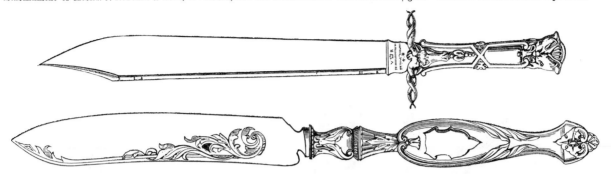

The Milanese sculptors, who, though under the political government of Austria, and exhibiting their productions in the Austrian department, have a closer affinity with the arts of Italy, contribute well and largely to the Exhibition. M. SANGIORGIO has sent four figures, from which we select one, called "L'ALMA," re-

presenting a soul ascending to heaven. The subject is one not easily susceptible of illustration; the figure is, nevertheless, very graceful.

We introduce here the central design of a COVER for a child's cradle or bassinet, manufactured and exhibited by Messrs. D. & J. MACDONALD, of Glasgow. The material whereof it is made is cambric, the plain ground of which, by the ingenuity and skill wherewith the needle

has been applied, is transformed into "point," most perfectly executed. The establishment of Messrs. Macdonald is among the most extensive in Glasgow, employing thirty thousand hands.

The manufactures of M. VAN KEMPEN. of Utrecht, gold and silversmith to the King of the Netherlands, manifest great beauty of design. and very excellent workmanship; examples of lands, William II.; in the niches are statues of six of the most famous princes of the houses of

some of his contributions appear on this and the next page. The first is a CASKET, in the pseudo-antique style of the Renaissance; it is bold in its design. The next is a table INKSTAND, in the

Orange and Nassau, from 752 to 1544; the lid is surmounted by that of Adolphus of Nassau,

style denominated Louis Quatorze; the attitude of the figure on each side is not less novel than pleasing. The TEA-SERVICE, in the same style, may claim a similar remark. The HAND-BELL

at the head of the next column also shows the Louis Quatorze ornaments and form. The VASE underneath is of Gothic style; it was made by M. Van Kempen for the late King of the Nether-

who became Emperor of Germany; this cup is a very beautiful specimen of silver-work. The

HAND-BELL on the next page is another example of the Louis Quatorze style, and the CUP that

follows it shows that of the Renaissance to great

advantage : it is exceedingly graceful in form.

The annexed engraving is from one of the few ornamental objects of industrial art contributed by the Swiss Cantons ; it is a lady's ESCRITOIRE, manufactured of white wood by M. WETTLI, of Berne, and is so constructed that it may be used at pleasure for a writing-table in a sitting or a standing posture. The ornamentation is unique and characteristic ; the figures which appear in the different parts represent the rustic economy and Alpine life of the inhabitants of Switzerland ; many of whom, while tending their flocks, amuse themselves with carving various objects.

The CABINET underneath is manufactured by M. FOURDINOIS, of Paris ; the material of which it is made is ebony, the moulding and ornaments are of brass gilt, the panels of tortoiseshell, inlaid with buhl. In this, as in many other objects of French cabinet-work, we cannot but

notice the purity of style that exists throughout the entire design, by which its true nature is so much enhanced. Ornament, like extravagant colouring in a picture, only attracts observation to its defects, unless it be accompanied by taste in its selection, and great skill in its adaptation.

The light PHAETON, by Messrs. BROWN, OWEN, & Co., of Birmingham, possesses all the requisites of convenience and elegance which characterise modern carriage-building, in England: the shafts are made of steel.

The noble old romance, the "Nie-belungen Lied," has furnished FERN-

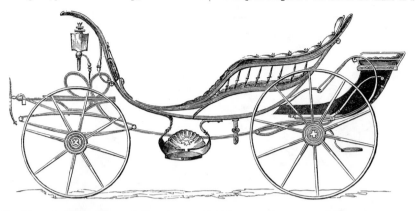

The SHAWL by Messrs. KEITH & SHOOBRIDGE, of London, is a tasteful and elaborate design, remarkable for harmony of colour, as well as for intricacy of composition. It is printed by Mr. Swaisland, of Crayford.

KORN with subjects for characteristic

statues, executed in bronze at the foundry of the Prince of Salms, at Vienna.

The MARLBOROUGH TESTIMONIAL, one of the striking groups by Messrs. HUNT & ROSKELL, represents John, Duke of Marlborough, writing the despatch of his great victory at Blenheim on the drum-head brought to him on the battle-field, as the only available desk on which to announce the important event to Englishmen at home. The note written on this occasion still exists among the family archives. The group surmounting the pedestal is modelled with great truth and spirit; the pedestal itself is a bold example of the Louis Quatorze style of ornament.

A SIDEBOARD, carved in walnut-wood, is the entire work—design and execution—of Mr. H. HOYLE, of Sheffield, a young man who is largely indebted to the Sheffield School of Design, of which he is a pupil, for the great ability displayed in this production. It has been executed under considerable difficulties, the producer having to labour at one of the manufactories in the town three days in the week for his maintenance, while he devoted the remaining three to the sideboard here engraved. It is a well-studied and very beautiful example of carved wood-work.

The CHAIR engraved below is made by Mr. G. COLLINSON, of Doncaster. Independent of its merits as an example of rustic furniture, there is a little history attaching to it, which enhances its interest. About three years since, two oak trees, measuring together two hundred feet of timber, were found below the floor of the river Dun out-fall drain, then being dug at Arksey, near Doncaster, by Mr. W. Chadwick, of that place, for whom, we believe, the chair has been manufactured. It is presumed, by those acquainted with the locality where these trees were found, that they must have been buried in the soil upwards of two thousand years.

Mr. AMOS HOLD, of Ardsley, near Barnsley, in Yorkshire, contributes an object of manufacture which proves the spread of artistic knowledge; it is a FRAME, elegantly carved in pine-wood.

The engraving underneath represents a portion of a CARPET, manufactured by Mr. B. H. WOODWARD & Co., of Kidderminster, and designated a "five-frame carpet." The advantages which we understand this peculiar fabric offers, are warmth, cleanliness, and durability; the capability of being made either in Brussels, Tournay, Wilton, or velvet-pile qualities; and facilities

for change of colours in the same design. The pattern we have engraved is one especially adapted for effecting these desirable results.

The illustration placed across the top of this page represents the upper part of a FRAME, carved by Professor ALBERTY, Member of the Berlin Academy of Arts, from a design by M. Stüler, principal architect to the King of Prussia. The design is successfully executed.

The CABINET, which appears beneath, is engraved from one manufactured and exhibited by Mr. J. W. INGRAM, of Islington, Birmingham; it is made of wood, decorated by the enamel process, with electro-gilt metal mouldings, forming a chaste and somewhat unique object of cabinet-work. The decorations are of a description to tell more effectively in the original, than in any illustration, however carefully executed.

The FENDER is another of those exhibited by Messrs. ROBERTSON, CARR, & STEEL, of Sheffield, and, like most of the productions of this firm, is characterised by a judicious combination of elegance with utility: it is of polished steel.

A WINDOW of stained and painted glass is exhibited by Mr. G. HEDGELAND, of London; its style harmonises with the decorated period of Gothic architecture; the background is executed with reference to the peculiar character-

The engraving underneath is somewhat of a deviation from the plan we have adopted with reference to machinery of every description; but the MILL here represented may be accepted as proof, that even to machinery may be given elegance of form and character. The manufacturers are Messrs. S. ADAMS & CO.,

of Oldbury, near Birmingham, whose object has been, in their invention, to construct a mill, more durable, yet not more expensive, than those in ordinary use.

istics of that style, as existing in the best examples of ecclesiastical decoration. The work is, in all respects, one of considerable merit.

A LACE SHAWL is manufactured by Mr. W. VICKERS, of Nottingham, from what is termed the "pusher bobbin net machine;" the work is exceedingly delicate.

Mr. PENNY, of London, whose mountings for carriage harness we have engraved elsewhere, exhibits some elegant heraldic SKEWERS; the handle of one is seen illustrated underneath.

Among the beautiful shawls and scarves exhibited by Mr. BLAKELEY, of Norwich, of whose contributions by the way, we gave specimens in an earlier number of our Catalogue, is an elegant SCARF of Cashmere, of which a portion is here engraved: in its simple yet elegant design, and

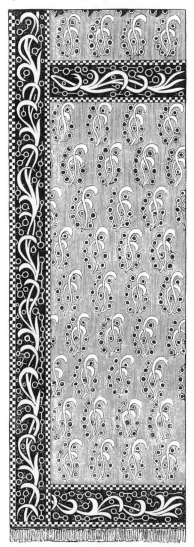

in tasteful arrangement of colour, it is every thing to be desired. We understand the scarf has been purchased at the Exhibition by the Queen.

Mr. SANGSTER, of London, exhibits some very beautiful WHIP-HANDLES, displaying an amount

of fancy and picturesque applicability to their uses which evince a well directed taste and

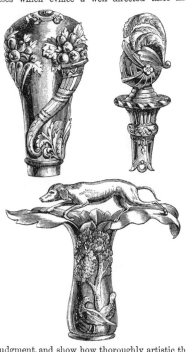

judgment, and show how thoroughly artistic the most ordinary article of use may be made. An

UMBRELLA-HANDLE and PARASOL-TOP concludes our series, which exhibit much originality.

The exhibition of LADIES FANS by M. DU-VILLEROI, of London and Paris, is unique; all that taste and ingenuity can devise in the way

of ornament may be seen among the variety contributed, any one of which is worthy of the ladies who graced the courts of Queen Anne or Louis XIV., to whom fans were always indispensable.

THE INDUSTRY OF ALL NATIONS.

A decorative picture for a CEILING is exhibited by Mr. HERVIEU, of London. Britannia is personified in her Sovereign leaning on Peace, and supported by Religion. She presides at the convention of Agriculture, Commerce, Science, and the Arts, and has called around her the representatives of all nations. The genius of Immortality bears a crown to Britannia, and other genii offer palms to the various representatives of the Industrial Arts: it is a spirited composition.

The two objects underneath are from the productions of Messrs. MARREL, Frères, of Paris: one is a MINIATURE FRAME, in gold and oxydised

silver the other a large VASE with silver ornaments, executed for the Duc d'Aumale.

The annexed illustration is from a CASHMERE DRESS, manufactured by Messrs. T. GREGORY, Brothers, of Halifax, by direction of Prince Albert, for the Queen. It is made from the wool of a favourite goat, belonging to her Majesty. The design, which is simple but elegant, is by Mr. G. Odely.

Mr. THORNYCROFT has realised the tale of the youthful KING ALFRED TAUGHT BY HIS MOTHER, who places the illuminated book before him as an inducement to cultivate that knowledge, for which he ultimately became conspicuous; the composition of the group is spirited and clever.

The PIANOFORTE here introduced is manufactured by M. PAPE, of Lon-

Messrs. CLABBURN & Co., of Norwich, exhibit a large variety of the textile fabrics for which this city is famous; shawls, poplins, brocades,

hunting-wrappers, &c. We engrave here one of their POPLIN patterns, of an exceedingly neat and pretty design, that is most effective in the fabric.

don, Paris, and Brussels; it is made to serve as a table when shut down.

A SALVER is termed by Messrs. R. & S. GARRARD, the manufacturers, "The Great Railway Salver;" it being a testimonial presented to Mr. Brassey, (the famous and universally-respected railway contractor) by the sub-contractors and workmen in his employ. It is of silver, and in the compartments around are enamel portraits of the chief railway engineers; above each, respectively, is a view of his principal work.

The GROUP OF STATUARY is a most spirited production, by M. JERICHAU, of Copenhagen. It represents a man

We have already had occasion to notice the contributions of Messrs. FEETHAM, of London, who exhibit various works in iron of a very artistic kind; we here engrave one of their principal works, a FIREPLACE of great beauty, displaying a large amount of ornament of a well-studied character. The sides are decorated with slabs

defending himself from a tigress, whose cub he has taken.

of china designed in an elaborate interlaced pattern, enriched with coloured studs in raised work, similar to the old jewelled porcelain.

The group of ECCLESIASTICAL VESSELS, &c., are | selected from a large variety of those quaint and | beautiful works, designed by Mr. Pugin, and exe-

cuted by Messrs. J. HARDMAN & Co., of Birming- | ham. They fully realise the style and artistic | feeling of the best works of the middle ages

The CABINET here engraved is one of the most | important pieces of furniture in the Medieval | Court; it is executed by Mr. CRACE, of London.

The furniture of the Medieval Court forms one of the most striking portions of the Exhibition, and has attracted a large amount of attention. The design and superintendence of these articles are by Mr. Pugin,

an artist who has studied the leading principles of medieval composition, and ornamental design, until his works are identified whenever they are seen. He has been ably seconded by Mr. Crace, who has

executed his designs. The two specimens on this page are their joint productions. The Prie-Dieu is very elegant, and is enriched with painting and gilding. The Cabinet is of oak, richly carved, and is decorated with characteristic brass-work of exceedingly bold design.

On this and the succeeding page are engravings from the Monumental Cross, designed and executed by the Hon. Mrs. Ross of Bladensburg, Ireland. It is sixteen feet high, and measures more than six feet across the arms. The object of this lady's design has been to illustrate, on one side of the

cross, the chief features of the Gospel, as typified in the Old Testament. The subjects selected for this purpose are "Moses and the Brazen Serpent," "The Translation of Elijah," "Noah entering the Ark," "Abel's Sacrifice," with busts of the prophets Isaiah, Jeremiah, Ezekiel, and Daniel, from each one of whose writings an appropriate text is introduced. On the opposite side, the same idea is maintained, by sculptures selected from New Testament history; "The Crucifixion," "The Resurrection," "The Return of the Prodigal," "The Good Shepherd," accompanied by busts of St. Peter, St. John, St. James, and

The LECTERN, of bronze, is the work of Messrs. HARDMAN, of Birmingham. It is an exceedingly beautiful production; a truthful rendering of the best antique style in all its varied enrichments.

The CABINET of oak, decorated with carving of the richest descrip-

St. Paul, with texts from their writings also. The north and south elevations of the cross are ornamented with busts, and the circle with emblematic grapes and wheat. The design, object, and execution of the entire work are equally honourable to the accomplished lady by whom it has been produced.

tion, is by Mr. MYERS, of Lambeth, who has contributed a large number of the finest articles in wood and stone to the Medieval Court.

The CHANDELIERS and LECTERN are executed

by Messrs. HARDMAN, of Birmingham, in brass-

work. They are excellent examples of modern

manufacture, unsurpassed in careful fabrication.

Mr. MYERS, of Lambeth, has contributed the very beautiful FONT which forms the centre of the group of Ecclesiastical Objects gathered in the Great Exhibition. The Font is sculptured

in stone, and stands on three steps. It is elaborately and beautifully enriched; the canopy above is of wood; the cover to the font rising into it when the sacred ceremony is performed.

The canopied STATUE OF THE VIRGIN AND SAVIOUR is entirely of stone, also executed by Mr. MYERS,

of Lambeth. We engrave beneath it the top of a

Gothic SCREEN, of the Flamboyant style, in oak.

The engraving on this column is from an ornamental GOBLET, modelled by M. CONRAD KNOLL, of Munich, and intended to be cast in bronze. It is in the true German style of the earlier period.

The merits of Mr. W. HARRY ROGERS as a designer we have long recognised, and have repeatedly availed ourselves of his talents in connection with our Journal; we were, therefore, pleased to see in the Exhibition a large number of ornamental works, manufactured from the designs he has furnished to the producers, as well as many subjects from his pencil applicable to future manufactures. Whatever Mr. Rogers puts forth is characterised by the purest taste, a taste which is fostered by an intimate acquaintance with the best works of the medieval ages. We introduce here a design for a KEY, in the Italian style; other illustrations from his hand will be found on the last page of our Catalogue.

The annexed illustration is also from a GOBLET, modelled in plaster of Paris, by M. J. HALBIG, of Munich; it is in the German Gothic style.

The contributions of M. FROMENT-MEURICE, of Paris, include a magnificent BRACELET, presented by subscription to her Royal Highness the Countess of Chambord, one of the old Bourbon family, by the ladies of Marseilles. In the centre are the arms of the city, surmounted by a mural crown; on each side are portraits, in enamel, of characters celebrated in the history of Marseilles, supporting a warrior in the

costume of the period, and a female, also accoutred, as indicative of the courage displayed by the women of the city when it was besieged in 1524. This unique article of jewellery is executed in the highest style of ornamental Art.

The engraving underneath represents a CHILD'S ROBE, of muslin, richly embroidered, from the extensive manufactory of Messrs. S. & T. BROWN, of Glasgow; the pattern is elaborate and beautiful.

Among the statuary in the Sculpture Court, stands Mr. THEED'S life-size statue of NARCISSUS; he is represented leaning on his hunting-spear, and contemplating his reflection in the stream.

Messrs. MARREL, Frères, of Paris, exhibit, among other objects, a beautiful VASE, of gold

A DRESSING-CASE, made of yew-tree wood, is exhibited by Mr. STRUDWICK, of London. The

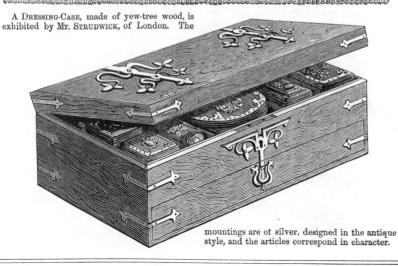

mountings are of silver, designed in the antique style, and the articles correspond in character.

and enamel, designed in the purest Venetian style, and most artistically executed throughout.

The Jewels of the Queen of Spain are exhibited by M. LEMONIER, of Paris: we have engraved such of them as we consider most suitable for

illustration; it is almost unnecessary to add that all are of the most costly

description, and exquisitely set. Our first illustration is a TIARA, or

head-dress, of sapphires and diamonds; the next is an ORNAMENT for the

head, of emeralds and diamonds. most elegantly arranged as a bouquet; an AIGUILLETTE, or shoulder-knot, of diamonds, pearls, and a large emerald follows, by the side of which is a BROOCH, of pink pearls and diamonds; a BRACELET, of emeralds, and diamonds, completes the series.

Among the most successful productions in decorative furniture contributed by continental artisans may be classed the TABLE AND CHAIR we here engrave, and which are designed and executed in strict accordance with classic models; indeed there is no portion of these articles without

strict adherence in form and enrichment to antique authority. Ebony and ivory enter into their material as lavishly as they did into the furniture of the higher classes of Greece and Rome. They have been executed for the King of Sardinia by G. CAPELLO, of Turin, and are deserving of a

place in the palace of any sovereign. The Curule Chair is a really fine work, graceful in its general form, and enriched by the ornament of the best period of Grecian taste; when decorative Art received from that wonderful people an impetus and an ultimate perfection which has stamped it with an individual character of the most unmistakeable kind.

The proprietors of the GRANGE-MOUTH COAL AND FIRECLAY WORKS exhibit a large number of useful

articles, constructed in their improved material, which contains a

large amount of silica and alumina, both of the most essential use in the

production of an infusible fireclay. The VASES which fill our column are

made from this material. and are, therefore, well adapted for gardens.

The elegant CASKET we have here engraved. is of ivory, with or-molu mountings, by M. MATIFAT, of Paris.

An octagon TABLE, of which the top is here engraved. is an elaborate specimen of marquetrie, executed by Mr. G. WATSON, of Paddington, who has exhibited extraordinary taste and perseverance in its production.

M. GASSER, of Vienna, exhibits a FLOWER-VASE of metal.

Mr. J. BELL, the sculptor, exhibits the group engraved underneath; the subject is "Una and the Lion," to which the title of PURITY is given. It is a highly poetical work.

The figure in a devotional attitude is by Mr. P. MAC-

A rich and costly BEDSTEAD, carved in walnut wood, is exhibited by Messrs. ROGERS & DEAR,

DOWELL, R.A., who calls it "MORNING PRAYER."

of London; with its magnificent and costly hangings, it presents a most splendid appearance.

The display of jewellery in the Exhibition, whether of English or of foreign manufacture, naturally attracts no little attention. Whatever

is costly in itself, without any especial reference to the amount of human ingenuity expended upon adding to its primary value, is generally a matter of interest; thus the great Koh-i-noor

diamond finds crowds of admirers, though its brilliancy is unaided by the hand of the goldsmith; still it must be acknowledged that precious stones of every description lose much

of their splendour when seen apart from their settings; and on the taste of the jeweller, his knowledge of the qualities each jewel possesses, and his capability to draw out these qualities to

We introduce on this page an engraving from a rich figured CASHMERE SHAWL, manufactured by Messrs. CLABBURN, SONS, & CRISP, of Norwich, which, we understand, was purchased by

the best advantage, mainly depends the beauty of the stone, presuming it to be properly cut, which also is an operation requiring considerable skill and judgment. The jewellery engraved on

the Queen. It is a first attempt, in Norwich, at shawl-weaving in a Jacquard loom. For fineness of texture, variety and beauty of colours, and elegance of pattern, it cannot be surpassed.

this page is contributed by Messrs. PHILLIPS, Brothers, of London, and is very elegant. Of the BROOCHES, the first consists of diamonds set in gold and green enamel; the next is a cameo

surrounded with diamonds, on blue enamel; the eagle is also of diamonds; the third is of diamonds alone. The first BRACELET has diamonds and amethysts set in green enamel, with golden links; the other is of blue and white enamel, on which musical notes are represented.

An INKSTAND, in the cinque-cento style, is exhibited by M. F. SCHNEIDER, of Berlin. It is an elaborately ornamented and most beautiful work of art, full of subject which would occupy a large space to describe fully; our explanation, therefore, must necessarily be brief. It is made partly of gold, and partly of silver, gilt and enamelled; the extended wings of the Prussian eagle in front serve as pen-holders; the bird is overcoming the dragon, the source of all evil; behind this is the vessel for ink, over which preside two winged figures, emblematical of Peace and Happiness. The groups in the framework at the back signify the moral and Christian Virtues, and scenes of a domestic character, &c.: the design and execution are alike excellent.

The magnificent JEWEL-CASE engraved underneath is exhibited by the QUEEN, whose property it is, and who has, with great kindness and condescension, permitted it to be placed in the Crystal Palace. Like the preceding object on this page, it is in the cinque-cento style, and executed by Messrs. Elkington, of Birmingham, from a design by Mr. L. Grüner. The material is bronze, gilt and silvered by the electrotype process; upon the front of the case are enamel portraits, by Bone, of her Majesty, Prince Albert, and the Prince of Wales, copied from miniatures by R. Thorburn, A.R.A., besides small medallions, representing profiles of the other juvenile branches of the Royal Family, modelled from life by Mr. Leonard Wyon. At the top are two Cupids, bearing the royal crown, surmounted by the British lion. On the back, which is represented in our engraving, are the royal arms, and those of Prince Albert, surrounded by wreaths of laurel, &c.; the caryatides at the angles of the case are novelties in an object of this description, but they impart great elegance to it. The whole of the ornamental work is in the purest taste, and most exquisitely engraved.

From the designs exhibited by Mr. W. HARRY ROGERS we select three specimens exhibiting much ability in their composition, and an intimate knowledge of the peculiarities of the Italian

artist, of thorough applicability to the uses of the workman and the necessities of the fabric he

and another, the centre one, of a similar character. The remaining designs for manufacturers by this artist are for bookclasps, encaustic tiles, pipes, gold spoons, keys, a crozier, and a

style of the sixteenth century, in which some of his happiest efforts appear, and to which few have given so much attention and study. There is the great advantage in the designs by this

employs. We engrave two views of a SPOON for a tea-caddy intended to be carved in box-wood,

royal cradle. We may add, the head and tail-pieces which decorate our present Catalogue, are from the pencil of Mr. Rogers; they manifest his fertility of invention and the suitability of his designs.

By ROBERT HUNT, Esq.,
Keeper of Mining Records Museum of Practical Geology.

PART I.

T is a noble object to test by actual experiment to what extent the ingenuity and skill of the nations of the earth has corresponded to the intentions of their Creator, and to improve the advantages which each country can offer the other in supplying the wants, and adding to the happiness of mankind."

The depth of meaning which is in this passage, part of an address delivered by Sir Robert Peel, at one of the Metropolian festivals, in honour of the progress of this Industrial Exhibition, admirably fits it for the motto of an essay, the purpose of which is to examine the progress made by the industry and intelligence of man, in rendering useful the raw materials of the several kingdoms of nature, and moulding its productions into forms of beauty.

Man—placed upon a strangely constituted globe, covered with all that is necessary for the sustenance of life—is compelled by the necessities of his condition, to exert his intellectual powers in devising means by which he may be sheltered from the summer heats and the winter colds. This impulsive power drives him to the study of nature—he cannot create, but everything which is created he can fashion to his desire; but to do this he must obey the great physical laws, by which the conditions of all matter is determined, and to obey them they must be known, and to be known, natural phenomena must be attentively observed.

Every step made by man has ever been an example of induction, often obscure, and scarcely traceable as such; but upon close examination such it will be found to have been.

Man witnesses a fact, it recurs again and again, experience thus gives him information concerning the things around him, and eventually,—the progress is commonly slow,—he perceives that by the knowledge of that one fact, he may improve upon nature to his own advantage. Some baked clay taught the potter his useful art, and the *accidental* fusion of sea-sand instructed man in the manufacture of glass. By a similar

class of observations man has ever advanced his knowledge. Science has been the staff by which he has been helped forward, but for many ages he was ignorant of the nature of his aid. This progress, as Coleridge says, was not like that of a Roman road, in a right line; it may be more justly compared to that of a river, which both in its smaller reaches and larger turnings, is frequently forced back towards its fountains, by objects which cannot otherwise be eluded or overcome; yet with an accompanying impulse that will ensure its advancement hereafter, it is either gaining strength every hour, or conquering in secret some difficulty, by a labour that contributes as effectually to further it in its course, as when it moves forward uninterruptedly.

It has been by such a devious course as this that man has advanced to his present position; like the river, he has cut out his way through the plains of nature, and in his further advancement he must toil in the same field, but he has all the advantages of that knowledge, which has been gained by other labourers, who having finished their work, rest from their exertions.

We have long boasted of our age as a most remarkable one; the number of useful applications which we have made within a comparatively limited period, are no doubt more numerous than were ever before made within the same time. What has been the cause of this? Why have we such vast improvements in steam machinery? Why the electrotype, the electric telegraph, and the other aids of which we are so justly proud. Watt observed a small fact connected with the expansion of steam; Daniel noticed a peculiarity in copper precipitated under certain conditions; Œrsted studied the movement of a magnet, in the proximity of a wire, through which an electric current was traversing; and from the observations of simple facts great laws were deduced, and great ends have been attained.

The Exhibition exhibits the beautiful results which have been derived from the study of science, and it will also exhibit some—we trust not many—of the mistakes which are made from the attempt to apply physical force without a knowledge of the laws by which it is regulated. The inventive genius, being closely allied to imaginative power, must be restrained by a philosophical education to become of value to its possessor, or available for the benefit of his race.

Let us examine the four great sections of the Exhibition—Raw Material and Produce, Machinery, Manufactures, and Fine Arts—and see how completely, in every stage of progress, Science lends her aid to Art and Manufacture, confining our attention, however, principally to the mineral kingdom, since the other departments will fall more properly into the hands of those, whose studies have rendered them high authorities.

The development of our lithological treasures is materially aided by geology. The beautiful limestones of Derbyshire, and its fluor-spars, which have been by the ingenious workmen of that county, wrought into almost every form of article for house decoration. The less known, but even more beautiful serpentines of Cornwall and of Ireland, of which are displayed obelisks, columns, candelabra and vases; the marbles of Devonshire, the porphyries and granites of Scotland, of Ireland, and of south-western England, chiselled into highly ornamental decorative forms, at once speak of the advantage of geological science in developing the native resources of a country.

These pages exhibit many illustrative examples of the perfection of metal-casting in bronze, brass, iron, silver, and other metals. Having passed into forms which attract attention as works of Art, we are too apt to forget that the very perfection we admire is due almost entirely to the condition of crude ore, as we find it exhibited in Class I. To take bronze and brass as our example, amidst the raw materials of the mineral kingdom, we find Cornwall, the most ancient mining district of which history records the fact, or tradition supplies the tale, exhibiting its tin ores in all their variety, oxide of tin, and sulphuret, tin as mined from the lode, and as it is found amid the débris of the primary mountains, and the metallurgical process is displayed in model by which this mineral is reduced to the metallic state. Copper ores from the almost pure metal as found deposited in the serpentine rocks of the Lizard, and the whinstone of the North, to the double sulphuret of copper and iron, are abundantly displayed; and the large copper smelters of Swansea exhibit illustrative specimens of every stage of a process, regulated at each step by a knowledge of physics and chemistry, which is necessary for the production of copper, in such a state of purity as to be fit for the use of the manufacturer, or for the purposes of that most permanent form of Art—bronze statuary. Zinc ores in the same way tell their own instructive story. If we take the trouble to examine the stages of reduction and manufacture and thus trace the metal from the ore to the finished work, the value of mineralogy, of chemistry, and of natural philosophy will be seen. The same may be said, even more strongly, of iron. The iron ores of the United Kingdom, collected with infinite labour by Mr. Blackwell, show the variety we possess, and in the large contributions of iron ores from Canada, Nova Scotia, and the United States, from Prussian Germany, Sweden, and Russia, we have such means of comparison as never before could be obtained. Our own iron-masters have fully illustrated the processes of iron smelting; and our manufacturers have exhibited every form of iron-work from the saucepan to the sword-blade; from the candlestick to the ornamental casting. Swedish and Russian iron, in all stages, are shown; and the Berlin castings, so long famous, are abundantly displayed. Mineralogy will here have its work of classification; chemistry its important business of analysis; and physics is called into full play in the arrangements of the blast and puddling furnaces, in the economy of fuel, in the application of the gaseous products, and in the new process of using gas in the operation of puddling. Upon the character of the ore, and the perfection of the processes of reduction, depends the condition of the finished work.

At present, it is impossible to do more than indicate the illustrations of science which are spread around; but we can return to the subjects, and explain fully all that is novel and instructive in each particular class, as it falls legitimately under consideration in a close survey. In that chemical department which connects itself with the mineral kingdom, we find illustrations of white lead manufacture, and also the processes of obtaining white zinc—of the preparation of Prussian blue—soluble and insoluble, and, indeed, all those pigments which result from the combinations of oxygen, sulphur, arsenic, or other substances, with the metallic bases. We have the separation of wolfram from tin ore, which is sadly injurious to it—and the conversion of the tungsten into an oxide, and into tungstate of soda, forming a new mordant for the calico-printer, and also the production of a new colour from the same substance: we believe by passing coal gas over the oxide, by which the metallic tungsten is reduced in a peculiar condition, probably mixed with carbon. Then we find all the products from peat—which, if the question of economical production can be satisfactorily answered, promises to convert the bogs of Ireland and Dartmoor, into sources of much wealth;—and many other illustrations of the available application of substances which have not been hitherto employed.

Many remarkable examples will be found in the China clays (Kaolins) of the St. Austle district, and from Dartmoor; the clays from other localities are also shown in considerable variety, and we shall find specimens of each form of the ceramic art, resulting from the use and mixture of these materials.

As we expected, the potteries have made a display in every respect creditable to England. Not only have we our old familiar earthenware somewhat refined, but we have "hard porcelain" in a state of great perfection, and some beautiful examples of egg-shell china. In decoration, too, the stimulus which has been applied has evidently produced a considerable advance in the right direction. We have colours which are new or revived, and a considerable improvement in many which have been long employed. Among the revivals, we cannot but notice the beautiful Rose Dubarry, which is certainly an exceedingly beautiful example of the old Sèvres colour. In glass, whether we linger over the sheet glass prepared by Messrs. Chance for the Industrial Palace itself, or the enormous shades, the largest ever made by man, or pass on to the plate and flint glass, it will be found that

a considerable improvement has been effected; since the restrictive duties have been removed, manufacturers being enabled, without the annoying interference of the Excise, to try an experiment, it will be seen that the quality of our crystal—flint glass with lead—has been improved, and that the colours imparted by the metallic oxides are far more brilliant, transparent, and intense than before.

The subject of silvering glass is a curious one—and the examples of the most recent improvements of precipitating silver with grape sugar, found in the contributions to the Exhibition, are excellent. We are not, however, sure that the silvering of coloured glass, and thus depriving it of transparency, is altogether what we desire, although we freely admit that many new and not unpleasing effects can be produced by the process. We are very anxious to see the process extended to silvering plates of glass, as, by the application of such a method, the sad effects which are known to arise from the absorption of quicksilver by the skin would be got rid of. Humanity calls for an extension of the application in this direction, and we trust the very enterprising patentees will prosecute their experiments with this view.

In immediate connection with the process, because illustrated by it, we may refer to the brilliancy of colour produced in our English flint glass. Since the glass-maker has succeeded in rivalling the Bohemian in his tints, the reflection through these from the silvered surface, teaches us that colours are produced which are curious in their effects, and physically interesting. It has been proved that almost every variety of colour can be produced in glass by very dissimilar agents; that, indeed, charcoal, iron, gold, &c., may be made to impart to glass nearly all the colours of the chromatic scale, by modifying the amount of heat to which the composition is exposed. It will, however, be found that, if the colour transmitted is the same, the colour reflected is different. There is, in nearly every variety of coloured glass, to be detected a certain dichroism. We often find a glass, yellow by transmitted light, which exhibits a blue colour at certain angles of reflection, and the same is often, although less frequently, seen with the ruby glasses. By the silvering process, this reflected colour is considerably exalted, and this dichroism is very pleasingly illustrated.

The southern wall of the building is covered with such a display of Decorative Art as we have never witnessed, and there is scarcely a specimen of Art or Manufacture there which is not an illustration of the present subject. Numerous specimens of gypsum, both amorphous and crystalline, as nature gives it to us, will be found in the various departments; the resulting plaster of Paris—so called from the circumstance that it is found in great abundance in the neighbourhood of the French capital, being largely worked at Montmartre—forms also an article of exhibition; but to the various means which have been adopted to give hardness and durability to this material, so exceedingly valuable for procuring casts, we would particularly direct attention. Plaster of Paris casts, it is well known, are porous and absorbent, and hence the necessity of painting them to preserve their surface, and even this has proved exceedingly inefficient. Among the beautiful specimens of Art adorning the southern walls of the English division—which extend from the sculpture court immediately adjoining the transept to the western end—will be discovered several examples of processes by which the plaster of Paris is hardened to such an extent that a high polish can be given to its surface. In some cases where these cements have been employed, it has been found that the effect of them has been materially lowered by a constant efflorescence over the surface. This would appear to arise from the presence of soda, which it is well known is liable to efflorescence, and it is prevented by giving an acid rather than an alkaline reaction to the composition. The silicate of potash, formed by dissolving flint in caustic potash under pressure, has the property of cementing sand into a very solid stone: this preparation has also been employed for covering fresco-paintings; giving to them, by the application of this soluble glass, a very perfect impervious glazing by which they are protected from the influence of the atmosphere. Messrs. Ransom, of Ipswich, exhibit some specimens of their siliceous artificial stone; but we desire to see the result of its combination with either the sulphate or carbonate of lime as imitating marble.

Artists will find in the metalliferous minerals, and in that section of the same class—chemical manufactures, most unfortunately somewhat too widely separated, one being on the floor and the other in the gallery—some very beautiful illustrations of the processes of preparing their pigments from the raw material. As illustrations, numerous specimens of cinnabar—sulphuret of mercury,—from Spain and California, will be found. It may be explained that this ore is vermilion in its native state, but it is usually prepared for artists by thoroughly blending sulphur and mercury together, and then exposing them to a moderately high temperature in close vessels. The French exhibitors of pigments have a choice display; many of the colours which they manufacture, from the extreme care with which every part of the process is conducted, being superior to those made in England: this particularly applies to their Mars colours and their lakes. Cobalt and smalts are well illustrated by Goodhall & Reeves, who display the Norwegian cobalt and nickel ores, and a beautiful series of smalts. The discovery of this metal is of very modern date: the ore being used long before the metal was separated. About the end of the fifteenth century the cobalt ore was found in large quantities in Bohemia. It was long thrown aside as useless; the miners had an aversion to it, as it gave them much useless labour, and from proving also prejudicial to their health, they gave it a name which was odious to them. The Germans called supposed evil spirits, hags and witches, *kobolt* or *kobel*, which is probably only another form of expressing *covalus* and *gobelinus*, both terms employed in the tenth and eleventh centuries to signify a phantom. Hence the Bohemian miners named this glistening ore which produced them no profit, but gave them on the contrary much annoyance, a *kobel*, and hence our modern term cobalt. As the manufacture of this colour, and its use in the arts of the potter and glass-maker, in addition to its use to the artist, involves much scientific skill, a brief space may be afforded to its history.

Christopher Schurer, a glass-maker at Platten, in Bohemia, being at Schneeberg, collected some fine pieces of cobalt ochre. He tried them in his furnace, and finding that they melted, he mixed some of it with his glass, and obtained a beautiful blue colour. For a long time he prepared a smalt, a cobalt glass, ground into a fine powder, for the use of the potters only; but the use of it rapidly spread, and, eventually, it became greatly in request in Holland. Some artists in coloured glass windows, repaired to Nendeck, in order that they might learn the process of preparing this new colour; they persuaded Schurer to remove to Magdeburgh, where he also made the same material. At this period, the colour was worth seven dollars and a-half per hundred-weight, and in Holland from fifty to sixty florins. Eight colour-mills for grinding smalt, which was procured in a roasted state from Schneeberg, were soon constructed in Holland. The manufacture of cobalt blue, was extended over many parts of Europe, and our Industrial Exhibition affords us the means of comparing the smalts of Saxony, of Norway, and of other districts. Some specimens from Cornwall, from Cumberland, and, we believe, from Cheshire, show the extent to which this mineral is produced in this country.

Smalts are combinations of silica and oxide of cobalt, and cobalt blue is a compound of the same oxide with alumina.

Prussian blue is another pigment upon which a large amount of science has been expended, and the result has been the production of most beautiful colours, and the formation of a soluble, as well as the old insoluble Prussian blue. Our chemists have furnished the Exhibition with some magnificent specimens of a yellow salt—the result of a combination of the nitrogen and carbon obtained from animal matter; the compound being *cyanogen* with potash. This is called the ferro-prussiate of potash, and it is of the utmost importance for dying various shades of blue. If this salt is added to sulphate of iron, Prussian blue is precipitated—its colour gradually improving by the absorption of oxygen from the air. This being the insoluble Prussian blue. If, however, as the Rev. Mr. Reade has shown, we combine the per-oxide of iron

with a solution of this salt, a Prussian blue is formed, which is soluble in water, and of which an ink is prepared; this process, and others analogous to it, has been patented by the discoverer, who exhibits the results of his experiments.

In commencing with a hasty outline of this Exhibition, we have purposely confined our attention to leading features which go to show that the Exhibition *is* what Prince Albert stated it *should* be, "a true test and a living picture of the point of development at which the whole of mankind has arrived in the great task, and a new starting-point from which all nations will be able to direct their further exertions." Recurring back to another passage in the same address, we feel how entirely the result conforms to the design. "The products of all quarters of the globe, are placed at our disposal, and we have only to choose which is the best and cheapest for our purposes, and the powers of production are entrusted to the stimulus of competition and capital. So man is approaching a more complete fulfilment of that great and sacred mission which he has to perform in this world. His reason being created after the image of God, he has to use it to discover the laws by which the Almighty governs his creation, and, by making these laws his standard of action, to conquer nature to his use — himself a divine instrument. Science discovers these laws of power, and motion, and transformation; Industry applies them to the raw matter, which the earth yields us in abundance, but which becomes valuable only by knowledge; and teaches us the immutable laws of beauty and symmetry, and gives to our productions forms in accordance with them."

In the production of the precious metals there are some peculiar processes well deserving of attention. Silver, gold, and platinum are only obtained in a state fitted for man's use by very elegant processes, involving a profound knowledge of chemistry and of physics.

Nearly all our silver is found in combination with ores of lead, principally the sulphuret, and known as argentiferous galena. Some of these ores contain as much as 60 ounces of silver to the ton of ore, whereas others do not give more than from 6 to 10 ounces from the same quantity. The process of separation was originally a very tedious and wasteful one. The lead being reduced to a metallic state, still holding the silver mixed with it, was remelted in a reverberatory furnace, and kept for a long period in a melted state, a strong current of air being made to play constantly over the surface, which is kept disturbed until all the lead is oxidised, converted into litharge or red lead, the silver being left at the bottom of the furnace, silver being less easily oxidisable than lead.

Another process was patented some years since by Mr. Pattinson, by which the process of separation is greatly facilitated, and in the Exhibition we have the Duke of Buccleuch, Mr. Sopwith, and Mr. Pattinson, himself, giving exemplifications of the method adopted, and the results. These commence with samples of the lead ore as taken from the mine, and end with cakes of silver, weighing from 8000 to 10,000 ounces.

The process is founded on the fact that, in slow cooling, the lead crystallises, or becomes coherent much sooner than silver does; consequently many tons of the melted metal being placed in large iron pots, is kept at a temperature but just sufficient to maintain it in a semi-pasty state. Men are now employed with rakes and strainers to collect and separate, as they form, the small crystals of lead, and these are found to be entirely free from silver. This being carried on for some time, the metal left at the bottom of the pot is lead, excessively rich in silver. The whole of the lead might be thus separated from the silver; but the result of practice has shown that it is more economical to remove the last portion of lead by oxidation. The beautiful purity of the masses of silver exhibited, will show the perfection of Mr. Pattinson's method, and we have only to pass into some of the other departments and examine the beautiful works of Art in silver, to learn how very completely man has here achieved a victory, and moulded nature to his will.

In the small but valuable case exhibited by Messrs. Johnson and Mathey, we have very complete illustrations of the processes discovered by Dr. Wollaston, of separating platinum from the metals with which it is combined, and reducing it to the metallic form. This is one of those very curious and unique processes by which a metal, which will not fuse in the highest temperature of our ordinary furnaces, is brought into metallic coherence by mechanical force acting in conjunction with an elevated temperature. Mr. Matthison of the Royal Mint refinery, also illustrates the processes of refining employed in his establishment :—processes so delicate that one ten-thousandth part of gold can be separated with facility.

The Exhibition is a reflex of the book of Nature, as translated into human language, and to be made beneficial it must be carefully studied. Having rapidly turned over a few of its pages illustrating raw material and produce, we shall, if we proceed to finished manufacture, find a most abundant study, proving most completely that Manufacture cannot advance a step without the aid of her hand-maiden—Science ; and that Art is nearly as dependent for the means of completing and multiplying her works.

The porcelain manufacture, to which we have already alluded, and to which we shall again return, exhibits the degree of perfection to which a material, the discovery of the geologist, has been brought. It is but a few years since Mr. Cookworthy, of Plymouth, experimented on the Cornish clay, and then established his small china-works at Plymouth, which were subsequently removed to Worcester. From this beginning the advance has been most rapid, and a survey of the contributions from the Potteries, glancing back occasionally to Class I. with its illustrations of the raw material, will satisfactorily prove the energy of our manufacturers when once set upon the right track.

In our woven and felted materials, and in the illustrations of the processes to which the raw material is subjected, and in the exhibition of the machines by which the finished fabric is produced, we have a yet more remarkable illustration of the power of human intelligence.

Leaving the consideration of the vegetable and animal products to abler hands, we would very briefly intimate the wonders of the steam-engine, by which the coarse blanket, or the most costly silk, is produced. The impulsive force of steam is as old as Hero of Alexandria, but the world waited for Watt to develope its powers. Men had done before his time, what men are doing now, in relation to other physical forces ; they had gone empirically to work, they had speculated without experiment, and they constructed machines on the strength of their speculations. These, like the electro-magnetic engines, and the electric light of our own day, failed ; as to apply the great forces which nature employs, without first learning how nature employs them, will always fail.

The pseudo-magician destroyed by the spirits he has evoked but knows not how to control, is a picture of the inventor, who builds his invention on a system of blind guesses.

Watt observed the laws of expansion in steam, determined the force exerted at different temperatures, and thus discovered the secret of controlling the giant in his power. That force which is sufficient to lift the most ponderous weight above the highest towers, is also applied to weave the silk gauze for the neck of beauty, without the risk of fracture to the most attenuated thread.

The dyes of some of the beautiful fabrics before us must receive some special examination. Many of the combinations of colours are new, and some of the results are exceedingly pleasing. In dyed and in printed goods we have a very great variety, and we are convinced, that the care and skill which has been devoted to the object of producing colours, which should bear comparison with the best works of the Continent, has resulted in the production of colours, and combinations, which are highly creditable to English science, and to British taste.

The Foreign Exhibitors' contributions are most numerous, and we shall return to the consideration of a great number of the articles which they exhibit.

Prussian Pottery and Metallurgy in particular will claim large notice, and the numerous articles of taste which come within the extensive compartments of France, show equally the attention of our French neighbours to the science of manufacture ; but Russia and Sweden, Holland and Belgium, Italy and Spain, have examples of human industry, which may be studied with profit. America charters a ship of war with the trophies of peace, and from the abundance of the stores, both natural, and such as her artisans have transformed, which are presented to the "World's Fair," as our brothers of the West delight to call it, many subjects of great interest at once strike us, which must form subjects of separate consideration in this Essay. From the Brazils and Chili, to the Canadas, and even further North than these, Hyde Park has received examples of mineral, vegetable and animal produce. Many of them still waiting for the exercise of man's industry, to develope their probably high value.

From South Australia the mineral specimens are very remarkable. The native copper from the Burra-Burra mines, and the beautiful malachites now so extensively used for ornamental purposes, rivalling the long famed malachites of Russia ; and the other specimens of the green and blue carbonates of copper, this last in a state of purity and beauty, which at once fits it for a pigment, claim very particular notice. The contributions from the East would of themselves form subjects for a most instructive volume, but we hope to do some small justice to a section of them by devoting to them an especial examination.

It is not now desirable to do more than direct attention towards those points of interest which are illustrative of the position we maintain, and which, in the future pages of this Essay, it is our intention to explain, *seriatim*. On all sides new features are rapidly being developed—the chrysalis state is nearly over, and the bright creation working its beautiful form forth into the sunshine, appears to be a full realisation of the most sanguine hopes of those who nursed the embryo.

Of the examples of the direct application of the physical powers to the purposes of use and ornament, we have some most interesting specimens. Electricity performing its wonderful work of decomposing and recomposing has, in the processes of the electrotype, and in the operations of electro-plating, been rendered familiar to the public. Seeing the beautiful productions of the Messrs. Elkington—their electrotype copies from the antique—preserving all the vigour and the high perfection of those beautiful exponents of the Greek and Roman Art, we have been disposed to think the process could not be extended beyond this point of excellence. Nor, indeed, do we conceive that, in this direction, there is much room for improvement. We have, however, here some beautiful examples of the applicability of the galvano-plastic Art, as our Continental friends delight to call it, to the production of large works, many of them very remarkable examples of modelling. But there are smaller applications of the electro-chemical deposit which promise to open up new branches of Art : these are the productions of British and Continental manufacturers and artists, and from an examination of them we shall exhibit satisfactory proof—that much may yet be done in ornamental Art, by the agency of the electrical elements, at a comparatively small cost, which could not, by any of the old processes, be obtained, except at an enormous expenditure of time, and, consequently, of money. Desiring to sketch out, in the first instance, the strong features of the scientific value of this great industrial gathering, another very remarkable exemplification is found in the numerous specimens of the daguerreotype, the calotype, and other photographic processes which are assembled here, from our own artists, and those of the old Continent and of America. In these we have evidences of the advantages arising from the study of abstract science ; and there are yet other examples no less striking, which remain to be examined, and popularly illustrated.

In returning to the subject, we already feel ourselves like Medora, when gathering flowers for Conrad ; perplexed amid the immense variety ; and discover, we must adopt that lady's plan, of guessing at the fairest. We hope, however, that without much difficulty, a tolerably complete examination of the SCIENCE OF THE EXHIBITION may be instituted, which shall not be valueless, as the contribution of one who desires only to be an interpreter of facts.

PART II.

THE civilisation of the world has advanced to a certain point which is marked by the triumphs man has achieved over nature and the applications, to use and ornaments, of the crude material which he derives from their native source. The Great Exhibition stands a striking record of all that the world has done—it marks the point to which mankind has arrived—and indicates what he has yet to subdue.

The accumulated thoughts of thousands of years are expressed in this gathering. No truth—being born unto man—is ever suffered to perish; it may be hidden for a season, but like the seed buried in the soil, it gathers strength and eventually springs forth all vitality upon the world. All noble growths are slow, and those things which are now common to us in their perfection, it should be remembered, required ages to mature them—and the efforts of thought of many generations. For example: how long a time has passed away since the fusion of a siliceous sand and an alkali led to the discovery of glass! Yet all that time has been required by man to produce those beautiful examples which we see in the crystal fountain, so charmingly marking the centre of the Industrial Palace of Glass, and in the lenses arranged for the humane purpose of indicating through the long nights the dangers of a lee shore. Such is also shown to be the case in the processes of metallurgy, and in metal manufacture. The ancients knew but few of the metals, which we now employ; copper and tin and iron and lead, with silver and gold, appear to have been all with which they were acquainted. Zinc is found in the antique brasses, but metallic zinc was quite unknown until about the middle of the last century: the ancient brasses being made by combining copper with calamine—an ore of zinc regarded by all as an earth—but it was not until 1735 that Brandt separated the metal.

Albertus Magnus thought iron an ingredient of zinc ore—Paracelsus called calamine a spurious son of copper—Lemery held it to be a kind of bismuth—Glauber conceived it to be an immature solar sulphur—Homberg said it was a mixture of tin and iron—Kunckel declared it to be a coagulated mercury—and Schluter believed it to be tin made brittle by sulphur.

Yet now we employ the metal zinc for a great variety of useful and ornamental purposes, and we use it for multiplying works of high Art. Of this application the Amazon of Kiss, and Baily's Eve are fine examples; and the colossal statue of Her Majesty, by the Ville Montagne Company, shows the applicability of this metal to large works.

It appears important in considering the scientific value of the Exhibition to indicate, in the first place, the examples which it contains of the raw material; and secondly to describe the more important applications of science in the processes to which it is subjected under the transforming hand of man. Attention is confined to the Mineral world. Professor Edward Forbes having undertaken the task of describing the value of the Vegetable productions here displayed.

Class I.—is devoted to the earthy and metalliferous minerals of the United Kingdom. As we have to consider those only which are of industrial value, we omit from our consideration such as are merely curious. Building and road-stones are exhibited in considerable quantities—the granites of Cornwall and of Scotland—the serpentines of the Lizard and of Ireland—the limestones of Plymouth and of Derbyshire, and many other of our lithological treasures are here accumulated. If from this section we pass into a compartment on the north side of the nave, those stones will be seen in their manufactured condition. The red and green serpentine is wrought into vases—candelabra—obelisks and tables—granites and porphyries are chiselled into chimneypieces, and many other articles for ornament; and on the outside of the building, on the west end, stands a beautiful Ionic column, the tall shaft of which is a single stone procured from the Cheesewring granite quarries near Liskeard, in Cornwall. Other examples of the same durable stone will be seen near this. The works in Derbyshire marbles are of the most beautiful description, and numerous specimens of manufactured slate will, we are certain, be much admired. The science of this may not be, at the first glance, apparent; but a mo-

ment's reference to the beautifully coloured Geological Map which hangs on the south wall, will show how Science aids in tracing out the localities within which certain rocks are found, and thus ministers directly to the economical uses of mankind.

In connection with these, the various kinds of clay employed in our potteries are exhibited, and in most cases samples of the pottery produced from them. The clays are, in all cases, the result of the decomposition of the older rocks, and in chemical composition are,—variable quantities of alumina, silica and lime—with an alkali in small proportions. The varieties of sands employed in glass-making are instructive—some are from Lynn, in Norfolk, and some from the Isle of Wight,—each glass-maker usually regarding one variety as superior to another. In all cases it must be remembered the sand employed is purely siliceous; and it is in the process of glass-making always combined with an alkali and some metallic oxides, such as the oxide of manganese, or lead.

In the department devoted to the glass manufacture will be found examples of all the materials which are employed in the process. In addition to the sands already named, we find a very beautiful sand sent from the Wenham Lake, and by its side are some specimens of glass made from it. These examples are remarkable for the purity of their colour, and their extreme transparency. There are other sands from Aylesbury and from Ireland. Here are also collected the various alkalies which are employed, and specimens of red lead and oxide of manganese which are so largely employed in all the finer kinds of modern glass.

Simply to fuse sand and an alkali produces the common kinds of glass; the combination with lead produces that brilliancy which is the peculiar feature of flint-glass. The black oxide of manganese is employed to prevent the peroxidisation of any iron which may be present in the materials employed, but it has the peculiar property, if used in any quantity, of changing, under the influence of light, to a fine pink colour; hence great care is necessary in employing this remarkable agent.

Plumbago, or graphite, has for the artist a peculiar interest; the largest quantity is obtained in this country from the Borrowdale mine in Cumberland, in which mine it occurs in masses of varied and most uncertain size. The value of this black lead, which is of a very fine quality, is great; and from this mine alone about £5000 or £6000 worth is sold annually. It is a curious circumstance in connexion with this that the discoveries of plumbago have been made at somewhat wide intervals, but the market has been regularly supplied—the proprietors refusing to sell more than a certain quantity annually. Plumbago must be regarded as carbon in a peculiar condition, and as being in all chemical characters identical with the Koh-i-Noor Diamond, which glistens so brilliantly in its safety cage at the commencement of the nave proceeding eastward. Charcoal is readily combustible; graphite is so incombustible that it is employed for making crucibles which will stand the highest temperatures of our furnaces, and the diamond can only be burnt by procuring the most exalted artificial temperatures. The two former are dense black opaque bodies—the last is perfectly transparent, refracting light in a remarkable manner, yet science has demonstrated that this is due to a change in molecular arrangement merely. We have other examples of similar phenomena, but none of them are so striking as the allotropism, as this peculiar state has been called by Berzelius, of charcoal, plumbago and the diamond.

Our mineral fuel may be regarded as one—perhaps the greatest source of our national prosperity. Every coal-field in the country presents an accumulated mass of human industry; and associated with the coal formations we find almost every variety of process carried on, which requires the use of coal in any considerable quantities. The formation of coal may be studied from the examples here exhibited, in many cases with the associated fossils and the rocky strata.

It is most satisfactorily shown, that coal is of vegetable origin. Certain fern-like trees grew luxuriantly upon large swamps. For ages, perhaps, they grew and decayed upon the same spot, forming thus a large accumulation of carbonaceous matter. A geological change occasioned this mass to be covered with water, and in the course of time a sandy bed was deposited, which again rose above the water, and then a new vegetation commenced, to undergo the same process. Thus bed after bed of coal was formed, by a series of oscillations, at irregular periods, of land and water. The peat products present to us some such conditions as those which may be supposed to have prevailed in the formation of coal. Peat is, however, formed from the *sphagnum*, or peat-moss; whereas coal is due to the decomposition of *sigillaria*, and other allied plants, which assumed a character much resembling that of the vegetation of the tropical deltas of the present day.

Those who may desire to learn something of the forms of organic life which existed during the formation of the coal, will here find the means of acquiring that knowledge. Here they may learn to correct a popular error—originating in the first place in the speculations of an eminent geologist. The theoretical views of Brongniart were that the coal-plants were designed for the purpose of removing from the atmosphere that excess of carbonic acid, which he supposed to exist at the carboniferous period, and which rendered the earth unfit for air-breathing animals. A popular and poetical writer has but recently given additional strength to this speculation, by his eloquent description of the fern-forests existing in the full luxuriance of vegetation, but without the stir and animation of animal existence. Geological science has proved the incorrectness of this. Animal life existed long before that geological period, distinguished as the carboniferous. These ancient forests were probably filled with insect life, the remains of them having been discovered; and the vestiges of a huge frog-like animal prove the incorrectness of this theory. Every fact in physics—and there are many showing the mutual dependence of the Animal and the Vegetable Kingdoms on each other—tends to prove the impossibility of one form of organic life existing without the other, under the present physical constitution of creation.

Iron ores, as associated in nature with coal—all the argillaceous, or clay-ironstones, being found in the coal-fields of Great Britain,—are very properly associated with the coal in the arrangements adopted.

The gross annual production of iron in Great Britain is now upwards of 2,250,000 tons. South Wales furnishes 700,000 tons, and South Staffordshire rather more than 600,000 tons. Scotland producing about the same quantity.

In addition to the iron-stone beds of the coal measures, the mountain limestone series of Lancashire, Cumberland, Durham, Derbyshire, Somersetshire, furnish beds and veins of hæmatites; and the older rocks of Devonshire and Cornwall contain many important beds of black hæmatite, and magnetic iron ore. All these varieties are here well arranged, and may be studied with advantage. The most curious are, perhaps, the iron-stone formations from the green sands of Sussex. At one period this was the principal source from which we derived iron in this country; but the forests becoming exhausted, the iron-workings of Sussex were abandoned. It is now, however, probable that the railroads will again open up this unworked field, which may at no distant date furnish the iron trade with additional supplies.

Many of the exhibitors of iron ores have associated with them examples of the iron manufactured from them; thus we are enabled to judge of the general character of the metal produced from any given variety of iron. There can be no doubt but the chemical constitution of the iron ore materially influences the physical character of the metal; it therefore becomes very important that the chemical analyses of each variety should be afforded.

The processes of reducing the ores of iron to a metallic state involve many very peculiar chemical changes, particularly under the improved processes, which our own iron-masters have adopted. The ores of iron are either oxides of iron, or carbonates of the oxide; and the difficulties of the metallurgical processes rest in the eagerness with which the oxygen and the carbon are retained by the metal. It would occupy too large a portion of this essay to describe the processes of iron-smelting. Good illustrations of the conditions under which iron is found, and of the mode of reduction, are afforded in

one group by the Ebbw-vale Company, who exhibit a model of this important mineral district, another, of their blast furnaces, and of the numerous arrangements required to secure a successful result. Manufactured iron of various kinds have a place on the adjoining counters, so that passing from the collection of all the iron ores of the United Kingdom, as brought together by Mr. S. Blackwell, of Dudley, to the models just alluded to, and onward to the samples of manufactured iron shown by the Messrs. Birds and others—a very complete view will be obtained of this most important branch of British industry. Mr. Morries Stirling has introduced some novelties in iron manufacture. He alloys this metal with lead and tin, and arsenic, and many of the results obtained are stated to be in the highest degree favourable. Several other alloys introduced by the same patentee exhibit certain peculiarities, which, whatever may be their merits in a commercial point of view, go to prove that very perfect combinations of metals may be obtained. By alloying iron in this way, bells have been produced at a considerably less cost than bell-metal, which is a compound of copper, tin and zinc, in varying proportions. One very large bell placed in the nave is certainly exceedingly musical—its full, deep tone occupying the whole space west of the transept, when it is set in vibration. This is a point of much interest. Iron bells have been occasionally employed, but never very successfully, the chief objection to them being the want of a pleasing tone in them. That a small quantity of another metal added to iron should effect so great a difference is not a little remarkable, and it proves that a very slight cause alters the order of molecular arrangement.

The fine iron castings of Berlin have been long celebrated throughout Europe; and their extreme sharpness has been thought to depend upon some peculiar condition of the bog-iron ore which is usually employed in Prussia. Within the Zolverein department, will be found good exemplifications of all the ores of iron employed in the German states, the iron manufactured from them, and examples of the perfection to which iron-casting has been carried. We think an examination of the Coalbrook-dale ornamental rustic dome, and the other iron castings which they exhibit, will show that British manufacturers can produce ornamental works in iron, which are in no respect inferior to those for which some places on the Continent have been famed. It would not, therefore, appear that the supposed superiority was due to any chemical difference, since we find that careful manipulation alone is capable of producing works of equal excellence.

The opportunity now afforded of examining the various iron ores of the world, is, in itself, a proof of the value of the Exhibition. The United States, Canada, and Nova Scotia, are large exhibitors. Trinidad sends her magnetic iron from the Maraccas Valley, and hæmatite from Gaspari Island. New Zealand contributes a rich iron sand; and Tasmania, also, shows the varieties of this valuable ore, which that interesting colony produces. The continental kingdoms have seen the importance of collecting their native stores; and the iron ores of Sicily, of the Italian peninsula, of Spain, of Austria, Germany, Russia, Sweden, Belgium, Holland, and France, instruct us in the various characters of the different formations. That chemist who would collect specimens of each variety, and subject them to a careful analytical examination, particularly with a view of determining minute differences in the constituents, would be performing a work of the utmost value to his country. Numerous specimens of sheet-iron are exhibited; but even the finest varieties of English iron in sheets have not that uniformity of surface, that evenness of texture (if the expression may be allowed), which the Russian sheet-iron possesses. We heard an iron-master say that in comparison with English iron, the Russian possessed the fineness, flexibility, and surface of India-rubber.

In pursuing our scientific examination of the Great Exhibition, steel naturally occupies the next place to iron. Sheffield, with her cutlers' trophy, and the fine display of almost every kind of steel manufacture, may be regarded as the exemplar of this branch of English industry. From all parts of the world we find examples of steel weapons. The showy arms of the chiefs of the tribes of India, the swords of the Africans, and the scimitars of the Turks, the true Toledos, and the beautiful blades of Damascus, all show the attention which man has given to the production of the implements of war. The superior temper of many of these swords appears to be due to the circumstance that the steel is manufactured in comparatively small quantities, from iron obtained directly from magnetic iron ore, which variety we only find in two localities in this country, and, even in these, in exceedingly small quantities.

Steel, it is tolerably well known, is iron combined with a small quantity of carbon. The mode in which this is effected is, usually, by a process called *cementation*. Bars of selected iron are stratified in a furnace with charcoal, and the whole maintained at a high temperature for some time. The chemical or physical changes which take place are imperfectly understood; but the association of a small quantity of carbon with the iron, in the process, is certain. In some instances, steel is made at once in the furnace, by smelting it with charcoal; and to the circumstance that most of the iron produced in Russia and Sweden is smelted with wood, has been referred, with some degree of probability, the superior character of the iron of those countries.

The mines of Danemora, in Sweden, so renowned for yielding the finest iron in the world, the greatest part of which is sent to this country, were discovered in 1488; since which time they have been constantly worked. The richest ore raised from these mines contains 70 per cent. of iron, and the poorest 30 per cent.; the quantity raised is about 12,000 tons annually, which produce about 4000 tons of bar iron. These are rather quarries than mines, being worked open to the day. They sink pits, which form so many gulphs, into which the miners descend in baskets; in these they also send up the ore produced. The ore is only worked in the summer months, and is laid out in heaps and divided in the winter months, from November to March, when it can be conveyed in sledges. About 300 persons are employed in mining and transporting the ore, and as many more at the forges belonging to the proprietors.

In the Sheffield department will be found an instructive series of models, showing the mode adopted for preparing and working steel.

We pass from iron to some of the other metals. Cornwall exhibits the various forms in which tin is found in that county; and Bohemia, in which country tin mines have been worked from a very remote antiquity, exhibits that metal; and the islands of the Indian Archipelago have forwarded specimens of this useful mineral. Associated with the Cornish produce, a model of a furnace, for smelting the ores of tin, is shown; and by a short study of this, a very perfect idea of the easy process by which this ore is reduced, may be obtained. Tin has been worked in Cornwall from the earliest periods. That the Phœnicians traded with Cornwall for this metal appears certain; and, from time to time, indications of the old workings are discovered. There is exhibited a specimen of a very ancient block of tin, found in ploughing a field; these blocks are usually called "Jew's tin;" and, from time to time, many of them have been discovered, and often associated with the furnaces in which the ores were smelted. These remains prove the early period at which the tin-mines of Cornwall were worked; the probability being that the ancient Britons were taught mining by the merchants of Phœnicia.

One of the valuable applications of chemical science has now to be considered. Mr. Oxland exhibits a case containing illustrations of tin ore containing wolfram, and this substance separated from it. Wolfram is a tungstate of iron, and, when combined with the tin, it is of so deteriorating a nature, that the market price of such tin is very low. It is a very intractable substance, not attacked by any acids; and although pure tungsten has been prepared, it is very unusual to see it in anything like a coherent form. Mr. Oxland's process for its removal from the tin consists in roasting the impure tin ore with soda, the result of which is the formation of a tungstate of soda, which is dissolved out, leaving the tin pure. The tungstate of soda being treated with an acid, the oxide of tungsten is separated; and this is likely to be extensively employed as a mordant base for some of the processes of calico printing.

In the Chemical Department, Mr. Young exhibits some remarkable crystals of stannate of soda, formed by combining the tin directly with the alkali; and this preparation is also largely employed in fixing scarlet and other colours.

Copper ores form a very extensive and important section of the British and Foreign departments of the Exhibition. The Redruth Committee have exhibited some remarkably fine masses of the ordinary yellow ore of the kingdom;—the double sulphuret of copper and iron—and also some beautiful examples of the grey sulphuret. The native copper from the serpentine rocks, near the Lizard, is exhibited in pieces which rival the enormous lumps obtained from Lake Superior. We observed that three specimens—one from the Lizard, Cornwall, another from the trap rocks, near Glasgow, and an American mass—are placed together, to show the peculiarities of those remarkable mineral formations.

The process of copper-smelting has been well illustrated by the Swansea Committee; all the copper produced in this country, and all that is imported, being smelted at that town. Messrs. Bankart and Sons exhibit their new process, in which, by roasting, the ore is converted into a soluble sulphuret; this is dissolved, and the copper precipitated by throwing iron into the solution. Mr. Longmaid, another exhibitor, adopts, in the process which he here illustrates, the principle of roasting the ore with common salt, by which he obtains a sulphate of soda: any silver which may accompany the ore is converted into a muriate, and the copper is rendered soluble. It is stated that this process, which is now being tested by practice, is capable of separating exceedingly small portions of silver from the ores; and it thus renders available a substance which has hitherto, unless the combined silver was in considerable quantities, been wasted. Science, in this manner, goes on ministering; thought is for ever exerted on means for improving our Arts and Manufactures, and the reward is certain to those who advance to the work with that preliminary knowledge of physics and chemistry which should form a portion of all practical education. The mineralogist will be delighted to trace from table to table, in the collection, fine examples of the ores of his own country, of the Colonies, and those of other States. The Australian colonies are, as might have been expected, large exhibitors of copper ore, the Burra Burra Mines, near Adelaide, in particular, showing some of the finest examples of carbonates and oxides of copper ever seen. These mines are exceedingly curious, both in the character of the ore raised, in the conditions under which it occurs, and it is singular in the history of mining. In 1845, from indications which were considered favourable, this mine was started by a few adventurers in Adelaide; and since that time the following quantities of ore have been raised:—

		Tons.
1846	. . . .	6,359
1847	. . . .	10,794
1848	. . . .	12,791
1849	. . . .	7,789
1850	. . . .	18,692
		52,428

tons of copper ore in five years, the market value of this being 738,108*l.* The Canadians send to us many examples of their copper ores. It appears, however, from the reports of Mr. Logan, the government geological surveyor, who has been a most indefatigable investigator, that the mineral deposits of all kinds are most extensive. The Canadian Collection, which is due principally to the exertions of this geologist—show gold and silver, iron, copper, and lead—human industry alone is wanting to develope fully the native wealth of this interesting country. Science has been working over her plains, and through her forests, with zeal, and numerous most valuable discoveries have rewarded the geologist. The miner and the metallurgist should follow and profit by the discoveries, the examples of which are laid before the world for the first time in the Exhibition.

Tin and copper—Bronze forms a valuable alloy which was employed at a very early period. The celts of the ancient inhabitants of these islands, and the swords of the Romans, were made of bronze: we have substituted steel for all the purposes to which they applied it, and have allotted this metal chiefly to ornamental purposes.

Several very fine examples of bronze castings may be examined in the British and Foreign departments. The bronzes of the Coalbrook-dale Company may fairly compete with those of Austria and France, and they stand a fair comparison with those beautiful productions for which Munich has been so long celebrated. The George and Libusa are examples of fine bronze castings, but these are not equal to the Lion which stands untouched by any tool since it was removed from its sandy mould in which it was cast. We would dwell on many of the exquisite works in bronze with pleasure, but it would lead us from our subject, and take us into the domain of art, when our object is only to show how far science has aided in giving permanence to its high creations. One bronze casting of a group of flowers, in an ornamental stand, stated to be cast into moulds formed by the flowers themselves is very remarkable. The producer is Clement Papi, of Florence. It would appear to be the result of some such process as Chantrey recommended, which was to take any delicate branch with its leaves, and, having lightly suspended it in a box, to pour in very liquid plaster of Paris. When this—which would find its way into every part—was perfectly set, the mass was exposed to a heat sufficient to char the vegetable matter, without in any way altering the mould. The ashes being shaken out, the metal was poured in, and then an exact *fac simile* of the object was obtained. Many other plans may be devised, but this is recommended as a practical one.

We are enabled however by the processes of electrotype deposit to produce, very easily, results which might be rendered very far superior to this. As one of the most important exemplifications of the useful applications of science, the electrotype claims particular attention. The source of power being the voltaic battery, it is necessary to examine in the first place the extent to which this variety of apparatus is exhibited. The ordinary forms of battery are all shown. Smee's battery is presented under various modifications—from the common laboratory one, to a beautiful battery by Messrs. Horne and Thornthwaite, which is really too elegant for use. The advantage of Smee's battery is, that one fluid alone is employed. The plates are silver covered with platinum, in a state of very fine division, and zinc; by the action of the sulphuric acid the zinc is oxidised, and sulphate of oxide of zinc is formed; by the chemical excitement, electricity is disturbed, and the platinised silver plate, from which hydrogen is freely evolved, becomes the collector, as it were, of this subtile agent. According to the intensity of chemical action, so is the amount of voltaic electricity developed; hence, in any battery arrangement, if we secure the first condition, we obtain a greatly increased action. This is exemplified in Grove's batteries, also exhibited amongst the philosophical instruments. In Grove's battery two fluids and two metals are employed; the latter are platinum and amalgamated zinc, the former dilute sulphuric acid and strong nitric acid. A porous cell is placed into one of glass or glazed earthenware, a cylinder or plate of amalgamated zinc is placed in dilute sulphuric acid in the outer cell, and platina in strong nitric acid in the inner one. Here we have the chemical action of the acid on the zinc, and the action of the platinum on the nitric acid, which is rapidly decomposed. The result is the continuation of the excitement, and the development of a largely increased amount of electric force. In many respects similar to Grove's battery, we have also the carbon battery, introduced by Bunsen, and much employed on the continent. In these the carbon supplies the place of the platinum, and in all respects the form of action in the cells is the same. Daniell's battery is also exhibited: this, it will be remembered, is remarkable for the constancy of its action, and it is important as having led to the discovery of the electrotype. It, like Grove's, consists of two cells; in that one which contains the copper-plate, a strong solution of sulphate of copper is put, and in the other diluted sulphuric acid. The zinc, as in the other examples, is oxidised, and for every equivalent of zinc dissolved, an equivalent of copper is deposited from the cupreous solution. There are several other forms of battery modified to meet the requirements of the electric telegraph; in these the object is duration of power and permanence of action. This is secured by the employ-

ment of sand in some, and by the additional security of a system of percolation in others, by which the exhausted acid is removed from the battery. The tin and iron batteries may be ingenious, but they do not appear to offer any advantages over those we already possess. Since any two bodies, upon which the chemical action is different, may be employed to form a voltaic pair, it is evident that a great variety of batteries might be constructed, but to improve those we already possess is of more importance. The great disadvantage under which we labour in our voltaic arrangements, arises from the loss of electricity as it passes from a solid to a fluid medium, or from a fluid to a solid one. Nearly as much electricity is developed from a single pair of plates, as from a dozen; but the eleven are required to urge it to a higher intensity, to develope it with more force.

Electro-Metallurgy, or the electrotype, receives its best illustrations from the hands of Messrs. Elkington, who exhibit some choice productions of art and art-manufacture.

The principle upon which the electrotype is based has been already intimated in our remarks on Daniell's battery, but it will be well to consider it a little more closely. Under any form of battery the conditions are these:—We produce or develope electricity in the battery by chemical excitement, and according to the quantity of matter which changes form within the cells, is the quantity of electricity set free, and if by wires this is conveyed to another cell, we discover that the operation of the force is such, that as much metal is deposited, as is equal, in chemical relation, to that dissolved in the battery. We have therefore only to form a surface which shall equally diffuse the electricity, to produce a uniform deposit. We may get the copper, for example, to collect in a mass around the end of a wire, or by presenting sufficient surface, diffuse over a large space, and form a very attenuated film. In copying of statues the most satisfactory mode of proceeding is to form a mould of either gutta percha, or in the elastic compound of glue and treacle; then to well cover it on the inside with plumbago, pure black lead: this forms a good surface for diffusing the deposit, and we obtain, if proper care has been taken, a perfect copy of the original. Engraved plates may be thus multiplied, the first copy from the original plate would have a raised impression, but any copy taken from this one in relief would be a *fac-simile* of the original. The ordnance maps, suspended at the western end of the building, and the geological maps against the southern wall, are mostly printed from electrotype plates. Many of the ornamental blocks employed in the works of the Messrs. De la Rue, have had no less than 3,000,000 impressions taken from them, and they show but slight indications of wear. These are all produced by electrotype deposit.

Electro-gilding and plating are most important applications of this beautiful process, of which numerous illustrations are afforded. The most remarkable being those of Messrs. Elkington, particularly the examples forwarded to the Exhibition by her Majesty. The action is of a character precisely similar to that by which copper is deposited; but the solutions of gold and silver are more easily decomposed than those of copper, and hence less battery power is required to effect the revival of the metal. The solutions usually employed are formed by dissolving the oxides of gold and silver in the cyanide of potassium; other solutions may, however, be employed.

The applications of electricity to useful ends are numerously illustrated, and they solicit close attention from those who would learn what science is doing for manufacture. In proceeding with our examination of the other applications of this great power, we shall have to return to the consideration of the philosophy which has guided our experimentalists, and by attention to which, we can alone hope to attain to any extension of its economical value. We have subdued the elements of a thunder cloud to aid us in our metallurgical operations; to manufacture for us vessels of utility; and to decorate for us the choicest productions of artistic taste. These illustrations, as afforded by the Exhibition, advancing from the almost primitive mode of reducing tin, to the scientific one of gilding a richly chased vase, are of the most instructive character, to which each visitor may return again and again to find them suggestive of new trains of thought.

PART III.

THE processes of the electrotype very naturally conducts to the consideration of that section of the Exhibition within which are exhibited an application of a still higher order of science. Electricity—that singularly subtile and diffusive power, which is perhaps, of all the physical agents, the most active in nature—is now chained and made to do the bidding of its subduer. The marvel of modern experimental science is, beyond all question, the Electric Telegraph, by which we are enabled to convey instantaneously our thoughts to the most distant point. The flight of Ariel is slow compared with the speed of this physical agent, which (the mechanical difficulties of placing the wires below the reach of the action of breakers, when crossing seas, being overcome,) would enable us to convey our desires round the world in an instant of time. Those who are unacquainted with the peculiarities of arrangement which lead to the effective production of this result will do well to study the instruments in the Exhibition of Industry by means of which telegraphic communication is now effected. It may not be regarded by our readers as out of place if we endeavour to render the mode by which electricity is generated and employed familiar. The relation between voltaic currents and magnetism must be understood. It is, therefore, necessary that this should be clearly but succinctly described. Voltaic currents are generated by chemical action. An acid, usually sulphuric, is made to act upon zinc plates, which are placed in juxtaposition with, and connected by, a wire to a copper plate. The electric action is dependent on the different chemical affinity of the liquid for the respective metals: it will dissolve the zinc, but not the copper. Water is decomposed during the action. *Hydrogen* makes its escape at the surface of the copper plate, and the *oxygen* combines with the zinc to form oxide of zinc. The law of action as established by the researches of Faraday is, that the quantity of electricity liberated is exactly equal to that which was necessary to hold together in their original states the substances undergoing chemical change. During this disturbance of the electrical equilibrium, a portion passes through the liquid to the copper plate, and back through the connecting band to the zinc plate. Howsoever great may be the length of the connecting wires between the plates, the disturbance is communicated along the whole length of the line. The difference between the result, when the distance is but a few inches, and when it is extended over many miles, is only lessened by the degree of resistance offered by the metallic wires to the propagation or onward movement of the disturbance. We speak of a current traversing the wires. Our language, here imperfectly applied, is often very incorrectly understood; an idea of something flowing is usually conveyed to the mind by this form of expression. This is not the case,—a motion is communicated to one point of the mass, which is transmitted to the other, or rather is sensible at that extremity. At the time of this electrical progression, the wire is magnetic,—that is, it will attract iron in the same manner as a magnet does. If we hang up a magnetic piece of iron, so that it swings parallel to, and over or under the wire, this iron is unmoved if an electric disturbance is not circulating; but the moment that the force moves, from connexion being made with a battery in action, the iron is swung round at right angles to the direction of the wire. When contact is broken, and no electricity is traversing, it returns to the line of the wire; connection being made, it is again deflected. Having a power of thus moving a magnetic needle at any distance from the battery, we obtain the means of giving signals and of conveying signs. For the purpose of increasing this effect, the wire is bent many times around a magnetic needle, so that the current passing frequently along the length of the helix produces an increased effect. In this manner the weakest disturbances are rendered sensible. Upon this principle the needle telegraphs are constructed. These needle arrangements are of several kinds; the great object being to obtain rapidity of deflection and freedom from oscillation. The compound needle is that which is most frequently employed, and it consists of a very thin ivory disc, which sustains several highly magnetised short needles, firmly secured to it. This compound arrangement is placed between the wires and the index-needle beyond them. It will be evident, upon considering the construction, that by such an arrangement, the index-needle must come to rest almost immediately after it has been moved. Another method for moving the index is to attract or repel the support placed upon its axis by means of an electro-magnet. When we coil around a piece of soft iron a quantity of copper wire covered with silk, and connect the ends of those wires with a voltaic battery, the iron becomes powerfully magnetic. The moment contact is broken the magnetism is destroyed; or, by reversing the direction of the current, the poles of the magnet are rapidly changed. Thus any series of attractive or repulsive influences can be obtained with much facility. Brett and Little's patent electric telegraph is of this order. The magnet is in the form of a ring or horse-shoe, and is suspended in the centre of the helices of copper wire, which are double, and of a circular form. This magnet is deflected either to the right hand or to the left, according to the direction of the current. The indicators are not magnets, but are moved by the agency of the magnets, by which a distinct and certain indication is insured. In the electric printing telegraphs, similar means are employed to effect the desired end of printing the intelligence communicated. In some, inked types are actually employed, and brought into contact with the paper by the force of an electro-magnet. In others, whenever connection is made, the electricity effects chemical decomposition. When it is interrupted, no change takes place. Thus any number or variety of marks can be impressed at any distance from the communicator with great rapidity. The chemical agents usually employed to produce the marks on the paper are the ferro-cyanide of potassium, which, being decomposed, gives rise to the prussiate of iron, and makes a deep blue impression; or the iodide of potassium and starch, which is white,—but by the battery action, iodide of starch, a very dark purple substance, is produced, so that the letters or signs are impressed in a dark colour. All that is here attempted is to give an outline of the processes adopted; with the modifications of these, and the details which are introduced for the purpose of facilitating communication, space prevents our dealing.

Bakewell's Electric Telegraph possesses the peculiarity of transmitting *fac-similes* of the hand-writing of correspondents, so that their signatures can be identified. This is so ingeniously effected, that we must endeavour to render the arrangements adopted intelligible. The transmitting and receiving instruments are of the same description. Trains of wheels moved by weights impart uniform motion to each; these are allowed to act, or are checked, by the action of electro-magnets, in connection with a voltaic battery. As the power is derived from the same source, the machinery, at whatever distance the two arrangements may be from each other, is equally affected; the movement of the wheels and weights being isochronous. On each instrument is a metal cylinder, and over each cylinder metal styles, which press lightly on the cylinders from end to end. One of the poles of the voltaic battery is connected with the cylinders of the instruments, and the other with the styles. Thus those two systems of arrangement are always in precisely the same electrical condition; this being clearly understood, the following mode of electro-printing, or writing, will be intelligible. The message to be sent is written on a sheet of tin-foil with sealing-wax varnish, this is placed on the transmitting cylinder, all the lines covered by the varnish serve to break the connection. On the receiving cylinder a sheet of paper moistened with acidulated ferro-prussiate of potash is placed, when the connection is completed, electro-chemical decomposition is effected, and where any interruption occurs no change takes place. Now the cylinder carrying the inscribed tin-foil and that on which is placed the prepared paper, moving at the same rates, the current is interrupted by the varnish-writing in both at the same time. All the parts of the paper on which the metal styles press, when they are in connection with the tin-foil, become blue, all those corresponding with the varnish on the foil remain white. Hence the writing, signs, drawing, or whatever it may be, on the tin-foil, are faithfully represented on the prepared paper, hundreds of miles from it.

The application of the subtile power of electricity to

measure the tread of time, is another of the beautiful applications which have been made of this agency. Mr. Shepherd's clocks in the Exhibition present many novelties, the general principles of which we must endeavour to describe. It has been already explained that electro-magnets give us the power of changing the direction of a current at will, and of exerting a large amount of attractive force and suddenly suspending it. It will be evident, when the subject is considered, that magnets may be thus employed to attract and repel a pendulum which shall give motion to a clock, and that the force may be communicated to any number of clocks. But when this method is adopted, any irregularity in the action of the battery produces a corresponding irregularity in the motion of the pendulum. To obviate this, Mr. Shepherd, who exhibits the large electric clock in the transept of the Exhibition Building, gives impulse to the pendulum by means of a *remontoir* escapement. The pendulum under any circumstances of battery action, moves through the same arc in the same time, and thus uniformity of action is secured; the electro-magnets being the motive instruments of the whole. They are also employed to lock up the escape-wheel, to prevent motion being communicated by the action of the wind upon the large hands on the outside. In the striking arrangements much ingenuity has been exerted, the electro-magnets moving the hammer by the means already explained, and also regulating the number of blows to be struck by a very ingenious mechanical contrivance shown in a skeleton clock.

The arrangements for regulating the polar termination of wires of the batteries in the apparatus for the electrical light are exceedingly ingenious, and they appear to secure as far as it is practical to do so, the uniform distance of the charcoal points from each other, upon which entirely depends the constancy of the illumination. It is of course understood that whenever there is any interruption to the passage of the electric current, or where it has to move from a good conductor through an imperfect conductor, there is a manifestation of other forms of physical force; heat and light are developed. If we connect the two poles of a powerfully excited voltaic battery by a continuous wire, forming what is called a closed circuit, everything progresses quietly, there is no evolution of either heat or light. If, however, we cut the wire in any part, there will be developed between the parts so cut, both calorific and luminous agencies; the rush—to use a poetic form of expression—from one end or pole to the other, of electricity, by some mysterious action, gives rise to light and heat. Thus is produced the *electric light*, to increase the intensity of which poles of the hardest and purest charcoal are introduced; these have generally been manufactured for the purpose, by powdering the best coke that could be obtained, pressing it in moulds with some cementing material, and re-coking it with care. However hard the charcoal may be, it undergoes a change; particles are constantly carried off from one pole and deposited upon the other, thus altering their distances apart, and interfering with the uniformity of the light. The difficulties which arise from this cause may without doubt be overcome by mechanical adjustments; but there are other considerations, of an economic character, which appear of a more serious kind. As they apply equally to the applications of electro-magnetism as a mover of machinery, the consideration of the question may properly follow the notice of the electro-magnetic machines exhibited.

When it is shown that a piece of soft iron, around which is coiled a quantity of copper wire, through which an electric current is circulating, can be made to sustain the weight of many tons, or to exert an enormous pulling force, it appears natural to suppose that an agency so manageable as this might be applied with the greatest advantage to moving machinery. Numerous attempts have been made, and the applications of the power in several different ways attempted, but hitherto without any successful result. The power of electro-magnets, it is believed, may be increased without limitation. A voltaic current produced by the chemical disturbance of the elements of any battery, no matter what its form may be, is capable of producing, by induction, a magnetic force,—this force being always in an exact ratio to the amount of matter (zinc, iron, or otherwise) consumed

in the battery. The greatest amount of this magnetic power is produced when the chemical action is the most rapid. Hence, in all magnetic machines, it is more economical to employ a battery in intense action than one in which the chemical action is slow. It has been most satisfactorily proved that a one-horse power is obtainable in an electro-magnetic engine (the most favourably constructed to prevent loss of power), at the cost of 45 pounds of zinc, in a Grove's battery, in twenty-four hours; while 75 pounds of zinc are consumed in the same time, to produce the same power, in a battery of Daniell's construction. The cause of this is referred to the necessity of producing a high degree of excitement to overcome the resistance which the molecular forces offer to the electrical perturbations on which magnetic force depends. It is contended, that although we may not have arrived at the best form of voltaic battery, yet that we have learned sufficient of the law of electro-magnetic forces to declare, that under any conditions, the amount of magnetic power would depend on the change of state,—consumption of an element,—in the battery, and that the question resolves itself into this—What amount of magnetic power can be obtained from an equivalent of any material consumed? The following are regarded as the most satisfactory results yet obtained:—1st. The force of the voltaic current being equal to 678, the number of grains of zinc destroyed per hour is 151, which raised 9000 pounds one foot high in that time. 2nd. The force of current being relatively 1300, the zinc destroyed in one hour was 291 grains, which raised 10,030 pounds through the space of one foot. 3rd. The force being 1000, the zinc consumed was 223 grains; the weight lifted, one foot, 12,672 pounds. One grain of coal consumed in the furnace of a Cornish engine lifted 143 pounds one foot high; whereas one grain of zinc consumed in the battery lifted only 80 pounds. The cost of one hundred weight of coal is under 9d.; the cost of one hundred weight of zinc is above 216d. Therefore, under the most perfect conditions, magnetic power must be nearly twenty-five times more expensive than steam power. But it is an impossibility to reach even this, owing, in the first place, to the rate with which the force diminishes through space. As the mean of a great many experiments on a great variety of magnets, of different forms and modes of construction, the following results are given:—Magnet and armature in contact, lifting force 220 pounds; magnet and armature distant 1-250th of inch, 90·6 pounds; distant 1-125th of an inch, 50·7 pounds; distant 1-63rd of an inch, 50·1 pounds; distant 1-50th of an inch, 40·5 pounds. Thus, at 1-50th of an inch distance, four-fifths of the power is lost. From an examination of all these results, I am disposed to regard electro-magnetic power as impracticable, on account of its cost, which must necessarily be, under the best conditions, fifty times more expensive than steam power, and it is at present at least one hundred and fifty times as costly.

These remarks apply with equal force to the Electric Light. It must always be borne in mind that no physical power can be produced without a change of material somewhere. Steam is generated by the consumption of a certain quantity of coal; electricity by an equivalent weight of zinc, or some other metal on which chemical action takes place. Thus the question resolves itself into the simple one of, Is the light produced from the gas obtained by the destructive distillation of coal, or that developed by the consumption of zinc in the voltaic battery, the most effective and economical?

Other applications of electricity have their exemplification in this gathering of the results of human thought. One among others of the utmost importance, occupying no very prominent position, deserves our especial notice. Amongst the minerals in Class I. will be found two obelisks of coal, and one of an exceedingly hard stone, surrounded by miners' tools; and against the wall a drawing of a plan (now in most successful operation at Abercarne, in Monmouthshire) for blasting rocks at the bottom of a shaft by voltaic agency. In the ordinary mode of sinking through hard rocks, one hole only can be fired at a time. The miners then have to leave the shaft, and remain absent until the gases formed by the explosion are sufficiently cleared away to allow of their returning. In this way much time is lost. By galvanism any number of holes can be fired at the same time; and thus we obtain the cumulative force of simultaneous explosions. The mode of proceeding at the colliery of Sir Benjamin Hall is, in the first place, to bore three holes, forming the points of an equilateral triangle, which are inclined inwards towards the lower part. Fuses are prepared by passing the wires from a galvanic battery to the bottom, and there interposing a small piece of thin platinum wire. The wire is continued on to the next, or any number of holes; platinum being interposed at that point which is to be brought in contact with the gunpowder. The three holes being properly charged in this manner, the miners leave the pit, and, coming to the surface, make themselves the connection with the battery, and thus, out of all chance of accident, fire the holes. The moment the circuit is completed, all the platinum wires become white hot, and the powder is exploded. The first action is to rend out the entire centre of the shaft. Six or seven holes are next prepared in a similar manner, and also fired by the battery simultaneously, by which the whole of one surface of the shaft is heaved out. It is stated that the application of this power, in this instance, will lead to the happy result of sinking the shaft, and improving the ventilation of the coal-mine, in one-third the time which would have been occupied in the usual mode, with a very considerable saving of money at the same time.

Although satisfied that, with our present knowledge of electrical forces, we can scarcely hope to adapt the electric light to any useful purpose, within the limits of any ordinary economy, or to apply electro-magnetism as a motive power; it is quite possible that we may, by a careful study of the primary laws of these forms of electrical force, arrive at new conditions which may enable us to apply them. The empirical mode of proceeding at present adopted is of the most hopeless character. The models of electro-magnetic engines exhibited have much in them which is exceedingly ingenious; but, although working well as models, they do not promise to work with regularity or economy on the large scale; and for the present we must rest content to burn coals in our furnace rather than zinc in our batteries.

Electricity—that power which, from its fearfully destructive force, was regarded as the manifestation of Almighty power, and which was placed as the emblem of might in the hands of the Olympian Jove—from which men still retreat in terror, has, by the force of human intelligence, directed in a philosophic spirit, been subdued to perform the most important tasks for man. Through space it passes, without note of time, to convey the expression of our thoughts and feelings. India by its means will soon be united with England, and the merchant in London may instantaneously communicate with his agent in Calcutta, or the lover with his mistress. Thus, breaking through the barriers of distance, remote lands will be united together. The march of civilisation is in unison with the advance of science; and few things prove more convincingly the harmonious arrangements of Universal rule than the fact, that the physical agents which determine the condition of matter, which regulate the structural arrangements of the earth's crust, its rocks and its metalliferous deposits, and which mysteriously influence every organic change, are destined to work upon the spiritual part of creation, and to produce psychological phenomena,—which shall result in the production of order and the spread of peace. Bring people together,—let them know one another,—they develope the latent good which is in every human breast. Thus the gathering of nations in the Industrial Palace of Hyde Park cannot but be for good; and those small instruments which are exhibited in its north-western gallery are world-embracing in their influences, and must assimilate more closely the thoughts of those nations which they may bring into communion.

Electricity, again, has been made to perform for us more humble tasks,—to work in metal, and to measure the progress of time. Within the Exhibition all these appliances can be studied, and from the study of them much good must result.

In connection with this order of application, by interest, and also by position in the building, are the numerous contrivances adopted for ascertaining the laws which regulate terrestrial magnetism, and the adjustments by which the mariner, guided by the magnetic needle, is enabled to traverse the pathless ocean, with the utmost certainty of arriving at his destination. The magnetic forces of the globe are subjected to constant variations, principally owing to the changes of temperature. The lines of equal magnetic intensity around the globe are very irregular, and are evidently the result of heat. At the same place it is also found that monthly and daily variations occur; and it is important, in connexion with the elucidation of the great phenomena of nature, that these should be accurately determined. Several instruments are exhibited which are employed for determining the variations over different parts of the globe; the most important being those of Mr. R. W. Fox, exhibited by Mr. Wilton. In those instruments the power exerted by the magnetism of the earth is weighed off in parts of grains with the most surprising accuracy; and by them Ross, Stanley, Belcher, and others, have determined, in the most satisfactory manner, the magnetic intensity of those countries they visited in their surveying expeditions. The variations detected at the same spot have usually been determined by attentive observation; the number of vibrations made by a needle on either side of its zero point in a given time determining the force exerted by the earth's magnetism on the freely suspended magnetic bar. These researches were of exceeding delicacy, and even with the most practised observers they were liable to some errors. In the gallery of the Exhibition is an arrangement of the utmost ingenuity, in which the magnets are made to register their own movements. This is effected by reflecting a concentrated pencil of artificial light from the end of the bar upon some sensitive photographic paper placed between glass cylinders. The light makes a dark impression on the paper, and therefore any movement is very distinctly indicated. The oscillations of the magnet are horizontal; the motion of the cylinders, determined by a small clock arrangement, are vertical. A zig-zag line is therefore produced,—the variations of these from a standard line indicating the amount of disturbance. By means of this instrument, thus arranged, many magnetic perturbations, which would otherwise have passed unnoticed, have been detected. By an analogous arrangement, the conditions of the barometer and thermometer, for every moment of the day or night, are faithfully recorded. All errors of observation are thus avoided; and the same agency which produces the disturbance is made to record it. Light, the radiations from the sun, or any incandescent source, mark the movements; and to solar influence we are referred, by all the facts of science, to the probable cause for producing them. The consideration of this very beautiful application of our knowledge, that the radiations associated with light produce chemical change, naturally leads to the Photography of the Exhibition. Spread over various departments, Daguerreotypes and Calotypes, and other examples of the art, are to be found. England, France, Germany, Austria, and America, are equally ardent cultivators of photography. In the English department are a very extensive series of Daguerreotypes; possessing, however, but one novelty, which is to be discovered in the enamelled Daguerreotypes of Mr. Beard. The metallic tablets in these are covered with a transparent lacquer. The process of effecting this is not developed; but it is evident that heat is employed in diffusing the "enamel,"—and it certainly renders the picture permanent against the action of any ordinary mechanical force. For some years past, the Daguerreotype processes have advanced but little. The modes of manipulation have been somewhat improved, — the celerity of production slightly quickened, — many important physical facts discovered; but the art stands much where it was. Not so, however, with the processes on paper, and those on glass. In these a most marked improvement has taken place. Some examples of forest scenery, and picturesque bits, selected with artistic taste from "the ancestral homes of England," are perfect studies for an artist to dwell upon. The blending of the lights and shadows are more harmonious than usual, and the darker portions of the pictures are developed with much beauty of detail. These are the productions of Mr. Shaw, of Birmingham, who unites the skill of an artist with the experience gained by the long study of chemical science. The positives from glass negatives, executed by Ross and Thompson, of Edinburgh, are remarkable examples of the delicacy of this variety of sun-painting, and the artistic groups, by Mr. Hill of Edinburgh, of the Newhaven fishwomen, &c., together with many admirably selected bits, cannot but be admired for their truthfulness—they exhibit nature in those charming aspects the selection of which proves the ability of the artist and the refinement of his perceptions. In the French departments, M. Martens is the exhibitor of some photographs prepared by a process of his own on albuminised plates, which are first-class works of Art. The process employed is a modification of the Calotype as applied to glass tablets by the agency of albumen. The German and Austrian productions have each their beauties of a peculiar kind; but they have no novel features requiring any especial notice. The American Daguerreotypes are certainly very beautiful; the general tone of these productions being more of the mezzotinto style than those produced in either France or England. Many of the groups are exceedingly characteristic, and some of the selections of the scenery are remarkable for the perfection of their detail. The Hyalotypes, or photographs on glass, both positive and negative, (many of the positive pictures being coloured for magic-lantern slides), are a very pleasing application of the art. On the whole, we may regard the examples of sun-drawing exhibited as a very complete exemplification of the state of the art up to the present time.

Amongst the instruments which possess any character of novelty, those of M. Claudet, for determining the focus of lenses, and for adjusting the camera to the chemical focus for photographic purposes, and his arrangement for examining the quality of the solar rays, deserve especial notice. The peculiarities of these cannot be understood by descriptions merely; but by their adjustments, it is quite possible to determine with accuracy the action of the sun-light for so short a period as the thousandth part of a second of time. This zealous Daguerreotype artist has appreciated the value of imparting visible information; and in many examples amongst his collection, he has given illustrations of the operation of the chemical, as distinguished from the luminous, rays of the sun,—the influence exerted by media,—and the dissimilar action of the most and the least refrangible rays of the solar spectrum.

From these we learn many very important facts, which appear to support the view that the luminous power and the chemical power (*actinism*) of the solar radiations are agencies united in action, but balanced against each other in the effects which they produce on natural phenomena.

Of late years much attention has been paid to Meteorological phenomena, with the hope of determining the laws by which the apparently inconsistent winds and the resulting weather are regulated. We have established observatories in all parts of the world in which records are carefully kept of almost every passing cloud. The temperature of the air, the pressure of the atmosphere, the hygrometric state of the gaseous envelope, the electrical condition of it, the directions of the winds, and many other points of importance are registered under the direction of competent observers. From the results thus obtained, Professor Dove has already deduced some important facts, and determined the existence of fixed laws regulating at least some of the atmospheric phenomena.

Instruments have from time to time been devoted for registering the above points. Professor Whewell of Cambridge and Mr. Follett Osler of Birmingham, have devised very complete anemometers and rain-gauges; Mr. Osler associating also some other registrations with his very complete instrument. In the Hall of the Polytechnic Institution, and at the Philosophical Institution of Birmingham, an opportunity is afforded of examining what has been done, and of comparing it with the very complete "Atmospheric Recorder," of Mr. Holland, which registers every breeze that blows, or shower that falls, upon the Industrial Building in Hyde Park. Without drawings it is quite impossible to describe, so as to be understood, the details of the arrangements. But some of its principles may be rendered easily intelligible. In the first place it will be understood that every fact is recorded by the machine itself, by means of a pencil passing over a regularly moving piece of paper, which is carried onward by an attachment with an eight-day clock.

The barometer is of the siphon form, of large bore, and upon the mercury in the shortest leg is a float very accurately counterpoised, leaving only sufficient weight to enable it to follow the mercury in its rise and fall. It will be readily conceived that many plans might be adopted for correcting this with a pencil, which should mark every variation. The thermometric arrangement consists of ten mercurial thermometers, of a peculiar form, very accurately balanced, so that the slightest movement of the mercury gave at once a given degree of preponderance on one side or the other. A slip of wood is employed as the hygrometer; this is placed in a tube, through which the air passes freely; every elongation or contraction of this, indicating an excess or deficiency of moisture in the air, is in like manner registered. It will be, of course, understood that a piece of wood forms a very good hygrometer by absorbing moisture or parting with it readily. The electrometer is an insulated conductor, fixed on the highest convenient place, from which a wire is brought down to the instrument, and connected with a fixed disc, near which is placed a moveable one. When a cloud charged with the electric fluid comes within the range of the conductor, the moveable disc begins slowly to pass from the fixed disc to a spring, discharging each time a portion of its electricity; it then falls back to the first disc, and remains quiet until another electric cloud approaches; the moving disc carrying a pencil, records every disturbance.

The rain-gauge is placed on the top of the building; it is a foot square. The rain collected in this passes through a pipe into the building, and a float indicates the height of the water and regulates the motion of the pencil. The amount of evaporation going on is by a similar contrivance registered. The direction of the wind is recorded by another pencil which marks the course upon the paper throughout the whole circle of the horizon, or that portion through which it passes, and the force of the wind is indicated by the action of the aërial current upon a board one foot square fixed to the vane, and accurately counterpoised, so that the slightest pressure is at once indicated by the movement of the counterpoise. Thus is afforded a means of determining, with the utmost accuracy, every change in the weather, and by thus avoiding all the errors which arise from the carelessness or inaptitude of assistants, we may expect to arrive more satisfactorily at some important facts in climatology beyond those which we already possess. It is interesting to watch the little pencils moving to and fro, marking their zig-zag or curved tracts upon the paper, and to observe the peculiar association of one phenomenon with another. The very remarkable groups of instruments which we have been describing are amongst the most striking evidences of Science in the Great Exhibition. By appliances such as these we advance our knowledge and gain power over the phenomena of nature. An instrument by which the navigator is, by a very easy method, enabled to determine the position of the centre of a storm, called by the inventor, Lieut.-Col. Lloyd, Typhodeictor, or storm-pointer, appears to be exceedingly useful. It is now fully determined that the great storms of the tropics are revolving masses of air, moving onward at a great rate. If a ship becomes involved in one of these, she is soon disabled, but by the investigations of the law of these storms by Lieut.-Col. Reid, an easy method of determining the direction of their movement is given, and thus the mariner is enabled to sail out of their influence. It is to facilitate this that Colonel Lloyd has constructed his storm-pointer. Strange things though meet us here; we have a Storm Indicator, in which leeches crawling out of the water, as is their habit when there is much free electricity, are made to ring bells; and we have Count Demni's Man of Steel, composed of many thousand parts, and these so contrived that from a figure of about five feet in height, it may readily be converted into one of eight. The ingenuity of these cannot be doubted; but we fear their utility is questionable. They are among the things which sometimes cause us to marvel at the variety of ways to which human invention is frequently applied without the probability of any satisfactory practical result.

THE SCIENCE OF THE EXHIBITION.

PART IV.

IN our rapid glances at the developments of science, as they are manifested in the efforts of thought and industry now gathered within our "palace all of glass," we have confined our attention principally to the productions of British skill. Much has been done towards the extension of abstract science to the useful purposes of life, but still more remains to be done; and we should learn to look upon the Great Exhibition as one of the resting places, from which in our ascent we can contemplate the triumphs of the past, and meditate upon the labours which yet remain to try the human mind. The ocean of knowledge has been ventured upon in frail, but skilfully managed barques, and some of the isles of truth, which stud its surface like stars of light in their beauty, have been discovered; but "a wilderness of heaving waters" is beyond the horizon; and from the crest of the wave upon which we rest, we see mirages of glorious promise for those who will essay the untracked space from which yet higher treasures may be gathered to improve the condition of toiling humanity.

It now becomes an equally pleasing task to contemplate the Eastern side of the industrial palace, within which space those, whom we, from long habit, call foreigners, have so liberally displayed the evidences of their industry. If no other good were to result from the Exhibition, than that of bringing the nations closer together, of making man better acquainted with his fellow man, and thus destroying those national prejudices which are so many barriers against human progress, it would have done much towards the advancement of civilisation.

In passing carefully through the labyrinthine ways, between Tunis and Turkey on the one side, and the United States on the other, we have diligently sought to discover some novel application of science—something peculiar in its way—illustrative of some branch of study to which England might yet be a stranger. But we have found it not;—we confess to some disappointment, and we acknowledge some amount of pleasure. It proves, that notwithstanding the barriers of language—that in spite of still existing prejudices—the truth diffuses itself like an atmosphere over the old and the new continents.

Whether any law regulates the progress of human knowledge is a question of interest, which, however, we are not in a position to answer. There are nevertheless many curious phenomena connected with the advance of truth which appear to indicate psychological effects to be determinable in obedience to some general cause. When we find the electrotype developed at the same time by Jacobi in St. Petersburgh and by Spencer in Liverpool; the mystery of sun-drawing being discovered by Daguerre in Paris and by Talbot in this country; and many other examples of the publication of new truths at nearly the same time in countries widely separated from each other, and where previous concert was impossible, we are compelled to admit, at least, the general operation of almost occult powers, inducing to the development of facts new to human knowledge. Be this as it may, it is certain that no one country amongst those exhibiting their works, can claim priority on account of any new application of science. For varieties of industry, and for perfection in those varieties, the international juries were appointed; they have completed their labours, their reporters are now at work on their respective reports, and it will not be long before the world will know how they have performed their responsible duties.

Commencing our review of the continental section of the Exhibition, we are met first by the productions of the most singular people on the face of the earth—the Chinese. The inhabitants of the celestial empire had a science—probably an empirical science—in a high degree of perfection, while yet Europe was enveloped in the night of ignorance. The manufacture of porcelain, which is only now in its perfection familiar to ourselves, was amongst the earliest of their industrial Arts. Metallurgy, particularly mixed metal casting, has been practised by them with great success for many thousands of years. They have taxed and tortured nature to minister to their wants, and yield fresh food for their luxuries for ages, and yet now they figure amidst the gatherings of the earth, the exemplars of a people who have stood still while all the world has been moving. In manufacture and in art they have great capabilities, but they have made no progress. Their vases are of the same kind as adorned the halls of the wealthy in the Si-Hang dynasty. Their ivory carvings are similar to those of Tai-tsong in 626, and their paintings are such as in the very infancy of art are to be discovered in other lands. Yet in one little corner of the area, occupied by China, is a little picture of a female bather, doubtless a copy, in which there is a degree of perfection in drawing, in knowledge of colour, and in artistic effect, which proves how easily they could excel if they were stimulated to the trial. There is much of considerable scientific interest in the contributions from China. We learn something of the mineral produce of that country in the collection of the various materials from the great porcelain works of Kiang-tiht' Chin near the Poyang lake, employed in the manufacture of porcelain. We have a beautiful exemplification of their process of making pottery. We find that all the materials they employ are such as we possess, and judging from the appearance they are, most of them, inferior in quality to those which our potters employ. The naturalist might glean much information from the study of the series, but the products of the vegetable and animal kingdom are beyond our province. However, in the metal tea-pots, *lined* with earthenware, we see that our process, recently introduced, of enamelling iron utensils is familiar to the Chinese. Their paper-hangings should be inspected, and we should remember that we owe this branch of manufacture entirely to the Chinese, and that the first attempts made in Europe were with a view merely to imitate those papers which were then imported and sold at an enormous price. The Chinese metal castings are most ingenious; they make their model of wax, place it in a box and cover it with sand, tightly packed on every side; the whole is then exposed to heat sufficient to melt the wax, and bronze is run in to supply its place. The Chinese compasses are curious, seeing that with this nation the use of the magnet as a guide over the ocean or the desert, had probably its origin; and the models of pumps shown are interesting as illustrating the knowledge of hydrostatics possessed by the inhabitants of the flowery land.

Tunis has many remarkable features; rough manufacture united with beautiful form and an harmonious arrangement of colours, being curiously displayed. The Tunisian dyes have long been celebrated, particularly their red dye, as shown in the celebrated caps called *Beretti*. The mordant they employ is alum: much merit is attributed to the waters of a river, but it appears that the whole secret of their process consists in fixing their vegetable dyes by means of the sulphate of alumina, exposing the dyed goods to the chemical agency of their southern sun, and then streaming out, by immersion in the river, everything which is not chemically combined with the wool, cotton, or silk. It is interesting to examine the earth, rich in iron, and the lead ore from the mountains of Slata, and the copper ore from the mountain of Gerisa; we gain thus knowledge of the distribution of minerals, which can rarely be obtained; and if instead of being dispersed in areas, representing kingdoms, the articles exhibited had been gathered into natural groups, the kingdoms being subdivisions, the educational character of the great Exhibition would have been increased a hundred fold. Incidentally, while dealing with the minerals of Asia and Africa, we should refer to a recent addition in Class I., on the English side, of copper ores, and iron, of remarkable character, from some barren mountains in the depths of the deserts of Arabia Petræa, which have only once been passed by an English traveller. The gypsum, the limestones, and the salt of Tunis are all deserving the attention of those who would really profit by this great gathering.

Persia contributes little of scientific interest; but Greece, in addition to a valuable collection of vegetable products, including a jar of honey from Mount Hymettus, sends a series of lithological specimens, which have much importance and classic association. The priors of the monasteries of Hymettus and Pentelicon contribute specimens of the marbles from those quarries on which the great sculptors of Athens exerted their genius. Upon such stones as these Phidias worked, and from these quarries came the wonders of the Parthenon. There is also the Cipolino marble, from which the Columns of Antoninus and Faustima were built; and there are numerous examples of variegated limestones, many of which are very beautiful.

Some specimens of puzzolano, which is much used for hydraulic architecture, are important; and particularly as these are said to be equal to the celebrated lime cement of Italy.

The first paragraph in the Catalogue of the Turkish contributions truly bespeaks their importance: "This collection of upwards of three thousand three hundred objects is arranged under the several divisions of Vegetable, Animal, and Mineral Kingdoms, and into two general classes, of Raw Materials and Manufactures." Under the head of manufactures again, we read: "The articles of manufacture, the produce of Turkish industry, forwarded for exhibition by the Turkish Ministry of Commerce, comprises about one thousand three hundred items; and the articles themselves illustrate, under the simple and intelligible conditions of this arrangement, the industrial progress, the arts, the costumes (and the varied materials of which these are composed), as they at present exist in some of the extensive dominions of the Sultan."

The inductive system thus adapted by an Oriental people, might have been worthily imitated by other nations. This series can be read with facility, and instructive are the tongues of the trees and the sermons of the stones of the Ottoman empire. The dye woods are numerous. The grains and other vegetable produce are varied; and their balsam, resins, and pharmaceutical preparations of considerable value. The essential oils of Turkey are familiar to all; and the perfume of the "Attar Gul," while it has been the poet's theme, has been a mystery to the perfumers of all Europe. Here we have the otto, and the oils of cedars and sandars, and violet and jessamine, and those fragrant essences, which combined, form the attractive scents of British dealers.

We scarcely knew the mineral riches of Turkey before; but she brings us gold, silver, copper, iron, lead, and salt. The alums exhibited are exceedingly curious and interesting; and the coal, pitch, bitumen, and liquid naphtha, are equally important. The clays are numerous, and to the lovers of the fumes of tobacco the original *meerschaum*, poetically called the "foam of the sea," will have a peculiar value. Amongst the large group of manufactured articles, we find numerous examples of weaving and felting, of tanning, and or dyeing, which should be carefully examined. The works in gold and silver, particularly the "tarfs," are curious examples of the delicate chasing and filagree work in which many of the oriental nations excel. The spoons in amber, the cup of Calcedony, the narguilles in silver, and the glass and china porringers, show much perfection in this character of manufacture. The iron manufacture of the East has been long celebrated; the Turkish scimetar has taken its position amongst the most celebrated weapons of oriental warfare, and some good examples of these blades are exhibited. On the whole the present condition of Turkish industry is well represented; but regarded with a view to elicit the aids derived from science, we are bound to declare that these are few. The perfection shown has been the result of slow gathered experience, a sort of traditionary code which has passed from father to son through many generations. The systematic arrangement adopted proves, however, that the Turk might become an apt student in inductive science; and it is not improbable but that the interest felt in the city of the Sultan in this gathering under the auspices of the consort of the Queen of England, may have its influence in leading back to the East that kind of learning which has had a general bearing towards the western regions of the earth.

Nor are the productions of Egypt of less interest than those of Turkey. The beautiful vase of stalagmitic arragonite, and the blocks of the same, called in the Catalogue by the general term of alabaster, displays an ornamental stone of much beauty and novelty. The petrified wood, part of those forests in the neighbourhood of Cairo, which have, buried in the sands for ages, yielded up the carbon they once contained, to be replaced by silica, has much that is instructive in connection with the chemistry of natural substitution.

The natron of Lower Egypt and the native and prepared alums are alike illustrations again of nature's chemistry. In the manufactures we discover much of the same character as in Turkey—indeed, they may properly be included in the same list.

The contributions from Algeria are chiefly from the vegetable kingdom, but we have also some specimens of red chalk, of coral, and the Commission of Mines of Algiers and of Constantine have sent samples of various ores, and geological specimens and mineral products. There are yet three other portions of African produce in the Exhibition, but these have their place amongst the British Colonies. Western Africa has many curious products: lime made from bones burnt to ashes mixed with water and dried in the sun, used by those who spin, to keep their fingers dry, is one of those distinguishing characteristics which should not be unobserved; this is of course a phosphate of lime. The earthenware and the metal manufactures, and the bottles of galena and of antimony used to dye the eyelids, are peculiarly African. The copper figures of the Ashantees, the gold ornaments from Cape Coast, and the glass beads from the same locality, are curious, though we suspect the glass beads to be of Birmingham manufacture, the trade for these with the western coast of Africa being very large. The Cape of Good Hope contributes skins, and ivory, and pearl; there is lead ore from Port Elizabeth, iron from Uitenhage, and graphite from the neighbourhood of Cape Town. In thus rapidly sketching off the characteristic productions of each country, it is hoped that it is understood that it is with reference to their value—scientifically—as pointing to new localities in which known substances are produced, and to their value as sources upon which the industry of the native population of each locality might with advantage be exerted.

We return to Europe, and here, in Spain, we have abundant examples of scientific application. There is much for the mineralogist and the botanist to study; for the practical miner to contemplate, and for the manufacturer to consider with care. The marbles contributed from the Royal Library of Madrid are numerous; here are the finest statuary marbles, and the Sierras produce many beautifully marked varieties. The Directors of the Mines are large exhibitors, and enlighten us on many of the products of the Spanish mines. Antimony, and silver, and lead, and copper are sent from several districts; amongst these are some good examples of the process of converting the double sulphuret of iron and copper (*copper pyrites*) into soluble sulphate of copper, by slow roasting: the process consists in stratifying the sulphur ores with carbonaceous matter, and setting fire to the pile; both the sulphur and copper combine with oxygen in the process, and sulphate of copper (blue vitriol) being formed, it is dissolved out, and the metal precipitates from the solution by the electro-chemical action of iron. The ores of iron exhibited are numerous, and some of them are remarkably fine specimens. The most interesting, however, of the mineral products of Spain are the ores of mercury.

The mines of the Asturias and of La Mancha, particularly of Almaden, yield the largest quantity of cinnabar, sulphuret of mercury. Almaden is stated to furnish annually upwards of one thousand tons of ore. These are the most extraordinary formations of quicksilver in the world; the mines produce native mercury and the sulphuret, and, notwithstanding the mines of La Mancha have been actually worked for many centuries, they are still exceedingly productive. Black-lead, *plumbago*, or graphite, is produced in considerable quantities; and nickel and cobalt ore, the demand for which is every year increasing in this country, is found in some abundance in Grenada and Malaga. The *phosphorite* of Estremadura, of which good specimens are in the Exhibition, is of high scientific interest. A mountain of phosphate of lime exists in the wild part of this district. It was visited by Dr. Daubeny, some few years since, with a view of ascertaining the capabilities for transporting a substance so valuable to this country. It was found to have very nearly the composition of the earth of bones, viz:—81·15 of phosphate of lime, and 14 of fluoride of calcium, it is, however, quite useless, the cost of carriage being far too great to render its use possible.

The vegetable products of Spain are largely shown, and many of the manufactures of that country. The wine and oil jars will render the young some information on that mystery, the thieves of the Arabian Nights and the wine jars. Amongst the most attractive of the many displays of arms in the Exhibition, those furnished by the Royal Ordnance of Toledo are the most interesting. The swords of Toledo have long been celebrated, and some of those now exhibited display all the perfections of that celebrated manufactory. They are engraved, enamelled, and gilt, many of them most elaborately so, and it is said that the temper of the blades now in the Exhibition, is equal to any ever made. There are many other examples, involving a very considerable amount of science, as the illustrations of dyeing, of the preparation of leather, of chemical and of metal manufacture, but our space forbids our dwelling on these.

Portugal comes forward, rich in vegetable products, particularly in woods and dye drugs. Their mineral products are few, but some of them of much interest. Their woven materials and dyed fabric exhibit much manufacturing skill, and their fictile manufacture show that much attention has been paid to the chemistry of pottery and of glass.

Rome contributes many objects of much interest, but an interest rather belonging to Art than to science. We have some examples of a vitrification effected by some chemical process, but this is not explained. Natural and manufactured asphalt, and specimens of the alum formations of the Roman States, are in this series.

Tuscany contributes many things of much scientific interest. The marbles, alabaster and lithographic stones of the states, together with the ores of copper, lead, and mercury, are well selected. The examples from the celebrated Boracic Lagoons, of Tuscany, which produce so largely the Boracic acid, and its salt, borax, are of much interest. New colours for encaustic painting are shown, but these are secret preparations, the scientific or practical value of which we cannot learn. The terra-cotta, and paintings on that ware, is curious, and the china from the manufactory near Florence, with the chemical glass, well illustrates the condition of these manufactures. Tuscany has ever been celebrated for her works in marbles, and these are well displayed, the celebrated *lumachelli* marble, and the marble of Cipollino, together with a table from the brocatello of Caldana, and columns of the same, with the capitals of the yellow marble of Sienna, are much admired. But that which gives a preeminent scientific interest to the contributions from Tuscany, is the series of beautiful wax models, illustrating most perfectly the galvanic system of the torpedo, or electric ray. These are most exquisitely copied from some of the most careful dissections which have ever been made of this extraordinary electrical arrangement. The beautiful arrangements of the cells, and their connection with the nervous system, may here be studied with the greatest advantage; rarely has so fine an opportunity presented itself, for acquiring a knowledge of that minute anatomy, which appears to lay open to us the processes of electrical excitation as connected with the phenomena of vital action.

Sardinia contributes many chemical products of much interest, amongst others quinine, beberine, morphine, glucosate of soda obtained from the syrup of mulberries, and ergotine, the active principle of the ergot of rye, may be named. Some of the mixed metal castings are of an admirable character; and the bronze medals exhibited, which are stated to contain a tenth part of pewter, appear to show that there is as stated by the exhibitor, an advantage in employing this admixture: it is not however uncommon to use lead with bronzes to make the metal flow readily.

Switzerland exhibits in a most satisfactory manner its tributes to the competitive display of industry. There are not many of its works which require any especial notice in connection with science. Their clocks and watches, their woollen and other woven manufactures, their embroideries, etc., are admirable illustrations of the applications of prior knowledge with all the advantages of native skill and industry. The specimens of their metal works, particularly their steel manufacture, is good; and the ingenuity displayed in the watch escapements and compensating balances is exceedingly great. Their musical boxes are well known, but these are rather illustrative of mechanical skill than of the science of acoustics.

To attempt to do justice to the numerous beautiful applications of science which are exhibited in the departments of France is not possible within the limits of our essay. In their dyes they have availed themselves of all the knowledge which chemistry has afforded, and in the results we see the advantages of placing such men as Berthollet and Chevreul to preside over special departments of industry. The rich hues of the French silks, the brilliancy of their pigments, and the intense colours of their tapestries, are evidences of the most exact attention to the investigations of science. In ceramic art, again, we have the same evidence afforded us; the Sèvres porcelain displays the results of the investigations of Brongniart, and attest to the skill of Ebelman, who has at present the direction of that national establishment. In ornamental metal manufacture the celebrity of the French is great, and in the evidences afforded by the Exhibition we learn that it is not merely to the works of elegance that they have devoted their attention; in their larger works, as machines and manufacturing tools, they have displayed their sense of the importance of applying scientific knowledge to a useful end. The philosophical apparatus from France are numerous; the electrical and magneto-electrical apparatus are excellent; their optical apparatus, in many respects superior to our own, in proof of which we have only to refer to the beautiful dioptric apparatus for light-houses, exhibited in the west main avenue, and to the apparatus of Soliel for investigating the remarkable phenomena of the polarisation of light. Their optical glass is of the first class, and this superiority is dependent entirely on attention to chemical and physical laws, which the British glass manufacturer has, unfortunately, not yet learned fully to appreciate. We hope, however, the Exhibition will lead to greatly improved results in this respect. While on the subject of glass we must not forget the great novelty of flint glass, in which zinc takes the place of lead; it is exceedingly transparent, and in many respects a beautiful manufacture. The daguerreotype was a French discovery; all the great improvements in this photographic process have been made in this country. The calotype is an English discovery, and it would appear that the greatest improvements in this process have been made in France. The results exhibited by Le Gray, Niepce, Martin, and others, are of the most artistic character, and many of them exhibit effects which we have never before seen produced. The chemical preparations of France are too well known to require any notice beyond the fact of their being fairly exhibited, although some of the first class manufacturers have not contributed to the series. There is not, that we are aware, a department of industry which is not well represented, and there are several special applications of science which we hope yet to make the subject of especial attention.

Our remarks on France apply with equal force to the Zollverein. Within this great commercial union we find evidences of extensive progress in the Industrial Arts, the applications of science are numerous, and the results most satisfactory. Whether we examine the products of Prussia, or those of the smaller states, we must be struck with the marked attention which has been paid to the improvement of the more useful branches of manufacture. The character of education within those states is such that every child is made familiar with the great truths of science, and taught to apply the facts afforded by experiment to the improvement of the great realities of manufacture. Of the more refined application, the electrotype, their galvano-plastic, of photography, and of the other applications of the discoveries in physical science, Germany in no respect falls behind.

The collection of minerals from Hungary, which are within the Austrian areas, are of much interest. The metallurgical processes exhibited are no less instructive. In chemistry the exhibitors from Austria are numerous, and many of the chemicals are of a very superior character. It is a curious circumstance that there are a great many exhibitors of lucifer matches. Here we have an illustration of the advantages of a scientific discovery. Schrœder, of Vienna, discovered that he could, by a certain process, alter the physical character of phosphorus without in any way producing a chemical change. The phosphorus which he prepares is but slightly combustible, but the great advantage of the discovery is that it has removed from the manufactories of instantaneous lights the liability to a frightful disease to which the men and women employed formerly were much subject. This allotropic phosphorus is now becoming an article of considerable importance in this country. The beet-root sugar—the ultramarine and numerous other chemicals attest the attention paid to the science of chemistry in Austria. The manufacture of machinery has not been hitherto a branch of industry much cultivated in Austria; but the few articles exhibited show the capabilities of the mechanist of that country. Natural history would find the Austrian contributions furnishing a large field for study. Metallurgy and metal manufacture is fully illustrated, and the finer kinds of Art-manufacture show the attention of the manufacturer to the teachings of Art and science. Bohemian glass is too well known to require a word beyond a renewed one of admiration at the exquisite colours produced in much of the glass exhibited.

Russia sends produce which is peculiar and interesting. The extraordinary display of malachite manufacture as doors, chimney-pieces, tables and vases, present a feature of a most remarkable character. In connection with this we have some beautiful sheets of copper, and beyond all question the most perfect sheet-iron that was ever manufactured. Amongst other characteristic manufactures, a series of ewers, jugs, etc., made of felted rabbits fur, should not be passed unnoticed; and their tanned skins of the Russian wolves, etc., the fur or hair being still preserved, are remarkable instances of a peculiarity in a scientific process which we have not yet reached.

Holland and Belgium, particularly the latter state, present numerous fine examples of their peculiar forms of scientific application to industrial purposes. In every example afforded by these countries we see the evidences of a thinking people. Denmark is a small exhibitor, but scientific application is particularly shown in a process called "Stylography"—a process bearing much analogy to our glyphography—and an electro-magnetic engine, of certainly a most ingenious construction. Norway contributes chrome-iron ores. Sweden maintains her position as the producer of iron of the finest quality; and cobalt and nickel are amongst the most important productions of these northern states. There are several of the independent states of Europe we would desire to examine with attention, but we must include them in the general expression of admiration at the zeal which has led our continental neighbours to incur the risk, the cost and the labour of transporting to our shores such valuable exemplifications of the efforts of thought exerted on the raw materials which nature has furnished to them in their respective localities.

The United States occupy the eastern end of the building, at which our imperfect sketch must end. Within the areas devoted to these important contributors it has been said as a reflection, there is a poverty displayed. If the articles are examined with proper views, it will be seen that they are rich in promise. The collections of metalliferous and of earthy minerals show that one of the most extensive mining districts in the world remains to be developed. Iron, plumbago, copper, lead, zinc, await the evocating power of Saxon industry, and coal comes ready to aid the labours of the evocator. Whether we examine the mass of red oxide of zinc sent with much labour and at an expense of 200*l.* to the Exhibition from the Sterling Hill Zinc Mine in New Jersey, or the collections of minerals which Dr. Feutchwanger of New York exhibits, we see these evidences. Beyond this exhibition of natural products, we find in the manufacturers every indication of the exercise of original minds, which must eventually exert a mighty power over the productions of nature. As the most striking exemplifications of science shown by the United States exhibitors, we cannot but refer to the daguerreotypes, which are certainly superior to any others in the exhibition; and those beautifully perfect pictures on glass, to which the name of hyalotypes has been given.

In proof of the good feeling of the exhibitors from the United States, even as the Exhibition is advancing to a close, they send us fresh contributions. Science and its useful applications are well illustrated in these; numerous agricultural implements of improved construction, and peculiarly fitted for the country in which they are to be employed, have been forwarded; a most ingenious adjunct to the ruling machine for ledgers, by which the pens are lifted, and a paging-machine, printing the numbers on both sides at once, are exceedingly valuable. From the vegetable kingdom they contribute a peculiar moss, found in the Southern States, which is of exceeding toughness and strength; this is employed for all the purposes of the upholsterer for which hair has been generally used, and it appears capable of being manufactured into ropes and matting, which quite equal the cocoa-nut fibre; it is found most abundantly in the southern parts of the Union, completely involving the trees in its wild growth. In addition to these stores, the lard-oil and the stearine manufacture, which is carried on so extensively in the United States, is well illustrated, as is also the manufacture of soap. We have omitted all notice of the variety of fossil remains, which illustrate many of the rock formations in America, of great scientific interest; these can scarcely be regarded as industrial, and are not to our present purpose.

The imperfections of this review of the Science of the Exhibition, arise from the numerous subjects laid out for examination. Many of much importance have necessarily escaped the attention they deserve, and some have been entirely missed in the process of selection, which are of high merit. Even now some are remembered which we could still desire to include in our essay. This is not now possible, suffice it then that we solicit all to believe we have made our selections without favour, and where we may have failed to be judicious in our choice of examples, the imperfections of our knowledge must be the excuse we offer. In the Exhibition we perceive the germs of lasting good. Believing that the entire world, from China in the east to Chili and California in the west, will feel the exciting tremors of vitality which spring from the industrial heart of the world in 1851, beating within the Crystal Palace of Hyde Park, we content ourselves, in conclusion, with that excellent maxim chosen by the Illustrious Prince, with whom the good, and being good—great thought—had birth, to teach to man exertion, and to temper it with humility.

"Say not the discoveries we make are our own; the germs of every art are implanted within us, and God, our instructor, from hidden sources, develops the faculties of invention."

THE HARMONY OF COLOURS.

The Harmony of Colours as exemplified in the Exhibition

By Mrs. MERRIFIELD.

ADDISON observes, in one of his Essays on the Pleasures of the Imagination, "Our sight is the most perfect and delightful of all our senses." "There is nothing," he remarks in another essay, "which makes its way more directly to the soul than beauty, —among the several kinds of beauty, the eye takes most delight in colours," and he even thinks "the ideas of colour are so pleasing, and so beautiful in the imagination, that it is possible the soul will not be deprived of them after its separation from the body, but perhaps find them excited by some other occasional cause, as they are at present by the impressions of the subtle matter on the organs of sight."* Although we may not feel disposed to adopt these opinions, in their fullest extent, the delightful and fascinating power of colours must be acknowledged by all. Their influence upon the English school of painting has been most decided, and has imparted to it its distinguishing characteristic. The English painters have long been colourists, but English manufacturers, as a class, have yet to learn that the laws relative to the harmony and contrast of colours are of universal application; that whether a picture is to be painted, or a few pieces of coloured silk or cloth are to be exposed for sale, the favourable impression made on the spectator or purchaser is in proportion to the extent to which these laws have been observed, and that the beauty of a colour depends less, perhaps, upon its individual purity and brightness, than upon the skill with which it is contrasted with others.

When the impressions of wonder and delight, which we feel on the first view of the interior of the Crystal Palace, have passed away, and the mind becomes capable of attending to details, we are sensible of a more pleasing and tasteful arrangement of colours in that part of the building appropriated to foreigners, than in the department assigned to the exhibition of native and American productions. The object of

* See the Spectator, Nos. 411, 412, 413.

all the exhibitors is the same, namely, to set off the articles exhibited to the greatest advantage, and to attract the attention of the spectator; but where coloured goods are displayed, we find the efforts of the various parties have been attended with different results. The harmony and good taste, as regards colour, with which many of the foreign productions are disposed, suggest the prevalence of some system by which the exhibitors have been guided in arranging the space allotted to them.

In point of elegance of design, harmonious arrangement of colours, and tasteful display, the French, considering the variety of works which they exhibit, excel all others. The Austrians (under which term the inhabitants of the Lombardo-Veneto are not included) and other Germans, although in advance of the English, have not yet attained the harmony of the French in the arrangement of colours. In all these countries we know that schools of design have long been established, and the scientific arrangement of colours is an object of sedulous study among all persons connected with the arts of design. But it is somewhat surprising to observe the harmony of colour which prevails in the productions of Turkey, Tunis, and the Asiatic nations; for, taking into the account the state of education in those countries, we cannot ascribe this harmony to a scientific knowledge, but to the custom which obtains generally in the East, of following the traditions of their ancestors. The fact is, however, a proof that the harmony of colours—of the more simple and positive colours, at least—was formerly well understood, and the perfect harmony of the architectural paintings of the ancient Egyptians, of the tombs of Xanthus, and Etruria, and the decorations of the Pompeian Villas, show that this knowledge has existed from a very remote period.

Excellent as the English have proved themselves to be, not only in the sciences but in the arts, it is universally, although reluctantly, admitted, that in the arrangement of colours they are not equal to their continental neighbours. This is apparent on a cursory inspection of the Great Exhibition, where the English goods appear to be arranged generally without any regard to the harmony of colours. The trophy of Messrs. Keith & Co., in the nave, is very defective in harmonious arrangement, and the defects are rendered more apparent by its prominent situation. In the first place the colours are all bright and positive, and the eye finds no neutral or quiet hues on which to repose. In the second place, the arrangement itself is bad; for we have the disagreeable impression of light blue next to crimson. Defects like these would have been obviated by a knowledge of the laws which govern the harmony and contrast of colours.

The harmonious arrangement and contrast of colours is not arbitrary, or absolutely dependent upon taste, but is governed by fixed laws, in the same manner as the other branches of natural philosophy. A "good eye," as it is called, may, indeed, greatly assist, but nine times out of ten the *good eye* will be found to mean the *educated eye*. All persons have not equal power of analysing their thoughts, so as to perceive accurately the whole chain of ideas which have led to certain conclusions; they are scarcely conscious of the intermediate state between the first impressions and the ultimate decision, and the "good eye" frequently receives credit for what has been, in fact, a mental operation.

The laws relating to the harmony and contrast of colours have been developed by M. Chevreul, professor of chemistry to the French national establishments of the Gobelins, Beauvais, and La Savonnerie, and they have been studied in France, less or more, by all connected with the arts of design; and, judging from the specimens we have seen, with more success by the industrial artist, than by the student of the Fine Arts.

It is much to be regretted that the subject is not more studied in England, where the arrangement of colours is too frequently looked upon merely as a matter of taste; and when we consider the large class of persons to whom this knowledge would be useful, it really appears astonishing that it should be so little cultivated. Not only would the manufacturers of articles of clothing and furniture benefit by this knowledge, but the wholesale and retail venders of the goods,—a very numerous class of persons,—as well as the upholsterer, house-painter, decorator, and paper-hanger. To these may be added the large class of artisans employed in these trades, all of whom would profit by attending schools of design, or where that is impracticable, by learning the principles of the harmony of colours from their employers, together with the mechanical part of the different trades.

The good influence of the Schools of Design established in this country is, however, in spite of the defects alluded to as regards colour, clearly perceptible throughout the English department, and if, in some things, the execution falls short of the design, it must, in many cases, be attributed to the nature of the materials employed, to the deficient education of the artisan, or to a false taste in the manufacturers, which is shown by changing the design, or adopting part of it only under the idea that by so doing, they are conforming to the taste of the public. But the public taste is, perhaps, better than is generally thought. At all events, a fair trial should be given it, by presenting to it only what is good and excellent of its kind. There is, in fact, no better way of improving taste than that of placing good examples constantly before the eyes. The influence of habit is everywhere felt and acknowledged, and the eye, accustomed to contemplate the best productions of art, will not tolerate those of an inferior order.

Unlike most other buildings, the beautiful edifice of Mr. Paxton, from its vast extent, the lightness of its construction, and the quantity of light which it admits, does not interfere with the arrangement of colours on the walls and counters. For practical purposes the effect of the interior of the building resembles that of the open air. It is perhaps the only building in the world in which *atmosphere* is perceptible; and the very appropriate style of decoration adopted by Mr. Owen Jones has added greatly to the general effect of the edifice. To a spectator seated in the gallery at the eastern or western extremity, and looking straight forward, the more distant part of the building appears to be enveloped in a blue haze, as if it were open to the air, the warm tint of the canvas and roof contrasts with the light blue colour of the girders into which it is insensibly lost, and harmonising with the blue sky above the transept, produces an appearance so pleasing, and at the same time so natural, that it is difficult to distinguish where art begins and nature finishes. The busy groups in the nave below, while by their movement they give life to the scene, contrast by their broken and motley colours with the cool and aerial effect of the upper part of the edifice.*

The quiet and retiring colour of the edifice allows full scope for the introduction of lively and powerful, and especially of warm colours, into the lower part of the building, but much of the agreeable impression made on the spectator, and in some degree the interest of the exhibitors themselves, depend on the judicious arrangements and distribution of the colours. Let us see now in what manner this has been accomplished.

To prove the importance attached by some of our continental neighbours to securing the best possible disposition of the articles exhibited, it will only be necessary to mention, that in the Zollverein, and some of the other foreign departments, the arrangement of the different articles was entrusted to the superintendence of a decorative artist and his assistants.† The successful results of employing a person conversant with the subject are apparent throughout the Zollverein courts : and the prevalence of a system of arrangement based on scientific

principles is everywhere perceptible, from the display of the most costly velvets and brocaded silks, to the tasteful disposition of gloves and balls of cotton. It is probable that the same kind of superintendence was also observed in the French and Austrian departments.

In order to trace out the system on which the arrangements of the continental decorative artists were founded, I made notes of the succession of colours in the spaces allotted to nearly 200 exhibitors, foreign and British, and from many of these notes, I afterwards made coloured diagrams. I shall endeavour to place before the reader the result of this investigation, and to show the principles by which the foreign decorative artists were guided.

Although the principles relating to the harmony and contrast of colours are equally applicable to the highest branches of Art, and to the arrangement of a few skeins of coloured silk, there is an important difference in the position of a painter and a decorative artist, which must not be overlooked. The former selects the whole of his colours, and arranges them according to the effect he wishes to produce, and the laws of good colouring. The task of the latter is in some respects more difficult, inasmuch as he frequently finds it already begun by others before his services are required. The apartments, for instance, may be papered or painted, or certain furniture may have been purchased. In this case his skill must be exercised in harmonising what remains to be done with the part already executed. The decorators of the different counters in the exhibition are in this predicament; —they are furnished with materials of certain colours which they must not only arrange so as to display their beauties of colour and texture to the greatest advantage, but must take care that they are not injured by the proximity of other coloured objects. In this respect their task resembles that of the "hanging committee" of an exhibition of pictures. Our good or bad opinion of an artist's colouring will frequently be influenced by the pictures which hang near his work. It is well-known that if a picture with a very warm effect is hung next to one of a colder tone, the latter will appear still colder to a person who has been contemplating the former. On the other hand, if the cold picture is looked at first, the other will appear unnaturally warm. In the exhibition of the foreign productions, and of many of the British, any injurious effect which might arise from the vicinity of the coloured articles belonging to other persons, is obviated by isolating the spaces appropriated to each exhibitor, by means of canopies and draperies, which in the foreign departments, are of rich or subdued colours, according to the nature of the goods to be exhibited.

All arrangements intended to attract the eye must be, in some degree, symmetrical. "The principle of symmetry," observes M. Chevreul, "has much influence on our judgment in many cases in which we do not recognise its operation," and this symmetry of form may be affected by light and shade, and colour. The consideration of form, independently of these two influences, is foreign to the present subject. I have before alluded to the good taste with which some of our continental neighbours, especially the French, have arranged the different articles they exhibit. In one respect, however, the English have an advantage over the foreign exhibitors on the ground-floor of the building, namely, in the superior height of the cases, or stalls, in which the dress and furniture fabrics are displayed. By this arrangement a greater quantity of light is admitted; and, where goods of large patterns, such as furniture damasks, are to be exhibited, the designs are in consequence shown to much greater advantage.

With regard to light and shade, it may at first sight be thought that they have no claim to consideration, when treating of the arrangement of colours. They however comprise an important part of it; for all colour is to some extent a deprivation of light—light colours are allied to light, dark colours to shade. To be satisfied of this fact, it is merely necessary to view colours contrasted with white, in a declining light, when the degree in which they are removed from light, and approach to darkness or shade, will be apparent. The attainment of the power of judging to what extent colour is a diminution of light, is an object desired by all engravers; and it is to an

---

* Mr. Owen Jones's coloured decorations of the building in Hyde Park are a convincing proof of his intimate knowledge of the laws regulating the harmony and contrast of colours. It will be observed that, in painting the roof, he has not introduced yellow which, next to orange, is the most exciting colour to the eye, and should therefore be admitted in small quantities only. The proportions in which the primitive colours are found to neutralise each other are—3 of yellow, 5 of red, and 8 of blue. The pale sky blue on the upper part of the building would neutralise but a small portion of yellow or orange. Mr. Jones, therefore, placed white of a warm tint next the blue, knowing that in conformity with the laws of the simultaneous contrast of colours, the white stripes by their opposition to the blue, would be slightly tinged with the complementary colour (pale orange) and thus perfect harmony would be produced, by one of the most beautiful contrasts in nature—namely, sky blue with the warm tint of delicate orange, which is frequently seen in clouds. The red stripes beneath the girders are only seen on looking upwards from below, and from being in shadow they do not strike forcibly on the eye.

† Mr. Chas. Müller, and Mr. Franz Köhler.

accurate perception of this, that the superior excellence of the best modern engravings is to be attributed. In the arrangement, therefore, of goods of different colours, and of different shades of colour, due regard should be had to the symmetrical dispositions of the lights and shades; that is to say, to the agreeable arrangement of the light and dark colours. This point has received no less attention from the foreign exhibitors than the arrangement of their colours. By some of them, the different pieces of goods are disposed alternately, so as to present the effect of dark and light: this arrangement prevails very generally, and may be traced from the richest and most expensive fabrics to the specimens of coloured leather, wools, and threads, and to the paper-hangings, and carpets on the walls. In other arrangements, black and white are disposed at regular intervals, the coloured goods being placed between them, as in some of the cases in the Austrian department. Sometimes the dark fabrics are suspended at the ends, the lighter and brighter goods being arranged in the centre. Again, where the greater part of the goods consist of dark colours, such as broad-cloths, a few pieces of lively colours are placed at regular intervals. The same arrangement may be seen in the kerseymeres, the greyish white tint of which is alternated with a few bright colours. When the general colour of the fabric is dark, relief is given by light coloured canopies; where, on the contrary, the general colour is light, or figured designs are exhibited, the arrangement is reversed, and the light colours are surrounded with dark and rich velvet canopies. Some of the articles, perhaps, consist of fabrics of one uniform colour, some of figured goods on light grounds, these are arranged with very pleasing effect, alternately, the plain (*i. e.* not figured) goods being considered as darks, the figured as lights. Sometimes the rich effect of velvets is increased by their being canopied with shawls of light and elegant designs.

The value of the quiet and semi-neutral colours in giving repose to the eye, and enhancing, by contrast, the beauty of rich and bright-coloured silks and velvets, is fully understood by the French, whose splendid display of Lyons silks and velvets, in the gallery, appears to the greatest advantage.

The beautiful Genoa velvets are, from the deficient quantity of light admitted into the cases in which they are displayed, not seen to such advantage as the French.

The velvets of the Zollverein are arranged with a very happy effect, somewhat on the principle of the rainbow or prism, thus:—

Deep crimson.	Mixed.	Geranium.	Red.	Orange.	Yellow.	Green.	Blue.	Violet.	Dull red.	Grey.	Mulberry.

and, with a little variation, thus:—

Pale yellow.	Amber.	Orange.	Red.	Blue.	Violet.	Other pieces of stuff, having the effect of dark and light, figured and plain.	Claret.	Dark green.	Puce.	Scarlet.	Violet.	Orange.	Violet.	Yellow.	Brown.

Among the most elegant and harmonious arrangements, both with regard to form and colour, may be mentioned that of M. Terrier, in the French department. The goods are suspended in three rows around the three sides of the case; the upper row consists of light and dark, but lively, colours, alternately; the second row consists of quiet semi-neutrals; in the third and principal row, the dark colours are arranged at the sides, and the more brilliant colours in the front and centre; but they are disposed with so much attention to gradation of tint, from the dark colours at the side, to the lightest in the centre, and, at the same time, with so much harmony, as to attract general admiration. Many of the cases in the Zollverein are also worthy of attention for their graceful disposition, and for the harmony of the colours.

In speaking of the harmony and contrast of colours, as exemplified in the Exhibition, the arrangements have, in many cases—especially where they have been illustrated by diagrams—been considered merely as abstract colours, without a polished surface, and without reference to form; it will, however, be easily understood that the effect of the colours may be much modified by the judicious disposition of folds, which not only produces variety, but adds to the beauty of the stuff, by the play of light and shade, and reflection.

The foreign decorative artists have availed themselves constantly of the harmony of contrast; where, for instance, the goods are each of a single, lively colour, they have produced variety by means of figured canopies and draperies: where, on the contrary, the goods are of light materials (such as muslins) and are covered with floral designs, plain-coloured canopies and fittings (sometimes of rich materials) are employed; and occasionally the colours are concentrated and brought to a focus by the judicious introduction of a well-assorted pile of plain merinos and crapes, of pure colours, the surfaces of which, having no lustre, are seen in their proper colours.

In the gallery there is an assortment of French muslins, very tastefully arranged under a lofty canopy of blue (nearly the colour of the girders), combined with a little red and white. Considering its vicinity to the blue in the roof of the building, the proportion of blue in the canopy, appears to me too great. The arrangement would, I think, be much improved by making the principal part of the canopy white, and enlivening it by a small quantity of blue, and a little red.

Another instance of the care taken by the French in the arrangement of their goods to the best advantage, is to be found in an assortment of black silks, also in the gallery. In order to obviate the sombre appearance of the black, variety and vivacity have been given by the introduction of a few pieces of orange-coloured silk. The French, in their most trifling arrangements, never seem to lose sight of the principle of the contrast of colours. The feather brushes, for instance, are coloured and arranged with artistic skill. In some, the outside feathers are red, while those in the centre are green; in others the outside is green, and the middle red; in others again, blue is contrasted in the same manner with orange. It is curious to contrast these harmonious arrangements of colour with the crude and unpleasant combinations on some English sheepskins.

Harsh and inharmonious contrasts of colour are, in the foreign departments, sometimes avoided by the interposition of rich figured or striped goods of different, but friendly colours, which conduct the eye agreeably, and gradually, from one contrasting colour to the other.

The arrangement of different pieces of plain coloured goods, so as to present an agreeable assortment of colours, is not attended with the same difficulties as those which are experienced in decorating buildings, or in the manufacture of carpets, or printing of fabrics, because the piece goods being separate and movable, their arrangement may be varied at pleasure.

As an instance of defective arrangement of British plain coloured stuffs, where there was ample room for improvement, may be mentioned that in the following diagram. The shaded parts represent the dark colours:—

Dark blue.	Scarlet.	Green.	Buff.	Violet.	Green.	Pea green.	Black.	Dark green.	Scarlet.	Blue.	Scarlet.	Violet.	Orange.	Cool Green.	Brown.	Salmon.	Sea green.	Blue.	Black.

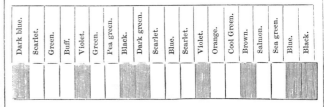

Here we have black, dark blue, and sea-green, in succession; sapphire blue between two scarlets, pea-green between black and blue,—all unpleasant combinations of colour. The dark and light colours also are arranged indiscriminately without any regard to effect.

The following arrangement of the same colours will be found more agreeable :—

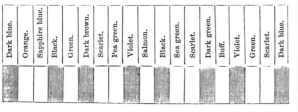

Dark blue. | Orange. | Sapphire blue. | Black. | Green. | Dark brown. | Scarlet. | Pea green. | Violet. | Salmon. | Black. | Sea green. | Scarlet. | Dark green. | Buff. | Violet. | Green. | Scarlet. | Dark blue.

In this arrangement the darks and the brilliant colours, such as orange and scarlet, occur at regular intervals ; all the inharmonious contrasts of the first diagram are avoided, and the colours are arranged, as nearly as the materials will permit, according to the laws of contrast. Light and dark blue are opposed to orange ; scarlet is contrasted with green, and green with violet.

Another defective arrangement consisted chiefly of reds and blacks with one green, yellow, and russet ; the last three of which are, with very bad taste, placed in one corner. The following would be an improvement :—

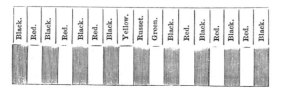

Black. | Red. | Black. | Red. | Black. | Red. | Black. | Yellow. | Russet. | Green. | Black. | Red. | Black. | Red. | Black. | Red. | Black.

Not only is the effect of dark and light obtained by this disposition, but symmetry also, from the central position of the isolated colours, which are so arranged as to offer no inharmonious contrast. These examples are sufficient to show how much the arrangement of goods of different colours may be improved by a little attention to the contrast of colours, and to light and shade.

Besides form, light and shade, and colour, there are other principles which must be considered in the decorative arts, namely, fitness for the end proposed—repetition, and variety. With the first, the subject now under discussion, has little or no connexion ; the importance of the second and third has been always acknowledged by all who study design.

The principle of *repetition* is observed in architecture, when both sides of a building, of a door-way, or of a window, correspond ; it is observed in pictures or coloured decorations when the same colours are repeated in different parts of the design : if, for instance, the north and south sides of the Crystal Palace had been different, the general effect would have wanted the symmetry which is found in the uniformity of the building by the repetition of the lines. In the same manner, the repetition of the colours in a picture adds greatly to its beauty and harmony ; a single spot of colour is looked upon by artists as a blot. The last diagram will show the advantage of attending to this principle in decoration.

If the repetition of forms and colours in works of art is considered a beauty, perfect uniformity is, on the contrary, a defect. The eye requires *variety* also. How much less beautiful would the Crystal Palace have been, had it consisted of the nave or transept only ! Whereas, by placing these at right angles to each other, the principle of repetition is kept in sight, sufficient uniformity is preserved, and variety is obtained by the open space in the centre of the cross occupied by the sparkling glass fountain. And here it may be observed, that, whenever it is wished to give one part prominence over others, that object should not be repeated either in form or colour. In the exposition of goods for sale, this should never be the case ; the object in all arrangements of this kind being to place the *whole* of the goods exhibited in the most favourable point of view.

In pictorial arrangement variety of colour is obtained by the introduction of different hues of the same colour, and of different degrees of brightness. For example, although it is proper to repeat certain colours, as red, for instance, it is not necessary that all the reds in a picture should be of a bright vermilion colour ; on the contrary, the picture will gain in beauty if one should be of a dull earthy red, another bright red, a third crimson, and so on through all the scale of colour. This principle is acted upon by all the best colourists. I will mention one instance only among the old masters. In a very fine picture by Titian in the Church of Sant' Afra, at Brescia, there are eleven figures or parts of figures ; The Saviour is dressed in a lake-coloured drapery, the lights of which are pink,—he has loose upper drapery of dark rich green. The figure on his left is dressed in light warm green. The dress of the woman is light yellow shaded with blue, her ample upper drapery is a rich and dark maroon. Another figure is dressed in green, and two others in different shades of red, inclining to maroon and crimson. The blue shades of the woman's dress are repeated in a blue sash over the red drapery of another figure, and in the dark blue of the sky. The light yellow is also repeated in two other parts of the picture. Thus, out of the eleven figures, four are dressed in red, and three in green ; and yet, while the principle of repetition has been acted upon, a due regard to variety has been observed. Among modern artists we need only refer to Sir Charles Eastlake's beautiful scripture-piece in the Vernon Gallery, in which some part of the drapery of six figures out of the eight, which the picture contains, is of a red hue, and yet great variety is preserved. We find this principle carried out in the foreign arrangements, in which red is frequently the prevailing colour ; but while the red tint is clearly perceptible at proper intervals, the individual hue of each piece of stuff is so varied that all monotony is avoided.

The manner in which the principles of repetition and variety are recognised and acted on in the foreign departments, will be seen by the following diagram. In the space allotted to a manufacturer of Klagenfurt, the principal colours are scarlet, orange, black, white, blue, green, and some of the semi-neutral colours ; they are arranged with excellent effect thus :—

Blue (dark.)	Scarlet.	White.	Black.	Blue.	Brown.	Scarlet.	White.	Black.	Light Drab.	Black.	Orange.	Black.	Light Drab.	Black.	White.	Black.	Claret.	Orange.	Grey.	White.	Scarlet.	Dark Green.	Crimson.	White.	Dark Grey.	Dark Red.	Black.

In another arrangement the pieces of cloth are so disposed that the blacks and very dark colours occur about every fourth piece, the lighter broken colours being arranged at the ends, the brightest and lightest in the centre.

Another means of producing contrast and variety, of which some of the exhibitors in the Zollverein department have availed themselves, is that of the opposition of cold with warm colours. These are further contrasted by the cold colours being treated as lights, and the warm colours as shades, and *vice versâ.* The broadcloths of Messrs. Keltwig & Co., are thus arranged :—

Warm dark Colours, and cool light Colours alternately.	Cool Colours, Dark and Light alternately.	Warm dark Colours, and cool light Colours alternately.

The same attention is paid to the proper contrast of colours, by avoiding harsh and inharmonious oppositions, and while sufficient bright colour is introduced to produce a rich effect, the value of this bright colour is enhanced, and repose is given to the eye, by the introduction of dark and semi-neutral colours. Addison remarks in the essays before quoted, that " where the colours of a picture are well disposed, they set off one another, and receive an additional beauty from the advantage of their situation." The same remark is applicable to all the decorative arts which depend upon colour for their effect ; the degree of pleasure received in contemplating them is, as has been before observed, regulated more by their arrangement with regard to each other, than by the absolute beauty and purity of the colours themselves.

After a general survey of the arrangements of coloured goods in the French, Austrian, and Zollverein departments, some of the principles by which the decorators have been guided become apparent. The principles of symmetry, repetition, variety, and harmony in the contrasts of colours, can be traced by an educated eye.

The general colour of the building being light and cool, it contrasts well with the positive colours of many of the articles exhibited. The prevailing colours of the fabrics exposed to view are rich and warm, and these are set off by the strong darks and semi-neutral colours with which they are surrounded. The favourite contrast, and that which pervades all parts of the building, is green and red; even in the Chinese department the pictures with ruby-coloured grounds are hung on a green paper, and the counter is covered with red. In the Indian department, also, the same contrast is found; on the carpets crimson is contrasted with green; the furniture of one of the beds is scarlet lined with green, the quilt is green lined with scarlet. In the French and Austrian departments the red harmonises with the green; this is not always the case in other parts of the building, where crimson is frequently placed by the side of cool green, and Mr. Monteith presents us with a piece of cotton print in which scarlet is contrasted with very warm green, the effect of which upon the eye is so dazzling as to be almost painful. Indeed, the general appearance of the court in which the cotton goods of this manufacturer are exhibited is far too red, and his combinations of red with green are generally inharmonious. The brilliant colour of the Turkey red dye, which Mr. Monteith produces in such perfection, would appear to greater advantage if contrasted with green of a colder and more subdued character.

Some of the combinations of colour in the Tunisian department are very harmonious. We see dresses of crimson lined with dark green, others of green lined with crimson; here a lilac dress contrasted with green; there a crimson dress lined with citrine.

If, however, the general impression is that the British goods are not arranged with as much taste as the foreign, we are happy to say there are among the former, many instances of tasteful arrangement, and of well-assorted colours. Among the best may be mentioned the mixed fabrics of Messrs. Brown, and Messrs. Akroyd of Halifax; and of Messrs. Schwann, Kell & Co.; the furniture prints of Messrs. Swainson & Dennys, of Ripley & Sons, Fry & Co., Crocker, Law & Sons, Englis & Wakefield, and Mr. C. Hooper's broadcloths, in which blacks are disposed alternately with colours. The space occupied by Mr. Winfield's (of Birmingham), hardware, is also arranged with much taste, and attention to effect.

If the task of the decorative artist is attended with difficulty, that of the carpet weaver is so in a greater degree. The former may alter his arrangement if he finds it inharmonious, but the latter has no resource but to let his work remain as it is, or to begin it again. The circumstance of a single thread being a little too dark or too light, will be sufficient to destroy the harmony of the design.

The effect of many of the carpets of English manufacture when viewed from the opposite side of the building is rich, but—

"'Tis distance lends enchantment to the view:"

a nearer inspection—and it is to be remembered that carpets are intended to be placed near the eye—destroys, in many cases, the pleasing effect, and the arrangement of colours is found to be harsh and discordant, wanting in that which contributes so much to the beauty of all colouring, the presence of middle tints, and of those soft and agreeable broken colours which give repose to the eye, uniting the extremes of light and dark, and harmonising the contrasting colours. The great difference between the pleasing arrangements of colour in the French carpets, and the harsh combinations in the British, appears to me to arise not only from the more skilful contrasts of colour in the former, but also from a mechanical

difference in the mode of execution, which I shall endeavour to explain.

If the same design were furnished to a French and to an English carpet weaver, it would be more than probable that the production of the former would possess the harmony of the design from which he worked, while that of the latter would be wanting in mellowness. The reason is this: in the best Brussels carpets of British manufacture, it is seldom that more than three or four shades of the same coloured wool are employed;* while the weaver of the carpets of Beauvais and La Savonnerie is furnished with between twenty and thirty shades; even for furniture carpets, the number of shades is generally ten. The weaver is consequently able to unite his colours by an almost imperceptible gradation, and thus to prevent the harshness which arises from colours or tints far removed from each other in the scale of harmonic gradation being brought into close contact. This may be explained by the following diagram:—

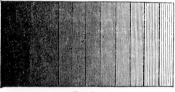

FIG. 1.

FIG. 2.

FIG. 3.

The first figure is supposed to represent a portion of the design for a carpet, which is to be shaded gradually from the darkest tint downwards, to the lightest tint of the same colour; the gradations of tints being twelve in number, the variations are slight, and the effect is very soft. The second figure is to be graduated in a similar manner, but the number of shades of colour, instead of being twelve as in the first, are only six; the gradations of tint, which must be selected at regular intervals, will be more abrupt, and the effect less soft. Now, suppose the same space in the third figure is to be shaded in the same manner, but four shades only are to be employed, in this case the transitions will be still more abrupt, and the general effect will be harder, and less pleasing than the second figure. It will thus be readily understood that the more numerous the gradations of colour, the softer and richer will be the effect.

Not satisfied with possessing a greater number of gradations of colour, the French weaver compounds others: for example, let us suppose that he has ten shades of colour given to him, that the wool with which he works is composed of three threads, he can, by mixing two threads of No. 10, with one of No. 9, form an intermediate tint which may be more suitable to the design than either of the others; in the same manner, by mixing threads of different colours, he can form those broken tints, which add so materially to the mellowness and harmony of the design. Thus, two threads of green and one of red (properly contrasted), will form a useful broken or shadow tint; and two threads of red and one of green, will form another shade, different in its effect from the first; both of

* It is said that seven colours only can be introduced into a Brussels carpet.

these may be found useful in carpets containing much red and green.

From the appearance of the coloured design on paper for a carpet, it is scarcely possible to judge of its effects when worked; for, as the weaver has no means of imitating the softly blended tints of the original design except by stitches, which are in fact a succession of small squares, the transitions of colour (which are also dependent on the number of shades to be employed) are necessarily more sudden and abrupt; and he cannot, as M. Chevreul observes, be said to *copy* the design, but to *translate* it; the peculiar manner of weaving the carpet, and the want of the requisite number of shades and broken colours, preventing his imitating it with greater exactness. Much, however, will depend on the skill of the weaver, and his knowledge of the principles of the harmony and contrast of colours; the artist who makes the design then, is not chargeable with those abrupt transitions of colour, which so frequently shock the educated eye in the finished carpet.

These remarks do not of course apply to Mr. Whytock's patent tapestry carpets, in which the wool being dyed of the *exact* tint required by the coloured design, all hardness occasioned by the want of intermediate tints, is avoided, and a rich effect is easily produced. In this case the beauty of the carpets depends upon the harmony and contrast of colours in the design, and upon the accuracy with which the tints are imitated by the dyer.*

The designs of the greater part of the carpets exhibited consist of a centre variously ornamented, surrounded with a border of a rich design. Carpets of this description are not adapted for apartments in which the furniture, according to the modern fashion, is disposed all over the room. The carpet is intended to be placed in the centre of the room, and no furniture but a table should be placed on it; the border should be visible in its whole extent, except at the fire-place, where it is concealed by the rug. The space beyond the ornamental border may be filled up with a carpet of quiet colours, inlaid boards, or encaustic tiles, according to the purpose for which the room is designed, and on this the chairs and other furniture should be placed. The effect of the rich border would be entirely destroyed by placing furniture on it.

These carpets suggest another observation. They are most of them of gorgeous colours. In order therefore to preserve a due harmony and balance of colours, the walls of an apartment containing one of these carpets should be covered with some quiet tints which harmonise with the colours of the carpet; and the chairs and curtains should be of one uniform colour.

The selection and contrast of the colours of carpets are governed by the general laws relative to the contrast and harmony of colours.

Although the English carpets, as a class, are justly charged with an inharmonious arrangement of colours, there are, nevertheless, some to which this defect cannot be imputed; and which, as regards the disposition, and assortment of the colours, are fully equal to those of any other nation. The limits assigned to this esssay do not permit a detailed description of the best carpets; but I have great pleasure in mentioning among the most successful exhibitors of carpets the names of Messrs. Wright, Crump, & Crane; Messrs. Tuberville & Smith; Mr. Lapworth; Messrs. Watson &

Bell; Mr. Humphries; Mr. Harris; Mr. Templeton; Messrs. Newcomb & Sons; Messrs. Jackson & Graham; Messrs. Henderson & Widnell; and Mr. Pugin. Mr. Woodward also, exhibits a stair-carpet, which presents a very pleasing arrangement of quiet colours.

The French exhibit some carpets and hearth-rugs of great beauty, which are deserving of study for the harmony and contrast of the colours, and the softness with which the different tints and shades are blended. In the large carpet with the elegant arabesque design the contrast of the deep rose colour with its complementary pale warm green, is very beautiful and quite novel, but the general effect of the carpet is too brilliant, the eye requires repose, and the introduction of a little more of the quiet semi-neutrals would have been a great improvement. The coloured flowers on the large industrial carpet are exquisitely wrought, the gradations of colour have all the harmony of the natural flowers; but the general effect would have been improved had the ground been of less positive colours.

The arrangement on the wall of different breadths of French carpets is dictated by the same good taste for which the French are generally distinguished. A single breadth of carpet, of two shades of dark crimson, dark green, or dark blue, is contrasted with two breadths of carpet of floral design, of the brightest colours on white grounds, the two breadths of the latter being necessary to show the beauty of the design. The arrangement produces the effect of light and shade.

The German carpets are not, on the whole, equal in the harmonious arrangement of the colours to the French, there are, nevertheless, some which are excellent. A carpet of Belgian manufacture, in which a claret-coloured ground is enlivened by a design in amber colour, relieved with a little white, lavender, and coloured flowers, is very handsome. In the Zollverein department is a carpet by M. Dinglinger, which has, also, a good effect. The good effect of a carpet, covered with a small design in red, dark blue, yellow, green, and white, is injured by the somewhat glaring colours of the border, which do not harmonise with the centre. Upon the whole, some of the richest effects of colours on carpets are those on a claret-coloured or russet ground, enriched by a design in oak colour, and enlivened by coloured flowers. Claret, or russet, is, in general, a better colour for the extreme darks of a carpet than black, for it harmonises with colours partaking of red, and it contrasts well with the cool colours. Black, besides, being too cold, frequently presents too great an opposition to the other colours.

Although the Turkey and Persian carpets do not emulate ours in the brilliancy of the colours, or the elegance of the design, they are generally far superior to them in the harmonious combination of the colours. The designs, if such they can be called, are generally small, and the beauty of the carpet consists chiefly in the arrangements of small portions of colour, which are disposed rather with a view to their general harmony than to the formation of any design. Occasionally, however, an arabesque or geometrical pattern may be traced. The prevailing colours are reds and greens, strengthened occasionally with deep indigo blue, and enlivened with a little orange or yellow. The scale of colour comprises yellow of two shades, orange, red, crimson, and russet, two shades of green, two of blue, black and white,—a sufficiently extensive scale to produce good and rich effects of colour, where a pictorial design and chiaroscuro effects are not attempted. The colours in the Indian carpets are, perhaps, brighter than in those of Turkey, and are contrasted with great skill. One carpet, in which the colours are very beautiful, is of silk. Some of the Indian prayer carpets, with deep gold borders and fringes, are extremely rich; in these, repose is obtained by making the rug of plain crimson silk,—persons with less taste would have covered it with an ornament.

Among the French carpets is an imitation Turkey carpet, which presents a very harmonious combination of colours. Mr. Lapworth has, also, a Turkey carpet, in which the colours are well arranged.

With regard to those libels on pictures, executed in Berlin wool, which are now unfortunately so common, and some of which have found their way into the Great Exhibition, it is

* In the Brussels carpets, wool of different shades and colours is employed, those required to produce the pattern being thrown upon the surface, while the others are passed at the back; by this means more wool is used than is necessary, and, as the shades of colour are limited in number, the transitions of colour are more abrupt. In the patent tapestry carpets, the wool is in one continuous length, which, by exact calculation of the quantity of each tint that is required to complete the pattern, is dyed of various colours before it is woven. The weaving of a carpet of this kind is, therefore, a simple process; the workman has nothing to do but to weave the tinted wool as it is delivered to him, and as in this kind of carpet, no wool is passed at the back, the material is economised. When the carpet is finished, the pattern is in every respect, except in the square form of the stitches, equal to the painted design (provided that the calculations have been made correctly), and the gradations of colour may be as numerous and as complicated as those of the original. The greatest nicety and accuracy is however required in making the calculations of the different lengths of colour with which the wool is stained, any error in this respect would of course distort the pattern.

lamentable to think that ladies should, with a patience and industry worthy of a better object, spend so much time upon them. It is impossible to see these caricatures of human nature without applying to them the words of Shakespeare,— "One would think that some of nature's journeymen had made them and not made them well, they imitate humanity so abominably." If half the time that young ladies devote to these useless labours were devoted to the acquirement of a knowledge of the principles which govern the harmony of colours,—a kind of knowledge which is very easily attained,— the good effects would soon be apparent, not only in the more appropriate choice of subjects on which to display their skill in needlework, but in better and more tasteful work applicable to domestic purposes.

The subjects adapted to this kind of industry are flowers, birds, arabesques, and other objects which admit of the introduction of lively colours. Subjects which involve the combination of tints, requiring the nicest gradations of colour and the most faithful observance of the chiaroscuro, such as occur in figure-subjects, should be always avoided.

The observations of M. Chevreul, in his excellent work on colour, with regard to the representation of the human figure in tapestry, are deserving the attention of those ladies who exercise their ingenuity and patience on Berlin wool work. M. Chevreul observes that, from the nature of the materials and the method of working, a coloured image is formed by two threads cutting each other at right angles, and consequently producing an uneven surface; whence it follows, that tapestry will never produce the effect of a picture (the surface of which is quite even), unless it is viewed by the spectator from such a distance that the lines are no longer visible; he also observes that, from the necessity that the interstices between the stitches should disappear from the sight before a piece of tapestry can produce the effect of a picture, it is essential that the objects represented should be of large size, and of a variety of colours, which present harmonies of contrast rather than those of analogy. "Every example," he continues, "which does not fulfil these conditions, is bad, and as it is very difficult to find shades of colour sufficiently numerous and properly contrasted to match the various tints in pictures which have not been painted for the express purpose of being re-produced in tapestry; it would be for the advantage of the art if pictures were executed purposely to serve as models for this kind of work: these models should be painted in a broad manner, without those delicate gradations of tint which distinguish the higher class of art." If such then be the opinions of one so well acquainted with the subject as M. Chevreul, with regard to the representation of figures in tapestry, with how much more force do they apply to Berlin wool work, in which the stitches are so much larger. Young ladies' should consider this before they attempt to represent with their needle Sir Edwin Landseer's "Bolton Abbey," or the young Prince of Wales as a sailor.

The oil-cloths appear, with some exceptions, to be open to the same objections as the carpets, namely, the prevalence of harsh oppositions of positive colours, and the want of middle tints. Some, however, exhibited by Mr. Nairn of Kirkaldy, are very harmonious. The colours in these are generally of quiet and broken hues. In one of his specimens more lively colours are combined with a graceful design and equally harmonious effect. An oil-cloth, exhibited by Messrs. Smith and Baker, has a very agreeable effect: in this, the colours are bright pure green; dark ultramarine blue, inclining to purple, and made to appear still more purple by its contrast with green, which in its turn receives a warm tint by the contrast; oak-colour, which here represents subdued orange, the third of the secondary colours; dark brown, and white. In another specimen, coloured black, white, and red, the black pattern on the red acquires, by contrast with the latter, a dark green tint. A well coloured design of an oak-colour, with coloured flowers on a white ground, is exhibited by Mr. Wells.

The arrangement of colours in encaustic tiles and other compositions for pavements and mosaic work, is in general better than in carpets. These, however, are not attended with the same difficulties, the designs commonly consisting of geometrical patterns in few colours.

As the last-mentioned arts must be considered rather as revivals than as new inventions, the manufacturers have shown much good taste in adopting not only the mechanical part of the arts, but the style of design, from examples of acknowledged excellence. The advantage of studying the principles of design and colour observed in the ancient and medieval works of this class is apparent in these modern imitations, which are comparatively free from those violent oppositions of colour so apparent in some of the other branches of Art-manufacture. The success of these designs therefore, affords a presumption of the perfection which may be attained in decorative Art, when the true principles become familiarly known and practised.

In the encaustic, and pavement tiles, and mosaic flooring, the colours are generally of the subdued or broken kind; deep and dull blue, quiet greens, buff or yellow ochre colour, dull red (the colour of terra cotta), chocolate brown, black, and slate, with white of a warm cream colour, are the usual colours. Bright and positive colours are by no means necessary to produce harmonious and agreeable effects—it is the just balance and contrast of colours which causes harmony. Among the best examples of mosaic pavement may be mentioned, copies of portions of the pavements in San Bartolomeo, and Sta. Maria Maggiore, at Rome, and in the cathedral at Naples; also of some Etruscan and Pompeian designs.

The arrangements of colour in the specimens of metallic lava are not so good: the harmony of the quiet and more subdued colours is broken by the abrupt transition to bright vermilion, or yellow, which overpowers the rest. Although this pre-eminence of one colour over the others, may produce an excellent effect in painting by calling the attention of the spectator to the principal object, it is not so with respect to the kind of decorative Art we are now considering, in which such an arrangement would be misplaced. In a design of this kind, it is intended that the eye should embrace the whole of the subject at once, and a general balance and harmony of colours should pervade the whole design; the prevalence, therefore, of one colour over the others, either by its brightness or its undue proportions, destroys the unity of effect, and is clearly a blemish.

It is much to be regretted that the papier-mâché and japanned goods should present so few examples of good taste in colouring. In these, the glitter of metallic colours is too frequently mistaken for richness, and violent contrasts for harmony. The artist seems to run riot in the riches of his palette, and to endeavour to dazzle if he fails to please. In speaking of the want of harmony in the colouring of carpets, due allowance has been made for mechanical defects, which render the adoption of certain designs a matter of some difficulty, but none of these defects can be imputed to the painting of papier-mâché works. With an almost unlimited scale of colour, and obedient materials, which are capable of producing the richest and most harmonious effects of colour, these works by the bad taste too often perceptible in their decorations, contrast disadvantageously with the Indian articles of the same nature, in imitation of which they were originally manufactured. The Indian principle of ornamentation deserves as much attention as the material, and the examples of the tiles and mosaic pavements may be adduced as instances of the advantage attending the study of the principle of decoration adopted in national manufactures, as well as the materials employed.

The same abruptness and crudity of colouring which are perceptible in the English carpets, are also too often visible in the printed table covers, the dyed sheep-skins, the designs for silk handkerchiefs, and the furniture chintzes and damasks. In many of the latter the designs are very beautiful, but the colours are frequently ill-assorted, as well as harsh from the extreme strength, and in some cases *blackness*, of the shadow colour, especially when contrasted, as frequently happens, with regard to furniture-prints, with a white ground. A design of holyhocks on a white ground among the furniture chintzes of Messrs. M'Alpin, Stead, & Co., is, however, exempt from these defects, and is very beautiful. Messrs. Swainson and Dennys have some excellent and well-executed designs upon white, pale green, and claret-coloured grounds. The general arrangement of the space allotted to these manufacturers is also very tasteful.

It is much to be regretted that the very elaborately decorated bed exhibited by Messrs. Rogers & Dean should not display a more chaste and harmonious assortment of colours. The designer appears to have mistaken gaudiness for splendour. The colours of the bed are scarlet, bright green, white, and straw-colour; the colour of the canopy is green, trimmed with gimp of various colours, among which are red and yellow, while the curtains are of deep blue and orange-coloured flowers with green leaves on a white ground !

The gorgeous medieval court of Mr. Pugin demands a few words. While acknowledging the beauty and richness of many of the objects with which it is decorated, it must be confessed that in general harmony of effect the court is inferior to the beautifully arranged French court containing the Sèvres china and Gobelins tapestry. In the former there is too much ornament; too much positive colour; too much unsubdued splendour; scarlet and gold meet the eye in every direction, and overpower it with their brilliancy.

The painted glass is too important a subject to be dismissed in a few words. It should furnish the text of a separate article. It may, however, be observed, while admitting the great beauty and excellence of the magnificent window by Bertini, of Milan, in the nave, that in this Art the English need not fear to enter into competition with foreigners. Even in this department, however, some contrasts of colour, which might have been avoided by a better knowledge of the principles by which the harmony of colours is regulated, may be detected by a practised eye.

The observations in the preceding pages will, it is hoped, have shown the utility and advantages which may be derived from the study of the harmony of colours, to those even who are not actually engaged in the production of coloured goods.

The man of taste, and even the casual observer, can judge whether the general arrangement of colours is pleasing or displeasing to the eye; but the artist and the scientific man take a more comprehensive view; they would ascertain how an effect had been produced, in order to be able to repeat or avoid it at pleasure. By means, therefore, of comparing and analysing, it is found that the contrast of colours, which, to the superficial observer, appears to be merely a matter of taste, is, in fact, governed by fixed laws; and that "good taste," and "a good eye," are but common terms for that almost instinctive perception which some persons possess, of what is in harmony with these laws or contrary to them, and which is only acquired by others after long and assiduous study.

That the British painters have "an eye for colour" is uniformly admitted; how is it then, that the same cannot be said of the British manufacturers? The answer is because the eye is *educated* in the one case, and *uneducated* in the other. The first attempts of our painters in colours were not attended with the successful results of their riper years. Neither do the early pictures of the great Italian colourists exhibit the harmony of the works executed in the prime of their artistical career. The attainment of a good and harmonious style of colour in painting is the result of much observation and study, not only of nature, but of the works of other artists: the same steps must be followed in Art-manufactures, or the same results will not be attained. When the principles by which the harmony of colour is regulated are clearly understood, they are easily carried into practice. Although, as has been justly remarked, the British manufacturers are inferior in colouring, and frequently in design, to the continental exhibitors in decorative art—for under this term we must include those elaborately ornamented carpets, dress, and furniture fabrics, exhibited in the Crystal Palace—there is evidently an improvement upon former designs; and when the subject of colour has received the attention which it deserves, we may confidently reckon on a still greater improvement. The elegant designs, and the harmonious colouring of the French and Italians in their Art-manufactures, has been the subject of general commendation; but neither of these nations acquired their good taste in design and colour in a day, or without study. In former times, it is well known, the best

Italian artists did not think it beneath them to make designs for Art-manufacturers; hence the good taste of the Italians in the lower branches of Art. The French have had schools of design for more than a century, and in consequence of the attention paid in these schools to the harmony of colours, their Art-manufactures exhibit a better and more harmonious style of colouring than many of their works of the higher classes of Art—a convincing proof of the success attending the study of the subject, and the advantages to be derived from the contemplation of good examples. When the British manufacturers study colour with the same earnestness as the British artists have done, the happy results will be visible in their productions; and not until then can they successfully compete in the decorative arts with their continental neighbours.

In conclusion, I must observe, that if, in the preceding pages, foreigners have been commended at the expense of the British for their skill in the arrangement of colours, it has been done in the full confidence that it was merely necessary to point out the defect in order to induce our enterprising manufacturers to overcome it. The superiority of our countrymen in so many branches of industry—in those especially which are most essential to the interests and comforts of mankind—is so manifest, that we can afford to acknowledge our inferiority as regards the arrangement of colour. But the British are not content with mediocrity, and I feel assured that if another exhibition of the industry of all nations should ever take place, the same defects will never again be imputed to us.

I have mentioned that the taste and skill of the Italians and French in the arts of design were not acquired in a day, but that they have been the growth of years; I am satisfied that time only is wanting to render the British fully equal to them in these arts. It has been urged by some that the superiority of the latter consists in the production of what is useful, and that they *cannot* attain eminence in the ornamental arts; but the word "impossible," as Lord Brougham says, "is the mother-tongue of little souls;" and the word "cannot" has had no place in the national vocabulary since the day when Robert Bruce watched the repeated, and at length successful efforts, of the spider to reach the wall of the hovel in which he lay concealed.

On the VEGETABLE WORLD as contributing to the GREAT EXHIBITION:

BY EDWARD FORBES, F.R.S.,

Professor of Botany in King's College, London, &c.

I.

EAUTY and utility are equally attributes of the vegetable kingdom. The natural ornaments and clothing of the earth are the herbs and trees that conceal the nakedness of her soil, and garb her with a robe of verdure. Her mountain peaks, that tower amid the clouds, and her rocky ledges, that stretch into the sea, alone are bare. The continents repose on their planet's surface, like mighty statues of the ancient time, whose lofty heads of snowy whiteness rose skywards uncovered, and whose ivory feet rested naked amid the ebb and flow of the tide of worshippers, pouring through the temple gates; whilst their massive bodies were invested with many-hued draperies, rich in embroidery, and thickly garnished with flowers. But the earth's clothing is no holiday vestment. Man wraps himself in its shreds, and derives nourishment from its countless products. Out of stem and leaf he constructs the implements of peaceful toil, the furniture of luxurious ease, the weapons of deadly warfare; and builds himself hut and house, palace and ship. From bark and fibre he manufactures fabrics, surpassing in beauty the tissues out of which they have been woven, and, staining them in symmetrical or fanciful devices with hues supplied by the saps of plants, emulates the brilliancy and variety of nature's own painting. Out of their vital juices he extracts healing medicines and virulent poisons, or, changing the flowing sap to purposes strangely foreign to its original destination, converts its concreted and flexible essence into graceful vases and endless tubes, vessels and vestments; or belts and valves of wonderful machinery that in its actions and operations dares to rival the untiring energy and productive power of Nature herself.

The investigation of the various vegetable products that have been used for purposes of manufacture, clothing, ornament, food, and physic, is a part of the science of the Botanist.

By him are determined the structure and affinities of the plants from whence they have been derived, and through his enquiries we are made acquainted with the relative value of substances already known, and the probable sources of new and sometimes better materials. He looks with hope to the influence which the Great Exhibition will assuredly exercise upon the economical bearings of his science. Through it he is enabled to see and examine the innumerable bodies of vegetable origin that find their way into commerce almost without notice or examination, except by those who employ them, without caring to enquire whence they come, and what they really are. Manufacturers have much yet to gain from science, and this great opportunity of bringing the student into contact with the practical man will doubtless benefit both. For the naturalist interested in the manifold applications of his favourite studies, now for the first time collected within his view, will mingle philanthropic aims with the somewhat selfish pleasures of purely scientific enquiry. And the manufacturer, quick to appropriate new fields for the exercise of his skill and profitable employment of his capital, will learn to value the accurate and minute information concerning the sources and capabilities of unused or imperfectly applied products, which so many of our philosophers possess without caring to communicate, unless where it is sure to be understood and appreciated.

The works of botanists contain minute descriptions of more than eighty thousand distinct kinds of plants. Each member of this vast assemblage has a name assigned to it, and a "character" by which it may be distinguished from every other known vegetable. The name is composed of two latin words, one significant of its genus, or relationship with plants very near it in structure and aspect, the other expressive of some peculiar feature of its own, or merely serving to designate it distinctly among the several species or kinds composing the genus to which it belongs. Out of this simple proceeding a scientific language results, comprehended by botanists all over the world. Thus, when we write of the *Populus tremula*, all botanists in all nations understand by the generic word *Populus*, a plant presenting an assemblage of characters of organisation, such as are common to all poplars and are combined in poplars only; and by the specific epithet *tremula* they understand that particular kind of poplar to which in England we familiarly give the name of *aspen*, and that kind only. The word *tremula* stands as a sign for a certain combination of characters distinctive of the aspen, among plants of the poplar group or genus. By this simple scheme of nomenclature, devised by the illustrious Linnæus, we are enabled in few words and within limited compass to refer every known plant to its recognised place in the great army of the vegetable kingdom, and the extent to which scientific labelling has been attempted among the collections of vegetable substances in several departments of the Exhibition, is a pleasing indication of the recognition of the definite language of science by not a few of the commercial exhibitors. In the end it will be found that this precise, though technical nomenclature, is really easily learnt and much more convenient for business use, than the vague, unmeaning, and often false terms in popular use.

Of all the natural history sciences, botany is that in which systematic research has been prosecuted with most industry and completeness. The facility with which large collections of preserved plants can be accumulated and kept in order by private individuals, and the comparative small expense at which assemblages of living vegetables can be brought together, have been the chief causes for this high state of botanical knowledge. It is out of the power of the student, unless vastly richer than students generally are, to accumulate within his reach a collection of great or sufficient extent of creatures even of any one division of the animal kingdom; a nation only can approach to completeness in the formation of a museum illustrative of animal life, and as to gathering together an ark-full of living animals, such as is essential for complete study, the greatest of zoological gardens can make but little way; and all the power, resources, and science of a Zoological Society can only succeed (inestimable is that success) in assembling the living representatives of a portion of one of the four great divisions of the animal kingdom, an effort impossible of imitation by an individual philosopher, unless he combine the love of science, the energy and wealth of an Earl of Derby. Of living plants on the other hand, not a few private persons have valuable collections, and the vast assemblage within the precincts of the Royal Gardens, at Kew, presents an opportunity for botanical study, such as can be met with nowhere else; whilst among the many and extensive herbaria of dried specimens belonging to lovers of botany and scientific societies in Britain, that of the illustrious botanist who presides, to the great benefit of the public, over the Gardens at Kew, is probably unequalled in the world, although it be a private collection.

Yet with all these facilities for the acquiring of botanical information, and with all the advantages of an extensive and constantly increasing literature in this department of science, it is astonishing to find how large is the number of vegetable productions used in the arts or manufactures of which our knowledge is very imperfect; the sources of many of them indeed are, scientifically, unknown. If we visit the workshop of the cabinet-maker, we find him using ornamental woods, known to him by some euphonious savage or uncouth English appellation, but of which the ablest of botanists cannot tell the name of the trees that furnished them, or state more than the great class, or the possible natural family to which such trees belong. If we explore the laboratory of the chemist, whose business it is to compound the prescriptions of the physician, or the stores of the druggist who supplies our manufactories, we are shown substances whose precise sources have escaped all the searching enquiries of a Royle, a Christison, or a Pereira. Even the yards of our ship-builders contain not unfrequently vast beams and planks of unknown or doubtful trees. All the light that pours so gloriously through the transparent walls of the Crystal Palace cannot, in the present state of our knowledge, enable us to determine with certainty the origin of many of the beautiful and curious vegetable productions so admirably arranged within them. But out of this ignorance knowledge will spring, for now, in this great gathering and comparison of things used and things useful, we shall have the means of knowing from whence many a substance really comes, that hitherto in its mystifying course through the labyrinths of commerce, has defeated all attempts to ascertain its birthplace.

In illustration of these remarks we may refer to the collections of vegetable substances employed in manufactures displayed in various parts of the Exhibition, and more especially to those sections of them devoted to ornamental woods. The admirable and most interesting series of specimens illustrative of imports of raw produce into the port of Liverpool, in the getting up of which the greatest pains have been taken by the gentleman who superintended it and carried out the idea of forming such a collection, contains not a few imported woods used for furniture-making in this country, derived from undetermined trees. This is also the case with almost all, if not all, the collections exhibited professing to display foreign ornamental woods in British use, such as the beautiful and most curious series collected at great cost by Mr. Wilson Sanders, a naturalist of well-known acquirements; the tastefully mounted set of specimens contributed by the Messrs. Harrison, of Hull; the foreign hardwoods of Messrs. Fauntleroy; the collections from India, and the Indian Isles; and those from some of the colonial possessions in America and the Southern Hemisphere.

Even in instances where the collections have been made expressly for this great display of the useful products of nature, and superintended on the spot by men possessing all the requisite scientific skill and acquirements, the difficulty of obtaining information respecting their sources sufficiently minute for scientific information has been insuperable within the limits of time permitted. The display of vegetable products from British Guiana may serve as an example. It is a very curious and instructive collection, prepared with great knowledge and care, got together in a colony, having the good fortune to number in its committee men of high scientific reputation; among others, Dr. Campbell, well-known for his botanical researches, and not forgetful in his adopted country

of his earlier pursuits. Yet not a few of the vegetable substances used for building or clothing in the colony, forming part of this collection, and enumerated in the admirably prepared document that accompanies it, are known only by their Indian names. Once, however, (as is now, indeed, sure to be done,) the attention of botanists is directed to these deficiencies, we may hope before long for systematised catalogues of the useful and ornamental timber of each country, as well drawn up as that accompanying the attractive series of English-grown woods exhibited by Mr. Cross.

There are few tracts of land, however limited their extent and barren their surface, that have not yielded to man some vegetable productions adapted for food, clothing, or ornament. Even on the seemingly naked and isolated rock, he gathers the crust-like lichen for the sake of its vivid dye; and on the sandy sea-side waste collects saliferous herbs from which to extract alkalies. Each belt of climate, each natural province, has its characteristic vegetation; and there is scarcely a region marked by the presence of a distinctive flora, which does not yield some peculiar plants, furnishing, or capable of furnishing, substances adapted for economical or decorative uses. The forests of temperate climates abound in trees, inestimable for their qualities as building timber, or their beauty as ornamental woods. The luxuriant vegetation of the tropics, where often a small space of ground is thickly studded with a vast variety of arborescent plants, rejoices in woods of exquisite colour, and is prolific in trees and shrubs whose juices, seasoned as it were, by a vertical sun, are rich with valuable oils, gums, and dyes. In both tropical and temperate zones grow, spontaneously or cultivated, numerous plants of very different structure, whose fibres supply materials from which to weave cloth or twist cords. Some of them have been under cultivation ever since the remotest antiquity, some have had their properties made known and developed within the memory of the present generation, and, possibly, some will date their history as articles of economic value from the passing and memorable year.

Around the poles, indeed, vegetable life is at its minimum. Among the realms of everlasting ice and snow there are no trees nor aromatic herbs. The people of the frigid zone can contribute no raw vegetable produce or articles manufactured from it to the great fair of the world, unless they adopt for the moment occupations unusual with them. In this way the Esquimaux have indicated their existence among the assembled races in Hyde Park, who have shown what they can do, or have done, by a few rude carvings in imported wood. But, in the boreal regions that belt the Arctic circle, vast forests of pines spread their dark, needle-shaped foliage, uninterrupted over the land. The axe of the woodman has there need of frequent sharpening. The trunks of giant pines are prostrated by thousands, and yet the forest seems as dense as before. The foaming torrent bears them down towards the sea, where once more they are destined to raise on high their taper forms, divested of spreading boughs and dark green leaves, yet clothed with a new and snowy foliage of sails, woven from the slender stems of delicate herbs. The herb, through man's transforming power, becomes master of the tree, and the tall monarch of the woods, so lately rooted firm in the deep earth, must obey the guidance of the wide-spread canvas woven from the tender blue-eyed flower, that seemed too frail to play any greater part beyond decorating the meadow where it grew, and feeding the wild birds with its oily seeds.

The people of all countries and climates, from the first appearance of the human race, have applied to use their vegetable productions. The spreading tree and its leaves seem symbolical of shelter and clothing, whilst its fruit is among the most natural of sorts of food. Everywhere do we find erections of timber and fabrics woven of vegetable fibre. However far we carry back researches into national antiquities, we can discover no traces of an epoch when the textile and colouring uses of plants were unknown and unapplied. It is an instinct of man's nature to subdue the vegetable kingdom to his service. A minute acquaintance with the qualities and properties of plants is deemed even a more necessary accomplishment by the savage than by the civilised man. With the latter, however, in the division and distribution of the various branches of knowledge, it becomes confined to a few, who make it their business or their pleasure, whilst among the former the well-being of every individual too intimately depends on its possession to admit of his dispensing with it.

The vegetable world is eminently suggestive even to savage man, of tasteful ornament. The graceful curves and elegant shapes of foliage, the droop of a peduncle, the symmetry and harmonious colouring of a flower, all sow the seeds of taste wherever there is intelligence to warm them into germination. The stately trunks of towering palms furnish the simple yet majestic pillars of his temple, or support the canopy of fan-like leaves that he erects to overshadow the resting-place of his ancestors. The interlacing boughs of congregated forest trees teach him to rafter the roof of his dwelling, and arch his store-house. The twining vine, the creeping ivy, the trumpet-sheathed arum bid him imitate in rude, but effective sculptures, their graceful outlines. He decorates his canoe with imperfect images of the wild flowers that star the thickets around his hut; he stains his body in tendril-like patterns with the bright coloured juices of the herbs that cluster spontaneously about his doorway; of their crimson berries and speckled seeds, strung on the fibres of a lily or a grass, he makes necklaces and armlets for festal decorations; the hollow of a gourd, filled with pebbles from a brook, yields a rude music in cadence with his less rude dancing; their brilliant hues of white, blue, purple, and gold, attract him to gather freshly blown and odorous flowers, which delight him with their brightness and sweetness, and serve as temporary adornments of his person.

Civilised man, whose observing and reasoning powers have ripened through the genial influence of centuries of education, sees in the humble effort and simple taste of his savage brother, the indications of paths leading to art, skill, and discovery. The rude yet not ungraceful house-post, hewn out of the forest-trunk, suggests the elegant column. The foliage clustering under the lintel that caps its truncated summit, becomes moulded into the sculptured capital. The avenues of the forest are petrified into pillared aisles. The greensward and its starry flowers, are pictured on the woven carpet. The herbs themselves yield up their filmy skeletons, to become the threads of flowing tunics and damasked cloths. The fleeting blossoms of delicate flowers are gathered, not merely for their own immediate beauty, but to serve as patterns for lasting and skilful imitations, which need but scent and honey, to deceive the wisest of bees, even though perchance the wax itself had manufactured has shared in producing the beautiful deceit.

Not without interest do we mark the display of barbarous and untrained skill amid this vast assemblage of workmanship by the nations of civilised regions. Not a few half-savage tribes have sent, either of their own will, or through the agency of enlightened friends, articles of no small ingenuity and skill, a great part of which are fabrics and instruments manufactured from the stems and leaves of plants. It is curious to notice how the uncivilised man of the tropics, the region of luxurious vegetation, derives his clothing and weapons mainly from the vegetable kingdom, whereas when we approach the poles the barbarian covers his body in the skins of wild beasts, and arms himself with mineral weapons. The native Africans of Ashantee, and the gold coast, send their ropes woven of grass and cotton. The intrepid survivors of the unfortunate Niger expedition, unwilling that their sable friends, of whom, among many sorrowful, they yet retain some pleasant recollections, should be unrepresented, have sent in their name curious and well-woven dresses of the silk-cotton furnished by the gigantic bombax, and beads constructed from palm-fruits, the ornaments of jetty belles. The Arab, more ambitious of European fame, contributes directly and with no small art and taste of workmanship, though most of his manufactures are derived from animal materials. Our deadly enemy at the southern extremity of Africa has no other plant-representative saving those fitting emblems of war, the bow and arrow. The exiled negro, naturalised in tropical America, sends fantastically ornamented calabashes and ingenious baskets. The aboriginal Indian of Guiana, and the Carib of the West Indian Islands, remnant of a once powerful race, display mats made of the cabbage-palm, and samples

of their primitive wardrobe. The North American Indian has his birch bark canoe, a simple and rapid, yet efficient construction. The wilder tribes of Asia exhibit more abundant evidences of their ingenuity in turning the flora of their beautiful countries to account. These are woods curious in themselves, and curiously carved; ingenious cigar-cases, and hats, made of the leaves of screw-palms, evidently more comfortable, and unquestionably more elegant, than the barbarous head-gear of the west; fans, and mats from that mightiest of grasses, the bamboo; floor-cloths of rattan; fishing-nets of cotton; cloths of cotton, and others woven from the fibres of pine-apple and papyrus. The New Zealander contributes his fabrics woven or plaited from the so-called flax of his country; a valuable contribution to the list of textile materials now in European use. Most interesting among all these simple manufactures, are the mats of Pandanus, coronets of Tacca, and cloths of bread-fruit tree, sent from the Society Islands, by their Queen Pomare: thus are the first efforts of infant civilisation contrasted with the grandest display of perfection of skill, and luxury of refinement ever exhibited by man.

II.

TO understand the part played by the vegetable kingdom in contributing substances fit for the use of man, or materials from which constructions and manufactures may be derived, it is necessary that we should regard it under two very different aspects—the one scientific, the other economical. The first shows to us the comparative amount of used and unused, and of useful and useless plants, included in each great natural assemblage; by it we are enabled to ascertain the probability of procuring new substances, for similar plants have often similar properties, and when this usefulness depends on their minute organisation, as is the case with vegetables furnishing textile materials, we may fairly expect to find many species adapted to our purpose in a tribe of which one or two members only may at present be employed. It is through the precise determinations arrived at by botanical science, that we can gain this knowledge, and though by blind trial and empirical experiment, valuable results are occasionally obtained, after much loss of valuable time, the great importance of sound scientific knowledge, when brought to bear on economic and commercial objects, and the far greater probability of our attaining the end of such researches, rapidly and surely, by scientific means, cannot be doubted by any person whose acquirements are sufficient to warrant his pronouncing a judgment on this sometimes, though ignorantly, disputed question. This first aspect under which we may view plants, with reference to the purposes of the Great Exhibition, may be regarded as one exhibiting their capabilities; the other point of view in which they are presented, is one that regards their uses, as already arrived at, in most cases through the experience of ages. It is curious to observe, that vegetables used for various purposes by man, are either such as have been employed from time immemorial, or such as have been turned to account since natural history became a science; the fruits either of that first instinct that directs the savage to seek among the productions of nature assembled around him, for food and clothing; or, of that refined knowledge which, acting by a purely intellectual process, induces man when he has attained the high stage of civilisation marked by the logical prosecution of scientific research, to seek for new and better materials than those transmitted to him by the experience of his less thoughtful ancestors. It seems consistent with the high purposes contemplated by the illustrious projector of the World's Exhibition, to regard our subject first in its most scientific aspect.

All plants have been grouped under two great assemblages; the one developing distinct flowers, and the other apparently flowerless; the former propagating themselves by seeds, the latter by spores. The flowering plants are regarded as of higher organisation than the flowerless; their tissues present vascular structures, which are but imperfectly developed in flowerless plants, and only among a few, and those the higher tribes of them. A great part of the substance of every plant is made up of little membranous vesicles, or cells; and the lower tribes of flowerless plants, such as mushrooms, lichens, and sea-weeds, are entirely made up of cells. Hence the lower plants are styled *cellular*, the higher ones *vascular*. A large proportion of the former division are minute, and often microscopic vegetables, and even in the present advanced condition of botanical science, numberless kinds of flowerless plants remain to be discovered. Their direct value to man is but small as compared with that of the flowering tribes; comparatively few of them are employed for purposes either of food or clothing. Out of these, however, some have found their way to the Crystal Palace, and are deserving of notice.

The most rudimentary forms of flowerless plants are exceedingly minute, and approach so nearly the nature of the lowest forms of animal life, that botanists and zoologists, even after the closest investigation, are in doubt respecting their true position. Yet, diminutive as they are, they are often invested with beautiful and symmetrical cases of siliceous matter secreted within their microscopic tissues; and being produced in myriads, their powers of multiplication compensating for their minuteness, they become accumulated, when they die, into masses of such quantity as in many places to form a stratum of considerable thickness. In that condition they have served occasionally for food, as in the instance of the famous Berg-mehl of Sweden, but more frequently are employed as a polishing-powder, and so become of commercial value. As such we find them exhibited; and in the Canadian collection considerable masses of this substance are displayed, which none but the naturalist could recognise as derived from so singular a source. Sea-weeds are some steps higher in the scale of cellular plants. Their elegant forms and brilliant, though, in their dried state, faded colours adapt them for ornamental work. At our sea-side watering-places they are often combined as decorations for baskets and boxes, and as pictures in frames. They are thus contributed to the Exhibition from Hastings and other sea-ports. Made up as books into small herbaria, properly arranged and accurately named, they would be more elegant and instructive, and probably more remunerative, than in the form in which they are usually presented. Several varieties of algæ, preserved mostly by drying, are forwarded as articles of food; among others, the so-called Irish moss, which is the *Chondrus crispus*, and the *Ulva* or sloke, both British plants. The Agar-Agar, a substance exhibited from the Indian Archipelago, where it is used for making jellies and stiffening silks, is very similar to the Irish moss; and the qualities which give value to both are those that are so highly prized by the Chinese in the edible birds'-nests, constructed of a sea-weed, probably a species of *Gelidium*, and exhibited in the Singapore collection. The ashes of fuci form kelp, which, with iodine, derived from various sea-weeds, is displayed in the collection of chemical products by both English and Scotch manufacturers.

Lichens are terrestrial algæ, mostly presenting the appearance of variously-coloured leathery crusts investing trees and stones. A few are used for food, such as the Iceland moss, *Cetraria islandica*. More important are those which furnish dyes, especially the different kinds belonging to the several genera and species that supply the Orchil, Litmus, and Cudbear of commerce, yielding valuable red and blue pigments. As these plants are generally diffused all over the world, we find them exhibited by countries very far apart,—from the far North and from the Tropics. The islands off the western coast of Africa have furnished the most valuable and abundant supply; and Portugal, as their possessor, exhibits many varieties.

The two great classes of Endogens and Exogens, into which the flowering plants are divided, offer a vast number of valuable products. Of the families of endogenous plants, the Grasses hold a pre-eminent position among sources of food; for to them the invaluable assemblage of *Cerealia* belongs. Nor should the sugar-cane be forgotten. Among substances adapted for manufactures, not a few come from this great family. The bamboo, a giant among grasses, some of its species attaining the height of one hundred feet, is one of the

most useful among the tropical genera; from it we have timber and cordage, baskets and flutes, fans and toys, paper and pickles. Deliciously fragrant screens are made by the Hindoos from khus-khus, the *Andropogon muricatum*; and from Indian plants of the same genus aromatic oils are distilled, especially the grass-oil of Namur, yielded by the *Andropogon calamus aromaticus*, shown by Royle to be the plant so named by Dioscorides, and also the sweet cane of Scripture. The native perfumers of India have contributed these delicious oils to the Indian collection,—probably the most complete and interesting, as well as one of the most beautiful, compartments, in the Crystal Palace. From the stems of maize excellent brooms and brushes are constructed, and displayed in collections belonging to both Old and New World countries. The stalks of many kinds of grasses have been used from time immemorial for platting into head-coverings; and England fairly competes with Tuscany for elegance and skill in platting straw. The family of Sedges, so closely allied to grasses in their structure, play a less important economical part. The sedge of most ancient fame, the *Papyrus*, no longer makes a conspicuous figure among Egyptian materials. Species of the same genus have furnished, however, mats and cloth, sent from the Indian Archipelago; and cordage, twisted of kinds of *Cyperus*, are exhibited by several countries. Among our native plants of this order is the cotton-grass, *Eriophorum* of botanists, whose heads of snowy hair, gracefully drooping and waving to and fro with every breath of wind, are the ornaments of boggy meadows and peaty moors. Vain attempts have been made from time to time to convert this beautiful substance, apparently so well adapted for textile purposes, into a cloth. A Scottish exhibitor claims to have succeeded in this desirable experiment, which, should it prove profitable as well as practicable, may give value to much boggy land at present of little worth.

That family of Endogens, to which the *Arum* gives its name, contains many plants remarkable for beauty or interesting for their singularity, but few are useful. Among them is the great bulrush, *Typha latifolia*, the creeping stems of which are exhibited on account of a novel application of their substance, a flour of pleasant taste and convertible into a kind of bread being made out of their central portions, whilst the more fibrous tissues are proposed to be used as a substitute for lint. Allied to the Arum-tribe is the family of Screw-pines, natives of the tropics, and many of them turned to good account in the manufacture of matting, sacking, and cordage. One of them, the *Pandanus odoratissimus*, is immortalised in the lays of Eastern poets on account of the exquisite fragrance of its flowers, whose perfume has been distilled into an "attar," and exhibited by the perfumers of Benares. The true palms, constituting the natural order of *Palmæ*, are the aristocracy of this section of the vegetable kingdom, and as such, the most useful of all aristocracies. To enumerate their uses would be to name almost all the purposes to which a plant can be applied. In the gatherings from the East and West Indies especially, do they play a conspicuous part. In the collections of ornamental woods beautiful sections of palm trees may be seen, and several kinds, especially species of *Cocos* and *Borassus*, are employed for cabinet-making. Canes and rattans, the stems of species of *Calamus*, are displayed in multifarious forms of furniture, cordage, weapons, and walking-sticks, and even woven into articles of clothing. The leaves of the *Borassus flabelliformis* are constructed into fans and punkhas. The leaf-stalks of various species of *Phœnix*, including the date tree, are converted into baskets and boxes. Beautiful ornamental baskets and artificial flowers are exhibited from the Seychelle Islands, ingeniously cut out of the leaves of the double cocoa-nut, *Laodicea seychellarum*, one of the most remarkable palms in the world, and characteristic of these islands. The hairy investment of the Gummuti palms is twisted at Singapore, into cables of peculiar excellence, and fibres from the Palmetto of the Bahamas are sent, converted into serviceable ropes. The dwarf-palm of the Mediterranean has been turned to account by M. Flechey, who exhibits paper and pasteboard made by a peculiar process from its leaves. M. Averseng transforms them into a vegetable hair. The vegetable ivory nut is the product of a palm of the genus *Phytelephas*. The ivory-like substance so much used by turners, and converted into beautiful toys and carven ornaments, is the stony albumen of its seed stored up for the use of the embryo plant. The hard pericarp of the fruit of *Attalea funifera* is the Coquilla nut of commerce, so much used for similar purposes with the vegetable ivory, and especially for the handles of canes and umbrellas. The fibrous rind of the cocoa-nut furnishes the valuable substance known as Coir, equal to hemp in strength, and extensively used for the manufacture of cordage, matting, rugs, and brooms. Palm oil is the product of an African species of *Elais*. Not a few valuable articles of food are contributed by this order. Among the most interesting of those exhibited are the sago cakes from the Moluccas, prepared from the pith of a kind of sago palm, and used by the natives as sea-biscuits are by our sailors. Far removed in appearance, but having considerable structural affinity with the palms, are our native rushes. The pith of rushes has been employed for centuries as a primitive form of candle-wick. In the Exhibition it holds an honourable place, having been used as materials for the construction of some ingenious and elaborate models. The Lily tribe is most familiar as furnishing not a few of the beautiful ornaments of our gardens, and when we look upon the tulip and the martagon we are apt to regard them as belonging to a family of useless though splendid idlers. Not to speak of onions, squills, and aloes, there are in this family plants of the greatest economical importance. One of these, though but a recent introduction into our list of materials for manufactures, increases in value and estimation every day; we allude to the *Phormium tenax*, or New Zealand flax, a singular misnomer. The so-called African hemp is derived from another liliaceous plant, and fabrics and even artificial flowers are exhibited from several tropical countries constructed out of the fibres of species of *Yucca*. Plants of the Pine-apple tribe furnish fibres of value for the weaving of cloth and manufacture of cord, and are represented in collections from both East and West. The Amaryllis family in like manner contains fibre-furnishing plants, especially the *Agave*. It is curious to note the exhibition of cloaks and bags, and even paper manufactured at Algiers of the fibres of Agave, insomuch as this singular vegetable, now so abundant in the Mediterranean region as to give a character to its vegetation, especially on the African side, is not a native there, but an American plant, introduced since the conquest of Mexico, and one, the uses of which were well known, and are still to the Mexicans, who, however, have displayed none of their manufactures from it. Incidentally we may remark the singular fact that there are more native Arabs of Barbary, exhibitors on their own account, than there are persons belonging to many of the South and Central American States. Fibres valuable for fine muslin textures are procured from members of the Banana tribe. The Arrow-root and Ginger tribes are fully represented by their peculiar product in the shape of food and condiments, contributed by tropical regions. The Orchids, very few kinds of which now extensive and most beautiful tribe were known to Linnæus, make but a poor figure amongst an assemblage of vegetables intended for use, and are represented by some vanilla pods and packets of salep. In another form, however, they have contributed conspicuously to the beauty of the Exhibition, since they have served as models for some of the most exquisite imitations of flowers that have ever been displayed. Accurate models of *Orchideæ* are of more consequence than might seem at first glance. It is not merely the extreme beauty of the subjects that gives them value and attraction, though none can fail to be struck by the chaste colouring and graceful outlines of some, and the gorgeous hues and almost grotesque shapes of others, or by the strange imitations of the aspect of living insects presented by the blossoms of many kinds, some of them indigenous to Britain. It is their importance as subjects for scientific study, combined with the excessive difficulty there is in preserving them so as to exhibit their original features and characters, that leads a botanist to examine with curiosity modelled imitations of these plants. The manner in which they are represented in wax by Mintorn, and in cambric by Constantin, is worthy of the warmest praise; and very

curious are the specimens of the flowers themselves, rendered indestructible through the ingenious method by which Captain Ibbetson has coated them with copper.

The great majority of European trees belong to the lower or apetalous sections of Exogenous plants. Among them, those of the Pine tribe stand apart, on account of singularities presented by their anatomical structure and mode of production of seed. Their wood has qualities peculiar to itself, and constitutes one of the most useful kinds of timber. Many of them yield valuable resinous secretions, such as turpentine, Canada balsam, Dammar, Sandarach, Thus, and Burgundy pitch. This tendency to deposit resin gives peculiar qualities to the wood, and sometimes, as in the case of the juniper and certain pines, flavours the fruit. Sections of coniferous wood are displayed in great variety in the collection of woods exhibited; and its applications to the construction of furniture meet us at every turn. Some of the exotic species are of sufficient beauty to be turned to good account for ornamental woodwork, and are likely to prove of considerable value to our southern colonies. The Huon pine of Van Diemen's Land is excellently fitted for this purpose; and some highly ornamental tables, chiefly constructed from it, are exhibited. It is well adapted for inlaying in combination with other woods, especially that of the *Casuarina quadrivalvis*, a Tasmanian tree, belonging to a natural family nearly allied to the pines. The celery-topped pine, *Phyllocladus aspleniifolia*, a native of the same region, is a magnificent tree, growing to a great height, and producing timber of much beauty and durability. The trees of the Walnut family furnish valuable wood as well as fruit; and much of the most beautiful furniture, especially carved sideboards, in the Exhibition, is made from the wood of the common walnut. The black walnut of North America produces a wood of a rich purple-brown hue, but little employed by cabinetmakers in this country. Its capabilities are well shown in the chairs and tables made of it, exhibited by the Canadians, and highly creditable to their taste and skill. It can be obtained in very large planks, and is sure to find its way into general use. The hickory is also a tree of the walnut tribe. The handles of axes and other tools, in the collections from the United States and our North American colonies, are mostly made of the wood of the white hickory, and are remarkable for their excellence. The great group of catkin-bearing trees supplies a vast number of valuable products, especially varieties of timber, pre-eminently the Oaks, Beeches, and Birches, the uses of which are almost countless, and the beauty inestimable. When looking at the furniture and section-specimens made from these valuable trees, we must bear in mind that there are many very distinct plants bearing these names, and that the American woods exhibited, although they bear the same denominations with European and Asiatic sorts, are derived from different species of the same genera. This is of consequence, since it does not follow that because two kinds of trees belong to the same genus, and closely resemble each other, they have therefore the same properties and economic value. Rich and varied in colour and grain as the numerous exotic woods now employed in cabinet-making are, few, if any of them, are so pleasant to the eye, when used in house-decoration, as our old and familiar acquaintance, the oak of England. Nor is its more ancient neighbour, the bog-oak of Ireland to be slighted,—that semi-fossil veteran, whose dark and tanned complexion reminds us of the countless centuries that have rolled away since his sturdy stem and stately arms reared a dense mass of waved foliage over mountains and plains that are now barren and treeless. The Irish furniture made from this primeval timber is admirably adapted for library equipments; and very elegant and tasteful are the little articles of jewellery carved out of the finer portions of it by Irish workmen. Indeed, for mourning ornaments, there are few more elegant and appropriate than the shamrock bracelets and harp-shaped brooch carved in the sister-island from its bog-woods; and with commendable taste the jewellers of Dublin have sought, in national emblems and antiquities, models that are as graceful as they are unhacknied. In the Willow we have another amentaceous tree, furnishing materials of value for domestic purposes, especially the osiers and the chip-yielding willows.

The bark of numerous catkin-bearing trees is of value either for direct use or on account of furnishing tanning or dyeing substances. The outer bark of the paper-birch is stripped away in large sheets, and rapidly converted into excellent and graceful canoes by the Canadian Indian, who sews together the fragments with thongs cut from the hide of the moose-deer; whilst of the white-birch bark, trays, baskets, and ornaments, embroidered with the hair of the same animal, are made, pleasing in colour, light and pretty. The uses to which cork, itself the outer bark of a species of oak, indigenous in Southern Europe, are applied are too many and familiar to be enumerated here. In the Exhibition several ingenious models are constructed of it; and a novel application is shown in exceedingly light hats made of cork cut into thin sheets. The bark of an Indian species of birch is used as a substitute for writing-paper. The peculiar smell of Russia leather is derived from an oil distilled from our common birch, and used in the dressing of that material; and from its sap, a kind of wine, sparkling to the eye and agreeable to the palate, is produced by fermentation; whilst several species of the same tree yield sugar. The bark of the aspen is exhibited by the Russians, converted into mats.

The nettle-tribe, regarded in its widest extension, is a fruitful source of valuable vegetable products. It furnishes fibrous substances of great value; above all hemp. The *Urtica tenacissima* of India yields a fibre used for ropemaking and the construction of nets, and the *Bœmeria nivea* or China-grass is a nettle imported of late years in considerable quantities from China into England, for the manufacture of yarn and fine cloth. The fibre of the *Artocarpus* is exhibited among Indian products. The yellow dye-stuff, fustick, is the wood of a species of mulberry. The beautiful snake-wood is the timber of a *Brosimum*. Many of the figs yield caoutchouc, furnished also by several other plants of this order, and by members of the neighbouring tribe of *Euphorbiaceæ*, the spurges. This substance is yielded by the milky juices of several plants belonging to very different natural orders. Useful as it is, but few nations have applied it to manufacturing purposes; and the display of india-rubber fabrics is almost entirely, in the Exhibition, confined to the departments of Great Britain and the United States. The spurge-family supplies some serviceable medicines, especially the croton, and castor-oils, and food, as the cassava; but with these also not a few poisons. The tallow-tree of China, the seeds of which furnish a fatty matter manufactured by the ingenious celestials into candles, belongs to this group as well as our own box, the wood of which is prized by engravers, and has been applied with success to ornamental carving; and turnsole, a blue dye, is the product of *Crozophora tinctoria*. Sandalwood, from which such exquisite boxes and cabinets have been carved by the natives of India, is the timber of certain trees of the order *Santalaceæ*. Fibrous tissues capable of being woven are furnished by several plants of the Daphne tribe, and the inner bark of one of them, the *Lagetta lintearia* is a natural lace in itself. The laurel and nutmeg families, chiefly composed of tropical plants, yield not a few of the best of spices. The greenheart wood, exhibited in the Guiana collection, belongs to a tree of the former tribe. In the family of docks and buckwheats, the *Polygonaceæ*, we find rhubarbs, the product of various species of *Rheum* chiefly inhabitants of temperate and cold climates. The remaining families of exogens, deprived of a corolla, produce a few medicinal or food-plants, but none remarkable for their value in the Arts.

Among the tribes of exogens that possess a monopetalous corolla, the first which attracts our attention as furnishing substances for use, is one familiar to the lovers of gardens, because it includes and is named after the verbena. In an economical point of view it derives its value, not from such small herbs, however pleasant to the eye, or sweet their scent may be, but because it boasts of one of the most valuable of timber trees, as well as one of the most gigantic in the world, —the teak tree of India. The neighbouring family of labiate plants is remarkable for the sweet scents and aromatic herbs, the lavenders and rosemarys, hyssop and peppermints, patchouli and thyme, all yielding volatile oils, and many among the most favourite subjects of the perfumer's skill.

The foxgloves and the figworts, like doctors, ready to kill or cure, stand beside them, and not far off the nightshades and tobacco-plants, with their associates the capsicums and love-apples; a strange mixture in one family of man's deadly enemies, with several of his valued friends. The borages bring alkanet; the bindweeds, scammony; the trumpet-flowers, sesamum; the gentians, bitters; thus do we find among the most beautiful of flowers, physic and food, poison and tonics, associated with elegant shapes and brilliant colours. The olive tribe gives us the oil from the fruit of its typical tree, and the wood of our own ash. Many of the exotic *Sapotaceæ* also furnish oil; and one of the most interesting examples of vegetable oils in the Exhibition, is the Shea butter, contained in the Niger Collection, since it calls up our recollection of the adventurous and unfortunate Mungo Park, and his account of its importance to the tribes of central Africa.

To us, however, a plant belonging to the same natural order, but whose value was unknown in the days of the explorer of Negroland, is of far more consequence; I allude to the *Isonandra gutta*, the source of the gum-elastic, known as gutta-percha, one of the most useful substances introduced into the arts during the present century, and only a very few years ago. The ebony-trees belong to another of this group of families; the ebony is the hard or old wood, the dusky beauty of which is fully developed in the exquisite cabinets scattered through the Exhibition. The heaths, beautiful as they are, do not offer much that is useful; the wood of the strawberry-tree is, however, not without merits, and can be employed for small articles of furniture with effect. From the vast order *Compositæ*, with its fearful array of ten thousand species,—food in many shapes, and physic in more, are the chief contributions; the safflower, yielding a dye which appears disguised in the shape of rouge, and the chicory, exhibited in all its stages, until, as with commendable truth and simplicity the labelling of the specimens assures us, it is "ready to be made into coffee," have their due places in the Crystal Palace. The madders have had no small part in giving beauty to the fabrics there, and their tribe can boast in coffee, of its services as furnishing the source of a beverage with which few civilised, and even uncivilised, nations could now conveniently dispense.

The exogens with flowers, the petals of which are constantly separate, number among them many families serviceable to man. Valuable food-plants and gum resins are supplied by the too-much-abused umbelliferæ. The gourds furnish both food and vessels adapted to hold it. The myrtles, under strange and unaccustomed shapes, arrest the attention of visitors to exotic and colonial collections, some as sections of trees of astonishing size, such as the great blue gum-tree (*Eucalyptus globulus*) from Van Diemen's Land, — or as polished woods of rare beauty; others among the spices and condiments in the shape of cloves and pimento, or as dried fruits, such as pomegranates and Brazil nuts. The rose tribe is represented, in the home department, by its pleasant array of native fruits, and in the Indian bays, by richly-scented attars. The pulse tribe has a greater and more conspicuous share of space, and very various are its products. Those valuable for agriculture and food, many in number, are sufficiently familiar. From it we derive many valuable woods; some of them are sought after for dyes, as Brazil-wood, log-wood, and Japan. Of all dyes indigo is that most valuable as an article of culture. Another herb of this tribe furnishes the Bengal hemp or sun, a fibrous substance of great strength. Catechu and divi-divi are imported from the East for tanning. Many and curious are the gums and balsams of the family; among others, gum-arabic, tragacanth, animé, kino, and Balsam of Peru. Nor must we omit such old acquaintances as Tonkin beans, tamarinds, and senna, all of which may be met with in their proper compartments. The family of balsam-trees has its place here, supplying myrrh and olebanum, and in a neighbouring group we find mastic and terebinth, with the trees that furnish the brilliant varnishes of the East, and those that bear mangoes, cashew-nuts, and pistachio-nuts.

From the *Zygophylleæ* we get the lignum-vitæ wood of the West Indies. The *Linaceæ*, small though the family be, hold a high place on account of including the flax plant; now, if the invention of Chevalier Claussen, one of the most novel features of the Exhibition, confirms by experience the promise which it holds out, it is likely to prove of greater value than ever. In a tribe not far removed, we find the vine, and next to it the mahogany tree, a collocation in natural affinities confirmed by artificial customs. The soapworts, mostly tropical, appear in the shape of the curious Litchi fruit, sent from the Indian Archipelago. The maples present themselves as beautiful furniture woods, several varieties being sometimes derived from the same tree. The wood of the sugar maple of Canada is the bird's-eye and also curled maple of the cabinet-maker. The gamboge trees furnish well known resins and curious butters and oils, as well as the world-famed Mangosteen. The orange tribe manifests itself in fruits and perfumes. Tea is the product of plants very nearly allied to *Camellia;* in the Exhibition the tea-growers of India compete with those of China. Camphor is a secretion of a tree of the order *Dipterocarpeæ,* a native of the Indian Archipelago. Cotton is the hair of the seed of certain plants of the mallow tribe, of which some other kinds produce useful, though less known fibres. Weld and arnotto are products of families in this section of the vegetable series. The great tribe of *Cruciferæ* is remarkable for the number of valued food-plants, the kaleworts, that it includes; in it too, we find the dye-plant woad, with which our British ancestors were content to decorate their shivering bodies. Opium is the chief representative of the poppy family. The water-lilies, though not present in person, exercise no small influence on the ornamental departments of the Exhibition; for their newly cultivated chief, the *Victoria regia,* one of the most wonderful, as well as beautiful, of flowering plants, has, with singular propriety, been the chosen model of not a few objects of manufacture woven, carven, or worked in metal, sometimes with admirable success, sometimes without a just understanding of the grace and delicacy of this exquisite plant. The *Anona* tribe, a group yielding several prized fruits, of tropical regions, furnishes the valued lancewood. The few remaining families of note are chiefly marked by medicines or poisons.

III.

WHEN we wander through the avenues of the Crystal Palace, charmed and interested by the manifold proofs of man's skill that attract us on every side by their ingenuity, beauty, or usefulness, we are apt to forget and overlook the materials that have been furnished by nature to serve for the construction of our fabrics and manufactures. The main purpose of the Exhibition is certainly to display the results of man's workmanship, and to convert any part of it into a vast museum of natural objects would be foreign to the great design that animates the whole. Wisely, however, it was resolved not altogether to overlook the unchanged elements of the products of skill, and the more important raw materials have their places in the arrangement. Those which are derived from the vegetable world occupy considerable space, and are, in many instances, classified with much thought and science.

There is one collection of vegetable substances in the Exhibition, pre-eminent for scientific and instructive arrangement, that of the vegetable productions of Scotland; it is a museum in itself, and worthy of a place in a national institution. It has been devised and carried out with equal skill and science, and reflects the highest honour on its authors, the Messrs. Lawson of Edinburgh. The several plants are classified according to their uses; a well preserved herbarium specimen exhibits the form and characters of the growing plant; if the product valued be a fruit, a root, a tuber, or a seed, it is exhibited not merely in its dried or preserved condition, but if unpreservable or incapable of retaining its first appearance, is carefully modelled of the natural dimensions, aspect, and colour; the valued substance produced by it, whether grain or flour, or dye, or extract, is displayed by its side; a carefully prepared label informs respecting its names, popular and scientific, its class and order, and other particulars of consequence to be known. Now the idea of this collection is one that might easily be developed into its full dimensions; what has here been done for Scotland might be done for the world, and most worthy would such a display be in the national museums of an empire like ours, seeking, as we do, all over the globe for materials to supply the enterprise of our manufacturers, and to extend the commerce and increase the wealth of Great Britain. Such collections carried out to their full development, scientifically and commercially, would be in the highest degree instructive, and most certainly would meet with the warmest appreciation from the productive and intellectual classes of the British community. A spacious room devoted to the display of animal products used in the fine arts and manufactures would add to the attraction of the British Museum: the Kew Collection should be enlarged so as to illustrate in their utmost extent the value and applications of the vegetable world: the Museum of Practical Geology has already undertaken, with the prospect of much public benefit, the display and illustration of the useful and ornamental applications of the mineral kingdom. Now is the time, when this unprecedented accumulation of materials has been brought together, to commence or complete such worthy projects.

The world of plants has its place and representatives in the congress of use and ornament, now holding its sitting within the new Palace of Hyde Park, under various and very different forms. Honest, hearty food-plants have come without veil or disguise, proud of their own wholesome natural aspect, and disdaining to appear otherwise than that which they are. Plump white wheat sits beside substantial, and pompous cobs of Indian corn; its plain dress, and orderly ears, albeit though it appears for the most part in collections from ancient monarchies, contrasting severely with the ruby and gold uniform of twelve-rowed maize that glitters beneath the republican starred and striped banner. More humble oats and barley, peas and beans, range themselves for the most part on the benches of temperate states; whilst the bays devoted to the products of warmer climes, contain rice, meek and pale, though coming from the sunny tropics, and grains with strange names and unfamiliar aspect. The coffee grains of Arabia seem in opposition to the hops of Kent; and the "Tick beans, with white eyes, grown at Hengrave," may well stare when they find themselves in the neighbourhood of sugar-canes and sugar-loaves from Surrey. Like severe and lucid critics are the vegetables in vinegar, that look so pulpy and tempting in their clear and acid envelopes, contrasting with the strange fruits and curious spices that are ranged in symmetrical compartments beneath them.

Balsams and resins, oils and gums, sugars and starches, the products of the chemistry that is at work in the minute tissues of plants, directed by the mysterious agency of the vital influence, are exhibited in wondrous variety, and many from strange and unexpected sources. The more we know of botanical science, the greater will be the number, and more certain the sources of these vegetable secretions capable of being turned to useful account. But a few years ago, and caoutchoucs and gutta-perchas were scarcely recognised, and almost unapplied. Now our manufactures would suffer materially were the supply of these substances to cease. When we consider what the gum-elastics essentially are, when we regard them by the light of vegetable physiology, we cannot doubt but that many more plants, yielding valuable products of a similar nature, will be brought to light, especially in the unexplored regions of the Indian Archipelago. It is the same with the vegetable dyes, at present few in number to what we have a right, reasoning from analogy, to expect. Cordage and clothing materials furnished by plants, occupy, as they justly should, a conspicuous place in the collections from every land; yet many known to be used, and of considerable value, are either absent or imperfectly represented; though, as if to compensate, not a few now or as yet only partially employed textile fabrics, suggest to us that we are far from having obtained a full knowledge of the resources in this department of the vegetable world. For when the origin of a substance so beautiful and common as the rice-paper of China is still a matter of discussion and enquiry, we may fairly hope for new information respecting old, and fresh discoveries of new materials. Great and successful attempts have been made to exhibit the variety of useful and ornamental woods now selected for building and cabinet-making; and no one can glance at the beautiful collections exhibited in the south-western galleries without perceiving that, however exquisite the furniture so profusely displayed on the ground-floor may be, there are ample resources remaining unemployed that will render such manufactures, sooner or later, yet more admirable than they now are. The numerous proposed devices for seasoning and preparing woods are all so far successful that we may look forward to the employment in furniture-work of many kinds of curious grain and colour at present seldom, and not always successfully, employed. Much of the furniture in the Exhibition, upon which infinite labour and marvellous skill have been bestowed for the production of sculpturesque effects, is constructed of woods chosen without regard to the character of the carver's design, which consequently materially suffers. A more minute knowledge of the colour, qualities and capabilities of ornamental timber, would prevent such mistakes.

The indirect influence of the vegetable world upon the Arts and Manufactures, must not be passed over without a remark. The share that it has had in giving origin to the beauty and variety of furniture, ornaments, and fabrics, displayed under so many and admirable forms in the Great Exhibition, is too important not to be strongly insisted upon here. Our silks and cottons, our muslins and poplins, our shawls and damasks, our sideboards and cabinets, our porcelain and glass, would make a comparatively graceless array, were the infinite variety of design and colour suggested by flowers and fruits, leaves and stems, herbs and trees, taken away. Yet, when these representations are scanned by a botanist, he is apt to regard them with a dissatisfied eye, not because they do not fulfil the requirements of scientific accuracy—that would be absurd to exact—but on account of the ignorance they too often make manifest of the riches suited to his purpose lying almost within the designer's grasp, had he known where and why to seek for them. A small amount of botanical study would prove a profitable capital to the ornamental draughtsman. Science would teach him how every stem is adapted for its own peculiar style of foliage, and how an incongruous mixture of leaves, fruits, and flowers, cannot give the pleasure to the eye that, even when it is uninstructed, it so rapidly and delightfully derives from the contemplation of combinations, the elements of which are truthful. The leaf of a mono-cotyledonous plant attached to the flower of a dicotyledon strikes the spectator who has no knowledge of botanical science as unnatural, for the eye learns, and compares, and recollects, even when the understanding is obscure and cloudy. To the botanist, who sees in all the structures and stages of vegetable organisms heaven-devised beauty, and the manifestations of Divine foresight and love, such mistakes become still more offensive. The mere literal copying of nature is not what is demanded; that would be contrary to nature's own plan. The value to a designer of a scientific comprehension of his models, is the insight it gives him into the possible variations of the original, and the inexhaustible sources of grace and beauty, whence so much that is new, and yet consistent, may be derived, towards the following out of Nature's own idea.

All substances in which vegetable forms have been imitated, whether by modelling, carving, casting, printing, painting, or inlaying, are not equally well adapted for representations of all kinds of ornamental plants. Leaves with broad and coriaceous lobes, borne on stout and stiff-jointed peduncles, suit castings in bronze and iron, or carvings in low relief on wood, but delicate and pinnated foliage, or slender fern-fronds requiring high or complete relief, and intended to stand out light and prominent, require hand-workmanship in the more precious metals, and can neither be carved nor cut with natural effect.

Perhaps a portion of the unpleasant effect produced by such experiments, depends upon the extreme difficulty of imitating, very perfectly, the minute features of the parts of plants. For, in the exquisite metal castings of bramble and other leaves, done from the plants themselves with a perfec-tion so extraordinary that, even under the lens, the minutest hairs and finest venations of their surface are seen projecting, executed by some novel process, invented by Captain Ibbetson, and placed in the Exhibition along with the electrotype plants to which we have already alluded, the effect to the eye is exceedingly pleasing. These castings suggest the probability of an extensive use of living plants, well selected, with reference to their capabilities for decorative effects, depending entirely on form and surface, becoming a new and delightful sort of furniture ornament. Thus, climbers remarkable for elegance of foliage, might be twined round the frames of mirrors, and along the cornices of rooms, the flowers and leaves of real plants becoming perpetuated in metal, never more to droop or wither. The choicest leaves might be converted, with little labour, into silver and golden dishes surpassing the craft of the cunningest goldsmith, and our dessert might be spread under the shadow of metallic fruits and flowers as true to nature as if the transforming touch of Midas had collected them.

One word more, for the plant's own sake, before concluding. When we rest on the velvety grass, under the shadow of some spreading tree, whose gnarled and sturdy trunk was stout and strong whilst our great-great-grandfathers were little boys; when we idly play with the painted and sweet-scented blossom of some summer flower that we have plucked in the sunny meadow, pulling sepal from sepal, and petal from petal, shaking the pollen from the stamens, and cutting open the pulpy germen to note the nascent ovules, let us not merely bless the tree for its shadow, or the flower for its curious beauty, but look upon them affectionately as living beings whom the one great Creator has placed in the same fair world with ourselves, to pass, even as we do, their lives freely and yet in continual accordance with His allwise designs; each leaf, each petal, each stamen, each pistil, playing its separate part in the vegetable commonwealth to which it belongs; some industrious and perpetually striving for the good of the whole, some seeming to lead a fleeting existence of brilliant display—the leaves provident for the coming day, the flowers provident for the next generation; all working, not merely for themselves alone, but forming wood, and fibres, and nutritious food for man, a being of whom in their passive undreaming life they take no note and have no knowledge. There is a deep lesson and politic meaning contained in the scientific idea of a plant—a lesson and a meaning not dissimilar from those that constitute the true moral of the Great Exhibition.

AS APPLIED TO TEXTILE MANUFACTURES.

BY LEWIS D. B. GORDON,

Regius Professor of Mechanics, University of Glasgow.

THE term manufacture is no longer confined to its original signification—the production of human manipulation—but is now generally applied to articles made by machinery, from raw materials, supplied by a beneficent Providence, for adaptation by the industry and ingenuity of man for the wants and enjoyments of civilised society.

To some minds manufacturing has lost its dignity by the substitution of the iron arms and fingers of machinery, for the bone and sinew and nerves of the cunning artificer who, within little more than a century, produced all that then existed of manufacture. But this is surely a misconception; and a very different impression will, we conceive, be left on the minds of all who have had an opportunity, however cursory, of contemplating the tools and machinery applied to manufactures, so liberally displayed in the Exhibition of the Industry of all Nations, and which we are now to endeavour briefly to elucidate and explain.

The object we have in view is to convey to general readers such information on the principles and exact functions of manufacturing machinery, as will increase their interest in what they may have seen for the first, and, in many cases, it may be for the last time, in the Great Exhibition, and enable them to carry away with them truer impressions of the amount of thought and ingenuity that has been expended in the creation of the automatic fabricators of the most complex as well as simplest necessaries and conveniences they find in use in their routine life, than they otherwise could do. It is not our intention to describe this manufacturing machinery in detail, suited for the instruction of manufacturers; we shall only attempt to give a correct account of the mechanical processes exhibited, sketched with the view of making their characteristic excellencies understood, but without any pretension to set forth their comparative merits further than mentioning those features that display the progressive improvement of the various processes selected for our purpose.

As in the labour of the artificer there is combined a physical exertion and a manual dexterity,—the latter an emanation of mental exertion, the former requiring a regular supply of food and raiment to the body, in order that the "right hand may not lose its cunning,"—so in manufacturing machinery, there are two great principles developed; there are machines which are adapted to *receive and modify the powers of nature*, and machines which are contrived *for the transport and for the change of the form or texture* of materials.

Every machine is contrived to perform some given mechanical process, which supposes the existence of two other things besides the machine, namely, a *moving power* and *work to be done*, i.e., an object subject to the process in question. Machines, in fact, are interposed between the *power* and the *work*, for the purpose of adapting the one to the other.

As an example connected with our subject, the old spinning-wheel may be cited, in which the spindle and fly are made to revolve by application of the foot to a treadle. Here the motive power is derived from muscular action: the operation of spinning is carried on by drawing out the fibre from the *rock*, and supplying it regularly to the fly, which is caused to turn rapidly and twist it into a thread or yarn. The arrangement of the form of the fly and spindle, and its connection with the foot in such a manner that the pressure of the latter shall communicate the required motion to the former, is the function and object of the machine.

This machine, we see, consists of a series of connected pieces, beginning with the treadle, the construction, position, and motion of which are determined by the nature of the moving power, and ending with the fly and spindle: but this is, in fact, the description of every machine. There is always one or more series of connected pieces, at one end of which is a part especially adapted to receive the action of the *power*—such as a steam-engine, a water-wheel, a horse-lever, a handle or a treadle. At the other end of each series will be found a set of parts determined in form, position, and motion, by the nature of the work they have to do, and which may be called the working pieces: between them are placed trains of mechanism, connecting them so that, when the first parts move according to the law assigned to them by the action of the power, the second must necessarily move according to the law required by the nature of the work.

There are, we thus see, three classes of mechanical organs independent of each other, inasmuch as, on the one hand, any set of *operators* or working parts may be put in motion by power derived from any source. Thus, a fly and spindle may be turned either by the foot, by water, or by steam. Again, a given steam-engine, or water-wheel, or any other *receiver* of power, may be employed to give motion to any required set of working parts for any process whatever. Also, between a given *receiver of power* and set of working parts the interposed mechanism may be varied in very many ways. Moreover the principles upon which the construction and arrangement of these three classes of mechanical organs are founded are different. The receivers of power derive their form from a combination of mechanical principles with the physical laws which govern the respective sources of power. The operators derive their form from a combination of mechanical principles with considerations derived from the processes to be performed. The principles of the interposed mechanism are purely geometric, and may be developed without reference to the powers employed or transmitted. Mechanism is a combination of parts connecting two or more pieces, so that when one moves according to a given law, the others must move according to certain other given laws. A train of mechanism is composed of a series of moveable pieces, each of which is so connected with the framework of the machine, that when in motion every point of it is constrained to move in a certain path, in which, however, if considered separately from the other pieces, it is at liberty to move in the two opposite directions, and with any velocity. Thus, wheels, pulleys, shafts, and revolving pieces, generally are so connected with the frame of the machine, that any fixed point is compelled, when in motion, to describe a circle round the axis; sliding pieces are compelled by fixed guides to describe straight lines, and so on. These pieces are connected either by contact or by intermediate pieces, so that when the first piece in the series is moved from any external cause, it compels the second to move, which again gives motion to the third, and so on.

The act of giving motion to a piece is termed *driving* it, and that of receiving motion from a piece is termed *following* it. The *follower* receives motion from the *driver*.

In the view we are about to take of the Manufacturing Machines of the Exhibition, we exclude any reference to the *receivers of power*, important as is the part they play in the history and economy of manufactures. Our object is specially to record mechanical processes, and to give some idea of the mechanism of the machines applied to textile manufactures exhibited. We have chosen an order for treating of the mechanical processes by which textile fabrics are produced, which leads from the simple to the complex, and which shows the origin of the improvements that led to the wonderfully perfect machinery exhibited as applied to each and all textile fabrics.

These processes depend primarily on the nature of the materials—the raw materials to be worked up. *Silk, Cotton, Flax,* and *Wool,* require different methods of preparation for being *spun* and *woven,* the ultimate processes in the union of all textile fibres.

Silk Manufactures.—It would be out of place to enter into any details in regard to the little worm which produces the millions of pounds of raw silk annually produced and worked up on the continent of Europe, in India and China, and imported into Great Britain to supply this branch of industry.

In the French, the Milanese, the Piedmontese, the Tuscan, the Roman, Neapolitan, Algerian, Chinese, and Indian departments of the Exhibition, samples of the cocoons, and of the *reeled* or raw silk of these countries may be seen and examined.

The weight of cocoons varies according to the climate and management of the worms. About two hundred and thirty to a pound may be taken as an average, and twelve pounds of cocoons make a pound of raw silk. Thus 2760 worms are required for every pound of raw silk! For every *million* pounds weight of raw silk produced in France, it is reckoned that two hundred and fifty *million* pounds weight of mulberry leaves are consumed, and that five million of trees, of the average age of thirty years, are stripped to furnish them! Upwards of five million pounds of raw silk are now imported into Great Britain annually. In Britain the silk factories are almost confined to England.

The process of *Reeling the Silk from the Cocoons* is carried on in Europe in the months of July, August, and September, in establishments called *filatures,* and in the cottages of the peasantry of the countries where the silk is produced. The cocoons become an article of trade as soon as the insect inside has been killed by exposing them in an oven, or to the steam of boiling water: they are now to be *wound* off, or reeled. In the commencement of the operation, the cocoons, having been for a short time in a trough of hot water to soften their gum, the loosened ends are then taken (four together generally), twisted with the fingers, then passed through an eye on the end of a wire, and thence to the reel. Two *skeins* are generally thus formed at the same time, a child turning the reel, and a woman attending to mend the threads or fibres. The reel is so constituted, that while revolving it has communicated to it by wheel-work, a *lateral traverse* from right to left, and from left to right. The amount of traverse for each revolution being regulated so that the thread of one revolution does not overlay the other, for if it did, the natural gumminess would cause these threads to adhere. The extent of traverse is about three inches, and in the time employed in reeling this breadth of threads, the gum dries sufficiently to prevent the threads from sticking to each other at the points of crossing.

All kinds of silk which are simply drawn from the cocoons by the reeling, are called *raw silk,* but are denominated *fine*

or *coarse,* according to the number of fibres of which the thread is composed.

The factories in which raw silk is spun into silk-thread for weaving are called *throwing* mills, the term *throwing* being formed from the word "throw," in the obsolete sense of "to twist," "to twine."

In 1719 a silk-throwing mill was erected at Derby. This was the first in England, and it still exists.

Winding is the first process which the raw silk undergoes.

Winding—that is, transferring the silk skeins on to bobbins, was formerly done by hand, on machines carrying four or six reals and as many bobbins. The winding machines now are driven by power of steam or water, and are arranged in frames carrying as many as one hundred *swifts* or reels. The winding requires the unwearied attention of children to mend the threads that break as well in this process as in the next. There are about eight thousand children under thirteen years of age employed in British silk factories.

Our drawing represents the winding machine as made by Mr. Frost of Macclesfield, the skeins of raw silk are put on to the *swifts* which are *six-armed reels,* with string cross bars to form the fork in which the skein lies. The axles of the swifts lie loosely in centres, and the framing descends no lower than this centre, so that there is very little liability to knocking. The thread is passed through glass guides, arranged on a traversing guide bar, to the bobbins.

The bobbins are turned by double wooden rollers, turned out of one solid piece of wood causing them to run with greater truth than ordinary rollers : and by their being covered with leather, the use of chalk or rosen, to get adhesion is unnecessary, and thus a source of *soiling* the silk is avoided. By working with double rollers as is done in the machine, it is impossible that the *cheeks* and *spindles* of the bobbins can wear out.

The motion of the guide bar is produced by oval toothed wheels. The object of this motion is to *cross the threads* diagonally on the bobbins in order to prevent the threads from sticking together, that is to ensure that the unwinding them shall take the least possible force, and proceed without entangling. The drawing No. 1 represents only a small part of the length of a winding machine.

Cleaning.—The silk having been transferred from the skeins to the bobbins has to undergo a process of cleansing. This process is performed in transferring the silk from the bobbins produced on the last machine, to the bobbins or trams in the machine represented in the accompanying drawing.

The silk has to be cleaned to rid it of adhesive gummy matter and dust. For this it is passed through a cleaner knife or double knife placed on the guide rail, by the motion of which the thread is uniformly distributed on the new bobbins. If by any accident a thread be left out of the knife, the fault is easily detected by the ridge which will appear on the bobbin. The cleaner knife rail is fitted up so as to move in a slot, and thus the degree of separation of the knife edges is adjustable to the quality of the thread or silk to be cleaned. This operation was formerly combined with a doubling of the threads, and a system of *drop wires* was introduced for stopping the bobbins when threads broke. This is now dispensed with, and *the spinning and doubling* frame in the annexed drawing performs the

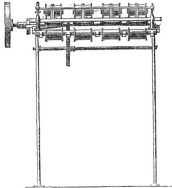

operation by one process and dispenses with the *stoving* of the silk, which was formerly necessary.

The silkworm-threads, perfectly cleaned, and become of a brilliant glossy appearance, are transferred to the spinning and doubling frame. In this machine, the threads from two or three of the bobbins from the cleaner are not now only wound together in contact upon another set of bobbins, but they are at once *spun* together. The lower set of bobbins are

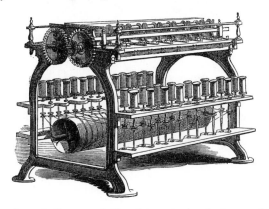

placed vertically on spindles driven by bands from a large drum, and then, in being transferred from one set of bobbins to the other, two or more threads are laid together. The *twist*, or, more correctly speaking, the angle of lay, is kept exceedingly uniform, the *bobbin going slower as it fills*, by working an intermediate friction roller (not seen in drawing). The guider is, of course, attached to this machine again with a very slow motion, so that the doubled and spun thread is laid very uniformly and closely on the bobbins, which are now transferred to the *throwing mill* or machine. On this machine

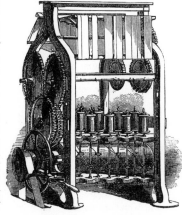

the doubled and spun threads are transferred from bobbins on to swifts or reels, and thus become *hanks* of silk in the state in which they are sent to the weaver. In this state, it is called *singles, tram,* or organzine, according as it has been made into hanks after being simply cleaned and twisted, after being doubled and twisted, or after being spun into thread by a second spinning operation.

The fineness of the silk is determined by the number of warp lengths, measuring seventy-two yards, in the ounce;

fine warp silk, for instance, runs about eight score threads. That is to say, there are upwards of six miles of thread nearly in an *ounce*, or one hundred miles in a pound weight.

The mechanical processes of preparing and spinning silk are of a very simple character, and form a striking contrast to the processes to which cotton, flax, and wool have to be submitted ere they are fit for the loom. Silk-*weaving* is, on the other hand, attended with difficulties which are not met with in weaving the yarns spun from the other textile fibres of which we are to treat.

The machinery of cotton-manufacture has its application even before the "raw material" is brought to the factory.

The "cotton-wool" has to be separated from the seed. The machine now almost universally used for this purpose is the *saw-gin*, the roller-gin having been supplanted even in India. The best example of this machine is exhibited in the United States department. Till 1793, when Eli Whitney invented the saw-gin, the wool of the green-seeded cotton could only be separated from the seed by an amount of labour very discouraging to the growth of that hardy and productive article. By this invention, one man was enabled to do the work of a thousand, and there was no limit to the cultivation of the cotton save the limits to the acreage of suitable soil.

The quantity of raw cotton consumed in the cotton manufacture of Great Britain, in the year 1850, was 584,200,000 lbs., or nearly 835 tons per diem.

The machinery for manufacture of cotton—for performing the various operations that *prepare* the cotton wool, as imported from the countries where it is grown, for being spun and woven—are liberally displayed in the Exhibition by leading British manufacturers and by the French.

There are few things more interesting in manufacturing processes than the progress of the soft downy substance of the interior of the cotton-pod, with all its fine filaments and delicate colour, through its various stages, until it becomes a useful fabric for the daily wear of the industrious classes, or assumes those beautiful forms in which Art has added grace to mechanical skill and ingenuity. These gradations are at once so perfect and complete, while they are based upon the most admirable system of orderly progress, that cotton-spinning becomes a science of no ordinary character when it is carried to the perfection to which we see it here displayed. The examples exhibited illustrate the various gradations of the coarse and fine manufacture—there are cases commencing with a specimen of Sea-Island cotton, and having every stage of progress up to nine-cord sewing thread, and muslin and figured lace. The only drawback to their great interest is the crowding together of so many specimens in so small cases, since there is some difficulty in distinctly separating them. This is the more to be regretted, as the connection of the raw material with the examples around is so admirably illustrated, and, if studied in connection with the machinery, is capable of affording valuable lessons.

The yarns, exhibited as the basis of other products, show to what an extent the ingenuity of man can be carried, when employed in a given direction. There we have specimens of yarn spun by machinery, which is of so delicate a character, that the fibres of cotton can only be discovered in the fabric by the aid of the microscope; and so delicate is it that it falls to pieces by handling. This curiosity of manufacture is exhibited by Messrs. Thomas Houldsworth & Co., of Manchester, and is the result of the energy and enterprise of Henry Houldsworth, Esq., of that firm. In the contributions of this establishment we find specimens of cotton yarn ranging from No. 100 to No. 700, in single yarn; and No. 100 to No. 670, in double yarn, or lace thread. These figures express the number of hanks to a pound weight, each hank being 840 yards; and the last named number of 700 in single, and 670 in double yarn, is the triumph of cotton-spinning for all practical purposes, since we find that a pound weight of cotton is elongated, in the first instance, to a length of 338 miles; and, in the other, to a double thread 324 miles, at a cost of 28*l.*, as the price of a single pound weight. The most remarkable example, however, is the specimen shown as

No. 900, both of yarn and thread, as a curiosity, by which a single pound of cotton is extended to 430 miles. So late as 1840, 350 was the finest yarn attempted. In 1841, Messrs. Houldsworth spun 450, which was then considered as the limit. Another still more astounding specimen exhibited by Messrs. Houldsworth is that of 2150 yarn, in which we may fairly presume that they have reached the limit at which the fibre will at all cohere. A single pound of this yarn would yield the extraordinary length of 1026 miles!

The first operation of a *cotton mill* is to open up the cotton into its original spongy state and shake out any earth or vegetable matter accidentally mixed with it.

In order to mix the cotton, several bales of the same, or of different kinds, are put together in a " bing." A tool, like a hay-rake, is employed to draw down and tear asunder the agglomerated mass of cotton as it is wanted for the picking, and other cleaning processes. Fine cotton, such as the best Sea Island, is still sometimes cleaned and opened at first by the hand-labour of women and children ; but various machines for accomplishing the same object have been contrived and applied to all qualities of cotton wool.

The *willow* is the machine in general use for opening out the entangled flocks of cotton.

A cylindrical cage, made of *willows*, with an axis carrying cross arms, and having a rotatory motion, was employed of old in Normandy for cleaning cotton-wool, under the name of *le panier de Normandie*. This simple machine is undoubtedly the original of the modern English willow, which has undergone various modifications, *retaining*, however, the essential features of its type.

We do not think it necessary to describe the willow properly so called, although the " conical willow," the most improved machine for this process, is exhibited both in Britain and in France. We take Calvert's patent machine for *opening* and *cleansing* cotton, as exhibited by Messrs. Hibbert, Platt, & Sons, as the most recent means of effecting this operation. This is, in fact, a scutching machine, so arranged that the preliminary process of willowing is performed within it.

The beating action is produced by rollers with long projecting wedge-edged teeth. The cotton is taken, in weighed quantities, from the bing, spread very uniform by hand on a feeding apron, which presents it to fluted rollers. These rollers present it to the toothed beaters, revolving at great speed, and so arranged that all the coarser impurities fall through. From these *beaters*, or *scutchers*, the cotton is taken up by fluted rollers, which, in their turn, pass it on to a hollow, serrated cylinder, revolving at great speed, and by which the fibre is drawn out, while the minute seeds pass through apertures left by the saw like teeth on the cylinder ; and the interior of this being in communication with a fanner, which sucks through the air, the dust and fine impurities are almost completely got rid of. This cylinder is cleaned of the teazed cotton by means of brushes, which deliver the cotton on to *fluted rollers* so regularly, that it comes out of the machine *lapped* into the form of a broad, felt-like *web* of cleaned cotton.

The web of cleaned cotton thus obtained is passed through a *lapping* machine, and in this machine it undergoes a further teazing, in such manner that several laps of different qualities of cotton from the scutcher may be mixed in this machine, so as to obtain a uniform quality of *staple*. The cotton, once more formed into a fleecy lap, is brought out by rollers, and delivered on to wooden *lap cylinders*. This makes the third mechanical process to which the cotton fleece has been submitted.

The scutching machine was originally invented by the late Mr. Snodgrass, of Johnston, in Renfrewshire ; and afterwards improved by Mr. Cooper, of the same place. Mr. Calvert's scutcher is, perhaps, the most perfect machine of the kind in use in any country.

From the lap machine, the cotton passes to the *carding engines*, or *cards*. The object of the carding operation is to separate or comb out the fibres of the cotton, which are still entangled in small tufts, so as to bring them into as perfect parallelism as possible. For this purpose the cotton is put through a long series of combings, which are effected by the reciprocal action of two surfaces which are mounted with slightly bent elastic wire points.

To Arkwright belongs the honour of having made the cylinder card a practical machine. This was about the year 1770.

Carding engines, says Dr. Ure, may be defined to be brushes of bent iron wire fixed in leather, applied to a set of cylindrical and a set of plane surfaces, the former being made to revolve so as to sweep over the surfaces of the latter at rest. Sometimes large cylindrical cards work against the surfaces of smaller cylindrical cards moving at a *less* speed; and sometimes both plans are combined in the same engine. The tufts or knots of cotton are held fast by the stationary or slow moving cards, while the quick moving cards teaze out the fibres, and gradually, very gradually, disentangle them. Thus we can understand how fixed cards, in which the cotton is exposed to an uninterrupted course of teazing, disentangle the long-stapled cotton better than the *squirrel* or secondary revolving cards, which bring the tufts under the action of the great drum-card only once in each of their own revolutions. They exercise a greater tearing force, and are therefore used for coarser and shorter stapled cottons, with which rapidity of work is an object of importance; in fact, much more cotton can be passed through in the same time, when both the main card and the counter cards revolve ; and as the latter require less frequent cleaning than what are called the *flat-top* cards, this system is generally used in preparation for the lower counts of spinning ; and occasionally in combination with fixed tops in that of the middling fine yarns.

The filaments, after emerging from the *flats*, lie in nearly parallel lines among the card teeth of the drum, when they are removed by a smaller drum card which turns in contact with it, called the doffer (stripper) or doffing cylinder, and is covered spirally with fillet cards. By its slow rotation in an opposite direction it strips the loosened filaments from the drum, and thus clothes itself uniformly with a fine fleece of cotton, which is shorn or combed off from the opposite side of the cylinder by the vibratory action of the doffing knife.

This knife is a blade of steel, toothed at its edge like a fine comb, and it is made to comb downwards with a rapid shaving motion along the edge of the cards. This is Arkwright's justly celebrated *crank and comb* contrivance. This admirably designed instrument doffs the cotton in a fine transparent fleece, and is beautiful to look upon. It is gathered as it comes off the whole width of the card, and passing through a funnel-shaped piece is gradually compressed into a riband and drawn through rollers in front of the engine. These rollers form the *card end* or *sliver*, which remains to be treated by the next process—viz., to be *doubled*. This is nothing more than a laying of forty slivers into one *fresh lap*. These forty slivers being the products of as many carding engines, and sometimes containing the fibres of many different varieties of cotton of various staples.

Uniformity and parallelism in the fibre are the great objects to be sought for in preparing cotton for the process of spinning.

The laps from the doubling machine are worked through a set of what are termed *finishing cards* which are used in many *coarse* and in all *fine* spinning factories. The finishing card does not differ in any essential respect from the *breaker card*. The large card-drum is generally surmounted by *urchin* or *squirrel* cards instead of tops, such as are used in the preparation of inferior cotton wools for spinning coarse yarns.

In a *fine* spinning mill, seven finishing cards will turn off 160 pounds of Sea Island cotton in sixty-nine hours (one week). Three yards of the lap presented to these cards weigh only four ounces. These *seven finishers* correspond to *six breaker cards*. For a *preparation*, as it is termed (one set), twelve card-ends go to form the first drawing. In the breaker-cards, 1600 grains weight of cotton are spread out upon seven feet of the apron-cloth to form one lap.

In such an establishment, 160 pounds constitute a preparation, which is confined to a given set of cards, drawers, and roving frames. One man *superintends* four such preparations.

In a *coarse* spinning mill (No. 30 and No. 40), the carding engines being surmounted with urchin cards, each does about 1000 lbs. per week. The drum makes 180 revolutions per minute.

The next process in cotton preparation is drawing out and elongating the downy slivers or ribands, to straighten the filaments, and lay them as parallel to each other as possible.

Before passing to a description of the process of drawing on the drawing frame, we must allude to the process of making *card cloth*, as exhibited in the Exhibition.

We have already indicated how much pains is taken to perfect the carding process of preparing cotton. It is the same for wool; and, in some respects, for the tow of flax. The carding depends more on the quality of the cards than upon any attention or skill in the operatives or *card-tenters*.

To make *card-cloth*, hides of leather are cut up into strips, varying in breadth according to the purpose to which they are ultimately to be applied. These strips are passed between iron rollers, adjustable to different distances, and furnished with a sharp-cutting edge below, by which, in the passage, the leather is shaved off in its thickest parts, and made uniform throughout. These stripes, thus reduced, are joined by bevelling off the ends for about an inch in length, applying to the bevelled surfaces a thin solution of glue, made of acetic acid and isinglass, and then subjecting them to a powerful press. The union is made so perfectly, that it is scarcely possible to distinguish the joint. A number of such pieces being united together in one length, the leather is fit for the operations of the card-making machine.

This machine delights all who look at its rapid and wonderfully accurate operation.

The card-making machine is an American invention; but the first patent for it was taken by Mr. Dyer, of Manchester. This was in 1811. Many patents have been taken for improvements since, Mr. Dyer himself having taken not fewer than five.

The mechanism is simple, and yet so complicated that no drawings, such as could come within the scope of this Essay, could represent it. The machines are variously arranged. In most machines the leather is placed vertically, as in that exhibited; in others, it is stretched horizontally. The process is the same in both. A hank of fine wire is put on a reel turning horizontally, at a short distance from the machine, and the end of the wire introduced into the frame. The machine being now put in gear, the wire is slid forward about an inch, and is instantly cut off at that length. Two side pieces of steel now press on the projecting ends of the wire, and bend the wire to the staple form, like a two-pronged fork. In the mean time two fine steel prickers are pushed forward to form two holes in the leather. These are below the two ends of the staple, and on the instant they are withdrawn the staple is thrust forward into the holes, while a pair of nippers takes hold of the back of the staple, and gives it that slight bend which we have described as necessary. The staple entering in one operation is pushed home; at the next at the instant the new holes are made. The whole of these operations is performed in *less* than half a second. A slight movement of the leather sideways, after each insertion, provides for the continuous progress of the operation.

Hundreds of these machines are at work in Manchester, in Leeds, in Glasgow, and elsewhere. *Miles*, many miles, of wire, are worked up by these machines daily. The difficulty of making card cloth increases with its fineness. The French have carried this manufacture to great perfection, as exhibited in numerous cases of samples in the Exhibition.

The Drawing Frame. The drawing out of the cotton slivers is effected by revolving rollers, and to use the words of Dr. Ure, it can only be clearly understood by an attentive and minute consideration of the operation of such mechanism upon textile fibres. Arkwright was so impressed with the importance of his drawing-frame in automatic spinning, that when any bad work was turned out he immediately desired his people to "*mind their drawings.*"

The cards straighten many of the filaments, but they also double not a few by catching them by the middle. The drawing undoes all these foldings of the fibres when it is well conducted, and is, therefore, the most curious in a philosophical point of view, which factory genius displays.

The drawing-frame produces a succession of *slivers* which pass to the roving-frame.

Six slivers from the finishing cards are presented through the *curved guide-plate* to a first drawing-frame roller. The compound or sextuple sliver, in passing between the roller series, is drawn out principally by the front roller into a uniform attenuated and much elongated sliver, and two of these are generally drawn together through a conical mouth-piece, which delivers the new sliver into a revolving *can*.

The rate of the surface speed of the front roller to that of the back roller varies from four, or six, to one; and that rate may be modified by changing certain wheels according to the size of the sliver that is desired. The difference between the speed of the two back rollers is no more than one tenth part; the middle roller serving rather as a guide in leading the filaments to the front roller.

The sliver thus drawn with multiplied doublings acquires a regularity of texture which, if not impaired in the subsequent processes, ensures a level yarn to the cotton spinner.

The sextupling of slivers is generally continued through two drawing-frames, and then twelve slivers are put into one, and drawn by a frame which feeds the *slubbing* machine.

The number of doublings varies according to the fineness of spinning for which it is a preparation.

The process of drawing being finished, the next process is *the twisting the slivers*—that is, *laying the fibres* together by torsion.

It were vain to attempt an account of the expenditure of thought which the production of the roving frames at work in the Exhibition has occasioned in the progress of the arrangement of the mechanism to the state of perfection there exhibited.

This beautiful machine, consists of several pieces of mechanism, which may be separately considered. There is a set of rollers, a *roller-beam* similar to that in the drawing-frame, and there are *vertical spindles*, bearing on their tops a forked piece, called a "Flyer," of which one leg or branch is tubular, and serves to conduct the soft roving from the hose of the spindle to the bobbin. By the revolution of the spindle and flyer the cotton *slub* receives its twist, and by the difference of the rotation of the flyer and bobbin it is wound upon the latter exactly in proportion as it is given off by the rollers. This gives the *torsion*. The *winding-on* takes place in a ratio compounded of the difference of the speed of the bobbin and flyers, and of the circumference of the bobbin.

"Were the winding on to be a constant quantity, like the motion of the delivering rollers, the product of the two numbers would remain the same; but when one of them alters, as happens to the diameter of the bobbin, which is constantly increasing, the difference between the number of revolutions of the bobbin and flyer must be decreased; a change produced by increasing the speed of the bobbins while the flyers revolve uniformly, in order to give a uniform degree of torsion to a definite length of the delivered slub. As, therefore, the up-and-down motion of the bobbin, in the distribution of the roving over its surface, must be decreased in a constant progression, according to the grist of the roving, so the rotation of the bobbin is increased by a motion compounded of the regular speed of the driving-shaft of the machine, and the decreased speed of the other parts. We cannot attempt more minute details of description of this machine."

The process of spinning thus commenced is finished on the stretching-frame—the throstle and the mule. The cotton from the roving-frames is *pieced* up to either the *mule* or *throstle*, and spun into yarn, according to the quality of yarn intended to be produced.

We have been so minute in our account of the preparation of cotton, that we have only space left for a very brief account of mule-spinning. The stretching-frame is, in fact, a mule without the second draught and second speed. In the bobbin and fly-frames, the amount of lay, or quantity of twist given to the roving, is as little as is compatible with their being unwound without impairing their uniformity. The object of the throstle is to extend the rovings into fine threads at the same time that it twists them by the rotation of spindles or flyers, and winds them upon bobbins, somewhat resembling what we have endeavoured to describe in speaking of the bobbin and fly-frame.

The most interesting and perfect illustration of the throstle is that termed the *Danforth*, exhibited by Sharp Brothers of Manchester. There are various modifications of it; but we have not space to do more than name the machine.

The manufacture and improvement of the form of spindles and flyers has occupied the attention of many machinists, and specimens are to be seen from Manchester, Salford, Lille, and elsewhere, of the exquisite workmanship put upon these vital elements of modern spinning machinery. When it is

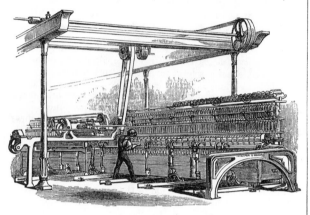

considered that these spindles and flyers revolve from 1000 to 2000 times in a minute, the perfection with which they must be finished and hardened, in order that they may move steadily and without self-destruction, and the consumption of power, may be easily conceived.

The Mule, or Mule Jenny, consists of four distinct sets of parts:—

1. The *drawing* rollers, already fully explained. 2. A *moveable carriage*, of a length equal to the roller-beam, mounted with as many spindles as there are threads to be spun. This carriage runs upon wheels upon edge-rails laid in the floor of the factory, which allows the carriage about five feet of forward and backward motion, relatively to the roller-beam. 3. The *headstock*, or the mechanism, by which the carriage is moved to and fro. In some Mules the head-stock is placed in advance of the roller-beam, towards the middle of its length. In others, the headstock is put behind the roller-beam, so as to leave the whole length of the roller-beam and carriage without interruption.

The general action of the mule may be stated as follows:— The rovings being passed forwards from their respective bobbins, set upright in the creel, through between the rollers, and their ends being attached to their respective spindles, the rollers, and carriage with its spindles, are all set in motion simultaneously: the carriage being made to recede from the roller-beam at a somewhat quicker rate than the surface-speed of the front rollers, or the delivery of the soft threads. This excess of velocity is called the "gain" of the carriage, and is intended to render the thread *level*, upon the principle above explained—namely, that the greater quantity of twist runs into the slenderer or weaker parts of the yarn, and obstructs their due extension; whereas, if the quantity of twist be skil-fully adapted to the occasion, the thicker portions of the thread will have time to be acted upon by the gain of the carriage, till their substance is reduced somewhat nearer to the average thickness required. When the carriage has moved out about 45 or 50 inches, according to the fineness of the work, a general change takes place in the operation of the mule. The rollers suddenly stop, the spindles begin to revolve with nearly a double velocity, and the carriage slackens its space to about one-sixth of its previous speed. This stage of the process is called the stretching, or the draw. The exten-

sion of the filaments, performed in part by the twin-roller system, is by this action carried on and completed in their softly twisted state. When the carriage, by its advance, has stretched the threads to the full extent they will bear without breaking, the second draw ceases by the stopping of the carriage, while the spindles still continue to revolve till the requisite quantity of twist is communicated, which is regulated by the twist-wheel having completed a certain number of turns. Upon the twist-wheel shaft a finger is usually fixed, which at each revolution disengages a catch, whereby the driving-strap is allowed to pass to the loose pulley, and the whole machinery stands still. In the hand-mule the spinner now puts down with his left hand the faller, or guide-wire, to the level requisite for guiding the threads into the proper winding-on position upon the caps of the spindles. In putting down the faller-wire, he at the same time unwinds that portion of the thread which is coiled spirally round the spindle, from its point to the nose of the cap, which he does by causing the spindles to turn the backward way, with his right hand working their main driving-pulley. This operation of undoing the coil is called *the backing-off*.

Whenever the faller has arrived at the degree of depression suited to the winding-on of the yarn, the spinner now reverses his backward motion, and winds on the yarn by causing the spindles to turn the forward way, while, at the same time, he pushes in the carriage at a rate commensurate with the revo-lution of the spindles. As the carriage approaches the roller-beam, the spinner gradually raises the *faller-wire*, to allow the last portion of the threads to be coiled again in an open spiral, from the nose of the cap up to their points. One operation being thus completed, another is immediately begun.

By winding successive portions of thread upon the spindle, a conical-shaped coil of yarn is formed, which, when sufficiently large, is slid off the spindle, in which state the article is ready for the market, under the denomination of Cop yarn. A considerable quantity of it, however,—particularly of that destined to be dyed or shipped to foreign countries,—is unwound from the cops upon reels, and thereby made up into skeins or hanks.

The rendering the machinery which performs all these processes automatic was first accomplished by Richard Roberts, of Manchester, between 1830 and 1835, and his headstock is still unrivalled. The late Mr. Smith, of Deanston, and Mr. McIndoe, of Glasgow, have modified the headstock in various ways, and their *self-actors* have earned great reputa-tion for excellence. The self-actor of Mr. McIndoe has much to recommend it, and has been applied to spinning numbers as high as 150 with success, whilst self-actors in general are not applied to higher numbers than 120. The hand mule has still to be used in spinning finer numbers of cotton, and in spinning wool.

Weaving.—If we take the term, weaving, in its most comprehensive sense, as applying to the process of combining longitudinal threads into a superficial fabric, it will have relation to the whole series of textile fabrics; not only those woven in the loom, but likewise net-work, lace-work, and hosiery.

First, of plain weaving.—By this term we mean the weaving of all varieties of lathe manufacture; whether of silk, cotton, woollen, or linen, in which the weft threads interlace uniformly among the warp threads without producing twills, checks, stripes, sprigs, or any variety of figures.

Calico, Irish linen, and plain silk, are good representations of this kind of weaving. If we examine any of these, we find that the cross threads pass alternately *over* and *under* the long threads, no one thread passing over or under two other threads at once.

The long threads are called the warp-twist, or organzine; while the cross threads are called *weft, woof, shoot,* or *tram.*

Twist is the term usually applied to the kind of yarn used for cotton warp; organzine to that for silk warp: and some of the other terms have, in like manner, only partial applica-tion. We shall speak simply of *warp* and *weft* to avoid ambiguity. The *warp* is always attached to the loom, or weaving machine, while the *weft* is contained in the shuttle— a small, canoe-like instrument. The winding of the weft on the spindle, which runs through the shuttle, is a simple matter; but the arrangement of the warp in the loom is very important, and must be understood, before we can follow the details of weaving.

In the process of the cotton manufacture before the yarn comes to the warping-machine, it is wound from the cop on to bobbins about four inches long, and about three inches diameter: these bobbins of yarn are then taken to the warping-machine, for the purpose of the threads being laid parallel to each other, to make them into a *beamed warp*, and to facilitate the arrangement of them after being *sized* and placed in the heads or 'heddles' of the loom in weaving. In the old system of preparing the yarn, before its being placed in the loom, a cumbrous machine, called the warping-mill, was used instead of this improved machine of

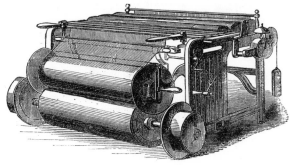

Mr. Kenworthy's, which warping-mill was worked by hand. After the yarn had been made into a balled warp, it was then taken to the old kind of sizing-machine, which soaked the yarn into the warm size (a kind of paste), then dried it, then squeezed it between iron rollers, and next it was reballed. The warp was then taken from this machine to a machine for winding it on a roller-beam, after which it was taken to the looming-frame, and next to the loom to be woven into cloth. But now, by the connection of Mr. Kenworthy's warping-machine, with the sizing-machine of Messrs. Hornby & Kenworthy, the process is made much shorter and more simple, and is withal systematic and mechanical.

It will be seen, on reference to the drawing, that the bobbins containing yarn are placed in a wooden frame called a 'creel,' so that they will revolve; the threads are then passed through a 'wraithe' on to a roller-beam. The 'wraithe' is for the purpose of keeping the threads separate and uniformly in the order in which they are intended to be wound off (after having passed through the size) on to the weaver's yarn-beam. In this machine is a beautiful adaptation of mechanism, by which the yarn may be backed off the beam, if by chance any broken thread has escaped the eye of the operative and got on the beam. This motion consists of a series of small cylindrical rods, so arranged that the threads of yarn pass under them; and supposing none of the threads had to break during the process, the beam would get filled without any necessity for calling this inven-

tion into action. But it so happens that breakages often do occur, and, as the machine works at a rather quick speed, those dissevered threads get on to the beam before the operative has sufficient time to stop the machine. The machine is provided with two sets of driving-pulleys, one pair at each end of the driving-shaft: that pair which drive the backing-off motion work at one half the speed the others do. The leathern straps or bands which connect these pulleys with the main shaft of the factory, are so arranged by the one (that which drives the backing-off motion) being crossed and the other being open, that the motion of the machine can be reversed whenever the threads are broken. The series of cylindrical rollers perform their office by moving down slots made in the framing of the machinery, in their progress bearing down with them the threads backed off the beam, until the severed thread is discovered and united, when the operative sets on the machine as before the breaking took place, and the cylindrical rollers return to their former position. After the beam is filled by this machine, it is placed, along with five others, in the improved sizing-machine. These beams are placed in bearings so that they will revolve at the left end of the machine, and weights are placed upon their pivots, so that they are kept in their places; the six threads of yarn are then passed through an ordinary comb-bar or 'wraithe,' and thus divided equally until passed through the healds, which, in this machine, are situated at the left end, for the purpose of effecting the cross shed, and thereby taking the 'lease' previously to the yarns being submitted to the sizing process. The 'lease' now being taken, and the cross band or threads being introduced for the purpose of 'looming,' or drawing in of the weaver's beam, the threads of yarn are passed over a 'wraithe' or comb-bar, formed by a row of teeth or pins of intervening spaces, for the purpose of laying the threads in parallel breadths side by side, and forming each division or band of threads (of any required number) into separate and distinct tapes or sheets (of any desired width), each thread being laid parallel side by side, and thus in lateral contact, the 'wraithe' or comb-bar being allowed to vibrate or oscillate freely as the threads proceed. The continuous threads now being thus made or separated into breadths or bands, are now passed over a conducting roller and immersed into the trough containing the sizing material, which is here kept in a heated state by steam passing through a pipe into the trough, and thus boiled into the warp-threads as they pass through it and under the adjustable tension roller, which can be adjusted to any required degree of tension at pleasure, or can be raised up, when necessary, entirely out of the trough by means of a winch, worm, and rack, with which the pinions of the rollers are connected. The threads are then passed forward through a pair of squeezing rollers, and again similarly immersed in the trough containing the size, to finish the yarn; from thence they are passed around the drying cylinder, also heated by steam, and now assume the form of tapes or bands, the sizing material, by its slightly adhesive properties, causing the threads thus to adhere slightly together, and thus proceed in a tape-like form, being of course much stronger, more regular and even, and less likely to be broken or

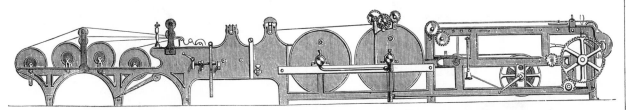

disarranged than in the old mode of sizing. A circular revolving brush is placed over the threads as they proceed over the drying cylinders, for the purpose of dressing or laying the fibres, and making the tapes or bands more compact and even. They now proceed in a sized, dried, and finished state, being conducted by two rollers through a similar 'wraithe' or comb-bar, but of a much finer pitch, and by passing through which the bands of threads are passed edges

wise, and again similarly divided by the oscillating or vibratory action of the comb-bar, and laid over the tension roller at the right-hand end of the machine, in a proper state to be received and wound upon the warp-beam, ready for the operation of drawing in, after which operation it is taken to the loom and woven.

The warp in the last state described is received by the *weaver.*

We shall not do more than direct attention to the numerous power-looms exhibited, to the Jacquard looms, and to the machines for making the *healds* or *heddles*—for making reeds, for cutting cards, and for making other appendages to weaving machinery. Weaving in almost every fibre—cotton, flax, silk, worsted, and wool—may be learned in the department of Machinery in Motion.

We must suppose our readers already acquainted with the process of weaving by the hand-loom. Nor can we enter into the description we intended to have done of *Pattern-weaving*, from the simple but effective "shot" patterns—the stripes and checks, the twills and all its varieties—as dimities, dornocks, bombazeens, satins, kerseymeres, &c., to the more complicated, embracing damasks and brocaded silks. By means of the *Draw*-loom, the order in which the warp threads are depressed or elevated, varies continually; strings being so arranged that the *Draw-boy* can draw down the requisite warp threads preparatory to the movement of the shuttle. The warp threads pass through the eyes or loops in vertical strings, each thread having one string, and these strings are so grouped that the attendant boy, by pulling a handle, draws up all those warp threads which are required to be elevated for one particular shoot of weft; and when a different order of succession is required, he pulls another handle. Hence it follows that the arrangement of the strings and handles must be preconcerted with especial reference to one particular pattern, and this is called "cording the loom." The *cording* used to occupy a skilful thoughtful man *several months*, and would then of course serve for only one particular pattern.

The first step in improving the *draw-loom* was the substitution of mechanism for the handle and boy called a *draw-boy*, and then the adoption of Duncan's automatic carpet loom or barrel loom, in which pins inserted in a rotatory barrel, like an organ barrel, moved a reciprocating lever, as in the draw-boy, and thus the way was paved for Jacquard's most perfect invention in 1800.

In all the kinds of weaving hitherto noticed, whether of plain goods, figured goods, bobbin net, stockings, or other fabrics, we have alluded to the weaving machine as *worked by hand*—or, more correctly speaking, by hand and foot—for the treadle is invariably the receiver of power in these machines.

So early as 1678 M. de Gennes invented "a new engine to make linen cloth without the aid of an artificer," and at various times during the last century, M. Vaucanson, Mr. Austin, and Mr. Miller, contrived looms which were to be worked by a winch, by water power, or some power extraneous to the common hand loom.

As Arkwright's and Watt's inventions were perfected and

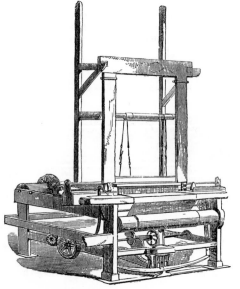

extended in their applications, the necessity for having weaving machinery became more urgent. In 1802 the power-

loom had not produced important saving in the expense of weaving, as a man had to be employed about each loom.

The power-loom of the present day is one of the most remarkable machines of the age we live in.

Mr. Harrison exhibits a power-loom made in 1798 or 1800

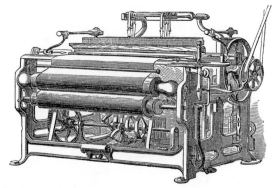

[it is engraved on the preceding column] alongside of the most improved looms of the present date, engraved on this column. How great the difference! Yet the honour due to Robert Miller, who commenced to introduce power-looms of the same construction as this old loom in 1796, is perhaps greater than to those who have produced the improvements, because his was the *beginning*.

The old machine can be worked to advantage at 60 picks per minute, requiring one person to each loom, or five persons to six looms. The new looms can be driven at 220 picks per minute, and are to be seen working at that speed in the Exhibition, and in all the best power-loom mills in England and Scotland. One person can attend two of these, and in many instances three looms.

An experienced operative of the manufacturing district, working the modern looms, produces 26 pieces of printing cloth, 25 inches wide, 29 yards long, and 11 picks per $\frac{1}{4}$ inch, in a week of 60 hours. The cost of weaving each piece is $5\frac{1}{2}d.$—less than $6d.$! If the same cloth were woven on the old loom, one operative would produce only four pieces, and at a cost of $2s.\ 9d.$ each; or the weaver's wages in 1800 were as much as is the entire value of the *cloth* in the Manchester market at present. Wonderful mechanical result! What are the moral results?

AN ESSAY ON ORNAMENTAL ART AS DISPLAYED IN THE INDUSTRIAL
EXHIBITION IN HYDE PARK, IN WHICH THE DIFFERENT STYLES
ARE COMPARED WITH A VIEW TO THE IMPROVEMENT OF
TASTE IN HOME MANUFACTURES.*

BY RALPH NICHOLSON WORNUM.

"It is known that the Taste is improved exactly as we improve our judgment; by extending our knowledge, by a steady attention to our object, and by frequent exercise. They who have not taken these methods, if their taste decides quickly, it is always uncertainly; and their quickness is owing to their presumption and rashness, and not to any sudden irradiation." BURKE.

"Conamur tenues Grandia."

I.—*Introduction.*

THERE is perhaps no province of industry, in which the advantages of an intercommunication of ideas are more direct, than in that of Art-manufacture; and this must be more especially the case when the means of production of the various parties are pretty nearly mechanically equal. The differences of results arise purely from differences of degrees of artistic skill, depending on the greater or less cultivation of those faculties of the mind which conduce to that species of judgment termed Taste.

It is evident that Taste must be the paramount agent in all competitions involving ornamental design, where the means or methods of production are equally advanced; but where this is not the case, the chances are still very greatly in the favour of Taste over mere mechanical facility, provided low price be not the primary object.

Thus, the Great Exhibition in Hyde Park is of all things the best calculated to advance our National Taste, by bringing in close contiguity the various productions of nearly all the nations of the earth in any way distinguished for ornamental manufactures. The

distinctive characteristics of each are so many elements of novelty of arrangements which every nation may appropriate according to its own views and practice.

Our present subject of consideration is how far British manufacturers may derive advantage from this congress of national peculiarities of design.

Ornament is essentially of the province of the *eye*; it is beautiful appearances that we require, not recondite ideas, in works of Ornamental Art: these may be associated with ornament, but they must be kept perfectly subject to the mere principles of beauty of arrangement of the material forms. Dramatic, allegoric, and ornamental art are totally distinct in their development; they may be combined, but one can never be the substitute of another. If dramatic or allegorical compositions are introduced as portions of an ornamental scheme, they must be treated upon the symmetrical or ornamental principle. Whatever other principle we may associate with the ornamental, must be kept secondary to *effect*, if we are desirous of making a good design: introduce what symbols we will, they must be made subject to the ruling principles of ornament itself, or, however good the symbolism, our design is a mere crudity in Art.

Some general examination of ornament in its characteristic developments of various times and nations, or what are technically called *styles*, must necessarily precede our examination of the modern expressions of ornamental art as now displayed in the Great Industrial Exhibition.

We shall find that the elements of form are constant in all cases; they are but variously treated: this, in fact, must be so, if a Style be founded upon any principles at all; and all those styles which have carried with them the feelings of ages, could not be otherwise than based upon some fixed natural laws. How certain variations of form and colour happen to be so universal a desire, that the varieties of their arrangements have occupied all people from the remotest times, is a question of both material and psychological interest.

Universal efforts show a universal want, and beauty of effect and decoration are no more a luxury in a civilised state of society than warmth or clothing are a luxury to any state: the mind, as the body, makes everything necessary that it is capable of permanently enjoying. Ornament is one of the mind's necessities, which it gratifies by means of the eye. So it has been discovered to be again an essential element in commercial prosperity. This was not so at first, because in a less cultivated state we are quite satisfied with the gratification of our merely physical wants; but in an advanced state, the more extensive wants of the mind demand still more pressingly to be satisfied. Hence ornament is now as material an interest in a commercial community as the raw materials of manufacture themselves.

In early stages of manufactures, it is mechanical fitness that is the object of competition: as society advances, it is necessary to combine elegance with fitness; and those who cannot see this must send their wares to the ruder markets of the world, and resign the great marts of commerce to those of superior taste who deserve a higher reward.

This is no new idea: let us take a lesson from the experience of past ages,—the various coloured glass of Egypt, the figured cups of Sidon, the shawls of Miletus, the terra-cottas of Samos, the bronzes of Corinth—did not command the markets of the ancient world, either for their materials or for their mechanical qualities; not because they were well blown—cleverly chased—finely woven —ingeniously turned—or perfectly cast:—these qualities they had only in common with the similar wares of other nations; but in the gratification of one of the most urgent necessities of the mind in an advanced social state, they were pre-eminent—they were objects of a cultivated refined taste. And it is by this character alone that manufactures will ever establish that renown which will ensure a lasting market in the civilised world. The great object of attainment is Taste, which is not a mere impulse of the fancy, but dependent upon the operations of reason as completely as any other conclusion respecting good or bad, or right or wrong, to which we attain by the mind's experience. To demonstrate this truth is the chief aim of the following Essay, in which the various species of ornamental art exhibited will be examined with respect

* To this Essay has been awarded the prize of one hundred guineas, offered by the Proprietors of the ART-JOURNAL, for "An Essay on the best mode of rendering the Exhibition of the Works of Industry of All Nations, to be held in London in 1851, practically useful to the British Manufacturer."—ED. A. J.

to their quality, wholly regardless of magnitude or quantity; for a single good work is worth a whole museum of mediocrity, in an educational point of view, and this is the bourn of our inquiry—How far our manufacturers may improve their taste through the present Great Exhibition of Works of Industry now established in Hyde Park?

It is only by an analysis of the principles and styles of ornament that such an inquiry can be practicable, and only by testing the works exhibited by these principles that any sound or useful conclusions can be drawn.

II.—*The Styles.*

Style in ornament is analogous to hand in writing, and this is its literal signification. As every individual has some peculiarity in his mode of writing, so every age or nation has been distinguished in its ornamental expression by a certain individuality of taste, either original or borrowed. In a review of this kind, however, when we speak of the styles, we can comprise only the broad distinctions of ornament itself, the kinds or genera, not the mere specific varieties. There are, of course, many varieties of every great style; but so long as the chief characteristics remain unchanged, the style is the same. From this point of view, therefore, the styles become comparatively few. We shall find that nine will comprise the whole number of the great characteristic developments which have had any influence on European civilisation: namely—three ancient, the Egyptian, the Greek, and the Roman; three middle-age, the Byzantine, the Saracenic, and the Gothic; and three modern, the Renaissance, the Cinquecento, and the Louis Quatorze.

All styles are only so many different ways of using the same language, that of ornament; some expressing one sentiment, some another: the various expressions do not depend so much upon the details themselves as upon their mode of treatment. In the Egyptian, the earliest historic style, we have the conventional and the symbolic elements paramount, in a simple symmetrical treatment, combined with a very positive expression of colour.

The Egyptian is literally a hieroglyphic style: as a rule the Egyptian elements have a particular meaning, even to the geometrical patterns; few, if any, are arbitrarily chosen for the sake of beauty of effect only; the style is accordingly very simple and limited in comparison with later styles, in which mere symbolism was superseded by the pure principles of Art.

But many Egyptian ornaments are still popular ornaments, and have been so through all times; as the fret or labyrinth, wave-scroll, spiral, zigzag, water-lily, the palm, and the star. The arrangements are almost exclusively a mere symmetrical progression, and always of a very simple order, though of gorgeous character; for precious stones and metals, and the richest materials generally, seem to have been abundantly used. The frieze is the commonest form of these decorations, and the details are generally some of the more important symbols; as the Lotus or water-lily of the Nile, the type of its inundations, from which Egypt derives its fruitfulness; and the zigzag, the type of water itself.* The Winged Globe, however, or the Scarabæus (the Beetle) is the most prominent of all Egyptian ornaments; it was a species of talisman, an invocation of the good spirit, *Agathodemon*, and was used universally as both architectural and personal ornament, in almost every kind of material, wood, metal, or stone; from the largest block of granite of Syene to the diminutive proportions of the rarest precious stones. The Asp, and the cartouche containing hieroglyphics, are other important materials of Egyptian ornament.

We find mixed up with these more characteristic details almost every natural production of Egypt, conventionally treated; not mere crude imitations from nature, but natural types, selected by symbolism, and fashioned by symmetry into ornamental decorations.

In viewing the character of Egyptian Art, then, besides its conventionalism and symbolism, which are expressions of details, we have a general expression—namely, its grandeur of proportion, simplicity of parts, and splendour or costliness of material: gold, silver, and ivory, precious stones, and colour. Its great prevailing characteristic, like that of all Oriental Art, is sumptuousness.

Jewish and other Asiatic ornament, like the Egyptian, appears to have been purely representative: the only elements mentioned in scripture, are the almond, the pomegranate, the palm-tree, the lily or lotus, oxen, lions, and the cherubim.*

It is not till we come to Greece that we find the habitual introduction of forms for their own sake, purely as ornaments, and this is a very great step in art. The Egyptians produced many beautiful useful forms, but the Greeks not only improved these forms, but decorated them with appropriate and beautiful ornaments, designed solely for their effect as delightful objects to the eye; they paid the same attention to architectural and general decoration.

If we consider the Greek as one great historic period of ornament, the following are its chief characteristics, with some of which Egypt has already made us acquainted :—the fret, the wave-scroll, sometimes called the Vitruvian scroll, the echinus, or horse-chesnut (vulgarly called the egg and tongue, and egg and dart), the astragal, the anthemion (commonly called the Greek honey-suckle, because some examples resemble that flower), the guilloche or plat, and the volute: the ordinary scroll and the acanthus are very partially developed in the pure Greek, compared with what they were in later times among the Romans; they both belong, nevertheless, to Greek Art, especially the acanthus which distinguishes the last and richest of the Greek orders—the Corinthian. These three orders, as regards their ornamental qualities, are better described as the Echinus—the Voluted—and the Acanthus—Orders, than by their national designations. They are not so much distinct as successive orders, each adding something to that which preceded it; for instance in the Doric, or early Greek order, we have the echinus as the only ornament; in early times it was painted, in later it was cut on the capital: in the Ionic, or second Greek order, we have the addition of the volute, or ram's horn, to the echinus; and in the third order, or the Corinthian, we have the addition of a row of acanthus leaves below the volutes, of the second order, but which are here modified into stems, or *cauliculi*. How all these various Greek elements were treated it is not expedient to explain here; space precludes it, if nothing else; but there is always a great simplicity both in the details and in the arrangement of the materials of Greek ornament; it is generally the various elements arranged in simple horizontal series, one row above another.

In the Roman, the third and last ancient style, we have, as the chief characteristic, a gorgeous magnificence; but this magnificence was accomplished only by an enrichment and a profuse use of Greek details; the scroll and the acanthus, however, being predominant over all others, so much so, that the acanthus scroll alone when in anything approaching magnificence of development, is sufficient to stamp a design as Roman in character, and it is the chief distinction between Greek and Roman work.

The Romans used the Greek orders, but they added to them one of their own, which is, however, a simple mixture of the three Greek orders into one—an echino-voluted-acanthus order; the original modification of the volutes in the Corinthian acanthus order being restored to a complete Ionic capital in the Roman. Besides this great richness of detail, the mixture of grotesques such as human, animal, and vegetable forms combined, is a common characteristic of Roman Art, as, for instance, the sphinx, griffin and others; these elements were likewise Greek, but not of such frequent occurrence in Greek examples: † the Romans, in fact, added no element, except perhaps the shell, to the materials of Greek ornament.

With the Roman ends what may be technically termed ancient ornament; the change of religion which ensued, through the adoption of Christianity by Constantine, totally revolutionised Ornamental, as well as all other Art.

During the first and second centuries, Christian works of Art were limited to symbols, and were then never applied as decorations, but as exhortations to faith and piety. And all Christian decoration rests upon this foundation; the same spirit of symbolism

---

* This ancient signification of the zigzag is still preserved in the Zodiac sign of the Water-Carrier or, Aquarius.

* See the visions of Ezekiel, 1 and 10, from which are derived the four symbolic images of the Evangelists—the angel, the lion, the ox, and the eagle.
† The sphinx was also Egyptian, but there is a great difference between the Greek and Egyptian sphinxes: the first is human-headed, ram-headed, and hawk-headed, and is always male; while the Greek is female, with the head of a woman, and always has wings, which the Egyptian never has. See Sir Gardner Wilkinson's account of the sphinx.—*Manners and Customs of the Ancient Egyptians, &c.*

prevailing throughout, until the return to the heathen principle of beauty in the period of the Renaissance.

The early symbols were the monogram of Christ, variously written—the lily—the cross—the serpent—the aureole, or *vesica piscis*—representing the acrostic symbol, the fish, from the common Greek word for fish—ἰχθύς, containing the initials of the following sentence—Ιησους χριστος θεου υιος σωτηρ, Jesus Christ, of God, the son, the Saviour ; and the circle or *nimbus*, the glory of the head, as the *vesica* is of the entire body. These are all very important elements in Christian decoration, especially the *nimbus*, which is the element of the trefoil and quatrefoil and analogous forms, so common in Byzantine and Gothic Art ; the trefoil having reference to the Trinity ; and the quatrefoil to the four evangelists, as the testimony of Christ ; and to the cross, at the extremities of which we often find the circle, besides the circle or *nimbus* in the centre, signifying the Lord : the circles of the extremities, which are the *nimbi* of the evangelists, often contain their respective symbolic images, the angel, the lion, the ox, and the eagle ; thus making their signification palpable.

Why the beautiful and accomplished styles of the ancients, then, were discarded for such comparatively crude elements of ornament, needs no other explanation than that they were pagan. Paganism consisted, however, solely in forms, not in colours, and therefore in respect of colour there were no restrictions. But ancient forms also, as paganism itself gradually disappeared, were slowly admitted among the elements of Christian decoration ; and the scroll, under certain modifications, became eventually a very prominent figure in Byzantine ornaments ; and under a similar modification, the anthemion and every other ancient form was gradually adopted after a systematic exclusion of four or five centuries.

But all Byzantine decorations are strictly conventional, a trefoil leaf or a lily form being the ordinary foliation for a scroll : and every form, whether from nature or from earlier styles of Art, was always treated in a peculiar manner ; more skill, on the whole, being displayed in the general effects than in the details, and owing to the richness of material used, which was characteristic of Byzantine taste, a very gorgeous style was ultimately developed upon the mere foundation of a rude symbolism.

The leading forms of Byzantine or Romanesque architecture are likewise due to the same influence ; the cross, the circle, and the dome pervade everywhere. Both the Lombard and the Norman styles may be considered as mere varieties of the Byzantine. All are comprised in the term Romanesque, which comprehends the round-arch style of Middle-Age Art, as distinguished from the Saracenic and the Gothic, which are pointed-arch species.

Indeed the Byzantine was so widely spread and so thoroughly identified with all Middle-Age Art, after the first few centuries of the Christian era, that its influence even in Italy did not wholly decline before the fifteenth century, until the establishment of the *Quattrocento*, by Lorenzo Ghiberti. Both the Saracenic and the Gothic proceeded from the Byzantine. The Greek missionaries carried its influence into the extreme north ; and while the artists of Syria were accommodating their style to Mohammedan exclusiveness in the south, in the colder regions of Europe the mysteries of Mount Athos were freely mixed up with the fables of Scandinavian mythology. The Scandinavian soldiers, also, of the imperial body-guard at Constantinople, made, on their return, the talismans of Christian mythology almost as familiar in their native homes, as the gods of their forefathers. The cross planted on the serpent is not an uncommon image on Mount Athos ; and the cross surrounded by the so-called Runic knot, is only a Scandinavian version of the original Byzantine symbol of the redemption—the crushed snake curling round the stem of the avenging cross. The same mixture of Christian and Northern mythology characterises the portals of Lombardy.

As the peculiarly Norman style, such as it is best known in this country, was originally developed in Sicily, it contains many Saracenic features, of which the pointed arch and the zigzag are the most characteristic. The original Norman was not national, but simply Romanesque or Byzantine ; and the decorated or pointed zigzag Norman is, strictly speaking, Siculo-Norman ; there is no other peculiar Norman style.

The principles of the Saracenic are soon stated . the conditions of the new Mohammedan law were stringent ; there was to be no image of a living thing, vegetable or animal. Such conditions led of course to a very individual style of decoration, for vegetable forms were now excluded for the first time. However, by the eighth century, when the richer works of the Saracens commenced, the Byzantine Greeks who were pressed into the service of the Arabian Caliphs and generals, were already sufficiently skilful to make light of such exclusions, and the exertion of ingenuity which they impelled gave rise to, perhaps, a more beautiful simply ornamental style than any that had preceded it, for there was no division of the artistic mind now, between meaning and effect ; and although the religious cycles and other symbolic figures, which had hitherto engrossed so much of the artist's attention were excluded, the mere conventional ornamental symbolism, the ordinary forms borrowed from the Classic period, and geometry, left an abundant field behind, which was further enriched by the peculiarly Saracenic custom of elaborating inscriptions into the designs. Mere curves and angles or interlacings were now to bear the chief burden of a design ; the curves, however, very naturally fell into the standard forms and floral shapes ; and the lines and angles were soon developed into a very characteristic species of tracery or interlaced strap-work, very agreeably diversified by the ornamental introduction of the inscriptions. The Saracenic was the period of gorgeous diapers ; but like the Byzantine, it was more remarkable for its general effects than for any peculiar merit of the detail, or of its combinations—it is made up of an infinite number of minute contrasts of light and shade and colour ; something like a formal flower-garden, wanting the simplicity and grandeur of natural scenery. But no details are so applicable for mere *fillings* as the Saracenic, and hence we find them constantly occurring in the designs of the Renaissance.

The last great middle-age style the Gothic, like the Saracenic, grew out of the Byzantine : it flourished chiefly on the Rhine, in the north of France, and in England ; it was developed in the thirteenth century, was perfected in the fourteenth, and in the sixteenth became extinct.

The Gothic is essentially a pointed and geometrical style in its general forms, though all the symbolic elements of the Byzantine are preserved in it ; its details appear to be an infinite repetition of its greater architectural features, by which it is distinguished ; as the spire in the place of the dome, and the pointed, in the place of the round arch, compared with the Byzantine or Romanesque. The pointed arch, however, it has only in common with the Saracenic and the Siculo-Norman.

As an ornamental style, it is an excessive elaboration of the pointed and geometric element, vertical and diagonal lines prevailing over the others. It is further peculiar in its combinations of details, at first the conventional and symbolic prevailing, and afterwards these combined with the elaboration of natural objects proper to its localities. We find in Gothic examples, not only the traditional conventional types, but also in the later periods, mixed with them, exact imitations of the plants and flowers growing in the neighbourhood. This is a great feature, but still always secondary to its elaboration of geometrical tracery—vesicas, trefoils, quatrefoils, &c., with many other geometrical combinations, —which always remains the main characteristic of the style, whether the so-called early English, the decorated or the perpendicular, French or German.

In ornament, therefore, as in architecture, it is the geometrical tracery which stamps a design with a Gothic character ; mixed with natural flowers only, it is still Gothic ; but the example is more characteristic when it contains also the historic ornaments of the style—as the Tudor-flower, the fleur-de-lis, the crocket-leaf, trefoil-leaf, vine-scroll, and other familiar details. The Gothic scroll always preserves the character of its early Byzantine type, namely that of a foliated serpentine rather than a succession of spirals.

The *Rinascimento* or *Renaissance*, as the ultimate revival of classical art in Italy is termed, dates from about the Venetian conquest of Constantinople, in the year 1204. This revival, best known under its French name of the Renaissance, was long strictly but a revival of the classical orders of architecture ; there was no revival of classical ornament itself in its completeness before the sixteenth century, until the style known as the *Cinquecento*,* the real goal of the Renaissance. There are four distinct varieties of the Renaissance, independent of the Cinquecento. In its earliest character, the *Trecento*,† in the fourteenth century, it is chiefly a mixture of Venetian and Siculo-Norman ornament, the Venetian being purely Byzantine in its origin, consisting for the most part of conventional foliage and scroll forms, such as the decorations by Giotto in the church of San Francesco at Assisi, or the mosaics of the Baptistery of San Giovanni at Florence.

In the fifteenth century, or in the *Quattrocento*, the influence of tradition was wholly superseded by selection, and a gradual recurrence to ancient examples; with a mixture of original arbitrary forms and natural imitations. The introduction of exact natural imitations was the great feature of this new stage of the Renaissance, as displayed by Lorenzo Ghiberti at Florence, in his magnificent gates of the Baptistery of San Giovanni.‡ Still all details were ornamentally treated, strictly in accordance with the laws of symmetry in their arrangement. It was in this period that were gradually introduced also those peculiar arbitrary forms, pierced and scrolled shields, or cartouches, and tracery, or strap-work, which eventually became the most characteristic details of the styles of the Renaissance, except during the short period of the prevalence of the Cinquecento in the earlier half of the sixteenth century, when they were very generally discarded, as was every element not found in ancient examples.

A design containing all the elements indiscriminately, can be designated only by the vague term Renaissance; and such a design may contain the classical orders and ornaments combined with conventional Byzantine scroll-work, Moorish tracery and interlacings, scrolled shields, fiddle-shapes, and strap-work, natural imitations of animal or vegetable forms of every description, and the grotesque arabesques. Such is the mixture we find in the works of Benvenuto Cellini, and also in the great majority of the foreign cabinet and silver-work in the Exhibition.

This peculiar style flourished in the sixteenth century, simultaneously with the more definite Cinquecento, which was, in fact, an attempt at purification of style by the great artists of that period, who excluded every element not warranted by ancient examples, and accordingly in this style, which must be considered as distinct from the ordinary Renaissance, we have an endeavour to restore ancient ornament to its original purity and splendour, and even to develop it to a still greater degree of variety, and a more chaste magnificence, than is exhibited by ancient examples.

The Cinquecento, therefore, in a critical distinction of styles, does not imply merely sixteenth century Art, but a particular art of the sixteenth century. The term Renaissance is sufficiently definite for the mixed style, more especially as this style belongs to several ages and countries, though more peculiarly to France, where it has prevailed almost to the exclusion of every other style; but it is of strict Italian origin. There are, accordingly, four Italian styles of the revival—the Trecento, the Quattrocento, the pure Cinquecento, and the mixed Cinquecento, or Renaissance; there is one French style of the period—the Renaissance, the same as the mixed cinquecento of Italy; and there is one English style—the Elizabethan, which is the English Renaissance: minor modifications it is unnecessary to notice here. We have made this cursory enumeration for the sake of defining the Cinquecento itself, as practised by Agustino Busti, and others, more particularly in the north of Italy, towards the middle of the sixteenth century; the school of Julio Romano, at Mantua, developed it in painting.

The prevailing spirit of this style, aiming at a revival of the gorgeous decorations of Rome, naturally threw out all those peculiar arbitrary forms, which are never found in ancient examples, as the scrolled shields and tracery; and, on the other hand, elaborated to the utmost the most conspicuous characteristics

of Greek and Roman Art, especially the acanthus scroll, and the grotesque arabesques, abounding with monstrous combinations of human, animal, and vegetable forms, in the same figure or scroll-work; but always characterised, whatever the materials, by an extreme beauty of line: every natural form, and every conventional or ornamental form of antiquity, is admissible in the pure Cinquecento; it has also this feature, a beautiful variation of ancient standard types, as the Anthemion, &c., which occur not only as we find them in ancient examples, but as Italian plants also, treated in the order of the ancient examples.

The Cinquecento is considered the culminating style in Ornamental Art, as presenting the most perfect forms, and the most pleasing varieties; Nature and Art vieing with each other in their efforts to attract and gratify the eye. It appeals only to the sense of beauty; all its efforts are directly made to attain the most attractive effects, without any intent to lead the mind to an ulterior end, as is the case with the Byzantine and other symbolic styles. The Cinquecento forms are supposed to be symbols of beauty only, and it is a remarkable concession to the ancients that the moderns, to attain this result, were compelled to recur to their works. And it is only now, in the contemplation of this consummate style, that the term "Renaissance" becomes quite intelligible. The Renaissance, or Re-birth, of ornament is accomplished in the Cinquecento; still the term is not altogether ill-appropriated to the earlier styles, as these were really the stepping-stones to the Cinquecento. We now come to the consideration of the last of the historic styles—the Louis Quatorze with its variety, the Louis Quinze, and its final debasement, the Rococo.

The great medium of the Louis Quatorze was gilt stucco-work, which for a while seems to have almost wholly superseded decorative painting; and this absence of colour in the principal decorations of the period seems to have led to its more striking characteristic, infinite play of light and shade. Such being the aim of the style, exact symmetry in the parts was no longer essential, and accordingly in the Louis Quatorze varieties, we, for the first time, occasionally find symmetry systematically avoided. This feature was gradually more and more developed until it became characteristic in the Louis Quinze, and ultimately led to that debased style, or rather variety, the Rococo, in which symmetry either in the balance of the whole, or in the details of the parts, seems to have been quite out of place.

The characteristic details of this style are the scroll and shell; the anthemion treated as a shell by being made concave, and a small acanthus scroll; it is a variation of the most common decoration of the ancient funeral tiles; all classical ornaments are admitted in the Louis Quatorze, but they are confined to the mere accessory details: all elements of the Cinquecento also from which the Louis Quatorze proceeded, are admissible under peculiar treatment, or as accessories to the scroll and shell as principal features: the very panels are formed by chains of scrolls, the concave and convex alternately, some clothed with an acanthus foliation, others plain. A fiddle-shape combination of such scrolls is very characteristic even for various purposes; a legacy probably of the ordinary Renaissance.

The broad acanthus foliations of the scroll in the Louis Quatorze, became much elongated, resembling more commonly the flag-leaf, in the Louis Quinze.

As long as these various elements were treated symmetrically, and with attention to the masses, good effects were not uncommon, but when, in the time of Louis Quinze, symmetry was wholly disregarded, and the acanthus scrolls degenerated into the *coquillage*, a species of crimped conventional shell-work, the designs became a mere mass of vagaries of indescribable forms, and the Rococo was displayed in the perfection of the bizarre in ornament. The play of light and shade is so essentially the element of the Louis Quatorze styles, that every other motive yields to it; and it is carried out to such an extent that they scarcely admit of a flat surface in their details; all are either convex or concave, and hence also the prevalence of the wave-line in their general forms. This constant varying of the surface gives every point of view its high lights and contrasts, and for this reason stucco has superseded decorations in the flat and gold colour in all characteristic Louis Quatorze and Louis Quinze designs. But the mere general aim of these styles gradually led to so great a neglect of the details, that eventually all individuality was lost, and with it all study: hence, in the absurd Rococo, the very natural result of this general neglect, we have designs made up of details so without meaning and individuality as to defy description.

Such is a review of the great Historic styles of ornament, and, having thus defined the peculiar distinctions of the styles, we may now examine in detail the various objects exposed in the Exhibition, with a view—by critical comparison—to draw what lessons we may from this great industrial competition of nations.

III.—*The Exhibition.*

Once the overwhelming impression of admiration and wonder at the unparalleled collection, and the admirable arrangement of the whole, subsided, the inquisitive mind naturally turns its attention to the details in the mass, and in classes more or less definite according to its own objects and pursuit. In our instance, the mind intent on Art-manufacture, naturally turned its attention only upon such objects as were of an ornamental character. The first general impression is one of bewildering magnificence and endless wealth; as the particular classes are gradually separated in the mind, a process of comparison commences between the objects before the eyes and the vague anticipations of the mind previous to entering the building, with results more or less satisfactory according to individual knowledge and experience.

Definite ideas now arise in the mind, of dissatisfaction or approval as it may be, at the various impressions from the different departments, and then the operation of criticism in detail commences, followed by individual comparisons of the relative display of the various countries.

In examining minutely the results of these two last operations, the following are the conclusions we must draw from them:—

That there is nothing new in the Exhibition in ornamental design; not a scheme, not a detail that has not been treated over and over again in ages that are gone; that the taste of the producers generally is uneducated, and that in nearly all cases where this is not so, the influence of France is paramount in the European productions; bearing exclusively in the two most popular traditional styles of that country—the Renaissance and the Louis Quinze—with more or less variation in the treatment and detail. There are few designs of any country that do not come within the range of these two styles—from the Italian Renaissance to the French Rococo, or debased Louis Quinze. The few Greek, or so-called Etruscan specimens, and the Gothic examples, in the singularly styled Medieval Court, are almost the only exceptions as regards European design. The best understood style is that which we have been obliged to designate the mixed Cinquecento or Renaissance; the apparently most able designers of Italy, France, Austria, Belgium, and England, have selected this style for the exhibition of their skill; if, therefore, the Exhibition can be considered as a test of the favourite style of the day, it is evidently the Cinquecento Renaissance, or the style which was developed in the second half of the sixteenth century in Italy. The Louis Quatorze varieties perhaps prevail in quantity, the Louis Quinze, and the Rococo: the Gothic is evidently in little requisition in foreign countries, and is only very partially cultivated in this, as is evident from the very small number of exhibitors who have contributed to what is very strangely misnamed the Medieval Court, as if the Gothic were the only medieval style, or even the medieval style *par excellence.* The Romanesque, Byzantine, and Saracenic, and several Italian varieties, were infinitely more extensive in their influence in the middle ages than the Gothic, which was almost limited to the neighbourhood of the Rhine and bordering countries, and it endured only for a comparatively short period, and in point of time scarcely belongs to the middle ages at all, as it was not completely developed until the fourteenth century, and was contemporary only with the Renaissance styles of Italy, which, however, nearly everywhere superseded it in the sixteenth century.

With regard to classical or Greek and Roman ornament, it is astonishing to find so little of it. The taste so active fifty years ago, in this country at least, appears to have spread no further than its original promoters could extend it; in furniture it

is scarcely represented, and in pottery it is still seemingly the great prerogative of Messrs. Wedgwood to exhibit pure specimens of the Greek style; and still for the most part in the exquisite productions of Flaxman, which appear more beautiful than ever, surrounded as they are by such endless specimens of the prevailing gorgeous taste of the present day, which gives the eye no resting-place, and presents no idea to the mind, from the want of individuality in its gorged designs.

The stall of Messrs. Battam* is devoted to the, so-termed, Etruscan taste, but so exclusively in one class of fabric, uniform in character and material, that it conveys only the notion of copying a design, not the revival of a simple and pure taste. The mere red and black are not essentials of the taste, but accidents of material; the materials further might be applied to modern uses, and the ancient forms and ideas expressed in other materials; this would be adopting a taste, a very different thing from merely copying designs.

The Medieval Court is open to much the same objection, though not so entirely so. We have in this collection not an evidence of the application of a peculiar taste to modern and ordinary wants or purposes, but simply the copy of an old idea; old things in an old taste. Byzantine or Gothic symbolism, in as far as they generate beautiful forms, may claim our admiration, and Mr. Crace's table in inlaid wood shows that such a result is quite possible out of such materials. But where the thing is made not for its own sake or the use it may be of, but purely as an embodiment of the old bygone idea that originally caused it, it is only a cowl to smother all independent original thought or ingenuity, and by preserving symbolism as principal in all efforts would reduce Art much to what we find it in India, or rather China. Indeed, except in the most obvious forms of superstition, this court already presents a striking similarity of taste to that of the Indian works, in its rude undefined details, and in richness of material; as in the stuffs and carpet exhibited by Mr. Crace; in the wood-carving of Mr. Myers; and in the ecclesiastical vessels and robes exhibited by Mr. Hardman: all showing the strong analogy with the Oriental types, and the Byzantine origin of the style. This is the fact however which explains the similarity of the two developments, their common source, the Byzantine symbolism; the triangles, trefoils, squares, and quatrefoils and various Romanesque adaptations of the old Byzantine Greeks: spread on one side by the Christians of the west, the Latins, and on the other by the Mohammedans of the east, the Arabs. Much scroll-work in Indian and Gothic is identical; and the Byzantine standard, the horns of plenty, have given rise to a very similar treatment on both sides. As individual designs, however, this court offers some very fine samples of Gothic, as the mantelpiece by Myers, with the clever adaptation of the dove and olive as a crocket.†

Such being the relative proportion of the styles, what is the general conclusion that we are to draw from this evidence? We have ventured to assert, that the best specimens of ornamental design as a class, are of the Renaissance, but that the great bulk of the specimens are of the Louis Quatorze varieties; that Classical Art is scarcely represented, and that the Gothic, is only very partially so. Setting aside the Gothic, which owes what we have of it to sentiments distinct from ornament, we have only three decided expressions of taste, the Greek, the Italian, and the French; or the Classical, the Renaissance, and the Louis Quinze. These three tastes are very distinct; we have in the first a thoroughly well understood detail, with a highly systematic and symmetrical disposition of these details, always arranging them upon such forms and at such intervals as shall fairly display the article and its ornaments in due proportion; in fact a faultless taste: in the second, in the Renaissance, we have also a well understood detail, but a prevalence of the bizarre, and a love of profusion of parts; great skill of execution, but upon the whole a bewildering and fantastic effect, still one more agreeable to the generality than the simple purity of the Greeks: in the third taste, that best illustrated by the Louis Quinze, in every variety, we have a total disregard of detail, therefore exclusively a general effect; individuality of parts, beauty of execution, anything that can possibly display any merit in itself as interfering with a purely general effect, is not only

* See Cat., p. 247.   † See specimens eng. pp. 317—320.

superfluous but detrimental to the design, which aims only at a gorgeous effect as a whole. We have in this last essentially a superficial style aiming at a glittering or attractive display; hence it is best exhibited in gilt-work or silver, or where there is at least a uniformity of colour; reflection, or mere play of light and shade being its element. The very nature of this style offers a premium to the neglect of detail; those practising it therefore soon neglect everything of the kind, and thus the whole province of ornament is degraded, and where such a style prevails the paramount impression conveyed to the critical mind must be a general want of education in taste, just such an impression as the Great Exhibition gives at this moment.

Now it is not a desirable thing that we should find the best talent of Europe devoted to the taste, having profusion of detail and mere skilfulness of execution as its great characteristics; yet if one style is to be chosen, considering its general nature, no more pleasing one could be adopted: we have both an understood detail, and a general effect at the same time, free from the prevalence of any particular kind of forms or lines, which gives the Renaissance an infinite superiority as an ornamental style over the Gothic, in which the profusion of vertical and diagonal lines, in the same relation, is fatiguing and palling to the mind, as is well illustrated by the peculiar assemblage in the so-called medieval court, which stands there as a warning to us against making this style familiar in our dwelling-houses. It is essentially an architectural style, and is applicable only when it can be applied on a great scale, so that the eye does not at once comprise in a small compass its peculiar angularity and formality.

To bring the reader to a more exact comprehension of this prevailing style of the Renaissance, we will instance a few of the principal works exhibited, and which are its best exponents. To commence with Italy, the original arena of the style, there are the plaster mantel-piece by G. Bottinelli, of Milan, and the painted ceiling in the same room by A. Montanari, of Milan; and also the walnut cabinet exhibited by Angelo Barbetti of Florence, but this borders on the pure Cinquecento: among French works, the Fontaine à Thé, silver, exhibited by M. Durand, of Paris;* the specimen of room decoration by Cruchet, wood and carton-pierre combined, in the nave †; and the magnificent side-board exhibited by Fourdinois. ‡ From Austria, the bedstead exhibited by M. Leistler, of Vienna.§ From Stuttgard, a dressing table, and ward-robe by J. F. Wirth, in mahogany, in exquisite taste. From Belgium, a large marble mantel-piece by J. Leclercq of Brussels.|| Of English specimens may be mentioned her Majesty's cradle by Rogers,¶ though this specimen also borders closely on the pure Cinquecento; and the table of gold and silver electro-plate, exhibited by Elkington: also the large silver centre-piece in the nave, exhibited by Hunt & Roskell; the walnut bedstead by Rogers and Dear;** a drawing-room fire-place by Yates, Haywood & Co., of Rotherham;†† and a parian chimney-piece exhibited by Minton and Co.

These works are not mentioned as of extraordinary merit, but as combining with general excellence the most decided expression of this particular style, which, at the present moment, appears to engross the chief attention of the more able designers, whether English or foreign: and many of them are of a character approaching the best Cinquecento taste.

It will be observed, on examination, that cartouches or scrolled shields, and tracery, prevail more or less in all the above-mentioned works; except for these features several of them would be admirable specimens of the Cinquecento in its purity, of which however the Exhibition also affords a few fine specimens, some of which we may mention here for the sake of clearly separating these two styles. Her Majesty's cradle, as already observed, for the general character of its ornaments belongs to this style; as does also the book-case exhibited by Holland & Sons,‡‡ and the sideboards by Levien, and by Johnstone & Jeanes,§§ and likewise the bold sideboard in the south gallery, by Henry Hoyles, of the Sheffield School of Design,|||| also a grate by Baily & Sons, and

some decoration by Morant. Of more delicate work may be mentioned the crystal vase and dish belonging to Mr. Webb, exhibited by Morel & Co.; a vase in silver, gilt, and enamel, by Hunt & Roskell; a large gilt bronze vase and dish,* adapted from the shield and helmet of Francis I., in the Louvre (both exhibited likewise in bronze), by Villemsens of Paris, the last an exquisite and genuine example; and a very beautiful specimen, a ewer and dish, in parian, exhibited by Minton & Co.; also a carved frame in walnut by Pietro Giusti, of Siena; and a frieze, an admirable specimen of one development of the mere scroll-work, exhibited by J. Harmer, jun., in sculptured plaster.†

The above specimens are noticed for mere distinction's sake, for they are rather exceptions to, than examples of, a prevailing taste. It remains yet to point out specimens of the third taste alluded to, the Louis Quinze. As a general reference, English silver-work, and carving and gilding, as a whole, will represent this taste, and exhibit it often in its worst shape. The bad effect of the Louis Quinze, however, as mostly displayed, is not so much an inherent defect in the style as it is the fault of treatment of the elements by the designer. Hence we find a wide difference in the merit of two designs of the same style, where the same materials are used, without descending to the Rococo, of which a large mirror frame in Dresden porcelain,‡ exhibited by the Royal Factory at Meissen, is a sufficiently characteristic specimen. Some of the Austrian furniture is Louis Quinze, as are also some of the handsomest chairs in the Exhibition, Austrian, Belgian, and English; and there are some pianos in the same style, as, for instance, one in the Belgian department, heavy Rococo scrolls, with large bulrushes, which belong to the worst examples of ornamental design exhibited.

The Russian malachite doors are of an intermediate degree between these two extremes. On the English side the style is well illustrated by the sideboards by Gillow,§ or Rivett & Sons, or the glass frame by T. Ponsonby; or, in its best development, the Louis Quatorze, by the gilt beadstead, by Faudel & Phillips;|| in silver work, by the testimonial to the Marquis of Tweeddale,¶ exhibited by Hunt & Roskell, from a design by A. Brown.

The wide-spread influence of France, therefore, in spite of the most debased taste in design ever tolerated, is one curious picture presented to the mind by this assemblage of the world's industry; and this influence, as the American examples show, is not even limited to Europe, or the Old World. Another great fact displayed, perhaps unavoidable where true education is absent, is the very general mistake that quantity of ornament implies beauty, many objects being so overloaded with details as to utterly destroy the general individuality of expression of the object, and even to render it at first doubtful what the object can be.

In the Oriental works, where quantity of detail also is the chief characteristic, it is of a kind so generally unassuming in its details, and harmonious in its effect and treatment, that the impression of quantity itself is the last that is conveyed, though the whole surface may be covered with ornament. The general form or effect of the design is never interfered with; and by the uniform delicacy of the detail, though it may often have no other merit, a vague trail for the most part, it allows only of a general expression, and we have the happy combination of simplicity and richness at once.

In comparing the Indian shawls with their European copies, and how purely they are copies is very satisfactorily shown, a most remarkable phenomenon develops itself; that is, that the skilled and educated designer of Europe should devote some of his most elaborate efforts in design to the imitation of the crude patterns of the hereditary weaver of the East. The skilful designer of Paris, London, or Vienna, could produce patterns infinitely more beautiful than the most gorgeous specimens of the East, with half the trouble it costs him to make his spurious Cashmeres; but as they could then be no longer mistaken for Cashmeres, their highest merit would be lost.

Often in the best of Indian specimens the details will not bear looking at; much of the design is put in to fill a space, the whole being generally only an infinite combination of minute portions of different colours, aiming at a purely general effect. The merits of

* Engraved in Cat., p. 105.   † Engraved in Cat., p. 60.
‡ Engraved in Cat., p. 285.   § Engraved in Cat., p. 178.
|| Engraved in Cat., p. 227.   ¶ Engraved in Cat., p. 10.
** Engraved in Cat., p. 325.   †† Engraved in Cat., p. 205.
‡‡ Engraved in Cat., p. 22.   §§ Engraved in Cat., p. 16. |||| Engraved in Cat., p. 309.

* Engraved in Cat., p. 19.   † Engraved in Cat., p. 201.
‡ Engraved in Cat., p. 30.   § Engraved in Cat., p. 203.
Engraved in Cat., p. 41.   ¶ Engraved in Cat., p. 58.

the best are negative, rather than positive ; there is an absence of glaring faults, but no one feature of beauty ; if we except the general harmonious colouring and uniform unobtrusiveness of detail, which last, however, is in itself a great quality.

To return to Europe. It is a fact well worthy of being pointed out to the attention of designers and manufacturers, that they should still suffer themselves to be so much under the influence of the French taste at the period of the first revolution. The fashionable popularity of Watteau seems to have first established this taste, and the vast amount of emigration which was the consequence of the revolution, particularly to this country, seems to have firmly planted it here, and here in silver-work it is still paramount, though it has been long discarded by the French themselves, as a school, for the earlier style of the Renaissance, which superseded the Gothic in the time of Francis I.

But why this popular style should be so invariably characterised by the incessant shields or cartouches, it will be very difficult upon any reasons of taste to explain. In wood, marble, and in silver, we constantly find graceful curves and forms suddenly interrupted by a large pierced shield, with its projecting edges and angles, and which, so far from performing a service to the design, or of being in any way necessary to it, is in direct antagonism to the whole spirit of the forms with which it is united, except in our own Elizabethan, where it is, on the contrary, valuable, being in perfect sympathy with the ruling features of the design : of the flat strap-work of which it is a simple aggrandisement.

By the separation of the Renaissance as developed in the examples we have pointed out, into its two distinct elements of curved and angular forms, we do actually resolve it into two distinct and popular styles, the Cinquecento and the Elizabethan, for it amounts in nearly all its great examples to a mixture of these two, although generally neither style is well expressed in the combination, one necessarily neutralising and supplanting the other. As an illustration, this value of the individuality of expression in design is very well shown, in the variety of papier mâché specimens exhibited by Walton & Co., of Wolverhampton ;* or in some of the papers by W. Woollams & Co., of London.†

Abstaining from further details at present, having explained the general impressions, as regards ornament, of the most prominent classes of manufacture, we may venture upon some comparison between English and foreign specimens in the respective classes.

First, generally, the English side does not betray that great inferiority of taste which has been so long prognosticated of it ; on the contrary, in some respects, there is a palpable pre-eminence, on the part of this country, in many articles of general use ; but on a more careful investigation, turning our attention to abstract taste in design, a very decided inferiority must be admitted.

This is not in the application of design, but in ornamental design itself ; nor is it so much in the absolute work as in the taste which guides this work. However, in the more magnificent foreign productions, especially those of France, besides the excessive mannerism of working only in one style, however cleverly, there is a disregard to usefulness, or the general wants and means, which essentially detracts from that high credit which the mere design or artistic execution of the work would otherwise ensure. It is very much easier to produce a successful result with ample than with contracted means, and infinitely more meritorious in the manufacturer to produce a simple beautiful work, which shall be within the reach of the world of taste in general, than the accomplishment by an extraordinary effort of an extraordinary work, which he cannot easily repeat, and which it is beyond the pale of all but regal or princely means to derive gratification or benefit from. It would be no distinctive feature of an age to work well for princes ; princely means have secured princely works in all ages, of different quality at different times, and according to the varieties of taste ; some being gratified by rare and exquisite Art, others by minute elaboration and expenditure of labour, and others again by an ostentatious display of precious metals.

The Exhibition will do nothing for the age if it only induce a vast outlay of time and treasure, for the enjoyment of the extreme few who command vast means.

This we take to be no object of the Exhibition ; and although

we must admire for themselves such productions as the great French sideboard, or some of the Gobelins carpets, or the larger Sèvres specimens,* or the Austrian furniture,† these are not the fruits which will bring about the great results which should accrue from this unexampled event, though they may aid them negatively by rather warning us that beautiful effects may arise from infinitely less outlay of either time or substance. And one great source of congratulation to ourselves is, that by the evidence of the Exhibition, this is a result far more likely to be accomplished first in this country than in any other. While England has been devoting nearly all its efforts to the mere comfort of the million, France has expended its energies, for the most part, over luxuries for the few ; it is an amalgamation of the two that we require, fitness and elegance combined ; recreation for the mind as well as comfort for the body. It is perfectly right that there should be single works of great cost and magnificence, both because there is a demand for them, though limited, and as a means of inducing the utmost efforts of Art, and to serve likewise as a key or standard by which mere ordinary works may be tested, and artists stimulated to legitimate rivalry commensurate with a humbler class of production. However, when a costly work is distinguished by exquisite taste, it is something more than a specimen of costliness, which is sufficiently distinct from taste or beauty, and a skilful work will be beautiful, not by virtue, but in spite, of its materials. Good taste is a positive quality, however acquired, and can impart such quality in perfection to even the rudest materials ; it is taste, therefore, that must ever be the producer's most valuable capital ; and this, in our opinion, is the capital which the English manufacturer may acquire in the Exhibition from a careful study of many foreign productions.

In silver-work, for instance, the inferiority of the English manufacturer to the French is very striking, though, perhaps, the most beautiful work of this class in the Exhibition is German,— namely, the table ornament in oxidised silver, by Albert Wagner, of Berlin.‡ But the stalls of Froment-Meurice, Durand, Rudolphi and Gueyton, display many examples of exquisite taste, and at the same time of a simple character.

In wood-carving, but more particularly in its treatment, there is an equal superiority of French and German work over English ; and, indeed, foreign carving and modelling generally are of a better quality than the home specimens.

The same superiority is evident in the printed cottons and muslins, though the Scotch dispute pretty equally with the French prints from Mulhouse. In silks and satins, ribbons, and in shawls, there does not appear any very evident disparity, but it is notable that many of the best Lyons specimens are manufactured expressly for English houses.

The British, French, and Austrian Cashmere shawls seem of nearly equal merit ; the houses of Morgan, and Kerr, of Paisley ; of Blakeley, of Norwich ; of Duché ainé, and Deneirouse, and Boisglavy, of Paris ; and of Martinek, and Berger & Son, of Vienna, exhibit many magnificent specimens of this class, which it would be difficult to distinguish in point of merit.

In lace the finest specimens of design are English, Mrs. Treadwin's Flounce § being, perhaps, unrivalled in this respect, though Vanderkelen-Bresson, of Brussels, is superior to all competitors in delicacy of fabric. The specimens from Ireland are likewise conspicuous, and considerable taste is displayed in some of the Swiss, Scotch, and Irish embroidered muslins, and in the damasks of Dunfermline and Belfast, ‖ many of which are excellent.

In general hardware—especially grates—England has no competitors, and the Exhibition seems to indicate more unusual efforts in this manufacture than in any other : some of the specimens in burnished steel and ormolu, from Sheffield, Rotherham, Birmingham, and Coalbrookdale, and of London, indicate a great advance in the appreciation of Taste, and are a certain evidence of its soon very materially influencing the more ordinary classes of grates in common demand.

In ornamental bronzes no country shines : candlesticks are not creditably represented, and candle-lamps are much in the same obscurity ; the larger candelabra also are confused and tasteless :

* Engraved in Cat., p. 98.   † Engraved in Cat., p. 129

* Engraved in Cat., pp. 169-72.   † Partly engraved in Cat., pp. 177-80.
‡ Engraved on a small scale in Cat., p. 149.
§ Engraved in Cat., p. 143.   ‖ Specimens engraved in Cat. pp. 62 4, and 165 68.

the chandeliers and other works by Potts,* and by Messenger † of Birmingham (which town shows altogether with surprising force in the general quality and in the variety of its contributions), are perhaps the chief exceptions to the comparative inferiority of this department of manufacture.

In other respects, in works of a more purely ornamental character, in metal work, MM. Falloise of Liège, André of Paris, Jacquet of Brabant, Barbédienne, Matifat, Vittoz, Villemsens, Mène, Elkington, Winfield, Hatfield, and the Coalbrookdale Company, exhibit much beautiful work.

In carpets, there is a decided superiority on the side of home productions; notwithstanding much that is staring and inconsistent. The carpet is, however, an article of comfort that is scarcely yet in general use on the continent of Europe. Hence the French specimens are of that impracticable costliness which betrays at once that they are made for show rather than use; although the mere pattern carpets are anything but successful in this respect even : the French designer's skill in a paper-hanging seems to forsake him when he transfers his labour to a carpet pattern. Impracticable costliness appears to hang also over Sèvres porcelain, for in the adaptation of the beautiful to the useful in this department, as well as in that of glass, the English manufacturers are pre-eminent. The English ornamental works in pottery or porcelain do not yield to the French either in elegance of shape or in decoration, while at the same time they are far less costly. The specimens exhibited by Messrs. Copeland, Minton, and Wedgwood, place England in the highest rank in this manufacture, in spite of the fostering patronage of royal factories abroad. In glass, England appears to be almost unrivalled, not only in the purity of its crystal, but in the manufacture and application of this invaluable material; to instance only the matchless specimens of Messrs. Osler ‡ and Apsley Pellatt,§ and the magnificent slabs of coloured glass of Swinburne & Co., of Newcastle-upon-Tyne, or the ornamental panes of Chance Brothers, of Birmingham.

We will now proceed to review *seriatim* the principal classes of ornamental manufacture in detail, always limiting our remarks in accordance with the prescribed object of this essay, to the development of Taste, in order, by this analysis of designs, to endeavour to draw the attention of our manufacturers and designers to the source of all beauty of effect—the elements of design itself.

IV.—*The precious Metals.*

We commence with gold and silver-work,—not as the most important branch of manufacture, but, as being purely ornamental, it is the most prominent object for ornamental criticism, and that to which perhaps the greatest skill has been devoted from the earliest times. Though the Exhibition affords a vast display in amount, there is no great variety or choice of taste ; the Louis Quinze, prevailing, and in every phase of its development, from the symmetrical variety proceeding immediately from the Louis Quatorze, to the most bizarre vagaries of the Rococo ; which last very much predominate.

Though the English silver-work exceeds in quantity, by several times, all that is exhibited by other nations, it displays far less variety of taste ; it is clearly under the absolute control of trade conventionalities, which, from the character of the prevailing style, appear to have been imported with it, in the latter part of the last century. Besides, the interminable coquillage of the Rococo, the constant contrast of dead and burnished silver, making up the chief feature of so many works, is absolutely fatiguing to the mind that seeks, or can receive, any impression of delight from an ornamental composition.

The system of *boiling out*, to produce the whitest possible appearance of the silver, seems to be one essentially opposed to the display of excellence of design ; and when the dead white thus produced is combined only with burnished portions, the sole effect of a work is a mere play of light without even the contrast of shadow. The result is a dazzling whiteness ; pure flashiness, in fact, such as precludes the very idea of modelling—for this can only be displayed by a contrast of light and shade, which, in so uniform a dazzling

mass as an ordinary piece of dead and burnished silver plate, is impossible.

Flashiness may be a natural refuge for vague undefined forms, to the deformities of which it is an effective cloak ; and so long as our silversmiths adhere to their Rococo scrolls, and other inanities of the Louis Quinze, its aid will be indispensable. Immediately the details of design, however, are substantially reformed, frosting and burnishing, except as occasional incidental aids, must go together with the preposterous forms to which alone they owe their present popular development. If we turn from the English to the foreign silver-work, the contrast in this respect is surprising ; frosting and burnishing seem to be unanimously banished from all high class design, whether French or German, and oxidising substituted in their places ; and the consequence is, that in many foreign examples we have specimens of the most elaborate modelling, most effectively displayed as works of Art ; the minutest detail fully asserting its own merits, and at the same time, contributing its portion to the general expression of the whole, in all the oxidised specimens. The process of oxidation, as it is termed, not only protects the silver from further tarnishing, but can convey every variety of tint from white to black, so that it is particularly well calculated to display fine modelling or chasing, which would be utterly thrown away in a dazzling white material. The merits, therefore, of the two methods depend on the object of the silversmith, whether it be his desire to display silver as a mere noble metal, or to exhibit a work of Art in a noble metal ; whether the metal be paramount in his estimation, or only a noble tribute to a noble Art—doubtless, many can only look at a silver ornament as a work in precious metal, just as they value precious stones for their sterling worth, not for their beauty. But there is an extreme distinction between the sentiments with which we ought to view a diamond and a piece of plate ; the first we admire for its refractive power, and as a rare mineral, that is, as a natural curiosity ; the second, on the other hand, is to be looked at purely as a piece of human ingenuity ; their only common field is that both delight us through the sense of vision.

If we exhibit silver-work for the reflective power of the material, we should treat it exactly as we do glass, display it for its physical properties only, and shape it accordingly ; but even the most inveterate froster and burnisher would hardly admit that his labours had no other end in view than a display of catacaustics, in a friendly, though hopeless, rivalry, with the diacaustics of the lapidary—for such effects every material must yield to the silvered glass of Messrs. Varnish, of Berners Street.

We hold it to be proved by the Exhibition, that all frosting and burnishing, except for occasional relief or variety among the minor details of a design, are fatal to silver-work as Art, however they may enhance its effects as specimens of a noble metal.

The most striking piece of silver-work in the Exhibition is the large Vase or table ornament, by Albert Wagner, exhibited by Wagner & Son, of Berlin * ; it is in oxidised silver, and is about four feet six inches high. The design is an allegory of the gradual civilisation of man ; the allegory, however, be it ever so good would be quite out of place, were not the whole composition admirable as a work of formative Art, both in design and execution ; in the disposition of the whole, in the treatment of the figures, and in the elaboration of the ornamental details. As regards ornament, the style is a mixture of natural and conventional forms in the spirit of the *Quattrocento,* as represented in the gates of Ghiberti. In the lowest position, we have the Lion and the Serpent, indicating man's victory over the animal world, ingeniously combined into an elegant and masterly tripod support of the circular base, which is decorated with a rich moulding of fruit arranged in a running vortical around it ; above this we have at the lower portion of the stem, man in the nomadic state, represented by the huntsman, the fisher, and the shepherd, with their attributes, both means and results ; and immediately above these, decorating the upper part of the stem are, Pomona, Ceres, and Flora, in reference to the second stage of civilisation ; over their heads are hanging rich clusters of grapes : the Vase itself is ornamented on the underside with a conventional treatment of the acanthus, and a chased frieze in bold relief, representing the cultivation of the liberal arts and

* See Cat., pp. 23-5. † See Cat., pp. 184, 185.
‡ Engraved in Cat., p. 206. § Engraved in Cat., p. 174-5. * Engraved in Cat., p. 149.

sciences, indicating the third stage of civilisation ; on the upper edge is a rich border of foliage in high relief, likewise arranged in a running vortical, with an anthemion series as the decoration of the edge itself. From the centre of the Vase proceeds a palm, on which is a winged genius, having reference to man's triumph over evil, and consequent final victory over himself. All the details of this beautiful work are executed with strict attention to natural truth, and at the same time disposed with the closest adherence to ornamental symmetry. But, we notice it far more for its value as an example of how the most comprehensive notions may be made perfectly subordinate to the principles of ornamental design, than for the ideas themselves, or as a mere specimen of silver-work, admirable though it be as such ; its highest merit is its excellent *ensemble* as a specimen of Ornamental Art, irrespective of material, whether for its general effect or its treatment of detail. Yet had this fine work been in dead and burnished silver, it might have been entirely overlooked, for its exquisite details of modelling would have been indiscernible, and its style is such, that its catacaustics would have been of a very unpretending character compared with those of the rampant Rococo.

Turning now to the French department, we find very many exquisite specimens of silver-work, and in different tastes, but those of the highest class invariably oxidised, as the admirable *Milieu de Table* exhibited by Froment-Meurice, belonging to the Duke de Luynes ; a table in extremely delicate Renaissance work, with a prevalence of natural details, altogether admirable in execution and tasteful in design, by Rudolphi ;* and some equally good specimens by Gueyton, where the effect of oxidation is very well illustrated, as it is so variously applied †—in boxes, cups, coffres, swords, statuettes, and in the fine group of the "Horse and Slave." There is not one specimen of frosted or burnished silver on either of these two stalls, and the advantage of the effect of the oxidised may be well seen by comparing the Table, or a Covered Dish by Rudolphi, or the Slave and Horse by Gueyton with the frosted and burnished examples exhibited by M. Odiot, of Paris, of which the magnificent Louis Quatorze dinner service is the finest of its class in the Exhibition.‡

The modelling of the details and animals in this service is excellent, but their value is lost through the merely dazzling effect of the combination of matting and polishing, which transcends every other consideration. There is something positively vulgar in such a mere metallic blaze as a service of this kind displays ; had the various pieces been only slightly oxidised, as the equestrian statue of Napoleon, by Nieuwerkerk, in the same stall, or the centre-pieces by Wagner and Froment-Meurice, or the group of Queen Elizabeth and Leicester, by Jeannest, exhibited by Messrs. Elkington, the effect would have been most imposing in comparison : the impression of the nobility of the metal would have still been there, and every group and object, whether natural or ornamental, would have attracted its due share of admiration ; for the modelling of the various natural types is excellent, and the treatment of the mere ornamental elements of the style is as tasteful, and as skilful, perhaps, as the elements themselves admit ; superior, probably, to any genuine elaboration of the style in its own period ; and this set is, perhaps, on the whole, the most complete representative of the prevailing modern taste in silver-work exhibited, for it has all its merits of design and characteristic conventionalisms of execution combined at once.

There are several other specimens on a similar scale, and in the same style, which equally suffer from the fashion of frosting and burnishing. The pure colour of the silver, unaided by boiling out or burnishing, provided a difference of texture be observed in different objects, would have an infinitely more artistic effect, without having recourse to oxidising, if the dulness thus produced should be an insurmountable barrier to a public taste too far compromised with frosting and burnishing. Still that oxidising does not altogether destroy a certain metallic brilliancy, those specimens more delicately oxidised, already pointed out, are sufficient proof ; and the group of Queen Elizabeth and Leicester, by Jeannest, is of that excellent intermediate character, that it may safely be referred to as a model for the mere treatment of the silver as a material of Art ; it is not sufficiently oxidised to

suggest dirt or dulness, but quite enough so to admit of any display of the most elaborate execution, and it at the same time is a fine example of variety of texture, in accordance with variety of substance represented.

Before leaving the French department there are a few objects to be pointed out, and yet one or two general impressions to be recorded. All the works of the greatest pretensions of design are oxidised ; the prevailing style is the mixed Renaissance that we have already had occasion to explain, and it is evident that still the great model of the French silversmiths is Benvenuto Cellini, notwithstanding several important specimens of the Louis Quatorze.

One of the most striking examples of the influence of Benvenuto is the very magnificent Fontaine à Thé, exhibited by M. Durand, of Paris ;* it is entirely of silver, but by recourse to gilding, burnishing, oxidising, and niellos, a most beautiful variety of effects is produced ; the varieties of effect aiding the design. Though a complete tea-service, it is designed to constitute a *Milieu de Table;* the general effect is that of a vase and pedestal, the vase being the urn, and the tea-pots, cream-jugs, sugar-basins, bread-baskets, &c., being placed on four several stages on the pedestal below. The design represents admirably the mixed Renaissance of the sixteenth century, and is beautifully executed. The various elements of the style are very well expressed,—the cinquecento grotesque scroll-work, the scrolled and pierced shields, and the conventional Saracenic foliage in relief, illustrating the origin of Elizabethan strap-work, and at the same time by the beauty of its effect, the value of the Saracenic element. This work is further a good example of the mixed Renaissance being virtually a combination of the Cinquecento and the Elizabethan.

In the stall of Froment-Meurice, of Paris, are likewise many prominent specimens of exquisite taste, in jewellery and in oxidised silver, in various styles, comprising some animal groups (for salts) of surprising effect, in oxidised silver. The most important, though not the most beautiful, work is, however, the magnificent toilet-table and glass, with ewer and basin, candlesticks (girandoles), and jewel caskets, in silver-gilt and enamelled, a present from the legitimists of France to the Duchess of Parma.† Silver-works of such magnitude, even though presentation pieces, belong rather to the province of the ostentatious than the beautiful, and the general style of this service certainly makes it no exception : it is another of those examples of somewhat impractical costliness for which the French have distinguished themselves in the Exhibition. In style it is mixed, of the natural school, but a Gothic character prevailing, as shown in the pointed arches of the glass frame and of the jewel caskets, in the ivy stem and leaf, and in the general vertical treatment of the lily and fleur-de-lis elaborated as emblems, but rather in the German than the French taste. The ewer and basin and the caskets contain much admirable work in the details, but as a whole it is rather a display of magnificence than of that exquisite artistic taste which characterises nearly all the other works exhibited by M. Froment-Meurice ; the legs of the table particularly are wholly objectionable to criticism.

The *Milieu de Table,* belonging to the Duke de Luynes, is a noble example of *repoussé* work or embossing with the hammer, and it displays some fine modelling of the figure by M. J. Feucheres ; it is an allegory of the world—four giants or Titans support the globe, above which are Bacchus, Ceres, and Venus, with other symbolisms : it is in oxidised silver. Another beautiful object is a vase, also in oxidised silver, offered by the City of Paris to the engineer, H. C. Emmery, in exquisite Cinquecento taste in spite of its Renaissance cartouches. Here are likewise a magnificent shield in oxidised silver and iron ; a Gothic chalice, silver gilt and enamelled, designed as a present for the Pope : on the foot are figures, in oxidised silver, of Faith, Hope, and Charity ; also a Cinquecento tea-service of very good effect ; and a hunting-knife, of great beauty, with the handle composed of game, and which, contrary to the general rule of such devices, is well adapted to the hand. M. Gueyton also exhibits several swords of this character, which, though good as designs, are of very doubtful propriety considering their ostensible destination, even though they be really made for show rather than the hand.

* Engraved in Cat., p. 244. † See p. 283 of Cat. ‡ See specimens in p. 287. * Engraved in Cat., p. 105. Engraved in Cat. p. 130.

IX***

M. Marrel also exhibits many minute objects of taste. In German silver-work there is little beyond the large vase, by Wagner, if we except, perhaps, the hunting-cup in the Cinquecento style, by Jacobi, of Brunswick, and a vase of flowers more curious than beautiful,* in the octagon room, by Strube & Son, of Leipsic ; the same must be said of the gilt and enamelled chessmen, in the same compartment, by Wieshaupt & Sons, of Hanau.†

The Russian is in a similar taste with the English, the Louis Quinze being its archetype ; but nearly all the specimens exhibited are as good samples of the style as any in the Exhibition ; they never descend to the Rococo. There are, besides these, some copies of old works, as a hanap, of the seventeenth century, and a Cellini vase, silver-gilt ; and several specimens of the natural school of ornament, some of humorous character—as the Bear candelabra. But the principal effort is the large centre-piece, consisting of an historical group under a fir-tree ; the composition and modelling are highly effective, and wholly without the aid of either frosting or burnishing, but by the pure naturalism of the design, we have the anomaly of a dish placed on the top of a tree ; a trifling inconsistency, however, compared with what we have on the English side of the Exhibition.

Spain, faithful to its historically ecclesiastical taste, exhibits a magnificent gilt Gothic tabernacle, by Moratilla, of Madrid. And the Italian contributions are nearly all comprised in the filagree work of Loleo, of Genoa.

In passing from the foreign to the English silver-work, the general change of taste is very decided, and though there are some exceptions, the general inferiority is not to be overlooked. The first work which attracts our attention is the large centre-piece, a candelabrum, and flower-vase, designed and executed by A. Brown, in dead and burnished silver, in the nave, exhibited by Hunt & Roskell. This piece, though displaying the characteristic flashiness of the prevailing home taste of the present day, possesses also many merits of design, which are conspicuous in spite of boiling out and burnishing, though the modelling of the high reliefs in dead silver, in the centre, displays only half its merit, through the want of shadow in detail.

The design is somewhat complicated, and in two distinct parts, Candelabrum and Plateau ; the candelabrum is decorated, at its base, with groups of the four quarters of the Globe, with an alto-relievo of Apollo and the Hours, or Day and Night, as a frieze, around the stem ; on the plateau below are groups of the Four Seasons. The style is of the mixed Renaissance, with rather a prominence of the more characteristic Cinquecento details, as griffins terminating in vegetable forms, and mere conventional scrolls ; but sufficiently mixed with the ordinary details of the Renaissance. The want of variety of texture, a characteristic defect of English silver-work, is much felt in this great piece, though its large size renders many delicacies of detail, which would be otherwise desirable, comparatively unimportant, and it has altogether a magnificent effect, and is, doubtless, the finest centre-piece exhibited on the English side. Still, if the figures, especially the groups, had been only slightly oxidised, instead of dead white, the effect would have been immensely enhanced, in our opinion. No better evidence of the value of oxidation need be pointed out, than the shield and the vase, by Antoine Vechte, though, perhaps, overdone, exhibited also by this firm, in their stall in the gallery ; the vase with the Battle of Jupiter and the Titans ; and the unfinished shield, with Shakspere, Milton, and Newton, and the genius of the Arts in the centre. The shield exhibits some chasing of unequalled beauty and delicacy, and owing to the oxidised surface shows with all the vigour of a fine proof engraving. There is, in this stall, also a Cinquecento vase in silver, gilt, and enamel, which is conspicuous among so many others in a very different taste, chiefly the Rococo, of which Mr. Brown's candelabrum for the Marquis of Tweeddale,‡ is a fair example. The general want of the variety of texture, is further well illustrated by the two small gilt equestrian statues of Napoleon and the Duke of Wellington, which though well modelled, are wholly wanting in effect.

In the stall of Morel & Co. a superior taste prevails.§ There are here several good specimens of the Cinquecento, but some of them appear to be injured by the enamels, which are too varied and too strong in colour for such objects ; otherwise the following are excellent—a vase and dish in crystal of exquisite form, an oriental agate cup, a lapis-lazuli cup, and a gilt vase, with a frieze in relief in oxidised silver, representing a boar-hunt in German Cinquecento ; also a gilt sugar-basin, and a few other objects insignificant but tasteful, as a stork and a marabout paper-weight.

A toilet-glass * on this stall, in silver, from its tasteful and symmetrical arrangement shows that even the Louis Quinze is capable of agreeable effects ; its shape is such that the details used are in exact sympathy with the form of the whole.

The large equestrian statue of Queen Elizabeth, exhibited by this house, by Cavalier, is another fine example of *repoussé*, or hammer-work ; and in colour is another good illustration of how wholly superfluous is the process of frosting. We have in this group the simple colour of the metal, and it shows that, saving the prevention of tarnishing, there is no real necessity for oxidising, though it indisputably enhances the effect of the forms.

Mr. Joseph Angell also exhibits several specimens of delicate taste, chiefly in the style of the Renaissance, but with a sufficient mixture of Rococo : a claret jug, in Etruscan or early Greek taste, is a notable exception,† as in a style hitherto very rare in modern silver-work. Of more modern taste is conspicuous a jug with vine-twig twisted round it, which, with its frosted leaves and burnished fruit, gives a rich variety to the vessel ; and this application to distinct minute details, as mere accessories, is a legitimate mode of introducing frosting and burnishing.

Mr. George Angell also exhibits some extremely beautiful classical jugs, and some good Renaissance specimens, and also a very superior candelabrum, with a lioness defending her cubs against a boa-constrictor.

Messrs. Watherston & Brogden exhibit a very effective design by Mr. A. Brown, a gold vase in the Renaissance taste, with scrolled and jewelled base, surmounted by an emblematical design of Great Britain.‡

Messrs. Garrard have two stalls ; amongst the most conspicuous objects in the smaller, containing several good specimens of modern taste, is a large Moorish candelabrum of some pretensions, but indistinct in the details owing to the brightness of the metal ; and also a good Renaissance tea-set of a Moorish character ; there is no Rococo on this stall.

Lambert & Rawlings exhibit a handsome pair of wine flagons § of unusual shape.

Mr. Hancock exhibits two race cups—the Warwick and the Goodwood—distinguished for the fine modelling of the dogs and horses, &c., from designs by Mr. M'Carthy ; the effect, however, is very materially injured by the bright scratching of the figures, and the attempt at rendering the hair of the horses, not here and there, but uniformly ; the object is in itself puerile, for the hair is not so conspicuous upon a horse that it need be prominently elaborated in a small silver model ; we see the shape of a horse not his hair, and on the small scale of these models a much more delicate indication is required.

In this respect the horse of M. Jeannest, in the Elkington Group, or that of M. Gueyton, may serve as a model of treatment ; the animal's coat is sufficiently represented without the artifice of a palpable elaboration of hair coarse enough for an animal of the natural size.

A Greek vase and ebony table, with an anthemion inlaid in silver, and also an ebony and silver cigar box, on this stall, are worthy of attention as out of the ordinary taste.

Mr. Thomas Sharp also exhibits a candelabrum in electro-plate, with a group of St. George and the Dragon, which is in very superior style to the average of such designs.

Payne & Sons, of Bath, exhibit a beautiful vase from an old Roman marble.||

Smith, Nicholson, & Co. appear as the most decided representatives of the "naturalist school," as we must term this taste ; but there are evidences besides in this stall of an appreciation of classical ornament. This firm exhibit a very striking dessert service, designed by Mr. J. S. Archer, and made for the Duke of

---

* Engraved in Cat., p. 47.   † Engraved in Cat., p. 301.
‡ Engraved in Cat., p. 58.   § Engraved in Cat., pp. 112-13.

* Engraved in Cat., p. 113.   † Engraved in Cat., pp. 162-3.
‡ Engraved in Cat., p. 281.   § Engraved in Cat., p. 140. || Engraved in Cat., p. 104.

Roxburgh,* which, though possessing great beauty of general arrangement or grouping of the forms, is open to the theoretical objection that we have natural objects performing impossibilities; the fuchsia, the lily, the thistle, and the vine, are, respectively, without any artificial or mechanical aid, made to support dishes upon their delicate flowers or tendrils; the simple contrivance of a central support to these dishes, would, with an imperceptible alteration of the several groups to render them accessory instead of principal, have most certainly added to the beauty of effect, and obviated a very great offence to sound criticism. There are several other similar designs, graceful in their general forms, but open to the same objection; and here, too, the inveterate frosting and burnishing everywhere obtrude themselves.

Collis & Co., of Birmingham, exhibit two services, for Mehmed Pacha, and for the Prince of Nepaul, in very appropriate styles of design; and also a tea-urn, with dragon handles, of an Elizabethan character, in good style.

Dixon & Sons, of Sheffield, exhibit a chaste classical soup tureen.†

Harvey & Co. exhibit some graceful forms, several of which are from classical models; and also some Renaissance and Gothic specimens. The classical forms of this stall, as well as those of the Messrs. Wedgwood, George Angell, and a few others, show that beauty can never really be antiquated, or old fashioned, whatever the conventionalities of the day may be. An essentially ephemeral taste, which has owed its popularity to some incidental circumstances or caprice of the moment, can never be a subject of revival, however it may itself interfere with the establishment of a purer taste. What is inherently beautiful is for all time, and the repeated attempts at the revival of classical forms, with a steadily increasing interest on the part of the public in spite of fashions or conventionalisms the most opposite, is at least one sure test of the inherent beauty of form of these vessels of the ancients, and an earnest of their eventual triumph, and, it is to be hoped, the banishment of all others from the market that cannot boast an approximate, if not equal merit, whether in a different or a similar taste. It is a morbid taste to hunt after variety purely for variety's sake; and it is perfectly legitimate to preserve all that is beautiful, however we may continue to prosecute the search of the beautiful in other provinces; it is doubtless in itself inexhaustible.

The stall of Messrs. Elkington is another justification of our adhering to what is beautiful for its own sake, independent of all other considerations; the reproductions of Pompeian and other ancient forms in this stall, and other repetitions in bronze and silver from the Cinquecento treasures, (the table in electroplate, by G. Stanton, of the Birmingham School of Design, is a beautiful adaptation of the Cinquecento,) old as they are, strike the eye with an extraordinary degree of freshness after the vast collection of Baroque and Rococo varieties of the novelties of the day, displayed by English silversmiths in the aggregate.

Efforts at variety, unless founded on the sincerest study of what has already been done, not by our own immediate rivals in our own time, but by all people at all times, are at most but assumed novelties; but, if such, the chances are that it is their only recommendation, as their novelty represents the exclusion of all the beauty of the past; which will leave little enough behind; and he must be indeed fortunate who alights upon a valuable system of forms or combinations which have escaped all the eager searchers after beauty of the last 3000 years.

The very vague taste displayed generally in modern silver work, is the pure result of this injudicious hankering after something new, without the justification of a sound study of the old to warrant it. Each beautiful form will of itself admit of a thousand variations of detail without interfering with its essential form or properties; as, for instance, the common pitcher: nearly all countries, from the time of Abraham, have used the same species of vessel for carrying water—the Egyptians, the Greeks, the Etruscans, the Romans, the Chinese, the Hindoos, all down to the present day, have preserved in constant use a pitcher form of jug identical in its essential shape; it is, in fact, the most convenient adaptation of form or capacity to use—a curved, narrow neck, and comparatively broad body, the foot and handle varying according to circumstances. All are absolutely mere varieties of the pitcher

of the *Nepenthes distillatoria*. Many of the most beautiful ancient jugs or vases are nearly fac-similes of this form, with the mere addition of a foot; but nothing will ever make such a form old-fashioned or distasteful, if for no other reason, simply because it is a form essentially adapted to its use. What is recommended by use never grows old; it is only what is fostered by fashion that will be superseded as a new fashion arises. So it is with the terms of the styles; some are characterised by mere local peculiarities or special objects, others by abstract principles. Local peculiarities, and all specialities, when their causes cease, must die out, and cannot be revived except by a revival of the cause; and so, if their causes cannot be recalled, it will be impossible to revive several of the historic styles; but where the causes of styles still exist, the styles themselves are as much of this age as of the past. The Classical and Renaissance styles are founded on abstract principles, and therefore may and will be revived when their motives are once understood, and their restoration will then not be a copy, but a genuine revival of the taste itself. It is not so much the business of criticism to create taste, as to destroy what is vicious in it; the critic judges, and he fulfils his functions if he only condemn the bad, without lauding the good; to laud the good and pass over the bad in silence may be more generous, but it is certainly less sure; and if the critic be not allowed to freely criticise what is exposed to public criticism, better that his functions cease altogether; for of all evil genii, the most mischievous are those who only flatter or bepraise our follies and our vices. Our observations on this department of Art-manufacture have been restricted rather to principles, or general expressions, than devoted to individual details; and it would be utterly impracticable to review the Exhibition otherwise, especially in an essay of this character, which attempts to be suggestive, by comparing and making prominent the ruling ideas which influence a taste.

V.—*Carving and Modelling, &c.*

One of the most important branches of ornamental manufacture in the Exhibition is that of carving and inlaying in wood. This branch of industry, as more generally accessible and applicable, and accordingly in far more extensive demand, than manufactures in the precious metals ever can be, is one of the best fields for the spread of taste, and although nobly represented in the Exhibition, perhaps better than any other branch of Art-manufacture whatever, is still capable of a much more widely extended use than we find here displayed.

The good specimens are mostly of a very costly kind, and the others are generally rather distinguished for quantity of detail than propriety of application. This is a feature to which we wish particularly to call the attention of our manufacturers, whose productions, with only few exceptions, are generally very inferior to those of the French and German carvers, and, in some cases, the Flemish and Italian.

As the very essence of this essay is the expression of opinion, without assuming any special value for our opinion, we find three great objections to the character of English carving in several of its specimens of most pretensions; such as are exceptions we shall presently specify. These objections imply every want but those of mere mechanical skill and means:—in the first place, there is a want of definite design, and disregard of utility; in the second, an overloading of detail; and, in the third, a disagreeable inequality of execution, one part destroying the effect of the other. For example, in some instances, where the human figure or animals are mixed up with mere conventional ornament, as strap or shield-work, the last is perfectly well designed and executed, while the former are absolutely barbarous in conception and in execution, effectively betraying the weakness in design and the absence of taste. Other specimens found their pretensions solely on abundance of detail, every other quality being overlooked; and there are others again that are conspicuous only for their bad style, or their ill conceived mixture of styles. We lay prominent stress upon these defects, as they are really the sum of the causes of all those various faulty results which so infinitely disfigure the majority of the specimens of this beautiful Art.

The general superiority of the French in wood-carving (at once the most mannered, and at the same time the cleverest artists), is as decided as it is in silver-work; but there are also some exquisite German, Flemish, and Italian specimens. Of these, the Austrian, though the most conspicuous, are far from being the best; but as having attracted more general attention than any others, we may as well turn our attention also first to the magnificent furniture exhibited by M. Leistler & Son, of Vienna, from designs by the architect Bernardo de Bernardis.* We have here the furniture for four rooms, but in three styles, mixed and distinct, Renaissance, Louis Quatorze and Louis Quinze. The Gothic bookcase does not belong to the suite.

In the Ladies' Library, we have besides the Gothic oak bookcase of the "Decorated" taste,† with some illustrative figures beautifully treated, also a Renaissance bookcase of novel and simple character,‡ but somewhat mixed with the Louis Quinze, like most of the designs by M. de Bernardis here exhibited: also a table in inlaid wood, Louis Quatorze.

In the drawing-room we have some very massive specimens of furniture, the taste of the Louis Quinze prevailing, as in a sofa, but it is symmetrically treated, with an agreeable prominence of natural flowers and great freedom of execution and general fulness of curves, the elongated acanthus foliations of the Louis Quinze. In the large sofa, and in the fauteuils, we have the Louis Quatorze. The chairs are more developed, perfectly symmetrical, and have a broader treatment of the acanthus; the arm chairs, enriched with bouquet centres, are altogether excellent. The miniature stand, also,§ displays an exraordinary fulness of style, Cinquecento scrolls and monsters being mixed with the Louis Quatorze; the frames are Louis Quinze. There are also Louis Quinze and Rococo side tables, which, however, through their positive symmetry, are not disagreeable. A small table with Elizabethan marquetry and Rococo feet is the only objectionable piece of furniture in the room; the large and small round tables in Louis Quinze have a good effect.|| The furniture of the dining-room is in similar taste; the sideboard, a marble slab, has some extremely massive carving, and the festoons of fruit are elaborately and boldly treated at the same time.¶ The legs of the dining table are a magnificent example of the Louis Quatorze. But perhaps of the whole of this suite of furniture, the finest designs are the chairs of the bed-room, which are very beautiful specimens of the purest Louis Quatorze, the shell as a centre, rich acanthus scrolls combined with fiddle-shape members, a Renaissance feature. The sofa and looking-glass frame are similar in taste, a Louis Quatorze treatment of Renaissance scrolls and shields, the various parts being rounded instead of flat. The sofa has more of the Cinquecento character of design, though still with Louis Quatorze treatment; the boys holding the acanthus scroll have a rich effect, and are admirably treated. Some of our upholsterers would do well to take a lesson from the furniture of this room, which, with the exception of the gorgeous Renaissance bedstead,** it would be difficult to surpass in any sense; it combines both utility and beauty in this style, in the highest degree.

Such praise may seem inconsistent with the mixture of style described; but there is no mixture of incongruous elements; the Renaissance and the Louis Quatorze varieties are closely connected in their elements, though they have their own proper treatments. But the Louis Quatorze can appropriate any curves, provided they have given them the characteristic roundness of members of this style; the introduction of the shell, and the rounding of the details of the Renaissance, comprise almost the whole process of transition from the Renaissance to the Louis Quatorze, which originally sprang from it. Of course, there is no impropriety in Louis Quinze and Louis Quatorze mixture, for the former is but an inferior variety of the latter, and where the treatment becomes masterly, there is not the slightest symptom of incongruity. The whole originality of this furniture, however, consists purely in these limited mixtures of style; but in some instances, as in the chairs and sofa of the bed-room, we have a more beautiful development of the Louis Quatorze than perhaps could be shown in any original example of the style in its own period. The various woods used are tulip-wood, walnut, and lime-tree.

* Engraved in Cat., pp. 178-80, 262, 286, 296. † Engraved in Cat., p. 280.
‡ Engraved in Cat., p. 180. § Engraved in Cat., p. 262.
|| Engraved in Cat. pp. 178-9, 296. ¶ Engraved in Cat. p. 286. ** Engraved in Cat. p. 178.

The Austrian furniture is the chief contribution of Germany in wood-carving; but there are some other specimens of the highest merit, of which a dressing and writing table, and a wardrobe, in mahogany, by J. F. Wirth, of Stuttgard, literally in the style of the Renaissance, but in a decided Cinquecento taste, the whole exquisitely disposed and executed, are altogether of the utmost elegance as pieces of furniture, and of the highest class as specimens of wood-carving. This is the style and taste which has commanded the greatest ability throughout every branch of ornamental manufacture; as we found in silver generally, and as we shall find in other departments as we proceed; but by our own manufacturers it has been comparatively seldom had recourse to.

Belgium also contributes some fine specimens of this Art to the Exhibition; and well applied: but here, again, the Louis Quinze is the prevalent taste, with little, however, of the coquillage in the best examples, and they are symmetrically treated; as some chairs by J. T. Colfs, of Antwerp, in which some delicate natural scroll-work is ingeniously mixed; but the masses are very slender compared with the Austrian. Compare also these chairs with such a work as the piano by Deffaux, with the coquillage scrolls and bulrushes, and you see the two extremes of this style; and this comparison will show how very much more a work depends upon the treatment of elements than upon the mere elements themselves.

Two other Belgian works—an oak gun-press, by A. Beernaert of Brussels, and a wardrobe by Hooghstoel, of Ghent, are good illustrations of the pleasing variety of effects attained by a cultivation of the styles—the former Cinquecento, the latter Romanesque; in sentiment they are opposites, and contrast well: the delicate richness and gracefulness of the Cinquecento also here compare with great advantage with the formal geometrical figures of the angular Gothic.

There is something quite refreshing, from its rarity, in the Romanesque oak cabinet by Hooghstoel, with its round arch and simple grandeur of style relieved by a mere contrast of zigzags and what appears to be a somewhat original plum or apple moulding; the whole moderately enriched by statues and high reliefs in panels.

The press, by Beernaert, is enriched with panels, containing hunting scenes; a stag's head and boys make a very appropriate top; and the scrolled frieze and the capitals of the acanthus order are in genuine taste. The capitals are novel: they are decorated with goat's heads, instead of the cauliculi or spiral stems of the plant, in the original Corinthian, or the volutes of the Roman composite, to which order the echinus ornament between the heads shows that it belongs. All is in good taste, with the exception of the introduction of boys as the supports of the pillars, which they carry on their heads; though these things occur in old examples, they are the blemishes—not the beauties, of the style.

The samples of wood-carving from Italy are very few; but these are distinguished for delicate workmanship, and are in the ordinary Italian Renaissance in their general character; the large and elaborate Louis Quatorze frame in the Milanese room is an exception. The most exquisite Italian specimen is perhaps the small frame in pure Cinquecento taste by Pietro Giusti of Siena, in walnut: the more important specimens, however, are those by Angelo Barbetti of Florence; but these are distinguished more for their abundance of minute detail, especially of the Cinquecento arabesque, than for general taste or effect; the minutiæ are overdone, while some of the most conspicuous portions of the design are worse than ordinary—as the lions in the cabinet or writing-table, which are wholly unworthy of the design and execution of the minor ornamental details. This work, otherwise, would be one of the most beautiful specimens of wood-carving in the Exhibition, and, but for the delicate shield-work introduced, would be also one of the best examples of the Cinquecento; it is pure in style, with this exception.

In passing to the French wood-carving, we first meet with the Art in all its multiform bearings, and displaying its own proper capabilities. All the French works of merit would be far too numerous to mention here; but there are several which may be taken as types of classes and models of treatment, not to dwell upon laborious trifles that stand entirely upon their own merits as such—as the, what we may term, landscape carving of M. Lienard, in pear-tree, representing sporting scenes* and a boar hunt,† in

* Engraved in Cat., p. 74. † Engraved in Cat., p. 73.

exquisite finish. This is a class, as unapplied to any direct use, and therefore quite secondary in our present object, which we must, with a few exceptions, generally pass over,—though such works are quite suitable for the ornamentation of mantelpieces or even clock-stands. But this is certainly not the class of labour that will either improve manufactures or advance taste, and may perhaps be not inaptly termed laborious idleness. The English side exhibits its share of such things; but we do not include among them Mr. T. W. Wallis's two groups of birds, notwithstanding in tasteful and elaborate finish, they may rival anything in the Exhibition.

A very prominent feature in French wood-carving is the skilful adjustment of the relief to the situation or use of the object decorated; and, further, the generally very careful grouping of the details, so as to enable them, as it were, by their position, to provide their own protection against injury: both qualities, in fact, tend to one and the same end—the preservation of the work. This is beautifully illustrated in a large frame, in the nave, carved in pear-tree by M. Lechesne, in the Cinquecento taste; though the relief in this work is comparatively low, all the numerous details are sufficiently detached and prominent; but, notwithstanding the delicacy and number of these details—vine-tendrils, foliage, snakes, birds' nest, &c., the artist has never once lost sight of the durability of his work: this frame will bear dusting without danger— an assertion which we would not hazard with respect to many similar works of English manufacture. There is the same judicious degree of relief in the magnificent sideboard by Fourdinois—all the various groups of fruit, fish, or implements, are so arranged as to be of mutual protection to each other, and are tolerably secure against any ordinary accident, which is a virtue the more estimable in proportion to the value of the article.

This great French sideboard* is in every respect one of the noblest works in the Exhibition: its decorations are completely typical of the relations of the uses of the object. The entire food of man, both meat and drink, and the means and localities by and from which it is procured, are all charmingly expressed, and disposed in exquisite ornamental symmetry.

The style is Renaissance, of noble design, and of a strong Cinquecento feeling: in the upper part, agreeably interspersed with architectural features, is Ceres, with the inexhaustible horns of Amalthæa, one on either side, as the centre group; the side groups of boys and fruits have reference respectively, one on the right to the harvest, and the other, on the left of the centre, to the vintage. Below, on the right hand, is a terminal figure representing fishing, with a group still lower, showing the locality, or source of the operation implied; on the other side is a corresponding figure, representing the chase, with its illustrative group below indicating the woods as the seat of game. In the front of the sideboard are allegorical figures of Europe, Asia, Africa, and America, with characteristic attributes in the province of food and drink, and further, each figure is illustrated by panels containing the fruits or products of the four quarters, with the implements of their acquisition grouped with them. All these panels are exceedingly effective: and just above the board itself is a magnificent group of game and fish, &c., of several kinds, most admirable in its arrangement, and masterly in its execution; beneath the board in front are four large staghounds, in couples, reposing, arranged symmetrically and formally before four bracket-trusses: the mouldings, and other details, are all valuable specimens of the Cinquecento Renaissance. The dogs, by their formal position immediately under and before the trusses, appear, on a careless view, to support the sideboard on their heads; but this is done by the pierced trusses above and behind them; were it not so, this would be a capital error of material consequence in so magnificent a work; the very formal position of these dogs, however, is, perhaps, the only weak portion of the design.

On the whole, this work must be admitted to be an extraordinary masterpiece of wood-carving; and the idea of making a sideboard express at once in so palpable a manner, the fruits of the four quarters of the Globe, and of the four seasons, with the means and manner of their gathering, is as happy and intellectual as comprehensive. The picture, however, in the centre, is much too light

* Engraved in Cat., p. 285.

and clear in colour for the tone of the wood, to which it gives a dirty appearance.

There are many other first-class cabinets, book-cases, and others, exhibited by French manufacturers, but almost exclusively in the styles of the Renaissance, which it is high time for the French to vary; to the English eye they are fresher; among these are conspicuous the medal cabinet of M. Ringuet-Leprince in ebony and pear-tree, ornamented with stones;* a somewhat similar case by M. Tahan,† in a fine Cinquecento taste; and several elegant book-cases by Messrs. Durand,‡ Krieger, Leclerc, and Cordonnier, in oak, rosewood, and mahogany: besides several billiard-tables of a magnificent character, as one enriched with buhl-work by M. Bouhardet; and some fine chairs, Cinquecento, Louis Quatorze, and Louis Quinze, by MM. Rivart and Andrieux, and M. Verge.

M. Cruchet exhibits some remarkable specimens of carving for room decoration, but displays the same mannerism in taste, which detracts seriously from the merit of the French contributions to the Exhibition; and this artist shows far greater skill in the execution of his work, than in its distribution; the specimen exhibited is excessively overloaded with detail,§ but it contains, perhaps, the best example of mere wood-carving in the Exhibition, in the two groups of fruit and game hanging from the brackets of the lower portion; the upper part is chiefly in carton-pierre, which, with some specimens exhibited by M. Hardouin, are good examples of the application of this material to something more than mere picture-frames or mouldings. M. Hardouin exhibits a very excellent frieze-scroll, containing a boar-hunt and other sport, in the Cinquecento taste.

Of the more delicate French work we must not omit to mention a group of the "Virgin and Child," by M. Knecht, of Paris; it is placed in a niche, which is adorned with a canopy of a rich Gothic character of design, but composed of the vine, treated after the manner of the German stump, or knüttel tracery,|| a taste not much expressed in the Exhibition,¶ though of this class there are two magnificent specimens in inlaid metal-work, a cabinet and chair, in the German octagon room, exhibited by F. X. Fortner, of Munich.

Before passing to the English furniture, there are some specimens of general decoration in carving, or analogous work, in the Nave and in the Fine Arts Court, which demand our notice; in this court are also some of the most delicate specimens of English carving, as the Birds by T. W. Wallis, of Louth; and the Cradle exhibited by Her Majesty, carved by Mr. Rogers, from a design by his son; and a case containing some elegant Renaissance specimens by the same carver.**

The cradle in Turkey boxwood contains much admirable carving, and the scrolls are in the taste of the best Cinquecento scroll-work; this is altogether the best specimen of Mr. Rogers's carving. Many of the others, more particularly the large frames, are overcrowded, and have a mere general effect that might be produced with very much less labour, and in a more durable form, as in the works of Grinling Gibbons. That practical quality of relief which we had occasion to praise in some of the French works, is here absent. However, much of the superiority of the cradle, as also of a Cinquecento bracket and canopy, is owing purely to the excellence of the design, and it is another illustration of the paramount value of taste, with which no mere mechanical skill can ever come into competition. There are some good specimens here also by J. Mitchell, and by C. De Groot, of Dublin. The so-called Kenilworth buffet,†† by Cookes & Sons of Warwick, is a massive and handsome piece of furniture, but it suffers materially in effect by the purely dramatic treatment of the figures, and the consequent sacrifice of symmetry; for which we have only a very feeble expression of a doubtful idea:—Ornamental Art, to be perfect, must engross the whole ability of the designer, it admits of no division of attention.

The leather flowers, and relievo hangings,‡‡ by Esquilant, and Leake & Co., are very excellent examples of a style of ornament or decoration which might be infinitely more developed than it has

* Engraved in Cat., p. 297.   † Engraved in Cat., p. 228.   ‡ Engraved in Cat., p. 251.
§ Engraved in Cat., p. 60. || Engraved in Cat., p. 73.
¶ The Coalbrookdale garden-house is a striking exception.
** Engraved in Cat., pp. 8—10.   †† Engraved in Cat., p. 123.
‡‡ See specimens in pp. 33 and 74 of Cat.

hitherto been; stamped leather hangings were an important feature of the decorations of the middle ages, and even of the Cinquecento period; to book-binding, of which Leake & Co. exhibit some excellent examples, it is particularly applicable.

There are here exhibited some very chaste and delicate specimens of decoration by J. W. Ingram of Birmingham, in white enamel and gold, gilt wood-carving, with ormolu mouldings; and also some very elegant Cinquecento arabesques for pilasters. The enamelled door, on deal, with the gilt mouldings and painted figures in the centre of the panels, has an exquisite effect, and for which it owes much to its simplicity; the enamelled Commode in deal, with gilt Renaissance scrolls in carved wood, is likewise a chaste and simple piece of furniture.* This is a style well calculated to display the finest delicacies of design.

This court also contains many well-expressed efforts for carpets, table-cloths, and others, by the students of the Government School of Design, Somerset House.

On the north side of the transept are many elaborate specimens of furniture from the provinces, but few are distinguished for any thing beyond profusion of detail; the styles of decoration being mostly of that class we have termed natural, that is, with no definite idea, or of the Louis Quinze. Some good exceptions are a frame by A. Hold, Barnsley; a black oak chair by Collinson, Doncaster;† and a bog-oak chair by Curran and Sons, Lisburn, Ireland.

The works in carton-pierre, or papier-mâché, by Jackson & Sons,‡ and Bielefeld, show well the great capability of the material. But still more remarkable capabilities are displayed in the specimens exhibited by the Gutta Percha Company;§ the discovery of a "non fragile pendant" is doubtless of the highest value in Decorative Art; and the specimens of Hunts, &c., in imitation of bronzes, show its almost universal applicability for decorative purposes. Some gilt specimens are exhibited by Thorn & Co.; and its advantages over wood or composition, and other materials used for picture or looking-glass frames, considering its ductibility and comparative indestructibility at once, must be almost incalculable in all delicate work.

The specimens of Jordan's machine-carving are another promise of the unexampled facilities of the coming age in all mechanical resources, and if we can but establish the essential quality of all decoration, taste, the rising generation will have nothing to fear from the rivalry or the prestige of past ages. These specimens of machine-carving,‖ the most delicate touches only being given by the hand, are quite equal to the general average of that executed wholly by hand; and where many examples of one design are required, as in church-carving, the saving of labour and expense must be enormous. The colossal gilt looking-glass frame and console-table by M‘Lean in the western avenue, is an extraordinary piece of carving and gilding, were it only for size; but this appears to us its worst feature; the intent, however, of the designer is well expressed. The forms and groups are Renaissance in spirit, and thoroughly Louis Quatorze in treatment, but the merits of the design would have been much more conspicuous had it been executed on a smaller scale; the parts by their great size are separated and viewed successively, while the nature and execution of the design demand a simultaneous view of the whole. This is an important point in Decorative Art; where a design is seen only in detail, the details themselves should have an individual completeness independent of what they contribute also to the general effect.

The London furniture-court contains many fine examples of decoration and carving, and exhibits, except perhaps pottery alone, on the whole, better average taste than any other branch of English manufacture; though in comparison with some of the French examples, not taking into consideration the greater variety of style, none can be instanced as remarkable specimens of carving.

The work of greatest pretension in the collection is certainly the book-case, or side of a room, exhibited by Holland & Sons, from designs by Macquoid;¶ the ornamental details are in the Cinquecento taste, and are beautifully executed, but as a whole the design expresses much more the feeling of the ordinary Renaissance, notwithstanding the absence of the cartouches and strap-work;

the somewhat Moorish feeling of the tracery of the doors supplies the place of the latter.

Mr. Levien's sideboard, opposite to this great work, is a better example of the Cinquecento, and certainly also one of the finest pieces of English furniture in the Exhibition, though it is not pure in style, and is weakest in its most prominent details; the large scroll with nymphs and satyrs, is confused and heavy; there is too much leaf, and too much uniformity of shape in the leaf, and it shows too little ground; the figures also admit of much improvement. The smaller scroll-work is excellent; and a very good general effect is produced by the variety of woods. Messrs. Johnstone & Jeanes also exhibit a sideboard in the Cinquecento taste.* The boldest specimen, however, of this style, Roman in its taste, is the magnificent sideboard, in walnut, in the south-west gallery, by Henry Hoyles, of the Sheffield School of Design;† near this is also a fine Cabinet, in the same style, by Arthur Hayball, likewise of the Sheffield School of Design.‡

J. Thomas, further exhibits the side of a room, in Cinquecento; and Morant, of Bond Street, exhibits some similar decoration, and furniture,§ altogether in excellent taste; and the same feeling prevails in the contributions of Snell & Co., Albemarle Street. It is highly gratifying to see the decided progress this most finished taste in design is making with our manufacturers, and those who still adhere to the Rococo Louis Quinze, or vague natural groups without design, will do well to compare their own contributions with those we have selected as evidence of a more cultivated taste.

Our catalogue of good works, however, does not end here; as in most other parts of the Exhibition, here too, the Renaissance has occupied some of the best skilled hands, and we have some good specimens of the Elizabethan, our version of the Renaissance.

This collection of furniture may be of some aid to us in pointing out more nearly the distinctions of these styles which we have already spoken of generally. It shows sufficiently well for an understanding of the distinctions, that the very popular Renaissance, so characteristic of the present day, is virtually a combination of the Cinquecento and the Elizabethan, or, perhaps, rather, that the two are a very judicious separation of the incongruous elements of the Renaissance into its two distinct expressions of forms. The Cinquecento we have pointed out: the Elizabethan are the sideboard by Caldecott;‖ the bedstead by Durley & Co., and the bookcases and very elegant sideboard by Jackson & Graham;¶ but the last is of mixed style rather, especially in the lower portion. Of the mixed style the examples are more numerous and decided, though not so well expressed as in foreign examples; as the magnificent bedstead by Rogers & Dear;** another by Dowbiggin & Co.; the sideboard by Trollope & Sons;†† a sideboard and cellaret by Hunter, and some chairs by Gillow and Hunter: the last exhibits two of the most elegant chairs in the Exhibition,‡‡ one of a Louis Quinze character. The sideboard exhibited by this house is elaborately executed, but the legs are in position, shape, and design, extremely objectionable.§§ A satyr, or any figure proceeding from the cornucopia or Amalthæa's horn, is not a happy idea; and as the horn in this instance terminates in a dolphin's head, we have the very great anomaly of a figure with a head at both ends, and made use of as a leg; and in addition expressing weakness in its very form.

A sofa by Gillow is open to a similar objection; the leg is of a winged griffin, with one large foot, out of all proportion to the figure; the very disagreeable effect produced might have been avoided by the simple contrivance of giving it two feet of proportionate size. A simple green sofa by Jackson & Graham, with a species of caryatid terminal figure of elegant design, applied to the same use, is in very superior taste; the same house exhibits a very beautiful chair in the Louis Quatorze style.‖‖ Pratt, of Bond Street, exhibits a commode which is a fine example of buhl-work, in tracery of a very tasteful Louis Quatorze design. And there is much good marquetry, or similar work, in inlaid wood, but we have not space to specify examples. Hanson & Sons exhibit some delicate wood-carving for frames.

---

* Engraved in Cat., p. 311.   † Engraved in Cat., p. 310.   ‡ Engraved in Cat., p. 237.
§ Partly engraved in Cat., pp. 222-23.
‖ Engraved in Cat., p. 132.   ¶ Engraved in Cat., p. 22.

* Engraved in Cat., p. 16.   † Engraved in Cat., p. 309.   ‡ Engraved in Cat., p. 271.
§ See specimens in p. 34 of Cat.   ‖ Engraved in Cat., p. 118.
¶ Engraved in Cat., p. 186.   ** Engraved in Cat., p. 325.   †† Engraved in Cat., p. 70.
‡‡ Engraved in Cat., p. 160.   §§ Engraved in Cat., p. 160.   ‖‖ Engraved in Cat., p. 186.

We must now pass rapidly over the remaining objects, which come under the class of carving, modelling, or inlaying, exclusive of metal. To these belong the Italian ornamental mosaics, of which Rome sends a beautiful table, by the Cav. Barberi; and a magnificent example of this species is exhibited by Speluzzi, of Milan, in metal, wood, and pearl, but in the taste of the Louis Quinze; this is in the Milanese room, containing a painted ceiling by Montanari, and the plaster mantel-piece and frame by Guiseppe Bottinelli, both effective, and the latter an admirable example of the Renaissance, and more complete than any of the English carving. The same may be said of the similar piece in marble by Leclercq, in the Belgian division, which is a still more valuable example of style, and, perhaps, on the whole, the best work of its taste and class in the Exhibition.*

Mosaic and marquetry seem to be especially the province of Italy, or, rather, the relative proportion of this class to others is unusually great in the Italian specimens from Rome and Tuscany, among which is conspicuous the table in Pietra Dura, by Bianchini, from the Royal Factory of this branch of industry at Florence; also a beautiful scagliola table, by the brothers Della Valle, and many other specimens of merit. There appears to be something very much more rational in these marquetry, pietra dura, or scagliola examples, than in the laborious and minute mosaic specimens of Rome and other places, which seem to be valued infinitely more from the number of pieces they contain, than for any intrinsic merit of an ornamental quality. One hundred handsome tables in any of the above three styles might be produced with less labour and at less cost, perhaps, than a single one of these extravagant trifles.

Mr. Stevens' glass mosaics, after the manner of the old Byzantine mosaics, are another example of a style in which many beautiful works might be produced at a comparatively small cost.† It is, however, a matter of congratulation that the examples of inordinate waste of labour over trifles, such as was so very characteristic of the middle ages, in their manuscript illuminations and others, are very few in the Exhibition. The "Chinese ivory ball, containing fifteen separate balls," is now known to be no curiosity at all, but a very simple specimen of machine carving or turning. Curious ivory carving seems to be now almost limited to the East and it is still more curious than beautiful, as the ivory throne, or chair, and footstool, in the Indian collection, which does not exhibit one well expressed form either in the design or the execution.

Of European ivory carving a fine Gothic pokal is exhibited by C. Frank of Fürth, with illustrations from the Lay of the Nibelungen;‡ a rich vase by Heyl, of Darmstadt; another goblet with bacchanals, by M. Hagen of Munich; and several specimens, including another large cup, by Geissmar & Co., of Wiesbaden. R. C. Lucas, on the English side, exhibits some very minute and elaborate copies of old pictures in ivory, which must be classed among the curiosities of carving.

Of Indian carving, which demands a few words, the specimens are not all of one description; some carved chairs and other furniture in black, and sandal wood, from Bombay and Madras, show a strong European character, vine-scrolls in exact Gothic or Byzantine forms: an ebony screen from Madras has even a Cinquecento character in its elements, though not in treatment; but the Byzantine of the middle ages is the prevailing taste. A more national character is displayed in the minute details of some of the small boxes carved in various woods, and the samples of this class exhibited by Mr. C. W. Reade, are the best specimens of Indian carving exhibited; they have the same general effect arising from a mass of minute detail which characterises most Indian work, but they display good general design, and are carefully and uniformly executed.

Some excellent general decoration has been applied to bookbinding by Messrs. Leighton,§ Westley, Macomie, Barritt & Co., Tarrant,‖ and others, on the English side; and by Hanicq of Belgium, Leisegang and Schœning of the German Zollverein; and by Gruel,¶ Lortic, and Niedree, of France.

VI.—*Bronzes, Hardware, &c.*

Ornamental bronzes constitute a very small portion of the Exhibition, which, considering the great fitness of the material to many articles of constant use, is somewhat remarkable. This is however greatly owing to the introduction of several new materials applicable to the uses which have been hitherto reserved as in the special province of bronze; as for instance, candlesticks, inkstands, and various ornaments for the writing table or mantel-piece, which are now made in zinc, iron, or gutta-percha.

Some fine examples of purely ornamental bronzes are exhibited by M. Barbédienne, of Paris, including small copies of the celebrated gates of the Baptistery of Florence by Lorenzo Ghiberti; and the various reliefs and ornaments of these gates, with some bronzes from the Medici monument by Michelangelo, are very skilfully applied as the decorations of a large ebony book-case, in the style of the Renaissance, constituting a magnificent piece of furniture, and one of particular interest as actually containing the most celebrated genuine works of the Italian Revival. Some of the bronzes also exhibited by Villemsens of Paris, are likewise genuine examples of this interesting period of Art, but in the pure Cinquecento style, being copies of the shield and helmet of Francis I., the originals probably genuine Milanese work. The large ewer and basin* gilt, which we have already mentioned, on this stall, is an adaptation of the details of these beautiful pieces of armour. In the French bronzes generally, there seems to be something exceedingly trifling in the designs; whims and oddities prevailing in the purely fancy pieces, as those of M. Cain, and gilt and confusion disfiguring nearly all the candelabra. The Art-groups of MM. Vittoz and Susse, and the animals of M. Mène are excellent, but the candelabra, generally, are of a very cumbersome character; species of conventional trees, with knights taking shelter under them; altogether puerile in design. And the specimens of MM. Miroy, Boyer, and Lerolle are disfigured by the same bad taste and confusion of parts. The articles exhibited by M. Matifat † are distinguished for much better taste, a chaste pair of candlesticks of a Greek pattern on this stall, are attractive through their pure simplicity amongst so much extravagance. A fountain exhibited by this manufacturer is also a beautiful though fanciful design.‡

The trophy seems to be the leading idea in many of the best French Candelabra; a remarkable pair of this class is exhibited by M. Marchand. We find the same objection to the clocks; the majority are over-crowded and many are outrageous designs; this is the more to be regretted as the modelling is generally good, and the casting almost always excellent, but the effect is often destroyed by plating and gilding, or the mixing of ormolu portions with the bronzes. Of Art-bronzes the groups of M. Jacquet of Shaerbeek, Brabant, are perhaps the best in execution.

The contributions of Mr. Potts of Birmingham, are distinguished most conspicuously for their elegant and varied taste;§ we have here candelabra and chandeliers admirably expressed, in several of the most studied historic styles, as the Classic, Gothic, Renaissance, and Cinquecento; and there are several good natural designs.

The Apollo and Daphne candelabrum, though in French taste, may safely challenge on its own merits any of the French specimens; the old fable is most happily made use of, but the idea is a painful one. Messenger & Sons of Birmingham likewise exhibit some well understood forms in bronze and ormolu, in Greek, Roman and Gothic taste: a Greek scroll for a gas-bracket is of a very elegant design.‖ The bronzes of Messrs. Elkington, Mason & Co. of Birmingham, are also highly creditable to their taste, and by their perfect execution are a strong advocacy for the electro process by which they are executed. The Hours Clock-Case, by John Bell, is in design and execution a fine specimen of ornamental bronze; and we have in the oak sideboard by John Guest, a similar application of bronzes as decorations, as in the book-case by M. Barbédienne, and with the extraordinary facilities which the electro process offers for the production of beautiful

---

and durable designs, we may hope to see a comparatively new order of decorative furniture; and if produced at a moderate price, a widely extended one, which might be the means of effectively multiplying and publishing the various master-pieces of past ages: and of this valuable application of the process a very fine example is here exhibited in the reduced copy of the Theseus by Mr. Cheverton, for the Arundel Society. A cast from an original by Fiammingo is another instance of this application; its sphere is boundless if not negatived by costliness—however this may be for a time, the galvano-plastic art is destined eventually to perform a great part in the dissemination of taste, and in general education.

J. A. Hatfield also exhibits some tasteful bronzes; and Wertheimer two very elegant caskets in ormolu*.

The Coalbrookdale company also are distinguished contributors, and are evidently making great efforts to render their name and productions a sufficient guarantee for good taste; they exhibit several good designs by John Bell, C. Crookes, and B. W. Hawkins. But we could wish to see much more attention paid to the production of ordinary articles of use, as candle-sticks, ink-stands, and such works, embodying beautiful designs, than to deer, and dogs, or vases, or mere Art-groups, made simply to be gazed at. This is too much the fault of the French bronzes, and our ordinary grates are not of that beauty that we can afford to give all our extra efforts to burnished steel and electro-gilt, lacquered brass, or ormolu. This company exhibits a magnificent grate in these materials, somewhat in the taste of the Cinquecento; but we have seen no good design applied to a simple cast in iron for this purpose; and here, in exception to the general rule, a French manufacturer, M. André of Paris, the exhibitor of the large Cinquecento fountain in the East nave, sets us a fine example, in his Louis Quatorze chimney-piece as a simple iron casting.† Ornamental grates of this character are quite within the capabilites of iron and the province of good taste, and though London, Sheffield, Rotherham, and Coalbrookdale, shine conspicuously in ornamental specimens of a costly description, indicating an immense advance of taste of late years, the idea of applying the finest design to a simple iron casting does not appear to have occurred to any manufacturer. One of the noblest specimens of this class is the grand Elizabethan grate, manufactured by Pierce of London, for the Earl of Ellesmere.‡ Evans of London exhibits also an elegant grate in the Cinquecento taste; and Baily & Sons also of London, another in the same style, of very elegant character, besides a beautiful piece of iron railing, in the Fine Arts Court.§

The proportion of Cinquecento design in stove-work is unusually great; but the Renaissance and the Louis Quatorze are likewise sufficiently represented, and some of the latter style with its imperfections abounding. Jobson, of Sheffield, exhibits, with other good specimens, an elegant grate of this style. A stove, somewhat of Romanesque or Byzantine taste, is exhibited by Jeakes, of London; ‖ W. S. Burton exhibits a fender with a good adaptation of a natural type, the snake, by J. W. Walton;¶ and several good common-sense grates are exhibited by Mapplebeck & Low, of Birmingham. Hoole, Robson, & Hoole, of the Green Lane Works, also exhibit some very good examples of the ornamental and practical combined.** Gorton, of Birmingham, and Deane, exhibit some elegant forms, also Glenton & Co; Yates, Haywood, & Co.; and Stuart & Smith, of Sheffield, who make by far the greatest display in this class of manufacture, comprising several good expressions of various styles—Cinquecento, Renaissance, and Gothic, besides some good simple specimens;†† showing altogether great efforts at effect, and not unsuccessful ones: the combination of burnished steel, ormolu, and porcelain is very effective.‡‡

Of more purely ornamental iron-work, some of the Coalbrookdale specimens are very beautiful, not to mention the noble set of park gates, or the very elegant but somewhat large garden-house; and a very elegant iron vase in a Byzantine or Norman Romanesque taste, is exhibited by Mr. Handyside, of Derby;§§ another beautiful work, of a similar class, but more of a Fine Art character,

is sent by the Berlin foundry, remarkable for the beautiful execution of a small copy of Thorwaldsen's celebrated "Triumphal Entry of Alexander into Babylon." And among the most tasteful works in the Exhibition, are the contributions in damascened iron by M. Falloise, of Liege,* consisting of a shield, vases, and other articles in iron with Renaissance tracery, somewhat of the Cinquecento scroll-work and Henry II. tracery combined, with Moorish arabesque inlaid in silver: the mixture itself of the two metals so combined, and the whole feeling of the designs, produce a delightful effect, strongly recommending by its own merit this old style of decoration, which modern Europe has hitherto seemed disposed to resign to the East. The display of "Bedry work" from India comprises many beautiful vessels of this class, though not to be compared in workmanship with the contributions of M. Falloise. The Moorish details in these works, though superior, resemble the Indian, and the whole stall presents another capital example of the value of the Moorish element in Cinquecento or Renaissance design.

There is also some excellent French iron-work exhibited by M. Potonié, of Paris; and a very interesting, though fanciful, iron bedstead by M. Dupont, of Paris;† and some others of more conventional character by M. Leonard, of Paris, in good Renaissance and Cinquecento taste. This is evidently a branch of manufacture to which iron castings are very applicable; it is an application of Art scarcely represented on the English side, except in the costly brass specimens of Winfield, of Birmingham, who exhibits one magnificent bedstead of this description. ‡

VII.—*Pottery, Porcelain, and Glass.*

In this department of industry, more especially in the province of uses, the contributions of British manufacturers show an immense improvement in design upon the ordinary standards of former years; the very long unrivalled preeminence of the Messrs. Wedgwood in classical taste only proves how difficult it was to impress the mass of the master potters with even the belief in the real existence of such a quality as Taste. The material prosperity, however, of those who have taken the lead in cultivating this tardily-acknowledged essential element of manufacture, must establish now and for ages the absolute necessity for its cultivation as one indispensable foundation of success.

To limit fine taste or design to such works as the more magnificent productions of Sèvres, which from practice we may assume to have been a rule, is a now admitted folly, which individual pecuniary interest, if no higher motive, is likely effectually to correct for the future. If in expensive productions the relative high price may be said to secure a return for the extra outlay consequent on employing higher talent, the same cause restricts the manufacture; and where the same high talent is employed over the low-priced article, the remuneration is secured by the increased attractiveness and consequent greater demand. This was formerly discredited, but the general movement of late years in this direction, encouraged by the increased facilities of education offered by the Schools of Design, have proved its practical reality; and we can but hope that nothing will deter our manufacturers from pursuing this enlightened course.

Form is the great element of pottery, porcelain, and glass, as applied to domestic uses, and should command the first consideration; a vessel, even should it have no other attraction than an agreeable shape, or, in other words, be wholly without decoration, may still be a beautiful and delightful object to the cultivated eye, and will itself eventually educate the uncultivated. Shape is the element of beauty; decoration may enhance it, if judiciously applied, and may do much towards destroying it if had recourse to in too great proportion; but it is this more or less, which tests the quality of taste. We cannot illustrate better what we mean than by referring to the stall of Messrs. Wedgwood, where we find only exquisite shapes just sufficiently decorated to enhance their effect.§ Though the designs of Flaxman for the most part, these are the revival of an old taste, or rather the utmost development of taste, after an uninterrupted education of many centuries; no parallel opportunity has ever offered itself to Christian Europe;

* See specimens in Cat., p. 64. † Engraved in Cat., p. 75.
‡ Engraved in Cat., p. 134. ‖ Engraved in Cat., p. 233.
‖ Engraved in Cat., p. 198. ¶ Engraved in Cat., p. 77.
** Engraved in Cat., p. 71, and a fender, p. 55.
†† See two examples in Cat., p. 35. ‡‡ See Cat., p. 35. §§ Eng. in Cat., p. 6.

* Engraved in Cat., p. 82, 83. † Engraved in Cat., p. 13. ‡ Engraved in Cat., p. 244.
§ See specimens in pp. 14, 15, of Cat.

mere symbolism and religious dissensions have rendered it hitherto impossible. In comparing, therefore, the modern with the old, we compare the crude and unfinished productions of a divided attention, constantly interrupted by one whimsy or another wholly irrelative to the purpose, with the last and crowning efforts of the most cultivated people of the ancient world, after the successive and undivided attention of whole generations of educated designers in the attainment of beauty.

Repudiate the idea of copying as we will, all our vagaries end in a recurrence to Greek shapes. All the most beautiful forms in the Exhibition, whether in silver, in bronze, in earthenware, or in glass, are Greek shapes ; it is true, often disfigured by the accessory decorations of the modern styles, but still Greek in their essential form.

In adopting Greek shapes, we are not restricted to either Greek materials or Greek colours, nor are we limited to their details ; but if their principles are true, we can but work upon them, and whatever variations we adopt there is sure to be a beautiful effect in the arrangement. If reproductions in the Greek taste have hitherto had a general monotony of effect, it is because the materials themselves have been imitated, rather than the taste of form and decoration ; let the materials and colours be properly varied, and all that sameness of effect which too often characterises these reproductions will disappear ; this is sufficiently evident by a mere reference to silver, bronze, or glass, where the shape is the same, but where the idea of mere imitation or monotonous repetition never occurs.

Though the Sèvres porcelain* takes the lead in point of pretensions, it is not superior in taste, and is certainly inferior in matters of utility, to the specimens of Alderman Copeland,† of Stoke-upon-Trent. We have in this stall much of that variation of classical models which appears to us to constitute the true use of these ancient remains, and the best evidence of a refined taste. There is besides on this stall much handsome porcelain of modern design, rich in decoration, without being gaudy ; and in several styles, all well expressed, as the Indian, Moorish, Cinquecento, and the Louis Quatorze, and Louis Quinze ; but the Greek justly prevails over all the others.

Minton & Co., also, of the Staffordshire Potteries, make likewise a magnificent display, especially in a dessert service in Parian and Porcelain mixed, in turquoise, white and gold, purchased by Her Majesty.‡ The designs comprise many statuettes of an allegorical character, but in the ornamental details the Louis Quinze has been allowed too conspicuous a part ; the centre piece, a wine-cooler,§ is a good example of general skilfulness of treatment of relief, and of that class of design of which the ornamental details illustrate the uses, or ideas and customs, associated with the object of the design. On this stall is a beautiful Cinquecento ewer and basin, in Parian, which is one of the most tasteful specimens of this class of design in the Exhibition ; and in much the same style is a magnificent mantelpiece of exquisite design, but of more ordinary Renaissance character : many of its details, however, are admirable, as the scrolls and centre of the frieze ; and the general style of the terminal pilasters, a nymph and faun so adapted, is perfect in character, except that the lintel or architrave is made to rest on the flowers which these figures carry in baskets on their heads, which, though not without a precedent, is an outrageous idea; the wreath round the heads of the figures would have made a better capital, and would have obviated this anomaly.

This firm exhibits also a pair of magnificent vases, of which the handles, in metal, are extremely beautiful ; a ram's head, scrolls, cornucopia, and infant boys, ingeniously grouped into a convenient and ornamental handle-shape ; and there are also some clever imitations in Parian of the delicate trifles of old Dresden china, in flowers and fancy figures, of the school of Watteau. The colours generally, and the ordinary services of this firm, are extremely good ; and its encaustic tiles are a very important contribution towards the general cultivation of Taste.

The Louis Quinze is still the prevailing style in porcelain, as in many other manufactures ; and, generally speaking, profusion of ornament is the rule. Much beautiful work, however, rich and simple, is exhibited by Ridgway & Co.,* whose conservatory fountains and stair rails are very agreeable novelties: also by Alcock and Co., Burslem ; Messrs. Boote, of Burslem ;† Meigh & Sons, of Hanley ;‡ Dimmock, of Shelton ; Rose & Co.,§ of Coalbrookdale ; Bell & Co.,‖ of Glasgow ; and Grainger & Co., of Worcester,¶ who contribute in their semiporcelain some minor works in excellent taste.

The famed Dresden porcelain seems to exhibit the atrophy which not seldom is induced by a just consciousness of superiority at one time, ending in an assumed incontestable pre-eminence for all time : thus while other fabrics have steadily progressed, that of Meissen has unconsciously remained stationary, and its specimens are in the Exhibition merely to astonish us how it ever attained its former notoriety.**

There is, indeed, very little in German pottery or porcelain to attract attention. The Berlin specimens take the highest position; the Austrian is of a very ordinary character, and the beer-mugs of Neureuther, of Munich porcelain,†† or the terra-cottas of E. March, of Charlottenburg,‡‡ or the stone-china of Villeroy and Boch, are among the most prominent German efforts in this class of industry.

England holds, perhaps, a still higher position in glass than it does in pottery or porcelain. Though the English manufacturers may yet find some difficulty in competing in cheapness with Bohemia, the Islington glass-works of Rice, Harris, & Son, of Birmingham,§§ seem to have surpassed this famed manufacture in every other respect ; they exhibit an equal beauty of colour with the Bohemian, a general superiority of taste, and uniformly superior workmanship ; and this notwithstanding Bohemia displays some very beautiful examples, for they often owe more of their beauty to their decoration than to their shape or colour. Many beautiful specimens also in coloured glass are exhibited by Bacchus and Sons ;‖‖ by Davis, Greathead, & Green ; and by Lloyd and Summerfield, of Birmingham.¶¶ It is, however, in pure white crystal glass that this fabric, now as of old, displays its highest sphere of beauty and usefulness, and in this department Messrs. Osler, of Birmingham, and Apsley Pellatt & Co., of London, besides numerous articles of ornament and domestic utility, exhibit some candelabra chandeliers and lustres of unexampled magnificence, as displaying the refractive beauties of the metal ; the world-celebrated crystal fountain in the centre of the building, and the very elegant candelabra in the gallery, belonging to Her Majesty,*** by Mr. Osler ; and many chandeliers, some of extraordinary size and magnificence, by Mr. Pellatt.††† Mr. Osler exhibits also some beautiful lustres, and some griffins, in dead glass, which have an excellent effect.

Mr. Pellatt exhibits a great variety of articles, both of use and ornament, in cut, engraved, and frosted glass, and curious imitations of Venetian frosted and gilt glass. The frosted glass, though it may be a revival of an old taste, is now not only a novelty, but has a unique and beautiful effect.

There are here, also, some lustres of great beauty, and by the partial hollowing of the drops, a very rich and uncommon effect is produced ; the exquisite purity of the metal used is shown by some very interesting models of diamonds, among which is the Koh-i-noor itself, and nothing inferior in brilliancy to the original below. This stall contains likewise many beautifully engraved jugs and glasses, and many specimens of simply cut wine-glasses, of solid character and admirable design.

Messrs. Richardson, of Stourbridge, likewise make a magnificent display, comprising many wine-glasses and decanters of beautiful shapes, most tastefully cut and engraved,‡‡‡ but the introduction of the painted or enamelled glass, appears to be an attempt at combining two antagonistic elements, the opaque and the transparent ; the best of colours, not viewed as transparencies, must appear dull, and even dirty, when compared with the brilliant refractions which constitute the chief charm of glass ; and the specimens of

---

* Engraved in Cat., pp. 162, 179.
† Several fine specimens engraved in Cat., pp. 1—4.
‡ Engraved with other specimens, in Cat., p. 114.   § Engraved in Cat., p. 116.

* Engraved in Cat., pp. 86, 87.   † Engraved in Cat., pp, 218-19.
‡ Engraved in Cat., pp. 240, 241.   § Engraved in Cat., p. 258.
‖ Engraved in Cat., p. 236.   ¶ Engraved in Cat., p. 76.
** Specimens engraved in Cat., pp. 30, 31.   †† Engraved in Cat., pp. 34, 35.
‡‡ Engraved in Cat., pp. 46, 47.   §§ Various specimens engraved in Cat., pp. 182-83.
‖‖ Engraved in Cat., p. 32.   ¶¶ See specimens, p. 270.   *** Engraved in Cat., p. 206.
††† Engraved in Cat., pp. 174-75.   ‡‡‡ See specimens in Cat., pp. 138-39.

this new application of enamel here exhibited, are sufficiently dull in effect to be a warning against its repetition or imitation, except upon opal or opaque glass ; and then it will always require great delicacy, and it is, to say the least, an aid that glass does not require. Of this, no stall is a better proof than Messrs. Richardsons' own, which is conspicuous for its very beautiful crystal metal, delicate colours, and variety and general skilfulness of design. Stourbridge is further distinguished by the contributions of J. Webb, of Platts' Glass Works.

The stall of J. G. Green, London, displays, perhaps, the most delicate engraving in the Exhibition, and upon some of the most exquisite shapes ; constituting another illustration of the accomplished finish of Greek forms. This judicious choice has resulted in the production of several jugs on this stall, which are exquisite works of Art ;* and the Greek details of the engraving of a portion of them has rendered these very adequate illustrations of Greek taste equally interesting with the Wedgwood specimens in earthenware, and of some value in showing the very different general effect produced by a simple change of material.

Much admirable work, also, is exhibited by Molineaux, Webb and Co., of Manchester,† Powells, Conne,‡ Rose & Co., Naylor,§ Sharpus & Cullum, and others, all showing the high condition of this manufacture in England. Sharpus & Cullum exhibit some extremely handsome shapes for wine-glasses, white and coloured, plain and cut ; some of them after the taste of the old Dutch glass ; with green and purple bowls and white stems, and exhibiting the comparative novelty of plain bowls and cut stems, the bowls being tulip and chalice shaped, and the stems straight, polygonal, plain, and cut—altogether displaying a novel and noble effect. Of purely ornamental glass, coloured or etched, for windows or general decoration, there is also much that is new and of a high class, as the magnificent coloured slabs by Swinburne & Co., of Newcastle, with some admirable imitations of marbles ; and the etched and painted glass of Cogan & Co., and the enamelled glass of Chance & Co., of Birmingham.

Some very tasteful and historical ornament is displayed among the stained and painted glass by the Royal Patent Decorative Glass Works, S. K. Bland, Jackson, Hetley, and some very good Norman patterns by Wailes of Newcastle ; and some similar ornament‖ and other tasteful details in the lower frames of a figure window by Gibson of Newcastle.

Some curious Venetian glass is exhibited by P. Bigaglia ; and, in other styles, by Hall & Sons of Bristol, and by the St. Helens Glass Company.

But in painted glass generally, the display is unaccountably small and insignificant, considering the character and capabilities of the Art ; the too prevalent notion that glass-painting is peculiarly an ecclesiastical province of decoration, unless shortly exploded, promises to be fatal to the Art, under the very restricted development which ecclesiological prejudices are disposed to allow it in this country. The fine window by Bertini, of Milan, is a wholesome innovation upon such morbid pretence.

VIII.—*Woven and Printed Fabrics.*

This department of ornamental manufactures, though perhaps less generally attractive than many others, is of greater commercial importance than any, owing to its universal extent ; and probably there is no class of manufactures which good design is better calculated to encourage than the infinite variety of pattern goods of this description, which, when the quality of the fabric itself is decided upon, must be in nearly all cases chosen for the pattern.

When, therefore, a general standard as regards the substance and texture of a fabric has been attained, which is pretty well the case with the woven goods of Europe at the present day, design becomes the sole field of competition. Even in this respect also one general average of merit is now pretty well attained, the excellence of French designs has at last forced other countries to turn their energies to the same province, and the vast strides of England in the last few years aided much by Schools of Design,

have been not without their rewards. In shawls, silks, damasks, lace, carpets, &c., it would be difficult to pronounce any decided opinion as to respective superiorities ; we venture to assert, however, that Spitalfields silks are not inferior to those of Lyons ; that no ribbon in the Exhibition can compare with the "Coventry ribbon," * from a design by Mr. Clack of the Coventry School of Design ; and that if the lace, damasks and carpets, of British manufacturers are not decidedly superior to the similar productions of the Continent, they betray, certainly, no shadow of inferiority : in printed muslins, however, and in chintzes, and in shawls, we do not venture to claim that equality which we believe to be established in other branches.

The printed goods of Glasgow, or of Dalgleish, Falconer & Co., of Stirling, may compare with those of Mulhouse ; and of the English prints generally, those of Thomson, of Clitheroe, come, perhaps, nearest to their foreign rivals ; the similar goods of Manchester, with some few exceptions by Hargreaves & Co., and Nelson, Knowles & Co., are heavy and stiff, and display too many browns and greys or lilacs ; the trails are too close, and there is a want of flow in the curves ; they are like the chopping sea of the Nore compared with the waves of the Atlantic. In damask, brocaded, and embroidered silk, Manchester is far more successful ; the contributions of Messrs. Houldsworth, and of Winkworth and Procters, are equal to anything in the Exhibition ; and may, with the silks of Campbell, Harrison & Lloyd,† of Spitalfields, compare even with the admirable specimens from Lyons, exhibited by Candy & Co., which to surpass would be almost impossible.

As a spur to our manufacturers it may be worth pointing out that the best of the Mulhouse prints exhibited, as well as other goods, are manufactured for London houses ; a circumstance that can only possibly be accounted for by the superiority of design, and it shows that English ladies are judges of what is tasteful, if English manufacturers are not. Some of the most beautiful specimens exhibited by Koechlin, of Mulhouse, Gros Odier, Roman & Co., of Wesserling, and several others, have been expressly manufactured for Howell & James, Sewell & Co., Williams & Sowerby, Swan & Edgar, Lewis & Allenby, or Hitchcock & Co., of London. The Mulhouse prints are nearly all trails, no one colour particularly prevailing, as in the greys or browns of Manchester ; there are some extremely small trails in pink and lilac, of great elegance ; they are mostly on white grounds, but there are also blue, brown, green, pink, and drab grounds. The tints are generally delicate, and all large masses of colour seem to be systematically avoided ; entirely opposite in fact to chintz patterns in their character, between which and these prints for dresses, the French manufacturers observe a very wide and very proper distinction. To fully particularise, however, in this vast range of fabrics, would occupy more space than has been allowed for the whole of this essay. The gauze tissues of Vatin, of Paris, and similar fabrics of Bertrand, Gayet, and Dumontat, of Lyons, seem to leave little to be desired ; and the same may be said of the cashmere prints of Depoully, Boiraux & Co., Choqueel, Damiron, and others.

The prints of Depoully, Boiraux & Co., for Candy & Co., are extremely beautiful, and as swerving somewhat from the conventional Cashmere patterns, deserve more than a mere mention ; they consist of light patterns of tropical foliage, and flowers in various colours, and in several of them the conventional shawl pine is wholly dispensed with, in others it is treated with great freedom. Similar patterns are exhibited by English manufacturers, and some of the prints of Messrs. Swaisland of Crayford, fully rival the French,‡ but they are in the same conventional style of Cashmere pattern, which it would seem our manufacturers, or rather the whole body of the manufacturers of the west of Europe, dare not deviate from. The introduction of the palm is nearly the extent of the variation of even the best French designs. Doubtless, gracefully grouped tropical plants or flowers, have an extremely beautiful effect, and may be most applicable for the shawl, which is more characteristic of Oriental than of European costume ; but this much cannot be said in favour of that very peculiar figure which so very decidedly disfigures so many of these magnificent examples of manufacturing skill ; it cannot be excused, for it

---

* Engraved in Cat., p. 91.

† Engraved in Cat., p. 290.　　　　　‡ Engraved in Cat., p. 62.
§ Engraved in Cat., p. 70.　　　　　　Engraved in Cat., p. 72.

* Engraved in Cat., p. 13.　　　　† See engraved specimen in Cat., p. 125.
‡ Engraved in Cat., pp. 157, 308.

cannot be explained, and, certainly, it does not recommend itself by any inherent beauty of shape. There are several Spitalfields patterns in the Exhibition, of tropical and European flowers,* which, if skillfully followed out, and enlarged in style, might, without any very extraordinary effort, be adapted into an appropriate filling for shawls, by scrolling in masses, and still allowing the corners to preserve some of their conventional character, as has been very well done in a shawl † exhibited by Mr. Blakely, of Norwich, without giving any prominence to the offensive pine; European and Indian details are combined, and the same has been done with good effect, by Towler, Campin, & Co., of Norwich.‡ Many of the Indian specimens themselves, however, are wholly free from the pine, and have little of that conventionality which seems to be an indispensable characteristic in the west.

It is a somewhat remarkable fact, but the Exhibition clearly shows that the whole European shawl trade of the highest class, is engrossed in the manufacture of a spurious article, the imitation of an Oriental fabric, so that European skill and taste are virtually withdrawn from this branch of manufacture; and this is the result of the love of ostentation, the reputation of possessing something rare and costly, without any reference to taste.

The whole onus of this state of matters is accredited to public prejudice, but it originated in the primary attempt at counterfeit, and the result is, as the Exhibition shows, that there is now no choice, that Europe has not yet produced a genuine sample of one of the most important and at the same time most ordinary articles of female costume—it has yet to make its shawl. What is remarkable, however, there is much more variety of pattern in the genuine Oriental fabrics than in the European imitations, which aim almost exclusively at the counterfeit of the most elaborate specimens from Cashmere or Lahore, but these they leave far behind them as mere designs, though they are often inferior in colour, and generally of a much coarser texture. The oriental fabrics indeed, more especially from the British colonies, make a display in draperies which seems to gain rather than suffer by comparison with the similar productions of Europe; and this appears to be chiefly from the minute nature of Indian ornamental detail which precludes all possibility of those outrageous exhibitions which the fabrics of the west so incessantly display. The Indian shawls have two conditions at least, which are demanded by criticism, namely a general harmonious effect of the whole, and such a choice and disposition of detail that the part never interferes with the whole by attracting any particular attention to itself. Some Indian specimens are actually covered with the so-called pine, and yet it is so unobtrusive in its treatment that many or most people even would overlook its presence. And the simple and charming effect of the woven fabrics of India, shows how much may be accomplished with the simplest materials, that is of ornament, if only this one point, that the detail must be entirely subservient to the general effect, be attended to. These manufactures have a value which their mere materials could never give them, and yet as works of ornamental design themselves they belong in all other respects to the humblest class; the details are either diapers or scrolls of the rudest kind, or a simple trail, or the interminable pine, as we must call it, in which the original type is neither approached nor even intelligibly expressed; and it is far too irregular in its treatment to be admitted as a recognised conventional type.

Many of these pines remind us of the horns of plenty of the Romans and Byzantines; we have a treatment much resembling what we find also in the mosques of Cairo, a pair being arranged in symmetrical contrast; others again are so much elongated that they resemble the flag leaf, or the leaf of Indian corn. Mixed with this figure we occasionally find the palm or aloe, and even the anthemion and fleur-de-lis, but executed in the oriental manner of an infinite combination of minute portions of different colours, aiming at a purely general effect. There are however patterns from which it is wholly absent, as scarfs in silver and gold, and in colour; sometimes a simple diaper of a conventional bush or tree, or a mere geometrical figure with a scroll border;

sometimes an alternation of stripes and scrolls arranged diagonally, with a much larger scroll for the borders; the scrolls being invariably of a Byzantine character, such as we find them in the manuscripts of the middle ages; and like the decorations of Cairo, most probably having their source in Dasmascus, the common nursery of Mahometan art: the zigzag too is a common element in these Indian works.

The embroidered cloths of Ahmedabad offer some of the most varied examples of Indian design; one of these, a magnificent scarf, a blue centre with a red border, embroidered in gold, is a characteristic specimen of its class. The centre pattern is a diagonal succession of a flower in a wave-scroll, alternated with a mere succession of flowers in a uniform line; the broad border at the ends consists of three rows of pines one above another. In these pines is foliage interspersed with an animal and two birds; the birds look like the peacock or dodo, and the vulture; the animal is something between a bull and a stag. The space around the pines is likewise covered with a trail of foliage, among which are an elephant, a lion, and the same two birds that are within the pines: the whole is surrounded by a border of a foliated serpentine. The same details spread over various kinds of manufactures;* the silver decorations of the iron vessels, the so-called "Biddur or Bedry work" are identical with the diapers and other details of the scarfs of Ahmedabad, or the Kincobs or Brocades of Benares.

By far the finest specimens as works of Art are the large shawls from Cashmere and Lahore; though they are very much less showy, by the absence of the gold and silver embroidery or tissue, which constitute the chief attraction of the majority, or even the pearls and tinsel which constitute the only merits of others.

The details of the Cashmere patterns are generally light pines, dispersed with considerable freedom, aud a figure resembling the aloe or the tuft of leaves which grows from the top of the pine-apple; it may be supposed also to represent the palm-tree, and it sometimes looks like a vase of flowers, or like the Greek anthemion. The pines are rarely solid, but generally contain scroll-work, and all the figures are made up of infinitely small conventional flower forms, such as we see on a large scale in Turkey carpets, and certain colours are constant, and always of a clean pure character, even bright in themselves, but being dispersed in small quantities they have a very good effect, and it is worth noting that the red is generally embedded in green, a point which, in their imitations, our shawl-makers have overlooked.

The chief variety of effect produced in these shawls is by varying the predominant colours; for in all some colours prevail, and they further observe a good practice of following the great outlines of the pattern with white; that is, a delicate white fringe separates the details from the ground, which obviates a heaviness, which so much work would otherwise involve, without the white relief; this, too, is neglected in many imitations.

The saddles, howdahs, parasols, and such fabrics from India, are more decided in their details than the shawls; they show also a more decided European influence, and have much similarity with the specimens from Constantinople, many of the details of which are pure Byzantine ornaments, and it would be very remarkable were it not so.

On a gold embroidered saddle-cloth from Madras, and on a large parasol of similar character, we have an anthemion such as we have on the vases, and also a simple floral arabesque on the latter Byzantine scroll-work is also the common feature of decoration of howdah and elephant cloths, as it is of the horse-cloths of Constantinople; on one of these last a rich wave-scroll, with a bunch of flowers proceeding from the eyes of the scroll, in the reverse direction of the scroll, embroidered in gold on blue cloth, is a good design and a very elegant decoration.

The great features of Indian work are shown to be, by this exhibition, general richness of material and unobtrusiveness of detail: deprived of their richness many of the embroidered fabrics would have nothing left but their unobtrusiveness, for absolute merits of design are in most cases altogether out of the question: we often hear of the love of finery in Europe, but it is quite evident that it is only in the East where this taste is carried out in perfection.

---

* See specimen by Stone & Kemp, p. 149, and another by the committee of the School of Design, p. 100., and another by Redmayne & Son, p. 202 of Cat.
† Engraved in Cat., p. 103.　　　　　　‡ Engraved in Cat., p. 151.

* See specimens in Cat., p. 28.

In comparing the spurious with the genuine Cashmeres, we find the genuine more minute and delicate, more general, less showy, and inferior in design, yet by no means inferior in effect. The European Cashmeres have often staring grounds, and sometimes, which has a very bad effect, a different coloured ground for each corner of the shawl; this, though it occurs, is rare in genuine work, but must be bad everywhere. We have also in the European shawls the same pattern without the slightest alteration, worked upon different coloured grounds; this exhibits a fundamental error in design: for instance, if a pattern be elaborated for a red ground, the pattern should display a predominence of green in the details, and the effect would be good; but if this same pattern be simply transferred to a blue or a yellow ground, the effect would be destroyed; yet this has been done in several instances by the most eminent manufacturers of France and Great Britain; the complementary colours must be observed in these matters if we desire beautiful and tasteful effects. In European shawls the pine is elaborated *ad nauseam*, while other Indian details are neglected. Our manufacturers further seem to have selected their colours from the sombre class of Turkey carpets; but to apply such colours to shawls, in which the details are so extremely minute, amounts to a total annihilation of colour in the finished work; the most brilliant hues when dispersed in such minute portions as Cashmere patterns display will scarcely attain a secondary degree of colour when worked up, and this choice of colour may in a measure account for the very great superiority of the shawls exhibited by Duché ainé, and Deneirouse and Boisglavy, which are of Indian workmanship, the workman probably using his own wools; but the patterns of these shawls are also superior, especially the contributions of M. Duché, though the French shawls generally are poorer in effect than the English; but their imitation is closer, their details are very good, and they are free from that stariness which ours too often exhibit. The Austrian shawls are quite on a general equality with French or British.

In lace and embroidery, and analogous work, the Exhibition makes no such display as to demand any detailed examination. A vast improvement has of late years been made in the character of English lace, especially that of Nottingham; but as yet it may safely be asserted, that high class design has been little identified with the manufacture of lace in any country.

The specimens exhibited by Mrs. Treadwin, of Exeter, and Mr. Gill, of Colyton, from designs by Messrs. Slocombe & Rawlings,* of the School of Design, Somerset House, are of a far higher order of taste than any others exhibited. Videcoq & Simon exhibit some good specimens of French; but viewed with reference to design, the Exhibition really contains very little that is good.

In embroidered or sewed muslin, the case is very similar. A rich dress is exhibited by Brown, Sharps & Co., of Paisley;† and there are several good specimens of curtains exhibited by J. J. Sutter, of Buhler, in Switzerland.

The damasks of Dunfermline and Belfast make a more gratifying display; some of these exhibit a high class of design, as several manufactured by Mr. Andrews, of Belfast;‡ and here again we find the value of the School of Design, in the patterns of Mr. Mackensie and Mr. Blain.§ The coloured cloths and damasks of Mr. Beveridge, of Dunfermline,‖ display skilful and well-studied design.

Milligan's patent embroidered Alpaca is another class of manufacture displaying much beautiful design.

In another important fabric, carpets, English manufacturers make a very distinguished display, though the most essential feature, æsthetically, is uniformly disregarded, namely, that a carpet is made to be trodden upon. This is the great point from which every carpet designer should view his subject; let him put nothing down that a man would object to, or could not, tread upon. What does it serve us to study the theory of design, if we make no distinction between ceilings and carpets? We find here water-lilies floating in pretty pools, shady recesses, and overhanging branches, with pleasant little peeps of blue sky, or hillocks of flowers, and basket-loads of fruits, Rococo scrolls, or a spread of hippopotamus tusks; all strewed before us to be trodden upon. As

well might a man counterfeit the bottomless pit, and expect people to walk into it, as think to attain the approval of men of taste by such designs as these. But neither is a pot-pourri from Italian ceilings the kind of thing that is required; what is good for a ceiling cannot be good for a floor, where a decoration is made with the slightest reference to the use of the two structures.

These discriminations may be considered as mere æsthetical niceties; they, are, however, important essentials of design, and may be made a valuable element in the cultivation of the mind, as well as the taste, if properly attended to.

The great feature required of a carpet is, that it express flatness; this was well done very generally by the ancient and middle-age mosaic or marquetry designs; and it is really not imposing any material limits to the subject if we exact this as a primary condition. Every species of foliage, or floriage, or even of fruit, may be rendered suitable by choosing the form only of the natural type, without any attempt at imitation of its actual appearance; its shadow rather than itself; in fact, a skiagram: all natural design that goes beyond the imitation of a natural floor is inadmissible for a carpet; these, however, we should soon exhaust, but conventional design never can be exhausted. There is besides something puerile in imitating a floor for a floor; we have a good floor already in our wooden boards, and our object is to decorate this in so tasteful a manner, that it shall suggest comfort and elegance, without giving offence to the sense or perception.

The oil-cloths exhibited by Hare & Co., of Bristol; and Barnes,* and Smith, and Baber, of London, show a far better perception of what is required for a floor than the carpets; there are, however, happily, some carpets which are of a very different character from those we have been referring to—as some of those manufactured by Gregory, Thomsons & Co., Kilmarnock; Henderson & Widnell, Lasswade;† Lapworth & Co., London; Blackmore Brothers, Wilton; Templeton & Co., Glasgow; ‡ Crossley & Sons, Halifax; White, Son & Co., London; § Dove & Co., Leeds; and Humphries and Sons; Kiteley; and Brinton & Sons, of Kidderminster; still many of these are on thoroughly wrong principles of design; the majority of them being mere reiterations of ceilings or walls, and crowded with flowers and scroll-work in high relief. Some are, of course, less objectionable than others, and compared with the average of this class of patterns, the following are distinguished for beauty of design:—An Axminster carpet, with interlaced tracery and scroll work, and flowers, by Lapworth and Co.;‖ the worked carpet, from a design by J. W. Papworth, exhibited by Her Majesty; two tracery and Louis Quatorze scroll patterns, by Watson, Bell¶ & Co.; a tasteful panel carpet, with Roman and Cinquecento scrolls and natural flowers, by Morant; another, somewhat similar, red in red and black, with Roman scroll-work of a magnificent character, by Templeton and Co.; and a more simple specimen, by Gregory, Thomsons and Co., from a design by J. Lawson; a magnificent Louis Quatorze pattern, by Jackson & Graham;** and a somewhat similar design, by Crossley & Sons. An extremely rich carpet of the same class is exhibited by the Royal Factory at Tournay; and the chief contribution of the Gobelins is likewise of the same description, containing much delicate work, but very much better fitted for a ceiling than for a floor, a judgment that might be justly passed upon most of these carpets, including also the large Windsor carpet, from Mr. Gruner's design.

There are designs of another character which appear to us more appropriate: as the beautiful carpet manufactured by Lapworth and Co. for Buckingham Palace; †† or the carpets in an Oriental taste manufactured by Blackmore Brothers, for Watson, Bell & Co., from designs by Messrs. Arbuthnot & Crabb; and if natural foliage or flowers are essential to some tastes, they should perhaps be rather dispersed with a mere studied carelessness, than in systematised groups, as in a diaper or trail, or spread over the surface as in the fern-pattern‡‡ manufactured by Henderson & Widnell, for Turberville, Smith & Co., from a design by Mr. E. T. Parris. The colouring of this last carpet is extremely good, the tints being the three tertiaries—russet, citrine, and olive; and no colours

* Engraved in Cat., p. 143.   † Engraved in Cat., p. 44.   ‡ Engraved in Cat., pp. 166-8.
§ Engraved in Cat., pp. 109, and 168.   ‖ Engraved in Cat., pp. 62, 63.

* Engraved in Cat., p. 214.   † Engraved in Cat., p. 107.
‡ Engraved in Cat., pp. 89, 153.   § Engraved in Cat., p. 101.
‖ Engraved in Cat., p. 161.   ¶ Engraved in Cat., pp. 79, 213.
** Engraved in Cat., p. 187.   †† Engraved in Cat., p. 146.   ‡‡ Engraved in Cat., p. 135.

could be more agreeable in themselves or more appropriate for a carpet, which should always be an accessory decoration, and aid in displaying the general furniture, rather than rival it, or, what is worse, destroy its effect by its own attractions. It would require gold and white, or something extremely rich and delicate as the prevailing tones of the furniture, to enable it to tolerate even some of the best of these carpets. If they are merely designed to be associated with crimson and gold, well and good; but this would amount to an admission that our upholsterers and manufacturers ignore the public and devote all their energies to the wealthy few, which would be both bad taste and bad policy at once. The real cause of their anomaly is simply and solely want of taste, the utter absence of propriety of design and critical judgment; making no distinction between a ceiling, a wall, or a floor. The convulsive movements of the fingers under a fit of epilepsy, have as much title to the credit of intelligent design as the pencillings of the hand that wanders over the paper uncontrolled by a cultivated taste.

IX.—*Ornament.*

Having now taken a general and, to some extent, detailed view of all the various branches of manufacture which more essentially depend upon ornamental design, we have yet a few remarks to make on the nature of ornament itself. Ornament is not a luxury, but, in a certain stage of the mind, an absolute necessity. When manufactures have attained a high mechanical perfection, or have completely met the necessities of the body, the energy that brought them to that perfection must either stagnate or be continued in a higher province—that of Taste; for there is a stage of cultivation when the mind must revolt at a mere crude utility. So it is a natural propensity to decorate or embellish whatever is useful or agreeable to us. But, just as there are mechanical laws which regulate all our efforts in pure uses, so there are laws of the mind which must regulate those æsthetical efforts expressed in the attempt at decoration or ornamental design.

There are two provinces of ornament, the *flat* and the *round;* in the flat we have a contrast of light and dark, in the round a contrast of light and shade; in both a variety of effect for the pure gratification of the sense of vision. In the first case a play of line is the main feature, in the second a play of masses; and colour may be an auxiliary to both, but it acts with far greater power in the flat, as it is entirely dependent upon light.

Ornament, therefore, is a system of contrasts; the object of study is the order of contrasts; the individual orders may vary to infinity, though the classes are limited; as right-line, or curved-line series, series of simple curves or clustered curves; series of mere lines or natural objects, as flowers, arranged in the orders of these different series. For example, the common scroll is a series of spirals to the right and left alternately; the Roman scroll is the acanthus plant, or brank-ursine, treated in this order of curved series.

Such a treatment of a plant is termed *conventional,* because it is not the natural order of the growth or development of the plant; where the exact imitation of the details and its own order of development are both observed, the treatment is *natural,* and an object so treated, independent of any application, is only a picture or model, not an ornament; to be an ornament it must be applied as an accessory decoration to something else.

The production and application of ornament are distinct processes, though they cannot be separated in applied design. A proper distinction between a picture or model and an ornament, is of the utmost importance to the designer, for the mere power of imitation of natural objects, and even their exact imitation, is perfectly compatible with the total ignorance of Ornamental Art; the great art of the designer is the selection and arrangement of his materials, not in their execution; there is a distinct *study of ornament,* wholly independent of the merely preliminary exercises of drawing, colouring, or modelling. A designer might produce a perfect arrangement of forms and colours, and yet show the grossest stupidity in its application.

Any picture, whatever the subject, which is composed upon principles of symmetry and contrast, becomes an ornament; and any ornamental design in which these two principles have been made subservient to imitation or natural arrangement, has departed from the province of ornament to that of mere imitative Art. And in all designs of this latter kind, where we have strict natural imitations applied to purposes of active use, to which the natural types can have no affinity whatever, notwithstanding our adherence to nature in little matters, we have committed a gross outrage upon her in great matters. What merit can we claim for our elaboration of fuchsias and tulips, if the only appropriation we can make of their delicate forms is to load them with heavy dishes of fruit or of trifle, burdens one hundred times more than enough to crush them in their natural state?

The artistic fault here committed, and the Exhibition affords many examples of it, is the using our imitations from nature as *principals* in the design, instead of mere accessory decorations, substituting the ornament itself for the thing to be ornamented: ornament is essentially the accessory to, and not the substitute of, the useful. Of course there are many natural objects which at once suggest certain uses, and we cannot be wrong if we elaborate these into such implements or vessels as their own very forms or natures may have spontaneously presented to the mind.

Every article of use has a certain size and character defined for it, by the very use it is destined for, and this may never be disregarded by the designer. It is in fact the indispensable skeleton of his design, and is wholly independent of ornament in its primary condition of a mere form of use. But it is upon this skeleton that the designer must bring his ornamental skill to bear, whether he use conventional ornament or natural, or both; and he is a poor designer if he can do nothing more than imitate a few sprigs or leaves wherewith to decorate it; he must give it character as well as beauty, and make it suggestive of something more than a cluster of weeds or flowers from the field, or this is mannerism indeed.

This naturalist, or, we may call it, horticultural school of ornament, has made rather inordinate progress of late, and unless at once contested by other styles, bids fair to constitute the characteristic mannerism of the Ornamental Art of the age; it seems alone to share the favour with Rococo in silver-work.

Natural floral ornament is a very beautiful kind of ornament, but it is but one kind; and an infinite variety of floral details, especially in the round, would have but a monotonous effect on the mind unless aided by Art,—by conventionality of arrangement. In no popular style of ornament have natural details ever yet prevailed; the details of all great styles are largely derived from nature, but for the most part conventionally treated, and theory as well as experience seems to indicate this as the true system.

In Egyptian, Greek, and Roman ornament, it is extremely rare to find any natural treatment of the details, that is, any mere imitation. The case is the same with Byzantine and Saracenic Art, and with the great styles of Italy in which all the most perfect schemes are purely conventional, or upon a strict geometrical basis.

Lorenzo Ghiberti has introduced exact natural imitations in his celebrated gates of the Baptistery of San Giovanni, at Florence, of which copies are exhibited by M. Barbédienne, but they are strictly accessory to a general plan, and symmetrically arranged, being neither negligently nor naturally disposed. They are bound in bunches or groups of various shapes and sizes, and disposed in harmony with the main compartments of the gate of which they are ornaments.

There can be no question that the motive of ornament is not the presentation of natural images to the mind, but the rendering the object ornamented as agreeable as possible to it; the details of decoration, therefore, should have no independent character of their own, but be kept purely subservient to beauty of effect. This technical limitation is quite compatible with the most complete symbolic or allegoric expression. Our symbols must be as amenable to the laws of symmetry and the general scheme of our design, as completely as the simplest detail derived from nature.

Symmetry is so important an element of decoration that there is no form or combination of forms whatever, that, when symmetrically contrasted or repeated, cannot be made subservient to beauty. We still use as our principal standards, the very details adopted by the artists of Greece or Egypt three thousand years ago ; not from their speciality of detail, but because it would be extremely difficult, if possible, to select others of a less decided individuality which would so well illustrate the principles of ornament—series and contrast : contrast of masses and contrast or harmony of lines.

There are few ordinary decorations for mouldings or borders, of which these ancient ornaments do not thoroughly express the principles, and there are no examples of them more happy in effect than such varieties as we find on the ancient monuments themselves ; the moderns, even the best artists of the Renaissance, have never improved upon their Greek or Roman types, and all the most beautiful ornaments of the Cinquecento are but varieties of Roman standards—as the guilloche, the scroll, the anthemion, the echinus, the astragal, the fret or labyrinth, and the zigzag.

To examine these several ornaments as to their principles, we have in the zigzag the simplest example of a right line series ; in the fret or labyrinth we have a more complicated example of right line variations ; in the guilloche* varieties we have simple curved line series ; in the scrolls, successions or alternations of complete curves in the place of a mere running curved line ; and in the anthemions, or the varieties of what is commonly called the honeysuckle ornament, we have a third order of curved line series, namely successions or alternations of regular clusters of curves, the unit in this case being itself a succession of curves in a certain order of repetition ; and lastly in the echinus or horse-chesnut,† and in the astragal and their variations, we have an alternation of round and sharp forms, giving a powerful contrast of light and shade, independent of a certain play of line.

Examining these ornaments, therefore, with reference to their principles, it is clear that, provided we keep these principles in sight, we may change the details at pleasure, whether symbolic or sensuous only, and thus produce that variety of effect so essential to the steady gratification of the eye : one ornament, in fact, suggests many. On the contrary, if we appreciate only the individual details of an ornament, a whole class or genus is represented by a single specimen, and our resources are reduced to the extremest poverty of expression. This has been actually the case as regards the genus of which the honeysuckle specimen is only a variety : instead of seizing the principle of this ornament, and treating almost any floral or vegetable, or even symbolic, form in that order of curved series, our architects have been engrossed by the details of an individual, and have acquired only one ornament in the place of thousands which must have suggested themselves, had the principle itself been grasped in the first instance instead of the details of only one of its illustrations. There is scarcely a weed in England that might not be treated, on the principle of the Greek anthemion, with nearly equal effect with the honeysuckle, which is only the nearest corresponding type of the ornament in Nature. The eye, however, does not admire the anthemion, the echinus, or the astragal, because they may be taken from the honeysuckle, the horse-chesnut, or the hucklebone, but because they are admirable details for the illustration of those symmetries and contrasts which, by the very nature of vision, must, by the gratification of this one of its senses, be delightful to the mind—just as harmonies and melodies delight it through another of its senses.

Where the mind views something more than the surface, or where the eyes are ancillary only to the mind, every natural object may be suggestive of some new essential form or combination of forms. The lotus, the lily, and the tulip, are but flowers to the many, but to the designer they must be something more ; every individual is

* Called by the Greeks Speira, signifying, literally, a plat or coil, which all the early guilloches are.
† The echinus, commonly called the egg and tongue, or the egg and dart, or sometimes the ovolo ; it is derived from the horse-chesnut, called echinus by the Greeks.

but an illustration of a principle, and it is to the constructive principles of his natural models that the designer should give his attention : by separating the minutiæ of individual development from the essential strength and elegance of the construction, he becomes a creator of new forms, and by this simple exercise of the natural faculty of contrivance, he combines with the beauty of nature the ingenuity of Art.

All established styles of ornament are founded upon the same principles, their differences are differences only of the materials— either the natural types or the artificial forms, the details of the several standards which each taste more or less partially developed, —some for one reason, some for another ; all arising from some one predominant sentiment. The peculiarity of Byzantine ornament, for instance, is owing to its prevailing Christian symbolism ; the peculiarity of the Saracenic, equally decided though opposite in its sentiment, is owing to its rigid exclusion of all imitation of natural types, whence its striking artificial character.

The time has perhaps now gone by, at least in Europe, for the development of any particular or national style, and for this reason it is necessary to distinguish the various tastes that have prevailed throughout past ages, and preserve them as distinct expressions ; or otherwise, by using indiscriminately all materials, we should lose all expression, and the very essence of ornament, the conveying of a distinct æsthetic expression, be utterly destroyed. For if all objects in a room were of the same shape and details, however beautiful these details might be, the mind would soon be utterly disgusted. This is, however, exactly what must happen on a large scale ; if all our decoration is to degenerate into a uniform mixture of all elements, nothing will be beautiful, for nothing will present a new or varied image to the mind.

It is under this impression that we have undertaken to analyse the various ornamental expressions, in this unexampled collection of the world's industry, to place them distinctly before our manufacturers, in order that they may make their own uses of them, towards the cultivation of pure and rational individualities of design, which will not only add to their own material prosperity, but will also largely contribute towards the general elevation of the social standard.

LONDON :
BRADBURY AND EVANS (PRINTERS EXTRAORDINARY TO THE QUEEN), WHITEFRIARS.

Dover Books on Art

AFRICAN SCULPTURE, Ladislas Segy. 163 full-page plates illustrating masks, fertility figures, ceremonial objects, etc., of 50 West and Central African tribes—95% never before illustrated. 34-page introduction to African sculpture. "Mr. Segy is one of its top authorities," NEW YORKER. 164 full-page photographic plates. Introduction. Bibliography. 244pp. 6⅛ x 9¼.

20396-4 Paperbound $5.00

CALLIGRAPHY, J. G. Schwandner. First reprinting in 200 years of this legendary book of beautiful handwriting. Over 300 ornamental initials, 12 complete calligraphic alphabets, over 150 ornate frames and panels, 75 calligraphic pictures of cherubs, stags, lions, etc., thousands of flourishes, scrolls, etc., by the greatest 18th-century masters. All material can be copied or adapted without permission. Historical introduction. 158 full-page plates. 368pp. 9 x 13.

20475-8 Paperbound $7.95

DRAWINGS OF MUCHA, Alphonse Maria Mucha. 70 large-sized illustrations (including 9 in full color) survey the surprisingly cohesive expanse of Mucha's draftsmanship. Original plans, ideas, etc., for such works as "The Seasons," famous poster for the St. Louis World's Fair, drawings of Sarah Bernhardt, etc. Adds new power to the resurgence of critical acclaim for Mucha's art. 75pp. 9⅜ x 12¼.

23672-2 Paperbound $4.50

FRENCH OPERA POSTERS 1868–1930, Lucy Broido. 53 posters (32 in full color) cover gaiety and epic passions of French opera of La Belle Epoque. Chéret, Steinlen, Grasset and 30 other artists create posters for Massenet, Offenbach, Delibes, Fauré, Février and others. Introduction, extensive notes by Lucy Broido. 96pp. 9⅜ x 12¼.

23306-5 Paperbound $6.00

DESIGN FOR ARTISTS AND CRAFTSMEN, Louis Wolchonok. Recommended for either individual or classroom use, this book helps you to create original designs from things about you, from geometric patterns, from plants, animals, birds, humans, landscapes, manmade objects. "A great contribution," N. Y. Society of Craftsmen. 113 exercises with hints and diagrams. More than 1280 illustrations. xv + 207pp. 7⅞ x 10¾.

20274-7 Paperbound $6.50

HANDBOOK OF ORNAMENT, F. S. Meyer. One of the largest collections of copyright-free traditional art: over 3300 line cuts of Greek, Roman, Medieval, Renaissance, Baroque, 18th and 19th century art motifs (tracery, geometric elements, flower and animal motifs, etc.) and decorated objects (chairs, thrones, weapons, vases, jewelry, armor, etc.). Full text. 300 plates. 3300 illustrations. 562pp. 5⅜ x 8.

20302-6 Paperbound $6.95

THREE CLASSICS OF ITALIAN CALLIGRAPHY, Oscar Ogg, ed. Exact reproductions of three famous Renaissance calligraphic works: Arrighi's OPERINA and IL MODO, Tagliente's LO PRESENTE LIBRO, and Palatino's LIBRO NUOVO. More than 200 complete alphabets, thousands of lettered specimens, in Papal Chancery and other beautiful, ornate handwriting. Introduction. 245 plates. 282pp. 6⅛ x 9¼. 20212-7 Paperbound $4.50

PRINCIPLES OF ART HISTORY, H. Wölfflin. This remarkably instructive work demonstrates the tremendous change in artistic conception from the 14th to the 18th centuries, by analyzing 164 works by Botticelli, Dürer, Hobbema, Holbein, Hals, Titian, Rembrandt, Vermeer, etc., and pointing out exactly what is meant by "baroque," "classic," "primitive," "picturesque," and other basic terms of art history and criticism. "A remarkable lesson in the art of seeing," SAT. REV. OF LITERATURE. Translated from the 7th German edition. 150 illus. 254pp. 6⅛ x 9¼.   20276-3 Paperbound $4.95

FOUNDATIONS OF MODERN ART, A. Ozenfant. Stimulating discussion of human creativity from paleolithic cave painting to modern painting, architecture, decorative arts. Fully illustrated with works of Gris, Lipchitz, Léger, Picasso, primitive, modern artifacts, architecture, industrial art, much more. 226 illustrations. 368pp. 6⅛ x 9¼.   20215-1 Paperbound $6.95

METALWORK AND ENAMELLING, H. Maryon. Probably the best book ever written on the subject. Tells everything necessary for the home manufacture of jewelry, rings, ear pendants, bowls, etc. Covers materials, tools, soldering, filigree, setting stones, raising patterns, repoussé work, damascening, niello, cloisonné, polishing, assaying, casting, and dozens of other techniques. The best substitute for apprenticeship to a master metalworker. 363 photos and figures. 374pp. 5½ x 8½.
22702-2 Paperbound $5.00

SHAKER FURNITURE, E. D. and F. Andrews. The most illuminating study of Shaker furniture ever written. Covers chronology, craftsmanship, houses, shops, etc. Includes over 200 photographs of chairs, tables, clocks, beds, benches, etc. "Mr. & Mrs. Andrews know all there is to know about Shaker furniture," Mark Van Doren, NATION. 48 full-page plates. 192pp. 7⅞ x 10¾.   20679-3 Paperbound $5.00

LETTERING AND ALPHABETS, J. A. Cavanagh. An unabridged reissue of "Lettering," containing the full discussion, analysis, illustration of 89 basic hand lettering styles based on Caslon, Bodoni, Gothic, many other types. Hundreds of technical hints on construction, strokes, pens, brushes, etc. 89 alphabets, 72 lettered specimens, which may be reproduced permission-free. 121pp. 9¾ x 8.   20053-1 Paperbound $3.50

THE HUMAN FIGURE IN MOTION, Eadweard Muybridge. The largest collection in print of Muybridge's famous high-speed action photos. 4789 photographs in more than 500 action-strip-sequences (at shutter speeds up to 1/6000th of a second) illustrate men, women, children—mostly undraped—performing such actions as walking, running, getting up, lying down, carrying objects, throwing, etc. "An unparalleled dictionary of action for all artists," AMERICAN ARTIST. 390 full-page plates, with 4789 photographs. Heavy glossy stock, reinforced binding with headbands. 7⅞ x 10¾.   20204-6 Clothbound $15.95

GRAPHIC WORLDS OF PETER BRUEGEL THE ELDER,
H. A. Klein. 64 of the finest etchings and engravings made from
the drawings of the Flemish master Peter Bruegel. Every aspect
of the artist's diversified style and subject matter is represented,
with notes providing biographical and other background information. Excellent reproductions on opaque stock with nothing
on reverse side. 63 engravings, 1 woodcut. Bibliography. xviii +
176pp. 9⅜ x 12¼.   21132-0 Paperbound $6.95

THE COMPLETE WOODCUTS OF ALBRECHT DURER,
edited by Dr. Willi Kurth. Albrecht Dürer was a master in various media, but it was in woodcut design that his creative genius
reached its highest expression. Here are all of his extant woodcuts, a collection of over 300 great works, many of which are
not available elsewhere. An indispensable work for the art his-
torian and critic and all art lovers. 346 plates. Index. 285pp.
8½ x 12¼.   21097-9 Paperbound $8.95

CHINESE PAINTING AND CALLIGRAPHY: A PICTORIAL
SURVEY, Wan-go Weng. Comprehensive survey of Chinese
painting from Northern Sung (960–1127) to early Ch'ing dynasty
(1644–1911). 149 reproductions from Crawford Collection, finest
private holding in the West. Emphasis on pivotal painters, callig-
raphers—landscapes from Ming, Sung eras, three classic styles
of calligraphy shown. 109 illustrations, including many two-page
spreads. Finest reproductions of any Dover book. 192pp. 8⅞
x 11¾.   23707-9 Paperbound $7.95

WILD FOWL DECOYS, Joel Barber. Antique dealers, collectors,
craftsmen, hunters, readers of Americana, etc. will find this the
only thorough and reliable guide on the market today to this
unique folk art. It contains the history, cultural significance, re-
gional design variations; unusual decoy lore; working plans for
constructing decoys; and loads of illustrations. 140 full-page
plates, 4 in color. 14 additional plates of drawings and plans by
the author. xxvii + 156pp. 7⅞ x 10¾. 20011-6 Paperbound $6.95

1800 WOODCUTS BY THOMAS BEWICK AND HIS SCHOOL.
This is the largest collection of first-rate pictorial woodcuts in
print—an indispensable part of the working library of every
commercial artist, art director, production designer, packaging
artist, craftsman, manufacturer, librarian, art collector, and
artist. And best of all, when you buy your copy of Bewick, you
buy the rights to reproduce individual illustrations—no permission needed, no acknowledgments, no clearance fees! Classified
index. Bibliography and sources. xiv + 246pp. 9 x 12.

20766-8 Paperbound $7.95

THE SCRIPT LETTER, Tommy Thompson. Prepared by a noted
authority, this is a thorough, straightforward course of instruction with advice on virtually every facet of the art of script
lettering. Also a brief history of lettering with examples from
early copy books and illustrations from present day advertising
and packaging. Copiously illustrated. Bibliography. 128pp.
6½ x 9⅛.   21311-0 Paperbound $3.50

VITRUVIUS: TEN BOOKS ON ARCHITECTURE. The most influential book in the history of architecture. 1st century A.D. Roman classic has influenced such men as Bramante, Palladio, Michelangelo, up to present. Classic principles of design, harmony, etc. Fascinating reading. Definitive English translation by Professor H. Morgan, Harvard. 344pp. 5⅜ x 8.
20645-9 Paperbound $5.00

HAWTHORNE ON PAINTING. Vivid re-creation, from students' notes, of instructions by Charles Hawthorne at Cape Cod School of Art. Essays, epigrammatic comments on color, form, seeing, techniques, etc. "Excellent," Time. 100pp. 5⅜ x 8.
20653-X Paperbound $2.25

THE HANDBOOK OF PLANT AND FLORAL ORNAMENT, R. G. Hatton. 1200 line illustrations, from medieval, Renaissance herbals, of flowering or fruiting plants: garden flowers, wild flowers, medicinal plants, poisons, industrial plants, etc. A unique compilation that probably could not be matched in any library in the world. Formerly "The Craftsman's Plant-Book." Also full text on uses, history as ornament, etc. 548pp. 6⅛ x 9¼.
20649-1 Paperbound $7.95

DECORATIVE ALPHABETS AND INITIALS, Alexander Nesbitt. 91 complete alphabets, over 3900 ornamental initials, from Middle Ages, Renaissance printing, baroque, rococo, and modern sources. Individual items copyright free, for use in commercial art, crafts, design, packaging, etc. 123 full-page plates. 3924 initials. 129pp. 7¾ x 10¾.
20544-4 Paperbound $6.00

METHODS AND MATERIALS OF THE GREAT SCHOOLS AND MASTERS, Sir Charles Eastlake. (Formerly titled "Materials for a History of Oil Painting.") Vast, authentic reconstruction of secret techniques of the masters, recreated from ancient manuscripts, contemporary accounts, analysis of paintings, etc. Oils, fresco, tempera, varnishes, encaustics. Both Flemish and Italian schools, also British and French. One of great works for art historians, critics; inexhaustible mine of suggestions, information for practicing artists. Total of 1025pp. 5⅜ x 8.
20718-8, 20719-6 Two volume set, Paperbound $15.00

AMERICAN VICTORIAN ARCHITECTURE, edited by Arnold Lewis and Keith Morgan. Collection of brilliant photographs of 1870's, 1880's, showing finest domestic, public architecture; many buildings now gone. Landmark work, French in origin; first European appreciation of American work. Modern notes, introduction. 120 plates. "Architects and students of architecture will find this book invaluable for its first-hand depiction of the state of the art during a very formative period," ANTIQUE MONTHLY. 152pp. 9 x 12.
23177-1 Paperbound $7.95

THE HUMAN FIGURE, J. H. Vanderpoel. Not just a picture book, but a complete course by a famous figure artist. Extensive text, illustrated by 430 pencil and charcoal drawings of both male and female anatomy. 2nd enlarged edition. Foreword. 430 illus. 143pp. 6⅛ x 9¼.
20432-4 Paperbound $3.50

Dover Books on Art

MASTERPIECES OF FURNITURE, Verna Cook Salomonsky. Photographs and measured drawings of some of the finest examples of Colonial American, 17th century English, Windsor, Sheraton, Hepplewhite, Chippendale, Louis XIV, Queen Anne, and various other furniture styles. The textual matter includes information on traditions, characteristics, background, etc. of various pieces. 101 plates. Bibliography. 224pp. 7⅞ x 10¾.

21381-1 Paperbound $6.00

PRIMITIVE ART, Franz Boas. In this exhaustive volume, a great American anthropologist analyzes all the fundamental traits of primitive art, covering the formal element in art, representative art, symbolism, style, literature, music, and the dance. Illustrations of Indian embroidery, paleolithic paintings, woven blankets, wing and tail designs, totem poles, cutlery, earthenware, baskets and many other primitive objects and motifs. Over 900 illustrations. 376pp. 5⅜ x 8.   20025-6 Paperbound $5.95

AN INTRODUCTION TO A HISTORY OF WOODCUT, A. M. Hind. Nearly all of this authoritative 2-volume set is devoted to the 15th century—the period during which the woodcut came of age as an important art form. It is the most complete compendium of information on this period, the artists who contributed to it, and their technical and artistic accomplishments. Profusely illustrated with cuts by 15th century masters, and later works for comparative purposes. 484 illustrations. 5 indexes. Total of xi+838pp. 5⅜ x 8½. Two-vols. 20952-0,20953-9 Paperbound $13.00

A HISTORY OF ENGRAVING AND ETCHING, A. M. Hind. Beginning with the anonymous masters of 15th century engraving, this highly regarded and thorough survey carries you through Italy, Holland, and Germany to the great engravers and beginnings of etching in the 16th century, through the portrait engravers, master etchers, practicioners of mezzotint, crayon manner and stipple, aquatint, color prints, to modern etching in the period just prior to World War I. Beautifully illustrated —sharp clear prints on heavy opaque paper. Author's preface. 3 appendixes. 111 illustrations. xviii + 487 pp. 5⅜ x 8½.

20954-7 Paperbound $7.50

ART STUDENTS' ANATOMY, E. J. Farris. Teaching anatomy by using chiefly living objects for illustration, this study has enjoyed long popularity and success in art courses and home-study programs. All the basic elements of the human anatomy are illustrated in minute detail, diagrammed and pictured as they pass through common movements and actions. 158 drawings, photographs, and roentgenograms. Glossary of anatomical terms. x + 159pp. 5⅝ x 8⅜.   20744-7 Paperbound $3.50

COLONIAL LIGHTING, A. H. Hayward. The only book to cover the fascinating story of lamps and other lighting devices in America. Beginning with rush light holders used by the early settlers, it ranges through the elaborate chandeliers of the Federal period, illustrating 647 lamps. Of great value to antique collectors, designers, and historians of arts and crafts. Revised and enlarged by James R. Marsh. xxxi + 198pp. 5⅝ x 8¼.

20975-X Paperbound $5.50

Dover Books on Art

THE FOUR BOOKS OF ARCHITECTURE, Andrea Palladio. A compendium of the art of Andrea Palladio, one of the most celebrated architects of the Renaissance, including 250 magnificently-engraved plates showing edifices either of Palladio's design or reconstructed (in these drawings) by him from classical ruins and contemporary accounts. 257 plates. xxiv + 119pp. 9½ x 12¾. 21308-0 Paperbound $10.00

150 MASTERPIECES OF DRAWING, A. Toney. Selected by a gifted artist and teacher, these are some of the finest drawings produced by Western artists from the early 15th to the end of the 18th centuries. Excellent reproductions of drawings by Rembrandt, Bruegel, Raphael, Watteau, and other familiar masters, as well as works by lesser known but brilliant artists. 150 plates. xviii + 150pp. 5⅜ x 11¼. 21032-4 Paperbound $6.00

MORE DRAWINGS BY HEINRICH KLEY. Another collection of the graphic, vivid sketches of Heinrich Kley, one of the most diabolically talented cartoonists of our century. The sketches take in every aspect of human life: nothing is too sacred for him to ridicule, no one too eminent for him to satirize. 158 drawings you will not easily forget. iv + 104pp. 7⅜ x 10¾. 20041-8 Paperbound $3.75

STYLES IN PAINTING, Paul Zucker. By comparing paintings of similar subject matter, the author shows the characteristics of various painting styles. You are shown at a glance the differences between reclining nudes by Giorgione, Velasquez, Goya, Modigliani; how a Byzantine portrait is unlike a portrait by Van Eyck, da Vinci, Dürer, or Marc Chagall; how the painting of landscapes has changed gradually from ancient Pompeii to Lyonel Feininger in our own century. 241 beautiful, sharp photographs illustrate the text. xiv + 338 pp. 5⅝ x 8¼. 20760-9 Paperbound $6.50

PAINTING IN ISLAM, Sir Thomas W. Arnold. This scholarly study puts Islamic painting in its social and religious context and examines its relation to Islamic civilization in general. 65 full-page plates illustrate the text and give outstanding examples of Islamic art. 4 appendices. Index of mss. referred to. General Index. xxiv + 159pp. 6⅝ x 9¼. 21310-2 Paperbound $7.00

THE MATERIALS AND TECHNIQUES OF MEDIEVAL PAINTING, D. V. Thompson. An invaluable study of carriers and grounds, binding media, pigments, metals used in painting, al fresco and al secco techniques, burnishing, etc. used by the medieval masters. Preface by Bernard Berenson. 239pp. 5⅜ x 8. 20327-1 Paperbound $4.50

THE HISTORY AND TECHNIQUE OF LETTERING, A. Nesbitt. A thorough history of lettering from the ancient Egyptians to the present, and a 65-page course in lettering for artists. Every major development in lettering history is illustrated by a complete aphabet. Fully analyzes such masters as Caslon, Koch, Garamont, Jenson, and many more. 89 alphabets, 165 other specimens. 317pp. 7½ x 10½. 20427-8 Paperbound $5.50

ART ANATOMY, Dr. William Rimmer. One of the few books on art anatomy that are themselves works of art, this is a faithful reproduction (rearranged for handy use) of the extremely rare masterpiece of the famous 19th century anatomist, sculptor, and art teacher. Beautiful, clear line drawings show every part of the body—bony structure, muscles, features, etc. Unusual are the sections on falling bodies, foreshortenings, muscles in tension, grotesque personalities, and Rimmer's remarkable interpretation of emotions and personalities as expressed by facial features. It will supplement every other book on art anatomy you are likely to have. Reproduced clearer than the lithographic original (which sells for $500 on up on the rare book market.) Over 1,200 illustrations. xiii + 153pp. 7¾ x 10¾.
20908-3 Paperbound $5.00

THE CRAFTSMAN'S HANDBOOK, Cennino Cennini. The finest English translation of IL LIBRO DELL' ARTE, the 15th century introduction to art technique that is both a mirror of Quatrocento life and a source of many useful but nearly forgotten facets of the painter's art. 4 illustrations. xxvii + 142pp. D. V. Thompson, translator. 5⅜ x 8. 20054-X Paperbound $3.50

THE BROWN DECADES, Lewis Mumford. A picture of the "buried renaissance" of the post-Civil War period, and the founding of modern architecture (Sullivan, Richardson, Root, Roebling), landscape development (Marsh, Olmstead, Eliot), and the graphic arts (Homer, Eakins, Ryder). 2nd revised, enlarged edition. Bibliography. 12 illustrations. xiv + 266 pp. 5⅜ x 8.
20200-3 Paperbound $3.00

THE STYLES OF ORNAMENT, A. Speltz. The largest collection of line ornament in print, with 3750 numbered illustrations arranged chronologically from Egypt, Assyria, Greeks, Romans, Etruscans, through Medieval, Renaissance, 18th century, and Victorian. No permissions, no fees needed to use or reproduce illustrations. 400 plates with 3750 illustrations. Bibliography. Index. 640pp. 6 x 9. 20557-6 Paperbound $7.95

THE ART OF ETCHING, E. S. Lumsden. Every step of the etching process from essential materials to completed proof is carefully and clearly explained, with 24 annotated plates exemplifying every technique and approach discussed. The book also features a rich survey of the art, with 105 annotated plates by masters. Invaluable for beginner to advanced etcher. 374pp. 5⅜ x 8. 20049-3 Paperbound $4.50

OF THE JUST SHAPING OF LETTERS, Albrecht Dürer. This remarkable volume reveals Albrecht Dürer's rules for the geometric construction of Roman capitals and the formation of Gothic lower case and capital letters, complete with construction diagrams and directions. Of considerable practical interest to the contemporary illustrator, artist, and designer. Translated from the Latin text of the edition of 1535 by R. T. Nichol. Numerous letterform designs, construction diagrams, illustrations. iv + 43pp. 7⅞ x 10¾. 21306-4 Paperbound $3.00

AN ATLAS OF ANIMAL ANATOMY FOR ARTISTS, W. Ellenberger, H. Baum, H. Dittrich. The largest, richest animal anatomy for artists in English. Form, musculature, tendons, bone structure, expression, detailed cross sections of head, other features, of the horse, lion, dog, cat, deer, seal, kangaroo, cow, bull, goat, monkey, hare, many other animals. "Highly recommended," DESIGN. Second, revised, enlarged edition with new plates from Cuvier, Stubbs, etc. 288 illustrations. 153pp. 11⅜ x 9.

20082-5 Paperbound $6.00

ANIMAL DRAWING: ANATOMY AND ACTION FOR ARTISTS, C. R. Knight. 158 studies, with full accompanying text, of such animals as the gorilla, bear, bison, dromedary, camel, vulture, pelican, iguana, shark, etc., by one of the greatest modern masters of animal drawing. Innumerable tips on how to get life expression into your work. "An excellent reference work," SAN FRANCISCO CHRONICLE. 158 illustrations. 156pp. 10½ x 8½.

20426-X Paperbound $4.50

ARCHITECTURAL AND PERSPECTIVE DESIGNS, Giuseppe Galli Bibiena. 50 imaginative scenic drawings of Giuseppe Galli Bibiena, principal theatrical engineer and architect to the Viennese court of Charles VI. Aside from its interest to art historians, students, and art lovers, there is a whole Baroque world of material in this book for the commercial artist. Portrait of Charles VI by Martin de Meytens. 1 allegorical plate. 50 additional plates. New introduction. vi + 103pp. 10⅛ x 13¼.

21263-7 Paperbound $6.50

HANDBOOK OF DESIGNS AND DEVICES, C. P. Hornung. A remarkable working collection of 1836 basic designs and variations, all copyright-free. Variations of circle, line, cross, diamond, swastika, star, scroll, shield, many more. Notes on symbolism. "A necessity to every designer who would be original without having to labor heavily," ARTIST AND ADVERTISER. 204 plates. 240pp. 5⅜ x 8.

20125-2 Paperbound $3.50

CHINESE HOUSEHOLD FURNITURE, G. N. Kates. A summary of virtually everything that is known about authentic Chinese furniture before it was contaminated by the influence of the West. The text covers history of styles, materials used, principles of design and craftsmanship, and furniture arrangement—all fully illustrated. xiii + 190pp. 5⅝ x 8½.

20958-X Paperbound $4.00

DECORATIVE ART OF THE SOUTHWESTERN INDIANS, D. S. Sides. 300 black and white reproductions from one of the most beautiful art traditions of the primitive world, ranging from the geometric art of the Great Pueblo period of the 13th century to modern folk art. Motives from basketry, beadwork, Zuni masks, Hopi kachina dolls, Navajo sand pictures and blankets, and ceramic ware. Unusual and imaginative designs will inspire craftsmen in all media, and commercial artists may reproduce any of them without permission or payment. xviii + 101pp. 5⅝ x 8⅜.

20139-2 Paperbound $2.50

ANIMALS IN MOTION, Eadweard Muybridge. The largest collection of animal action photos in print. 34 different animals (horses, mules, oxen, goats, camels, pigs, cats, lions, gnus, deer, monkeys, eagles—and 22 others) in 132 characteristic actions. All 3919 photographs are taken in series at speeds up to 1/1600th of a second, offering artists, biologists, cartoonists a remarkable opportunity to see exactly how an ostrich's head bobs when running, how a lion puts his foot down, how an elephant's knee bends, how a bird flaps his wings, thousands of other hard-to-catch details. "A really marvellous series of plates," NATURE. 380 full-page plates. Heavy glossy stock, reinforced binding with headbands. 7⅞ x 10¾. 20203-8 Clothbound $15.95

THE BOOK OF SIGNS, R. Koch. 493 symbols—crosses, monograms, astrological, biological symbols, runes, etc.—from ancient manuscripts, cathedrals, coins, catacombs, pottery. May be reproduced permission-free. 493 illustrations by Fritz Kredel. 104pp. 6⅛ x 9¼. 20162-7 Paperbound $2.75

A HANDBOOK OF EARLY ADVERTISING ART, C. P. Hornung. The largest collection of copyright-free early advertising art ever compiled. Vol. I: 2,000 illustrations of animals, old automobiles, buildings, allegorical figures, fire engines, Indians, ships, trains, more than 33 other categories! Vol. II: Over 4,000 typographical specimens; 600 Roman, Gothic, Barnum, Old English faces; 630 ornamental type faces; hundreds of scrolls, initials, flourishes, etc. "A remarkable collection," PRINTERS' INK.

Vol. I: Pictorial Volume. Over 2000 illustrations. 256pp. 9 x 12. 20122-8 Clothbound $15.00

Vol. II: Typographical Volume. Over 4000 specimens. 319pp. 9 x 12. 20123-6 Clothbound $15.00

Two volume set, Clothbound, only $30.00

THE UNIVERSAL PENMAN, George Bickham. Exact reproduction of beautiful 18th-century book of handwriting. 22 complete alphabets in finest English roundhand, other scripts, over 2000 elaborate flourishes, 122 calligraphic illustrations, etc. Material is copyright-free. "An essential part of any art library, and a book of permanent value," AMERICAN ARTIST. 212 plates. 224pp. 9 x 13¾. 20616-5 Paperbound $9.95

AN ATLAS OF ANATOMY FOR ARTISTS, F. Schider. This standard work contains 189 full-page plates, more than 647 illustrations of all aspects of the human skeleton, musculature, cutaway portions of the body, each part of the anatomy, hand forms, eyelids, breasts, location of muscles under the flesh, etc. 59 plates illustrate how Michelangelo, da Vinci, Goya, 15 others, drew human anatomy. New 3rd edition enlarged by 52 new illustrations by Cloquet, Barcsay. "The standard reference tool," AMERICAN LIBRARY ASSOCIATION. "Excellent," AMERICAN ARTIST. 189 plates, 647 illustrations. xxvi + 192pp. 7⅞ x 10⅝. 20241-0 Paperbound $6.00

PINE FURNITURE OF EARLY NEW ENGLAND, R. H. Kettell. Over 400 illustrations, over 50 working drawings of early New England chairs, benches, beds, cupboards, mirrors, shelves, tables, other furniture esteemed for simple beauty and character. "Rich store of illustrations . . . emphasizes the individuality and varied design," ANTIQUES. 413 illustrations, 55 working drawings. 475pp. 8 x 10¾.   20145-7   Clothbound $15.00

BASIC BOOKBINDING, A. W. Lewis. Enables both beginners and experts to rebind old books or bind paperbacks in hard covers. Treats materials, tools; gives step-by-step instruction in how to collate a book, sew it, back it, make boards, etc. 261 illus. Appendices. 155pp. 5⅜ x 8.   20169-4   Paperbound $2.50

DESIGN MOTIFS OF ANCIENT MEXICO, J. Enciso. Nearly 90% of these 766 superb designs from Aztec, Olmec, Totonac, Maya, and Toltec origins are unobtainable elsewhere. Contains plumed serpents, wind gods, animals, demons, dancers, monsters, etc. Excellent applied design source. Originally $17.50. 766 illustrations, thousands of motifs. 192pp. 6⅛ x 9¼.
20084-1   Paperbound $3.50

A DIDEROT PICTORIAL ENCYCLOPEDIA OF TRADES AND INDUSTRY. Manufacturing and the Technical Arts in Plates Selected from "L'Encyclopédie ou Dictionnaire Raisonné des Sciences, des Arts, et des Métiers," of Denis Diderot, edited with text by C. Gillispie. Over 2000 illustrations on 485 full-page plates. Magnificent 18th-century engravings of men, women, and children working at such trades as milling flour, cheesemaking, charcoal burning, mining, silverplating, shoeing horses, making fine glass, printing, hundreds more, showing details of machinery, different steps in sequence, etc. A remarkable art work, but also the largest collection of working figures in print, copyright-free, for art directors, designers, etc. Two vols. 920pp. 9 x 12. Heavy library cloth.   22284-5, 22285-3   Two volume set $40.00

SILK SCREEN TECHNIQUES, J. Biegeleisen, M. Cohn. A practical step-by-step home course in one of the most versatile, least expensive graphic arts processes. How to build an inexpensive silk screen, prepare stencils, print, achieve special textures, use color, etc. Every step explained, diagrammed. 149 illustrations, 201pp. 6⅛ x 9¼.   20433-2   Paperbound $3.50

STICKS AND STONES, Lewis Mumford. An examination of forces influencing American architecture: the medieval tradition in early New England, the classical influence in Jefferson's time, the Brown Decades, the imperial facade, the machine age, etc. "A truly remarkable book," SAT. REV. OF LITERATURE. 2nd revised edition. 21 illus. xvii + 240pp. 5⅜ x 8.
20202-X   Paperbound $3.50

THE AUTOBIOGRAPHY OF AN IDEA, Louis Sullivan. The architect whom Frank Lloyd Wright called "the master," records the development of the theories that revolutionized America's skyline. 34 full-page plates of Sullivan's finest work. New introduction by R. M. Line. xiv + 335pp. 5⅜ x 8.
20281-X   Paperbound $6.00